# America at War

# America at War

## An Anthology of Articles from MHQ: The Quarterly Journal of Military History

Edited and Introduced by
## Calvin L. Christman

Naval Institute Press
Annapolis, Maryland

Naval Institute Press
118 Maryland Avenue
Annapolis, MD  21402–5035

Book design by Mervyn E. Clay


Library of Congress Cataloging-in-Publication Data

America at war : an anthology of articles from MHQ, the
      quarterly journal of military history / edited and intro-
      duced by Calvin L. Christman.
           p.     cm.
    Includes bibliographical references (p. 627) and index.
    ISBN 1–55750–036–3 (alk. paper)
    1. United States—History, Military.  I. Christman, Calvin L.
II.  MHQ.
E181.A38  1995
973—dc20                                                95–11131


Printed in the United States of America on acid-free paper ∞

02  01  00  99  98  97  96  95        9  8  7  6  5  4  3  2
First printing

To Nina, Abbey, and Alex

# Contents

# Introduction

H istory has woven the threads of war into the very fabric of America. From the earliest settlement at Jamestown through the Persian Gulf War and beyond, armed conflict has been an inseparable part of United States history. In little more than two centuries of independence, this nation has fought ten major wars and numerous small ones; in the process, the blood of over a million of its sons and daughters has marked the soil and sea of the farthest corners of the world. If a person is truly to understand this country, then its military history dare not be ignored.

AMERICAN MILITARY HISTORY is marked by paradoxes. This fact is part of its inherent fascination. Despite the warlike nature of America's past, its populace is unmilitary. Throughout all of the nation's conflicts, the people of the United States have maintained a strange ambivalence toward those who sought to master the tools of battle. There exists a genuine historical distrust of a professional military and a deep reluctance to depend for security upon a military caste. After all, should not a republic be defended by its own citizens? Dare a democracy put its survival in the hands of a military institution that it viewed as inherently undemocratic? Would not a professional military be a threat to the people and government it was sworn to defend? Might not its very existence draw the nation into wars? And, even if tightly controlled, would not a permanent military structure be a needless and debilitating drain on the financial health and democratic spirit of the country? Thomas Jefferson, Woodrow Wilson, and others have pondered such questions. Thus, the image of the citizen-soldier, the heroic minutemen of Lexington and Concord and the Cincinnatus-like figure of George Washington, has remained a vital part of the ethos of the nation, even as the country has increasingly turned away from militias, national guards, drafts, and citizen-warriors and found itself embracing a professional military.

Added to these strong elements of antimilitarism have been currents of pacifism, whether religious-based, as with Quakers, or founded on personal beliefs. Perhaps nothing is more symbolic of that American ambivalence toward the profession of war than the fact that Sergeant Alvin York, the nation's most decorated soldier of World

War I, started the conflict as a conscientious objector.

Yet for all the currents of antimilitarism and pacifism, for all the perceptions of ourselves as a peaceful democratic people, the history of America has been a history of war. This American contradiction and experience cannot be ignored, though we might try. D.H. Lawrence, reflecting on this duality of the American character, discovered a harsh reality: "All the other stuff, the love, the democracy, the floundering into lust, is a sort of by-play. The essential American soul is hard, isolate, stoic, and a killer. It has never yet melted."

Given the diverse composition of this nation, perhaps such inconsistencies should not be surprising. In addition, war itself is replete with its own paradoxes and ironies. How can action so violent and destructive produce among its participants so many monuments to self-sacrifice, camaraderie, courage, and nobility of character, monuments that often seem missing in peacetime? How do warriors maintain their humanity while performing actions that must be, by their very nature, inhumane? Sometimes, of course, they do not. War brings out not only the best but also the worst in an individual and nation. For every monument to valor, there are also the stains of pettiness, mendacity, betrayal, and cowardice. War and the human character form a vicious and wondrous combination, and we must do everything possible to understand this union.

In *Gettysburg*, the movie adaptation of Michael Shaara's Pulitzer Prize–winning novel, Colonel Joshua Lawrence Chamberlain, reflecting on man's nature, recalls the lines from *Hamlet:* "What a piece of work is man! . . . in action how like an angel!" Former sergeant Buster Kilrain's reply recognizes the ultimate paradox of man: "Well, if he's an angel, all right then, but he damn well must be a killer angel."

WHEN BYRON HOLLINSHEAD, the publisher of *MHQ: The Quarterly Journal of Military History,* asked me if I would be interested in compiling an anthology of *MHQ* articles on American military history for the Naval Institute Press, I readily agreed. Since it began publication in 1988, MHQ has attracted articles from many outstanding historians, from both the United States and abroad. It is a publication of quality, and the Naval Institute Press has long been one of the world's most respected publishers on military topics. My role would be to choose the essays, write a short introduction to the volume, provide introductions to each piece, and assemble a brief bibliography of suggested readings that would conclude the volume. In doing so, I benefited from the suggestions of Bullitt Lowry, Allan Millett, Peter Maslowski, and William Snyder. All are outstanding historians and teachers, and I am appreciative of their counsel.

I found assembling *America at War* to be both a delight and a challenge. All of *MHQ*'s articles are outstanding examples of style and scholarship. Thus, if *America at War* were not to become enormous, I had to omit excellent articles that deserved inclusion. In reviewing and selecting the articles, I tried to pay particular attention to material that both recalled and clarified the American military experience, that gave insight into our national history and character, that explored the individual participation in and reaction to war, and that shed light on people or subjects that in the past have often been ignored or neglected. Some areas of American military history, such as the Second World War, have attracted the attention of many of *MHQ*'s authors, while other areas have not. I tried to maintain a rough chronological balance in the subject matter of the articles. That I could not do so completely, a quick perusal of the table of contents will demonstrate. Despite these problems of omission and balance, I am confident that the readers, whether they be interested laymen or serious students, will find these articles to be just as much a delight to read and study as I have found them to be.

*—Calvin L. Christman*

MARCH 1995
DeSoto, Texas

# America at War

# 1

# The Pequot Massacres

## By Neil Asher Silberman

*Few American-history texts mention or discuss the Pequot War of 1636–37 between the Puritans and the Pequot Indians of Connecticut. Neil Asher Silberman argues, however, that it deserves examination. In both its degree of violence and its covetous motivation, this conflict set the pattern of Anglo–Native American relations through 1890. Marked by racial and cultural differences and often fueled by the settlers' desire for more land, the Indian wars frequently concluded with the near or total extermination of their adversary. Although New England had seen nothing like the Pequot War before, the colonists to the south in Jamestown had already tasted the ferocity of the Indians wars when 350 settlers— the entire settlement numbered under 2,000—died from a surprise Indian attack in 1622. In this and in the Indian wars to come, neither side held the patent on brutality.*

*The Pequot War displayed another element of future Anglo–Native American relations: Both white and Indian combatants deliberately used the other for their own benefit. The Narragansetts and Mohegans willingly joined with the settlers in the war against the Pequots. They were quite content to use the Puritans to gain the upper hand against their traditional Indian rival, just as the colonists were pleased to use the various Indian tribes to their own benefit. It was a partnership that would continue for the next 250 years.*

The old grudge was to be settled decisively, or so the governor and magistrates of the Massachusetts Bay Colony hoped. Few could have predicted, though, that the hastily organized military campaign of fewer than a hundred Englishmen against a small tribe of Indians in southern New England would establish a pattern of violent settler-Indian confrontation that would spread across the entire North American continent during the next 250 years. Until the "Pequot War" of 1636–37, military conflicts in North America between Native Americans and arriving Europeans had been primarily local, meant to settle individual grievances or punish specific cases of kidnapping, murder, or theft.

1

Now, for the first time, not just individuals but entire nations were pitted against one another, with survival or extermination the ultimate stakes.

The explosive chain of events that sparked the first full-scale war between European settlers and Native Americans in New England began on September 5, 1636, when a convoy of three ships from Boston bearing a force of ninety musketeers, officers, and pikemen dropped anchor in Pequot Harbor (now the Thames River between New London and Groton, Connecticut), determined to make a military point. John Endecott, the commander of the Puritan forces, carried instructions from Governor Henry Vane to parley with the Pequots. He was to demand that they immediately hand over the killers of Captain John Stone, an English trader who had been murdered by local Indians at the mouth of the Connecticut River in 1633.

Because three years had passed and that crime had remained unpunished, the Puritans would also demand guaranties that no such incident would happen again. Endecott had further been instructed to demand a huge reparation payment—a thousand strings of the valuable shell beads called *wampum*—and to take several Pequot children back to Boston as hostages. If the Pequots proved so foolish as to ignore or refuse to comply with the Bay Colony's ultimatum, Endecott was authorized to engage their warriors in battle and take the prisoners and the booty by whatever force necessary.

When a Pequot ambassador paddled out in a canoe to find out why the Baymen had come into Pequot Harbor, Endecott instructed his interpreter to reiterate the charges that had remained unresolved since the first meeting between the two peoples in October 1634—almost two years before. In reply, Endecott once more heard the same excuses: that the men responsible for Stone's murder were members of the neighboring tribe of Western Niantics, not Pequots; that Stone had tried to kidnap those Indians and hold them for ransom; and that in any case most of the responsible parties in this unfortunate incident were now dead.

Endecott had neither the time nor the patience to listen to the Pequots' excuses; he had come to establish the Bay Colony's supremacy over southern New England's most powerful tribe. After suggesting to the Pequot ambassador that if his people "desire their own peace and welfare, they will peaceably answer our expectation," he sent the man quickly off to summon Sassacus, the most powerful Pequot sachem (chief). As the ambassador paddled back toward the wooded eastern bank of the river, Endecott ordered his own ship's boats lowered in order to ferry his well-armed forces ashore.

Several hours passed as Pequot messengers shuttled back and forth between the sachem's residence at the village of Weinshauks and the Puritan forces, who stood in a nervous cluster on the riverbank, sweating under their heavy helmets, corselets, and bandoliers. By afternoon it had become clear that the Pequots were merely delaying, and John Endecott resolved to prepare his forces for a fight. Like most of the other military leaders of the Massachusetts Bay Colony, Endecott had served in the English mercenary forces during the Dutch-Spanish wars in the Low

Countries, where he had learned the art of carefully choreographed European combat. Now the time had come for Pequots and Puritans to join in battle. Therefore, directing one of the ensigns to unfurl the colors and ordering the drummer to begin a steady beat, Endecott led his men to a grassy clearing by the river that he chose as a suitable campaign field.

Unfortunately, the Pequots didn't have the benefit of European training. A crowd of spectators soon gathered in obvious amusement at the edge of the clearing to watch the strangely attired Englishmen march to a drumbeat and wave their colorful flag. "None would come near us," complained Captain John Underhill, one of the Puritan officers, "but standing remotely off did laugh at us for our patience." Naturally the Baymen, tense and ready for battle, did not appreciate the Pequots' laughter. And as they angrily fired their muskets at the horrified spectators and relentlessly pursued them into the thick forests of the interior, a new phase of English-Indian relations in southern New England got under way.

"We spent the day burning and spoiling the country," John Underhill later reported with satisfaction, and "no Indians would come near us, but ran from us, as deer from the dogs." By the following day, when the Baymen returned to their ships and set sail for Boston, their demands were still unanswered, but they had learned an important lesson: Static battle formations would be of little use in this American wilderness; more flexible tactics would have to be used. And the Pequots, for their part, returning to their homes to find a grim landscape of burnt wigwams, plundered corn-storage pits, and lifeless bodies, had learned an equally useful lesson. Their conflict with the English would soon become a struggle for survival, and the presence of Puritan forces on their territory would never be a laughing matter again.

Relations between the Pequots and the Puritans of the Massachusetts Bay Colony had never been easy. Each side confronted in the other a more formidable adversary than either had ever encountered. The Pequots, unlike the small, plague-ravished tribes of eastern Massachusetts, were a powerful nation. They had enjoyed more than twenty years of lucrative commerce in beaver pelts with Dutch traders from Manhattan and had extended their authority over the other tribes of the Connecticut shoreline and far up the Connecticut Valley. The Puritans of the Massachusetts Bay Colony, on the other hand, were no less powerful in seventeenth-century New England politics. Unlike the few canny Dutch traders who cared only for commerce, or the few "Pilgrims" of Plymouth, these Englishmen had begun arriving in large numbers in the early 1630s, bringing along their wives, children, hogs, and cattle, to establish new "plantations" and to take over large amounts of land.

Only a sudden decline in the fur trade of the Connecticut Valley had brought the two peoples together. The Pequots, falling out with the Dutch in a violent trade dispute, sought an alliance with Boston in 1634. The leaders of the Bay Colony were wary, but intrigued by the possibilities for trade and settlement. The matter of Captain Stone's murder by Pequot tributaries, though never completely resolved in the treaty negotiations, was not brought up again for nearly two years. But by the summer of 1636, the unpunished death of an Englishman proved a useful pretext for solving an even more pressing problem. For by that time, the leaders of the Bay Colony were engaged in a struggle for power within the colony itself.

During the previous fall and winter, dissident groups from the Bay Colony towns of Dorchester, Watertown, and Newtown (later renamed Cambridge) had founded the towns of Windsor, Hartford, and Wethersfield in a massive westward migration (the first of its kind in American history) to the rich farming lands of the Connecticut Valley. Their aim was to escape the tight political and religious control of the Bay Colony's leaders, and they settled on land traditionally claimed by the Pequots, where English territorial claims were, at best, vague. The leaders of the Bay Colony were determined to maintain unquestioned legal control over the colonists in Connecticut, and that's apparently why they suddenly brought up the issue of Stone's murder. They believed that by conquering or establishing their supremacy over the Pequots, they would inherit a legal claim to the Connecticut Colony's land.

Endecott's hit-and-run attack on Pequot Harbor was, however, a disaster. The Pequots' military response was not long in coming, and it was directed squarely at the small garrison at the mouth of the Connecticut River—Fort Saybrook—which the Bay Colony had established to maintain at least the legal fiction of control over the rebellious plantations farther upstream. All through the fall and winter of 1636–37, Lieutenant Lion Gardiner and his garrison at Fort Saybrook faced the wrath of the Pequots, who monitored all English movements and attacked any Puritans foolish enough to wander beyond the fortifications or to sail up the Connecticut River alone.

As frantic messages from Fort Saybrook arrived in Boston, it became clear that something had to be done. If Fort Saybrook were to fall, the Connecticut settlements would be the next targets. And if the dissident colonists there were sufficiently provoked and defeated the Pequots in battle, they would have earned, by right of territorial conquest, complete freedom from Bay Colony control. So on April 18, 1637, seven months after Endecott's initial attack on Pequot Harbor, the governor and magistrates of the Bay Colony decided to put an end to the question of the rights to Connecticut once and for all. Meeting in General Court, the assembled magistrates and ministers planned not a raid but an enormous expedition, drawing troops from Boston, Plymouth, and Connecticut—under strict Bay Colony supervision—to deal the Pequots a fatal blow.

There might have been a way out of this looming conflict had the Bay Colony really desired peace and friendship with the Pequots, for by the spring of 1637—with the approach of planting season—the Pequots themselves were looking for a way out. After months of attacks and relentless siege tactics against Fort Saybrook, and having satisfied their injured honor with the deaths of thirteen Puritan colonists and traders, they sent three ambassadors to meet with Lieutenant Gardiner. "Have you fought enough?" they asked the English commander. They hoped that diplomacy would now take its course and the conflict would be resolved in the traditional Indian way.

But Gardiner, aware of the Bay Colony's preparations, was in no position to end the hostilities with the Pequots, and his evasive responses to their cease-fire proposal infuriated the Pequot emissaries. "We are Pequots and have killed Englishmen," they angrily responded, "and can kill them as mosquitoes, and we will go to Connecticut and kill men, women, and children, and we will take away the horses, cows, and hogs." Up to this point, they had centered their attacks on Fort Saybrook, but since they had now been dishonorably rebuffed by its commander, they decided to change their strategy. On the morning of April 23, 1637, they struck a more vicious blow against the English. A force of 200 Pequot warriors suddenly descended on the fields of Wethersfield—a village thirty miles upstream from Fort Saybrook—killing six men and three women, and taking two girls away.

In ordering this direct attack on English settlers rather than soldiers, the Pequot leaders ensured their eventual downfall. They had now provoked far more dangerous adversaries than the sedate ministers of the Massachusetts Bay Colony. As news of the attack on Wethersfield spread to the other towns of the Connecticut Colony, its outraged inhabitants recognized that they had finally gained a legitimate justification for independent conquest. Two weeks later, after the assembled leaders of the Connecticut plantations had authorized their own "offensive and defensive war" against the Pequots, a combined force of eighty Connecticut volunteers and a hundred Indian allies set sail down the river toward Fort Saybrook. The Pequot War would soon turn even bloodier. A race for the right of conquest was on.

Major John Mason, commander of the hastily assembled and poorly trained Connecticut militia, arrived at Fort Saybrook on May 16 with a detailed strategy. He was well aware that his force of farmers and tradesmen was not capable of organized battle, and that his erstwhile Indian allies—the inland Mohegans, led by their sachem, Uncas—sought only their own gain by taking advantage of the Pequots' misfortunes. Mason therefore planned to strike a blow at the Pequots that would not require his men to confront experienced warriors in a fair fight on a campaign field. Since terror had proved effective during Endecott's earlier expedition, Mason decided to launch a surprise attack on one of the Pequots' main villages; he believed he could "put them to the sword and save the plunder" for his men and the Connecticut Colony.

Mason, like Endecott, was a veteran of the wars in the Low Countries, yet he had perceptively recognized another European model as more appropriate for his military strategy. Southern New England was not, after all, the land of the Prince of Orange. It was much more like the uncivilized countryside of Ireland, where for the last half century English forces had been trying to subdue the local Irish population and establish their own colonies. In the course of that struggle between armies and clansmen, the English had learned that "uncivilized" enemies could be demoralized by

5

raiding and destroying their villages. Since the technique had proved so successful in the Old World, Mason decided to test it in the New.

Bay Colony leaders were already contemplating a similar strategy. They would attack one of the two main Pequot villages under cover of darkness, execute all its warriors, and spare only the women and children who might be useful as servants or slaves. On May 17—as it turned out, the day *after* Mason's arrival at Fort Saybrook—Governor John Winthrop finally ordered a large Bay Colony expedition to undertake this mission. Three days later he dispatched forty men under Captain Daniel Patrick to rendezvous with the Pequots' eastern neighbors—and longtime enemies—the Narragansetts, to prepare for the upcoming terror campaign. But Mason, it turned out, had departed from Fort Saybrook by sea and was also headed for Narragansett territory, with the same purpose.

When reports reached Boston of Mason's unauthorized expedition, Governor John Winthrop and his colleagues became justifiably concerned. Mason's anticipation of the Bay Colony's tactics, though aimed at the same military objective, would endanger the Bay Colony's territorial claims. So as Captain Patrick and his forces made their way southward through thick swamps and forests toward Narragansett Bay, they dispatched a runner to Major Mason to command him to wait. Mason, however, was intent on pursuing the claims of Connecticut, without any Bay Colony interference. After picking up Narragansett supporters, he crossed westward into Pequot territory at once, to attack where least expected.

The outcome was bloody beyond even the most sordid Puritan expectations. Two hours before dawn on Friday, May 26, 1637, the combined Connecticut and Indian forces reached a ford in the Mystic River, stopped to pray, and then proceeded southward to execute their bloody work. At the foot of a hill occupied by one of the two main Pequot villages, Mason divided his forces for the surprise attack. A sudden burst of English musket fire broke the predawn silence, and as Mason led one detachment of soldiers through a gate in the timber palisade that surrounded the village, they drew their swords, prepared to massacre every Pequot they could lay their hands on—in this case, several hundred women, children, and old men.

The Pequots, fearing an attack by the English in the direction of Fort Saybrook, had concentrated their main force of warriors at the other stockaded village, at Weinshauks, where their sachem, Sassacus, resided. The Pequot village of Mystic (in present-day Groton) was therefore ill equipped to defend itself. As terrified Pequot families began to flee down the main street of the village, they discovered that their only escape route was blocked by the other detachment of Puritans, who, with swords drawn and ready for action, were waiting for them inside the village's southern gate.

By this time Mason had realized that hacking so many terrified noncombatants would probably be too bloody for his inexperienced soldiers, and he ordered them to put their swords away. Making his way to the nearest wigwam, he grabbed a brand from a smoldering hearth fire. "We must burn them!" he screamed to his men. Panic gripped the villagers as Mason's soldiers set the highly flammable reed shelters alight. "And indeed," Mason later reported in his memoirs, "such a dreadful Terror did the Almighty let fall upon their Spirits, that they would fly from us and run into the very Flames."

As the fire spread quickly among the closely packed wigwams, Mason ordered his men to retreat. Once outside the wall, determined not to leave the work unfinished, he arrayed his troops in a tight ring around the burning village to prevent the escape of any of its inhabitants. While some tried desperately to climb over the high stockade wall, others resigned themselves to the flames. Only about forty managed to escape the inferno, but emerging from the gates of the stockade, they were met by a concentrated volley of musket fire. The few who survived the flames and the gunshots, according to one of the Puritan officers, were "received and entertained with the point of a sword." Never before had there been such a complete massacre of noncombatants. Within an hour approximately 500 Pequot men, women, and children were killed outright; only seven were taken prisoner, and not more than a handful escaped with their lives.

"Great and doleful," reported Captain John Underhill, a participant in both Endecott's and Mason's expeditions, "was the bloody sight to the view of young soldiers that had never been in war, to see so many souls lie gasping on the ground, so thick, in some places, that you could hardly pass along." Mohegans and Narragansetts who had joined the expedition in hope of inheriting the Pequots' power were now clearly horrified by the Englishmen's method of war. "It is naught, it is naught," many of them told Captain Underhill before they fled the scene of the killing, "because it is too furious and slays too many men."

But Major John Mason had achieved his objective, which, as a good Puritan, he saw as the work of Almighty God. "Let the whole earth be filled with his Glory," he proudly wrote many years later at the conclusion of his account of the Pequot War. "Thus the Lord was pleased to smite our enemies in the hinder Parts, and to give us their Land for an Inheritance."

The massacre at Mystic was not, however, the end of the smiting. The Massachusetts Bay Colony, determined not to allow the Connecticut forces to claim all the glory, went ahead with its own expedition against the Pequots. At the end of June, after a day of thanksgiving had been declared throughout the Bay Colony to celebrate the English victory over the Pequots, Captain Israel Stoughton arrived in Pequot Harbor with a force of 120 men. His main objective was to finish the killing, but the eradication of the Pequot tribe proved a more difficult task than it originally seemed. After landing his troops and reconnoitering the former heartland of Pequot territory, Stoughton found few potential victims. The village of Weinshauks, once the seat of the powerful sachem Sassacus, had been emptied of all its inhabitants and burned to the ground.

Mason's Connecticut troops were not responsible for this additional act of destruction. After the massacre at Mystic, they had made their way overland to the Pequot River and, running short of ammunition and attacked by hundreds of enraged Pequot warriors, barely escaped with their lives. It was the Pequots themselves who had put the torch to their village at Weinshauks, for in a tribal conclave hastily convened in the aftermath of Mason's attack, Sassacus had been powerless to persuade the other Pequot leaders to continue to fight. The English had shown that they had no standards of honor in combat, and most of the Pequot leaders, fearing that many more of their people would inevitably die in continued fighting, decided that they must now flee. Sassacus had no alternative but to do the same, and after setting fire to their fortress and wigwams, he joined a group of about eighty warriors and their families in a desperate flight westward along the coast toward the distant safety of the Hudson Valley. Another group of about thirty warriors and their families fled eastward to seek shelter with the Narragansetts, and a third group fled into a large swamp a few miles to the north that had long served the tribe as a secure place of refuge, a place they called Ohomowauke, the "Owl's Nest."

Determined to return to Boston with something to show for his efforts, and learning of the whereabouts of that group of fugitives. Captain Stoughton ordered his men to march northward toward the Owl's Nest under cover of night. Somewhere in the vicinity, they captured eighty Pequot women and children, more than half of whom were quickly shipped off to Boston as slaves. Twenty-four Pequot warriors who were also taken prisoner faced immediate execution, but two escaped beheading by promising to lead Stoughton's forces to an even more valuable objective: the hiding place of Sassacus.

The Connecticut colonists, in the meantime, were not willing to have their rights of conquest contested, and they dispatched Major Mason and a force of forty volunteers back to Pequot territory to join Stoughton's pursuit of Sassacus. Sailing westward along the coast, the combined Bay Colony and Connecticut forces finally located their quarry at a place called Sasco—later renamed Fairfield—where about 300 of the fugitive Pequots had taken cover, as was their custom, in a heavily overgrown swamp. The Puritans surrounded the Pequots, as they had at Mystic, but this time the massacre was not as complete. Nearly 200 frightened women, children, and old men surrendered to the English forces and soon followed the earlier Pequot captives into slavery.

The warriors, however, fought hand to hand for their freedom, and though twenty were killed, more than sixty others escaped. Much to the Puritans' disappointment, Sassacus, too, remained at large and, it was reported by reliable Indian informants, finally made his way safely—with only about twenty followers—across the Hudson River into Mohawk territory. But with the conquest and dispersion of his people, Sassacus could no longer depend on his wealth and reputation to protect him from danger. On August 5, 1637, several weeks after the demobilization of the Connecticut and Bay Colony forces, the scalps of Sassacus, his brother, and five other Pequot sachems arrived in Boston via messenger as a sign of the Mohawks' goodwill toward the apparent victors in the Pequot War.

With that symbolic action, the main fighting was over, though the matter of the legal rights of conquest to the Pequots' territory remained for a while unresolved. Connecticut's initial plan to establish a settlement at Pequot Harbor was firmly vetoed by the Bay Colony's leaders, who claimed that they were entitled to share in the spoils. Angry petitions flew back and forth between Boston and Hartford until eventually the two sides reached an uneasy compromise. After a long legal battle, title to the now largely depopulated Pequot territory was granted to the Connecticut Colony, though with a provision permitting a significant Bay Colony presence there.

In 1646 John Winthrop, Jr., the eldest son of the Bay Colony's governor, established a new settlement at the former Pequot village of Nameag, just across the Pequot River from the "campaign field" where John Endecott and the Bay Colony forces had struck their first violent blow. To wipe out all memories of the earlier Pequot presence in this region, Winthrop renamed the place "New London" and rechristened the nearby Pequot River "the Thames."

IT'S CLEAR TODAY that the Puritans of Massachusetts and Connecticut did not succeed in wiping out the Pequot tribe as thoroughly as they had hoped. Just off Connecticut State Route 214, about nine miles northeast of New London, the modern houses, clinic, and tribal offices on the Mashantucket Pequot Reservation provide ample evidence that the Pequot nation refused to die. The massacres of 1637, for all their savagery, killed only about a quarter of the Pequot population—primarily those in large villages along the coast. With the extermination of the old tribal leadership, scattered bands began a long struggle to survive.

One of the largest groups was slowly hemmed into the tract of forest and swampland known as Mashantucket, around their traditional place of refuge, the Owl's Nest. During the eighteenth century, much of that original 3,000-acre reservation was taken over by arriving Connecticut settlers, and by the middle of the nineteenth century, barely 200 acres were left. By 1910 only four Pequot families lived on the reservation, and by the early 1970s only three elderly women remained. But the old tribal traditions were never completely forgotten by the Pequot families who lived in other parts of southern New England, and when the state of Connecticut proposed that the last, tiny fragment of Pequot territory become a public park, the surviving Pequots were unwilling to see their claim to the land taken away from them.

In 1975 Richard Hayward, the grandson of one of the remaining residents of the reservation, began mobilizing his people for the legal and political struggle that eventually brought the Mashantucket branch of the Pequot tribe to life again. In 1983, with federal recognition and a cash settlement of $900,000 to compensate them for the lost lands of their original reservation, the Mashantucket Pequots began to buy back every available parcel of adjoining real estate. Even though the old tribal lands, now occupied by cities, towns, shopping malls, beach resorts, and even a nuclear submarine base, could never be fully reclaimed, the Mashantucket Pequots at least established their reputation as wronged parties in early New England history.

In the woods just beyond the tribal offices, on every new parcel of land added to the reservation, and along the nearby coast of Long Island Sound, Dr. Kevin McBride and a team of archaeologists from the University of Connecticut have begun a painstaking reconstruction of 10,000 years of Pequot cultural history. McBride and his staff, supported by funds from the tribe's annual budget, have already mapped and uncovered dozens of ancient Pequot sites, ranging from prehistoric rock shelters to seventeenth-century hunting camps and even apparently an early-seventeenth-century settlement thought to be the doomed Pequot village of Mystic. These finds provide modern Pequots with a powerful new connection to their land and traditions, but have also reawakened bitter memories of the Pequot War.

Hayward, now serving as tribal chairman, has a unique perspective on that tragic seventeenth-century conflict, and he spoke about it frankly in his office at tribal headquarters. "I can't help thinking about that old man," he said. "I mean that ambassador who paddled out in his canoe when the English soldiers first arrived here. What could he have said to avoid all the bloodshed? What could he have done? So much has changed here that it's probably impossible to guess how things could have been different. But we've got to keep on learning all we can about our history. And we've got to use the Pequot War as a lesson to ourselves and our children—about how important it is to keep our traditions alive."

The landscape of the Pequots' traditional tribal territory has changed dramatically since the early seventeenth century, but the sites of the major episodes of the Pequot War can still be found. At Saybrook Point, at the mouth of the Connecticut River, a small public park and a low timber fence mark the approximate location of the fort in which the small Puritan garrison was besieged and attacked by enraged Pequot warriors throughout the fall and winter of 1636–37. Nothing is left of the original Fort Saybrook; its remains were obliterated at the end of the nineteenth century by the construction of a railroad roundhouse and right-of-way. Today, the drifting scent of fried clams from the beachside drive-ins and the continuous hum of pleasure boats cruising up and down the Connecticut River make it difficult to visualize the complete isolation of Fort Saybrook when it stood at the edge of the tidal salt marshes as a lonely symbol of English authority.

A few miles to the east, Pequot Harbor—now the Thames River—is busy with seagoing traffic from the marinas and ferry dock of New London on the western shore and from the naval base at Groton on the east. The riverside "campaign field" where the Puritans, led by John Endecott, first challenged the Pequots is now covered by the sprawling modern warehouses, workshops, and dry-dock facilities of the Electric Boat shipyard, home and birthplace of America's nuclear submarine fleet. Farther east, the remains of the Pequot War's bloodiest battle lie buried in a quiet residential neighborhood of Groton. In the backyards and gardens of the expensive homes along Pequot Avenue, Dr. McBride has excavated portions of what seems likely to be the village destroyed before dawn on May 26, 1637, by Major John Mason and his force of Connecticut volunteers.

A larger-than-lifesize statue of Mason snatching his sword from his scabbard and striding manfully forward stands in the middle of a small traffic circle on Pequot Avenue. Erected by the state of Connecticut, belatedly, in 1889 to mark the 250th anniversary of the Mystic battle, its bronze inscription praises "the heroic achievement of Major John Mason and his comrades who near this spot in 1637 overthrew the Pequot Indians and preserved the settlements from destruction." But Mason's military achievement is no longer a cause for celebration in Groton; the Pequots' legal battle to regain their tribal territory has become a source of concern. In fact, many Pequot Avenue homeowners were reluctant to allow archaeological excavations on their property, fearing that the discovery of ancient Pequot relics would spark a modern Pequot land suit.

The Pequots, however, are realistic. They have abandoned their territorial claims along the coastline and are devoting all their efforts to the development of their small inland reservation. There at Mashantucket, contemporary town houses, tribal offices, a clinic, and a highly lucrative bingo hall—attracting eager gamblers from as far away as Hartford, Providence, and Boston—have sprung up on land cleared from the forest. But while the battle sites of the Pequot War are today largely obscured, the Pequots have not forgotten them. Just off Connecticut Route 2, near the thickly wooded swampland that once served as the Pequots' traditional place of refuge, stands a symbol of both modernization and continuity: an up-to-date restaurant built and operated by the Mashantucket Pequot tribal council and called, appropriately enough, "The Owl's Nest."

*SPRING 1989*

The author of *Between Past and Present: Archaeology, Ideology, and Nationalism in the Modern Middle East* (1989), Neil Asher Silberman is an archaeologist and historian. His latest book is *Invisible America: Uncovering Our Hidden Past* (to be published in 1995).

# 2

# Braddock's Defeat

## By Thomas Fleming

*Almost since the day the French and their Indian allies destroyed the army of Major General Edward Braddock along the steep banks of the Monongahela River, Americans have mocked the British effort to fight a European-style war in the heart of the American wilderness. With their colorful uniforms, massed troops, and rigid commanders, the British forces appeared destined to be ambushed, and the result seemed a case of British hubris and arrogance versus French savvy and courage. Yet Thomas Fleming contends that General Braddock deserves better from history. Personally courageous but ill served at critical moments by both his officers and men, Braddock was, in the last analysis, unlucky. That fact cost him his life and his reputation. For other figures in the battle, this clash in western Pennsylvania was merely their introduction to the pages of American history; the battle's roster—with such names as Washington, Pontiac, and Boone—reads like a who's who of early American history. And one cannot help wondering, if only for a moment, what role others might have played in the future had they not been among the fallen in this opening battle of the French and Indian War.*

No one in the raw new Potomac River port of Alexandria—indeed, in the entire colony of Virginia—had ever seen anything like it. From a fleet of Sixteen Ships came boatload after boatload of British regulars in red coats and buff breeches. A thousand strong, they marched from the waterfront up the town's only street, forty drums (twenty to a regiment) thundering, almost as many fifes shrilling. At the head of each regiment floated colors of fringed yellow silk, with rose-and-thistle-wreathed Roman numerals on them, announcing that they were the 44th and 48th King's Foot.

Three days later, on March 26, 1755, the regiments' commander disembarked from a fifty-gun warship. He was Major General Edward Braddock, a stout, sturdy, red-faced man of sixty who had spent forty-five years in the British army, most of them in the elite Coldstream Guards. The son of a major general, virtually born into the army, Braddock had a reputation for being bluff and often blunt to the point of rudeness. But Virginia's acting governor, Robert Dinwiddie, called him "a sensible moderate gentleman" after their first meeting, in which Dinwiddie informed him that the Americans had done practically nothing to prepare for the undeclared war that Braddock was about to launch.

Braddock and his soldiers had come to settle a quarrel between France and England about who owned most of North America. It was a dispute that had been sputtering for almost a century. The first shots in the latest round had been fired in 1754 by one of Virginia's own, a twenty-two-year-old militia colonel named George Washington. Leading a patrol through the western woods in June of that year, he had ambushed a party of French and Indians, killing their leader. The outraged French claimed the dead man was an ambassador coming to Virginia to negotiate peace. Backed by hundreds of Indian allies, they soon assailed Washington and his regiment of some 350 militiamen in a makeshift fort and forced him to sign a humiliating surrender, in which he admitted (in French, which he could not read) that he had assassinated the ambassador.

In London the French claims were greeted with more than a little skepticism. Since 1748, when the two great powers had signed a putative peace at Aix-la-Chapelle, ending the War of the Austrian Succession, commissioners had been meeting in Paris to iron out the details of the treaty. On North American matters, progress was zero. The French laid claim to everything watered by the rivers that flowed into the St. Lawrence, the Great Lakes, and the Mississippi. That gave them the right to build forts and station troops in the heart of New York on Lake Champlain and on the crests of the Allegheny Mountains.

The British countered by claiming, in the words of America's first historian of the quarrel, Francis Parkman, "every mountain, forest or prairie" where the wide-ranging war parties of their ferocious allies, the Iroquois, had taken a scalp. This entitled them to everything between the Alleghenies and the Mississippi, plus most of what is now the Canadian province of Ontario. The claims and counterclaims were almost mutually exclusive, and in 1755 the peace commissioners had abandoned their task, leaving four volumes of allegations, arguments, and so-called proofs for pamphleteers to chew on.

While the French talked for six years in Paris, they acted in North America. They built additional forts at key points along their riverine empire, sent armed parties swarming from Quebec to warn off American traders and settlers pushing west, and exhorted their Indian allies to support them, adding terror to their repertoire of intimidation. In Virginia these acts of aggression stirred outrage and alarm. Its charter entitled the colony to claim all the land between its northern and southern boundaries "from sea to sea." Far more influential were the claims of a number of its leading citizens, who in 1747 had formed a real-estate operation called the Ohio Company. Granted 500,000 acres of land by George II, they dreamed of owning and colonizing the Ohio River valley and becoming millionaires. Among the stockholders were Dinwiddie and young Washington.

Coolly dismissing the Ohio Company as agent provocateurs, in 1754 the French had banished a handful of frontiersmen Dinwiddie had sent to the forks of the Ohio to build a small fort on the site of present-day Pittsburgh. Within twenty-four hours after the group's departure, the French had axmen in the woods felling trees for a far more formidable fort, which they named Duquesne in honor of their royal governor. Dinwiddie had responded by sending Washington and his regiment of militiamen to expel them—with disastrous results.

The governor's agitation, which was probably multiplied by his Ohio Company shares, had failed to stir much response among the Americans in nearby colonies. Pennsylvania competed with Virginia for the Indian trade and had its own group of leading citizens with designs on the Ohio Valley's real estate. The southern colonies found it hard to grasp the idea of danger from distant Canada and were loath to vote money to protect frontiersmen, whom they considered largely disreputable. But Dinwiddie's letters to England did persuade the home government, irked by six years of verbal smoke screens in Paris, to dispatch Braddock and his two regiments to Virginia.

The general's orders seemed to show a surprising amount of sagacity in the somnolent administration of the lisping duke of Newcastle, a prime minister whose witlessness anticipated Gilbert and Sullivan. (A typical anecdote: Someone told Newcastle that Annapolis should be defended. He fluttered about his office like an agitated moth for five minutes, then asked, "Where is Annapolis?") In fact Newcastle had little to do with Braddock's orders; they came from the commander of the British army, Prince William Augustus, duke of Cumberland, the third son of George II. The gruff, rotund prince, sometimes called the boy general, was a professional soldier who had stopped the French-financed Scotch army at Culloden in 1746, saving his father's throne. For several years he had been saying France was plotting another war, and he had urged Britain to strike first.

Braddock was told to attack the French fort at the forks of the Ohio— and also to demolish five other forts in the North. Some historians have ridiculed the British government—and Braddock—for these orders, which supposedly were based on ignorance of the geographic realities of America. From a strategic point of view, however, the orders had much to recommend them. They gave Braddock the initiative—and did not, as some have assumed, require him and his two regiments to do the whole job. The directives included plans to raise two more regiments in America and allowed Braddock the freedom to deputize subordinates to handle the northern assaults, using these troops and American militia.

Cumberland also cautioned Braddock to be "particularly careful that the troops be not thrown into a panic by the Indians, with whom they are yet unacquainted." Both knew British regulars had a tendency to run away when frightened. That had happened at the Battle of Prestonpans in 1745, when howling Scottish Highlanders had routed an entire British army. The duke may have reminded Braddock that among the fastest sprinters that day were the men of the 44th and 48th regiments.

With a vigor few have given him credit for, Braddock went to work as a theater commander the moment he arrived in Virginia. He sent messengers pounding up and down the Atlantic coast to ask royal governors to a conference in Annapolis to work out plans for the general offensive. Executed with energy, the offensive would pin down the few regulars France had in America and take advantage of the enormous edge in manpower the million-plus Americans had over the 90,000 Canadian French.

Braddock also tartly reminded the governors that the king expected their assemblies to vote substantial sums to finance this campaign and provide men, food, and wagons to keep it going. Parliament had done its part: It had voted £50,000 to launch the assault—part of a £4-million increase in the military budget, which George II blandly explained in his speech to Parliament would be used to guarantee peace and promote the trade and prosperity of the colonies.

The French, after debating whether to call for another round of peace talks, decided on an armed riposte. They began building flatboats in the Channel ports for an invasion of England—and ordered eight regiments of regulars, 3,000 men, to America, under the command of one of their best generals, Baron Ludwig August Dieskau.

By the time Braddock arrived in Alexandria to take command of his troops, he had been in America five weeks and had already encountered enough frustrations to exasperate a far more patient man. There were no trustworthy maps of the wilderness he was about to invade. The recruits he was turning up to flesh out his regiments to their full strength of 700 each were, to the general's experienced eyes, "very indifferent men." Many of them were leftovers from the shiploads of convicts the British regularly sent to the colonies to keep Britain's prison population manageable. For extra irritation, someone stole one of Braddock's horses from the stables of the Raleigh Tavern just before he left Williamsburg.

On March 30, Easter Sunday, Braddock tried to boost the morale of his regulars by giving them each an extra twenty shillings to compensate them for their winter crossing of the Atlantic. They proceeded to buy up all the peach brandy in Alexandria's only tavern and go on a weeklong drunk. To restore order, the infuriated colonel of the 44th Regiment, Sir Peter Halkett, had to threaten to withhold rations.

Meanwhile, at his residence in one of the town's best private houses, with a guard of thirty privates commanded by an ensign at the gate, Braddock received the local gentry. He was agreeable enough to dinner invitations, but he retained his hard soldier's eye when someone asked to join his army. One of his harshest rejections fell on vain, lanky Richard Henry Lee, scion of one of the colony's most influential families. Braddock took one look and told him to go home, thereby incurring the Lee clan's enmity.

On the other hand, Braddock had responded enthusiastically to twenty-three-year-old George Washington. This strapping six-footer had drawn a hearty welcome from Braddock and an offer of a captain's commission with the flattering title of aide-de-camp. It was not only a case of one born soldier recognizing another one; Washington had been to the forks of the Ohio, could read a map—and could draw one.

Washington was touchy about plummeting from colonel to captain in less than a year. He had resigned in 1754 partly because he had found himself outranked by several officers with captain's commissions from the king. He negotiated laboriously—and lugubriously—until Braddock cheerfully agreed to let him serve as an aide without a commission. Braddock even agreed to let him stay home and put the affairs of his new estate, Mount Vernon, in order before joining the army at Wills Creek in western Maryland, the jumping-off point for the march to the Ohio.

Washington was not the only actor to step onto American history's stage under Braddock's aegis. The lieutenant colonel of the 44th Regiment was Thomas Gage. who was destined to send British regulars to fight embattled farmers in Concord, Massachusetts, twenty years later. And in one of the 44th's companies was a lean, voluble lieutenant named Charles Lee, a future major general in the Revolutionary army of the as yet unimaginable United States of America. Soon they would be joined by Captain Horatio Gates, who would humble a British army at Saratoga for this same improbable nation. He was leading a company of New York recruits to Virginia.

While his men drilled, got drunk, or chased the few available women in Alexandria. Braddock grappled with his major problems: food and transportation. He had to carry all his salt beef and flour with him into the wilderness—along with fourteen pieces of artillery. Fort Duquesne, with rivers on two sides, would require siege tactics. He had brought sixteen artillery wagons from England, but no horses. Braddock and his quartermaster, Colonel Sir John St. Clair, estimated they would need another 200 wagons and 2,500 horses to travel the 110 miles from Wills Creek to the Ohio. Governor Dinwiddie had flourished contracts guaranteeing delivery of these necessities by May 10. But as April ebbed away, few of them appeared, and even fewer were satisfactory. The horses, in particular, were the worst jades Braddock had ever seen.

Cheating the government was bad enough, but the Virginians carried things to excess by doing the same thing to Braddock's officers, who had to buy horses too. One officer wrote of visiting a plantation for a hearty supper, after which he was sold a horse that as "soon as it was cool, showed itself dog lame and moon-blind." Denouncing both the inhabitants and the weather, which went from hot to snowy in the same week, he wrote: "I reckon the day I bought my commission the most unhappy in my life excepting that in which I landed in this country."

After irritating delays, Braddock finally met on April 15 with Dinwiddie and the governors of Massachusetts, New York, Pennsylvania, Maryland, and North Carolina. He laid before them the plans for the general offensive and got an enthusiastic response. William Shirley of Massachusetts—whose moody son, William, Jr., was serving as Braddock's secretary—fancied himself a man of action, perhaps because he had married a French girl a third his age during the year he spent in Paris rebutting France's American claims. He eagerly accepted the responsibility for assaulting Niagara, a crucial choke point in the French network of forts. Braddock put him in command of the two regiments to be raised in the North and gave him money to build two sixty-ton warships on Lake Ontario.

Sir William Johnson, the Indian agent for New York, who had accompanied his governor, took charge of the attack on the fort at Crown Point, near the southern end of Lake Champlain, and promised to bring the Iroquois into the battle on the British side. A third expedition of New England men was to attack three forts in Nova Scotia and expel French power from that province.

On the surface the conference was a triumph of strategic planning. Braddock had no idea that the governor of South Carolina, the one man who could have brought the powerful Cherokees and Catawbas into his attack on Fort Duquesne, had not even been invited by Dinwiddie. The ambitious Scotsman wanted most of the credit for supporting Braddock. He had sent his own emissaries to the Cherokees, who ignored them. Hoping for the best, Dinwiddie smoothly assured Braddock that the savages always wanted to be on the winning side and would join them when they reached Wills Creek with their mass of men and cannon. Inexperienced in dealing with the Indians, Dinwiddie did not realize that the rout of Washington and his militiamen in 1754 had already swung most of the western tribes to the French side.

A more visible failure of the conference was the governors' rueful report that not one of their assemblies was willing to vote a shilling to support Braddock. While this lack of financial backing from the Americans was infuriating, it did not endanger the expedition; Braddock had a "contingent account" from the home government to meet expenses. Newcastle, obsessed with the fear that a war would bankrupt England, had urged him to count his shillings carefully. Now Braddock wrote the duke that the contingencies were going to be much more expensive than "Your Grace imagines."

Braddock continued to be far more worried about food and transport than about Indian allies. Over wretched roads his two regiments marched up opposite sides of the Potomac to Wills Creek. The governor of Maryland had promised that Braddock would find wagons and a generous supply of horses and cattle at Frederick. Braddock found nothing. St. Clair, who had gone ahead to Wills Creek, reported no sign of Dinwiddie's supplies there. Officers scoured the countryside but could not even find anything to commandeer.

For a few days Braddock considered abandoning the expedition. He might have done so if Benjamin Franklin and his son William had not ridden into Frederick to confer with him. As deputy postmaster general for the colonies, Franklin had been summoned to set up an express service that would enable Braddock to communicate as rapidly as possible with the home government and his deputy commanders in the North. When he heard Braddock raging about his lack of wagons, Franklin remarked that almost every farmer in Pennsylvania owned a wagon and would be glad to lease it to the government for the generous fee Braddock was offering, fifteen shillings a day.

The general seized on his suggestion like a drowning man clutching for a spar. He gave Franklin £800 and empowered him to advertise for wagons in Pennsylvania. Franklin went to work writing a clever proclamation that ended by warning the largely German farmers that if they did not accept the offer, "Sir John St. Clair, *the hussar,*" would come to get the wagons "with a body of soldiers." St. Clair was in fact an ex-cavalryman. The word *hussar* awakened memories of European pillagers and produced a magical flow of wagons and horses.

Franklin, who had an opinion about everything, asked Braddock if he worried about being attacked by Indians while his column, almost four miles long, toiled toward the Ohio. Couldn't this line of march be "cut like a thread into several pieces" and be unable to support the severed parts? Writing fifteen years later in his autobiography, Franklin remembered Braddock dismissing this possibility. "These savages may, indeed, be a formidable enemy to your raw American militia," Braddock supposedly said, "but upon the King's regulars . . . it is impossible they should make any impression."

There are strong reasons for doubting that Braddock ever said this. His discussions with Cumberland and his entire conduct of the expedition suggest that he and his superiors were extremely worried about the Indians. But he thought they could be beaten with the same massed firepower and bayonet charges that had defeated the wild Scots at Culloden Field.

Wills Creek and its fort did nothing to lighten Braddock's mood. The fort was a pathetic green-timbered affair, which one of Braddock's engineers saw no point in improving; he said it could be knocked to pieces by three six-pounders. Braddock named the shambles Fort Cumberland in honor of his patron and told the engineer to do his best. Nothing seemed to go right. Beef from Virginia had not arrived because the assembly had declined to pay for it and the contractor declared the deal null and void. The beef from Maryland was rotten. A raging Braddock sent officers to arrest the contractor, but he had taken to the woods.

Arriving on May 10, Washington found the general ready to damn the entire continent of North America. Washington defended his countrymen. In a letter to his friend William Fairfax, he described a typical scene: "Instead of blaming individuals as he ought, he charges all his disappointments to public supineness; and looks upon the country, I believe, as void of both honor and honesty; we have frequent disputes on this head, which are maintained by warmth on both sides."

But a genuine affection had taken root between the gruff general and the diffident young Virginian. It began to flourish even though Washington took issue with more than Braddock's opinion of Americans. At Wills Creek he watched the regulars drill each day and practice platoon firing—the standard European way to repel an attack. He told Braddock these tactics would not work in the forest. Years later a survivor of the expedition remembered young Washington in his blue uniform, "two thumbs [in] the armpits of his vest," lecturing Braddock on wilderness fighting. With a twinkle in his eye, Braddock growled: "What think you of this from a beardless boy?"

One of the reasons Braddock stayed with the standard tactics was a report from England warning him about the 3,000 French regulars heading for Canada. Another reason was that the gush of flame and smoke from 150 leveled muskets impressed the Indians at Wills Creek. About 100 had shown up, led by Pennsylvania trader George Croghan. Braddock gave them speeches, presents, and rum, and encouraged them to put on their war paint and dance and howl for the troops. He thought it was a good way to familiarize his men with their fighting style. The regulars watched the braves rush each other with raised tomahawks and go through the motions of scalping a victim. One flourished a real scalp, taken in an earlier battle. Many think this only tightened, rather than toughened, everyone's nerves.

Unfortunately, the Indians brought their wives and children. The wives—and perhaps a few daughters—were soon the rage of the camp, among both officers and men. The Indian husbands did not seem to mind, but Braddock disapproved mightily. Discipline was unraveling before his eyes. He told the Indians to take their women and children home. They obeyed, but few of the men returned. With their numbers shrunk to fifty, Braddock decided they were not numerous enough to help him but were too many to feed on the march. He sent home all but ten, who were retained as scouts.

Though still short of wagons and horses, Braddock had to march. Letters from the North reported that troops for the assault on Nova Scotia were at sea, escorted by three warships. William Shirley had recruited his regiment and was moving toward Albany to link up with a corps raised in New Jersey. At Albany, William Johnson was assembling a largely New England army to attack Crown Point. A wandering Delaware Indian brought a report from Fort Duquesne that the garrison numbered only 100 men but they were expecting another 900 soon. It was vital to beat these regulars to the site.

On June 7, with 300 sweating axmen ahead of them leveling a twelve-foot-wide road, the 2,200-man army slogged out of Fort Cumberland into the wilderness. The two regiments had been recruited to full strength. Some 1,400 of the men wore red coats, and there were also three companies of blue-coated Virginians, two companies of New Yorkers, and single companies of North and South Carolinians wearing the same color. Serving as a wagoner and blacksmith in the North Carolina company was the future founder of Kentucky, twenty-one-year-old Daniel Boone. Handling the reins of another team was nineteen-year-old Daniel Morgan, a future brigadier general in the Revolution.

No one was in a particularly happy mood. The bloody flux—dysentery—had begun to appear among the men, from the rotten beef and bacon. The regulars were not enthusiastic about being turned into road builders. The senior officers had become disenchanted with the whole expedition. Colonel Thomas Dunbar of the 48th complained about his health and threatened to go home. Sir Peter Halkett of the 44th exuded pessimism. Quartermaster St. Clair, whose temper was as short as Braddock's and whose tongue was even sharper, sulked because the general did not take his advice. In response, the general's military family, led by his chief aide, Captain Robert Orme of the Coldstream Guards, formed a protective circle around him. Orme insulted Dunbar to his face, and Braddock let him get away with it. He had decided that Dunbar was an old woman.

Too much should not be made of this bickering, which always goes on in the military. Soldiers are blunt. Far more serious was the pace of Braddock's march. The toiling axmen and the second-rate horses, hauling 1,300-pound cannon and tons of food, were moving only two miles a day. An exasperated Braddock, knowing his senior officers were looking for a chance to call it quits, sought Washington's advice. The big Virginian staggered from his tent. He was down with dysentery, feverish, his head splitting. He urged Braddock to leave most of the heavy artillery and food behind and push ahead with a picked force, traveling as light as possible.

This advice gave Braddock a chance to get rid of Dunbar. He put the colonel in charge of the rear echelon and took the best horses and troops for his flying column. Wagons were limited to thirty, and the number of horses per team was increased to add speed. Packhorses carried much of the equipment. St. Clair was sent ahead with 400 ax swingers to clear the road. The column, counting St. Clair's men, numbered 1,459 officers and men.

Washington was not among them. He was prostrate. He begged Braddock to send for him when they reached the fort so he could participate in the final assault. The general promised him on his word of honor.

The lightened column advanced at a respectable five or six miles a day. Often Braddock and his wagons caught up to St. Clair and his axmen and the two forces camped together for the night. The strictest security was maintained against surprise. Flanking troops prowled the woods a hundred yards from both sides of the column. As they drew closer to the Ohio, they slept with loaded guns at their sides. Whenever they halted, the men faced outward, two deep, with shouldered arms.

They had no contact with the enemy, except for obscene warnings scrawled in charcoal on random trees and one or two brushes with scouting Indians, who killed several stragglers. Braddock ordered redoubled vigilance and tried to persuade his ten Indians to range well ahead of the column. They declined to do so until July 5, when two of them prowled close enough to observe the French fort. They saw no sign of any plan to ambush the column along the twenty miles left to march. Christopher Gist, a Virginia frontiersman and friend of Washington's who had scouted on his own, confirmed their account.

The next day Washington rejoined the column. Too weak to ride a horse, he arrived in a wagon, determined not to miss the assault on the fort. He had a personal score to settle with the French commander, Pierre Claude Pecaudy, the sieur de Contrecoeur, who had accused him of assassinating the French ambassador.

Contrecoeur was no longer the commander of Fort Duquesne; he had been relieved at his own request by Canadian-born Captain Daniel Beaujeu. But he was still at the fort; he did not want to be accused of fleeing from the British. How to handle Braddock's attack, neither he nor Beaujeu could decide. Their scouts had reported Braddock's army at 3,000 men marching "so well on their guard, always ready for battle," that it seemed futile to attack them with small detachments. The fort's garrison consisted of only a platoon of regulars and about 200 Canadian militia. Encamped outside the walls was their only hope of victory—some 800 Indians. But the size of the British army and its train of artillery had profoundly discouraged the red men.

What to do? Surrender after a brief siege? Or blow up the fort and retreat? To Beaujeu and Contrecoeur, these seemed the only options. Just one subordinate captain, Jean Dumas, favored attacking Braddock on the march. By the time he talked the wavering Beaujeu into making the attempt, Braddock was only a day from the fort. But the Indians remained uninterested. "What, my father, do you wish to die and sacrifice us?" one warrior asked Beaujeu. He spent most of the day arguing with the chiefs, to no avail.

Eight miles away, on July 8, Braddock convened a final council of war. Sir Peter Halkett thought they ought to wait for Dunbar to join them for the final assault. Washington said that would take three weeks, because Dunbar's horses were used up. Braddock called Halkett a fool and told him they would attack with their 1,400 men. On the advice of his scouts, Braddock decided to avoid a final slog across some difficult ridges. They would approach the fort by two fords of the winding Monongahela, which would give them access to a trail that led along the east bank of the river directly to their goal. It was risky because the second ford was an ideal site for an ambush: The trees were thick and the riverbank was twelve feet high.

Again exercising maximum caution, Braddock ordered Lieutenant Colonel Thomas Gage and an advance party of 160 men to march at dawn on July 9 and seize both fords. If they were attacked, there would be plenty of time for the main force to come to their aid, or take defensive positions if the advance was driven back.

At Fort Duquesne the Indians had spent the night in council. When Beaujeu asked them to come with him to attack the British, they still said no. Undeterred, Beaujeu rolled barrels of powder and bullets to the gates of the fort and broke the barrels open. "Will you let your father go alone?" he shouted. "I am certain of defeating them." Several younger chiefs, notably an Ottawa named Pontiac, wavered.

Into the fort rushed a scouting party of thirty braves who had exchanged shots with the British advance guard at the upper ford. They gave Beaujeu the exact route of the British advance. No time was to be lost if he was going to ambush them at the lower ford. "You see, my friends, the English are going to throw themselves into the lion's mouth!" he shouted. "Those who love their father, follow me."

With wild yells, the Indians changed their minds. They crowded up to the barrels, scooping out bullets, filling their powder horns. But the frantic Beaujeu had to wait while they put on their paint and whipped themselves up with dances. He organized his white men—Dumas and another captain, four lieutenants, six ensigns, and about sixty cadets who were capable of functioning as junior officers, giving their force a remarkably high leadership quotient. With the platoon of regulars and the Canadian militia, they numbered about 250. The French officers stripped to the waist like their savage allies, cocked hats and silver gorgets around their necks as their only symbols of authority. Beaujeu led the way at a dead run to reach the lower ford before Braddock.

They were already too late. Gage and his men had done their job. As Braddock led the main army across the upper ford, with 400 men posted on high ground to cover their passage, a messenger from Gage reported that the lower ford had been seized without firing a shot. St. Clair and his axmen and engineers were leveling the twelve-foot banks for the wagons and were beginning to work on the final leg of the forest road.

The good news swept through the ranks. A captain's batman, who kept a journal of the expedition, wrote: "We began our march again, beating the grenadier's march all the way. There never was an army in the world in more spirits." One of the engineers noted in his journal that the men "hugged themselves with joy at our good luck." The batman milked a cow and fixed a milk punch for his captain.

Still Braddock was cautious. He crossed this second ford by the book, first drawing up his wagons and artillery on the riverbank and posting pickets on the high ground behind them. Then, with Washington and his other aides and senior officers beside him, he studied the opposite bank for a sign of danger. Shortly after noon, as the men began to grow restless in the hot sun, the grade was finished on the opposite bank. Braddock ordered St. Clair and Gage to advance through the forest until 3:00 P.M. and bivouac; they would invest the fort the following day. Braddock had finally accepted the universal assumption that the French, having failed to defend the ford, were going to stay inside Fort Duquesne.

Drums thundering, fifes shrilling, the army splashed through the shallow water and up the bank into the forest, following the axmen and Gage down the twelve-foot-wide road they were cutting. The woods were fairly free of underbrush. Horses and even wagons could pass among the trees. Flanking parties led by sergeants covered both sides of the column. Prowling scouts and a detachment of Virginia horsemen were at the head to sniff out an ambush. Behind them came an engineer, marking the trees to be cut for the road, and behind him two companies of grenadiers, the best and biggest soldiers from each regiment.

Suddenly the scouts and horsemen recoiled and went rushing past the engineer. Peering through the woods, he saw a man, probably Captain Beaujeu, running toward him, his silver gorget gleaming on his bare neck. The man turned and waved his hat to the right and left to send the Indians down both flanks of the column. They streamed past him, howling the war whoop.

Panic swept through the grenadiers. They almost followed the fleeing engineer, scouts, and horsemen, but a command to fix bayonets steadied them. They quickly formed into a line of battle and delivered a full volley, the front rank kneeling. Once, twice, three times their guns boomed, echoing through the forest like thunderclaps. A bullet from the third volley hit Beaujeu in the forehead, killing him instantly. The terrified Canadian militia fled screaming "Sauve qui peut!"—"Save yourself if you can!" A good many Indians followed them. Only the platoon of French regulars stood firm.

For a few seconds it looked as if Braddock's men were about to achieve a rout. "God save the king!" roared an ensign. The grenadiers huzzahed and surged forward, bayonets lowered. But Captain Dumas, now in command, proceeded to demonstrate how courage and daring can turn a battle around. With reckless disregard for his own safety, he steadied his platoon of regulars, and they stopped the grenadiers with a volley. He ordered the rest of the French officers to regain control of the Indians and lead them along the British flanks.

Lieutenant Colonel Gage, in command of the advance guard, now demonstrated his lack of military judgment. If he had reconnoitered at the head of the column, he might have seen there was only a platoon of Frenchmen, whom his 160 men could have demolished with a determined bayonet charge. But instead, he ordered his men to fall back. He thought the flanking Indians were going to cut him off. His panicky grenadiers blundered into the axmen behind them, who in turn recoiled on the column's 800-man center, which was advancing on the double to their assistance.

Simultaneously, the French and Indians on the British right seized a commanding ridge that Gage should have occupied as soon as he reached the east side of the ford. From it they unleashed a hail of musket balls on the red-coated men in the road. Lesser but still deadly fire poured from thickets between the road and the river on the left. Braddock, in the regulation position at the rear of the column, galloped forward with his secretary, William Shirley, Jr., Washington, Captain Orme, and another aide, Captain Roger Morris of the 44th.

A bullet in the thigh knocked Orme out of the saddle almost instantly. Colonel St. Clair staggered past them, his shoulder shattered by an early bullet. "For God's sake, the rising ground on our right!" he shouted, and passed out. Young Shirley went down with a bullet in his brain; then Captain Morris was wounded. Riderless horses plunged wildly through the forest. The British officers, proudly refusing to abandon their saddles, were prime targets.

Braddock found his men huddled in the road firing volleys at their invisible assailants. Artillerymen manning two six-pounders under Gage's command added to the thunder for a few minutes but soon abandoned these guns as their casualties mounted. The flanking parties had already been driven in or killed. Drifting clouds of gunsmoke added to the confusion. Braddock saw that he had to seize the high ground on the right and get the column moving forward. He ordered a lieutenant colonel to attack the ridge. On horseback, the officer led a hundred men up the slope and was promptly shot out of the saddle. The men straggled back to the road, and the Indians' war whoops rose to a new crescendo.

Displaying a courage that his terrified troops could not emulate, Braddock rode up and down the column, cursing, flailing men with the flat of his sword, trying to get them into line. Washington and several other Virginians begged him to let the Americans, at least, scatter behind trees and fight it out Indian-style. Braddock refused to listen to them. He did not want to fight the enemy their way. He roared curses at any man he saw crouching behind a tree. He wanted to mass his men and smash the enemy back with bayonets and volleys, but too many officers were dead or wounded to create the coherence he needed for these tactics.

The situation slowly disintegrated. Virginians under one of their captains disregarded Braddock and took a position behind a huge fallen tree on the slope of the ridge. Some British, seeing guns go off, fired a volley at them, killing many. Braddock ordered the rest to fall back to the road, and they were further decimated by the Indians. Sir Peter Halkett rode forward from the rear guard to try to help. At Prestonpans in 1745, he had been one of the few officers able to control the men around him. But now he was shot dead the moment he reached the battlefield. His son, a major in his regiment, tried to rescue him and fell dead with his father in his arms.

Royal artillerymen brought three twelve-pounders into action, cutting swaths through the forest with grapeshot. But these fresh gunners were also shot down by the steady fire of the invisible enemy. The infantry gave them no protection. Again and again, officers tried to rally the men and lead them up the slope of the ridge. They died gallantly, to no purpose. Officers, Captain Orme later wrote, were "absolutely sacrificed." Among the seriously wounded was Captain Horatio Gates.

Washington and Braddock seemed to have charmed lives. The big Virginian had bullets through his coat and hat. Two horses were shot out from under him. Braddock lost four horses. For another hour they struggled to rescue the situation, but their men became more and more incapable of obeying orders. They just kept shooting madly, blindly, sometimes killing their own officers by accident. Eventually they fired away all their ammunition. Braddock realized he had to retreat to save the army from annihilation. He decided to fall back to the wagons and make a stand there to protect the food and reserve ammunition. But a moment after he gave the order and began mounting his fifth horse, a bullet flung him to the ground, tearing through his arm and penetrating his lungs.

In the rear of the mile-long column, around the wagons, the situation was relatively stable. A company of South Carolina volunteers had beaten off an Indian attack. But when the survivors of the battle in the woods reached the wagons, panic became a rout. Wagoners such as Daniel Boone cut loose their horses and rode for their lives. Soldiers seized officers' bathorses and did likewise. Those without a horse threw away guns, knapsacks, and belts and fled across the ford. "Sheep pursued by dogs," Washington said. He helped load the wounded general into a little cart with a still-intact team. They forded the river under fire, with terrified soldiers running after them and Indians leaping into the water to tomahawk wounded men. Otherwise, there was no pursuit. The French were too few in number, and the Indians were too busy scalping the dead and wounded and plundering the wagons.

On the opposite bank, Braddock, whose mind was clear, ordered Washington to ride ahead and rally as many fugitives as possible. About 200 men had retreated in fairly good order. They would seize the nearest high ground and hold out until Dunbar's men reached them. Washington, reeling with fatigue and fever, obeyed. He found Gage beyond the upper ford with about eighty men. How the commander of the advance guard got that far back has never been explained. Some people later accused him of cowardice.

Washington told Gage to join them on the high ground and rode back to Braddock. He found the general and the rest of the army retreating. The regulars were too shaken to stay close to the battlefield. Those they had put out as pickets simply ran away. Braddock ordered Washington to ride on to Dunbar's camp, forty miles back, and tell him to rush forward food and liquor for the wounded. Washington and two guides rode down the darkening road, past wounded men begging them for help. The sounds, he recalled thirty years later, "were enough to pierce a heart of adamant."

In front of Fort Duquesne, meanwhile, the Indians celebrated the victory in their usual style: They tied twelve British captives to stakes and burned them alive. A young Pennsylvanian, taken prisoner by a raiding party a few days earlier, watched the first man die. The Indians "kept touching him with firebrands hot irons &c and he screaming." The French piously deplored such barbarities in their reports, but seldom stopped them.

When an exhausted Washington reeled into Dunbar's camp late the next morning, Dunbar, proving Braddock's doubts about him were correct, lost his head and beat "to arms" as if they were about to be attacked. Teamsters, soldiers, and even a few officers fled east. But as lightly wounded men began to show up, it became obvious that Braddock's survivors were between them and the enemy; Dunbar calmed down and sent Braddock the supplies.

Braddock arrived the next evening. He was in agony, but his mind was clear. He ordered Dunbar to retreat to Fort Cumberland. As they began the withdrawal, he turned over his command to Dunbar. He said little after that. Musing almost to himself, he sighed: "We shall know better how to deal with them another time." Later he told the wounded Orme to report that "nothing could equal the gallantry and conduct of the officers nor the bad behavior of the men." Around 9:00 P.M. on July 13, he died.

The next morning Washington superintended Braddock's burial in a trench at the head of the column. After a brief service, all the men and horses and wagons tramped over it, obliterating the grave. Washington knew the Indian habit of digging up corpses and abusing them.

The column staggered into Fort Cumberland with 387 wounded officers and men. Of the 1,459 men who forded the Monongahela in such high spirits at noon on July 9, an appalling 977 had been killed or wounded. French casualties were 16. The Indians reported 25 dead. Dunbar, although he still had almost 1,000 men under his command, once again confirmed Braddock's doubts about him—by retreating all the way to Philadelphia, exposing western Virginia and Pennsylvania to Indian scalping parties. Reappointed a Virginia colonel, Washington was left to defend a 350-mile frontier with a thousand militiamen, whom he was soon damning with a vehemence that matched Braddock's.

While the French exulted in the capture of Braddock's cannon, they were far more excited by his papers, with his secret orders from the duke of Cumberland for a general offensive. They rushed troops to the threatened forts in the North and tried to seize the initiative by attacking the New England army that William Johnson had assembled to assault Crown Point. Baron Dieskau led two crack French regiments and a force of Canadians and Indians to the assault. The New Englanders, fighting behind log barricades, met them with blasts of musketry, then charged, routing the lot. Dieskau, wounded in the leg, was captured.

Governor Shirley, faced with daunting numerical superiority at Niagara and a nearby fort that threatened his flank, abandoned his attack. But the assault on Nova Scotia was successful—and gave the modern world its first glimpse of total war. To guarantee their possession of the province, the British and their New England allies deported almost the entire French population of 6,000, burned their homes, and laid waste their farms.

There was no longer any doubt that General Braddock's undeclared war would soon become official. On May 18, 1756, England declared hostilities, and France replied on June 9. For the next six years, war raged around the globe. Although the French scored a few victories in the early years, the British never lost the strategic initiative that Braddock had so energetically seized. In 1758 another British army, again including George Washington, bulled its way to Fort Duquesne. This time the French blew it up and retreated. By 1762 France was beaten in America—and in India and Europe—and Britain was master of the greatest empire the world had ever seen.

This triumph of British arms had an oddly negative effect on Americans. They emerged from the conflict with a skeptical attitude toward the prowess of the mother country. Not a little of this opinion had taken root on that bitter, bloody July day along the Monongahela. In an age when news traveled largely by word of mouth, Braddock's defeat quickly acquired mythic proportions. The regulars supposedly ran at the first war whoop. Braddock blundered arrogantly, stupidly, into an ambush that any junior officer should have foreseen. Virginians such as the Lees gleefully

piled on the slanders. Gage, Dunbar, and other survivors, anxious to protect their own reputations, planted letters in newspapers smearing the
dead general's tactics and personality.

George Washington was among the few who never uttered any criticism
of Edward Braddock. Thirty years later, when a friend remarked that he had
always had a low opinion of the Coldstream Guardsman, Washington
replied: "He was unfortunate, but his character was much too severely treated." By then he knew that a general could do everything he thought right in
preparing for a battle and be undone by an inept subordinate or a single false
assumption or a collision with the enemy at the worst possible moment. In
the final analysis, Edward Braddock was the victim of all these vicissitudes.
He lacked the one ingredient every general needs: luck.

*Autumn 1990*

Thomas Fleming is both a historian and novelist. His books include *Beat the Last Drum: The Siege of Yorktown, 1781* (1963) and *1776: Year of Illusions* (1975). His latest book is *Loyalties: A Novel of World War II* (1994).

# 3

# George Washington, General

## By Thomas Fleming

*Thomas Fleming continues his exploration of early American military history with an examination of George Washington's generalship. Although Washington has long been an American icon for his service to his country and for his value as a symbol of the Revolution, Fleming believes that Washington deserves far more credit as a general than he has often received. Washington was the key to military victory, the sine qua non of the American cause, for he understood—when others around him did not—the strategy, imagination, and leadership that would be necessary if America were to gain the ultimate triumph.*

How good a general was George Washington? If we consult the statistics as they might have been kept if he were a boxer or a quarterback, the figures arc not encouraging. In seven years of fighting the British, from 1775 to 1782, he won only three clear-cut victories—at Trenton, Princeton, and Yorktown. In seven other encounters—Long Island, Harlem Heights, White Plains, Fort Washington, Brandywine, Germantown, and Monmouth—he either was defeated or at best could claim a draw. He never won a major battle: Trenton was essentially a raid; Princeton was little more than a large skirmish; and Yorktown was a siege in which the blockading French fleet was an essential component of the victory.

Most contemporary Americans, even if unacquainted with these statistics, are inclined to see General Washington as a figurehead, an inspiring symbol whose dedication and perseverance enabled his starving men to endure the rigors of Valley Forge and Morristown winter quarters. He wore the British out by sheer persistence, with little reference to military skill, much less genius. The recent spate of books devoted to how Washington's image was invented either by himself or by skillful propagandists bolsters this idea. Almost as misleading is our post-Vietnam fascination with guerrilla warfare and comparisons of our defeat in Southeast Asia with the British failure in America. If American guerrillas defeated the British, Washington the general seems almost superfluous.

A general's ability to inspire his men is not, of course, to be discounted, and Washington unquestionably had this gift. But in the final analysis, the great captains of history are rated on their ability to conceive a winning strategy and devise tactics to execute it. Does Washington, the man the British called "a little paltry colonel of militia" in 1776, belong in this select group? The answer is complicated by Washington's character. He was, as the historian J.A. Carroll has pointed out, "not an architect in ideas; he was essentially a man of deeds." He never set down in a neat volume his military (or political) principles. The best way to grasp his superior qualities, Carroll maintains, is to examine his thoughts and actions at climactic moments of his career.

To judge his generalship this way requires a look at the strategy of the Revolutionary Army when Washington became its commander on July 3, 1775. By that time the Americans had fought two battles, Lexington-Concord and Bunker Hill, from which their politicians and soldiers drew ruinously wrong conclusions. At Lexington-Concord they saw proof that militia could spring to the defense of their homes and farms and rout British regulars on a day's notice. At Bunker Hill they thought they had found a secret weapon, the entrenching tool, that would enable them to inflict crippling casualties on the attacking British even if, at the very end of the battle, the Americans ignominiously ran away.

In fact, the minutemen who fought at Lexington and Concord were a well-trained rudimentary army that had been drilling and marching for six months. They outnumbered the British five to one and knew it—a fact that added immensely to their élan. At Bunker Hill the overconfident British commander, William Howe, ordered a frontal assault on the entrenched colonials. Why the Americans assumed he would repeat this mistake in the future remains a mystery. As early as March 17, 1776, when the Americans outflanked the British defenses in Boston by seizing Dorchester Heights and fortified them with cannon dragged from Fort Ticonderoga in New York, Howe demonstrated he had learned his lesson by evacuating the city—something he had planned to do anyway.

A corollary to these ideas was the conviction that the war would be settled in one tremendous battle—what in the eighteenth century was called "a general action." Thus there was no need to sign men up for long enlistments—a year was considered more than enough time. There was even less need for a large regular army, which might endanger the liberties of the embryonic republic. Militia could operate as well as regulars from behind Bunker Hill–like barricades. As Israel Putnam, the commander at Bunker Hill, summed it up: "Cover Americans to their chins and they will fight until doomsday."

Still another corollary—though the term may be paying too much of a compliment to the Continental Congress's foggy military thinking—was the idea that if the Americans could push the British off the continent, the war would be won. So Washington obediently detached some of his best regiments and officers, such as Daniel Morgan and Benedict Arnold, to wrest Canada from royal control—a campaign that consumed close to half the 20,000 regulars Congress had empowered him to enlist. And the British evacuation of Boston was hailed as a stupendous victory, for which Congress issued Washington a medal.

Washington did not question these strategic assumptions—or Congress's order to abide by a majority vote of his generals in councils of war—until mid-1776, when the main theater of conflict shifted to New York. Congress told him to defend the city; he did it Bunker Hill–style. On Brooklyn Heights and at various points around Manhattan, his men expended immense amounts of energy building forts on which the British were expected to impale themselves. One, on the corner of Grand and Greene streets, was appropriately named Bunker Hill.

Meanwhile, in mid-July, William Howe proceeded to land 25,000 men unopposed on Staten Island, underscoring the idiocy of Congress's continental redoubt strategy in a war with the world's dominant sea power. Washington had only about 10,000 regulars to defend a city surrounded by rivers that permitted the enemy to land where and when they chose. The rest of his 23,000-man army was militia.

A few weeks later Howe shifted his field army to Long Island and defeated the Americans in a battle of feint and maneuver. Faking a frontal assault in order to pin Washington's men in their entrenchments, Howe swung half his army in a night march around the exposed American left wing, creating rout and panic.

A shaken Washington was able to move his surviving troops to Manhattan by night. But a few weeks later Howe outflanked the American forts on lower Manhattan, landing at Kips Bay (now Thirty-fourth Street) after a ferocious naval bombardment. The Connecticut Militia guarding the shore fled without firing a shot. Washington, watching this stampede, cried out, "Are these the men with which I am to defend America?" Again, mostly thanks to British sloth, Washington managed to extricate the bulk of his army, this time to strong positions on Harlem Heights, where a brisk skirmish with British patrols temporarily steadied their collapsing morale.

During "hours allotted to sleep," Washington began rethinking the strategy of the war in a series of letters to the president of Congress. Henceforth, he wrote, the Americans should "avoid a general action or put anything to the Risk, unless compelled by a necessity into which we ought never to be drawn." Their goal should be "to protract the war."

In cutting terms, Washington demolished congressional prejudice against a large standing army. It was imperative to recruit regulars committed to serve for the duration, and end their dependence on militia. "Men just dragged from the tender Scenes of domestick life, unaccustomed to the din of arms," had no confidence in themselves or their officers on a battlefield. They were impatient and impossible to discipline, and they infected the regulars with similar vices.

But Washington and his generals were themselves still infected with the Bunker Hill virus, which they now called "a war of posts." When Howe outflanked him again, landing troops on the Westchester shore of the

Hudson who threatened to trap the Americans on Manhattan Island, Washington retreated to the hills around White Plains. Behind him he left almost 3,000 regulars in Fort Washington, overlooking the Hudson at present-day 181st Street. These men were supposed to deny the British full use of Manhattan Island and the river.

At White Plains, Howe did little more than feint an attack, then detached a hefty portion of his army to assault Fort Washington. Masterfully combining artillery with flank and frontal attacks, the British took the fort in two hours, bagging irreplaceable regulars and scores of cannon. A chagrined Washington confessed there had been "warfare in my mind" about whether to evacuate the place. He had let Major General Nathanael Greene, at this point one of the leading Bunker Hillists, talk him into leaving them there.

That bitter pill purged the last vestige of entrenchment-tool illusions from Washington's mind. Two weeks later General Greene was across the Hudson River in Fort Washington's New Jersey twin, Fort Lee, when he learned from a local farmer that four or five thousand British troops had crossed the river at Dobbs Ferry, a few miles to the north, and were marching on the fort. Greene rushed a dispatch to Washington in Hackensack, asking for instructions. Should he stay and fight it out? Instead of a written answer, he got General Washington in person on a lathered horse. His instructions were one word: Retreat. Cannon, food, ammunition—everything was abandoned.

That was the day Washington began fighting a new kind of war in America. He was just in time, because in New Jersey the British, too, had some new ideas. Having demonstrated their ability to defeat the American army almost at will, they launched a campaign to win what post-Vietnam Americans would call hearts and minds. Along their line of march, they distributed a proclamation offering rebels pardons and guaranties against "forfeitures, attainders and penalties." All they had to do was appear before a British official within sixty days and sign a statement promising to "remain in a peaceable Obedience to His Majesty." New Jersey, the British hoped, would become a model of how to defuse the Revolution. It had a large percentage of Loyalists who would support a restoration of royal government and back the king's troops against "the disaffected."

At first Washington thought he had a good chance to defend New Jersey. He had brought 2,500 regulars across the Hudson with him, leaving some 7,000 men in Westchester to bar the British from the Hudson Highlands and New England. New Jersey had 16,000 militiamen on its muster rolls. He asked Governor William Livingston to call them all out. He told the commander of the Westchester force, Major General Charles Lee, to cross the Hudson and join him for a stand on the Raritan River around New Brunswick.

These hopes rapidly unraveled. The British reinforced their invading army until it was 10,000 men strong, under the command of one of their most aggressive generals, Lord Charles Cornwallis. Charles Lee, a headstrong compound of radical political opinions and careening military ambition, ignored Washington's request to join him. Meanwhile New Jersey's militia declined to turn out. Not a single regiment responded to the governor's call. Only about 1,000 individuals showed up at mustering sites, almost as useless as none at all. It was grim evidence of the power of Britain's shrewd combination of carrot and bayonet.

On November 29, Washington was in New Brunswick with an army driven by three months of retreat and defeat. Some militiamen broke into stores of rum and got drunk. Others, mostly Pennsylvanians, deserted in droves, although they had been paid to stay until January 1. Those whose contracts expired on December 1 announced they were going home then, no matter what was happening to the glorious cause.

Soon down to 3,000 men, and with the British crunching toward the bridges over the Raritan, Washington told Congress, "We shall retreat to the west side of the Delaware." Although New Jersey and the rest of the country saw this decision as mere flight, Washington was still thinking strategically. He wrote Charles Lee that he hoped the British would pursue him and attempt to pacify New Jersey by detaching garrisons across the state. He planned to "lull them into security" and, when he saw an opportunity, "beat them up."

The Revolution in New Jersey slid toward collapse. The legislature disbanded. As many as three to four hundred people a day flocked to British army posts to renew their allegiance. Brigadier General Alexander McDougall wrote from Morristown: "This state is totally deranged, without Government or officers, civil or military . . . that will act with any spirit." Another contemporary observer remarked that at this point the British could have bought New Jersey for eighteen pence a head.

Finally realizing that the fate of the infant nation was at stake in New Jersey, Charles Lee crossed the Hudson into Bergen County. He was not encouraged by what he encountered along his line of march: The mass of the people were "strangely contaminated" with loyalty to the king. He urged Congress to recruit a new army immediately by drafting every militiaman it could find. A few days later Lee was captured by a British cavalry patrol and the remnants of his force straggled across the Delaware to join Washington's handful.

Major General Israel Putnam, the architect of Bunker Hill, was also wandering through New Jersey telling everyone the war was lost. The current army was about to disband, he said, and even if Congress could raise another one, there was no hope of resisting the British "in the plain country to the southward." Without a hill to fight from, Putnam was devoid of ideas.

Washington took a different view. In a letter to General William Heath, who was guarding the Hudson Highlands, the American commander in chief wrote that "the defection of the people . . . has been as much owing to the want of an Army to look the Enemy in the face, as any other cause."

In this offhand, intuitive way, Washington enunciated the central idea of the strategy that would win the American Revolution. It merits his inclusion in the select circle of great revolutionary generals who invented a new kind of war—with an additional laurel for conceiving this winning strategy while most of the others around him were losing their heads.

This central statement coincided with the rest of the new strategic ideas Washington had enunciated in the previous chaotic months of defeat and disillusion: recruiting a regular army for the duration, protracting the war, never risking a general action, retreating until the enemy exposed a part of its army to insult or destruction.

Washington swiftly demonstrated his ability to implement tactics to match his strategy. He ordered General Heath to invade northern New Jersey from the Hudson Highlands, seize arms, and intimidate the many Loyalists the British had encouraged to come out of hiding there. He gave Alexander McDougall three of Charles Lee's Continental regiments to support a fairly good turnout of militia in Morris County. Finally, he marshaled the 2,500 shivering regulars under his command and led them across the ice-choked Delaware River on Christmas night of 1776 to kill or capture two-thirds of the 1,500-man royal garrison at Trenton.

A few days later, Washington again invaded New Jersey. Cornwallis came at him with 9,000 men. On January 2, 1777, Washington wheeled his army around the British left flank by night and chewed up three regiments at Princeton, then headed for the royal army's main base at New Brunswick. The frantic British abandoned west Jersey and marched all night to get there first. They flung themselves into defensive positions around the town—only to discover that Washington had slipped away to winter quarters in Morristown. There, he coolly issued a proclamation announcing that anyone who had switched sides could return to the cause by showing up at any American post and pledging fresh allegiance to the United States.

With an army to look the enemy in the face and British power reduced to a narrow enclave along the Raritan, New Jersey's revolutionary ardor underwent a magical revival. British commissaries and foraging parties were ambushed on the roads. Loyalism beyond the army's enclave collapsed. Brilliantly combining military force and patriotic persuasion, Washington had rescued the state—and the country.

Recruiting for a new army revived in the rest of the nation, and General Howe glumly reported to London that he now saw no hope of ending the war "but by a general action." Here was irony indeed: Washington had maneuvered the British into adopting the flawed strategy with which the Americans had begun the war.

Washington had already decided that a climactic battle was precisely what Howe was never going to get. And for the next five years he stuck to his strategy despite criticism from hotheads in Congress and in the army, who still envisioned a general action as the answer to everything. In early 1777 Congressman John Adams, who fancied himself a military expert, was still drinking toasts to "a short and violent war."

When the British tried to advance across New Jersey that summer to assault Philadelphia, they found Washington's army on the high ground in the center of the state, waiting to pounce on them—and absolutely declining to come down from the hills to give all-out battle. A disgusted Howe abandoned the stunned Loyalists of east Jersey as he had deserted those in the west after Trenton and Princeton, marched his army to Perth Amboy and sailed them down the coast, then up Chesapeake Bay to attack Philadelphia in a roundabout fashion.

Howe found the hard-marching American army waiting for him in line of battle on Brandywine Creek, apparently ready to offer him the general action he wanted. But Washington positioned his men to give them the whole state of Pennsylvania into which to retreat if—as it transpired—victory eluded them. He followed the same policy a few weeks later at Germantown. Retreat, a dirty word in the American vocabulary in 1776, was no longer considered disgraceful. When the frustrated Howe settled into winter quarters in Philadelphia, former Bunker Hillist Nathanael Greene exulted that British rule in America did not extend beyond "their out-sentinels."

Meanwhile, to make sure the British did not conquer America piece-meal, Washington was extending his central strategic concept of an army to look the enemy in the face. When a British army under General John Burgoyne descended from Canada in 1777, Washington sent some of his best troops, in particular a regiment of Virginia riflemen under Daniel Morgan, to help Major General Horatio Gates's Northern Army. These men played a crucial part in the victory at Saratoga, inspiring thousands of militiamen to turn out to support the regulars. Although the regulars did almost all the fighting, the militia blocked Burgoyne's line of retreat and destroyed his supply lines, giving him no alternative but surrender.

Washington followed the same strategy in the South when the British shifted their main effort to that region in 1779. They swiftly pacified Georgia and ensconced a royal governor in Savannah. Washington detached one of his most dependable generals, Benjamin Lincoln, and some of his best regiments to meet the threat, but the British trumped this hand by trapping Lincoln and his army in Charleston and forcing them to surrender—a victory that more than balanced Saratoga.

Grimly, Washington detached more regulars he could not spare and assigned them to an army led by Horatio Gates, the victor at Saratoga. They inspired another good turnout of militiamen, but Gates made the mistake of putting the amateurs into line of battle alongside the regulars at Camden. A bayonet charge routed them, exposing the regulars to defeat.

This time Washington riposted with his best general, Nathanael Greene, who had learned a great deal about the art of war at Washington's side since sponsoring the disaster at Fort Washington in 1776. Although he began with barely 800 ragged regulars, Greene adapted Washington's strategy to the South, summing it up admirably in a letter to the guerrilla leader Thomas Sumter:

> The salvation of this country don't depend upon little strokes nor should the great business of establishing a permanent army be neglected to pursue them.

Partisan strokes in war are like the garnish of a table, they give splendor to the Army and reputation to the officers, but they afford no national security. . . . You may strike a hundred strokes and reap little benefit from them unless you have a good army to take advantage of your success. . . . It is not a war of posts but a contest for States.

Greene soon demonstrated what he meant. He dipatched 350 regulars to South Carolina under Daniel Morgan when the state was on the verge of total surrender. These regulars rallied enough militiamen to win a stunning victory at the Cowpens and reverse the momentum of the war.

While Washington supported armies to the north and south, he never forgot New Jersey. The state remained the cockpit of the Revolution for him. In three out of five years, he made it the site of his winter quarters. In the other two years, the ones he spent at Valley Forge and at Newburgh in Westchester, he was never more than a day's march away. The payoff came in June 1780, when swarms of New Jersey militiamen turned out to join 3,500 Continentals in stopping a 7,000-man invading army. After two bloody collisions at Connecticut Farms and Springfield, the British withdrew and never invaded the state again.

One thing should now be apparent: Washington's strategy was far more complex than guerrilla warfare. Instead, it posited a regular army as an essential force to sustain a war, aided when necessary by guerrilla elements. In spite of his criticism of militia, Washington used them throughout the war. He had no other choice. He soon resigned himself to never achieving the 40,000-man army Congress voted him in the aftermath of Trenton and Princeton. For most of the war, he was lucky to have a fourth of that number under his command. He called out militia again and again to flesh out his forces, but he never depended on them the way he and his fellow generals had in 1776. In 1780 he told the president of Congress that militia were useful "only as light troops to be scattered in the woods and plague rather than do serious injury to the enemy." This kind of fighting, which he called *petite guerre*—a first cousin of the Spanish word *guerrilla*—was, as his lieutenant Greene made clear, never decisive.

In 1778 Washington met the greatest challenge to his strategy. It came from Charles Lee, who returned from British captivity with a plan to disband the regular army and commit the country to a guerrilla war. Washington rejected the idea as firmly as he turned aside proposals for summoning all the militiamen within reach and hurling them and the regulars at the British for the one big battle John Adams and other fire-eaters wanted.

Washington got the most out of his thin line of regulars because he seldom used them in a European way—and because he was generously endowed with a trait essential to a great general: audacity. It runs like a bright thread through his whole career, beginning with his dawn attack on a French patrol on Virginia's frontier in 1754, a burst of gunfire that started the Seven Years' War. Even in early 1776, during the stalemated siege of Boston, he startled his Bunker Hill–infatuated colleagues by proposing a dawn assault across the ice of Back Bay on the entrenched British—a gamble that might have ended the war on the spot. A council of war voted him down.

Trenton and Princeton were, of course, masterpieces of audacity, but not enough credit has been given to Germantown. Here, just four weeks after losing a major battle on the Brandywine, he hurled his entire army in four columns at the main British camp. Only the confusion generated by an early-morning fog prevented him from winning. In Europe, it was Germantown as much as Saratoga that convinced France the Americans were capable of winning the war and were worth the risk of an alliance.

Even after he went into winter quarters at Valley Forge, Washington's audacity continued to manifest itself. He insisted on constant skirmishing and harassment of the enemy in Philadelphia. Although driven to cries of exasperation and despair at the way Congress failed to feed and clothe the army, he found time to plan a winter attack on the British, which Nathanael Greene narrowly persuaded him was too "hassardous."

By this time Washington had stopped paying much attention to Congress's military thinking. He refused to split up his army to give various parts of the country an unfounded feeling of security. Not even the president of Congress could persuade him to station some units closer to the politicians' 1778 headquarters in York. "It would give me infinite pleasure to afford protection to every individual and to every spot of ground in the whole United States. Nothing is more my wish . . . [but] I cannot divide the army. If this is done I cannot be answerable for the consequences," Washington wrote. For the same reason he vetoed a plan to give the marquis de Lafayette a chunk of the main army and let him invade Canada in 1778.

But Washington never stopped looking for a chance to strike at an exposed British position. In July and August of 1779, when the war in the north seemed stalemated, he struck two ferocious blows. First, bayonet-wielding light infantry under Anthony Wayne killed or captured the entire garrison at Stony Point on the Hudson. A month later Washington's favorite cavalryman, Light-Horse Harry Lee, repeated the performance against the smaller British outpost at Paulus Hook in present-day Jersey City.

*Surprize* [*sic*] was one of the favorite words in Washington's military vocabulary, and he was constantly studying ways to improve his technique for achieving it. Because the enemy expected surprise attacks at dawn, he recommended midnight. "A dark night and even a rainy one if you can find the way, will contribute to your success," he told Anthony Wayne, advice Wayne put to good use at Stony Point.

But Washington tempered his audacity with caution. When Benedict Arnold wanted to organize an assault on British-held Newport in 1777, Washington told him to forget it unless he had "a moral certainty" of succeeding. More and more, as the war dragged on, he sought to avoid giving the British even the appearance of a victory. He was ever aware of the importance of maintaining popular support. This not only was important politically but was a vital part of his military strategy. Militia would not turn out for a loser.

In this context, Brandywine, which seems at first glance to contradict Washington's determination to avoid a general action, fits his strategy of maintaining an army to look the enemy in the face. He recognized that in the struggle for hearts and minds up and down a 2,000-mile-long continent, there were times when the Americans had to fight even if the odds were heavily against them. To have allowed the British to march into Philadelphia without a battle would have ruined the patriots' morale.

A similar blend of pugnacity and public relations motivated the last major battle under Washington's command—Monmouth in June 1778. The French had entered the war, and the panicky British abandoned Philadelphia to retreat to New York. Now more than ever Washington was disinclined to risk everything in a general action. But he sensed the need to strike a blow. After a day of ferocious fighting in nightmarish heat in the New Jersey Pine Barrens, satisfied that he had won the appearance of a victory, he let the redcoats continue their retreat.

To maintain civilian morale, Washington at one point suggested Congress provide the army with "a small traveling press" to supply "speedy and exact information of any military transactions that take place." When the bankrupt Congress refused, Washington did the next best thing. He furloughed an ex-newspaperman, Lieutenant Sheppard Kollock of the Continental artillery, and set him up as editor of the New Jersey *Journal,* which at least stabilized public opinion in the cockpit state.

On another front Washington displayed an audacity—and an imagination—few generals have matched. Throughout most of the war, he was his own intelligence director. He proved himself a master of the game, running as many as a half-dozen spy rings in Philadelphia and New York, and constantly urged his fellow generals to follow suit. "Single men in the night will be more likely to ascertain facts than the best glasses in the day," he wrote to Anthony Wayne in 1779.

One of the keys to his victory at Trenton was his use of a double agent, John Honeyman, to give him a thorough briefing on the enemy's defenses—and to lull the local commander with stories of the American army's collapse. At Valley Forge, Washington manufactured documents in his own handwriting full of returns from imaginary infantry and cavalry regiments. Double agents handed those documents over to the British in Philadelphia, convincing them that the main army had been reinforced with 8,000 men and was too strong to molest.

In July 1780 Sir Henry Clinton decided to launch a preemptive attack on a French army that had just landed at Newport. A brilliant idea, it might well have succeeded if one of Washington's best New York agents had not rushed him news of the plan. Clinton actually had his men aboard ships when he was distracted by the capture of some "secret" papers that showed Washington was planning an all-out attack on New York. The jittery British general reluctantly abandoned his coup de main.

The Yorktown campaign was the ultimate proof of the genius of Washington's generalship. The idea of trapping Cornwallis in the little

tobacco port came from the French commander, the comte de Rocham-
beau; Washington was skeptical of its chances for success. But the execution of the plan depended totally on Washington's tactics and strategy. First
he befuddled Sir Henry Clinton with a veritable blizzard of false information about an attack on New York. Then he took the huge gamble of marching his men south in a long, exposed line through New Jersey. Benedict
Arnold, by that time a British general, begged Clinton to attack, but Sir
Henry declined another encounter with "the bold persevering militia of
that populous province" and let Washington march to victory.

Perhaps the most appealing thing about Washington's strategy was its
strong link to freedom. It eschewed the militaristic idea of hauling every
man into the ranks at the point of a gun. It rested instead on faith in the
courage of free men. It was a realistic faith: He did not expect men to commit suicide in defense of freedom, but he did believe men would take grave
risks if they thought they had a reasonable chance of succeeding.

Looking back later, Washington, an innately modest man, was often
inclined to attribute victory to the "interposition of Providence." But those
who study the evidence, and ignore the statistics, are inclined to think
Providence wore the shape of a tall Virginian who had the brains to conceive a way to win a war when it was on the brink of being lost—and the
ability to provide the leadership that converted this strategy into a military
victory won by free men.

*WINTER 1990*

**Thomas Fleming is the author of the previous article on Braddock's defeat.**

# 4

# Transformation at Saratoga

## By Thomas Fleming

*The clash at Saratoga in the early autumn of 1777 was a crucial victory—some historians argue the crucial victory—on the road to American independence. As Thomas Fleming points out, it was not just a clash of arms, but also a clash of ambitions and personalities. On the British side, the competition among Generals William Howe, John Burgoyne, and Henry Clinton undermined the Crown's effort to invade from Canada and slice through to the Hudson River. Across the lines, the American leaders Horatio Gates and Benedict Arnold carried on a personal feud that threatened to vitiate the American effort. But one partnership did hold firm, and, Fleming reminds us, it was ultimately decisive: the partnership of the Continental Army and the patriot militia.*

The campaign that reached a historic climax in the two battles of Saratoga began with news that left George Washington temporarily speechless—and the rest of the fragile union known as the United States of America in a fever of anxiety: Fort Ticonderoga had fallen with scarcely a shot fired in its defense. America's so-called Northern Army had fled the place in headlong retreat before an 8,000-man British force commanded by General John Burgoyne, which had appeared as if by magic before their ramparts on June 30, 1777.

Incredibly, no one in the American army—or Congress, for that matter—had believed in the existence of this imposing host. American attempts to scout into Canada had been frustrated by the screen of Indians the British spread along the border. The Americans had remained convinced that the main British army of 25,000 men under Sir William Howe would soon sally from New York to attack Philadelphia—and Burgoyne, who they had known was in Canada, would assemble every man who could be spared from the defense of that colony and sail south to join him. That was why Washington had husbanded the 9,200-man main American army in New Jersey and more or less ignored worried letters from Major General Philip Schuyler about the weakness of his Northern Army.

More bad news cascaded south on the heels of Ticonderoga's collapse. The rear guard of the Northern Army had apparently been routed in a fire-fight at Hubbardton, Vermont, in which two militia regiments had run like proverbial rabbits. But this was merely dismaying compared to the coup de main the British had managed at Skenesborough (now Whitehall), to which some 600 refugees from Ticonderoga had retreated by water with all the food, ammunition, and movable cannon from the fort. The Americans had cruised down Lake Champlain, enjoying band music and a bit of tippling, secure in the illusion that the entrance to the lower part of the lake was blocked by a sturdy bridge and a massive chain across the narrows. But British sailors chopped down the bridge and broke the chain with a few well-placed can-nonballs. Descending on the stunned Americans at Skenesborough, the British captured most of their fleet and forced them to abandon all their can-non and staggering amounts of flour and salted meats.

With his retreat through Skenesborough blocked, the mortified com-mander of Ticonderoga, Major General Arthur St. Clair, had to lead his men on a seven-day detour into the wilderness to reach Fort Edward, on the east bank of the Hudson River. There he found a distraught Philip Schuyler with a paltry 700 Continentals and 1,400 jittery militia—all of the Northern Army's reserve.

No sooner had the disgruntled Ticonderoga fugitives, most of them New Englanders, arrived at dilapidated Fort Edward than they began accusing Generals Schuyler and St. Clair of treason. They claimed the British had fired "silver balls" from their cannon into the fort to bribe them into surrendering the bastion. In fact, St. Clair had made one of the most courageous decisions of the war: Knowing he was wrecking his military reputation, he had chosen to evacuate the fort to preserve his precious Continentals. Schuyler, once he calmed down, realized this and made no reproaches when they joined forces at Fort Edward. But in humid Philadelphia, reproaches filled the July air as Ticonderoga's previous commander, Major General Horatio Gates, loudly supported by New England delegates, blamed both men for the loss.

New Englanders did not like the aristocratic Schuyler. He was something of a martinet. He also owned huge slices of land along the Hudson and Mohawk rivers and found it hard to practice the rude and often crude democ-racy favored by the Yankees. But few men made a larger contribution to the American cause. His skillful diplomacy kept most of the Iroquois neutral for the first years of the war. Without his talents for organization and supply, the Northern Army would have collapsed long before.

Schuyler was soon reporting more bad news to Washington. "A very great proportion of the [local] inhabitants are taking protection from General Burgoyne." Worse, another British army was heading for Albany. Some 1,800 regulars, Indians, and Loyalists under the leadership of Lieutenant Colonel Barry St. Leger had sailed across Lake Ontario and debouched toward Fort Stanwix, the flimsy bastion that was supposed to guard the Mohawk Valley. The mere threat made it impossible to raise any militia from this populous region to defend the Hudson Valley from Burgoyne.

What to do? Washington dispatched two of his best generals, Benjamin Lincoln of Massachusetts and Benedict Arnold of Connecticut, to Schuyler's aid, hoping they could turn out New England's cantankerous militia. Arnold had been sulking in Connecticut because Congress had promoted five other men to major general over his head. The nervous lawmakers finally decided to give Arnold the coveted rank, though still leaving him junior to those previously elevated, presumably to teach him a lesson in humility. They also fired Schuyler and St. Clair and appointed Horatio Gates the commander of everything north of Albany.

Washington debated marching his main army through the Hudson Highlands pass known as the Clove to West Point. He and everyone on his staff now assumed the British commander in chief, Sir William Howe, planned to fight his way up the Hudson and meet Burgoyne in a pincer movement designed to cut off militant New England from the rest of the colonies. On July 24 Washington had most of his army in the Clove when he received the amazing news that the British fleet, with General Howe and most of the main royal army aboard, had put to sea and was last seen tacking south! On July 27, they were spotted off Egg Harbor, New Jersey. A bewildered Washington turned his footsore soldiers around and headed for Philadelphia. "Howe's in a manner abandoning Burgoyne," he wrote to Horatio Gates, "is so unaccountable a matter that . . . I cannot help casting my eyes continually behind me."

The Americans were only beginning to discern the rivalries dividing the British high command. Howe was determined to prove he had been right when he left detachments along the Delaware River at the end of 1776 to protect Loyalists in Pennsylvania and western New Jersey, even though the risky policy had given Washington his crucial victory at Trenton. Meanwhile Burgoyne had gone back to London and lobbied himself into command of the northern invasion without consulting Howe. They were competitors, not allies.

Horatio Gates, the new commander of the Northern Army, was one of the few generals on the American side who understood this tangled British psychology. This might explain the eagerness with which he sought the seemingly thankless job. Gray-haired, ruddy-faced, with thick spectacles that often slid down his long pointed nose to give him an old-womanish look, the fifty-year-old Gates had risen to major in the British army thanks to his talents as a staff officer. Frustrated by his failure to advance beyond that rank, he had moved to Virginia and ingratiated himself with George Washington, among others. As the American army's first adjutant general, he had proven himself an invaluable organizer and administrator in 1775. But his combat experience was almost zero—about fifteen minutes before being struck down by an Indian bullet in the 1754 debacle known as Braddock's defeat.

Gates's New England admirers ignored his shortcomings and attributed to him nearly miraculous powers. One declared that his mere arrival in Albany had lifted them from "this miserable state of despondency and terror." Unquestionably, getting rid of Schuyler and St. Clair eliminated the rampant paranoia in the New England Continental regiments. Gates was also the beneficiary of the first good news the Northern Army had received in a long time: On the left flank, Mohawk Valley militia marching to relieve besieged Fort Stanwix had fought a bloody drawn battle with St. Leger's army at Oriskany, inflicting particularly heavy casualties on his Indian allies. On the right, a 1,500-man force of Germans that Burgoyne had dispatched to Bennington to seize stores and horses had been attacked and destroyed by New Hampshire militia under Colonel John Stark and Continentals under Colonel Seth Warner.

Gates also benefited from Burgoyne's decision to rebuild a twenty-three-mile road through the primeval forest from Skenesborough to Fort Edward, a task that consumed three weeks and gave the Americans time to regroup. Schuyler skillfully impeded Burgoyne's progress, putting a thousand axmen to work felling huge pines and hemlocks in his path, destroying some forty bridges over the numerous creeks and ravines. Burgoyne made no attempt to interfere. One reason may have been that the Americans had mauled the light infantry at Hubbardton—inflicting casualties of 21 percent in the brief firefight. Relaxing in the fine stone house of William Skene, the principal citizen of Skenesborough, Gentleman Johnny, as his admiring troops called him, enjoyed a new mistress—the wife of his commissary—and remained euphoric over the easy capture of Ticonderoga.

Still another reason American morale rebounded was a resupply of cannon. Some had come from Washington's army, others from Portsmouth, New Hampshire, where a French ship had slipped through the British blockade with thousands of muskets and other war matériel, including fifty-eight brass cannon. By mid-September, the Northern Army had twenty-two big guns.

At this point, we encounter one of the myths of Saratoga, the story of Jane McCrea. The Americans withdrew from Fort Edward, except for a small picket guard. Two days before the British arrived at the fort, a party of Indians (there were some 400 in Burgoyne's ranks) attacked it. The pickets fled, and the Indians found Jane in the cellar of a nearby house. She greeted them warmly and made it clear that she was a friend. As the Indians led Jane off on a captured horse toward the British camp, some of the picket guard—whose commander had been scalped in the melee—drifted back through the trees and blazed away at them. Three bullets hit Jane, killing her instantly. One of the Indians, Wyandot Panther, decided to scalp her as well, to see if he could collect the bounty Burgoyne was paying for such grisly proofs of slaughter. (Other versions of the story say Panther was arguing with a fellow tribesman over whose prisoner Jane was when he brained and scalped her to prove his point. Years later, when Jane's corpse was exhumed, her skull was intact—and the three bullet wounds were still visible in her body.)

Back at the British camp, Wyandot Panther found himself accused of murdering the young woman. Burgoyne demanded that the Indians surrender him for trial and execution. The Indians threatened to go home en masse, and Burgoyne backed down. The next day, many of them went home anyway, perhaps because they were intimidated by the losses of their cohorts at

Oriskany. Some blamed it on their notoriously fickle habits of warfare, which made them unsuited for long campaigns.

Propaganda about Jane's death supposedly caused the New England militia to turn out in droves. In fact, on August 27, Gates was complaining to Washington that he had yet to see very many of them. Benedict Arnold, whom Schuyler had sent to relieve Fort Stanwix in late July, also tried to use Jane's death to arouse the Mohawk Valley militia—with almost total lack of success. On August 24, he was stranded at Fort Dayton, thirty miles from Stanwix, with 913 Continentals and "a fine militia, not exceeding one hundred, on whom little dependence can be placed."

Lacking manpower, Arnold used brainpower to rescue Stanwix. He sent a captured Dutch Loyalist named Hon Yost Schuyler (no relation to the general) to Stanwix, along with an Oneida ally, to spread lies and confusion in St. Leger's army. Hon Yost was supposedly somewhat crazy—which gave him great influence among the Indians, who regarded the insane as holy men. Wearing a coat that Arnold had shot full of holes to simulate hot pursuit, Schuyler rushed to Stanwix and told St. Leger's Indians that the fearsome Arnold was on the march with 3,000 men. The Oneida confirmed everything Hon Yost said, and most of St. Leger's Indians began vanishing into the woods. He had no choice but to follow them, abandoning his cannon and leaving his tents standing, with some of his men still asleep in them.

This news, which Arnold triumphantly announced when he returned from Stanwix in early September with 1,200 men behind him, probably had far more to do with turning out the militia than the murder of Jane McCrea. Another arrival had an equally large impact on their willingness to march. Into the American camp swaggered huge Colonel Daniel Morgan and his corps of 331 frontier riflemen. No soldier, except perhaps Arnold, was closer to a living legend in the American army. Morgan had slogged up the Kennebec with Arnold in the fall of 1775 and assaulted Quebec on the last day of that year. The attack had gone awry and Morgan had been captured—he was later paroled—but his performance only added to his fame.

Washington had sent Morgan north, demonstrating how seriously he took the maxim he had laid down in late 1776—that the militia required an army to look the enemy in the face before they could stand up to British regulars. Along with Morgan, he dispatched two Continental brigades from the Hudson Highlands, totaling some 1,500 rank and file—manpower he badly needed to defend Philadelphia from Howe. This generosity raised Gates's Continental strength to about 6,500. He also had about 1,500 militia.

When Gates took command of the Northern Army, Schuyler had retreated to Van Schaick's Island, at the mouth of the Mohawk River, nine miles north of Albany. There he was able to block the main road and stay in touch with operations in the vital Mohawk Valley. The New England officers told their hero the men were disgusted by Schuyler's constant retreating. Gates decided it would be good for morale if they marched north "to meet the enemy." Some say the aggressive Arnold had not a little to do with urging this move on Gates.

Beginning on September 8, the army marched thirteen miles north to rugged country overlooking the Hudson called Bemis Heights, after a tavern on the riverbank. There, the Polish engineering officer, Thaddeus Kosciusko, constructed an elaborate array of field fortifications on the 100-foot-high bluffs and the 500-foot-wide strip of level ground along the Hudson. To the west, in case the British tried to outflank the position rather than storm it, the ground was thickly forested, broken by occasional clearings, and cut by deep east–west ravines—ideal terrain for American light-infantry tactics.

If Arnold was responsible for this move, it was the last advice Gates took from his fellow major general. An intriguer himself, he saw conspiracies everywhere—though when it came to touchiness, Arnold was in a class by himself. As Gates began countermanding his routine orders and excluding him from staff meetings, the hot-tempered ex-apothecary grew surly and obnoxious in return.

In Burgoyne's camp at Fort Edward, after the disaster at Bennington and St. Leger's collapse at Fort Stanwix, second thoughts were the order of the day. In the flush times of July, Burgoyne had written Howe assuring him he would need no assistance to reach Albany. Now, with his army shrunk to 4,600 rank and file, as well as about 800 Tories and Canadians and a mere 50 dispirited Indians, Gentleman Johnny began to realize the road to Albany had some large, forbidding bumps in it. But he could not bring himself to abandon a scheme on which he had staked his reputation as a soldier.

Without his Indian scouts, Burgoyne had no idea where the Americans were. Crossing the Hudson on September 13 on a bridge of boats near Saratoga, the British commander groped southward in slow, cautious marches. Not until September 18, when an American patrol fired on a group of his soldiers who were digging up potatoes on an abandoned farm, killing or wounding twenty of them, did he realize the rebels were close. Although he still had only the dimmest idea of the American position on Bemis Heights, Burgoyne decided to attack it the next day.

Gentleman Johnny divided his army into three columns. On the right, Brigadier Simon Fraser, with about 2,000 light infantry of both the British and German regiments, swung wide in an attempt to outflank the American fortifications. Burgoyne stationed himself in the center, where Brigadier Gustavus Hamilton commanded four British regiments numbering about 1,100. Along the riverbank marched Baron Friedrich von Riedesel with about the same number of Germans, plus six companies of the British 47th Regiment to protect the supplies and bateaux.

It was a risky, even foolhardy plan, revealing the contempt in which Burgoyne and his senior officers still held the Americans. Separated by as much as a half mile of thick woods, the columns would be forced to communicate through messengers and signal guns. An alert, aggressive enemy could easily defeat them in detail. But if the Americans remained as passive as they had been at Ticonderoga, the scheme had its merits. Fraser and his men stood a fair chance of seizing undefended high ground to the west, from which British heavy guns—Burgoyne had forty-two of them—could wreak havoc on the American defenses.

If it had been left to Horatio Gates, this is what might have happened. He was in favor of sitting inside Kosciusko's works and letting the British attack where and when they pleased. Benedict Arnold, who had been given command of the army's left wing, argued furiously against this fatal idea. He urged a fight in the woods against any attempt to outflank them. Gates grudgingly consented to send Morgan's riflemen, as well as 250 light infantry under Major Henry Dearborn, to contest the British maneuver and agreed to let Arnold support them with more men from his wing if they were needed.

Around 1:00 P.M. Morgan's Rangers collided with scouts from Fraser's column and sent them flying with a volley that killed all their officers. Losing their heads, the riflemen pursued the British into a ravine not far from a clearing called Freeman's Farm, after a Tory farmer who had fled to Canada. The riflemen collided with four times their number of British, who blasted them with musketry from front and flank. Twenty were taken prisoners and the rest fled past Morgan—who burst into tears, thinking his regiment was ruined. But when he gave his signal, a perfect imitation of a wild turkey call, it soon regrouped around him.

Fearing Morgan was in trouble, Arnold sent two New Hampshire regiments, former fugitives from Ticonderoga, to his support. They spread out to Morgan's left as Burgoyne and his four regiments emerged from the woods on the north side of Freeman's Farm. By this time, Arnold was on the battlefield. With the instinct of a born tactician, he saw a chance to drive a wedge between Burgoyne and Fraser, wreck the British plan of attack, and possibly destroy the enemy army. But Fraser detached several companies to support Burgoyne, and in the center the 20th Regiment dropped back and swung west to counter the American thrust. The Yankees were beaten back, and the battle turned into a slugging match between Arnold's men and Burgoyne's regiments, with Freeman's Farm as the cockpit.

Within an hour, Arnold poured in seven Continental regiments and one of New York militia. Back and forth through the tall grass the two sides surged, the British trying to close with the bayonet, to be repeatedly beaten back by American musketry. The 62nd Regiment, exposed to fire from flank and front when the 20th fell back, took fearful punishment from both directions. On horseback, Burgoyne repeatedly rallied his men, ignoring whizzing bullets from Morgan's marksmen, even when they shot his aide out of the saddle a few feet away from him.

For the Americans, the prize was the British artillery, which filled the air with screaming grapeshot. Several times they seized the guns but were driven back by a bayonet charge before they could turn them on the enemy or drag them away. It was, Brigadier General John Glover of Massachusetts said, "one continual blaze [of musketry] until dark."

Arnold whirled up and down the line like a dervish, shouting encouragement, leading some of the charges personally. He was convinced that they had a chance to break the center and destroy the British army. By the end of the afternoon, Burgoyne and other senior officers were in panicky agreement. The 62nd Regiment was on the brink of collapse. In the artillery, every officer and four-fifths of the gunners were dead or wounded. At five o'clock Burgoyne sent a frantic call for help to Riedesel on the riverbank.

In the midst of this action, Arnold rode back to Gates's headquarters (a mile and a half away) several times to beg for reinforcements. Gates primly rejected his pleas and finally ordered him to stay inside the Bemis Heights fortifications, claiming his rashness was endangering the whole army. Only around four o'clock did Gates consent to send a brigade from the American right wing under the command of Brigadier General Ebenezer Learned of Massachusetts. Learned only marched his men in a wide semicircle around Freeman's Farm and skirmished with Fraser's column—which contributed nothing to the battle Arnold was trying to fight.

Baron von Riedesel marched to the rescue of the British. Taking over 500 men with him, the German major general stripped the right-flank column of its ability to defend the precious stores and bateaux on the riverbank. But Gates, who should have been watching closely for this opportunity, did nothing, and the 500 fresh Germans stormed into the American right flank at sunset, beating drums and shouting religious slogans. Even more useful were two six-pounders that Riedesel's artillery officer, Captain Georg Pausch, manhandled into action to belch grapeshot at the charging rebels.

Without Arnold's leadership the American attack faltered, and they began falling back through the woods. Retreating down a twilit footpath, Colonel Philip Van Cortlandt ordered his 2nd New York Regiment to direct their aim "below the flash" of the British fire, which soon discouraged pursuit. The dazed, exhausted British had no stomach for more shooting anyway. The four regiments in the center had lost over 600 men. Only 60 rank and file from the 62nd were still on their feet—the other 230 were dead or wounded. American casualties totaled 319, including 65 killed.

Captain Thomas Anburey, who had spent the day with Fraser and seen very little action, was put in charge of burying the British dead. This grisly task inspired him to confide to his journal the "astonishment" of the British at the ferocity with which the Americans had fought. "They are not that contemptible enemy we had hitherto thought them, incapable of standing a regular engagement." The words underscore the assumptions on which Burgoyne had based his tactics—and the crucial nature of Arnold's response.

The next day, Burgoyne startled everyone in his army by announcing that he wanted to attack again. All his senior officers advised against it—the men were too spent to obey the order. Burgoyne then resolved to resume the offensive the following day. Many in the American army later admitted that if he had done so, he might have won his gamble. Arnold's regiments were also shaken by their heavy losses, and there was an acute shortage of ammunition in the American camp. But Philip Schuyler rescued the situation. Swallowing his detestation of Horatio Gates, he went around Albany tearing the lead sashes out of windows and melting them into bullets, which he then rushed to the army.

On the same day—September 21—Burgoyne received a letter that changed his mind about another attack. The writer was Henry Clinton, the general whom Howe had left in command in New York. He told Burgoyne that he had received reinforcements from England and now had enough men to make a foray up the Hudson in Burgoyne's favor. Gentleman Johnny seized on the proposal as heaven-sent. "Even the menace of an attack" on the Hudson Highlands forts some twenty-five miles north of New York City would be of "great use," he replied. He begged Clinton to "do it my dear friend, directly." Burgoyne proceeded to entrench Freeman's Farm and the high ground north of it and wait for Clinton.

It took Clinton two weeks to get his expedition under way. With 3,000 men and a naval escort, he captured the thinly held forts with an ease that amazed him. Garrisoning them, he sent one of his brigadiers with 1,700 men up the river—past West Point, which was not yet fortified—with orders to "feel for General Burgoyne, to assist his operations, and even to join him if that general required it."

This looming British presence on the upper Hudson badly rattled the Americans. They had no idea of the exact size of Clinton's force. Adding to the American alarm was the news that, on September 11, Washington's army had lost a major battle with Howe at Brandywine Creek in Pennsylvania, and the British would soon be in possession of Philadelphia. It was logical to assume Howe might have sent Clinton substantial reinforcements to rescue Burgoyne.

Meanwhile, Burgoyne was forced on October 4 to cut by a third the rations of vile salt pork and moldy flour on which his army was living. Shivering in summer uniforms in the chilly fall nights, his sick multiplied until the hospital cases, including the wounded from Freeman's Farm, numbered 800. The Americans gave them no rest. "Not a single night passes but there is firing and continual attacks on the advanced picquets," Captain Anburey glumly noted. "The officers rest in their cloaths, and the field officers are up frequently in the night."

American militia, under the overall command of Major General Benjamin Lincoln, added to Burgoyne's woes. In three columns, 1,500 of them attacked Ticonderoga, the outpost guard at the vital portage between Lake Champlain and Lake George, and Skenesborough. They got nowhere at Fort Ti, but at the portage, the column under Colonel John Brown surprised and captured 243 redcoats, freed 100 American prisoners, and burned 17 sloops and 200 bateaux. Burgoyne's supply line to Canada went up in those flames.

On October 6, against the advice of all his senior officers, who urged him to retreat, Burgoyne decided on another attack. Gates predicted the move, calling him an "old gamester" who was likely to "risque all upon one throw." The next day, with 2,000 picked men and ten cannon, Burgoyne led a reconnaissance in force to explore the vulnerable American left. If he saw a chance of a possible breakthrough, he planned to attack the following day with every man he had left in his army.

In the American camp, a demoralizing quarrel had been raging between

47

Gates and Arnold. With malice aforethought, Gates had sent Congress a report of the Battle of Freeman's Farm that totally omitted Arnold's name, as well as those of his friends Morgan and Major Dearborn. Enraged, Arnold had burst into Gates's tent and exchanged insults with him. Gates had retaliated by removing Arnold from command of the left wing and offering him a pass to Philadelphia. Many of the army's senior officers were appalled. Several prevailed on Arnold to stay, hoping Gates would relent. But on the day Burgoyne marched out of his camp, the two men were still not speaking and Gates was in command of the left wing.

Arnold had used the news of Clinton's foray to taunt Gates for his failure to attack Burgoyne during the seventeen-day hiatus. "Let me entreat you to improve the present time," he wrote, claiming he cared neither for glory nor for credit but was deeply concerned that Gates was about to let a great victory slip from their grasp. When Burgoyne's reconnaissance in force appeared, Gates realized he could not hunker behind his barricades without losing face. "Order on Morgan to begin the game," he said.

The British formed a battle line on a long, low ridge about three-quarters of a mile west of Bemis Heights, while Burgoyne and his senior officers climbed to the top of a log cabin to peer at the American position through spyglasses. They could see nothing. The tall trees beyond Freeman's Farm were a wall of impenetrable fall colors, rendering the expedition pointless. While they debated what to do next, and camp women and foragers furiously harvested wheat on two nearby abandoned farms, Morgan's riflemen circled wide to hit their right flank.

Gates also dispatched Brigadier General Enoch Poor of New Hampshire with a brigade of Continentals and two Connecticut militia regiments to attack Burgoyne's left. Although the British had a clear field of fire in their front, both flanks rested on thick woods in which they distributed some German light infantry and American Loyalists. Poor, having less distance to traverse than Morgan, made contact first, about 2:30 P.M. His 800 men quickly cleared the woods on their side and attacked without waiting for Morgan.

The British left consisted of grenadier companies commanded by Major John Dyke Acland. When Poor's men burst from the woods and charged up the slope at them, the British blasted them with musketry and grapeshot, but most of the metal flew over their heads. Acland called for a bayonet charge, and the Americans replied with a decimating fire that sent the surviving grenadiers fleeing. Acland, shot in both legs, was taken prisoner. The Yankees seized two cannon and turned them on the retreating grenadiers and on the 400 Brunswick Germans who had held the center.

By this time, Morgan's men were attacking the light infantry on the other flank, charging from the shelter of the trees "like a torrent" while their sharpshooters did their usual deadly job of picking off officers. As the British light infantry changed front to meet them, Dearborn and his light troops appeared on Morgan's right and hit them with a destructive volley. The British broke and fled, leaving the Germans exposed to attack on three sides. Burgoyne's aide, sent to order a general retreat, was shot out of the saddle. The Germans fought on.

At this point Arnold appeared on the battlefield, in direct defiance of Gates's orders. Taking charge of Ebenezer Learned's brigade, who were just entering the battle, Arnold led them up the hill against the Germans in two furious charges. They were repulsed by musketry and grapeshot. Seeing the flight of the light infantry, Arnold quickly shifted men to the left and, with the assistance of Morgan and Dearborn, enveloped the Germans' flank.

The Germans began falling back, and the battle teetered toward total rout. Burgoyne, with bullet holes in his coat and hat, his horse shot out from under him, was helpless. Only Brigadier Simon Fraser showed any semblance of command, riding on horseback into the fleeing ranks of the light infantry and rallying them to make a momentarily successful stand. Arnold pointed to him and shouted to Morgan: "That man on the gray horse is a host unto himself and must be disposed of." Morgan passed the order to Tim Murphy, one of his best sharpshooters, who quickly climbed a tree and put a bullet through the brigadier's belly.

Fraser's fall took the heart out of the reconnaissance in force, and the survivors ran for the protection of their fortified camp. But Arnold was not satisfied. He wanted to destroy Burgoyne before Clinton arrived. For two years he had fought to eliminate the threat of an invasion from the north; he was not going to let the British break off the action again to fight another day while he listened to more lectures from Gates on rashness and insubordination.

Shouting "Victory or death!" he led the thoroughly aroused Americans in an assault on the British camp. An appalled Burgoyne, looking over his shoulder, told Captain Anburey, who was guarding a sally port: "Sir, you must defend this post to the very last man!" To Anburey's relief, Arnold's first target was the outlying redoubt commanded by the earl of Balcarres, in the center of Freeman's Farm. It was supported by Canadian irregulars in two stockaded cabins. Routing the Canadians, Arnold and parts of two Continental brigades hurled themselves at the light infantry and assorted other fugitives manning the walls of the redoubt. But cannon fire and musketry tore cruel gaps in the American ranks, and they were forced to retreat.

Looking around, Arnold saw another brigade of Continentals arriving on the battlefield, heading for the British right. Riding his horse the length of Freeman's Farm with several hundred British muskets and cannon shooting at him, Arnold seized command of the newcomers and swung them around another outlying redoubt, defended by Germans under Colonel Heinrich von Breymann. Gaining the rear, Arnold rode his horse into the sally port with the Continentals swarming behind him, shouting and shooting. Men from Morgan's and Dearborn's commands scaled the front walls. When Breymann started sabering men who tried to run away, one of his own men shot him dead. Another wounded German got off a final shot at Arnold, breaking the thighbone of the same leg that had been wounded in the assault on Quebec in 1775. In agony, Arnold was carried back to Bemis Heights in a litter.

By this time the British had abandoned the field. They had lost another 600 men and all ten cannon they had dragged along on their reconnaissance. American losses were around 150. Far more important than these statistics was Arnold's capture of the Breymann redoubt. On high ground, its cannon commanded the Balcarres redoubt and the rest of the British camp. This time, no matter what Gates thought of Arnold's performance, he tacitly confessed his approval by rushing orders from his tent to hold the little fort "at all hazards."

At 9:00 P.M. on October 8, after burying General Fraser, Burgoyne began a slow, agonized retreat, leaving 300 sick and wounded behind in the hospital, along with a letter begging Gates's mercy. Heavy rain turned the road into a quagmire, forcing the British to abandon wagons with their tents and baggage. Most of their bateaux, following along the riverbank, were eventually captured or destroyed by the Americans. It took the British twenty-four hours to cover the eight miles to their old camp north of Fishkill Creek, near Saratoga (now Schuylerville), where the exhausted men fell in the mud and slept in their sodden uniforms.

Gates made a feeble effort to cut off the retreat, rushing 1,500 militiamen along the east bank of the Hudson with orders to cross at Saratoga and set up a blocking position. But the Americans were much too weak to deal with the whole British army; when it appeared, they hastily fell back. The next day Burgoyne sent two regiments north to build a bridge across the river at Fort Edward. Again, the Americans were so beat up—or so timid—that the regiments marched all around them unchallenged.

The departure of these regiments upset Gates, who was still very tense about Clinton's whereabouts. He thought most of Burgoyne's army was retreating and, without sending out so much as a patrol to explore the situation, ordered an assault on their rear guard. Around daybreak on October 11, the Americans advanced in a heavy fog. Morgan crossed the upper reaches of the Fishkill to get to the British rear. Four brigades of Continentals crossed the river lower down. General Glover's brigade picked up a British deserter, who told them nine-tenths of Burgoyne's army was still in camp, hoping the Americans would be foolish enough to attack them.

The appalled Glover sent messengers racing back to Gates, urging the other brigades that had crossed the Fishkill to fall back as fast as possible. A few minutes later the fog lifted, and there was Burgoyne's army on their outworks, bristling with cannon. The Americans retreated under a hail of grapeshot and bullets, losing about twenty men.

That was Burgoyne's last chance to reverse his collapse. The two regiments returned to report that militia were swarming on the east bank of the Hudson around Fort Edward, so crossing the river was out of the question. Soon New Hampshire militiamen, led by pugnacious John Stark, the victor at Bennington, took up positions directly north of the royal army, sealing off the last escape route.

Including all his militia, Gates now had over 14,000 men. He saw that Burgoyne could not tell the difference between a Continental and a militiaman. Any American with a gun in his hand was a menace. But Gates anxiously—and wisely—kept his 6,000 Continentals together, lest Clinton appear to his rear, or Burgoyne turn on him for another assault out of desperation. He refused to detach even a company to defend Albany against Clinton. Instead he ordered a regiment from Fort Stanwix, along with the Albany County militia, to take on that responsibility.

Burgoyne's situation rapidly grew hopeless. While rations dwindled and horses starved to death, the surrounding Americans sniped by day and bombarded by night. The Americans also unveiled a new weapon, about 150 Mohawk Indians whom Schuyler had persuaded to join the war. These made life even more hazardous for British pickets and sentries. Desertions multiplied, and there was not a word from Clinton. Finally, on October 13, Gentleman Johnny asked Gates for a parley.

Instead of letting Burgoyne propose the first set of terms, Gates nervously asked for an unconditional surrender. When Burgoyne furiously rejected the idea and insisted on the full honors of war, Gates accepted without a murmur. Burgoyne, suspecting Gates knew something about Clinton's approach, sparred for time by insisting that the word "capitulation" be excised from the terms. Instead, he offered to sign a "convention" that would permit his troops to return to Europe, on the promise that they would not be used again in the war. The jittery Gates accepted this demand—which would permit the British to send fresh troops from England or Ireland, whom Burgoyne's men would replace. Perhaps he knew—or hoped—the Continental Congress would find ways to circumvent the agreement, which, to their dishonor, they eventually managed to do.

More suspicious than ever, Burgoyne noticed large bodies of militia marching off from Gates's army and wondered if Clinton's approach was causing panic. He suddenly demanded the right to count the American force to ensure it was the same size as when he had opened negotiations. Gates angrily rejected this, explaining that some militia were simply going home when their time was up, in their usual style, indifferent to larger matters. Burgoyne asked his senior officers if he could honorably break off negotiations at this point. They unanimously said he could not—and added that they no longer had any confidence in their men's readiness to fight. After a few more hours of hesitation, Burgoyne signed the convention on October 16, 1777.

That same day, Clinton's troops attacked and burned Kingston, where the New York state government had been meeting, and sailed up the Hudson to Livingston Manor, forty-five miles below Albany and eighty-five miles from Saratoga. Militia on both banks—and the uncertain navigation of the river—discouraged them from going farther.

Just how sincere Clinton had ever been about trying to rescue Burgoyne is open to doubt. He specialized in embroidering orders with "little hints" about what he really wanted his subordinates to do. If he had been serious about reaching Albany, Clinton should have embarked his men in bateaux. Instead he chose seagoing transports, which drew too much water to get that far, though they offered his men better protection from potshotting militia on the riverbanks. From the start, Clinton had neither the manpower nor a burning desire to risk much to rescue Burgoyne. He also knew he was in line to succeed Howe as commander in chief, an event that Burgoyne's surrender made almost inevitable.

On October 17, Burgoyne's men marched out and stacked their arms in a meadow north of Fishkill Creek. The gleeful Gates wrote to his wife that "Burgoyne and his great army have laid down their arms . . . to me and my Yankees." With New England's politicians behind him in Congress, Gates thought he was now in a position to supplant George Washington as the American commander in chief. He made this clear by reporting his victory directly to Congress, only casually mentioning it to Washington in a letter on November 6.

Gates did not seem to realize that his claim to victory at Saratoga was forever tainted by his failure to get within a mile of the actual fighting—and by the meanness and pettiness he had displayed to both Schuyler and Arnold. In the following year, when he tried to persuade Daniel Morgan to join him in a campaign to unseat Washington, Morgan told him never to mention "that detestable subject" to him again. "Under Washington and none but Washington, will I serve," he roared.

It has become traditional to point to Saratoga as a historic turning point that transformed the war by persuading France to become America's public ally. The victory unquestionably contributed to the French decision. But Louis XVI and his ministers were equally impressed by Washington's skill at keeping the main American army intact outside Philadelphia, aggressively staring the enemy in the face. His ferocious attack on Howe's army at Germantown on October 4, only three weeks after the defeat at Brandywine, was explosive proof that Britain's 1777 campaign had failed on all fronts.

At least as important as France's decision to intervene was the way Saratoga transformed the British attitude toward their American opponents. In a private letter after the surrender, Burgoyne told Lord George Germain, who as colonial secretary was the war's civilian commander, that "a near inspection of the rebel troops" had convinced him that "the standing corps [his term for Continentals] are disciplined." Burgoyne added that he was not using the word lightly. He was applying it "to the great fundamental points of military institution, sobriety, subordination, regularity and courage."

Saratoga demonstrated how an artful mix of regulars and militia could create mutual inspiration and support. As the Continentals marched south to rejoin the main American army, they knew that they now had a strategy for victory—if they had the perseverance and steady nerves to make it work.

*AUTUMN 1993*

---

**Thomas Fleming is the author of the previous essay on George Washington.**

---

# 5

# Mrs. Benedict Arnold

## By Willard Sterne Randall

*Since the earliest days of the Republic, Benedict Arnold has been the American phrase for traitor. Other villains from Aaron Burr to Aldrich Ames have come and gone through the course of American history, but none have quite matched Arnold's nefarious reputation. Willard Sterne Randall, however, notes that Benedict Arnold did not plot treachery alone. Instead, the general's wife, Peggy Shippen Arnold, carried the key to her husband's betrayal. With today's concern for gender equality, perhaps it is time to remember a woman as America's greatest traitor.*

Nearly all her life, Peggy Shippen was surrounded by the turmoil of an age of wars and revolution. She was born with the British Empire in 1760, only weeks before the French surrendered all of Canada. Before her third birthday, British America had grown by conquest from a strip of coastal colonies to nearly half of North America. The town of Philadelphia, where her father, Judge Edward Shippen, held a lucrative array of colonial offices, was the largest seaport in America. A center for trade and its regulation, it was a natural target for protests when resistance to British revenue measures flared in the 1760s. By the age of five, she had seen riots in the streets outside her father's handsome brick town house.

The revolutionary movement grew all her childhood. At fifteen she listened at her parents' dinner table as their guests argued politics: George Washington, John Adams, Silas Deane, and Benedict Arnold were among the patriots who dined at the Shippens'; British officials and officers included General Thomas Gage and the intriguing John André. By the time Peggy was seventeen, the British army occupied Philadelphia and she was being linked romantically with the young British spymaster. After the Americans reoccupied the city, and before she was nineteen, Peggy married Military Governor Benedict Arnold and helped him to plot the boldest treason in American history—not only the surrender of West Point and its 3,000 men but the capture of Washington, Lafayette, and their combined staffs.

Delicately beautiful, brilliant, witty, a consummate actress and astute businesswoman, Peggy Shippen was, new research reveals, the highest-paid spy of the American Revolution. Understandably, the Shippen family destroyed papers that could connect her to the treason of Benedict Arnold. As a result, for two centuries she has been considered Arnold's hapless and passive spouse, innocent though neurotic. But new evidence reveals that she actively engaged in the Arnold conspiracy at every step. She was a deeply committed Loyalist who helped persuade her husband to change sides. When he wavered in his resolve to defect, it was she who kept the plot alive and then shielded him, risking her life over and over. Ultimately expelled from the United States, she was handsomely rewarded by the British "for services rendered."

When Margaret Shippen was born, on June 11, 1760, her father, who already had a son and three daughters, wrote his father that his wife "this morning made me a present of a fine baby which, though the worst sex, is yet entirely welcome." Judge Shippen was usually cheerful about his large brood: The Shippens were one of colonial America's wealthiest and most illustrious families.

The first American Shippen—Peggy's great-great-grandfather, the first Edward—had immigrated to Boston in 1668 with a fortune from trade in the Middle East. He and his wife were granted sanctuary in Rhode Island by Governor Benedict Arnold, the traitor's great-grandfather. The couple resettled in Philadelphia on a two-mile-deep riverfront estate. Shippen later became Speaker of the Pennsylvania Assembly and the second mayor of Philadelphia.

Peggy's father, the fourth Edward in the line, was a conservative man who seemed constantly worried, usually about money or property. He followed his father's wishes and practiced law, also holding several remunerative colonial offices simultaneously—admiralty judge, prothonotary, recorder of deeds—and was at first firmly on the British side in the long struggle that evolved into the Revolution. His tortured reactions to the almost constant tensions that accompanied years of riots, boycotts, and congresses in Philadelphia were the backdrop for his daughter Peggy's unusual childhood.

When Parliament passed the Stamp Act in 1765, before Peggy's fifth birthday, her father read aloud about "great riots and disturbances" in Boston. He considered the act oppressive, but he opposed illegally destroying stamped paper. "What will be the consequences of such a step, I tremble to think. . . . Poor America! It has seen its best days." By the time Peggy was eight and learning to read leather-bound books in their library, her father's admiralty court had become the center of the storm over British taxation. When she was ten, his judgeship was abolished.

As the colonial crisis dragged on, Shippen lectured his favorite daughter on disobedience: Bad laws had to be repealed; simply to ignore or resist them would open the door to anarchy. Despite his drawing-room bravery, however, Shippen refused to take a public stand, careful to avoid offending radicals or street mobs that might attack his property or harm his daughters. He burst into a rare fit of rage at Thomas Paine's "book called *Common Sense,* in favor of total separation from England. . . . It is artfully wrote, yet might be easily refuted. . . . This idea of independence, though sometime ago abhorred, may possibly, by degrees, become so familiar as to be cherished."

Judge Shippen's only son, the fifth Edward ("Neddy"), had early shown himself to be inept at business, and he eventually squandered much of the family fortune. The judge decided to educate Peggy as if she were his son. Peggy curled up in a wingback across from her father to read Addison, Steele, Pope, Defoe, all the latest British writers. Her mother saw to it that she was instructed in needlework, cooking, drawing, dancing, and music, but in none of her surviving letters is there any of the household trivia of her time.

Peggy had a distinctive literary style and wit, and, like her father, she wrote with unusual clarity. A quiet, serious girl, she was too practical, too interested in business and in making the most of time and money, for frivolity. By age fifteen, as the Revolutionary War began, she was helping her father with his investments. She learned the finer points of bookkeeping, accounting, real estate and other investments, importing and trade, banking and monetary transactions—and she basked in her father's approval.

But she had also been studying her sisters' manners and social behavior. It was at the fortnightly dances in Freemasons Hall that young men who danced with them began to notice Peggy: She was petite, blond, dainty of face and figure, with steady, wide set, blue-gray eyes and a full mouth, which she pursed as she listened intently.

As far into the new politics as Judge Shippen would delve was to invite partisans of all stripes to his brick mansion on Fourth Street, in Philadelphia's Society Hill section, to air their views at his dinner table. In early September 1774, Peggy and her family entertained some of the delegates to the First Continental Congress. Few, if any, foresaw a war of revolution against the mother country; many expected to conciliate their complaints with Parliament peacefully. Of all the colonies, Pennsylvania was the most divided: The majority was made up of pacifist Quakers and members of the more than 250 German pietist sects, and there was the strong Penn proprietary party, loyal to the British.

That steamy September, Philadelphians agonized over the course of the New England radicals' confrontation with the crown in British-occupied Boston as post riders, delegates, militiamen, and redcoats came and went down the broad cobbled streets, making it increasingly difficult to remain neutral. Congressional delegate Silas Deane wrote to his wife that "this city is in the utmost confusion." Rumors of British invasion also were flying; during one panic, Pennsylvania militiamen drilled and marched past the Shippens' town house even as the last red-coated British regiment in the middle colonies strode to the waterfront and boarded troop transports taking them north to reinforce Boston.

One young British officer who could have chosen to join them was

Second Lieutenant John André of the 7th Foot, the Royal Welsh Fusiliers, who had arrived in Philadelphia just a few days earlier. Sent out from England to join his regiment, André was en route to Quebec. He had been a peacetime officer for five years and had never fought in battle but instead had pursued the life of a dilettante poet, playwright, and artist.

From the safety of England, André had taken the unrest in America lightly, but upon arrival he found Philadelphia in the grip of anti-British frenzy. It was not a safe place for a young, solitary British officer. Oddly, he decided to travel not aboard a British warship but on foot alone north to Lake Champlain. He sailed on to Quebec in a schooner, in the company of a black woman, an Indian squaw in a blanket, "and the sailors round the stove." It was the first of John André's strange and romantic journeys through an America he would never understand.

As André meandered north, thirty-three-year-old shipowner and revolutionary Benedict Arnold, who had arrived in Philadelphia with the Connecticut delegation to Congress, was accompanying his mentor, Silas Deane, to a series of political caucuses and dinners. A self-made man of means and long a leader of the radical Sons of Liberty in New Haven, Arnold was helping to plan the systematic suppression of antirevolutionary sentiment. The purpose of the Congress was to protest British oppression, but Sons of Liberty from a dozen colonies used the opportunity to discuss the elimination of Loyalist opposition.

Yet Arnold and Deane had time for dinners in Philadelphia's best houses. And one Loyalist family, the Shippens, stood out for their hospitality. Deane and Arnold were invited to the judge's dinner table, where Shippen introduced his daughters, including the youngest, the precocious Peggy. Although only fourteen, she was already one of the city's most popular debutantes. Flirtatious and quick-witted, she could talk confidently with men about politics and trade. Benedict Arnold met her for the first time at dinner that September.

Peggy heard Benedict Arnold's name frequently in the next few years as the Revolution turned to war and its leaders put on uniforms and fanned out to fight the British. Arnold's attack on Fort Ticonderoga, his heroic march to Quebec and his daring assault on the walled city, his naval campaign on Lake Champlain, his wounding, and his quarrels over promotion often put his name in the Philadelphia newspapers. A few blocks from the Shippen house, a new ship in the Pennsylvania navy was given Arnold's name, and that was in the papers, too.

News of the war often touched closer to home. Peggy's oldest sister's fiancé, a rebel, was missing and presumed killed in the American rout on Long Island. Her brother, Neddy, eighteen, on the spur of the moment decided to join the British army in Trenton for the Christmas festivities. When Washington attacked, Neddy was captured. He was freed by the Shippens' erstwhile dinner guest, George Washington himself. All of Judge Shippen's careful neutrality was jeopardized. Stripping the youth of any further part in family business affairs, the judge turned his son's duties over to Peggy.

When the Americans invaded Canada late in 1775, the British made a stand at Fort St.-Jean on the Richelieu River, surrendering only after a long siege. One of the officers captured was twenty-five-year-old Second Lieutenant André. Freed on parole, he was sent south with the baggage of his fellow officers to house arrest in Pennsylvania. In Philadelphia, while he attended to provisions for his fellow prisoners, André had time to explore "the little society of Third and Fourth Streets," the opulent town houses of Peggy's neighborhood. The romantic young officer was ushered into the Fourth Street home of Judge Shippen and introduced to fifteen-year-old Peggy Shippen. Before he left for an indefinite term in captivity on the Pennsylvania frontier, he played his flute and recited his poetry and asked to sketch her.

One year later André was exchanged for an American prisoner. Then, in the autumn of 1777, when Peggy was seventeen, General Sir William Howe's British army drove the Americans out of Philadelphia and marched up Second Street, two blocks from the Shippens'. André had recently given the orders for a British regiment to fix bayonets, remove the flints from their muskets, and attack a sleepy American unit at nearby Paoli. The increasingly callous André tersely described the massacre in his regimental journal, calling the Americans a "herd" as nearly 200 men were killed and a great number wounded. He noted they were "stabbed . . . till it was thought prudent to . . . desist."

As an aide at British headquarters in Philadelphia, André decided to follow the example of his commanders and seek diversions from the toils of killing. He and his elegant friends reconnoitered in the best society they could find, and André began calling on the Shippens, accompanied by his friends Captain Andrew Snape Hamond of HMS *Roebuck* and Lord Francis Rawdon, who considered Peggy the most beautiful woman he had ever seen.

Even a conquering officer, however, could not hope to escort a Philadelphia debutante to the incessant round of military balls without a prior round of introductions. The first step was the morning visit to the drawing room of the intended partner. André frequently showed up, sketch pad under his arm, for obligatory cups of tea and chaperoned talks about the latest books, balls, and plays. In the evenings André, who was now a major, and his assistant, New York Loyalist Captain Oliver De Lancey, were hard at work turning a former warehouse on South Street into a splendid theater.

Peggy Shippen probably fell in love that winter with the charming major. But he flitted from one drawing-room beauty to another, serious about none of them. Still, he liked to be with Peggy; he liked to sketch her, showing her as elusively elegant and poutish, sometimes turning away, sometimes fixing him with an enigmatic smile. He enjoyed breakneck sleigh rides with her at his side, her friends crowding in with them under heavy bearskin rugs.

But when Peggy stepped out for the evening, it was more often on the arm of Captain Hamond, who later said, "We were all in love with her." One of the season's highlights was a dinner dance aboard the *Roebuck*. Peggy was piped on board the ship, which was illuminated with lanterns for the occasion. She sat down at Hamond's right for a dinner served to 200 invited guests, then danced until dawn.

By late April 1778 the British learned they were to withdraw to New York City and prepare for the arrival of the French, the revolutionaries' new ally. Philadelphia was too exposed. A new British commander was coming; General Howe was being recalled. John André volunteered to prepare a lavish farewell, a Meschianza, including a waterborne parade, a medieval tournament, a dress ball, and an enormous dinner party. No other effort of André's ever approached this opulent festival. He designed costumes for fourteen knights and their squires and "ladies selected from the foremost in youth, beauty, and fashion." For the ladies, he created Turkish harem costumes evoking the Crusades. He designed Peggy's entire wardrobe and sketched her in it. André's own glittering costume featured pink satin sashes, bows, and wide baggy pants.

Peggy's father grumbled, but he shelled out enough gold to outfit three of his daughters. As Peggy rode home the next morning, a Quaker diarist wrote, "How insensitive do these people appear while our land is so greatly desolated."

Before John André left a few weeks later, he gave Peggy a souvenir that showed how close they had become: a locket containing a ringlet of his hair. Though parted, they wrote each other secretly through the lines, at great risk to Peggy, directing the letters through a third party.

In May 1778, as the British made ready to evacuate Philadelphia, George Washington's newly appointed military governor was preparing a peaceful takeover of the capital city. Benedict Arnold—the hero of Ticonderoga, Quebec, and Saratoga—had been shot twice through his right leg and was still unable to stand without a crutch. Washington had urged him to take more time to recover, but Arnold insisted on returning to the war, so Washington gave him the rear-area command—thus placing Arnold in the middle of a political cross fire between the Continental Army and Pennsylvania politicians. As the British sailed away, Arnold drove into the city in his coach-and-four with his liveried servants, aides, and orderlies. From their brick mansion, the Shippens could see the American light horse ride by.

Benedict Arnold's duties as military governor included social evenings arranged by his spinster sister, Hannah, who was also rearing his three young sons; Arnold's wife had died while he was attacking Canada. Once an impoverished orphan, Arnold now moved freely in Philadelphia's elite society, sipping tea with the Shippens, the Robert Morrises, and other wealthy merchants and lawyers, and playing host to members of Congress at lavish dinners in his headquarters mansion.

He often encountered Peggy Shippen at these gatherings. Frequently his carriage was seen parked in front of the Shippen house, where British officers had come to call only a few months earlier, and as the summer of 1778 progressed, Peggy became known as the general's lady. At first, resentment that the American hero of Saratoga was courting the Loyalist belle of British officers' balls was confined to a little sniping in Congress. Arnold's insistence on inviting Loyalist women to revolutionary social events brought increasing criticism, yet Arnold seemed oblivious as he spent more and more time with eighteen-year-old Peggy.

In September 1778 Arnold declared himself a serious suitor in two letters, one to Peggy, one to her father. A relative of Peggy's wrote that "there can be no doubt the imagination of Miss Shippen was excited and her heart captivated by the oft-repeated stories of his gallant deeds, his feats of brilliant courage and traits of generosity and kindness." Peggy seemed especially touched by his paying for the education and upbringing of the three children of his friend Dr. Joseph Warren, who had been killed at Bunker Hill.

But Peggy had other reasons for falling in love with Benedict Arnold: He was still young (thirty-seven), ruggedly built despite his wounded leg, animated, intelligent and witty, strongly handsome and sometimes charming. It was obvious a life with "the General," as she always called him, would not be dull.

The judge did not say yes, but he did not say no. He wrote to *his* father to seek advice. But the more Arnold was publicly criticized for his leniency to Loyalists and his quite open love of one, and the longer the judge balked, the closer the two lovers drew together. Arnold had come to appreciate her "sweetness of disposition and goodness of heart, her sentiments as well as her sensibilities." He had faced few more implacable adversaries than Judge Shippen, who worried about his daughter's marrying an invalid. Finally, however, relatives persuaded the judge that Arnold was "a well-dispositioned man, and one that will use his best endeavors to make Peggy happy." The judge also liked the fact that Arnold settled a £7,000 country estate named Mount Pleasant on her as a wedding present.

On the other hand, the judge didn't like what he was beginning to hear about Arnold's private business dealings; but months of attacks on Arnold in the press by radical political opponents had made Peggy all the more determined to marry him. In the end, Judge Shippen seems to have acceded to his daughter's engagement only when his continued refusal made Peggy, now thoroughly in love, hysterical to the point of fainting spells.

On April 8, 1779, Arnold's nine-month siege ended. He rode down Fourth Street with his sister, his three sons, and an aide for an evening ceremony in the Shippen home. In his blue American major general's uniform, Benedict Arnold, thirty-eight, married eighteen-year-old Peggy Shippen. A young relative wrote that Peggy was "lovely, a beautiful bride" as she stood at last beside her "adoring general."

IN MAY 1779, within one month of their wedding, the couple entered into a daring plot to make Arnold a British general who would lead all the Loyalist forces and bring the long war to a speedy conclusion. All through their courtship there had been a mounting furor in the press about Arnold's alleged profiteering as military governor. No proof has ever been found that, up to then, he had done anything more than use his office to issue passes that helped Loyalist merchants, who in turn cut him in for a percentage of their profits; and once he diverted army wagons to haul contraband into Philadelphia for sale in stores. Both were common practices, but Arnold was often stiff-necked and arrogant in his dealings with Pennsylvania revolutionaries.

When Pennsylvania brought formal charges against Arnold, George Washington refused to intervene and, far from supporting him, treated him with the same cold formality he reserved for all officers facing court-martial. Arnold had already endured years of censure and controversy, and Washington's aloofness, coupled with a ferocious attack from Congress and in the newspapers, evidently drove him over the edge. Peggy seems not only to have approved of his decision to defect to the British but to have helped him at every turn in a year and a half of on-again, off-again plotting that at least once she alone managed to keep alive.

When Arnold's prosecutors produced no evidence to convict him, and when Washington, whose generals were preoccupied, was unable to bring about a speedy court-martial to clear him, the proud hero could tolerate the public humiliation no longer. On May 5, 1779, he wrote a drastic letter to Washington: "If Your Excellency thinks me criminal, for heaven's sake let me be immediately tried and, if found guilty, executed."

Apparently that same day, with Peggy's assistance, Arnold opened his secret correspondence with the British, using Peggy's friends and Philadelphia connections. A china and furniture dealer, Joseph Stansbury, who was helping Peggy decorate the Arnold house, acted as courier through the lines to André at British headquarters in New York City, where Stansbury often went on buying trips. Peggy already had been sending harmless messages to André with Stansbury. She now worked with Arnold to encode his messages, using a cipher written in invisible ink that could be read when rinsed with lemon juice or acid; a symbol in one corner indicated which to use.

On May 21, 1779, Peggy sat down with Arnold in a bedroom of their Market Street house and pored over the pages of the twenty-first edition of *Bailey's Dictionary.* (André had preferred Blackstone's *Commentaries on the Laws of England,* but they had rejected it as too cumbersome.) According to Stansbury, they used one of two copies of the compact dictionary: "This I have paged for [them], beginning at A. . . . Each side is numbered and contains 927 pages." The Arnolds added "1 to each number of the page, of the column, and of the line, the first word of which is always used, too. Zoroaster will be 928.2.2 and not 927.1.1. Tide is 838.3.2 and not 837.2.1."

It usually took ten days for Stansbury to slip through to André in New York, and as long to return; late at night he would send a servant to the Arnolds, and Peggy would carefully decode the message and encode Arnold's reply. Only rarely did the Loyalist Stansbury see the general; almost always he dealt with Peggy. André had instructed Stansbury to deal with "the Lady." In October 1779, when the British at first failed to meet Arnold's terms, Peggy wrote a cryptic letter in code to André and kept the negotiations alive until the two principals struck their bargains. This time she sent her note with a British prisoner who was being exchanged and returned to New York. She had become far more than an unwitting go-between, as historians have tended to portray her; she was now an active coconspirator:

> Mrs. Moore [Moore was one of Arnold's code names] requests the enclosed list of articles for her own use may be procured for her and the account of them and the former [orders] sent and she will pay for the whole with thanks.

The shopping list, evidently not the first, included cloth for napkins and for dresses, a pair of spurs, and pink ribbon.

André, who had feigned indifference in recent messages, became alarmed. He saw through Peggy's list: Although the negotiations with her husband had been fruitless so far, she was telling André that they were not hopeless. He put aside her shopping list and informed Sir Henry Clinton, the British commander in chief, that Arnold had finally stated his price: As Stansbury had told André, £20,000 if he succeeded; £10,000 if he failed. What Clinton wanted was detailed plans of West Point, the new American stronghold fifty miles up the Hudson from British lines. André sent the proposal back to Peggy, referring to her list as "trifling services from which I hope you would infer a zeal to be further employed."

It was late October before André received another coded note from Peggy:

> Mrs. Arnold presents her best respects to Captain André, is much obliged to him for his very polite and friendly offer of being serviceable to her.

To entice the British, the Arnolds sent much vital military and political intelligence through the lines in the seventeen months from May 1779 through September 1780. In June 1779 they tipped off the British commander that Washington would leave his base at Morristown, New Jersey, as soon as the first hay was harvested and move north to the Hudson for a summer campaign. This leak gave Clinton time to strike first up the Hudson before Washington could reinforce his forts there. The couple disclosed that Congress had decided to all but write off Charleston, South Carolina, the largest and most important town in the South, if the British once again attempted to take it. (They did and succeeded.)

The Arnolds also informed Clinton about American currency problems and about congressional refusal to give agents in Paris full power to negotiate a peace treaty with Britain: The Arnolds believed the French alliance was shaky, and that if it fell apart, the Americans would have to sue for peace. Arnold thought he could then be useful in bringing about a reconciliation between responsible Americans and the British. "I will cooperate with others when opportunity offers," he wrote, adding a postscript: "Madam Arnold presents her particular compliments."

Ironically, one of the Arnolds' early messages to the British led to the interruption of his court-martial in June 17, 1779, soon after it finally began, when the British took his advice and attacked up the Hudson. As Washington and his army dashed north, Arnold lurked behind at headquarters, talking to other officers about Washington's plans for the season of war.

The Arnolds encoded top-secret information about American troop strengths, dispositions, and destinations. He was the first to warn the British of an American expedition "to destroy the Indian settlements" of Pennsylvania and New York. But his most devastating tips were dispatched on July 17, 1779: the latest troop strengths; expected turnout of militia; the state of the army; the location of its supply depots; the number of men and cannon on the punitive raid against the Mohawks; troop locations, strengths, and weaknesses in Rhode Island and in the South; the location and movements of American and French ships. Peggy Shippen met alone with Joseph Stansbury during these treacherous July 1779 negotiations as Benedict Arnold showed the British what he was willing to give in exchange for a red uniform and at least £10,000.

More months dragged by before Washington could spare general officers to reconvene Arnold's court-martial. Meanwhile, Arnold had resigned as military governor of Philadelphia. Not until December 1779 was he allowed to defend himself, and although the generals recommended a formal reprimand, the Arnolds did not learn of his conviction until April 1780, only weeks after the birth of their first child. He never forgave Washington for publicly censuring him in writing. But Washington considered it a minor affair and promptly offered Arnold another field command, this time as his number two general.

The Arnolds were determined to defect, and Arnold himself put it in writing to André and Clinton that West Point would soon be his to command and his to betray to the British. But Washington insisted that Arnold join him with his troops. Peggy was at a dinner party at the home of Robert Morris when news reached Philadelphia that Arnold had been appointed to command the left wing of the Continental Army, not West Point. She fainted.

What Peggy did not learn for three weeks was that Arnold, pretending his old injuries had flared up, had finally persuaded a puzzled Washington to rewrite his orders, installing him as the commandant of West Point and an enlarged New York command. Arnold arrived at West Point on August 4, 1780.

He sent word to Peggy in Philadelphia to leave his sons by his first marriage in the care of his sister and to come by carriage with the baby and her two servants. Meanwhile, he went about weakening West Point defenses (by deploying men so they could not defend against the British) and arranging the details of his defection with Major André, who had been promoted to chief of the British secret service inside New York City. Plans for a first meeting on the Hudson on September 11, 1780, miscarried, and Arnold was almost killed by gunfire from a British gunboat.

After two months apart from her husband, Peggy at last arrived at West Point, and their days and nights took on the added excitement of plotting their defection. Peggy's weeks without Arnold, the longest she had ever been away from him, had been one of the loneliest periods of her life, filled with desperate anxiety. But the same day she rejoined him, they received a letter cutting short the time they could expect together. Washington was coming north from his New Jersey headquarters, he wrote Arnold secretly. Arnold was to provide an escort and meet him as he rode without his army to confer with the French in Hartford.

Realizing how vulnerable Washington would be, Arnold sent off an urgent message to André: If the British moved quickly, their warships on the Hudson, helped by a few hundred dragoons, could capture Washington and his generals as he crossed the river with a few score troops. In a bold military coup, Arnold would seize Washington and negotiate an American surrender that would quickly end the war. If the plot succeeded, Arnold could expect a dukedom from a grateful king, and Peggy would be a duchess.

PEGGY'S FIRST AND only Sunday as the mistress of West Point, September 17, 1780, was a tense affair. Arnold's staff fled into the wainscoted dining room of Beverley, the commandant's house, to take their seats with Arnold's weekend Loyalist houseguests. It was an early dinner: Arnold was soon to go downriver to deliver Washington's hand-picked escort. They were hardly seated when a courier arrived with two coded letters for Arnold from André, who was aboard the *Vulture,* a British ship twelve miles downriver. Trying not to betray his excitement, Arnold pocketed the letters. After dinner he rode off with forty Life Guards to meet Washington.

Circling back alone that night after his last meeting with Washington, Arnold waited for the British attack, but Clinton procrastinated and it did not come. He had learned, however, that Washington would be inspecting West Point on September 23; the British would have a second chance. Three more anxious days passed at Beverley. Shortly before dawn on September 21, Arnold kissed Peggy good-bye and slipped off to meet André. Late that night an open boat bearing André, wrapped in a navy blue caped coat, thumped ashore two miles below Haverstraw. At last the two men met. Arnold turned over papers to André and returned to West Point on September 22.

While Arnold had been gone, Peggy, still exhausted from her nine-day journey to West Point in an open carriage in the summer heat, had stayed with the baby in Beverley's master bedroom, a sunny, quiet place with big open windows and balustraded porch. Now, on September 23, a Saturday, she stayed late in the room, planning to go downstairs later when Washington arrived. Arnold and his staff had just been served breakfast when a messenger, muddy and dripping, was shown in: John André had been captured!

His luck had run out half a mile north of Tarrytown that morning. Seven young militiamen absent without leave had banded together to waylay Loyalist travelers. As André rode up to Pine's Bridge, he was startled by three of them. John Paulding, in a captured Hessian's uniform, grabbed the bit of Andre's horse.

"Gentlemen," said André, who could see the British lines, "I hope you belong to our party."

"What party?" Paulding demanded.

"The lower party," André replied, alluding to the Loyalists. "Thank God, I am once more among friends. I am glad to see you. I am an officer in the British service." The exuberant André pulled out his gold watch "for a token to let you know I am a gentleman."

"Get down," Paulding growled. "We are Americans."

"My God, I must do anything to get along," André rejoined with a stage laugh, brandishing a pass Arnold had written out for him.

"Damn Arnold's pass! You said you was a British officer. Get down. Where is your money?"

When André began to argue, Paulding swore and pointed his weapon. "God damn it! Where is your money?"

After André protested that he had none, Paulding and his friends forced him into a thicket and ordered him to strip. André later said that the three men ripped up the housings of his saddle and the collar of his coat and were about to let him go when one of the party said, "He may have it in his boots." They threw him down, yanked off his English boots, and, in his stockings, found Arnold's report of West Point's fortifications and troop displacements, a summary of the American army's strength, and the secret minutes of Washington's latest council of war concerning combined Franco-American strategy.

"This is a spy," Paulding finally shouted to the others. They prodded him with their guns as he dressed and mounted. Then they tied his arms behind him and led him back over the roads he had just ridden, back toward the American lines.

At West Point, Arnold was handed a note informing him that a packet of papers in his own handwriting was on its way to Washington. He hurried upstairs to Peggy, locked the bedroom door, and whispered that the plot had been discovered. Washington was expected any minute.

Peggy must have reassured her husband that she and the baby would be safe; it is unlikely that she tried to talk him out of fleeing for his life. She agreed to burn all of their papers and stall for time. He embraced her, took a last look at Neddy, and hurried out, ordering an aide to saddle a horse. At the river, Arnold jumped into his eight-oared barge, drew his pistols, and told his crewmen he would give them two gallons of rum if they got him downriver. The boat lurched into the Hudson channel, Arnold in the stern. By the time Washington arrived, a few minutes later, Arnold was on his way to the *Vulture* and the British lines.

Peggy's years of studying theatrics now saved her husband's life, even if her performance could have cost hers. As Arnold was making his escape, she ran shrieking down the hallway in her dressing gown, her hair disheveled. Arnold's aides rushed up the stairs to find her screaming and struggling with two maids, who were trying to get her back into her room. Peggy grabbed one young aide by the hand and cried, "Have you ordered my child to be killed?" Peggy fell to her knees, the aide later testified, "with prayers and entreaties to spare her innocent babe." Two more officers arrived, "and we carried her to her bed, raving mad." The distraught twenty-year-old so distracted Arnold's staff that no one thought to pursue him until Washington arrived.

Peggy Shippen's world had been exploded by a plot she had encouraged, aided, and abetted, and sheer nervous tension on the day of discovery helped her to completely fool everyone around her. It would be the twentieth century before the opening of the British Headquarters Papers at the University of Michigan proved what the eighteenth century refused to believe—that a young and innocent-appearing woman was capable of helping Benedict Arnold plot the conspiracy that nearly delivered victory to England in the American Revolution.

When Peggy learned that Washington had arrived, she cried out again and told the young aides that "there was a hot iron on her head and no one but General Washington could take it off." The aides and a staff doctor summoned the commander in chief, but when Peggy saw him she said, "No, that is not General Washington; that is the man who was going to assist . . . in killing my child." Washington retreated from the room, certain Peggy Arnold was no conspirator. A few days later he sent her and the baby under escort to her family in Philadelphia.

When news of Arnold's treason spread throughout America, Peggy was ordered expelled from Pennsylvania. The same officials whose hounding of Arnold had provoked him into treason now unwittingly aided her escape through British lines to join the traitor in New York City. She arrived at Two Broadway, the house Arnold had rented next door to British headquarters, in time to learn that John André had been hanged by Washington after a drumhead trial for espionage. She secluded herself in her bedroom for weeks, rarely appearing with Arnold at headquarters functions.

Paid £6,350, Arnold was commissioned a British brigadier general. He raised a regiment, the American Legion, made up exclusively of deserters from the American army—no British officer would serve under him—and led it on bloody raids through Virginia. Arnold's troops sacked the capital at Richmond, nearly capturing Thomas Jefferson, and his native Thames River valley of Connecticut.

Peggy spent the last year of the Revolution, her last year in her native country, a celebrity in New York, pregnant much of the time with her second child. Some of her old Philadelphia neighbors were also Loyalists living in British-occupied Manhattan; her former Society Hill neighbors kept tabs on her and wrote back news to Philadelphia.

Peggy was grieving for André, even though her marriage to Arnold was serene. Mrs. Samuel Shoemaker wrote in November 1780 that Peggy now "wants animation, sprightliness and fire in her eyes." When she did appear in public, however, it was as the new favorite at headquarters balls. Peggy "appeared a star of the first magnitude, and had every attention paid her," especially after she received a personal pension of £500 a year from the queen.

After the British surrender at Yorktown, where American troops celebrated victory by burning Arnold in effigy, the Arnolds sailed for England in a 150-ship convoy. They arrived on January 22, 1782, and according to the *Daily Advertiser* took "a house in Portman Square and set up a carriage." She was, wrote one nobleman, "an amiable woman and, was her husband dead, would be much noticed."

The Arnolds' warmest reception was at the Court of St. James's, where they were introduced to the king and queen. Arnold, King George III, and the Prince of Wales took long walks together, deep in conversation. Queen Charlotte was especially taken with Peggy, and her courtiers, as one wrote, paid "much attention to her." The queen doubled Peggy's pension to £1,000 a year and provided a £100 lifetime annuity for each of her children. Peggy was to raise five, and eventually received far more from the crown than Arnold did. Her pensions guaranteed that she could bring up her children comfortably and that based on their mother's prestige alone they would be introduced into society as English gentry. All four of the Arnolds' sons became British officers; their daughter married a general.

Arnold never got another farthing. When peace came, he became a half-pay pensioner and had to strap family resources to build a ship and return to the life at sea that had once made him wealthy. As her husband sailed to Canada, Peggy, twenty-five years old, suddenly felt the loss of her American home and family. Arnold was gone for nearly a year and a half, during which Peggy ran their business affairs, collected and invested their pensions, and fought lawsuits. When he returned, she had to pack everything up again—this time they were moving to Saint John, New Brunswick, where Arnold had established a shipping business, was buying up land, and had built a general store. Late in 1787, only six weeks after they arrived in Canada, Peggy gave birth again.

For the first time since she left Philadelphia, Peggy was able to make close friends. She lived in a big gambrel-roofed clapboard house elegantly decorated with furniture Arnold brought from England. But the house was an opulent island in a sea of deprivation: The city was crowded with impoverished Loyalist refugees, and few people could afford to pay Arnold for his imported goods. He made new enemies as he faced frequent decisions about whether to sue or to put men in debtors' prison. When his warehouse and store burned, there were whispers that he had torched them for the insurance. A former business partner was one of his accusers, and when Arnold confronted him, the man said, according to the court record, "It is not in my power to blacken your character, for it's as black as it can be."

The insult directly resulted in the denial of Arnold's insurance claim—and in the first jury trial for slander in New Brunswick history. Arnold won, but instead of the £5,000 he sought, the judges based the award on the value of his reputation and gave him only twenty shillings, an unbearable insult. At the same time, a mob sacked the Arnolds' home. Peggy and the children were away at the time, safe. After five years in Canada, the Arnolds moved back to England.

Like many Loyalists, Peggy Shippen Arnold planned to return one day to live in the United States, where she kept her inheritance invested in Robert Morris's Bank of the United States. However, when she went to visit her ailing, aged mother, she was menaced by sullen mobs who refused to forgive her husband. The arrival of the traitor's wife in Philadelphia, even as Congress was deliberating the new Constitution, stirred controversy. Her brother-in-law recorded that she was treated "with so much coldness and neglect that her feelings were continually wounded." Old friends said her visit placed them "in a painful position." Others whispered that "she should have shown more feeling by staying away." After a five-month visit, Peggy left her family forever.

Benedict Arnold's final years were occupied with a long string of business misadventures and also with his obsessive defense of his reputation. He expanded his Caribbean operations, in his last eight years sending or sailing thirteen different ships on trading voyages. Often offended publicly, he fought a duel with the earl of Lauderdale, who had insulted him on the floor of the House of Lords. Peggy wrote to her father that the days before the duel were filled with "a great deal of pain." She "had not dared to discuss the duel with the silent general," fearing that she would "unman him and prevent him acting himself." When fought, the duel produced no casualties, but it "almost at last proved too much for me, and for some hours, my reason was to be despaired of."

As a new war with France spread over the world, Arnold outfitted his own privateering ship to attack French shipping in the Caribbean. This time he was gone eighteen months, agonizing months for Peggy, who learned that her husband had been captured by French revolutionaries and had managed to escape only shortly before his scheduled execution. When Arnold returned and she again became pregnant, Peggy's health began to decline. On December 5, 1795, she wrote to friends in Canada: "For my own part, I am *determined* to have no more little plagues, as it is so difficult to provide for them in this country."

For years Peggy lived in dread that the queen would die and her pensions would stop—a legitimate fear, made worse after her husband's captains defrauded them of some £50,000 and she had to sell her American investments to bail him out. In 1801, at age sixty, Benedict Arnold became dispirited and, after a four-month illness, died "without a groan." Peggy, oppressed by his creditors and stunned by his loss, lived for three more years, long enough to pay off all his debts "down to the last teaspoon."

"Years of unhappiness have passed," she confided in a letter to her brother-in-law. "I had cast my lot, complaints were unavailing, and you and my other friends are ignorant of the many causes of the uneasiness I have had." To her father she wrote that she had had to move to a smaller house, "parting with my furniture, wine and many other comforts provided for me by the indulgent hand of [Arnold's] affection." Arnold had paid a final compliment to Peggy's business acumen by making her sole executrix of his estate, an unusual step at the time. Once she had cleared up the mess he had left and could see that her children would be provided for, she thanked her father for her fine private education: "To you, my dear parent, am I indebted for the ability to perform what I have done."

Years of anxiety and illness had exacted a terrible toll, and Peggy Shippen Arnold's quarter-century ordeal in exile ended on August 24, 1804. She had, she wrote, "the dreaded evil, a cancer." She told her sister she had "a very large tumor" in her uterus. "My only chance is from an internal operation which is at present dangerous to perform."

Peggy died at forty-four. After her death, her children found concealed among her personal possessions a gold locket containing a snippet of John André's hair. Family tradition holds that Benedict Arnold never saw it.

*WINTER 1992*

Willard Sterne Randall is the author of *Benedict Arnold: Patriot and Traitor* (1990) and *Thomas Jefferson: A Life* (1993). He is currently working on a biography of George Washington.

# 6

# Winfield Scott's Brush with Disaster

## By Timothy D. Johnson

*When Congress declared war on Great Britain in June 1812, the United States Army was small in size and antiquated in leadership, and the state militias—the second line of defense on land—were erratic and poorly disciplined. The army not only needed fresh leadership, but also a greatly expanded number of well-trained soldiers. It took time for new leaders to rise to the top ranks and for the country to mobilize and train both more regular army troops and a substantial number of citizen-soldiers. Fortunately for the United States, the British were preoccupied early in the war with European affairs and could project but a small portion of their military power into North America. By 1814, American land forces began to flex their enhanced combat skill and muscle, as the Battle of Lundy's Lane demonstrated. Fought in late July against a more numerous British force, this bloody brawl was to be important for the development of both the U.S. Army and one of its greatest commanders, Winfield Scott. Yet the future of each, Timothy D. Johnson writes, was risked when ambition overrode judgment.*

Winfield Scott's military career spanned more than half a century, including twenty years as commanding general of the army. He was recognized as one of the most capable commanders of the nineteenth century, with abilities as a tactician and strategist that stemmed from an extensive knowledge of military history and the art of war. The Mexico City campaign in 1847 was Scott's crowning achievement. Its careful planning and brilliant execution demonstrated his maturity of judgment and accuracy of forethought. When it was over, the duke of Wellington proclaimed him "the greatest living soldier." As a young man in the War of 1812, however, Scott was ambitious and impatient, sometimes immature and impulsive—though inarguably brave in action. His often rash behavior was personally damaging and, on at least one occasion, Lundy's Lane, almost resulted in disaster for the men he commanded.

Accounts of the battle generally focus on the accomplishments of the American army and its ability to stand up to British regulars in an open-field fight. Plagued by humiliating defeats early in the war, the army acquitted itself well in July 1814 at both Chippewa and Lundy's Lane, on the Canadian side of the Niagara River. Historians usually characterize these battles, fought within three weeks of each other, as a watershed for the regular army, demonstrating its tenacious fighting spirit and elevating its prestige. Scott, the ranking commander on the field during the early hours of fighting at Lundy's Lane, has received almost unanimous praise for his role in training the army and leading it into battle. President James Madison's annual message to Congress, delivered in September 1814, commended Scott and other officers for the two "splendid victories." "These heroes," Madison added, "triumphantly tested the progressive discipline of the American soldiery." Despite the severity of the battle and the number of casualties, to most military historians Lundy's Lane has become a symbol of the American tradition of rising to the occasion to meet uncommon challenges. It was, many contend, due to Scott's foresight and guidance as well as the rigorous training he had put his men through the preceding spring that the army accomplished what it did during that bloody contest.

Lost in most accounts of the battle is Scott's recklessness in ordering his brigade to attack the British position without forethought or knowledge of the enemy's strength. He also rushed into battle while the rest of the army was too far away to give immediate support. A few writers have made passing statements suggesting that Scott may have acted hastily, but then they have offered no elaboration or reason for that haste.

WINFIELD SCOTT ENTERED the army in 1808, hoping that military service would provide a vehicle for advancement and fame. Like many others after the British frigate *Leopard* fired on the *Chesapeake* in June 1807, Scott expected war to break out between Great Britain and the United States, and he intended to make a name for himself on the battlefield. The twenty-one-year-old Scott was consumed with ambition, but his first assignment proved disappointing. Ordered to New Orleans to serve under General James Wilkinson, Scott spent the summer of 1809 in the now infamous army camp at Terre aux Boeufs, several miles away from the Creole City. In order to maintain his business and social interests in the city, Wilkinson defied a War Department directive to move to a healthier location. His 2,000 men bivouacked in a marshy quagmire, where sanitation was nonexistent and mosquitoes abounded. A diet of spoiled beef and sour, worm-infested bread, along with brackish drinking water, resulted in widespread dysentery and scurvy. Within three months, 127 had died.

After witnessing the careless way in which the army was handled, Scott altered his opinion of the officer corps; he particularly deplored Wilkinson for subjecting the soldiers to such unnecessary hardships. Fighting insects and disease had sapped his enthusiasm, and he realized that fame and glory could not be found on the swampy banks of the Mississippi River. Distressed by the faltering prospects of war, Scott considered resigning his commission—but not before he indiscreetly called Wilkinson a liar and a traitor, and asserted that serving under the general was as disgraceful as being married to a prostitute. Scott found himself court-martialed and suspended from the army for a year without pay.

In June 1812—after years of tension over British attacks on U.S. shipping and impressment of American seamen, as well as American expansionist sentiment aimed at Canada and the northwestern frontier—Congress eagerly declared war on Great Britain. The United States now needed all the soldiers it could get, regardless of past indiscretions. Having previously boasted of his desire to "write my history with my sword," Scott accepted a promotion to lieutenant colonel and the command of an artillery regiment. In the fall, Scott rushed his regiment to the Niagara River and persuaded General Stephen Van Rensselaer to let him participate in the attack on Queenston, along the Canadian shore. Scott was one of more than 900 Americans captured by the British, but up to that point he fought bravely, eventually becoming the ranking American commander on the field.

So courageous were his actions that the next year, following a prisoner exchange, he found himself serving as adjutant general on General Henry Dearborn's staff. Not only did he draw up the plans for an attack in May 1813 on Fort George, near Lake Ontario, but he also accompanied the assault force ashore and boldly led the pursuit of the fleeing British army. After being ordered to stop the fight, Scott chafed with anger, proclaiming that he could have captured the entire enemy army. Again demonstrating a lack of good judgment, he characterized one of his superior officers as "vacillating and imbecile, beyond all endurance."

Believing himself more capable than any officer he had ever served, Scott had been rash and insubordinate. Nevertheless, he had displayed the courage and boldness that were often missing in the struggling American army. By 1814, Scott's energy and aggressiveness had been duly noted in Washington, and President Madison promoted him to brigadier general. Scott, then twenty-seven, was the youngest general in the army.

That spring, he put the army through rigorous training at Buffalo, before turning command over to General Jacob Brown. On July 5, as a brigade commander in Brown's army, Scott led his unit onto a plain near the Chippewa (to the Canadians, Chippawa) River, facing the enemy. The steadiness and discipline that the Americans exhibited under fire surprised the British regulars, who were accustomed to routing their opposition in open-field battles. Within minutes, Scott gained control of the field by maneuvering his inferior numbers into a dominating position. The victory was quick and decisive. By the time General Brown arrived with the rest of the American army, the British had retreated from the field. Scott proved at the Battle of Chippewa that his aplomb was justified.

The British, commanded by General Phineas Riall, retreated north to Fort George. Brown followed and planned to assault the fort if he could get assistance from the navy; Scott, impatient and eager to enhance his growing reputation, urged that the Americans attack without the fleet. The navy never arrived, and on July 24 Brown took the army back to the Chippewa River, hoping to lure Riall out from his fortified walls.

This retrograde movement disappointed Scott and led to friction between him and Brown. In his unpublished "Memoranda of . . . the Campaign . . . ," Brown recalled what transpired. When the army arrived back at the Chippewa, "General Scott, ever ambitious to distinguish himself and his command," asked that he be allowed to take his brigade in search of Riall, but Brown refused to divide his army. Scott repeated his appeal in a "tenacious" manner the next morning, and he became "quite vexed" when Brown exhibited an equal degree of obstinacy. Brown, dubious of his brigadier's motives, noted that "Scott honestly believed . . . he could cover himself with additional glory." Scott need not have been impatient, for that very morning British troops were approaching nearby Lundy's Lane. Later in the day, he would have all the glory he could manage.

After his exchange with Scott, Brown received word that four enemy vessels had landed on American soil at Fort Niagara and that British troops at Queenston were crossing the river to Lewiston. This disturbing news meant only one thing to Brown: The British intended to capture his supply base at Fort Schlosser. He decided to divide his army after all, ordering Scott to take his brigade and all the mounted troops to Queenston in an effort to draw the enemy back across the river.

Meanwhile, Major Henry Leavenworth, officer of the day, looked through his glass from a picket station just north of the Chippewa. In the distance, around the bend of the Niagara River, were red-clad troops, including what he thought was an unusual number of British officers. He galloped back to Brown's headquarters to report the news and his belief that the main enemy force was still on Canadian soil a scant three miles away. Leavenworth was right: In fact, not only was Riall in the Americans' front, but also reinforcements under Lieutenant General Sir Gordon Drummond were on the way. Drummond had indeed sent a force of 600 over to the American shore, prompting the report that Brown had received, but he had quickly withdrawn it in order to consolidate his forces at Lundy's Lane. However, Brown persisted in the belief that Fort Schlosser was under threat of an enemy attack, and so he ordered Scott to advance.

When the van of Scott's 1st Brigade rounded the bend in the river later that day, several British dragoons quickly mounted and scampered away, narrowly escaping capture. Two American officers then rode ahead to Willson's Tavern, where the enemy had been milling about, to question the widow who owned it. Soon Scott and his staff arrived, and everyone went in to listen as he interrogated the woman. She reported the presence of over 1,000 British troops in the vicinity; but because of the earlier accounts of enemy crossings downriver, Scott was skeptical. Looking around the room, at length he fixed his eyes on Lieutenant David Douglass, whom he perceived to be the youngest officer present. "Would you be willing to return to camp, sir?" Scott asked. Not knowing if the general was testing his will to fight, the subaltern was momentarily speechless. Realizing what Scott wanted, Colonel Eleazer Wood, Douglass's friend, broke the silence: "Lieutenant Douglass will, no doubt, be happy to bear your commands to General Brown." Scott then instructed the lieutenant to ride back and tell Brown that the brigade might encounter a strong enemy force but was nonetheless pushing ahead.

Scott's decision not to await reinforcements invites criticism. Although he commanded about 1,000 men, he did not know the enemy's strength in his front. He probably thought that he would face the remnants of Riall's broken army, or perhaps only an oversize reconnaissance party screening the supposed British crossing at Queenston. Possibly he thought that if he did encounter an enemy force, he could claim the victory before other units arrived, just as he had done three weeks earlier. He never conceived that he would face the bulk of the British army. One contemporary observer wrote that Scott always acted with "alacrity whenever honour was to be courted, and whereever [sic] danger awaited him." Another way to put it is that Scott was aggressive—sometimes too aggressive. After the battle, Brown seemed irritated at Scott's independent action, writing in a summary of the events that Scott had taken time only to report the British position in his front but not to await instructions.

Late in the afternoon on July 25, the Americans advanced through a wooded area until the road emerged into a clearing. There, along Lundy's Lane, they first glimpsed the enemy—drawn up in battle line. Suddenly, the gravity of Scott's decision hit him: He had blundered into an enemy force about 1,800 strong, including reinforcements under Drummond who were just arriving on the field. He thought of the wild rumors of enemy crossings downriver that had circulated through camp all morning, deceiving him into complacency, and was outraged at that "stupid report made by the militia colonel to his confiding friend Major-General Brown."

He considered pulling back, but for Scott retreat was only a fleeting thought. Instead, he sent word back to Brown of his intention to hold his ground until the rest of the army could arrive. Later he justified engaging a stronger foe by explaining that because his soldiers were young and half-seasoned, ordering a retreat might have resulted in a rout. This was a valid point; retreating within sight of an enemy force always leaves one dangerously exposed to attack. But if he feared that his men were too inexperienced to handle a withdrawal, how could he expect them to hold up in the face of superior numbers?

The British opened fire with artillery before Scott could deploy his forward units in battle formation. Upon emerging from the woods, the Americans had to go over a fence before taking up their place in line, and many of them were shot off the rails as they climbed up. Scott struggled to get all his brigade through the woods and into the clearing. As the rear units marched toward the sound of the fighting, they met the wounded already filtering back down the road. A fourteen-year-old drummer boy, still a half mile from the battlefield, became unnerved when he met a trumpeter who had been shot in the head and had blood pouring down his cheeks. The boy thought twice but bravely marched on with his regiment. When he reached the clearing, he lifted himself up on the fence, and while he perched there, preparing to jump to the ground, grapeshot sprayed all around him. Pellets hit the rail on which his feet rested, splintered the rail on both sides of his hands, and severed tree branches overhead, but miraculously the youngster was not hurt.

While trying to rush his men into the clearing to take up their positions, Scott sent word to Major Thomas Jesup, whose 25th Regiment brought up the rear, to swing around to the right and try to turn the British flank. Scott liked Jesup and considered him an able regimental commander. A success-ful flank attack required skill and speed, and to execute it the general chose to rely on the same man who had so successfully carried out a similar move at Chippewa. "Pop through the wood," he instructed the major, "and be gov-erned by circumstances."

With all of his brigade in position, Scott, instead of simply holding his ground, ordered an advance into the most confusing and deadly carnage of the entire war. To his credit, he understood that going on the offensive can result in decisive victories, but in this instance he allowed the intensity of the mo-ment to force him into a rash decision. The Americans succeeded in pushing the British back, but additional reinforcements from Drummond's command continued to arrived, stabilizing Riall's line. With overwhelming numbers and a strong position, the British were able to beat back several sallies by Scott's regiments.

At 6:30 P.M., after close to an hour of fighting, Scott's brigade began to show signs of disintegration. Colonel Hugh Brady—commander of the 22nd Regiment, which was located on the right—was wounded, and his men began to run out of cartridges. Some of them panicked and ran to the rear, leaving a gap on the right of Scott's line. In the center, the 11th Regiment—its ammunition also depleted; its commander, Major John McNeil, wounded; and all its captains dead or injured—followed the ex-ample of the 22nd. But not everyone from these two units fled. The more resolute stayed on the field and replenished their ammunition from the car-tridge boxes of nearby corpses.

On the left end of the line, Scott instructed Major Henry Leavenworth's 9th Regiment to attack, but when he learned of the collapse on the right and in the center, he countermanded the order and told the major to hold his position until Brown arrived with the reserves. A lull in the fighting afford-ed Scott time to improvise a battalion made up of the 9th and remnants of the 11th and 22nd regiments. He instructed Leavenworth to take command of this provisional unit. While he was discussing the perilous situation with the major, Scott's horse was shot from under him.

Darkness and smoke began to enshroud the battlefield. Still there was neither news of General Brown's approach nor word from Jesup's 25th Regiment. The major had not been idle, however. His men had eased along the riverbank undetected and, around dusk, succeeded in capturing over

200 British, including Drummond's aide-de-camp and Riall himself. Many of the prisoners succeeded in escaping, but Jesup sent the rest to the rear while he continued to move stealthily on the enemy's left flank. When news of Riall's capture filtered through Scott's line, the Americans gave a cheer and renewed their resolve to hold their position.

Not until nine o'clock did Brown and the rest of the army arrive on the scene. The night was dark, but the flash from muskets made it easy to discern the location of the opposing lines. The British fired the new Congreve rockets, originally invented by the Chinese and improved by a British officer. The rockets' "red glare," which would later gain immortality during the shelling of Fort McHenry, illuminated the sky; their shrill whistle pierced the ears. Not very destructive weapons, they were used more to inflict fear than casualties. Under this brilliant display, Brown's brigades commanded by Brigadier Generals Eleazer W. Ripley and Peter B. Porter groped their way to the front to succor Scott's shattered command. Brown located Scott and ordered him to pull back what was left of his brigade in order to reorganize and act as reserves.

After taking command of the field, Brown quickly perceived the need to capture a British battery located on a rise in front of Lundy's Lane. It was an important objective that Scott either had failed to appreciate or had been unable to achieve. Brown located Colonel James Miller, commander of the 21st Regiment, and said, "Colonel, those British guns on the hill must be taken! Can you do it?" Miller gave a stern, laconic response: "It shall be done, sir" (or, according to some sources, "I'll try, sir"). The colonel formed his regiment, charged the battery, and captured all seven guns. Fighting on the hill continued to rage for two hours as the British tried several times to retake the position.

Next, Brown started up the river road toward Lundy's Lane in search of Jesup; neither he nor Scott knew the whereabouts of the 25th. After traveling a short distance, he spotted the shadowy outline of an enemy unit approaching. As he sat motionless on his horse, he heard a voice with a thick English accent shout, "These are the Yankees." At that instant, a deadly fire poured into the British column, which turned and fled. A bewildered Brown then watched as Jesup's regiment emerged from its concealed position along the side of the road. This action on the British left flank, coupled with the loss of their battery moments earlier, caused them to withdraw and brought a few minutes of calm as both armies regrouped. The Americans pushed their line forward to link on the right with Jesup, whose regiment now occupied the junction of Lundy's Lane and the river road.

Sensing that the battle was far from over, tired and hungry soldiers on both sides collected themselves during the short respite. An eerie quiet, broken only by the groans of the wounded, fell over the field. The tense Americans strained their eyes in the darkness, looking for movement in front of them. Soon their ears told them what their eyes could not, as the footfalls of hundreds of British soldiers interrupted the silence. Sitting motionless, the Americans waited until the enemy advanced to within thir-

ty yards. Then the captured guns roared, belching fire at their former owners with what Brown later described as "awful . . . effect." The battle raged
at close distance for several minutes before the British retreated, leaving the
American front strewn with bodies.

Brown's little army had held up remarkably well thus far, convincing the
general that he could maintain his position until dawn. But the most intense
fighting lay ahead. When the British advanced again, Brown ordered Scott
forward to help bolster the line. Scott, who had grown impatient in the rear,
eagerly moved his brigade up—but instead of waiting for the enemy
advance, he decided to attack first. Scott rode up to Leavenworth and shouted over the noise of musket fire, "Are these troops prepared for the charge?"
Without giving his subordinate time to respond, he said, "Yes, I know they
are prepared for anything." Scott resolved to attack the approaching British
line by forming his brigade in column (a heavy, more compact formation
numerous lines deep). By trying this "experiment," as Scott termed it, he
intended to pierce the long enemy line and get in behind it. To get his men
into position, however, he inadvertently marched them across the front of
other American units, resulting in friendly fire on his men. At the same
instant, the British unleashed a volley into his front, and the cross fire cut
his unit to pieces, forcing him to withdraw.

What followed was a series of attacks and counterattacks as the Americans beat back repeated enemy advances. One writer described the late-
night fighting as "pure anarchy—a confused mêlée in which friend and foe
. . . inextricably intermingled." For both sides, there was "struggling in the
darkness, clubbing one another to death with the butts of muskets, mistaking comrades for foes, stabbing at each other with bayonets, officers tumbling from horses, whole regiments shattered, troops wandering aimlessly,
seeking orders." At one point, Scott tried another flank attack, but General
Drummond had hidden the 89th British Regiment in a grain field to guard
against such an attempt. When the Redcoats fired a fusillade into Scott's
men from twenty paces, the Americans broke and ran. The British 103rd
and 104th regiments saw them go by but mistook them for their own 89th
and let them pass. On their way, the Americans stumbled into the Royal
Scots, and a bloody hand-to-hand struggle followed. Eventually, Scott's
exhausted men made it back to their lines.

Sometime during the fracas, a cannonball knocked a second horse out
from under Scott. He quickly mounted another steed and continued at the
head of his troops. Later a ricocheting ball struck him in the side, severely
bruising his ribs, but still he refused to leave the field. The bravery that he
exhibited at Lundy's Lane could not help but inspire his men to greater
exertions. He possessed the will or, as military historians call it, the moral
courage to persevere. In an age when an army's performance was in direct
proportion to the willingness of its officers to stand in front of the line and
lead the attack, Winfield Scott was a model of valor. He stayed with his
brigade and fought beside his men until the waning minutes of the battle.
He was on the right of the line, consulting with Jesup, when a nearby sol-

dier was mortally wounded. Both officers rushed to assist the injured man, and while he was kneeling over the body, a musket ball ripped into Scott's left shoulder, smashing the joint. He lay unconscious for a few minutes; then two of his men carried him to the rear and placed him behind a tree, where he would be safe from stray bullets.

At about the same time that Scott received his wound, Brown was hit in the thigh. Courageously, Brown remained in command until he was struck again, this time in the side by a ricocheting cannonball. The blow almost knocked him from his horse and made him so groggy that he had to relinquish command to Ripley. Both Scott and Brown were carried back to camp; before leaving, Brown sent word to Ripley to withdraw the entire army to the Chippewa River. It was nearing midnight when the weary Americans began dragging themselves back to camp. During the night, Drummond learned that the Americans had left the field, and at dawn he reoccupied the lane and claimed victory.

Although it took the initiative away from the Americans, Lundy's Lane was actually a tactical draw. The bloodletting lasted over six hours, at appalling cost to both sides: Each army had more than 800 casualties. Scott's brigade accounted for an inordinate proportion of the American total—out of 860 killed or wounded, 516 came from his command. Consolidated, the 9th, 11th, and 22nd regiments could not muster 200 men when the battle ended. These figures alone indicate which units bore the brunt of the fighting. It was, in the words of Brown's aide-de-camp, "a most severe conflict."

One can only speculate as to how many lives might have been spared had Scott waited for the rest of the army to arrive instead of rushing head-long into battle. Scott was personally ambitious, domineering, and aggressive, and these traits carried over to his generalship on the battlefield. His personality, and his ambition, dictated that he be assertive and forceful; he was not one to sit back and wait for an attack. He had advocated attacking Fort George, and later he had wanted to search out the British army and destroy it. At Lundy's Lane, he very nearly took on more than he and his men could handle, and the result was that in the first four hours of fighting his brigade was shattered.

Why Scott did not wait for support is not the only question that needs an answer. Equally curious is why he did not silence the British artillery that fired from the hill in front of the lane. When Brown arrived on the scene, he quickly realized the necessity of doing so, yet there is no indica-tion that Scott had made a concerted effort to capture the position. In the early hours of the fight, Scott's brigade was continually pounded by grape and shot; later, after the rest of the army arrived and captured the guns, American casualties decreased. Given his failure to seize the enemy can-non and his lopsided casualty figures, it is remarkable that Scott's men held their ground as long as they did. Without the confidence that had resulted from the quick, decisive victory three weeks earlier at Chippewa, the army probably would not have endured the prolonged carnage along Lundy's

Lane. Scott would never admit it, but he knew that he had risked too much at Lundy's Lane; otherwise, he would not have offered excuses in his *Memoirs* for his failure to withdraw.

Despite these criticisms, there was a positive side to Scott's behavior. His advance at Lundy's Lane was a result of his knowledge that benefits can accrue from aggressive action on the battlefield. He understood that the commander who takes the initiative is in a better position to dictate the course of events, and that is what Scott wanted—to be in control. What he had not yet learned, however, was that sometimes the fog of battle renders events uncontrollable.

The Americans could not rightly claim the Battle of Lundy's Lane as a military triumph, but they could call it a moral victory. The battle helped bring about a metamorphosis in the United States Army by showing what trained and disciplined troops could accomplish. The battles of Chippewa and Lundy's Lane were a source of pride for the nation. Their legacy endured for many years, making it possible for the military establishment to argue for continued reliance on the regular army rather than on the capricious militia. Scott was a key figure in bringing about this change, and in so doing he helped to enhance the army's reputation—but at an awful price. The young general obviously learned from his mistake: Although he maintained an aggressive spirit and always preferred the offensive, never again would he enter combat without exhaustive planning.

*AUTUMN 1995*

**Timothy D. Johnson is an assistant professor of history at Lipscomb University. He is writing a biography of Winfield Scott.**

# 7

# Checkmate at Mexico City

## By Thaddeus Holt

*Although historians sometimes picture the Mexican War as a case of American greed and bullying toward its far weaker neighbor to the south, they often slight the fact that the war's outcome was far from certain. America's military prowess lay well in the future. In 1846 its regular army numbered fewer than 10,000 men. The military's performance in its most recent international conflict, the War of 1812, had been less than sterling; it had been unable even to defend the White House and Capitol from a British raiding force. Now the army faced a nearly impossible task: transporting its troops to a foreign shore and marching them over some of the hemisphere's most rugged terrain in order to assault the enemy's major city and capital. Napoleon himself might well have recoiled from the task. But General Winfield Scott did not recoil, and in the maneuvering and combat before the gates of Mexico City in 1847, he and his small army proved themselves the master of Santa Anna and his more numerous forces.*

It was perhaps the last campaign in the classical style, with small, compact armies maneuvering for position amid a civilian population that cheerfully sold supplies to either side and was essentially uninterested in its master's bloody games. Turenne, Marlborough, Frederick the Great would have been quite at home in it. But it was played not on one of the ancient chessboards of war, Flanders or Silesia or the plains of Lombardy, but in the Valley of Mexico. There, in 1847, Major General Winfield Scott, commanding general, United States Army, and General de División Antonio López de Santa Anna Pérez de Lebrón, president of Mexico, faced each other in the climax of the war of 1846–48 between Mexico and the United States.

In 1847, Mexico City, with some 200,000 inhabitants, was a compact rough quadrilateral surrounded by marshes and shallow lagoons and accessible only by long, narrow causeways. North and east of the city was the lagoon called Lake Texcoco. South and southeast were Lakes Xochimilco and Chalco, separated only by a narrow causeway and in effect forming one lagoon. West of Xochimilco was another seemingly impassable natural obstacle, the Pedregal de San Angel, usually called simply the Pedregal. This was a roughly circular area about four miles in diameter, formed of coarse red lava from some ancient eruption that had cooled in jagged, bizarre shapes from which sprouted twisted, stunted bushes and occasional trees.

The two main roads from the east and south threaded their way among these obstacles to reach the *garitas* or guardhouses warding the entrances to the city. From Puebla in the east came the Camino Nacional. From the south the second major highway, from Acapulco, came down from the mountains at the village of Tlalpan (in 1847 often called San Agustín), ten miles south of the city. Subsidiary roads connected these two main highways and ran among the villages of the valley.

From one of these, the pretty town of San Angel, northwest of the Pedregal, a road ran eastward two miles to the lovely village of Coyoacán and then another mile to Churubusco, with its handsome stone church and monastery, where the Acapulco highway bridged the Río Churubusco. Another road from San Angel ran northwesterly through the village of Mixcoac, thence north to the village of Tacubaya. From there a causeway ran northeasterly for about a mile to the foot of the abrupt, steep, and commanding hill of Chapultepec, some two miles from the city.

Chapultepec was one of the dominant features of the region, set in a wooded park and crowned by its "castle"—not a fortification but a commodious former summer palace for the Spanish viceroys, and in 1847 a military college. From it two causeways with arched stone aqueducts down their centers ran toward the city.

So much for the game board. The opponents:

Winfield Scott was a sixty-one-year-old giant with a magnificent and inspiring presence: He was also a pretentious and pompous ass ("Old Fuss and Feathers," they called him) with a special knack for putting his foot in his mouth; but withal a consummately professional soldier and student of the art of war, the true father of the United States Army, and a very fine general.

With Scott when he crossed into the Valley of Mexico was an army of 10,738 officers and men, both regulars and volunteers, organized into four divisions under two regular officers and two volunteer officers. The regulars were Brevet Major General William J. Worth, an intelligent soldier and inspiring leader, and Brevet Major General David E. Twiggs, a warrior of the tough and unintellectual variety. The volunteers were Major General John A. Quitman, a talented man of parts, and Major General Gideon J. Pillow, a bungler who got his military experience in the Tennessee militia and owed his command to the fact that he had once practiced law with President James K. Polk and claimed credit for Polk's nomination at the 1844 Democratic convention.

Santa Anna was fifty-three, a paradigm of the Spanish-American caudillo and of the creole oligarchy that tragically misgoverned Mexico during its first generation of independence; a veteran of coups, countercoups, intrigues, and betrayals, ousted as El Presidente more than once, yet now back again; an accomplished *chaquetero,* as Mexicans call a man who shifts allegiance for his own benefit; unprincipled, corrupt, and thereby rich; a leader and organizer who could conjure an army seemingly out of thin air in a whirlwind of activity, but was then inept at using it.

For the defense of Mexico City, Santa Anna had an army of some 30,000, with many veterans but also many untried militia volunteers. Several of his commanders were politicians as well as generals. Notable among these was the ruffianly General Gabriel Valencia, his political foe. Valencia commanded a separate force called the Army of the North; Santa Anna had ordered it to join the main army, and Valencia had obeyed, but his obedience to Santa Anna was grudging at best.

The war was not the one-sided affair that today we might think. In the 1840s the United States was far from being a great power. The regular army was a frontier constabulary of 7,000 men or less and had performed wretchedly in the War of 1812; later, a handful of Seminoles had run rings around it for years. Though the regular army had been enlarged at the beginning of the war, more important in terms of numbers were the thousands of volunteers who rushed to the colors at the outbreak of hostilities. Except among Whigs of New England, and the "colonies" of New England in upstate New York and the Western Reserve of Ohio, it was a popular war; the myth that it was broadly unpopular and divisive stems from nineteenth-century writers for whom Boston State House was the hub of the universe.

But half-trained, ill-disciplined civilian soldiers did not impress most contemporary observers. The Mexican army was infinitely more impressive. The officers, though unevenly talented, came from the creole oligarchy with its strong military tradition, and the soldiers were mainly Indians, forcibly enlisted and held under brutal discipline, but brave, tough, fierce men inured from childhood to suffering and death.

Nevertheless, by late 1847 a series of American victories, often against odds, had confirmed Napoleon's dictum that in war, the moral is to the material as three to one. So Scott and his men brought a significant psychological ascendancy to the final contest in the Valley of Mexico. But Scott was also taking a go-for-broke risk. After landing at Vera Cruz and defeating Santa Anna at Cerro Gordo, he had marched on to Puebla, 130 miles from the capital, and there rested and refitted. When he left Puebla, he cut his communications. Every man lost would thus be irreplaceable, and, as a Mexican author wrote, "While a single defeat would be sufficient for the destruction of the American troops, ours might suffer several without deciding the fate of the contest."

So on balance, the contestants were at least equally matched as the deadly chess game began. The first move was Scott's.

*First move: Scott (August 7–14).* The gringo vanguard marched out of Puebla on August 7, and four days later crossed the mountains into the Valley of Mexico. By August 14 the whole army was encamped round the eastern shore of Lake Chalco.

*Second move: Santa Anna (August 10–14).* Santa Anna supposed that

81

Scott would either march straight up the main highway or perhaps cut across via Mexicaltzingo to the Acapulco highway at Churubusco—or, barely possibly, swing all the way round Lake Texcoco and attack the city from the north. He stationed Valencia with 4,000 men to cover the latter possibility, then focused his attention on the main highway. Some seven miles from the city, the highway was hemmed in between Lake Texcoco and a steep hill, called El Peñón Viejo. Santa Anna fortified El Peñón Viejo with some thirty guns (covering the Mexicaltzingo road as well) and 7,000 men, established his headquarters there, placed a small force at Mexicaltzingo, and awaited Scott's attack.

*Third move: Scott (August 15–18).* Scott had no wish to make a direct assault on either El Peñón Viejo or Mexicaltzingo; he had planned to pass south of Lakes Chalco and Xochimilco to Tlalpan and the Acapulco highway. Nevertheless, when intelligence reports told him this route was too crude to carry artillery and supply wagons, he briefly considered a direct attack against Mexicaltzingo with a feint against El Peñón Viejo. But reconnaissance soon showed that the reports about the Tlalpan road were wrong, and during August 15–18 he moved his army round to Tlalpan, where he set up headquarters. So much for Santa Anna's initial assumption.

*Fourth move: Santa Anna (August 16–18).* Santa Anna responded promptly and effectively. Shifting his headquarters to the monastery at Churubusco, he moved the Peñón garrison, augmented by about 3,000 men, to Coyoacán, ordered Valencia with some 5,500 men from positions north and east of the city to San Angel, and blocked the Acapulco highway at San Antonio, some two miles north of Tlalpan. With 20,000 men to Scott's 10,000, Santa Anna was thus effectively positioned to bar Scott's way even if the gringos should manage to cross the Pedregal.

Valencia arrived at San Angel on August 17. For some reason he at first thought the San Angel position too exposed and wanted to fall back; but the next day, August 18, he decided to move well forward instead. Between the road southwest from San Angel and the western edge of the Pedregal, there curved the deep ravine of a creek; above it on the westerly side was a prominent hill called by the Indians Pelón Cuauhtitla. Valencia seems to have concluded that from this hill he could prevent any American advance up the road if Scott did manage to cross the Pedregal, so he moved his force there and set up an entrenched camp.

By the time Scott was well established at Tlalpan, his reconnaissance parties were reporting the Mexican positions at San Antonio, the Río Churubusco bridge, the Churubusco monastery, Coyoacán, and San Angel. Because of marshes on the east and the Pedregal on the west, a major attack at San Antonio would have had to be made head-on, straight up the highway, and such an attack would have been suicidal. Santa Anna seemed to have neutralized Scott's move, unless a way could be found to turn the San Antonio position by crossing the seemingly impassable Pedregal.

*Fifth move: Scott (August 18–19).* On August 18, two of Scott's engineer officers, Captain Robert E. Lee and Lieutenant P.G.T. Beauregard, went reconnoitering beyond Tlalpan and climbed a hill called Zacatepetl, from which they had a panoramic view of the Pedregal and the villages and haciendas beyond it to the north and west. On the western edge of the Pedregal could be seen a farm called Padierna; beyond was the hill of Pelón Cuauhtitla. Lee and Beauregard could see Mexicans at Padierna; more significantly, their escort ran into pickets from Valencia's force—proof that a path across the Pedregal existed.

Based on their report, Scott ordered Pillow's division, supported by Twiggs's, to set to work enlarging the path into a road adequate for horses and artillery, while Worth demonstrated against San Antonio and Quitman guarded the base at Tlalpan. Work began on August 19.

*Sixth move: Santa Anna (August 18–19).* On the evening of August 18, Santa Anna ordered Valencia to rejoin the main army at dawn the next day. Valencia refused; he evidently thought that when his pickets drove back Lee's escort, he had repelled an American advance, and he scented the possibility of a victory that would redound to his credit rather than to Santa Anna's. Santa Anna disapproved of Valencia's conduct but said he could do as he pleased and take the responsibility. On the morning of August 19, Valencia sent infantry against the American road builders, and by midday not only was infantry skirmishing in the Pedregal but Mexican batteries on the hill had placed the Americans under fire.

Santa Anna's acquiescence in Valencia's insubordination—producing the two classic cardinal errors: divided command and divided army in the presence of the enemy—was the crucial blunder by which he lost the war.

*Seventh move: Scott (August 19).* Road building stopped as American artillery was brought up to duel unsuccessfully with Valencia's guns on the hill. Pillow sent two brigades to work their way round to the right and behind Pelón Cuauhtitla and try to cut off Valencia's line of retreat. A third brigade, which Pillow apparently had envisioned making an impossible frontal attack on Valencia, also moved round to the right and joined the others. They concentrated at the village of San Jerónimo, just north of Valencia's camp and separated from it by the ravine of a creek. When Scott learned that fighting had started, he joined Pillow on Zacatepetl to view the situation, and ordered another brigade from Tlalpan to San Jerónimo. That brigade, commanded by Brevet Brigadier General Persifor Smith, did not arrive there till midnight.

*Eighth move: Santa Anna (August 19).* Meanwhile, Santa Anna moved a force under his personal command down from San Angel to high ground north of San Jerónimo. Because of exposure to flanking fire from the Americans, he dared not try to join Valencia; but even so, it was Scott's army that was now divided, and had Santa Anna not lost unity of command, he could have crushed the American brigades at San Jerónimo between his troops and Valencia's. Instead, after demonstrating harmlessly against Smith, whom he concluded he could not reach, he withdrew to San Angel at nightfall and sent orders to Valencia to spike his guns and fall back to join him. Again Valencia disobeyed, declaring that "after a desperate combat with the Anglo-American forces" he had "put them to shameful flight," and needed only to mop up in the morning.

*Ninth move: Scott—and the Battle of Contreras (August 20).* At sundown that August 19 a rainstorm began. Scott returned to Tlalpan and spent an anxious evening; seven times he sent officers to try to cross the Pedregal and find out the state of Smith's force, and all failed. But toward midnight Captain Lee arrived from San Jerónimo with great news: A ravine had been found by which Smith thought he could make a night movement around Valencia and attack him from the rear at dawn; could Scott arrange for a demonstration in Valencia's front to distract his attention?

Lee had volunteered to bring this message to Scott, and had crossed the Pedregal alone and on foot through the storm and the dark with only lightning flashes to light his way. (Scott called this "the greatest feat of physical and moral courage performed by any individual, to my knowledge," in the whole campaign, and anyone who has seen the Pedregal would have to agree; even today, if you tried to cross it in broad daylight you would be risking a broken leg or worse.)

Scott ordered Twiggs to create the distraction at Valencia's front at 5:00 A.M.—now August 20—with what troops he could collect. Worth was ordered to attack San Antonio as soon as he learned that Valencia had been defeated. Lee once again crossed the Pedregal in the dark to guide Twiggs and his troops to Padierna.

Meanwhile, leaving one brigade behind to guard against Santa Anna, Smith's men set out from San Jerónimo at 3:00 A.M., slipping and sliding through the rainy darkness down and across ravines and up behind Valencia's camp. At daybreak the Americans at Padierna began their demonstration, scrambling across the ravine and fixing Valencia's attention—when as if from nowhere Smith's brigades appeared at the Mexicans' rear, firing one volley and then charging with bayonets. Within seventeen minutes by Smith's watch, the battle was over; Valencia's force fled toward San Angel, their general leading the flight, cavalry trampling infantry in haste to get safely past a gauntlet of fire from the American brigade at San Jerónimo.

*Tenth move: Santa Anna (August 20).* At daybreak Santa Anna had again advanced his force from San Angel, hoping to link up with Valencia. But with Valencia's force destroyed, Santa Anna saw that his defense had collapsed, and he ordered a general retreat back to the *garitas* except for a force to hold the crossing at Churubusco, with a reserve north of the river.

*Eleventh move: Scott—and the Battle of Churubusco (August 20).* Upon hearing of the success on the other side of the Pedregal, Worth, as ordered, struck at San Antonio, attacking in front with one brigade while another went around through the Pedregal to turn the Mexican position. When the Mexicans abandoned San Antonio in accordance with Santa Anna's order, Worth's flanking brigade cut them in two; the rear segment dispersed while the advance segment fled to the Churubusco bridge, where they mingled with the troops retreating from San Angel.

Scott himself crossed the Pedregal, took personal command of the troops pursuing from the Contreras battlefield, and directed them toward the key junction at Coyoacán. The night's rain had ended, and it was a fine sunny day with clear visibility. When they reached Coyoacán an engineer officer reported that from the tower of the church he could see a mass of soldiers struggling to reach the bridge. Scott ordered Twiggs to hasten to Churubusco to intercept them, and shortly ordered two more brigades to move north from Coyoacán, cross the Río Churubusco west of the bridge, and try to cut the highway from behind.

Unfortunately, fields of tall corn had masked the strength with which the bridge and monastery were held. The monastery was defended ferociously; it took several hours to beat the defenders down. Meanwhile, Worth, advancing up the Acapulco highway from San Antonio, reached and assaulted the fortified bridgehead. It, too, was bravely defended. Eventually Worth managed to get a force through the fields on his right and across the Río Churubusco to outflank the Mexican left, and the bridgehead was finally taken in hand-to-hand fighting.

As for the brigades Scott sent to try to cut the highway from the west—after passing the river, they cut across cornfields and neared the highway some three-quarters of a mile north of the bridge. Poorly handled, they were pinned down until near the end of the battle, when they finally made a costly but successful charge and met Worth's men on the highway. The Americans pursued the retreating enemy another couple of miles up the highway before calling it a day, except for a group of dragoons who reached the Garita de San Antonio Abad itself before turning back.

Santa Anna's loss in the double battle, including the men of shattered units that never re-formed, was some 10,000 killed, wounded, taken prisoner or missing; American losses were 173 killed or missing and 865 wounded. The war was effectively won. Yet in fact more tough fighting lay ahead.

*Endgame (August 24–September 14).* Scott's mission, in his words, was to "conquer a peace"—accompanying him was a high State Department official with authority to negotiate a treaty—and though now he could easily have taken the capital, he was concerned that if he did so there might be no Mexican government to make peace with. So he offered an armistice to enable negotiations to take place; it went into effect August 24. Meanwhile, he moved his headquarters forward to Tacubaya.

It eventually became apparent that Santa Anna's government was merely playing for time in its negotiations, so the armistice was ended as of September 7. While Scott waited for the results of reconnaissance of Mexican positions, he made his only real blunder of the campaign. Intelligence reports told him that cannon were being made in a group of stone buildings called El Molino del Rey, at the western end of the park surrounding Chapultepec. He told Worth to send a small party on a night raid to wreck the foundry, but Worth persuaded him to allow a major daytime attack. The result was the fierce battle of Molino del Rey on September 8. The Americans finally prevailed—a Pyrrhic victory, for American losses were substantial and no cannon factory was found.

After weighing the choices, Scott decided to attack Mexico City from the west rather than the south. On September 13, Chapultepec was taken by storm in the classic fashion, with scaling ladders and hand-to-hand fighting. Troops under Quitman then fought their way down the Belén causeway while the main attack, under Worth, swept down La Verónica causeway and then battled house-to-house down the Tacuba causeway. By nightfall, after fierce fighting, Quitman had made a lodgment at the Garita de Belén and Worth at the Garita San Cosmé.

Scott's army was down to about 6,400 effectives, and Santa Anna still had perhaps 12,000 men, but that night Santa Anna gave up and evacuated the city. Though minor hostilities continued and a peace treaty was not signed until the following February, as a practical matter the war was over. The next day, September 14, 1847, Old Fuss and Feathers, resplendent in full uniform, took the salute from his ragged gringos cheering themselves hoarse in the great public square. For the headquarters of his military government, he commandeered the Palacio Nacional, the ancient residence of the viceroys on the site of the palace of Montezuma, emperor of the Aztecs. A detachment of marines that had accompanied the army was detailed to police its halls. The marines have a song about that.

*SPRING 1990*

---

Thaddeus Holt, both a lawyer and author, is a former deputy undersecretary of the army. His current research centers on Allied strategic deception in World War II.

# 8

# What Took the North So Long?

## By Williamson Murray

*In 1861, any comparison of strength between the North and the South gave an apparent overwhelming advantage to the Union. The North had more states, more people, more industry, more railroads, more money; the list went on and on. Statistics doomed the Confederacy from the first day of the war. Yet the Union, with all its seeming strength, took four years of unprecedented effort and profligate bloodshed to subjugate the Confederacy. Why? Was it a case of inferior Union generals? Superior Confederate military skills? The inherent hardiness of a rural society versus the softness of its urban neighbors to the north? The energy and power of the Southern cause? Williamson Murray finds that the answer is none of the above.*

The Civil War devastated the South and savaged the armies of both sides, exacting a casualty toll that made it one of the costliest wars in modern times and the worst in American history. At the heart of the bloody struggle lay the grand strategy of the North. As so often has happened in history, Northern strategy emerged only gradually. The path to victory was not clear on either side in 1861. Nor was the outcome of the war preordained. Political and military leaders on both sides enjoyed few of the prerequisites in education, inclination, and background to wage a war of this magnitude and intensity.

The North was eventually victorious because its leadership learned from its mistakes and adapted to the "real" conditions of war. In particular, Abraham Lincoln, a backwoods Illinois lawyer with only ninety days of militia experience in the Black Hawk War of 1832, and Ulysses S. Grant, perhaps the clearest-thinking general in American history, solidified Northern strategy and grasped victory from the wreckage of the early days.

The North, of course, relied on its great superiority in population, industrial resources, financial reserves, and agricultural production. Why, then, did it take so long for the federal government to achieve victory? We might begin by examining several popular explanations for the length of the war. The most persistent is that Southern soldiers, largely drawn from a yeoman class of farmers, had spent their lives shooting game and inuring themselves to hardship in a healthy outdoor environment. The Northern population, on the other hand, condemned to work in dark, dank factories, supposedly had developed few of the attributes that an army requires. Such a view, however, flies in the face of social evidence and the testimony of those who fought. One Southern officer, writing to a Northern friend immediately after the war, put the case differently. "Our officers were good," he commented, "but considering that our rank and file were just white trash and they had to fight regiments of New England Yankee volunteers, with all their best blood in the ranks, and Western sharpshooters together, it is only wonderful that we weren't whipped sooner." The fact is that nearly 80 percent of the Northern population lived in rural areas, like their Southern counterparts, and it is hard to see much difference in the social composition of the armies.

A corollary argument holds that the crucial factor in the war's length lay in the natural superiority of Southern officers and generals, an aristocratic group of West Point cavaliers who had been raised in the antebellum South to appreciate warrior values. The legends surrounding Robert E. Lee, Stonewall Jackson, and Jeb Stuart lend a certain plausibility to the argument, and the dismal record of the Union Army of the Potomac in the eastern theater of operations supports it. With two victories (Gettysburg and Five Forks), twelve defeats, and one draw (Antietam), the Army of the Potomac had a record of unambiguous failure matched by no other unit of equivalent size in the history of the United States Army. But historians have for too long overemphasized the war on the eastern front.

In fact, in the West, the reverse was true: There, Confederate forces fared just as badly as their counterparts in the Army of the Potomac and as a result of the same kind of wooden-headed leadership. Floyd, Pemberton, Bragg, and Hood on the Confederate side in the West fully matched the incompetence of McDowell, McClellan, Hooker, and Burnside in the Army of the Potomac. In his memoirs, Ulysses S. Grant recounts one anecdote from the prewar army that captures the nature of Bragg's leadership:

> On one occasion, when stationed at a post of several companies commanded by a field officer, [Bragg] was himself commanding one of the companies and at the same time acting as post quartermaster and commissary. He was first lieutenant at the time, but his captain was detached on other duty. As a commander of the company he made a requisition upon the quartermaster—himself—for something he wanted. As quartermaster he declined to fill the requisition, and endorsed on the back of it his reasons for doing so. As company commander he responded to this, urging that his requisition called for nothing but what he was entitled to, and that it was the duty of the quartermaster to fill it. As quartermaster he still persisted that he was right. In this condition of affairs Bragg referred the whole matter to the commanding officer of the post. The latter, when he saw the nature of the matter referred, exclaimed, "My God, Mr. Bragg, you have quarrelled with every officer in the army, and now you are quarrelling with yourself."

One of the soldiers in the Army of Tennessee reflected a perfect under-standing of Bragg's leadership when asked whether he was in the general's army. "Bragg's army? Bragg's got no army. He shot half of them himself up in Kentucky, and the other half got killed at Murfreesboro!" The superior command skills of the Confederate generals in the East were more than counterbalanced by the quality of Union leadership in the West.

As for the romantic image that clings to eastern Confederate generals, one might well remember Jackson's and Lee's ruthless brand of leadership. The former's marches up and down northern Virginia were frequently punctuated by summary executions of deserters; under his cold-eyed Presbyterian command, there was nothing cavalier about serving in his army. As for Lee, he was as ferocious a combat leader as the American army has produced. At Malvern Hill he brashly threw his men against a Union artillery concentration deadlier than any in the war. He won the day, but only at tremendous cost. War is a nasty business, and the Confederate generals in the East were extremely good at it.

The length of the war has far more to do with the immensity of the geo-graphic arena and the complexities of modern war than with the supposed superiority of Southern manhood and the competence of Southern gener-als. Geography offers a major clue as to why the North found it so difficult to project its industrial and military power into the Southern states and end the rebellion. Taken together, Mississippi and Alabama are slightly larg-er than present-day West Germany. The distance from central Georgia to northern Virginia is approximately the distance from East Prussia to Mos-cow. The distance from Baton Rouge to Richmond exceeds the distance from the Franco-German border to the current Soviet-Polish frontier. Considering that it took Napoleon from 1799 to 1807 to reach the frontiers of czarist Russia, one should not be surprised that it took the North so long to conquer the South. Exacerbating the challenge was the fact that primeval wilderness covered substantial portions of the South, particular-ly in the western theater of operations. While the eastern theater was rela-tively close to the centers of Northern industrial power, the starting point for the western armies—Cairo, Illinois—was nearly a thousand miles from the North's industrial center. Without railroads and steamships, the North would not have been able to bring its power to bear and probably would have lost the war.

The first formidable problem confronting the North in the Civil War lay in mobilizing its industrial strength and population and then deploying that power into the Confederacy. The problems of mobilization were daunting. The regular army was little more than a constabulary designed to overawe Indians on the frontier; it was certainly not prepared for large-scale mili-tary operations. Nowhere was there a body of experience from which to draw in solving the issues that now arose; the armies and their support structure had to come from nothing. The politicians knew nothing about war. The military leaders may have read a little of Baron de Jomini's works on the Napoleonic Wars, but the knowledge they derived was probably more harmful than helpful. Certainly no one had read Clausewitz; and though by 1864 Lincoln and Grant were to evolve an approach resembling Clausewitz's, their success resulted more from trial and error and common sense than from military history or theory.

The South did possess one significant advantage at the beginning of the war. Since it had no regular army, officers who resigned their commissions in the federal army to return home and serve the Confederacy found themselves spread throughout the newly formed state regiments, where their experience could at least provide an example to others.

But in the North, since regular units continued to exist, the experience of those within the professional officer corps was not used to best advantage in creating the Northern volunteer armies. Grant records the value of just one experienced officer—himself—in training the 21st Illinois. "I found it very hard work for a few days to bring all the men into anything like subordination; but the great majority favored discipline and by the application of a little regular army punishment all were reduced to as good discipline as one could want." The 20th Maine, trained by another lone regular officer, Adelbert Ames, also suggests the importance of experience in the training process. Not only did Ames turn out one of the best regiments in the Army of the Potomac, but Joshua Chamberlain, second-in-command of the regiment and up to July 1862 a professor of Greek at Bowdoin College, arguably became the best combat commander in the Army of the Potomac by the end of the war. All too often Union regiments did not have that one officer and therefore had to learn on the battlefield—which was an expensive process.

The armies themselves, whichever side one describes, retained a fundamentally civilian character. Photographs of even the units of the Army of the Potomac, supposedly the most spit-and-polish of all the Civil War armies, suggest a casualness that perhaps only the Israelis have exemplified in the twentieth century. When properly led, however, these troops were capable of sacrifices that few units in American military history have equaled. The performance of the 1st Minnesota at Gettysburg is only one case among hundreds. Although it sustained 80 percent casualties on the second day, it was back in the line receiving Pickett's charge on the third.

The whole first year of the war largely revolved around the complex task of raising, equipping, training, and deploying the forces that the strategic and political requirements of the war demanded. These problems presented themselves concurrently, not sequentially. Nor could Civil War military leaders depend on former certainties of war. The rifled musket had drastically altered combat. With killing ranges extended by 300 to 400 yards, Napoleonic set-piece tactics were no longer valid. Through a process of learning on the battlefield, Civil War armies substantially changed the manner in which they deployed and defended themselves as the war proceeded. How to wage offensive warfare against modern long-range firepower, however, remained an unsolved problem. Ultimately it would require the four long years of the First World War before answers to this question began to appear.

The initial strategic moves of the war turned out entirely in favor of the federal government. Above all, Lincoln's political acuity brought the all-important border states over to the Union camp. Ruthless action secured Maryland and Missouri, while cautious maneuvering led the South to mistakes that tipped Kentucky to the North. Gaining Maryland secured Washington; Missouri represented the first step down the Mississippi; and the securing of Kentucky would in early 1862 allow an obscure Union brigadier general to move against Forts Donelson and Henry. The latter success may have been among the most decisive in the war; the Tennessee and Cumberland rivers were now open to federal naval power as far as they were navigable. In effect Grant not only captured an entire Southern army but also made Tennessee indefensible by the South, while affording the Union the opportunity to cut the only east–west railroad that the Confederacy possessed.

However, the North's grand strategy took considerable time to emerge, at least in its fullest, winning form. The federal government's senior commander at the start of the war, General Winfield Scott, had a three-point strategic framework, the famous Anaconda Plan: (1) to blockade the South, (2) to capture its capital, and (3) to open up the Mississippi. It was a start, but only a start; the North would have to add a number of elements to achieve victory. The Battle of Shiloh in April 1862, which underlined how drastically the tactical game had changed, should have warned how difficult this war would prove to be. The federal government was going to have to break the will of a population—a population, moreover, inflamed by nationalism and possessing both a huge territory on which to draw and a Confederate government willing to take drastic measures to keep shirkers in line. Little of that was clear in April 1862; thus Grant was widely criticized in the North when Shiloh's casualties became known. But Grant at least sensed the depth of Southern hostility and its implications after the slaughter of Shiloh:

> Up to the battle of Shiloh, I, as well as thousands of other citizens, believed that the rebellion against the Government would collapse suddenly and soon, if a decisive victory could be gained over any of its armies. Donelson and Henry were such victories. An army of more than 21,000 men was captured or destroyed. Bowling Green, Columbus, and Hickman, Kentucky, fell in consequence, and Clarksville and Nashville, Tennessee, the last two with an immense amount of stores, also fell into our hands. The Tennessee and Cumberland rivers, from their mouths to the head of navigation, were secured. But when Confederate armies were collected which not only attempted to hold a line farther South, from Memphis to Chattanooga, Knoxville and on to the Atlantic, but assumed the offensive and made such a gallant effort to regain what had been lost, then, indeed, I gave up all idea of saving the Union except by complete conquest.

Grant's emergence in 1862 was seemingly one of the great surprises of the war; certainly the vicious backbiting that characterized Major General

Henry Halleck's reports on the future Northern commander did little to speed the process. Nevertheless, one should not assume that Grant was entirely an unknown quantity. Confederate general Richard S. Ewell wrote in spring 1861: "There is one West Pointer, I think in Missouri, little known, and whom I hope the Northern people will not find out. I mean Sam Grant. I knew him in the Academy and in Mexico. I should fear him more than any of their officers I have yet heard of. . . ."

Grant, of course, exercised little influence over Union grand strategy at the beginning; that was left to supposed prodigies such as George McClellan, whose sense of personal importance came close to losing the war in the East. Grant's conquest of the Mississippi in 1862 and 1863 opened up the great inland waterway, split the Confederacy, and cemented the alliance of the eastern and western states that would ultimately crush the Confederacy. His opening move at Forts Donelson and Henry exposed the one crucial geographic weakness of the Confederacy: the fact that its rivers in the West allowed Northern armies to penetrate into the very heartland of the Confederate nation. Tennessee, northern Alabama, and northern Georgia were all now within reach of invading Union troops. But under the constraints of Halleck's insipid leadership and Brigadier General William Rosecrans's tardy drive, the Union push took a considerable length of time to develop. There were some in the Confederacy who recognized how dangerous this threat might become, but Jefferson Davis continued to emphasize the eastern theater at the expense of the West and to support the inflexible and incompetent leadership of Braxton Bragg.

Unfortunately, Grant's second great victory—and his second battle of annihilation—at Vicksburg never realized its full potential. Once the Mississippi had been opened, his victorious army dispersed; the Union high command wasted Grant during the summer of 1863. The humiliating September defeat at Chickamauga, however, forced the high command to reorganize the western theater under Grant's control, sending him considerable reinforcements from the East. Lincoln and Secretary of War Edwin Stanton redeployed two corps from the Army of the Potomac, moving 25,000 men, along with their artillery and horses, over 1,200 miles in less than two weeks. This awesome logistic accomplishment underlines how far the North had advanced in its ability to mobilize and utilize its resources. Grant more than repaid the trust of the Lincoln administration with his smashing victory at Chattanooga in late November. His devastating defeat of Bragg's army solidified the Northern hold over Tennessee and established a solid base from which the Union's western armies could break the South apart at its very heart: Georgia. None of this had been imaginable at the onset of war. By now the North could logistically deploy, maintain, and put into battle an army of 100,000 men in the very center of the Confederacy.

Chattanooga set the stage for the Lincoln-Grant partnership—and the full evolution of Northern grand strategy—that saw the war through to its victorious conclusion in spring 1865. By the beginning of 1864, the Anaconda Plan had for the most part been realized: The Mississippi was open; the blockade was largely effective; and only Richmond remained untaken. Northern strategy moved in new directions. Lincoln had seen early in the war that a concerted, concurrent Union effort in all theaters would be required to break the outer ring of Confederate resistance. But George McClellan had babbled about the foolishness of such an approach and had contemptuously dismissed Lincoln's proposal. McClellan, as a disciple of Jomini, could think only in terms of capturing the enemy's capital or seizing some central position that would lead to a decisive battle. Lincoln thought in far broader terms. He would learn, while McClellan, like the Bourbons who briefly regained power between Napoleon's two reigns, learned nothing.

Both Lincoln and Grant looked beyond the eastern theater. Grant's grand strategy for 1864, after he was made commander of all the U.S. armies, aimed to crush the Confederacy with thrusts from a number of different directions. His instructions to General William Sherman (similar orders were given to General George Meade) made his intentions clear.

It is my design, if the enemy keep quiet and allow me to take the initiative in the spring campaign, to work all parts of the army together and somewhat toward a common center. For your information I now write you my programme as at present determined upon.

I have sent orders to [Major General Nathaniel P.] Banks by private messenger to finish up his present expedition against Shreveport with all despatch. . . . With [his] force he is to commence operations against Mobile as soon as he can. It will be impossible for him to commence too early.

[Major General Quincy] Gillmore joins [Major General Benjamin F.] Butler with 10,000 men, and the two operate against Richmond from the South side of the James River. . . . I will stay with the Army of the Potomac, increased by [Major General Ambrose E.] Burnside's corps of not less than 25,000 effective men, and operate directly against Lee's army wherever it may be found.

[Major General Franz] Sigel collects all his available force in two columns . . . to move against the Virginia and Tennessee. . . .

You I propose to move against [Joseph E.] Johnston's army, to break it up and to get into the interior of the enemy's country as far as you can, inflicting all the damage you can against their war resources.

I do not propose to lay down for you a plan of campaign, but simply to lay down the work it is desirable to have done, and leave you free to execute in your own way.

Grant concluded by telling Sherman that Sigel probably had the smallest chance of achieving his objective, but, as Lincoln had suggested during the strategy briefing, "if Sigel can't skin himself, he can hold a leg whilst someone else skins." There is no clearer, more concise strategic conception in American military history. It spelled the end of the Confederacy by 1865.

Why it did not spell defeat for the Confederacy in 1864 is worth examining. Failure to achieve victory before 1865 reflected the extraordinary difficulty in planning, coordinating, and executing military operations, as well as the inevitable impact of political reality on the world of military operations. Unfortunately, two key elements in Grant's strategy—Banks's move against Mobile, and Butler's move from Bermuda Hundred to cut the Petersburg–Richmond railroad—failed to materialize. Banks remained tied to the disastrously inept Red River campaign; consequently, his move against Mobile, which would have tied one corps of the Army of Tennessee to Alabama, did not occur and that unit reinforced Johnston's defense of Atlanta. Butler's attack from Bermuda Hundred collapsed in a welter of incompetence rarely seen this late in the Civil War. As Grant noted in his memoirs, Butler "corked" himself and his army into a position where he could exercise no influence on the unfolding campaign. Had he succeeded, Lee would have been forced to divide his forces against two foes. As it was, Butler's army was simply subsumed into the Army of the Potomac. The results of these failures prevented victory in 1864. Sherman faced far more effective resistance in his offensive against Atlanta, while the Army of the Potomac confronted an Army of Northern Virginia that was able to devote full attention to the defense of northern Virginia.

Significantly, Grant did not complain in his memoirs that the great spring offensive failed because of the incompetent leadership of "political" generals. He was well aware that Lincoln needed the support of "war Democrats" in the upcoming presidential campaign and that keeping Butler and Banks in positions of high responsibility was therefore essential for political reasons; both were "war Democrats." Good strategy, as with all things in war, is a fine balance of choices. As the British commander James Wolfe commented before Quebec in 1757: "War is an option of difficulties." The delicate coalition that Lincoln was holding together in the North was essential to the successful settlement of a war that had opened wounds not only between the North and the South but also within the North itself. To risk damaging that coalition by removing Banks and Butler was to risk losing the presidential election, and defeat in November might well have eviscerated whatever battlefield successes the Union army would achieve in 1864.

In assuming his position as commander of all Union forces, Grant was initially inclined to remain in the West. But his justified trust in Sherman's competence led him to change his mind: He would accompany the Army of the Potomac. Meade's competent but hardly driving brand of leadership in the last half of 1863 suggests that the Army of the Potomac's commander required the support of a more senior officer upon whom he could rely in moments of crisis. Grant would provide that support. He understood, however, that as an outsider he was not in a position to replace that army's senior leadership. He therefore was compelled to fight the coming battles of spring 1864 with a fundamentally flawed instrument—a military organization whose cohesion, willingness to sacrifice, and dogged determination were second to none in American military history, but whose repeated failures to seize the initiative, incapacity to take risks, and sheer bad luck resulted in a long record of defeat and reversal.

Thus, the Army of the Potomac fought the spring and summer battles in Virginia at appalling cost to itself and the nation. As a brigadier in the

Army of the Potomac wrote his wife after Spotsylvania Court House: "For thirty days it has been one funeral procession past me and it has been too much." However, while Grant pinned Lee and the Army of Northern Virginia to Richmond, Sherman battled General Johnston back in Atlanta. The pressure on Lee prevented the Confederate government from reinforcing Johnston. Jefferson Davis then made the fatal mistake of replacing Johnston with General John B. Hood. Hood's slashing attacks from Atlanta wrecked his army, lost Atlanta, and opened the way for Sherman's March to the Sea. The march again allowed Union forces to bisect the Confederacy and further fragment the span of Southern control, while opening up the last undamaged areas of the South to attack.

It also opened the way for the final chapter in the evolution of the war's strategy: a straight-out Union policy aimed at breaking the will of the Southern population by destroying the property, homes, and sustenance on which the survival of the South rested. In May 1864 Sherman had already confided to his wife his perplexity that the Southern population had not yet given up: "No amount of poverty or adversity seems to shake their faith. . . . Niggers gone, wealth and luxury gone, money worthless, starvation in view, yet I see no sign of let up—some few deserters, plenty tired of war, but the masses determined to fight it out." Sherman's frustration in front of Atlanta had led to bombardment of the city irrespective of the danger to civilians or to its military usefulness. The March to the Sea had taken place soon afterward, and while Sherman's progress through Georgia was not aimed directly at civilian lives, its "collateral" effects—the ruthless destruction of homes and foodstuffs and the starvation and disease that followed in its wake—indicated how far the North was willing to go in this war. As Sherman warned in a letter to the citizens of northern Alabama in 1864:

> The government of the United States has in North Alabama any and all rights which they choose to enforce in war, to take their lives, their houses, their land, their everything, because they can not deny that war exists there, and war is simply power unconstrained by constitution or compact. If they want eternal warfare, well and good. We will accept the issue and dispossess them and put our friends in possession. To those who submit to the rightful law and authority all gentleness and forbearance, but to the petulant and persistent secessionists, why, death is mercy and the quicker he or she is disposed of the better. Satan and the rebellious [saints] of heaven were allowed a continuance of existence in hell merely to swell their just punishment.

Sherman then noted that the American Civil War, unlike traditional European warfare, was "between peoples," and the invading army was entitled to all it could get from the people. He cited as a like instance the dispossession of the people of North Ireland during the reign of William and Mary.

General Philip Sheridan's conduct of the Shenandoah campaign suggests that Sherman's treatment of Georgia, Alabama, and South Carolina was not a matter of idiosyncratic choice but rather represented a larger strategic and policy design of the authorities in Washington and the Union high command. Clearly indicating this were Grant's instructions to Sheridan to turn the Shenandoah into "a barren waste . . . so that crows flying over it for the balance of this season will have to carry their provender with them." Sheridan followed his orders. His remark to the Prussians during the Franco-Prussian War of 1870–71 that they were "too humanitarian" in their treatment of the French population suggests how far the Union's strategy had descended into a relentless crushing of popular resistance. As he added to his European listeners, "Nothing should be left to the people but eyes, to lament the war!" Admittedly, neither Sherman nor Sheridan reached the level of Bomber Command's "dehousing" campaign of World War II. But Northern military forces were on the ground; they could spare the inhabitants their wretched lives while destroying the economic infrastructure, homes, foodstuffs, and farm animals far more effectively than "Bomber" Harris's force could ever dream of in World War II.

The Civil War was the first modern war, one in which military power, built on popular support and industrialization, and projected by the railroad and steamships over hundreds of miles, approached the boundary of Clausewitz's "absolute" war. Neither the strategic vision nor the military capacity to win the war existed at the onset. The mere creation of armies and their requisite support structure created problems that were neither readily apparent nor easily solved. The Union leadership did evolve a strategy that at last brought victory, but the cost was appalling: somewhere around 625,000 dead on both sides, equaling the total losses of all our other conflicts up to the Vietnam War. A comparable death toll in World War I would have been about 2.1 million American lives. Given what we now know of the cost of war in the modern world, we should not be surprised at the cost of this terrible conflict. We should, rather, wonder how the leaders of the Union—unversed in strategy at the beginning of the war, masters by its end—were able to see it through to its successful conclusion.

*SUMMER 1989*

Williamson Murray is coeditor of *The Making of Strategy: Rulers, States, and War* (1994) and *Calculations: Net Assessment and the Coming of World War II* (1992). His latest book is *Air War in the Persian Gulf* (1994).

# 9

# McClellan vs. Lee: The Seven-Day Trial

## By Stephen W. Sears

*Until battle is joined, it is very difficult to predict who will emerge as a great captain. Were it not so, the pages of American military history would have no opportunity to pause momentarily to note such names as William Hull, James Fannin, John Pope, Lloyd Fredendall—all leaders who, despite abundant qualifications, failed in the final test of combat leadership. Perhaps the greatest disappointment was George B. McClellan. In training, knowledge, and skill, McClellan seemed the proper choice to lead the Army of the Potomac against Richmond in 1862. Facing him across the battle lines stood Robert E. Lee, McClellan's equal but not his superior in training, knowledge, and skill. Neither general, however, was tested in command, and both generals would make serious errors in the Peninsula campaign, errors that ultimately sapped the affair of its potential decisiveness. Nonetheless, Stephen W. Sears relates, this first meeting of Lee and McClellan foretold which of these antagonists would win the laurels of a great captain and which would not.*

When McClellan and Lee met in battle early in the Civil War, they were both novices at command. In terms of the war, the outcome of their encounter was inconclusive; but as a measure of the two generals, it was decisive. Learning in April of 1862 that he might soon meet Robert E. Lee on a peninsula battlefield, George B. McClellan was well pleased. General Lee, he assured President Lincoln, "is *too* cautious & weak under grave responsibility—personally brave and energetic to a fault, he yet is wanting in moral firmness when pressed by heavy responsibility & is likely to be timid & irresolute in action." McClellan was confident not only of success but of "brilliant success." When finally they met in the Seven Days' Battles before Richmond two months later, McClellan's assessment proved spectacularly wrong. Ironically, he had precisely predicted not Lee's response to the pressures of command but his own.

Although the classic duel of Civil War commanders is now recognized to have been between Grant and Lee, the war's early stages featured Lee and McClellan. Each general entered the contest the commander of his nation's principal army; each was seen as a great captain. Yet today no one would bother to compare the two. Lee is arguably the finest general America has ever produced. McClellan is now dismissed, in the words of one historian, as "merely an attractive but vain and unstable man, with considerable military knowledge, who sat a horse well and wanted to be President." How could the Union have so misjudged its champion?

Anyone comparing McClellan and Lee in that spring of 1862 was bound to be struck by the parallels in their military careers. Both had notable records at West Point, both ranked second in their class at graduation, and both elected service in the Corps of Engineers, the army's elite branch. They had served together in the Mexican War, where Lee, the senior by nearly twenty years, directed young Lieutenant McClellan in engineering operations during the Mexico City campaign. Lee compiled a brilliant record in Mexico (Winfield Scott, the Mexican War commander, called him "the very best soldier I ever saw in the field"), while in his subaltern's role McClellan won two brevets for gallantry.

During the 1850s, Lee served as the superintendent of West Point and also was posted with the 2nd Cavalry in Texas. McClellan's experiences were even better preparation for the war to come: He was assigned to a commission sent to observe the Crimean War. Although he arrived too late to witness the siege of Sevastopol, his analysis of the siege operations and of the Allies' seaborne logistics would serve him well half a dozen years later in the Peninsula campaign in Virginia. He went on to examine military establishments from London to St. Petersburg. In 1857 he resigned from the army to enter the railroad business, where he became one of the highest-paid executives in the country. By 1861 his combined army and corporate business background seemed the perfect preparation for military command.

By the standards of the day, both Lee and McClellan were well educated in their chosen field. For McClellan, the study of military history and theory was an avocation even in civilian life. "I find that the old profession stirs my blood & delights me more than any other pursuit," he wrote his wife-to-be in 1860. Both men were avid students of Napoleon's campaigns; indeed, McClellan owned all the works of Antoine Henri Jomini, then recognized as Bonaparte's chief interpreter, in the original French editions. Both credited Winfield Scott with teaching them the art of war, although Lee's knowledge was the more direct: In Mexico he had been a member of Scott's "little cabinet" and had participated in strategic decision-making.

By training, experience, and inclination, then, Robert E. Lee and George B. McClellan were the two American soldiers best prepared for high command when the Confederates attacked Fort Sumter on April 12, 1861. They appeared to be an even match, but in one critical facet of generalship they were untested: Neither had exercised command in actual battle. Lee had directed no fighting in Mexico, and his subsequent experience was limited to a small, uneventful frontier expedition and to leading the detachment of marines that captured John Brown at Harpers Ferry in 1859. McClellan's command experience was just as limited. He had acted as head of an engineering company on garrison duty and directed an exploring party in the Pacific Northwest. It is doubtful if their brief contacts with each other—they never saw one another again after 1855—had furnished either with insights into the other's military prowess. In fact, the dismissive characterization of Lee that McClellan gave the president is something of a puzzle—his tendency was to overestimate his foes.

Lee's reputation among army leaders, in fact, was such that, after the attack on Fort Sumter, Winfield Scott bypassed some twenty senior officers to offer Lee command of the principal Federal field army. Emotionally ambivalent, Lee declined. Although he disapproved of secession, he said, he could "take no part in an invasion of the Southern States." Instead, he took charge of the forces of his native Virginia. For his part, ex-Captain McClellan was pressed by no less than three Northern states—New York, Pennsylvania, and Ohio—to take command of their troops. He accepted the Ohio post. A month after Fort Sumter, as a major general in the regular army ranked second only to Scott, he was commanding the main Federal forces west of the Alleghenies.

During the first year of the war, the careers of the two men continued to run parallel. In the summer of 1861, McClellan mounted a successful campaign in western Virginia. Lee was afterward assigned to the same area, although he was unable to revive Confederate fortunes there. McClellan was called east and in due course replaced Scott as general-in-chief; for four months he directed and planned strategy for all the Federal armies. During the spring of 1862, Lee held a roughly equivalent post as special adviser to President Jefferson Davis, in effect acting as chief of staff of the Southern armed forces. Then, on June 1, 1862, Lee replaced the wounded Joseph E. Johnston in command of the Army of Northern Virginia. By that date, McClellan had advanced with the Army of the Potomac up the Virginia peninsula to within half a dozen miles of Richmond. When the two generals at last met in battle, their objective was the Confederacy's endangered capital.

In an age when simply the appearance of command counted for much, both men were impressive martial figures. "No one could meet Lee and fail to be impressed with his dignity of character, his intellectual power, and his calm self-reliance," a Confederate officer wrote. McClellan radiated the same aura of competent authority; he had "an indefinable *air of success* about him and something of the 'man of destiny,'" an observer remarked.

Although Lee was not yet as revered by his men as he would be, McClellan was already an esteemed leader when he embarked on the Peninsula campaign. He took pride in his newspaper appellation, "The

Young Napoleon." He was thirty-five, the age at which Napoleon made himself emperor—and he confided to his wife that he doubted if even Bonaparte had ever elicited the same degree of love and confidence from his men.

Despite their personal similarities and career parallels, Lee and McClellan also had crucial differences in their approaches to high command. Lee demonstrated a genuine talent for working well with his superiors. From the moment he assumed command, he won the confidence of President Davis and of George W. Randolph, then the Confederacy's secretary of war. He consulted with them and kept them informed of his plans and never attempted to subvert the principle of civilian control of the military. This harmonious partnership was essential to Lee's performance during the Seven Days.

George McClellan, by contrast, had proved himself incapable of getting along with virtually anyone of higher rank, military or civilian. In the prewar army and in his railroad career, he had been constantly at odds with his superiors. During the Civil War the only civilian authority with whom he had no dispute was Lincoln's first secretary of war, Simon Cameron, who was not interested in war planning and did not question anything McClellan did. In January 1862, Cameron was succeeded by Edwin M. Stanton, and within a month McClellan and Stanton were feuding bitterly. Even while Winfield Scott was still general-in-chief, McClellan vilified him as a dotard and even a traitor: "that confounded old Genl always comes in the way—he is a perfect imbecile." President Lincoln was "nothing more than a well-meaning baboon." So great was McClellan's mistrust of those in authority that by the time he reached the gates of Richmond he was persuaded that the government had an "abominable design" to hold back reinforcements so that he would fail. The Republican administration, he reasoned, dared not let Democrat McClellan win the war. "I would have been the most prominent & influential personage in the country," he later wrote in a draft of his memoirs.

This conspiracy was entirely imaginary—in fact, the government supplied McClellan with more men for the Battle of Richmond than he had originally requested—but to the general its consequences were very real. He had a particular faculty, an observer remarked, for "realizing hallucinations." McClellan complained he would be at grave risk in the coming battle because General Lee had 200,000 men, twice as many as he did, to defend the Confederate capital. In actuality, in the Seven Days' Battles McClellan's forces outnumbered Lee's 104,000 to 85,000; but his delusion prompted McClellan to take Richmond not by battle but by siege, as the Allies had taken Sevastopol in 1855. With his massive siege train of a hundred big guns and mortars (his one admitted advantage over the Confederates) he would pound the enemy host into submission.

General Lee viewed the military possibilities with a far more perceptive eye. He had carefully observed McClellan's cautious advance up the peninsula and his dependence on the region's single railroad to move his imposing artillery, and he took note of how quickly his opponent had resorted to siege warfare in the campaign's first confrontation at Yorktown. "McClellan will make this a battle of posts," he told President Davis soon after taking command, and he formulated a plan to abort any siege of Richmond before it could begin.

His first step was to call on his cavalry commander, J.E.B. Stuart, to pinpoint the enemy's dispositions. In a spectacular ride, Stuart led his troopers completely around the Army of the Potomac and returned with a full report. The Federals' railroad supply line was vulnerable, Stuart told Lee, and while the bulk of the Union troops were entrenched on the south, or Richmond, side of the Chickahominy River, a substantial force—Fitz John Porter's V Corps—was still north of the river, guarding the army's communications. Hoping to avoid the costly tactic of storming entrenchments, Lee found his alternative in Stuart's report.

He would concentrate the largest part of his army against his opponent's weakest point. A turning movement against Porter's corps would threaten both McClellan's communications and his isolated right flank. To concentrate as many men as possible for the offensive, Lee ordered Stonewall Jackson from the Shenandoah Valley, where for the past month he had been befuddling substantial Union forces. Jackson was to spearhead the attack against Porter's V Corps. "Unless McClellan can be driven out of his entrenchments," Lee explained, "he will move by positions under cover of his heavy guns within shelling distance of Richmond. I know of no surer way of thwarting him than that proposed."

This battle plan revealed much about Lee as a commander. He recognized that his sole hope of forestalling a siege of Richmond, with its inevitable outcome, was to take the tactical offensive, and he designed an operation that best enabled his small army to outmaneuver the larger one. The plan involved an enormous risk, however, one that he dared take only because of his previous observations of McClellan's methods. Lee was leaving fewer than 30,000 men to defend Richmond, only 21,000 of them in the lines facing almost 75,000 Federal troops on the Richmond side of the Chickahominy. Meanwhile, he took the rest of his army north to operate against Porter's troops. He was convinced that McClellan would not seize this opportunity to counterattack, to smash into Richmond and cut off the Confederate army from its base of operations. Lee was confident that "The Young Napoleon" lacked the boldness of his namesake, the general who had seized on just such an enemy turning movement to produce a spectacular victory at Austerlitz.

In the Seven Days, Lee would be experiencing battlefield command for the first time, and, despite his longer record in the field, so would McClellan. In the campaign in western Virginia, McClellan had been involved in one action, but only peripherally, as all the fighting was directed by a subordinate in a distant turning movement. In the first battle on the peninsula, Yorktown, his efforts had been confined to siege operations, while at Williamsburg early in May, he reached the battlefield after the fighting had ended. In the only other major action of the campaign, at Fair Oaks (where Joe Johnston was wounded), McClellan was ill with malaria and played no role beyond ordering up reinforcements.

McClellan did inspect the Fair Oaks battlefield afterward, however, and found the sight unnerving. "Every poor fellow that is killed or wounded almost haunts me!" he confided to his wife. He had certainly seen such grim sights before in Mexico, where he witnessed friends killed in action and was very nearly killed himself. But this was different. These dead and maimed were *his* men, and as their general he had been responsible for them. When he wrote, "Victory has no charms for me when purchased at such cost," he was revealing an unwillingness to accept a reality of battlefield command.

This sense of intense, personal responsibility—for his men, his army, indeed for the Republic—proved all but suffocating to McClellan during the Seven Days' fighting. On June 25, the first day of the week-long battle, he was opening his long-awaited final advance on Richmond when a report reached him that Stonewall Jackson was about to fall on his flank and that the enemy was bringing 200,000 men against him. "I regret my great inferiority in numbers," he telegraphed Secretary of War Stanton, "but feel that I am in no way responsible for it." He would do his best to save the army, "but if it is destroyed by overwhelming numbers [I] can at least die with it & share its fate." Even before he was attacked he was anticipating defeat.

Lee opened his offensive the next day, and it soon became apparent that he had accurately read his opponent's mind. There was no Federal drive on Richmond on that day or on any other. General McClellan, to be sure, glimpsed his opportunity for a telling counterstroke. "I think the enemy are making a great mistake," he assured his wife on June 26; "if so they will be terribly punished." His opponent was "falling into a trap. I shall allow the enemy to cut off our communications in order to ensure success." But that fleeting thought was as close as he ever came to recapturing the offensive.

On June 27, while fighting raged savagely on Porter's front at Gaines's Mill north of the river, McClellan remained at his headquarters south of the Chickahominy, anticipating the need to defend "against superior numbers" at every point along his lines facing Richmond. "You must beat them if I move the whole Army to do it & transfer all on this side," he signaled Porter, yet only a single division of reinforcements fought alongside the V Corps that day. Seven other divisions idled away the hours in their entrenchments. At dusk Porter was overcome, losing twenty-two guns and having 2,800 of his men taken prisoner, in addition to the dead and wounded.

That night, convinced that the rest of his army would soon be engulfed as well, McClellan issued orders for a retreat to the nearest haven, the James River, where the navy's gunboats waited to provide covering fire. The day's events left him distraught and demoralized. Now and in the days to come, he became obsessed with salvaging what he could from the wreck of his campaign. He told Washington his troops had been "overwhelmed by vastly superior numbers even after I brought my last reserves into action," and he charged the administration with deliberately conspiring to sacrifice the army. A War Department official was so shocked by this accusation that he censored the dispatch before giving it to Secretary Stanton.

McClellan might have been acknowledging defeat, but Lee was far from victory. His plan had gone badly awry. His tactics proved complicated, his staff inexperienced, and his generals—especially, and surprisingly, Stonewall Jackson—ineffective. Instead of turning the enemy out of their lines as intended, the movement had degenerated into a series of bloody frontal assaults, and after two days of such fighting Confederate casualties were more than 10,000. Yet despite all this, the Federals were in retreat. The victory of the Army of Northern Virginia over the Army of the Potomac at Gaines's Mill was at best a narrow one; the victory of General Lee over General McClellan was decisive.

Ostensibly, Lee and McClellan followed similar theories of command. As Lee explained to a foreign observer, for him to lead personally in battle "would do more harm than good." He had to rely instead on his field commanders to manage the actual fighting. "I plan and work with all my might to bring the troops to the right place at the right time," he went on; "with that I have done my duty." McClellan, too, left the tactical details of the fighting to subordinates. But there was one vital difference in their leadership methods. While delegating authority, Lee retained overall control of the command. He closely followed the course of the fighting, often by personal observation, and he sought to anticipate what decisions would be needed. At a critical point in the fighting, warned that he was approaching too near the enemy's guns, he replied, "I'm trying to find out something about the movements and plans of those people." McClellan lacked that same determination to follow through. On the last three days of the Seven Days he made his dispositions, then simply abdicated the role of commanding general.

On June 29, at Savage's Station, McClellan left his rear guard to fight an ill-managed battle while he was five miles away directing the movements of the supply columns. Fortunately for the Federals, this particular enemy attack, equally ill-managed, was repelled. The next day, June 30, promised to be decisive for the campaign. McClellan's retreating army would have to pass across the front of the advancing Confederates at a crossroads called Glendale, and Lee sought to strike McClellan's flank and rear simultaneously. The danger could hardly have escaped McClellan when he inspected his position that morning and gave his orders. As firing commenced, signaling the enemy assault, he rode off to the James River, five miles away. Then he distanced himself even farther from the battle by boarding the gunboat *Galena*, which steamed upriver to shell enemy troops on the bank.

McClellan left no one in overall command at Glendale, and so his generals, as one of them testified, "fought their troops entirely according to their own ideas." It was their good fortune that once again Lee's battle plan went awry. His attack, intended to be a double envelopment by 70,000 men, collapsed into a series of headlong frontal assaults by only 20,000. Even so, the struggle was bitter, and the Federals lost eighteen more guns before finally beating off their attackers. For the Confederates it was a great opportunity missed. "It was the bitterest disappointment Lee had ever sustained," wrote his biographer Douglas Southall Freeman, "and one that he could not conceal. . . . He had only that one day for a Cannae, and the army was not ready for it."

The unhappy record of Confederate tactical failures reached a climax the next day, July 1, at Malvern Hill. Columns went astray, artillery support failed, assaults were uncoordinated, and the result was a decided Federal victory. "It was not war—it was murder," wrote the Southern general D.H. Hill, who lost almost a third of his men in the attack.

This day also saw the climax of General McClellan's wretched performance as a battlefield commander. His demoralization was complete. "Never did I see a man more cut down than Genl. McClellan . . . ," wrote an officer who was with him before the battle. "He was unable to do anything or say anything." In spite of clear signs that the enemy was preparing an attack that morning, he set off in the *Galena* for Harrison's Landing, the intended next stop in his retreat, an hour and a half's voyage downstream. As it happened, the Confederates were so much delayed that he had returned to Malvern Hill by the time the attack opened in late afternoon, but he posted himself two miles from the scene and out of sight of the fighting. He did not wait to learn the outcome of the battle before ordering the retreat to continue to Harrison's Landing. There the Army of the Potomac would remain until evacuated from the peninsula six weeks later.

The record of the Seven Days' Battles is proof that Robert E. Lee did not enter the war a great captain. He was forced to meet the pressures of combat command during his first experience of it, and it was a costly lesson. Confederate casualties came to more than 20,600, exceeding those of the Federals by some 4,700. However, though his excellent strategic plan was weakened by failures of execution, he never wavered in his determined leadership. Later, Lee said forthrightly in his report on the campaign that, but for the mistakes that were made, "the Federal Army should have been destroyed." He did succeed in seizing and holding the initiative, and as a result, Richmond was saved from siege. Furthermore, General Lee learned well from the experience. Incompetent officers were soon weeded out, and command and staff procedures were improved. On future fields, Lee would better conform his tactics to his army's abilities. Never again would his army display the weaknesses that were revealed during the Seven Days.

As for General McClellan, his discreditable performance during that week of battle amply demonstrated that he was neither a great captain nor capable of becoming one. Consumed by delusions about the enemy and oppressed by the responsibilities of command, he had lost the will to fight. In fact, his abandonment of his army during successive days of battle made it clear that he had lost even the will to command. Had any of these battles ended in disaster for the Union, he almost certainly would have been charged with dereliction of duty. And, unlike Lee, McClellan gained no discernible profit from the experiences of the Seven Days. In his last battle, at Antietam, as in his first, he was as Lee described him—a timid general, too fearful of losing to take the risks of winning. Lee revealed his grasp of this truth when he remarked, on learning of McClellan's relief from command, "I fear they may continue to make these changes till they find some one whom I don't understand."

*AUTUMN 1988*

Stephen W. Sears is the author of *Landscape Turned Red: The Battle of Antietam* (1983), *George B. McClellan: The Young Napoleon* (1988), and *To the Gates of Richmond: The Peninsula Campaign* (1992).

# 10

# How Lincoln Won the War with Metaphor

## By James M. McPherson

*In the summer of 1940, when Britain faced Germany alone, Winston Churchill understood that words could be as powerful as bullets in war. As one British historian later recalled, Churchill "made exhilarating the prospect of peril." Churchill was not the only master of the wartime pulpit. Much of Abraham Lincoln's greatness as a leader, Professor James M. McPherson contends, came from his use of the American language. His tutors had been Shakespeare, Aesop's Fables, Pilgrim's Progress, and the King James Bible; his mentors had been the sights, smells, and sounds of rural America. In Lincoln's clarity of expression, in his ability to explain and teach, in his skill with apt metaphors and parables, in his ability to inspire, Lincoln was without equal. In many respects, the legacy of Lincoln's words was the very survival of the Union.*

I n an essay on the reasons for Confederate defeat in the Civil War, the Southern historian David M. Potter made a striking assertion: "If the Union and Confederacy had exchanged presidents with one another, the Confederacy might have won its independence." Is this rather dramatic conclusion justified? Most historians would probably agree with Potter's general point that Jefferson Davis's shortcomings as a leader played a role in the Confederate defeat. They would also agree that one of Davis's principal failures was an inability to communicate effectively with other Confederate leaders and with the Southern people. As Potter put it, Davis "seemed to think in abstractions and to speak in platitudes."

Abraham Lincoln, by contrast, most emphatically did not think in abstractions and rarely spoke in platitudes. We have not had another president—except perhaps Franklin D. Roosevelt—who expressed himself in such a clear, forceful, logical manner. It is no coincidence that Lincoln and Roosevelt were great war presidents who led the United States to its most decisive victories in its most important wars. Their preeminent quality as leaders was an ability to communicate the meanings and purposes of these wars in an intelligible, inspiring manner that helped energize and mobilize their people to make the sacrifices necessary for victory. By contrast, Jefferson Davis, as another historian, Paul D. Escott, has concluded, failed to do a good job "in eliciting the enthusiasm and energies of the people."

Wherein lay Lincoln's advantage over Davis in this matter? It certainly did not derive from a better education. Davis had received one of the best educations that money could buy in his day: He attended one "college" in Kentucky and another in Mississippi (actually secondary schools or academies); he went to Transylvania University in Kentucky, which was one of the best genuine colleges west of the Appalachians at that time; and he graduated from the military academy at West Point, the best American school for engineering as well as for military science in that era. From his education Davis acquired excellent training in the classics, rhetoric, logic, literature, and science. He should have been a superb communicator, and in many respects he was, by the standards of the time. He could write with vigorous logic, turn a classical phrase, quote the leading authorities on many a subject, and close with a rhetorical flourish.

Lincoln had only a year or so of formal schooling in the typical rote-learning "blab schools" of the day, schooling that he obtained, as he later put it, "by littles"—a month here, a couple of months there, spread out over a period of a few years. Lincoln was basically a self-taught man. Of course he later read law, which along with the practice of that profession helped to give him an ability to write and speak with clarity, a skill in logical analysis, and a knack for finding exactly the right word or phrase to express his meaning. But Davis also had most of these skills of expository writing and speaking. So we are still left with the question: Wherein lay Lincoln's superiority?

The answer may be found in a paradox: Perhaps the defects of Lincoln's education proved a benefit. Instead of spending years inside the four walls of a classroom, Lincoln worked on frontier dirt farms most of his youth, he split rails, he rafted down the Mississippi on a flatboat, he surveyed land, he worked in a store, where he learned to communicate with the farmers and other residents of a rural community. Lincoln grew up close to the rhythms of nature—of wild beasts and farm animals, of forest and running water, of seasons and crops, and of people who got their meager living from the land.

These things, more than books, furnished Lincoln's earliest education. They infused his speech with the images of nature. And when he turned to books, his favorites were the King James Bible, *Aesop's Fables, Pilgrim's Progress,* and Shakespeare's plays. All are rich in figurative language—allegory, parable, fable, metaphor—in words and stories that seem to say one thing but mean another, in images that illustrate something more profound than their surface appearance.

Here lies one of the secrets of Lincoln's success as a communicator: his skill in the use of figurative language, of which metaphor is the most common example. We all use metaphors every day. We tell someone to stop beating around the bush; we say that we have too many irons in the fire; we express a desire to get to the heart of the matter; we worry about fitting square pegs into round holes; we see light at the end of the tunnel; and so on. Most of these examples are "dead" metaphors—that is, they are so commonplace that we often do not realize that they are metaphors, and they thus lose their power to evoke a vivid image in our minds. The best "live" metaphors are those that use a simple, concrete figure to illustrate a complex and perhaps abstract concept, thereby giving life and tangible meaning to something that might otherwise escape comprehension.

One of the first things that strikes a student of Lincoln's speeches and writings is his frequent use of images and figurative language. His speeches and letters abound with metaphors. Many of them are extraordinarily well chosen and apt; they have the persuasive power of concreteness and clarity. By contrast, Jefferson Davis's prose contains few metaphors or images of any kind. It is relentlessly literal. It is formal, precise, logical, but also stiff, cold, and abstract. Davis's wartime letters and speeches bristle with anger and bitterness toward Yankees and toward his critics and adversaries within the Confederacy. But the few metaphors he used to illustrate his points are quite dead—references to sowing the seeds of discontent and thereby harvesting defeat, and the like.

To be sure, a number of Lincoln's metaphors were dead on arrival. He complained of dealing with people who had axes to grind; he said more than once that he wanted everyone to have a fair start in the race of life; he referred to the ship of state and its navigational problems during his presidency. But Lincoln could neatly turn a seemingly dead metaphor into a live one. In his first message to a special session of Congress that met three months after the war began, he critically reviewed the long and, as he put it, sophistic attempt by Southern leaders to legitimize their actions with arguments for state sovereignty and the constitutional right of secession. "With rebellion thus sugar-coated," said the president, "they have been drugging the public mind of their section for more than thirty years," and this war was the result.

Here Lincoln injected life into a rather tired metaphor, "sugar-coated," and used it to clinch his point in a luminous manner. This occasion also gave Lincoln an opportunity to define his philosophy of communication with the public. The government printer who set the message in type objected to the phrase about sugar-coating the rebellion. "You have used an undignified expression in the message," the printer told the president. "A message to Congress [is] a different affair from a speech at a mass-meeting in Illinois. . . . The messages [become] a part of history, and should be written accordingly. . . . I would alter the structure of that, if I were you."

Lincoln replied with a twinkle in his eye: "That word expresses precisely my idea, and I am not going to change it. The time will never come in this country when the people won't know exactly what *sugar-coated* means!"

Lincoln was right: People knew exactly what he meant then, and his metaphor retains its pithiness today.

Lincoln used a different but equally expressive metaphor to describe the threat of secession on another important occasion, his speech at Cooper Institute in New York in February 1860, a speech that gave him great visibility among eastern Republicans and helped launch him toward the presidential nomination three months later. This time he discussed Southern warnings of the dire consequences if a Republican president was elected. "In that supposed event." said Lincoln, directing his words to the South, "you say, you will destroy the Union; and then, you say, the great crime of having destroyed it will be upon us! That is cool. A highwayman holds a pistol to my ear, and mutters through his teeth, 'Stand and deliver, or I shall kill you, and then you will be a murderer!' "

No one could fail to understand Lincoln's point. And through his whole life, one of his main concerns was that everyone understand precisely what he was saying. A colleague who praised this quality once asked Lincoln where his concern with exact clarity came from.

"Among my earliest recollections," replied Lincoln, "I remember how, when a mere child, I used to get irritated when anybody talked to me in a way I could not understand. I don't think I ever got angry at anything else in my life. . . . I can remember going to my little bedroom, after hearing the neighbors talk of an evening with my father, and spending the night walking up and down, and trying to make out what was the exact meaning of some of their, to me, dark sayings. I could not sleep . . . when I got on such a hunt after an idea, until I had caught it; and when I thought I had got it, I was not satisfied . . . until I had put it in language plain enough, as I thought, for any boy I knew to comprehend. This was a kind of passion with me, and it has stuck by me."

Many contemporaries testified to this Lincolnian passion, and to his genius for using everyday metaphors to achieve it. Francis Carpenter, the artist who spent six months at the White House during 1864 painting a picture of Lincoln and his Cabinet, noted that the president's "lightest as well as his most powerful thought almost invariably took on the form of a figure of speech, which drove the point home, and clinched it, as few abstract reasoners are able to do." Lincoln was also famous for telling stories. Many of them were parables intended to make or illustrate a point, and a parable is an extended metaphor. "It is not the story itself," Lincoln once said, "but its purpose, or effect, that interests me."

When Lincoln said "Now that reminds me of a story," his listeners knew that they could expect a parable. Take, for example, this story that Lincoln told soon after he had gotten rid of his controversial secretary of war Simon Cameron. Since some other Cabinet members had also made enemies among one faction or another, a delegation of politicians called on the president and advised him that this might be a good time to make a wholesale change in the Cabinet. Lincoln shook his head and replied, "This reminds me of a story. When I was a boy I knew a farmer named Joe Wilson who was proud of his prize chickens. But he started to lose some of them to raids by skunks on the henhouse. One night he heard a loud cackling from the chickens and crept out with his shotgun to find a half-dozen of the black and white critters running in and out of the shed. Thinking to clean out the whole tribe, he put a double charge in the gun and fired away. Somehow he hit only one, and the rest scampered off."

At this point in the story, Lincoln would act it out by holding his nose and screwing up his face in a pained expression while he continued. "The neighbors asked Joe why he didn't follow up the skunks and kill the rest. 'Blast it,' said Joe, 'it was eleven weeks before I got over killin' one. If you want any more skirmishing in that line you can just do it yourselves!' "

The moral of the story was clear to all. But not everyone approved of Lincoln's habit of telling stories—a few of which were a good bit earthier than this one. Some people considered it undignified for the president of the United States to carry on in such a fashion. But Lincoln had a reply for them, as related by Chauncey Depew, a prominent lawyer, railroad president, and New York Republican leader. Said Depew:

I heard him tell a great many stories, many of which would not do exactly for the drawing room, but for the person he wished to reach, and the object he desired to accomplish with the individual, the story did more than any argument could have done. He once said to me, in reference to some sharp criticism which had been made upon his story-telling: . . . "I have found in the course of a long experience that common people"—and, repeating it—"common people, take them as they run, are more easily influenced and informed through the medium of a broad illustration than in any other way, and as to what the hypercritical few may think, I don't care."

This was something that Jefferson Davis never understood. He would never have been caught telling a story about skunks to make the point that solutions are sometimes worse than problems. He did not have Lincoln's concern for reaching the common people or his knack for doing so. Lincoln was especially fond of animal metaphors and parables, as in the case of the skunk story. This derived in part from his own rural background and also undoubtedly from the many boyhood hours he spent with *Aesop's Fables.* During one of those hours his cousin Dennis Hanks said to him, "Abe, them yarns is all lies." Lincoln looked up for a moment, and replied, "Mighty darn good lies, Denny." And as an adult Lincoln was aware that these "lies," these fables about animals, provided an excellent way to communicate with a people who were still close to their rural roots and understood the idioms of the forest and barnyard.

Some of Lincoln's most piquant animal metaphors occurred in his comments about or communications with commanding generals during the war. General George B. McClellan clamored repeatedly for reinforcements and understated his own strength while overstating that of the enemy. On one of these occasions Lincoln, who had already reinforced McClellan and knew that Union forces outnumbered the Confederates, said in exasperation that sending troops to McClellan was like shoveling flies across the barnyard—most of them never seemed to get there.

Later on, when Joseph Hooker had become commander of the Army of the Potomac, Lincoln visited him at the front. Hooker boasted that he had built this force into "the finest army on the planet." He added that he hoped God Almighty would have mercy on Bobby Lee because he, Joe Hooker, would have none.

Lincoln listened to this and commented that the "hen is the wisest of all the animal creation, because she never cackles until the egg is laid." And to be sure, it was Lee who could cackle when he beat Hooker decisively at Chancellorsville. Lee then invaded the North in the campaign that led to Gettysburg. As Lee began to move north, Hooker proposed to cross the Rappahannock River and attack his rear guard. Lincoln disapproved with these words in a telegram to Hooker: "I would not take any risk of being entangled upon the river, like an ox jumped half over a fence, and liable to be torn by dogs, front and rear, without a fair chance to gore one way or kick the other." Napoleon himself could not have given better tactical advice or phrased it half so well.

A week later, when the Confederate invasion force was strung out over nearly a hundred miles of Virginia roads, Lincoln telegraphed this message to Hooker: "If the head of Lee's army is at Martinsburg and the tail of it on the Plank road between Fredericksburg and Chancellorsville, the animal must be very slim somewhere. Could you not break him?" But Hooker seemed reluctant to fight Lee again. The president therefore replaced Hooker with George G. Meade, who won the Battle of Gettysburg, though he proved to be cautious and defensive afterward.

Thus in 1864 Lincoln brought to the East his most successful commander, Ulysses S. Grant, to become general-in-chief. In a private conference with Grant soon after the general arrived in Washington, Lincoln referred to the military situation and said that he could best illustrate what he wanted to say with a story.

There was once a great war among the animals, said the president, and one side had great difficulty finding a commander who had enough confidence in himself to fight. Finally they found a monkey, by the name of Jocko, who said he could command the army if his tail could be made a little longer. So the other animals found more tail and spliced it onto Jocko's. He looked at it admiringly, but said he thought he needed just a little more. So they found some more and spliced it on. This process was repeated many times until Jocko's tail was so long that when coiled it filled the whole room. Still he called for more tail, and they kept adding by coiling it around his shoulders and then around his whole body—until he suffocated.

Grant understood the point; unlike McClellan and other generals, he would not keep calling for more troops as an excuse for not fighting. Instead, he worked out a plan for the two main Union armies, in Virginia and Georgia, to advance simultaneously against the two principal Confederate armies while smaller Union forces elsewhere pinned down Confederate detachments to prevent their reinforcing the main Southern armies. This was the kind of coordinated offensive that Lincoln had been urging on his generals for two years, and he was delighted finally to have a commander who would do it. Lincoln's expressive description of the auxiliary role of the smaller armies on the periphery was "Those not skinning can hold a leg." Grant liked this phrase so much that he used it in his own dispatches.

Later on, when Grant had Lee's army under siege at Petersburg while Sherman was marching through Georgia and South Carolina destroying everything in his path, Lincoln described Union strategy this way: "Grant has the bear by the hind leg while Sherman takes off the hide." On another occasion Lincoln changed the metaphor in an official telegram to Grant: "I have seen your despatch expressing your unwillingness to break your hold where you are. Neither am I willing. Hold on with a bull-dog grip, and chew & choke, as much as possible." In the end Grant's chewing and choking while Sherman took off the hide were what won the war.

The principal cause of this war was slavery, and one of its main consequences was the abolition of slavery. This peculiar institution gave rise to many Lincolnian metaphors, animal and otherwise. One of them was a metaphor of snakes and children that Lincoln used in several speeches during his tour of New England in the late winter of 1860. The central tenet of the Republican party's policy was to restrict the spread of slavery into new territories while pledging not to interfere with it in states where it already existed and was therefore protected by the Constitution. Lincoln considered slavery a moral wrong and a social evil. He hoped that the South would eventually take steps to end it voluntarily and peacefully. In the meantime, he said, we must not introduce this evil where it does not now exist.

"If I saw a venomous snake crawling in the road," said Lincoln in illustration of his point, "any man would say I might seize the nearest stick and kill it; but if I found that snake in bed with my children, that would be another question. I might hurt the children more than the snake, and it might bite them. . . . But if there was a bed newly made up, to which the children were to be taken, and it was proposed to take a batch of young snakes and put them there with them, I take it no man would say there was any question how I ought to decide. . . . The new Territories are the newly made bed to which our children are to go, and it lies with the nation to say whether they shall have snakes mixed up with them or not."

In our day of thirty-second political spot commercials on television, this metaphor seems long and involved. But Lincoln's audiences understood it perfectly and appreciated it boisterously. The stenographic report of this speech at New Haven indicates prolonged applause, laughter, and cheering as he spun out the metaphor. A professor of rhetoric at Yale was so taken with Lincoln's speech that he followed him to another town to hear him speak again and then gave a lecture on Lincoln's techniques to his class.

The day after Lincoln spoke at Norwich, Connecticut, the town's leading clergyman happened to travel on the same train with him and talked with him, praising Lincoln's style, "especially your illustrations, which were romance and pathos, and fun and logic all welded together. That story about the snakes, for example, . . . was at once queer and comical, and tragic and argumentative. It broke through all the barriers of a man's previous opinions and prejudices at a crash, and blew up the citadel of his false theories before he could know what had hurt him."

Lincoln used a number of other metaphors to describe slavery, including that of a cancer that must be prevented from spreading lest it kill the body politic. His best-known slavery metaphor formed the central theme of the most famous speech he gave before the Civil War, the House Divided address in 1858. Here the house was a metaphor for the Union, which had been divided against itself by slavery and could not continue to be so divided forever without collapsing. Therefore the Republicans wanted to stop the further spread of slavery, as a first step toward what Lincoln called its "ultimate extinction."

This metaphor of a house divided became probably the single most important image of the relationship between slavery and the Union, and remains so today. It provided an instant mental picture of what Republicans stood for. It also helped provoke the South into secession when Lincoln was elected president, because no matter how much he professed his intention to tolerate slavery where it already existed, had not this Black Republican Yankee also called slavery a moral wrong and looked forward to its ultimate extinction?

In that same speech, Lincoln elaborated the house metaphor to illustrate another of the Republican party's favorite themes—that the Democrats were dominated by a "slave power conspiracy" to expand the institution of bondage over the whole country. "When we see a lot of framed timbers," said Lincoln, "different portions of which we know have been gotten out at different times and places by different workmen—Stephen, Franklin, Roger and James, for instance—and when we see these timbers joined together, and see they exactly make the frame of a house . . . we find it impossible not to believe that Stephen and Franklin and Roger and James all understood one another from the beginning, and all worked upon a common plan, or draft."

The point of this rather elaborate metaphor seems obscure today, but Lincoln's audience knew exactly what he was talking about. The four men he named were Stephen Douglas, leader of the Democratic party; Franklin Pierce and James Buchanan, the previous and current presidents of the United States, both Democrats; and Roger Taney, chief justice of the United States, also a Democrat. The house for which each of them separately framed timbers, but with a secret understanding to make everything fit together, was a conspiracy to expand slavery. The timbers were the Kansas-Nebraska Act, which repealed the Missouri Compromise and made possible the expansion of slavery north of latitude 36° 30', where it had previously been prohibited; the Dred Scott decision, which included the legalization of slavery in all the territories; the Democratic pledge to acquire Cuba as a new slave territory; and other items.

After the Civil War broke out, Lincoln's main problem—next to winning the war—was what to do about slavery. And by the second year of the war, the slavery issue had become bound up with the fate of the Union itself as Lincoln gradually came to the conclusion that he could not win the war without striking down slavery.

In his public and private communications concerning slavery during the war, Lincoln used a number of telling metaphors and similes. His first effort was to persuade the loyal border states to accept a policy of gradual, compensated emancipation. This proposal, he said in an appeal to the people of the border states in May 1862, "makes common cause for a common object, casting no reproaches on any. It acts not the pharisee. The change it contemplates would come gently as the dews of heaven, not rending or wrecking anything. Will you not embrace it?"

When the border states did not respond, Lincoln shifted from soft blandishment to blunt warning. In July 1862 he called border-state congressmen to the White House. By then the war had taken a harder turn. Republican congressmen had passed a bill to confiscate the property of those who rebelled against the government, including their slave property. Lincoln himself had just about decided to issue an emancipation proclamation to apply to the Confederate states. The impact of these measures was bound to spill over into the Unionist border states. Slaves there were already emancipating themselves by running away to Union army lines.

In these circumstances Lincoln now told border-state congressmen that his plan of gradual emancipation with compensation from the federal government was the best they could get. Otherwise, as the war continued to escalate in intensity, "the institution in your states will be extinguished by mere friction and abrasion." The image of friction and abrasion was a most appropriate one, but it left the border-state congressmen unmoved. Most of them voted against Lincoln's offer—and three more years of war did extinguish slavery by friction and abrasion, in the border states as well as in the Confederate states.

After his unsuccessful appeal to the border states, Lincoln made up his mind to issue an emancipation proclamation. He used a variety of metaphors to explain his reasons for doing so. "It had got to midsummer 1862," the president later summarized. "Things had gone on from bad to worse, until I felt that we had reached the end of our rope on the plan of operations we had been pursuing; that we had about played our last card, and must change our tactics, or lose the game!" Both of the metaphors here—"the end of our rope" and "played our last card"—are rather tired, almost dead, but the context and the importance of the issue bring them alive and make them effective.

Lincoln liked the cardplaying metaphor; in letters to conservatives who objected to the government's total-war policy of confiscation and emancipation, he wrote with some asperity that "this government cannot much longer play a game in which it stakes all, and its enemies stake nothing. . . . It may as well be understood, once for all, that I shall not surrender this game leaving any available card unplayed."

Lincoln used other, more original and expressive metaphors at the same time, asking one conservative if he expected the government to wage this war "with elder-stalk squirts, charged with rose water." To a Southern Unionist who had complained that emancipation of slaves owned by rebels would inevitably expand into emancipation of slaves owned by loyal Unionists as well, Lincoln replied with an angry letter denouncing those Unionists who did nothing to help the North win but expected the government to take time out to protect their property while it was struggling for its very survival.

The president spun out a metaphor of a ship in a storm to clinch the point. Do Southern Unionists expect, he asked, "to touch neither a sail nor a pump, but to be merely passengers—deadheads at that—to be carried snug and dry, throughout the storm, and safely landed right side up? Nay, more; even a mutineer is to go untouched lest these sacred passengers receive an accidental wound."

When the constitutionality of the Emancipation Proclamation was questioned, Lincoln defended it by citing his military powers as commander in chief in time of war to seize enemy property. He also used an apt metaphor to illustrate how a lesser constitutional right—of property in slaves—might have to be sacrificed in the interests of a greater constitutional duty, that of preserving the nation's life. "Often a limb must be amputated to save a life," Lincoln pointed out in this age without antibiotics when everyone knew of wounded soldiers who had lost an arm or leg to stop the spread of fatal infection. "The surgeon," Lincoln continued, "is solemnly bound to try to save both life and limb; but when the crisis comes, and the limb must be sacrificed as the only chance of saving the life, no honest man will hesitate. . . . In our case, the moment came when I felt that slavery must die that the nation might live!"

Yet another metaphor that Lincoln used to illustrate a point about slavery is particularly striking. This one concerned the definition of *liberty.* The South professed to have seceded and gone to war in defense of its rights and liberties. The chief liberty that Southerners believed to be threatened by the election of Lincoln was their right to own slaves. In a public speech in 1864 at Baltimore, in a border state where the frictions and abrasions of war had by then just about ground up slavery, Lincoln illustrated the paradox of conflicting definitions of *liberty* with an Aesopian fable: "The shepherd drives the wolf from the sheep's throat, for which the sheep thanks the shepherd as a liberator, while the wolf denounces him for the same act as a destroyer of liberty, especially as the sheep was a black one."

This image leaves no doubt which definition of *liberty* Lincoln subscribed to, or whose cause in this war—the Northern shepherd's or the Southern wolf's—was the nobler one. The passage comes as close to a lyrical expression of Northern purpose as anything short of poetry could.

And at times Lincoln's words became poetic. He liked to read poetry. His favorites were Burns, Byron, and above all Shakespeare. He knew much of Burns and Shakespeare by heart. As president, Lincoln liked to relax by going to the theater—as we know to our sorrow. He went to every play of

Shakespeare's that came to Washington. He especially enjoyed reading the tragedies and historical plays with a political theme. The quintessence of poetry is imagery, particularly metaphor, and this is true most of all in Shakespeare's plays. Lincoln's fondness for this medium undoubtedly helped shape his use of figurative and symbolic language. As a youth he had tried his hand at writing poetry, but the way in which we best know him as a poet is through several famous passages from his wartime speeches and state papers. In these he achieved unrivaled eloquence through the use of poetic language.

A rather modest example of this occurs in a public letter that Lincoln wrote in August 1863 to be read at a Union rally in Illinois—and of course to be published in the newspapers. This letter came at a major turning point in the war. Union armies had recently captured Vicksburg and won the Battle of Gettysburg, reversing a year of defeats that had created vitiating doubt and dissent. But even after these victories, the antiwar Copperhead movement remained strong and threatening. Its animus focused mainly on the government's policy of emancipation and the enlistment of black troops. By the time of Lincoln's letter, several black regiments had already demonstrated their mettle in combat.

Lincoln addressed all of these issues. In delightful and easily understood imagery he noted the importance of the capture of Vicksburg in opening the Mississippi River and credited soldiers and sailors of all regions, including black soldiers and loyal Southern whites, in accomplishing this result:

> The signs look better. The Father of Waters again goes unvexed to the sea. Thanks to the great North-West for it. Nor yet wholly to them. Three hundred miles up, they met New-England, Empire, Key-Stone, and Jersey, hewing their way right and left. The Sunny South too, in more colors than one, also lent a hand. On the spot, their part of the history was jotted down in black and white. . . . Nor must Uncle Sam's Web-feet be forgotten. Not only on the deep sea, the broad bay, and the rapid river, but also up the narrow muddy bayou, wherever the ground was a little damp, they have been, and made their tracks.

Shifting from these cheerful, almost playful images, the president turned to the Copperheads, who had been denigrating emancipation and calling the whole war effort a useless and wicked failure. It was not a failure, said Lincoln; the Union had turned the corner toward victory. And when that victory comes, he said,

> there will be some black men who can remember that, with silent tongue, and clenched teeth, and steady eye, and well-poised bayonet, they have helped mankind on to this great consummation; while, I fear, there will be some white ones, unable to forget that, with malignant heart, and deceitful speech, they have strove to hinder it.

Here Lincoln was writing primarily about a process—about the means of victory in the war for the Union. It was when he defined the *purpose* of that war—the meaning of Union and why it was worth fighting for—that he soared to his greatest poetic eloquence. "Union" was something of an abstraction that required concrete symbols to make its meaning clear to the people who would have to risk their lives for it. The flag was the most important such symbol. But Lincoln wanted to go beyond the flag and strike deeper symbolic chords of patriotism. And in so doing he furnished some of the finest examples of poetic metaphor in our national literature.

In the peroration of his first inaugural address, Lincoln appealed to the South with an evocation of the symbols of a common history and shared memories as metaphors for the Union. "We are not enemies," he declared. "Though passion may have strained, it must not break our bonds of affection. The mystic chords of memory, stretching from every battlefield, and patriot grave, to every living heart and hearthstone, all over this broad land, will yet swell the chorus of the Union, when again touched, as surely they will be, by the better angels of our nature."

Having summoned forth the past as a metaphor for Union, Lincoln invoked the future in the peroration of his message to Congress in December 1862. Now he added emancipation to Union as the legacy that the people of that generation would leave to their children's children. "Fellow-citizens, we cannot escape history. . . . The fiery trial through which we pass, will light us down, in honor or dishonor, to the latest generation. . . . We shall nobly save, or meanly lose, the last, best hope of earth. . . . In giving freedom to the slave, we assure freedom to the free."

Lincoln put these symbolic themes of past, present, and future together in his most famous poem, the Gettysburg Address. This elegy uses no metaphors in a conventional sense; rather, there are what two literary scholars have called "concealed" or "structural" metaphors—that is, metaphors built into the structure of the address in such a way that they are not visible but are essential to its meaning. The Gettysburg Address contains three parallel sets of three images each that are intricately interwoven: past, present, future; continent, nation, battlefield; and birth, death, rebirth. Let us disaggregate these metaphors for purposes of analysis, even though in the process we destroy their poetic qualities.

Eighty-seven years in the *past* our fathers *conceived* and *brought forth* on this *continent* a *nation* that stood for something important: the proposition that all men are created equal. *Now* our generation faces a great war testing whether a nation standing for such an ideal can survive. In dedicating the cemetery on this *battlefield,* the living must take inspiration to finish the task that those who lie buried here nobly advanced by giving the last full measure of their devotion.

Life and death in this passage have a paradoxical but metaphorical relationship: Men died that the nation might live, yet metaphorically the old Union also died, and with it died the institution of slavery. After these *deaths,* the nation must have a "*new birth* of freedom" so that the government of, by, and for the people that our fathers conceived and brought forth in the past "shall not perish from the earth" but be preserved as a legacy for the *future.*

Contrary to common impression, Lincoln's Gettysburg Address was not ignored or unappreciated at the time. Lincoln himself may have contributed to this legend, for he reportedly told his friend and bodyguard Ward Hill Lamon that the speech was "a flat failure." Mixing a live metaphor with a dead simile (as Lamon remembered it a quarter century later), Lincoln said that the address "won't scour"; it "fell upon the audience like a wet blanket." It is true that admiration for the Gettysburg Address grew over the years, but many listeners and readers immediately recognized its greatness. One of them was Edward Everett, the main orator of the day, who wrote to Lincoln the next day: "I should be glad, if I could flatter myself, that I came as near to the central idea of the occasion, in two hours, as you did in two minutes."

Jefferson Davis did not—and probably could not—write anything like the Gettysburg Address, or like anything else in the way of images and metaphors that Lincoln used to illustrate his points both great and small. Communication and inspiration are two of the most important functions of a president in times of crisis. Thus perhaps David Potter's suggestion that if the Union and Confederacy had exchanged presidents the South might have won the Civil War does not seem so farfetched after all.

*SPRING 1991*

James M. McPherson, professor of history at Princeton University, is the author of the 1989 Pulitzer Prize–winning history *The Battle Cry of Freedom: The Civil War Era*. This essay is excerpted from his *Abraham Lincoln and the Second American Revolution* (1991). His most recent book is *What They Fought For, 1861–1865* (1994).

# 11

# "Lord High Admiral of the U.S. Navy"

## By Joseph T. Glatthaar

*The Union campaign to take Vicksburg in 1862–63 ranks as the most stunning achievement of joint operations (the army and navy working in close conjunction as a nearly single force) in the Civil War. History might have given that accolade to the Peninsula campaign in 1862, but Union general George B. McClellan seemed hesitant to believe either in the concept or in himself. In his study of Admiral David Dixon Porter, Joseph T. Glatthaar shows what joint operations could achieve when the leaders involved—in this case Porter, William Tecumseh Sherman, and Ulysses S. Grant—believed in both the concept and each other.*

In early December 1862, during a dinner party on an army quartermaster's riverboat at Cairo, Illinois, Acting Rear Admiral David Dixon Porter was feasting on roast duck and champagne when a stir on deck disrupted the festivities. The host politely exited, then moments later returned with a surprise guest: a slightly built, shabby-looking fellow in a brown civilian coat and gray trousers bearing a fresh coat of dust. The quartermaster introduced the unimpressive visitor: "Admiral Porter, meet General Grant."

As the admiral and the general shifted to a table by themselves, Porter, attired in his military finery, felt a twinge of self-consciousness. A navy man who had continually bucked the system for over three decades, he would have preferred a different atmosphere for his initial encounter with Ulysses S. Grant. He feared that if the army general fell victim to first impressions, he might conclude that Porter was just another naval officer, full of himself and his pomp and ceremony, one who had forgotten along the way that a military man was here to fight. Grant's expressions failed to provide a clue about his inner sentiments. All Porter could detect in that "calm, imperturbable face" was an overpowering sense of "determination." No one could ever read the inscrutable Grant.

Porter's predisposition led him to look unfavorably on Grant. Before this gathering, he had studied the February attacks on Forts Henry and Donelson, and he admired Grant's "bulldog courage." He also had to admit that Grant had demonstrated a capacity to cooperate with the navy during that campaign. But from animosity between the services he inferred that Grant's attitudes toward the navy were no different from those of any other army officer. "I don't trust the Army," Porter had commented to the assistant secretary of the navy just three weeks earlier. "It is very evident that Grant is going to try and take Vicksburg without us, but he can't do it."

But the admiral had mistakenly prejudged the general. The two men spoke in earnest, assessing difficulties honestly and calculating how to overcome them most effectively. There was no hint of superiority, no evidence that Grant perceived the navy as a weaker sister service. Instead, his "bull-dog tenacity" convinced Porter that this chap Grant could accomplish great things.

For twenty minutes the two men discussed a plan of campaign against Vicksburg, the critical Confederate stronghold on the Mississippi River. Grant had advanced south toward Grenada along the railroads in northern Mississippi, but a long supply line and repairs to a railroad bridge currently delayed his march. Along the Mississippi River, the Federals had begun to accumulate manpower for a blow at Vicksburg. The problem was that Grant held its proposed commander, Major General John A. McClernand, in low regard and wanted his trusted subordinate, Major General William T. Sherman, to direct the movement. Since McClernand was dawdling in Illinois, Grant elected to seize the opportunity and implement his own plan. He would march along the Mississippi Central Railroad, holding the Confederates in his front, while Sherman slipped downriver and stormed the bluffs overlooking the Yazoo River outside Vicksburg. From the high ground Sherman could either sweep into Vicksburg or drive south to the railroad from Jackson, then march on the city. Grant needed Porter's gunboats to provide fire support for Sherman's landing and assault and to assist in the reduction of Vicksburg. Porter approved the concept, and the meeting adjourned as abruptly as it had begun.

Grant and Sherman could not possibly have done better than David Dixon Porter. Born the son of a famous naval officer, Porter lived only for the sea. He sailed on his first voyage at nearly thirteen. Over the next three years he joined the Mexican navy (commanded at the time by his father), fought in a battle against a Spanish warship, and suffered through six months in a Cuban jail as a prisoner of war. In 1829, the sixteen-year-old Porter joined the U.S. Navy. The bulk of his duty for the next thirty years consisted of coastal and harbor surveys, which paid great dividends along the shifting channels of the Mississippi River in the Civil War. During the conflict with Mexico, Porter exhibited courage and dash, sidestepping the orders of his superior and achieving considerable results. But his audacious performance did little for his career. In the postwar years, the navy lapsed into stagnation. Only a politically charged assignment in New York Harbor, where Porter successfully marked courses through the treacherous

Buttermilk Channel and Hell Gate, earned him public acclaim. As the 1860 election took place, Porter was weighing a lucrative offer to leave military service and sail vessels for a commercial firm.

When the war broke out, Porter bypassed the Navy Department and went directly to President Lincoln with a plan to save Fort Pickens, near Pensacola, Florida. It worked. Later, he masterminded a scheme to capture New Orleans, even overseeing the construction of some novel mortar boats for the campaign. Porter's contraptions lobbed huge shells into the forts below the Crescent City, damaged them heavily, and enabled his foster brother, Commodore David Farragut, to sail up the Mississippi River and compel the authorities to surrender the largest city in the Confederacy. Porter fell out of grace for indiscreetly criticizing General George McClellan and his Army of the Potomac—he had advocated an attack on Norfolk to seize the navy yard back in 1861—but he returned to duty as commander of the Mississippi Squadron in late October 1862, with a rank of acting rear admiral. He had entered the war sixteen months earlier as a lieutenant, his rank for the previous twenty years.

Though only five feet six inches tall (near starvation in prison during his teens may have stunted his growth), Porter projected a strong image. His slicked-down black hair, darting brown eyes, long, sharp nose, and dark, curly beard hardened his appearance. A high-pitched voice belied this imposing presence, unless it engaged in repartee or witticisms. Blessed with a photographic memory and keen analytic powers, Porter thought and reacted quickly, occasionally too quickly. His penchant for speaking his mind, at times rashly, provided immediate gratification but caused him subsequent grief. Often during his career, Porter occupied the seat of honor in the naval doghouse for blunt talk, and this doubtless retarded his progress on the promotion track. A tendency to lapse into exaggeration or sarcasm exacerbated this problem with superiors. Porter's unconventionality and peculiar assortment of qualities led many to undervalue him. Lincoln called him "a busy schemer" and underestimated his ability throughout much of the war. Secretary of War Edwin M. Stanton considered him "a gasbag, who makes a great fuss and claims credit that belongs to others," which some may have thought more true of Stanton than of Porter.

The most influential event in Porter's life occurred in his youth, when his father resigned from the U.S. Navy. The commodore had emerged from the War of 1812 as a national hero, one of a cluster of brilliant naval officers. Like his gifted son, though, he never walked away from a squabble. In a dispute with several congressmen in the mid-1820s, naval officers turned against him and in a court-martial suspended him without pay for six months. He served out the sentence and promptly left the service. His impressionable son never forgot or forgave. Throughout his career, David Dixon Porter challenged authority. He despised the stodgy navy leadership, with its fixation on mindless tradition and lack of progressive reform. In fact, his favorite hobby was poking fun at ranking officers who resisted change, through either indiscreet quips—he openly described them as "fogies"—or burlesque sketches. Porter's stance unquestionably earned him the wrath of certain "superiors." But David Dixon Porter refused to succumb to the dictates of the old guard. He battled the stagnation that so appalled him, and he endured the consequences. Young naval officers adored him for it.

Several days after the Cairo meeting, Grant notified Sherman of his new designs and asked him to visit that evening. Together they hammered out the details of the operation. While Grant organized his forces for an overland advance, Sherman would head back to Memphis to gather troops for the Vicksburg landing. That night, Sherman telegraphed Porter to meet him in Memphis. "Time now is the great object," he noted, and Sherman, a thorough planner, wanted everything arranged in advance.

For over a month, Sherman and Porter had exchanged numerous informative letters that pledged harmony of action and established a positive tone for joint army-navy operations. In mid-November, Porter advised Sherman that Grant ought to use his gunboats in any attack on Vicksburg, and added, "I wish to cooperate with the army in every way where I can be of service, and if you can get any message to or from General Grant on the subject, and give me an idea of what is going on, I shall be much obliged to you."

Sherman responded with maps and other information and a call for unity of command. "My opinion is that a perfect concert of action should exist between all the forces of the United States operating down the valley; and I apprehend some difficulty may arise from the fact that you control on the river, [General Samuel R.] Curtis on the west bank, and Grant on the east bank," Sherman explained. "Were either one of you in absolute command, all, of course, would act in concert."

Porter agreed. "I am ready to cooperate with anybody and everybody," penned the admiral, "and all I ask on the part of the military commanders is their full confidence and a pull together." Naturally, when Porter visited Sherman, he expected a warm reception, and as he entered the general's Memphis headquarters, what he saw reassured him. It reminded him a bit of McClellan's command post—officers waiting, clerks scribbling rapidly, orderlies racing about on horseback, and sentries pacing back and forth—but there was a striking contrast. No one wore lace and feathers, and there were no velvet carpets; it was a working headquarters, not a showroom. "Everything was rough and ready," Porter noted with satisfaction.

Some early confusion daunted the admiral's optimism, however. Staff greeted Porter and seated him in a waiting room, where he stayed for an hour, stewing. Finally Sherman appeared and apologized—no one had told him of the admiral's arrival. But then, when Sherman abruptly broke off the discussion to complete business with a subordinate, Porter nearly erupted in rage. Fortunately, he managed to control himself and, within a few moments after conversation resumed, was reassured by Sherman's directness. "He turned towards me in the most pleasant way," Porter recalled, "poked the fire and talked as if he had known me all his life." Sherman chatted openly about preparations he had completed and what steps he intended to take next, interrupting his monologue periodically to dictate some terse message to a subordinate. Porter marveled at this loquacious general whose mind danced from subject to subject with such facility. This was a working general—attired casually, informal in manner, and immersed in his labors. Within minutes, the two men behaved as if they had known one another for years.

By December 19, 1862, Sherman's troops had climbed aboard transports for the strike against Vicksburg. En route, they picked up another division at Helena, Arkansas. Porter's fleet had gained control of the Yazoo River, just north of Vicksburg, and Sherman hoped to land, drive on to the Vicksburg & Jackson Railroad, and force his way into the city. Porter's gunboats would provide an invaluable shield and soften defensive positions around Vicksburg. If Grant could just detain the Confederates to the northeast near Grenada, Sherman would encounter only token opposition.

But in no time the intricate scheme began to unravel. Rebel cavalry raids severed Grant's supply line and compelled his retreat. Rather than come out to block Grant's movement, the Confederates held tight in Vicksburg. And Sherman, wholly unaware of Grant's fate, attacked directly into the lion's mouth. Bayous so bogged the area that Sherman found just two routes to reach the base of the bluffs, only one offering any promise of success. On December 29, with Federal gunboats and mortars shelling adjacent woods to isolate the target area, he ordered his troops to storm the heights. The Federals charged Chickasaw Bluffs with a will, surmounting obstacles and groping up the slick slopes toward the Confederate line. But the fortified position proved too strong. Dissipated by heavy losses, the attackers never gained a foothold. That night, torrential rains drenched the troops and so slopped the assault route that operations there promised only failure.

The next day, Sherman and Porter gathered to assess their options. From this conference emerged a new plan: Sherman would maintain his current position and feign an attack, while Porter would lead his gunboats and 10,000 soldiers farther upriver. With close fire support from the vessels, these troops would storm the heights there. That night, however, a dense fog blanketed the region and precluded any movement by water. Porter canceled the operation. The attempt to carry Chickasaw Bluffs ended in utter defeat.

From the misery of the Yazoo, where over 1,200 Federals sacrificed their lives or sustained wounds and another 550 fell into Rebel hands, a burgeoning friendship formed between Sherman and Porter. Their respect for one another's military conduct cemented the personal rapport they had established in Memphis. Porter not only directed his naval forces skillfully, he cooperated wholeheartedly. The admiral provided sound advice and proved to be a resourceful leader. For his part, Sherman impressed Porter with his mastery of all aspects of the operation and with the way he drew Porter into his confidence. Sherman accepted Porter as a full partner, a refreshing change of pace for a naval officer. To Secretary of the Navy Gideon Welles on the last day of 1862, Porter expressed his complete confidence in the army commander. "General Sherman is quite equal to the emergency," he insisted, "and nothing daunted by his want of success."

Several days after the assault on Chickasaw Bluffs, General McClernand arrived at the mouth of the Yazoo River to supersede Sherman as army commander. A longtime political friend of Lincoln's, McClernand had served with Sherman as a division commander at Shiloh. He impressed neither Grant nor Sherman with his military talents. Porter, who had met McClernand in Washington a few months earlier, held him in even lower regard, calling him a "hybrid general" and interpreting his appointment as an insult to Grant.

Sherman immediately recommended that McClernand withdraw the army to Milliken's Bend, which the new commander did. He then suggested that McClernand employ the army in conjunction with the navy in a campaign against Arkansas Post, a Confederate bastion on the Arkansas River. During the fight along Chickasaw Bluffs, a Rebel vessel from Arkansas Post had descended the river and captured a steamer towing coal and ammunition barges. Unless the Federals silenced the fortress, it would harass traffic on the river and hinder any Union attempts to capture Vicksburg. At the time, McClernand had no specific plans and only a general one to seek the fall of Vicksburg; yet he hesitated to adopt Sherman's recommendation. Sherman then alerted Porter to the problem. Apparently, the two had discussed this as a possible course of action a few days earlier, and Sherman felt sure that "General McClernand will do anything you ask." When they arrived at Porter's flagship, McClernand presented the operation as his own conception. Porter was outraged. He had disliked McClernand beforehand, and now, because the political general had expropriated his friend's plan, Porter resented the man even more. Only a private conversation with Sherman convinced him to participate in the venture. But Porter insisted on a price: Sherman would command the assault force. McClernand concurred.

A massive convoy of Federal transports and gunboats ascended the Arkansas River. By January 11, the troops had disembarked and assumed positions for an assault. Porter's gunboats opened an impressive barrage, and field artillery and infantry joined the fray. In short order, even before Sherman could order an assault, the Confederates raised the white flag. Nearly 5,000 surrendered. McClernand assumed much of the credit, but according to Sherman it was Porter's gunboats that won the engagement. Porter merely chalked up the lack of magnanimity to army egoism. "I find that army officers are not willing to give the Navy credit (even in very small matters) they are entitled to," he commented with disgust.

When Grant linked up with the victorious joint command near the mouth of the Arkansas River, Sherman and Porter confirmed what he had already anticipated: McClernand was incompetent to lead an important expedition. Sherman, of course, would obey his superior officer's orders, but to reduce Vicksburg the army needed Porter's cooperation with McClernand as well. Porter looked upon McClernand with "distrust." He felt Sherman was "every inch a soldier," and had "the confidence of his men," but he believed McClernand was "no soldier," and had the confidence of "no one, unless it may be two or three of his staff." He grumbled that, since McClernand's arrival, "I have twice the work to do. . . . Sherman used to help me to think, but now I have to think for McClernand and myself." Both Sherman and Porter urged Grant to assume command. Their pleas were unnecessary; Grant had already decided to direct the operations against Vicksburg.

Over the next two months, Grant employed his forces in a host of projects that would enable him to strike Vicksburg without assaulting the bluffs. Each enterprise, regardless of the likelihood of success, received Porter's complete support. Grant attempted to dig a canal that would bypass Vicksburg. But the Confederates realized that by repositioning some guns they could shell the entire course of the man-made waterway, thus eliminating it as a worthwhile Federal venture. West of the Mississippi River, Grant ordered his forces to clear a passage from Lake Providence, in northern Louisiana, through a series of narrow bayous and waterways into the Red River. Yet slow progress and the length of this circuitous route, approximately 500 miles, limited its utility.

East of the Mississippi River, Grant undertook two difficult schemes to reach the upper Yazoo River and avoid the powerful positions near Vicksburg. By breaking the levee along the Mississippi River across from Helena, Arkansas, he hoped to restore an old channel to Moon Lake. From there, soldiers and sailors would wriggle their way through a series of waterways that form the Yazoo River. Confederates felled trees and prepared other obstructions to discourage the Union advance. After much labor, the army-navy contingent worked its way to the intersection of the Tallahatchie and Yalobusha rivers, where the Confederates had constructed a fort. Since there was no means of attacking from land, the job of eliminating the position devolved to the navy. Twice gunboats shelled it, and twice the Rebel gunners kept them at bay. An effort to flood the defenders from the fort also failed, and Grant had to seek a means of entering the Yazoo River west of this tiny bastion.

The other scheme called for soldiers and sailors to enter Steele's Bayou from the Mississippi River not far from Milliken's Bend, travel north into Black Bayou, east into Deer Creek, north into Rolling Fork, east to Big Sunflower River, and finally south into the Yazoo River, some ten miles above Haynes' Bluff. Porter personally supervised this March operation, forcing his gunboats along waterways at times barely several dozen yards wide. Limbs stretching over the water chewed up his smokestacks, and tree stumps below the surface scraped his hulls. Aggressively, Porter pushed on, plowing all obstacles from his path. Sherman, in command of ground forces, pursued slowly by land. As the gunboats worked their way along Deer Creek, approaching Rolling Fork and more open travel, the Confederates started cutting down timber to obstruct their passage. Several vessels stuck fast in submerged willow branches. In the distant rear, Porter and his sailors could hear locals chopping down trees behind them. Then Confederate snipers began taking potshots at his sailors. The admiral's mortars blindly tossed shells into the woods, to no avail. His situation had suddenly become critical; the Confederates had them trapped. On tissue paper he scrawled a plea for help and entrusted a freedman with its delivery to Sherman.

As darkness crept over his crafts, Porter loaded all guns, secured the portholes, and huddled his sailors belowdecks. Minute after minute ticked away; Porter agonized over the condition of his ships and crew. In the hours before dawn on March 21, he even prepared detailed plans for the destruction of his vessels rather than let them fall into the hands of the Confederates. Sunrise brought small comfort. His situation was unchanged. The mighty gunboats sat helpless with enemy all around.

Shortly after noon, Porter's men could hear the distant crack of rifles. Straining to detect any clues, the sailors finally deciphered the noise: It was Sherman's advance party, skirmishing with the Confederates. Ninety minutes later, Sherman himself, covered with mud, rode up on an old horse to the huzzahs of the seamen. Once he had received word of Porter's plight the day before, Sherman had immediately pushed forward the few troops at his disposal. That evening three boatloads of soldiers had arrived at Black Bayou, and Sherman had led them twenty miles by candlelight through the dense thickets.

Six weeks earlier, when the press had harangued Sherman for his assault on Chickasaw Bluffs, Porter had come to his rescue, releasing letters he had written to the secretary of the navy during the campaign, absolving Sherman of blame and even praising his talents as a general officer. Now Sherman was rescuing Porter. "Halloo Porter," he cried, "what did you get into such an ugly scrape for? So much for you navy fellows getting out of your element; better send for the soldiers always."

Porter took the ribbing good-naturedly. "I never knew what helpless things ironclads could become when they got in a ditch and had no soldiers about," he confessed. The sight of Sherman and the men of the Army of the Tennessee, whom he aptly described as "half horse, half alligator, with a touch of snapping turtle," utterly delighted him.

The failure of the Deer Creek expedition turned Grant back reluctantly to an assault on Haynes' Bluff, north of where Sherman had lost more than 1,500 men the previous December. He had run out of options. Then two trains of thought meshed in Grant's mind. Rear Admiral David Farragut had cruised up the Mississippi River and requested a party to assist in knocking out the batteries at Warrenton, about ten miles below Vicksburg. At the same time, Grant was searching for a means of shipping up to 20,000 men along a route west of the Mississippi River, crossing them over to the east side, and reinforcing Major General Nathaniel P. Banks's command around the Rebel stronghold at Port Hudson, near Baton Rouge. After its fall, Banks could march north on Vicksburg, hugging the river and receiving protection and supplies from the Union gunboats. It suddenly dawned on Grant that his best option might be to move troops, supplies, and transports along the western side of the Mississippi River, shuttle them to the eastern bank below Vicksburg, and then attack that city first, from the south rather than the north. As the winter floods receded and the rains subsided, roadbeds that could carry Grant's men and wagons dried. The only remaining problems were accumulating enough barges and transports and running a few gunboats past the Vicksburg gauntlet to get the soldiers across from the west bank. From despondency bloomed promise.

For Grant's new plan to work, he needed the navy's support. In communications with Porter, he revealed his intentions and requested gunboats. "Will you be good enough, admiral, to give this your early consideration and let me know your determination?" Only a week after his near disaster, Porter did not hesitate. "I am ready to co-operate with you in the matter of landing troops on the other side," the admiral committed, "but you must recollect that, when these gunboats once go below, we give up all hopes of ever getting them up again"—since, moving slowly against the current, his boats would be easy targets for the Confederate guns. If he sent vessels below, he preferred to employ his best craft, "and there will be nothing left to attack Haynes' Bluff, in case it should be deemed necessary to try it." Two days later, Grant, Sherman, and Porter reconnoitered the prospective attack site at Haynes' Bluff. The following day, Grant announced his decision. An attack there "would be attended with an immense sacrifice of life, if not with defeat. This, then, closes out the last hope of turning the enemy by the right."

Porter was lukewarm to the new plan. Yet he not only pledged resources, he consented to supervise the preparation and movement of all vessels that passed the batteries. He agreed simply because Grant had urged it. "So confident was I of the ability of General Grant to carry out his plans when he explained them to me," Porter told the secretary of the navy, "that I never hesitated to change my position from above to below Vicksburg." As Grant accumulated the boats and barges, Porter had them packed with grain sacks, heavy logs, and wet hay for protection and to conceal the fires under the boilers. He also assigned sailors to man several army boats on the hazardous journey.

But before Grant could bring down all the necessary transports and barges, Porter received a blistering rebuke from the secretary of the navy. Dismissing the worthiness of Porter's support for Grant's various schemes around Vicksburg, Welles announced the president's view that patrolling along the river between Vicksburg and Port Hudson "is of far greater importance than the flanking expeditions which thus far have prevented the consummation of this most desirable object."

Porter, who never dodged a fight, responded with clarity and force. "I am sorry the Department is not satisfied with the operations here, but you will please remember, sir, that I was ordered to cooperate with the army, and sagacious officers deem these flanking movements of great importance." Control of the river above and below Vicksburg, he reminded the secretary, would not necessarily lead to the fall of the city. "While it is my desire to carry out the wishes of the Department in relation to all matters connected with operations here, still I must act in accordance with my judgment and a more full knowledge of affairs than the Department could possibly have." Nevertheless, Porter immediately notified Grant that a Navy Department directive "will compel me to go below the batteries with the fleet sooner than I anticipated," with whatever vessels the army had on hand.

On the night of April 16, seven gunboats and several transports, with an assortment of steamers and coal barges lashed to the side, drifted quietly downriver. Detailed instructions that Porter had issued nearly a week earlier carefully outlined the order, fire direction and range, and spacing between boats. He even included contingency plans in the event a vessel sustained a serious hit. Porter personally led the convoy. At 11:16 P.M., the Confederates opened fire on his ironclad, the *Benton,* and within minutes the Rebels ignited huge bonfires on both banks to illuminate the river. For two and a half hours the Vicksburg garrison poured shells into his squadron. Almost miraculously, only one craft, an army transport, sank, although every one sustained some hits.

Just as Porter's gunboat passed out of range, he heard a cry from a small boat: "*Benton* ahoy!" It was Sherman. He pulled up alongside to check on the condition of Porter and his crew. After receiving the status report, Sherman could not resist a bit of needling. "You are more at home here than you were in the ditches grounding on willow-trees," he teased. "Stick to this, old fellow; it suits Jack better." Then off the tireless Sherman went, to examine each vessel as it emerged from the fire.

Throughout the staging process for the movement across the river, Porter regretted Sherman's absence. Everything was chaos; he needed an experienced officer to supervise the loading. "I wish twenty times a day that Sherman was here, or yourself," he complained to Grant, "but I suppose we cannot have all we wish." Within the army, Porter confided to a friend, Sherman "has more brains than all put together." But Grant had other duties in mind for Sherman. While the bulk of the army was embarking for the transfer to the east bank of the river below Vicksburg, Sherman led a feint at Haynes' Bluff to draw away the attention of the city's defenders.

Grant continually had to adapt to overcome problems. A drop in the water level prevented the army from drawing supplies through the swamps, so more vessels, loaded with supplies, had to run the Vicksburg gauntlet to feed the troops. The original landing zone along the east bank of the Mississippi River, Grand Gulf, proved unsuitable as well: Porter's gunboats could not silence the Confederate batteries there, and the secure defensive position on the bluffs precluded a frontal assault. The Federal troops had to trudge farther south. On April 30, 1863, Porter's ships began shuttling Grant's army across the Mississippi River, from Hard Times, Louisiana, to Bruinsburg, Mississippi. After fifteen weeks of toil, Grant finally had positioned his forces to operate against Vicksburg.

While Grant conducted a brilliant campaign against separate

Confederate forces to the northeast, Porter slipped down to the mouth of the Red River to relieve Farragut of some of his duties. He returned, however, in time to assist in the fall of the city of Vicksburg. On May 18, Porter could hear the pop of musketry from the area around Chickasaw Bluffs. It was Sherman's XV Corps. Several hours later, he received wonderful reports of a lightning operation that continually kept the Rebel armies off balance. Vicksburg was now completely cut off.

Throughout the siege that followed, the admiral secured the supply line and provided fire support for the army. On May 19 and again three days later, he employed his gunboats and mortars to cover initial, unsuccessful direct assaults on the city and to disrupt the Confederate defenses.

On May 27, Sherman requested a gunboat to attack the water battery that anchored the Rebel left flank. The vessel, the *Cincinnati,* closed on the target and fought aggressively. In the process it sustained numerous hits and in minutes plunged to the bottom of the river, with the loss of forty crewmen. Sherman, who witnessed the entire affair from the bluffs, felt horrible. But Porter chalked it up as one of war's misfortunes. He would agree to lose all his boats, Porter told Sherman, if they would secure Vicksburg. Porter meant it. Back in December, one of his gunboat commanders had struck a mine in the Yazoo River while maneuvering closer in order to fire on the Rebel positions. His vessel sank. When the commander, one of Porter's best, asked about the date of a court of inquiry, the admiral erupted: "Court! I have no time to order courts! I can't blame an officer who seeks to put his ship close to the enemy." Porter then ordered the fleet captain to find the officer another gunboat and chugged away.

When Vicksburg fell on the Fourth of July, 1863, Grant and Porter gathered briefly for some warm congratulations. Two days later, in his after-action report, Grant's acclaim for Porter's aid had not abated. He expressed "thankfulness for my good fortune in being placed in co-operation with an officer of the Navy" such as Porter. The admiral and his subordinates "have ever shown the greatest readiness in their co-operation, no matter what was to be done or what risk to be taken, either by their men or their vessels." Grant then concluded, "Without this prompt and cordial support, my movements would have been much embarrassed, if not wholly defeated."

Sherman, too, heaped praise on the admiral. He regretted that he could not meet Porter on a wharf in Vicksburg to celebrate. "In so magnificent a result," Sherman expounded, "I stop not to count who did it. It is done, and the day of our nation's birth is consecrated and baptized anew in a victory won by the united Navy and Army of our country. God grant that the harmony and mutual respect that exist between our respective commanders, and shared by all true men of the joint service, may continue forever, and serve to elevate our national character, threatened with shipwreck." From a more personal standpoint, Sherman admitted, "Whether success attend my efforts or not, I know that Admiral Porter will ever accord to me the exhibition of a pure and unselfish zeal in the service of our country." On July 18, in the governor's mansion in Jackson,

Mississippi, Sherman and a party of generals joined in a hearty chorus of "Army and Navy forever." The next day, after describing the scene the night before, Sherman pledged eternal support for his navy friend: "To me it will ever be a source of pride that real harmony has always characterized our intercourse, and let what may arise, I will ever call upon Admiral Porter with the same confidence as I have in the past."

EXPOSURE TO OFFICERS of Grant and Sherman's caliber transformed Porter's opinion of professionally trained army officers. Earlier in the war he had confessed to the assistant secretary of the navy, an old friend, "I don't believe in our generals any more than I do in our old fogies of the Navy." Interservice mistrust and rivalry and early war experiences had soured Porter's assessment of high-ranking army personnel. But Grant and Sherman won him over through their cooperation, professional conduct, and sensitivity to Porter's rank and position. "Grant and Sherman are on board almost every day," the admiral noted with pleasure in early March 1863. "Dine and tea with me often; we agree in everything, and they are disposed to do everything for us they can." More than anything, Porter feared "for the sake of the Union that nothing may occur to make a change here."

Porter accorded full credit for the Vicksburg campaign to Grant. In his report to the secretary of the navy, the admiral asserted that

> the late investment and capture of Vicksburg will be characterized as one of the greatest military achievements ever known. The conception of the idea originated solely with General Grant, who adopted a course in which great labor was performed, great battles were fought, and great risks were run; a single mistake would have involved us in difficulty, but so well were all the plans matured, so well were all the movements timed, and so rapid were the evolutions performed that not a mistake has occurred from the passage of the fleet by Vicksburg and the passage of the army across the river up to the present time.

To be sure, Porter liked this pleasant-looking man with an unobtrusive disposition, but his fondness for Grant derived predominantly from his enormous respect for the general's military talents. Grant's quiet confidence, aggressive approach to warfare, and doggedness earned Porter's deepest admiration. No one Porter had ever met could focus on a problem, such as the conquest of Vicksburg, and labor at it as relentlessly. Grant had attempted scheme after scheme just to gain a position from which to launch an attack. Clearly, behind his unaltering countenance worked an adaptable, resourceful, creative mind.

Grant, like Porter, refused to bind himself to conventional methods and thought. He had experimented with varying approaches to reach the high ground near Vicksburg. Once he had slipped below the city, he cut loose from his supply base—a bold decision that Sherman opposed—to speed his march and enhance his maneuverability. He drew skillfully upon the resources at hand, particularly the navy. Unlike most army generals, Grant grasped the possibilities of joint operations. Selflessly committed to victory, and convinced that an army-navy team offered the only hope of success, he had no qualms about dealing with Porter as a peer, something few army officers would do. And Porter proved himself more than worthy of coequal status.

By contrast, Sherman and Porter established a much more personal relationship. Both quick-tongued, energetic, extremely intelligent, and wholly devoted to their profession of arms, these two liked each other immediately, and within a week were fast friends. Whether they were telling jokes, teasing, or damning the world of politics, they were at ease with each other.

Like Grant, Sherman appreciated the navy. But while Grant's interest was utilitarian, the maritime had a special attraction for Sherman. Since his travels to California in the 1840s, sailors and the sea had intrigued him. With his unquenchable curiosity, Sherman enjoyed poking around Porter's gunboats and talking naval matters. He entered the admiral's world with enthusiasm, setting himself apart from most army officers and winning new friends within the sister service.

Sherman's relentless pursuit of mastery of the art of war appealed to Porter. A naval officer who had spent years charting channels, he appreciated Sherman's passion for maps and geographic features. "The General himself," Porter wrote with but slight exaggeration, "had one peculiarity and that was a very correct knowledge of the topography of all places he had operated in or was about to operate in. He never forgot a house, a road or a bayou—in fact he seemed to possess all the crafts of a backwoodsman and never even forgot a 'blazed' tree." During active operations or in preparation for them, the general was almost a man possessed. "Sherman's whole mind was so absorbed in whatever work he had before him," Porter observed, "that he never thought of eating, sleeping or his dress." Instead, his "great delight was to pore over maps and he seemed to take in all the roads, fields and rivers, as if they were good to eat and drink, or he would spend the night in writing out general orders, which were always very full and explicit."

Throughout the Vicksburg campaign, Porter noticed that he and Sherman agreed with each other time after time. They conceived problems similarly and generated comparable solutions. That same consensus existed in their fundamental approach to war. As they communicated more and more, it occurred to both men that their thoughts on how the Union should conduct the war effort converged. After eighteen months of observation, contemplation, and analysis, Sherman had concluded that mere occupation of Confederate territory squandered resources and did little to subdue the rebellion. The Union needed to gain control of the Mississippi River and use it as a springboard for raids directed at the interior of the Confederacy. Federal troops would eat the food, take away the slaves, destroy the railroads, and make life so miserable for the inhabitants that they would realize secession and war were not proper solutions to their political complaints. "The possession of the river, with an army capable of disembarking and striking inland, would have a mighty influence," he insisted to Porter. War's devastations had already sapped many Confederates of their passion for secession, and his new troops, the men of 1862, "came with ideas of making vigorous war, which means universal destruction, and it requires hard handling to repress excesses."

Porter not only vowed, "Whatever control I have on the river shall be exerted to help the army," but also endorsed Sherman's approach to the war. "I am of the opinion that there is but one way to make war, and that is to harass your enemy all you can. I have tried to be as unpleasant to the rebels on the river as possible, and hope that the new armies now going into the field will give them (the rebels) a taste of devastation that may bring them to their senses." The army general and navy admiral thought as one.

In comparing Grant with Sherman, Porter marveled at their marked differences. "I don't suppose there ever was a greater contrast between any two men," he averred, "than between Grant and Sherman." He described Grant as unimposing physically. Still, he was a congenial-looking fellow with agreeable features, simple in taste and calm in demeanor. Sherman, however, was "a hard weather beaten soldier, with naturally a corrugated face, a nervous, restless, active man." Grant resembled any private; Sherman looked "every much a general." Porter once doubted that he had ever held more than a twenty-minute conversation with Grant; Sherman gabbed almost incessantly. Grant chose good people and could delegate work, while Sherman "attended to all the details himself." In fact, Porter thought, "They were unlike in everything except in their skill as soldiers, yet they agreed perfectly." What made the tandem so successful, Porter concluded, was that "Grant and Sherman together combine qualities possessed by no one general that ever lived; what one wants the other possesses."

Porter shared characteristics with both men. Temperamentally more akin to Sherman, he could act decisively, a quality that most observers regarded as one of Grant's strongest features. Intellectually, Porter fit more comfortably with Sherman, and he certainly found Sherman's company more enjoyable and intimate. But there was something reassuring about Grant, his quiet confidence and serenity soothing the more mercurial admiral. Like Grant and Sherman, Porter possessed a resourceful nature, and results, not methods, dominated his approach to military service in wartime. Once, after responding to a series of hypothetical questions from a young officer, Porter snarled back with his biting sarcasm, "All I have to say is that when the time comes to use your judgment you must use it; and if you do it right, you will hear from me damned quick; and if you do it wrong, you will hear from me a damned sight quicker!"

The Vicksburg juggernaut brought Grant, Sherman, and Porter together as only such an operation could. From their difficult experiences, they learned to depend on one another, and they developed mutual respect as individuals and as warriors. With each man possessing different talents and skills, they fed off one another, exchanging ideas, each increasing his knowledge of the other service, and evolving and maturing as joint commanders. The Vicksburg campaign tossed the three together; and from it they emerged with powerful professional and personal bonds. In the years to come, rich and lasting friendships blossomed among them, but the heart of the relationship stemmed from the demanding service along the Mississippi River.

FIVE DAYS AFTER the surrender of Vicksburg, Port Hudson fell to Union control, and now the Mississippi River ran "unvexed to the sea." All three men received promotions for their invaluable services. Porter earned a commission with the permanent rank of rear admiral. Both Grant and Sherman had held the rank of major general of volunteers; now the War Department also elevated Grant from brigadier general to major general in the regular army and awarded Sherman a brigadier generalship in the regular army.

Although Sherman and Porter continued to communicate and cooperate, they never again joined forces for a large-scale operation. As Sherman commented in mid-October, "You have almost finished your job and can and will, doubtless with infinite pleasure, help us who must live whilst we penetrate the very bowels of this land." The intimacy between them never waned. When personal tragedy struck Sherman, he poured out his heart to the tough-minded admiral. "I lost, recently, my little boy by sickness incurred during his visit to my camp on Big Black," a heartbroken Sherman revealed. "He was my pride and hope of life, and his loss takes from me the great incentive to excel, and now I must work on purely and exclusively for love of country and professional pride." Sherman concluded by saying, "To you I can always unfold my thoughts as one worthy and capable of appreciating the feelings of a soldier and gentleman."

In Sherman's absence, Porter prepared chatty, informative letters of considerable length, which the admiral wittily justified by admitting that "sailors will spin long yarns—it is part of their nature." Porter continued the practice with periodic reports throughout the remainder of the war. The two friends could accomplish more through direct, personal communication, discussing ideas and solving problems as they had done at Vicksburg, than by working through official military channels.

After Grant was assigned to central Tennessee, his communication with Porter slowed to a trickle. Only terse, businesslike dispatches passed between them over telegraph lines. When trouble erupted back in the Mississippi River valley, though, Porter did not hesitate to bring the matter to Grant's attention, using a belated congratulatory message to write his friend a lengthy letter. "If I have not sooner congratulated you on your splendid victory at Chattanooga," explained the admiral, "it was not because I did not share in the joy of your triumph, for you have no greater well-wisher than myself. I congratulate you now with all my heart, and now that you have finished that business so well, I must tell you that the guerrillas are kicking up the mischief on the river." Grant replied that Sherman was returning there to quash the partisans and launch his raiding strategy along the river. Porter was delighted. "I was glad to receive yours of the

20th instant, and to hear that I was soon to see my old friend Sherman, whom I esteem as you do. Indeed," joked the whiskered admiral, "we have been so much together and in so many hard places that we look upon him as the property of the navy."

Time permitted Sherman to organize a march on Meridian, Mississippi, living off the land and demolishing the railroad as he traveled. But other pressing matters precluded his intended raid up the Red River in Louisiana. The president had elevated Grant to lieutenant general, and Sherman would direct one of the two major Union thrusts that spring, with his target the Confederate army in northern Georgia. The campaign up the Red River lapsed to Porter and, by default, to Nathaniel P. Banks.

Porter was worried. He feared the consequences of a volunteer commander directing a joint operation. Sherman allayed the admiral's uneasiness by assigning 10,000 of his own troops under a trusted subordinate, Brigadier General Andrew Jackson Smith, to assist in the endeavor. As it turned out, the Porter-Smith combination could not secure victory, only stave off a disastrous defeat. Three converging columns—one under Banks, another under Major General Frederick Steele that never materialized, and the third under Porter and Smith—were to link up at Alexandria, Louisiana, and then advance as far upriver as Shreveport, breaking up Confederate opposition and gathering valuable supplies of cotton. Alexandria fell to Porter and Smith on March 19; despite promises, however, Banks started late and arrived after the fight. At that point, low water nearly terminated the campaign. Sherman had authorized Porter to cancel operations if the gunboats could not pass up the rapids. They barely did. Banks then led the column on, but a Confederate command routed his forces at Sabine Cross Roads on April 8. Smith's two divisions, along with some other Union troops, abruptly halted the Rebel pursuit at Pleasant Hill the next day. Nevertheless, Banks had had enough, and his troops continued their precipitous retreat. Rebel batteries and dropping water levels made the withdrawal a living hell for Porter. Only the imaginative labors of a Wisconsin officer, who erected a dam to raise the water level and float Porter's fleet over the rapids by mid-May, saved the admiral from an utter catastrophe.

Porter laid full blame on Banks's doorstep. "You know my opinion of political generals," the admiral fumed to Sherman after the two battles. "It is a crying sin to put the lives of thousands in the hands of such men, and the time has come when there should be a stop put to it." Two days later, he approached the failure more philosophically, but his attitude toward Banks and officers of his ilk had not budged:

> You know I have always said that Providence was fighting this great battle its own way, and brings these reverses to teach us, a proud, stiff-necked, and unthankful people, how to be contented under a good Government if peaceful times come again. I hope it will teach us not to place the destinies of a great nation in the hands of political generals and volunteer admirals.

Porter survived the Red River expedition with his reputation largely intact, perhaps not with the public but certainly with the Navy Department. And as Grant locked up with Lee around Petersburg, and Sherman battled his way to the outskirts of Atlanta and eventually captured the city, Porter returned east. The secretary of the navy wanted Porter to head a flying squadron in the Atlantic that would chase blockade-runners. Porter respectfully begged off. Such mundane duties offered no appeal; he best served the nation as a combat commander. Some days later, the secretary proposed a joint army-navy operation to North Carolina to seize Fort Fisher, which controlled the blockade-runners' last haven, Wilmington. Porter leaped at the opportunity.

Immediately, he paid his old friend Grant a visit at his headquarters in City Point, Virginia. After lengthy discussions, Grant endorsed the concept and assigned Major General Godfrey Weitzel, a brainy engineer officer, to command the army. Soon, however, problems developed. Fort Fisher was part of Major General Benjamin Butler's department, and he proposed an idea that intrigued authorities in Washington: Butler suggested that they load an old vessel full of gunpowder and explode it near the fort, either demolishing the bastion or so stunning the garrison that an assault would carry the works swiftly. Porter, whose nature attracted him to fresh methods and bold ideas, thought it was worth a try. Grant considered the project ridiculous, but he refused to expend capital to block it. Then Butler, another political general who had tussled with Porter during the campaign for New Orleans in 1862, decided to head the army contingent personally.

Not until mid-December 1864 did the expedition get under way. Incompetence ruled the army operation. Poor preparations, inexcusable delays, and a lack of aggressiveness hounded Butler's command, and gale-force winds worsened its woes. The gunpowder-ship explosion proved a pyrotechnic spectacle, but it did no damage to the fort, and Porter had to rely solely on his naval gunfire to soften the enemy positions and support the landing on Christmas Day. Butler's men were thirty hours late, and only 2,500 soldiers went ashore. Weitzel reconnoitered and found the defenses too strong. Much to Porter's mortification, he and Butler canceled the attack. By imputation and later accusation, the naval bombardment had failed to dislodge enough cannon in Fort Fisher for an assault to succeed.

Porter was livid. To the secretary of the navy, he bemoaned the incompetence of the army officers who headed the expedition and beseeched the secretary not to withdraw his fleet until they had conquered the fort. All the army needed, Porter insisted, was a skilled commander. That day, he dispatched his top subordinate, Captain K. Randolph Breese, with a letter for Sherman to come up and take control of the affair. "This," Porter enticed his comrade, "is merely on your way to Richmond. Take this place and you take the 'crème de la crème' of the rebellion." Sherman's masterful handling of the operation would "let our people see the folly of employing such generals as Butler and Banks. I have tried them both, and God save me from further connections with such generals."

Sherman declined Porter's invitation; instead, he intended to take

Wilmington from the rear, after his march through South Carolina. It did not matter. The previous day, the secretary of the navy showed Grant the dispatches he had received from Porter. Butler had failed wretchedly, and the admiral insisted that a combination of army and navy forces under a good general officer could take the fort. Grant sided with his old friend. "I know Admiral Porter to be possessed of as fine judgment as any other officer and capable of taking as great risks," the lieutenant general informed the secretary of war. That day, Grant urged the admiral to hold fast. He would send the same troops, reinforced by a brigade. Brigadier General Alfred H. Terry would command.

With Grant's involvement, the new expedition functioned superbly. Grant had handed Terry sealed orders; not until he and his force had lost sight of land did they know their destination. Terry's written instructions could not have been more explicit. "It is exceedingly desirable that the most complete understanding should exist between yourself and the naval commander," Grant explained. "I suggest, therefore, that you consult with Admiral Porter freely, and get from him the part to be performed by each branch of the public service, so that there may be unity of action." After directing Terry to prepare a written plan of attack, the lieutenant general ordered Terry to subordinate himself to Porter. "I have served with Admiral Porter, and know that you can rely on his judgment and his nerve to undertake what he proposes. I would, therefore, defer to him as much as is consistent with your own responsibilities." To avoid any misconceptions, the lieutenant general also prepared a letter to Porter, introducing Terry and informing the admiral that "General Terry will show you the instructions he is acting under." He went on to discuss reinforcements that he held on alert in Baltimore and proposed some options for an attack. Then Porter's old friend concluded with the statement, "General Terry will consult with you fully, and will be governed by your suggestions as far as his responsibility for the safety of his command will admit of." Grant had established a unified command.

Together, Porter and Terry conceived and executed a brilliant operation. Porter reworked his gunfire plan, and on January 13, 1865, after an extensive naval bombardment, Terry and his men, augmented by more than 1,000 marines and sailors under Captain Breese, landed and dug in on the beach. The innovative Porter had requested Terry to assign a signal corpsman to his flagship. Thus, when the landing and attack took place, Terry and Porter had ship-to-shore communications. As the amphibious force maneuvered its way up to the Confederate fortifications, Terry and Breese could direct close naval-gunfire support through the wigwag system (signaling with flags). By midafternoon the following day, Terry gave the signal, and the ground troops stormed the walls. For nearly seven hours they battled, sometimes hand to hand. Finally, at 10:00 P.M., Terry lofted a signal flare into the sky. The Union had secured Fort Fisher.

For his role in the victory, Porter praised Terry effusively. "General Terry is entitled to the highest praise and the gratitude of his country for the manner in which he has conducted his part of the operations," the tough-minded admiral commented to Secretary Welles. "He is my beau ideal of a soldier and a general." Porter probably did not know that Terry, like Butler and Banks, was a citizen soldier.

Meanwhile, Butler had returned to Washington in failure. He placed the entire blame squarely on Porter's shoulders, and the politician-turned-general convinced some congressional friends to hold hearings on the matter; but the triumph at Fort Fisher with essentially the same resources pulled the rug out from beneath any damaging investigation. At Grant's request, Lincoln relieved Butler of command of the Department of North Carolina and Virginia and ordered him to return to Massachusetts and await orders. As Sherman crowed to Porter on January 17, "I am rejoiced that the current of events has carried Butler to Lowell, where he should have stayed and confined his bellicose operations to the factory girls." Butler acted as a thorn in Porter's side for the remainder of the admiral's life, attacking him publicly and both resurrecting incidents and conjuring up fictitious tales that portrayed Porter in a bad light.

Although the campaign concluded well for the navy and the army alike, Porter was furious with Grant. Twice in a row on major operations, political generals had caused disasters and squandered the lives of many fine soldiers and sailors. Grant had known of Butler's incompetence before the first attempt, yet he had refused to intervene and replace him with someone of talent, fearful of taking on a general with political clout. Porter and the men of the joint campaign had suffered as a consequence. Worse, Washington rumors falsely indicated that Grant and the army had assumed credit for initiating the expedition. In a war fought predominantly on the ground, army achievements vastly overshadow navy heroics. This stung high-ranking officers and political heads of the Navy Department, and they were particularly tender about the army stealing the applause for navy valor and success. In a confidential letter to Welles, Porter foolishly blasted Grant with broadside after broadside. He accused Grant of being "always willing to take the credit when anything is done, and equally ready to lay the blame of the failure on the navy." Porter reminded the secretary, "I have served with the lieutenant-general before, where I never worked so hard in my life to make a man succeed as I did for him." Yet, he complained, Grant paid little more than lip service to the navy's efforts. "He wants magnanimity, like most officers of the army, and is so avaricious as regards fame that he will never, if he can help it, do justice to our department." Grant displayed "indifference" toward the operation "until he found his reputation at stake." Meanwhile, Porter had risked his own reputation with the likes of Butler. "His course proves to me that he would sacrifice his best friend rather than let any odium fall upon Lieutenant-General Grant." Grant deserved blame, not credit.

As he had done earlier in the war when he disparaged McClellan and the Army of the Potomac, Porter let emotions rule reason. The invective acted therapeutically, releasing pent-up frustration and stress from the two ventures, and in a short time Porter felt as warmly as ever toward Grant. The letter, however, came back to haunt him. In 1870, after President Grant had issued a commission promoting Vice Admiral Porter to the rank of admiral, someone dug up the letter to influence the Senate confirmation vote. The harsh words stung the president. Since their days at Vicksburg, Grant had counted Porter among his closest friends. It was hard for the president to believe Porter had ever harbored such vicious thoughts toward him.

Porter reacted with honesty and speed. He immediately admitted authorship of the letter and publicly condemned himself for it. To demonstrate his true feelings, the admiral turned over his wartime journal to a newspaperman for publication. All of its passages regarding Grant indicated deep affection and admiration for the general and the man. Then, hat in hand, he went to the White House. Still too hurt to forgive, Grant declined to see him, so Porter wrote him a lengthy letter, explaining why he had acted and felt so foolishly after the battle for Fort Fisher and apologizing for his misdeed. Surely their deep friendship since the event, long before he had any hint that Grant would seek the presidency, indicated his genuine sentiments toward him, Porter contended. Nearly three weeks later, Porter received an invitation to visit the White House. The president and the admiral cloistered for an hour, and when they stepped from the room, all had been forgiven. Grant had accepted Porter's explanation, and the two friends put the letter behind them.

In the decades following the war, Porter retained a rich relationship with both Grant and Sherman. As president, Grant not only promoted Porter but even wanted him to serve as his secretary of the navy; however, Porter did not want a political job. Grant's fondness for the man and respect for his talents never diminished. Late in life, Grant wrote, "Among naval officers I have always placed Porter in the highest rank. I believe Porter to be as great an admiral as Lord Nelson." Grant was the first of the triumvirate to pass away, succumbing to cancer in 1885.

Sherman and Porter, the ranking officers of their respective services, led the drive toward professionalism in the armed forces. Their friendship, founded at the base of Haynes' Bluff, retained its strength throughout their declining years. "Lord High Admiral of the U.S. Navy" was Sherman's pet name for Porter. Sherman retired as commanding general of the army in 1884.

Porter, the eldest of the trio, outlasted his friends in service. A naval officer to the end, he sustained a massive heart attack in 1890. The tough old admiral hung on for some months, but his faculties degenerated, and on February 13, 1891, he expired at his Washington home—in an upright, seated position. Sherman, who had recently developed pneumonia, outlived his old friend by a single day.

*SUMMER 1994*

---

A historian at the University of Houston, Joseph T. Glatthaar is the author of *Partners in Command: The Relationships between Leaders in the Civil War* (1994), from which this article is adapted.

# 12

# The Rock of Chickamauga

## By John Bowers

*Although unquestionably Virginian in his lineage and status, George H. Thomas did not follow his fellow Virginians into the Confederate army in those confusing and uncertain days following Fort Sumter. Instead, holding firmly to the Union, he became one of the North's most steadfast and successful generals, but also one of its least remembered. Though Grant and Sherman might occasionally be unsure of this Southerner leading Northern troops, Thomas was always sure of himself, his purpose, and his men. At Stones River, at Chickamauga, at Missionary Ridge, at Nashville, Thomas prevailed. As John Bowers reminds us, "He opted always to fight, to punish his foe, to win." The Union could not ask more of this son of the South.*

George H. Thomas was a triumphant Civil War general who led his men to victory in some of the war's hottest battles. He was a true Southerner, a son of the Old Dominion—and he fought for the North.

He was born in Southampton County, Virginia, not far from the North Carolina border, on July 31, 1816. He was gentry and a West Pointer (class of 1840, which included William Tecumseh Sherman and Richard S. Ewell), someone whose family had owned slaves, someone who could claim Southern ancestry as far back as Robert E. Lee could. Never was there a question as to Thomas's bona fides—even his accent was pure Virginian, with broad vowels and soft placement. Never was there a question about the ties that should have bound him to his region. Yet the day after Fort Sumter was fired upon in April 1861, Thomas, then a major in the regular army, did not resign his commission as so many other Southerners did. At Carlisle Barracks in Pennsylvania, he reaffirmed his loyalty to the Union—and caused his family in Virginia to disown him. His maiden sisters turned his picture to the wall, burned all his letters, and wrote him later in life only to suggest he change his name.

Few, if any, of Thomas's Virginia brethren could understand a man going against his own people, particularly when the Federals "invaded" Virginia soon afterward—fighting at First Manassas (Bull Run) on July 21, 1861—and remained intent on her destruction until peace at Appomattox on April 9, 1865. Why, so many in the South wanted to know, did Thomas turn out to be such a dedicated and formidable foe? Why did he unrelentingly, wholeheartedly dedicate himself to keeping the Union preserved and putting the rebellion down? Why?

NAT TURNER'S REBELLION, which began on the night of August 21, 1831, may have been a pivotal event in Thomas's youth. This volcanic uprising, led by a firebrand slave, had no antecedent save for Indian raids a generation or so before. Turner's wild, marauding band wove at random through isolated farms in Southampton County, raping, plundering, ripping society apart at the seams. Fifteen-year-old Thomas was called upon to ride to neighboring farms and warn the incredulous that they were in peril. His own family barely escaped with their lives.

Some survivors feared the whole black race after that and believed Southern whites should leave the Union and band together for safety's sake. Not Thomas. What he had learned, after seeing this revolt, was that there is nothing much worse than chaos and a center not holding. Secession and the threat of disorder were not for him. George H. Thomas was everlastingly conservative, never the romantic cavalier for a "cause." There was nothing Hamlet-like about him. As a man and as a soldier, he was straightforward, unswerving, sure of himself.

As a West Point cadet, Thomas was meticulous and hardworking. Cadet William Starke Rosecrans, who would later command him in Tennessee, said the blue-eyed, square-jawed Thomas bore a remarkable resemblance to Gilbert Stuart's portrait of Washington. West Pointers actually dubbed him "George Washington," for manner as well as facial resemblance. Nervous, fidgety, redheaded William Tecumseh Sherman shared a room in the Old South Barracks with Thomas. "Cump" Sherman, only sixteen at the time and talking a blue streak, was sloppy in dress then as later and led the corps in demerits—one of the all-time great "hash makers" in Point history. As a plebe he garnered 109 demerits; Thomas in his whole four-year career attained but 87.

Thomas caused little fuss but gave anyone pause who was out to give him trouble. An early trait, and one he kept, was never to back down or cringe in the face of a threat. Cadet Stewart Van Vliet, who also shared the room with Sherman and Thomas, told a story years later about hazing:

> One evening a cadet came into our room and commenced to give us orders. He had said but a few words when Old Tom stepped up to him and said, "Leave this room immediately or I will throw you through the window." There were no more attempts to haze us.

Ulysses S. Grant spent a year with Thomas at West Point and later knew him in the old army. But he never fully appreciated Thomas, and possibly did not trust him. "Thomas's dispositions were deliberately made and always good," Grant wrote. "He could not be driven from a point he was given to hold. He was not as good, however, in pursuit as he was in action." During the all-important Nashville campaign in December 1864, Grant had urged Thomas in frequent dispatches to attack Confederate general John B. Hood at once so that Hood could not escape north into Kentucky (and later attack Grant in Virginia). In his memoirs Grant writes, "At last I had to say to General Thomas that I should be obliged to remove him unless he acted promptly. He replied that he was very sorry, but he would move as soon as he could."

What faced Thomas on the road to Nashville was not the enemy but frozen, slippery ground that would not permit the essential advance of his cavalry. He would not move precipitously, but stayed by his guns and waited for a thaw. Grant ordered General John A. Logan to go to Thomas and take command if Thomas had not advanced by the time he got there. Then Grant changed his mind and said he himself would go to Nashville and take command. Still Thomas waited. He wasn't budging. When the ice melted on December 14, he geared up his army, moved, and overwhelmed Hood in one of the Union's greatest victories. Grant himself wrote, "He did move, and was successful from the start."

The qualities that Thomas showed, time after time, were patience and calm. "He would never do to conduct one of your campaigns," Grant said to Sherman, Thomas's former roommate. Sherman was excitable, given to wild mood swings, and more than once was thought certifiably crazy. Grant and Sherman had much in common and complemented each other well through the war. Both were theatrical by nature, highly eccentric, and had known periods, in peace and in the early stages of the war, when they were held in quite low esteem. Americans always cheer for the underdog—and Grant and Sherman were certainly that. They were counted out early—and came back to be made into celebrities in their day. They liked each other enormously and supported each other's positions. Later, someone asked Sherman to try to change some of President Grant's Reconstruction ideas. "No," replied Sherman, according to General Richard W. Johnson. "Grant stood by me when I was crazy and I stood by him when he was drunk, and now we stand by each other."

Characterologically, Thomas was the opposite of Grant and Sherman—a methodical, level-headed tactician who never flew by the seat of his pants but just as impressively won battles. His men adored him. They called him "Old Reliable," "Old Slow Trot," "Old Pap," "Uncle George," and "The Rock"—a father figure to tie oneself to. He was incorruptible—indeed in his case the word seems an understatement. After the war Grant was given a $50,000 house in Philadelphia by a group of wealthy citizens, and Sherman received one in Washington for twice that amount. When Thomas was offered a reward for his war record, he turned it down flat, saying, "While fully apprehending the motives which induce these kind offers, I contend that I cannot accept them and be wholly independent."

When Thomas went to extremes, he went perhaps to the extremes of rectitude—which does not always make good copy. He was no George S. Patton. When Grant asked him to hold a surrounded and besieged Chattanooga, Thomas replied, "We will hold the town till we starve"—not flamboyant, like General Anthony McAuliffe's reply of "Nuts!" to the Germans at Bastogne, but dramatic in its own way, and to the point.

In all matters prudent, Thomas waited to marry until he was thirty-six and securely ensconced as an artillery and cavalry instructor at West Point. He had received his academic post through the recommendation of Rosy Rosecrans, who would figure as Thomas's superior officer at Chickamauga. The superintendent at the Point at that time was Robert E. Lee. Thomas was a distinguished veteran of the Mexican War—as were Lee and Rosecrans— and a position at West Point was a favored retreat for these veterans.

There is no record of Thomas having had any *affaire de coeur* before age thirty-six. Until then, he had apparently been as chaste as a monk. In the spring of 1852, though, he began checking out romantic novels and volumes of poetry from the academy library, in addition to his usual requests for work on military matters. It was not long until he became engaged, then married, to Frances Kellogg, whose widowed mother had been in the habit of bringing her along on visits to her nephew, Cadet Lyman M. Kellogg, class of 1852.

Frances Kellogg was tall and stately and five years younger than her husband. Due to the Civil War and the military life Thomas never left, the couple was separated for long periods. They were devoted, but remained childless. The Kelloggs were Yankees from Troy, New York, and some have speculated that being married to a Northerner may have influenced Thomas in renouncing the Southern cause after Sumter. Influence him she undoubtedly did—but something fundamental and unswerving in his own nature caused him to fight for the Union.

Although Thomas usually presented a stone-faced exterior of total probity and solemnity, he was not without humor, passion, and deep feeling. He knew how to take a drink, and when he felt slighted and wronged, he did not simply put up with it. A Union general who knew how to win, a distinct rara avis through much of the war, he bridled at his slow promotions in rank. He surmised (in all likelihood correctly) that his Southern background stood in his way, a permanent black cloud over his full acceptance by the Northern high command led by Grant and General Henry Halleck.

As for the South, during the all-important battle for Chattanooga in November 1863, Sherman asked Thomas if he had had any communication with General Braxton Bragg, who commanded the Rebel army that they faced. Suddenly Thomas's blue eyes flashed and emotion poured out. "Damn him, I'll be even with him yet."

"What's the matter now?" Sherman wanted to know.

Thomas explained that not long before, he had tried to send a letter through Rebel lines, under a flag of truce, and that it had come back with a note: "Respectfully returned to General Thomas. General Bragg declines to have any intercourse with a man who has betrayed his State." In more pleasant antebellum days, Thomas, Sherman, and Bragg had served together at Fort Moultrie, South Carolina. Sherman recalled that Thomas uttered many threats as to what he was going to do to his former friend Bragg—and that he was quite heated about it.

Bragg certainly suffered the effects of Thomas's intelligence and capability. It is probable that Chattanooga, gateway to Sherman's March to the Sea, would have fallen to Bragg and his army if not for Thomas. At the Battle of Chickamauga on September 19–20, 1863, the bulk of the Union forces fled in near panic into the city. Alexander McCook and Thomas Crittenden and even the redoubtable Rosecrans fled, their armies thrown into disarray by Hood, who broke through a quarter-mile gap and poured unexpectedly over Rosecrans's right wing.

The only one who held was Thomas. He rallied his corps and some survivors of Crittenden's command and stood on a steep, horseshoe-shaped elevation called Snodgrass Hill that protruded eastward from Missionary Ridge. He kept this position into the growing dark and bought enough time for most of Rosecrans's retreating troops to reach Chattanooga. General James Longstreet and his veterans of the charges at Gettysburg scaled Horseshoe Ridge, and it seemed they would easily grapple Thomas into submission. But he held—with some last-minute help from General Gordon Granger's reserve corps—and Old Pete Longstreet's men had to retreat down the ridge. The Confederates did win a massive tactical victory at Chickamauga—in 8,000 blue-clads captured, tons of their supplies taken, and a Union army bottled up in Chattanooga—but one thing they couldn't claim: subduing George H. Thomas of Virginia.

Actually, Chickamauga was not the only place where Thomas was a rock. The Battle of Stones River, fought around New Year's 1863, near Murfreesboro, Tennessee, had been a rehearsal for Chickamauga, as hapless Bragg tarried in his retreat from Nashville but suddenly stood to fight. Rosecrans, the Union commander, felt the sting of Rebel fire and considered retreating to Nashville but feared the Confederates might be blocking his way. He also had Thomas as a general in his army. Thomas spread calm among his troops. He stood patiently and firmly, saying, "This army does not retreat." In the end, Bragg did. At Chickamauga it happened again; Thomas could not be moved when the chips were down.

On the Confederate side, Chickamauga cost General Hood his right leg in the battle (his left arm had already been shattered at Gettysburg)—but dismemberment did not soften his rash and truculent nature. A short time after the leg was amputated—so close to the trunk that at first the battlefield surgeon did not think it could be done—Hood was back in the saddle, where he had to be strapped every morning in order to remain upright. His long, bearded face looks extremely dour and stern in the few photographs we have of him.

Braxton Bragg also would win no prize for cheerfulness. His visage reflects a woefully depressed personality. Unlike Thomas's men, Bragg's did not adore him, and his fellow officers were nearly always in open revolt. On paper, before a battle, he was a great tactician, but once the cannon boomed and muskets rattled and the fight took unexpected turns, he did as Rosecrans did—made a getaway, both to regroup and to rethink. He had few intimates and brooded alone. After the Union finally prevailed at Chattanooga, Bragg was kicked upstairs to become chief of staff for the Confederacy. Ironically, today the U.S. flag flies over Fort Bragg in North Carolina and over Fort Hood in Texas—but Fort Thomas, a small city in Kentucky, is no longer even a military installation.

Although Thomas was highly popular with his men, he was not friendly with them. He once said, "I am naturally reserved and have found it difficult to be on familiar, easy terms with my men." But his dignity, his steadiness, and his air of assurance aroused the affections of those under his command—as shown in the nicknames they gave him. "Old Slow Trot," a nickname he came by while an instructor at West Point, may be misleading at first: It did not denote a lack of alacrity in pressing for battle—as one might think after reading Grant on Thomas. It came from the care he took never to labor his mount unnecessarily. A fine equestrian since boyhood, he always showed the utmost consideration for a horse's welfare. When he led West Point cadets in cavalry exercises and they began to chafe in anticipation of a gallop, there inevitably came Thomas's deep, rolling Southern accent to cool them down: "Slow trot, gentlemen. Slow trot!"

The cavalry is ceremonial today, but in Thomas's day it was a prestigious and crucial branch of the army. Grant sat well in the saddle and enjoyed racing to and fro among his men in the field. When he reined in his horse, he sat relaxed, from all accounts, leaning forward to talk, his white socks drooping above his black shoes, a large cigar in his hand or jutting from his mouth. His preferred comrade-in-arms, Sherman, rode impulsively, intuitively, a raw exposed nerve. Thomas was another kind of rider, and this tells something of his character and the type of commander he was. Captain Henry Stone of Thomas's staff once noted:

> When under fire, his movements . . . were as deliberate as at any time. . . . He was never seen riding up and down his lines waving his sword, shouting, or going through ceremonies. . . . On the march nobody ever saw him, with an escort trailing, dashing past a moving column of troops, throwing up dust or mud and compelling them to leave the road. If any had the right of way, it was they. He would break through the woods or flounder across a swamp rather than force his men from the road and wear them out by needless fatigue.

Thomas was persevering and dogged in advancing himself and his troops, but there was never a recorded incident when he puffed himself up and showed unseemly ambition—as did McClellan ("Young Napoleon") in blue and P.G.T. Beauregard in gray. He would not step over someone to advance his career. When he was appointed to succeed Major General Don Carlos Buell as commander of the Army of the Ohio, Thomas, who was second-in-command, notified Buell that he was declining the promotion because he considered it unfair. He felt that Buell didn't deserve such treatment—and besides, looking realistically at the situation, he concluded that he was not quite ready for the assignment. (Buell soon lost his command anyway.) Thomas also at first refused to succeed General Rosecrans after the Battle of Chickamauga, but Old Rosy himself persuaded him to accept the appointment.

If Thomas could be said to resemble anyone, it was perhaps Robert E. Lee. Both were deeply Southern in temperament, both inspired unquestioning devotion in their followers, and, most striking, both were so modest that some thought it almost a weakness. There was never a hint of scandal in their personal lives, and both were exceptionally kind and courteous. Grant and Sherman could be brusque and sometimes brutal in personal dealings. Never Thomas; never Lee.

Yet some deep, dark force simmered low in both Lee's and Thomas's psyches, and this force came out unbridled in war. Both could be expert, devastating killers—no other word for it. When ammunition ran low at Chickamauga, Thomas didn't blink an eye about calling for the bayonet. He opted always to fight, to punish his foe, to win. It was Lee who said, at Fredericksburg, "It is well that war is so terrible. We should grow too fond of it." And at a war council in Tennessee, it was Thomas alone who voted to stand and fight. He rose by the firelight and said, "Gentlemen, I know of no better place to die than right here," and walked out of the room and into the night.

Lee, who fought against the Union, is universally honored today. Public buildings and avenues are named after him, and in Eisenhower's White House his portrait hung on the wall. Thomas, who fought to save the Union and was crucial to its preservation, is held in far less esteem—if, indeed, most people even know who he was. Lee's home on the rise above the Potomac in Arlington is a national tourist attraction. Thomas's commodious boyhood home near Newsoms, Virginia, is not marked; in fact, natives of the region are said to often shake their heads when the curious ask where it is. Could it be we collectively romanticize the Lost Cause and those who led it, while even today we distrust, if not dislike, those who supported the Union but had to fight their own people to do so?

Grant was only one of the many Northerners who never completely trusted the Virginian. Who could fight his own people? And this suspicion in the North was more than matched by Southern abhorrence for his actions in scything down their armies.

After Thomas's death, General Sherman spoke before a crowd of veterans at the unveiling of Thomas's equestrian statue in Washington, D.C. He prophesied that a day would come when Southerners would forgive Thomas, that they would make pilgrimages to this statue erected to his memory. As far as that prediction goes, it may be said that few have ever paid attention to the statue in the center of a busy traffic circle in the nation's capital. No Southern delegation, as far as we know, has ever laid a wreath there. Today cars whiz by it and through a tunnel beneath, and it is the unusual tourist or passerby who takes a moment to honor the hero of the Battle of Chickamauga.

Various libels have been directed against Thomas. Sherman—his West Point classmate and allegedly his friend—at one point said that Thomas and his Army of the Cumberland were addicted to the defensive and that a fresh furrow would stop the whole column. Today, however, long after the firing has died and records have been sifted through, Thomas's stature has grown among Civil War scholars to an almost towering presence. Bruce Catton writes:

> What a general could do, Thomas did; no more dependable soldier for a moment of crisis existed on the North American continent, or ever did exist. . . .
>
> Thomas comes down in history as the Rock of Chickamauga, the great defensive fighter, the man who could never be driven away but who was not much on the offensive. That may be a correct appraisal. Yet it may also be worth making note that just twice in all the war was a major Confederate army driven away from a prepared position in complete rout—at Chattanooga and at Nashville. Each time the blow that routed it was launched by Thomas.

Thomas, a Southerner, led Northern troops, and they revered him. They fought for him because, most important, he never asked them to do anything he wouldn't do. He did not lead a battle from a headquarters in the rear. He liked to sit astride his horse, reins in hand, while cannisters thumped and minié balls buzzed past. There was never a question as to his physical bravery. A short time before the war, on August 26, 1860, while on a military exploration of the Concho and Colorado rivers, his detail engaged in a sharp fight with some plundering Indians. Thomas was painfully wounded by an arrow that entered his chin and lodged in his chest. He pulled out the arrow himself and kept the fight going until he was sure the Indians had been vanquished.

While recuperating from this wound, in November 1860, on leave in his native Virginia, he suffered a worse injury. Alighting from a railroad train in the dark near Lynchburg, Virginia, deceived by the shadows of the moonlight, he believed he was stepping onto firm earth and instead plummeted down a deep ravine, severely wrenching his back. He was in great pain, and at the time, fearing he could never return to full duty, he looked around for an alternative way of life. The first job he sought was as commandant of cadets at the Virginia Military Institute. By the time he applied, however, the position had been filled and he just missed serving at the same seat of learning as an obscure and eccentric professor named Thomas J. Jackson, soon to be known as "Stonewall." Thomas remained in the army and suffered from his back for the rest of his life.

In the closing months of 1863, the decisive military action at Chattanooga signaled the Union's grasp at last on victory. Of the commanders, Thomas was most essential in that victory, which broke the Confederate siege of the town and started Sherman on his way to the sea.

The taking of Missionary Ridge in the late afternoon of November 25 was one of the war's most curious assaults—unusual in that Thomas's men had been ordered only to take the row of Confederate rifle pits at the base of the ridge, not the ridge itself. However, the inspired blue-clads, 20,000 strong, fought through an inferno, sometimes by bayonet, captured the fortifications, and, when they could have stopped and rested, kept up the pursuit of the Rebels until they had captured the ridge as well. They did all this without a direct order from Thomas or anyone. In fact, officers—from second lieutenant on up—tried to stay them. But they were Old Pap's troops and knew what to do.

For perhaps the first time in the war, common soldiers led a charge while officers took up the rear—finally yelling, inappropriately, out of habit, "Follow me! Follow me!" At his command post down below, Grant fumed. He said commands would be lost if the unauthorized charge failed—meaning the ax would fall on Thomas. But Thomas did not worry. Through field glasses he watched his troops scale the impossibly steep, fortified ridge. They screamed "Chickamauga, Chickamauga!" at the frightened, fleeing Rebels—and almost captured Bragg himself before it was over. It was a costly victory, though. When Thomas was asked if the dead should be buried by state, he replied, "No, no, mix 'em up. I'm *tired* of states' rights."

Charles A. Dana, who was there as an observer, wrote this report immediately afterward:

> Glory to God. The day is decisively ours. Missionary Ridge has just been carried by a magnificent charge of Thomas's troops. . . . The heights which Thomas carried by assault are at least 500 feet above Chattanooga Valley, with an inclination of at least 45 degrees, and exceedingly rugged and difficult. . . . The storming of the ridge by our troops was one of the greatest miracles in military history.

Thomas's Army of the Cumberland fought under Sherman through the bloody battle of Kenesaw Mountain and through the fall of Atlanta; and it was the impetuous Sherman who started the rumor of Thomas's "slowness" in a dispatch to Grant during the march to Atlanta: "My chief source of trouble is with the Army of the Cumberland, which is dreadfully slow." Thomas was anything but slow. His troops bore the brunt of the fighting to Atlanta—and were essential in its capture. Then it was Thomas and the Army of the Cumberland who pursued Hood from Atlanta, defeating him at Nashville—thus protecting Sherman's rear and allowing Grant to battle Lee into submission in Virginia.

After the victory in Nashville, the Army of the Cumberland performed mainly garrison duties during the few months left in the war, and Thomas was rewarded by promotion to major general. He served in Tennessee during Reconstruction, fighting any vestige of Confederate resurgence—guarding the polls, putting down the Ku Klux Klan—as if he had been born in Massachusetts. On the other hand, he went as far as anyone in obtaining pardons for former Confederate officers and their kin. He remained in the army and served on the Pacific coast in the first years of Grant's presidency.

Thomas died of a stroke on March 28, 1870, at age fifty-three, while stationed in San Francisco. His body was transported east in a crepe-festooned railroad car. Guns echoed in salute at every nearby army post, and in Chicago there was a great demonstration of pomp. At the funeral in Troy, New York, there were the bowed heads of President Grant; Generals Sherman, Philip Sheridan, and George Meade; and a host of cabinet members, governors, and former soldiers under Thomas's command. Twenty-five railway cars, hauled by a couple of locomotives, brought New York's National Guard. "Never before in the history of Troy were so many strangers in the city," the local *Times* said.

It seemed everyone was there save Thomas's family from Virginia. Not one of them attended. "Our brother George died to us in 'sixty-one," his sisters told their neighbors. All presents that he had sent to them through the years had been returned unopened—but he kept sending them. Till the end he knew how to do the correct thing.

*WINTER 1991*

---

John Bowers, whose grandfather fought for the Confederacy at Chickamauga, authored *Stonewall Jackson: Portrait of a Soldier* (1989). He is currently working on a book about the battles around Chattanooga.

# 13

# Civil War Cavalry: Missed Opportunities

## By Paddy Griffith

*Despite the glamour and romance that surround the cavalry, it played a rather paltry combat role in the Civil War. Whereas the Napoleonic Wars witnessed massive cavalry charges at the crucial moment of battles, the Civil War saw only small, unimportant charges that had a negligible impact on the battle, or far-flung, independent raiding parties that took the cavalry away from the battle itself. At Gettysburg, history remembers J.E.B. Stuart's cavalry only because it was not there when needed, while at Antietam, the war's single bloodiest day, the cavalry was essentially an observer. Paddy Griffith explores why, in so much of the war, cavalry played such an insignificant role. At the same time, he argues that the deployment of cavalry late in the conflict gave the hint of warfare still to come.*

It is not without reason that on the only occasion when cavalry appear in Stephen Crane's classic novel *The Red Badge of Courage*, they are behind the fighting line, creating a traffic jam. Many Civil War soldiers must have felt that this was really all the cavalry was good for, apart from raiding railroads or hanging up invalids to get their gold. While there was a certain failure to make the most of either field artillery or the bayonet in the battles of the 1860s, the record of the cavalry was at least a hundred times worse.

The participation of cavalry in the major battles of the Civil War was generally negligible. For example, at Antietam—"America's Bloodiest Day"—the Union cavalry suffered precisely twenty-eight casualties from all causes. At Fredericksburg they lost just eight men—less than one in every 1,500 of the total Union casualties. In the first three years of the war, the cavalry of the Army of the Potomac made only five mounted charges against infantry during a major battle—far fewer than Marshal Ney's cavalry had made in three hours at Waterloo.

The first of these Union charges was made on June 27, 1862, at Gaines's Mill in the Peninsula campaign, where the 5th U.S. Cavalry, 250 strong, counterattacked the Confederates at their moment of greatest success. The cavalry later claimed that their charge kept a Union reverse from degenerating into a disaster. The Union infantry, on the other hand, said the cavalry charge converted an orderly retreat into a disorganized rout. One thing is certain: The cavalry failed to make any headway against the enemy, and suffered 150 casualties. The charge was all over in a matter of moments.

At the end of the Battle of Cedar Mountain on August 9, 1862, the 1st Pennsylvania Cavalry charged against five somewhat disordered enemy regiments. It, too, was repulsed, with 93 casualties out of 164 men. At Chancellorsville yet another holding action was launched, this time with the 8th Pennsylvania Cavalry charging in columns of twos down a road flanked by woods full of General Stonewall Jackson's men at the highwater mark of their most spectacular victory. Surprisingly, there were only 30 casualties out of 400 men—but they were repulsed just the same, after having made but a minor impact on the battle.

At the end of the Battle of Gettysburg, General Judson Kilpatrick ordered two cavalry charges—one by the 1st West Virginia Cavalry Regiment and the other by the 1st Vermont—against the extreme right flank of the Confederate army. Both units charged across difficult, broken ground against well-emplaced Texas infantry, and both were easily repulsed. The day's cavalry losses totaled ninety-eight, of whom sixty-five belonged to the 1st Vermont. Hence, we may infer that the 1st West Virginia lost little more than twenty-five men in its attack, even though it came within striking distance of the enemy line twice.

In all, perhaps 1,400 Union cavalrymen in the East took part in charges on Rebel infantry in major battles during the first three years of the war, suffering 365 casualties—approximately a quarter of their strength. Although some positive results could possibly be claimed for each charge, the overall outcome can only be described as negative. This seems to suggest that the day of the cavalry charge had passed; that the rifle musket's improved firepower had given a new security to infantry, even if they did not form squares; and that the American cavalry had been wise not to charge more frequently, in view of the probable outcome.

A European cavalryman raised in the Napoleonic tradition of Marshals Murat and Nansouty would probably point out a number of significant factors in these charges—most notably their tiny scale. None involved even one full-strength regiment (about 1,000 men), nor even a force as strong as the depleted British Light Brigade at Balaklava. If the "gallant 600" on that occasion lacked sufficient numbers to make an impact, what chance did the 1st Pennsylvania have at Cedar Mountain? Napoleon's tactic had been to throw in dozens of regiments together in massed divisions and corps of cavalry, not one squadron at a time.

Our European commentator would probably not find fault with the timing of these charges. In accordance with classical theory, all of them were launched at the end of a hard day's fighting, either to cover a retreat or to make the first tentative probes of a pursuit. Noticeably missing, however, was any attempt to intervene during the climax of the battle, as part of the process of deciding winners and losers. The rearguard and pursuit functions of cavalry could not be expected to decide much more than the level of damage once a decision had been reached. Therefore, by limiting itself to those functions, the cavalry of the Army of the Potomac was abdicating its most important role.

Another significant feature of these charges was that only the first two, at Gaines's Mill and Cedar Mountain, seem to have taken place on unencumbered ground. The Chancellorsville action took place in a wood that allowed only a two-man frontage—scarcely a legitimate operation of war. At Gettysburg the terrain was only slightly more favorable. Our European observer might therefore conclude that the failure of these three charges probably owed more to obstacles than to firepower, particularly since their casualties were considerably less than those suffered in the first two charges over more open ground.

The fact is, no serious attempt was made to use cavalry in these battles at all, even where the ground was favorable. Such a use was alien to the whole outlook and ethic of the Civil War commanders, and we do not have to look very far to find the reasons.

For a long time after the war started, the number of cavalry available was meager by European standards. The Army of the Potomac rarely fielded more than two regiments per 10,000 men—9 percent of the total manpower as compared with Napoleon's 20 or even 25 percent. Cavalry was enormously expensive to feed and still more expensive to equip. A horse cost at least $110—ten times the monthly pay of a private soldier and five times the price of a rifle musket. Each cavalryman also required a saddle, a saber, riding boots, and a few pistols (preferably the latest Colts)—not to mention horseshoes and tack. The whole proposition was so complicated, compared with the simple needs of an infantryman, that it is scarcely surprising that few cavalry regiments were put into the field. When we read about a cavalry regiment that demanded eighty-one wagons to support it, while an equivalent 2,000 wagons for an entire army of 60,000 men would have been excessive impedimenta, we can begin to understand the scale of the problem.

Doctrinal resistance to battle cavalry was also very strong. American tradition simply had no place for such an animal; the first U.S. regular cavalry unit had not been authorized until 1792, and subsequent emphasis had been all on dragoons or mounted infantry—hybrids that promised a double return on the government's investment but in fact turned out to provide neither an efficient infantry nor an efficient battle cavalry. Certainly the influence of Dennis Hart Mahan and his West Point teaching appears to have been in the direction of light cavalry outposts and scouting rather than of heavy combat. It comes as no surprise that Mahan's baleful engineering view of the battlefield eclipsed the potential contribution of a large and energetic cavalry force. He had been influential in shaping the tactical thinking of the infantry, and there was a logical spiral at work: The greater the emphasis laid by the infantry upon firepower and protection, the less attention was paid to shock and mobility such as the cavalry could—supremely—provide.

Then again—as with the infantry, as with artillery—the excuse of the terrain was often invoked to show that things could not be done in the European manner. There was some justice in this, especially in the various wildernesses and the Shenandoah Valley, not to mention the rolling forests of the West. But in quite a few cases the terrain obstacles consisted of fences or ditches that well-trained cavalry should have been able to jump. The problem was often one of training rather than of terrain. In some accounts of successful charges, we hear of fences being thrown down by a regiment's advanced pickets or "ground scouts," and ditches being leaped at the gallop. At Brandy Station in 1863, the ground had been picked bare by several armies camping there over the previous two years, which showed that cavalry country could be created artificially.

The problem of training, however, remained central. It was not simply that good cavalry took many months longer to build than did good infantry, but that the awareness of this fact often deterred Civil War commanders from making the attempt at all. McClellan, for example, though notorious for his insistence on long and careful training before his army could take the field, seems to have done little about training his cavalry. He apparently felt that Americans could never hope to approach European ideals. As a result, a whole year was lost, while the cavalry was allowed to indoctrinate itself with the notion that it could never make use of European methods. In the Army of the Potomac, the standards of training and organization were starting to improve in the summer of 1863, but by then it was already too late to demand anything more than a hybrid "American" style of tactics.

The Confederate Army of Northern Virginia suffered from a similar problem, expressed in slightly different ways. Standards of horse care and horsemanship were generally higher, simply because each man had to bring his own horse. One need not invoke theories of "Southern cavaliers" or "innate equestrian skills"—any soldier will do better riding his own cherished four-legged friend than astride an anonymous item of government property. In addition, the principle of massing regiments into brigades and divisions was pursued earlier by the Confederate cavalry than by the Union, just as it had been by their artillery, due to a greater sense of urgency and military commitment. The well-earned reward was a two-year period in which J.E.B. Stuart's horsemen literally ran rings around their opponents.

The reverse side of these Southern advantages, however, was a shockingly high level of absenteeism and indiscipline. Because the soldiers brought their own horses, they saw themselves as voluntary "visitors" and accepted neither discipline nor any of the rest of the military contract. They felt free to go home when they felt like it, or to wander away looking for forage, for remounts (often stolen from the Yankees), or for meals (usually from distant cousins living in the area of operations). This was doubtless a highly agreeable and civilized way to fight a war, but it left the regiments present for duty lamentably weak. The extreme case came in the 1st Tennessee Cavalry, which unilaterally decided to disband completely except for sixteen men who preferred to stay in camp.

The principle of using cavalry en masse was a sound and highly "European" one, but in the hands of J.E.B. Stuart and his friends it became little more than a license to roam off into the enemy's rear areas searching for plunder and glory. The success of his early raids in 1862 encouraged Stuart to repeat the process on an ever more grandiose scale. This led to disaster at Gettysburg, where the cavalry was absent when most needed—although in fairness we can also see that Stuart's example infected the Union cavalry still more disastrously than it did the Confederate one. The Northern troopers were to base a whole alternative system of war upon their enemy's much publicized exploits, thereby perpetuating the removal of cavalry from the battlefields. One is reminded of the terror-bombing offensives in World War II, in which a temporary German diversion of air effort from battlefield to city-center targets (to Rotterdam and then London) inspired a massive and permanent Allied diversion of effort (to Cologne and, later, to Hiroshima).

As the Union cavalry gradually built up its numbers and its skills, it came to be used increasingly for raiding rather than for close support of the infantry. (At Chancellorsville, for example, General George Stoneman was sent off on a raid, away from the battle, with almost all the available horsemen. Though this was intended to divert the enemy away from a direct engagement, it achieved no major result save to deplete Union numbers.) The tempo of raiding was also starting to rise in the Western theater at about the same time. It continued to rise right up to the end of the war, which quite appropriately coincided with the culmination of General James Wilson's Selma campaign, a massive *chevauchée* by 12,000 horsemen supported by 1,500 wagoners—and not a single infantryman.

The general Civil War doctrine of raiding, particularly of raiding with cavalry, represented not a great innovation in the art of warfare—as critics such as B.H. Liddell Hart have claimed—but its abasement and corruption: a reversion to the fourteenth-century methods of the Black Prince rather than a step forward to the twentieth-century blitzkrieg. The use of cavalry for raiding not only was a deliberate turn away from hope of victory on the battlefield but virtually removed the means by which victory might have been won at the very moment when those means were at last starting to be properly efficient. If the slow development of high-quality cavalry during the first half of the war was a major missed opportunity, the diversion of it into raiding during the second half was a still greater one.

The picture is not entirely bleak, however, since the late-war cavalry did eventually develop a fighting style that gave it, at last, considerable combat power and an important role in the major battles. Whereas by 1864 the infantry had become largely demoralized and exhausted, the horse soldiers—especially on the Union side—were just starting to come into their own. They could be invoked as a fresh new force straining to take up the main burden of the war, a spearhead that could use revolutionary new tactics to tackle an old and intransigent problem.

Four major ingredients went into this new tactical mixture: fast operational mobility on horseback out of contact with the enemy; a willingness to take cover and fight on foot when the enemy was close; a mounted reserve ready to make a saber charge when the moment was ripe; and new repeating carbines like the Spencer and Henry (for which the technology was not developed until the war was in progress). Taken together and used correctly, these four elements could produce important improvements not only in the cavalry's earlier performance but in the infantry's too.

What these "mounted infantry" tactics actually produced was a mixture of fire and maneuver equivalent to what the chasseur school and Lieutenant Colonel William J. Hardee, its innovative American proponent, had been trying to give to the infantry. Whereas the chasseurs—light infantry trained for rapid maneuvering—had sought to achieve operational mobility by jogging around the battlefield on foot, the cavalry achieved the same result, more convincingly, on horseback.

The chasseurs also stressed marksmanship—accurate, well-placed shots—whereas in the cavalry the idea was to create a rapid-fire barrage, however inaccurate. The two concepts were admittedly rather different, but the hope was to create a similar result. The cavalry was simply lucky—chance placed in their hands an exceptionally fine weapon, the carbine, that molded the way they used firepower.

Finally, the chasseurs had hoped to close with the bayonet and destroy a shaken opponent in a melee with that arme blanche. There is today a distinctly patriotic flavor to the widespread denigration of the thrusting weapon as an alternative to modern firearms. American writers on the Civil War have formed a solid front against cold steel. We read that "any saber was culturally alien to most Americans" (although not, apparently, to their West Point–trained officers), while in many cavalry units it almost became a mark of frontiersman status to do without it. The same, to an even greater extent, can be said of the bayonet.

Despite early doubts about this aspect of their role, the cavalry came to accept it. Typically a regiment kept back a mounted reserve of about a quarter of its numbers, ready to charge when the moment was right. In these circumstances the saber charge was found useful. Regiments that disliked the saber used the Colt revolver charge to much the same effect.

These tactics were a mixture of true cavalry action in the mounted charge and "mounted infantry" action in the preparatory fighting on foot. It might have been possible to achieve a similar effect in the major battles by attaching a mounted company to each infantry regiment, creating an organic link between the two arms in order to draw the best from each.

This had actually been tried in some of the early "legions" formed in 1861, but as with so many other tactical experiments in the Civil War, it was not centrally directed or sustained. The cavalry and the infantry remained two separate and jealously independent services, and usually did not cooperate as closely as ideal low-level tactics demanded.

There were, of course, exceptions, particularly in small-unit vanguard or rearguard skirmishing. Samuel Baron's last fight in the 3rd Texas Cavalry seems to have been a model of the kind. It was a rearguard ambush of a Union column marching up a road across a creek. A Confederate infantry regiment lined the creek, concealed by heavy mist. When the enemy came close, the infantry opened the action and then the Texas cavalry charged in column from behind, pressing the enemy back two or three miles.

If cavalry more usually had to provide its own "infantry" to prepare its charges, it did at least enjoy close cooperation with horse artillery. Some of the most daring and aggressive artillerists came from this service, which naturally stressed mobility and opportunism. It was also a dangerous service, since the artillery was often expected to operate in small detachments very close to the enemy's cavalry scouts, where it could easily become involved in skirmishing. Indeed, cavalry generally posed a greater threat to artillery than did infantry, since it could charge to close quarters more rapidly. The large numbers of guns changing hands at the all-cavalry Battle of Brandy Station seem to make the point.

When cavalry was well armed with repeaters and horse artillery, and prepared to fight either on foot or mounted, it could perform all the functions of an all-arms force. In effect it could do without infantry altogether, thus turning on its head the prewar prediction that "infantry would make cavalry obsolete." The primary disadvantage of such a force was that it was enormously expensive, requiring a much greater "tail"—with its foragers and horse holders—than would otherwise have been needed. Another disadvantage was that cavalry formations could put far fewer men into the firing line than could infantry formations at a comparable level of command, and these men would tend to feel themselves rather lightly supported. Their forte would lie in staking claims and making rapid assaults rather than in the formal, heavy-duty combat of a set-piece battle. In this respect they might well be compared with the airborne infantry of more recent times.

Nevertheless, it was precisely in the area of staking claims and making rapid assaults off the line of march that most Civil War armies were deficient. Few commanders used their infantry as "foot cavalry" to hit the enemy at unexpected times and places, to hustle him away from key points before he had settled into his positions. This may have been a major reason for the apparent indecisiveness of Civil War battles as a whole. If there had been a few more Stonewall Jacksons to control the march maneuvers, the war might have been more quickly decided.

By the time the cavalry had come to understand its new role as an all-arms force, the need for foot cavalry was chronic. In the Wilderness campaign, Grant's infantry had suffered the heartbreaking ordeal of performing a sustained series of rapid marches around Lee's right flank, only to find that the Confederates had anticipated them and adjusted their positions each time. Fatigue and deep mud made it impossible for the Union maneuvers to reach their objectives before countermeasures were taken, and the result was a futile sequence of parallel battles leading to the siege of Petersburg itself. The failure to move an all-arms force around Lee's flank meant that Grant was condemned to suffer heavy casualties for no significant gain. He was forced to give up the attempt and settle down to ten months of siege.

By 1865, however, General Philip Sheridan was at hand with a powerful and well-indoctrinated cavalry force, which could be used as a flanking spearhead of precisely the type the infantry had shown itself unable to provide in 1864. In the Appomattox campaign this cavalry gave a classic demonstration of what could be done. But credit for the conception must go to Sheridan himself, who resisted Grant's habitual preference to send the cavalry off on an independent raid. Sheridan insisted it be kept with the Army of the Potomac and used for a truly decisive purpose. He saw his role as prolonging the army's left flank to force Lee to abandon his positions at Petersburg and Richmond, rather than simply making a sweep in the bad old way to tear up a few miles of railroad.

Ironically, the operation started badly because the cavalry corps was itself outflanked and surprised by a fast-marching all-arms force under the ill-starred General George Pickett. Sheridan suffered a setback at Dinwiddie Courthouse on March 29–31, 1865, but was eventually able to stabilize a line and call up reinforcements to crush Pickett's open flank in a fluid encounter battle. These reinforcements were already involved in a battle of their own on the White Oak Road, however, and failed to intervene before Pickett had made good his escape to previously prepared positions at Five Forks. Sheridan's opponents claim the whole sequence was an unfortunate diversion from the main business of crushing Lee's army in the White Oak Road battle, where an outright victory could have been won if the cavalry had not upset the infantry's operations. This may be true; but similar infantry operations had failed so often that there was ample justification for the decision to try a different approach this time.

What followed at Five Oaks was in any case a magnificent feat by any standards. Sheridan pinned Pickett's men frontally with his cavalry while General Gouverneur Warren's infantry executed a flank attack worthy of Frederick the Great. Despite the difficulties of terrain, of command liaison, and of Confederate fieldworks, the position was carried and 6,000 prisoners were captured. Admittedly, the cavalry attacks had been repulsed until infantry unzipped the position from the side, but it undoubtedly made a great contribution to the final success by its frontal demonstrations and sacrifices. Many of the cavalry units fired off all their ammunition and sustained heavy casualties, but Southern hopes were even more severely damaged.

Next came a race to Jeetersville Station. The Union cavalry won the race and established a blocking position there, heading off the Confederates toward the west. In the ensuing scramble, the cavalry once again proved they could outmarch the enemy's infantry. General George Custer cut off a third of Lee's shrinking army at Sayler's Creek on April 6–7, 1865, and, when infantry supports arrived, captured some 10,000 prisoners. In this battle the cavalry repeated the achievement of Napoleon's cuirassiers at Borodino when they carried a line of enemy breastworks by a mounted charge.

The Confederate cavalry was badly outnumbered and outgunned in this campaign, but it usually managed to extricate itself from the traps in which its infantry was ensnared. It continued an active and technically impressive resistance right to the end—indeed, the last man killed in the Army of Northern Virginia was a cavalryman.

The end, however, was not long in coming. A new race was won by Custer and Sheridan, this time to the four fat supply trains waiting for Lee at Appomattox Station. The Confederates once again found themselves confronted by a defiant line of Spencer carbines backed by counter-charging mounted troops. Their first attempts to break out to the west were again unsuccessful, and by the time they organized a major assault with heavy supports, it was too late—the Union cavalry had been stiffened by a strong force of infantry.

The Appomattox campaign does not show us that a battle group of cavalry, even when armed with repeating carbines, could overcome all obstacles. Admittedly, there had been some impressive assaults, both on foot and mounted, in which the rapid fire of the new weapons shocked the opposition and covered the troopers as they advanced. Some commentators have seen this tactic as the forerunner of the twentieth-century concept of "marching fire" or "assault fire." Yet the rapid-fire weapons also ran out of ammunition more rapidly than the slower rifle muskets, and Sheridan's men were repeatedly told not to waste their rounds. Conversely, the new carbines suffered from various technical teething problems, especially in the rimfire ammunition itself. (This was ammunition on which the ignition cap encircled the entire casing.) As a result, the volume of fire that could be developed in action fell far short of expectations. For example, in one intense firefight in May 1864, the 1st Pennsylvania Cavalry managed to fire only twelve to eighteen rounds per man per hour, which was theoretically the volume of fire they should have been able to produce in just one minute.

In the Appomattox campaign there were some failures that showed mounted infantry was not the "panacea weapon" its champions believed it was. At Dinwiddie Courthouse, Sheridan was badly mauled by Pickett's shrewd blow, and at Five Forks the cavalry could make no headway against fieldworks. At Jeetersville, Sayler's Creek, and Appomattox itself, the cavalry's resistance probably would have been overcome if infantry reinforcements had not arrived in time. Possessing technically advanced small arms did not ensure victory against all odds.

What the Appomattox campaign did show us, however, was that cavalry could add considerable extra zest and impetus to the normal operations of infantry. The high mobility of horsemen allowed them extra freedom on the battlefield, unsettling any Civil War commander accustomed only to the sedate evolutions of foot soldiers. Even if they did not arrive at the key point with the "mostest" combat power, the cavalry could at least get there "fustest." This made a magnificent multiplier of the infantry's natural force, so that when used in conjunction the two arms became far more formidable than either had been on its own.

It is greatly to Sheridan's credit that he was quick to understand this and pressed his ideas upon his more traditionally minded superiors. It is greatly to the discredit of many other Civil War commanders that it took so long for the all-arms battle group to enter their tactical thinking.

*SPRING 1989*

A free-lance author and publisher, Paddy Griffith is the author of *Battle Tactics of the Civil War* (1989). He is currently working on a study of the Viking art of war.

# 14

# The Fiery Trail of the *Alabama*

## By John M. Taylor

*The Confederate raider* Alabama, *an exceptionally fast steam- and sail-powered warship built in Great Britain, made her first kill in September 1862, when she burned and sank the Union whaler* Ocmulgee. *In the twenty-two months before the* Alabama, *in turn, became the victim of the Union warship* Kearsarge *off Cherbourg in June 1864, she destroyed or captured sixty-five Northern merchant ships. Although Alfred Thayer Mahan would later argue that a commerce-raiding strategy cannot be decisive in war—and indeed the* Alabama, *despite her success, was not— the saga of this Confederate ship touched the future. It would be difficult to read of the* Alabama *putting out from Cherbourg harbor, with the holiday-mood spectators on shore or in small ships straining to see the coming spectacle, and not to think of that December day in 1939 when the German Graf Spee put out from Montevideo to face the* Ajax, Achilles, *and* Cumberland. *And, of much greater significance, the commerce-raiding strategy so brilliantly carried out by the* Alabama *would return in the deadly guise of the submarine almost to defeat Great Britain in two world wars and help to destroy Japan in one.*

Workers in the John Laird Shipyard at Birkenhead, near Liverpool, watched attentively on the morning of May 15, 1862, as a handsome steam bark slid into the waters of the Mersey River. The vessel was known to them as No. 290, for hers was the 290th keel laid at the Laird yards. Upon launching, she was named the *Enrica*, but the identity of her owners remained a subject of speculation, for she was being built to the specifications of a Royal Navy cruiser. As May turned into June, the new vessel sprouted three tall masts that would enable her to carry a broad spread of canvas, and took on two 300-horsepower engines for steam propulsion.

In the waterfront bars of Liverpool, it was said with a wink that the actual purchaser of the *Enrica* was the Southern Confederacy, then locked in a war to establish its independence from the United States. For once, the tipsters were right on the mark. The possibility that No. 290 was destined for the Confederacy had not been lost on the U.S. minister in London, Charles Francis Adams, who was bombarding the Foreign Office with demands that the ship be seized. By mid-July, James Bulloch, the adroit Confederate naval agent who had supervised construction of the *Enrica* for the government in Richmond, knew that time was growing short.

The ever-imaginative Bulloch arranged for the *Enrica*'s departure from England in the guise of a gala trial run. On the fine morning of July 29, the new bark sailed down the Mersey with local dignitaries on board. At dusk, however, Bulloch and his guests returned to Liverpool on a tugboat, leaving the *Enrica* off the coast of Wales at Moelfra Bay. British authorities had in fact been attempting to detain the *Enrica,* and Bulloch had thwarted them by the narrowest of margins.

On Sunday, August 10, the *Enrica* arrived at the island of Terceira in the Azores. Eight days later the *Agrippina,* a tender under charter to Bulloch, showed up with equipment for the Confederate cruiser, including a 100-pound Blakely rifle, an eight-inch smoothbore, six thirty-two-pounders, and provisions. That afternoon a second vessel, the *Bahama,* arrived with officers and hands for the new vessel. Thanks to Bulloch, the complicated logistics of equipping and manning a cruiser outside British waters were carried out without a hitch. On Sunday, August 24, in the presence of the crews of the *Enrica* and the *Bahama,* the Union Jack fluttered down from the mainmast and was replaced by the naval ensign of the Confederacy. A band played "Dixie," and the mystery ship was officially christened the Confederate steamer *Alabama.*

The cruiser's designated commander was fifty-two-year-old Raphael Semmes, a Maryland native who had taken up residence in Alabama. Semmes had entered the U.S. Navy in 1832 and by 1861 had achieved the rank of commander. He was widely read in naval history and marine law and had written several books, including a lively narrative of his naval service during the Mexican War. A strong advocate of states' rights, Semmes had resigned his Federal commission even before the firing on Fort Sumter.

In April 1861, Confederate secretary of the navy Stephen Mallory gave Semmes command of one of the South's first warships, the 437-ton screw steamer *Sumter*. The *Sumter* and her more powerful successors were intended to tackle one of two missions that Mallory had established for the Confederate navy: to attack the North's merchant marine, so as to increase the cost of the war to the enemy and thus encourage Lincoln to acknowledge Southern independence. The navy's other mission—to construct a fleet of ironclads capable of breaking the Federal blockade—was beyond Confederate capabilities, but the first was not.

It had taken Semmes about two months to convert the *Sumter* into a warship, but he assembled a nucleus of able officers—no mean feat in the agrarian South, with its limited seafaring tradition. The *Sumter* broke the Federal blockade off New Orleans on June 30, 1861, and reached the open sea. Thereafter, during a six-month cruise, the little raider burned eight

Northern ships and released ten others on bond—a procedure under which the owners of an American ship's neutral cargo were expected to reimburse the Confederacy for goods not destroyed.

Eventually, boiler problems and a need for coal obliged the *Sumter* to call at Gibraltar. There she was blockaded by three Federal warships, with no prospect of escape. Having made the most of his ship's limited capabilities, Semmes directed that the *Sumter* be sold, and set out to Britain with most of his officers. There, to the disappointment of Bulloch, who had hoped for the command, Semmes was given the far more powerful *Alabama.*

Semmes's first challenge in the Azores was to persuade enough British sailors to sign aboard the *Alabama* so that he could take his new command to sea. He assured the hands of the *Alabama* and the *Bahama* that they were free to return to Britain if they chose, but he painted a glowing picture of life aboard the *Alabama.* He offered good pay—£4 10s. a month in gold for seamen, and £7 for firemen—plus grog twice a day and the prospect of prize money. He touched only briefly on the issues of the American war, but promised excitement and adventure. To his relief, he was able to sign on eighty British crewmen—enough to take the *Alabama* to sea. As time went on, he would supplement this nucleus with recruits from captured vessels.

Once Semmes had his officers and crew, he turned his attention to his ship. The *Alabama* represented the zenith of a hybrid marine form: ships powered by both sail and steam. She measured 220 feet in length, had a beam of 32 feet, and displaced 1,040 tons. She carried enough coal for eighteen days' steaming and had an innovation found on few ships of her day—a condenser that provided a gallon of fresh water per day for each man on board, enabling her to remain at sea for extended periods. Her two-bladed screw could be raised into a well when she was under sail, thus posing no drag in the water. She could make about twelve knots under sail alone, to which her engines could add another three knots. She came with a year's supply of spare gear. In the words of one of her officers, Lieutenant Arthur Sinclair, the *Alabama* "was at the same time a perfect steamer and a perfect sailing vessel, each entirely independent of the other." The ship's armament also was impressive: six thirty-two-pounders and two pivot guns. A visitor to the *Alabama* would comment, "What strikes one most . . . is to see so small a vessel carrying such large metal."

Semmes was under orders to avoid engagements with enemy warships. for his was a special mission. The *Alabama,* as her commander wrote later, "was the first steamship in the history of the world—the defective little *Sumter* excepted—that was let loose against the commerce of a great commercial people." And Semmes set to his mission with a vengeance.

The *Alabama* had been at sea for only ten days when, on September 5, she sighted the first of the sixty-five victims she would claim over the next twenty-two months. The ship was a whaler—the *Ocmulgee,* of Edgartown, Massachusetts—and the capture was easy, for the *Ocmulgee* had a whale lashed alongside when the *Alabama* approached. The raider had been flying the American flag—an accepted ruse in war—and in Semmes's recollection, nothing could exceed the Yankee skipper's "blank stare of astonishment" when the *Alabama* finally ran up the Confederate ensign.

The *Ocmulgee*'s crew was transferred to the *Alabama*, along with some provisions; officers were permitted to bring one trunk with them, others a single bag. Semmes prepared to burn the whaler, but with the guile that would become his trademark, he waited until daylight: Whalers operated in clusters, and he did not want to scatter them with an unexplained fire at night.

The *Alabama* spent two months in the Azores, burning eight vessels in all. The American whaling fleet—or what was left of it—returned to its home ports in New England, where shipowners filled the Northern press with tales of the "pirate" Semmes. The *Alabama*, too, worked her way westward. Semmes briefly considered throwing a few shells into New York City, but he thought better of it and instead seized several grain carriers off the Newfoundland banks.

The *Alabama*'s captures followed a pattern. The raider would hail a ship on sight. If she did not heave to, Semmes would fire a blank cartridge. If she still failed to respond, he would send a shot from a thirty-two-pounder across her bow, and that would bring her to a halt. While the prize was boarded, Semmes stayed in his cabin; the skipper of his victim was taken to him there. Any ship whose papers showed her to be of neutral ownership was released. If she was U.S.–owned, Semmes transferred her crew to the *Alabama*.

For a commerce raider, the *Alabama* operated under an unusual handicap: Because of the Federal blockade, she had no home port to which Semmes might send prizes. He thus had to burn most of the ships he captured. After appropriating any usable provisions, a Rebel boarding party would pile up furniture and mattresses, douse them with lard or some other flammable substance, and fire the ship. Semmes's first officer was another veteran of the "Old Navy," John McIntosh Kell. The tough, red-bearded Kell later wrote:

> To watch the leaping flames on a burning ship gives an indescribable mental excitement that did not decrease with the frequency of the light, but it was always a relief to know the ships were tenantless as they disappeared in the lonely grandeur, specks of vanishing light in the "cradle of the deep."

Between captures, the crew had ample opportunity to take the measure of their skipper. Semmes had just turned fifty-three and was not physically imposing; some thought him past his prime for sea command. His one idiosyncrasy was a carefully cultivated mustache that led his sailors to call him "Old Beeswax," but he was a tough disciplinarian; in his postwar memoir he outlined his command philosophy:

> On week days . . . about one fourth of the crew was exercised, either at the battery or with small arms. This not only gave them efficiency in the use of their weapons, but kept them employed—the constant employment of my men being a fundamental article of my philosophy. . . . My crew were never so happy as when they had plenty to do, and but little to think about.

Whatever the hands may have thought of Old Beeswax, Semmes appears to have enjoyed the respect of virtually all his officers. First Officer Kell worshiped his commander. And Lieutenant Sinclair later wrote that "Semmes [understood] just how to keep himself near the hearts and in the confidence of his men, without in the slightest degree descending from his dignity, or permitting direct approach." Semmes also impressed everyone with his professionalism. He was a student of every facet of seamanship—he digresses in his memoir to discuss how variations in temperature affect the currents—and he had a childlike wonder at the natural beauty of the sea.

Probably only Kell glimpsed the virulent hatred that Semmes nourished for his enemy, the Yankees. Of them Semmes had written in his journal, "A people so devoid of Christian charity, and wanting in so many of the essentials of honesty, cannot be abandoned to their own folly by a just and benevolent God." Yet not even his loathing for Northerners as a class could totally destroy his admiration for them as seamen, and as the war went on, the task of burning their ships became less satisfying to him.

Semmes dealt with his prisoners as humanely as conditions permitted. Captured crews were usually housed on deck but were afforded some protection from the elements. When the prisoners included women passengers, Semmes's officers turned over the wardroom for their use. Prisoners received full rations, and cooks among their number had access to the *Alabama*'s galley. Officers were occasionally placed in irons, generally after Semmes had heard reports of mistreatment of Confederate prisoners. Because prisoners were a nuisance, Semmes got rid of them as fast as possible. Sometimes he landed them at a neutral port, but more often he transferred them to a captured ship whose cargo he had bonded.

From Newfoundland the raider worked her way south to Martinique, where, on their first liberty, crewmen got so drunk that Semmes put some twenty sailors in irons. The incident was a reminder that while the *Alabama*'s officers were reliable seamen, committed to the Confederate cause, most of the British crewmen were not. Much as the duke of Wellington once called his army the scum of the earth, Semmes called his crew

> a precious set of rascals . . . faithless in . . . contracts, liars, thieves, and drunkards. There are . . . exceptions to this rule, but I am ashamed to say of the sailor class of the present day that I believe my crew to be a fair representation of it.

Kell, who supervised the boarding of every prize, had a firm rule that no member of the *Alabama*'s crew could board a captured vessel until any supply of spirits was thrown overboard. Even so, he and Semmes were constantly on the alert for smuggled liquor.

Semmes had passed up the temptation to show his flag off New York City the previous fall, but in the Caribbean he was inclined to stretch his orders and play a role in the ground campaign along the Texas coast. A Federal force under General Nathaniel P. Banks had captured Galveston in October 1862. Confederate forces had subsequently recaptured Galveston, but the city was blockaded by five Federal warships when the black-hulled *Alabama* arrived there on January 11, 1863.

Semmes considered his options. The city that he had contemplated bombarding was now in friendly hands, and he could hardly take on five enemy warships. While he deliberated, the Federals detached one of their fleet, the gunboat *Hatteras,* to check out the new arrival. It was a fatal error. Semmes set out toward open water, steaming slowly, luring his pursuer away from the other Federal warships.

Night had fallen by the time the *Hatteras* reached shouting distance of the *Alabama,* and Semmes, in reply to a hail from the Yankee, identified his ship as HMS *Petrel.* While the Federal captain dispatched a boat to check out his story, Semmes ran up the Confederate ensign and loosed a broadside at point-blank range.

The *Hatteras* was an underpowered side-wheeler that had no business engaging the powerful *Alabama.* The U.S. gunboat struck her flag after an exchange that lasted only thirteen minutes; a few minutes later she sank in the shallow waters of the gulf. Two of her crew had been killed and three wounded. Semmes rescued the survivors and set course for the Atlantic.

The *Alabama* stopped at Jamaica, where Semmes paroled his prisoners and partook of the hospitality that he would encounter in British possessions throughout the *Alabama*'s two-year cruise. Then he turned his ship southeast around Brazil to work the heavily traveled trade routes of the South Atlantic. Four more ships were stopped and burned in the first weeks of 1863, raising the *Alabama*'s total to thirty.

However, coaling the raider was proving to be a problem. She still had the services of the *Agrippina* as a tender, but it was difficult for Semmes to anticipate every supply requirement, and he had little confidence in the master of the *Agrippina.* In southern latitudes, moreover, coal tended to be scarce as well as expensive. Fortunately for Semmes, he had a generous supply of gold for payment of ship's bills in remote corners of the world.

In June 1863, off the coast of South America, Semmes captured the U.S. clipper *Conrad,* bound for New York with wool from Argentina. He had been waiting for such a prize, and rather than burning her, he commissioned her as a Confederate cruiser, the *Tuscaloosa,* arming her with guns captured from another ship. This was one more example of Semmes's creative approach to commerce raiding; but the *Tuscaloosa* had little success as a raider.

From South America, Semmes set sail for the Cape of Good Hope. In August 1863 the *Alabama* reached Cape Town, where Semmes supervised some badly needed repairs on his ship. The Confederate commander found himself a celebrity in the British colony, in part because his latest seizure— the *Sea Bride,* from Boston—had been within sight of the cape. As in Jamaica, the *Alabama*'s officers were exhaustively entertained. Semmes held a shipboard "open house" that produced, in his view, "a generous outpouring of the better classes." He also came within a day of encountering a Federal warship that had been dogging his trail, a well-armed paddle-wheeler, the *Vanderbilt.*

For all the outrage in the Northern press concerning the *Alabama*'s depredations, pursuit of the raider was disorganized and ineffectual. This was partly deliberate. The Confederacy never had more than a handful of commerce raiders at sea, and of these only the *Florida*—commissioned around the same time as the *Alabama* and destined to destroy thirty-eight ships—was in the *Alabama's* class. The Lincoln administration regarded the maintenance and strengthening of the blockade of Southern ports as its first priority; it was not willing to weaken the blockade to track down the *Alabama,* the *Florida,* or one of their lesser consorts.

Even making allowances, however, Federal pursuit of the *Alabama* showed little imagination. The U.S. Navy dogged Semmes's trail as if convinced that the raider would remain in the area of its most recent capture. Semmes later wrote that had Navy Secretary Gideon Welles stationed a heavier and faster ship than the *Alabama* along two or three of the most traveled sea-lanes, "he must have driven me off, or greatly crippled me in my movements."

From Cape Town, the *Alabama* worked her way eastward across the Indian Ocean. There, most of the ships encountered proved to be neutral, and friendly captains warned Semmes that the Federals had a warship, the *Wyoming,* patrolling the Sunda Strait between Sumatra and Java. Nevertheless, Semmes seized and burned a New York clipper, the *Winged Racer,* off Java, and set off in pursuit of another, the *Contest,* the following morning.

The pursuit of the *Contest* proved to be an omen. For the first time, the *Alabama,* employing both sail and steam, was initially unable to overtake her prey. But the sun rose higher, the morning breeze died, and the Confederate raider eventually closed in. The *Contest* was burned—not without regret, for several of the *Alabama's* officers vowed that they had never seen a more beautiful vessel. Only the failing wind had enabled the *Alabama* to make the capture, however, and Semmes realized that eighteen months at sea had taken a toll on his ship.

On December 21, 1863, the *Alabama* anchored at Singapore. There Semmes saw new evidence of the effectiveness of his campaign: Singapore harbor was filled with U.S. ships that had taken refuge there rather than chance an encounter with the *Alabama.* Within days of her arrival, about half of these were sold to neutral nations and flew new flags. The *Straits Times* estimated that Singapore was playing host to some seventeen American vessels aggregating 12,000 tons, some of which had "been lying there for upwards of three months and most of them for at least half that period."

On Christmas Eve 1863, the *Alabama* set course westward. Pickings were predictably slim, but the crewmen had their hands full with their own ship. The raider's boilers were operating at reduced efficiency, and some of her timbers were split beyond repair. First Officer Kell observed that the *Alabama* was "loose at every joint, her seams were open, and the copper on her bottom was in rolls." For all of Semmes's skill at improvisation, nothing but a month in dry dock could restore the raider to fighting trim.

By early March the *Alabama* was again off Cape Town, but because a belligerent vessel could provision at the same neutral port only once in a three-month period, she had to pass ten days offshore before docking. After coaling at Cape Town, Semmes turned northward. He intended to put his ship into dry dock in France, but he must have realized that the time necessary for repairs made it likely that the *Alabama* would be blockaded in port as the *Sumter* had been.

On April 22 the raider made the second of only three captures during 1864: the *Rockingham,* carrying a cargo of guano from Peru to Ireland. After the crew was taken off, Semmes directed that the prize be used for target practice—the raider's first live gun drill in many months. Sinclair later recalled that the sea was smooth and that the gun crews "amused themselves blithely" at point-blank range. Semmes thought his gun crews fired "to good effect," but Kell was less impressed: Of twenty-four rounds fired, only seven were seen to inflict damage. Ultimately, Semmes had to burn the *Rockingham.*

On April 27 the *Alabama* made her final capture, the *Tycoon,* out of New York with a mixed cargo. Semmes burned the Yankee vessel and resumed his northward course. He later wrote:

> The poor old *Alabama* was . . . like the wearied fox-hound, limping back after a long chase. . . . Her commander, like herself, was well-nigh worn down. Vigils by night and by day . . . had laid, in the three years of war he had been afloat, a load of a dozen years on his shoulders. The shadows of a sorrowful future, too, began to rest upon his spirit. The last batch of newspapers captured were full of disasters. Might it not be that, after all our trials and sacrifices, the cause for which we were struggling would be lost?

On June 11, 1864, the *Alabama* docked at the French port of Cherbourg. Word of her arrival was telegraphed all over Europe, and three days later the U.S. Navy ship *Kearsarge* appeared off the breakwater. Semmes had not yet received permission to make repairs at the French navy docks at Cherbourg, but he was allowed to disembark his prisoners and take on coal.

The Confederate commander faced a crucial decision. He knew his ship needed a refit, and he probably realized that the prudent course would be to do as he had with the *Sumter:* put her up for sale and fight another day. But his fighting blood was up, and he had no great respect for his enemies. Nor was he inclined to solicit recommendations from his officers; as skipper of the *Sumter* and then the *Alabama,* he was accustomed to making his own decisions. Shortly after the *Kearsarge* appeared, he called Kell to his cabin and explained his intentions:

> As you know, the arrival of the *Alabama* at this port has been telegraphed to all parts of Europe. Within a few days, Cherbourg will be effectively blockaded by Yankee cruisers. It is uncertain whether or not we shall be permitted to repair the *Alabama* here, and in the meantime, the delay is to our advantage. I think we may whip the *Kearsarge,* the two vessels being of wood and carrying about

the same number of men and guns. Besides, Mr. Kell, although the Confederate States government has ordered me to avoid engagements with the enemy's cruisers, I am tired of running from that flaunting rag!

Kell was not sure the decision to fight was wise. He reminded Semmes that in the *Rockingham* gun drill only one in three fuses had seemed effective. But Semmes was not to be deterred. He sent a message to Captain John A. Winslow of the *Kearsarge,* whom he had known in the Old Navy: He intended to fight.

Sunday, June 19, 1864, was a bright, cloudless day off Cherbourg. Aboard the *Alabama,* boilers were fired at daybreak, and Semmes inspected his crew at muster. Decks and brasswork were immaculate, and the crewmen were dressed in blue trousers and white tops. By 9:45 the cruiser was under way, cheered on by the crews of two French warships in the harbor.

The clash between the *Alabama* and the *Kearsarge* was, among other things, pure theater. It seemed that everyone in France wanted to watch what would prove to be the last one-on-one duel of the era of wooden ships. Excursion trains brought the curious, and throngs of small craft hovered outside the breakwater. Painter Edouard Manet, with brushes, paints, and easel, was on one of them.

The two ships were almost equal in size and armament. Both were hybrid steamers of about the same tonnage. The *Alabama* carried 149 crewmen and mounted eight guns; the *Kearsarge* had a crew of 163 and mounted seven guns. The outcome of the battle would depend largely on the skill of the gun crews and the condition of the ships, but the *Kearsarge* had an ace in the hole: The enterprising Winslow had made imaginative use of his ship's chains, draping them along vulnerable parts of the hull as impromptu armor and concealing them behind wood paneling. Semmes later denied knowledge of the chains, but there is evidence that he was warned about it.

After the *Alabama* entered the English Channel, Semmes steered directly for his antagonist, some four miles away. He rotated his two pivot guns to starboard and prepared to engage the enemy on that side. The *Alabama* opened fire at about 11:00 A.M., and soon both ships were exchanging shots from their starboard batteries. The *Kearsarge* sought to run under the *Alabama*'s stern, but Semmes parried this move by turning to starboard.

The two antagonists thus fought on a circular track, much of the time at a range of about 500 yards. They made seven complete circles during the course of the action, reminding one Northern sailor of "two flies crawling around on the rim of a saucer." Semmes may initially have wanted to put his ship alongside the *Kearsarge* for boarding, but the Yankee's greater speed ruled out this option.

From the first, the firing from the *Alabama* was rapid and wild. The Confederate cruiser fired more than 300 rounds, only 28 of which struck the *Kearsarge,* many of them in the rigging. In their excitement, the *Alabama*'s gunners fired some shot without removing the caps on their fuses—preventing them from exploding—and in other cases fired ramrods as well. It was not a disciplined performance. One of the *Alabama*'s crew conceded that the Confederate batteries were badly served: "The men all fought well, but the gunners did not know how to point and elevate the guns." In addition, the dark smoke emitted by the *Alabama*'s guns lent credence to Kell's fear that the raider's powder had deteriorated.

In contrast, Winslow and his crew fought with disciplined professionalism. Kell later conceded that the Yankee guns were "aimed with precision, and deliberate in fire."

"The firing now became very hot," Semmes related, "and . . . soon began to tell upon our hull, knocking down, killing and disabling a number of men . . . in different parts of the ship." Semmes ordered his gunners to use solid shot as well as shell, but to no effect. Meanwhile, the *Alabama*'s rudder was destroyed, forcing the Confederates to steer with tackles. In desperation, Semmes offered a reward to anyone who could put the *Kearsarge*'s forward pivot gun out of action.

Sinclair recalled how an eleven-inch shell from that weapon entered the *Alabama* at the waterline and exploded in the engine room, "in its passage throwing a volume of water on board, hiding for a moment the guns of [my] division." With his fires out, Semmes attempted to steer for land, only to have the *Kearsarge* station herself between the *Alabama* and the coast.

Shortly after noon, Semmes gave the order to abandon ship. The *Alabama* had suffered only nine killed in the battle, but some twenty others, including Semmes, had been wounded; twelve more would be drowned. Semmes and Kell, along with about forty others of the *Alabama*'s complement, had the good fortune to be rescued from the water by a British yacht, the *Deerhound*, which took them to England rather than turn them over to the *Kearsarge*. Seventy more were picked up by the *Kearsarge*, and another fifteen by excursion boats.

Semmes was lionized in England—British admirers replaced the sword that he had cast into the English Channel—but he was bitter over the loss of his ship, blaming the debacle on his defective powder and the *Kearsarge*'s protective chains. In point of fact, the battle off Cherbourg was the Civil War in microcosm: the gallant but outgunned South, ignoring its own shortcomings, heedlessly taking on a superior force.

During her twenty-two months at sea, the *Alabama* had burned fifty-four Federal merchant ships and had bonded ten others. When, after the war, British and U.S. negotiators determined that Britain owed the United States a total of $15.5 million for damage caused by ships sold to the Confederacy, the amount charged to the *Alabama*—$6.75 million—was much the highest. In addition to her remarkable toll in merchant shipping, the *Alabama* had sunk an enemy gunboat, the luckless *Hatteras*, and had brought untold embarrassment to the Federal navy. Semmes's record with the *Alabama* would not be approached by any raider in modern times.

Yet the raider's influence on the outcome of the Civil War was almost imperceptible. Its toll, however remarkable, represented only about 5 percent of U.S. shipping; the bulk of the U.S. merchant fleet stayed in port, transferred to neutral flags, or took their chances on the high seas. After all, the Confederacy's three or four commerce raiders could not be everywhere. Soaring rates for marine insurance added to the North's cost of waging war, but such economic damage was insignificant alongside the cost of the ground fighting in terms of either lives or matériel. The Northern states—economically self-sufficient—could ignore the depredations of Confederate raiders.

After the war, Semmes suggested that the North at first could not comprehend the threat posed by Confederate commerce destroyers. Yet when the threat materialized, he noted ruefully, the North was "too deeply engaged in the contest to heed it."

By the summer of 1864, there was no possibility of a replacement for the *Alabama,* and Semmes could have lived out the war comfortably in England. Instead, he made his way back to the Confederacy by way of Cuba and Mexico. In Richmond he was promoted to admiral and assigned to the command of the James River squadron in Virginia. Following the evacuation of Richmond, he burned his boats and formed his men into a naval brigade that served under General Joseph E. Johnston in the final weeks of the war. After the war Semmes was briefly under arrest, but he was never brought to trial and supported himself with a small law practice until his death in 1877.

Raphael Semmes was not the first commerce raider in the history of naval warfare, but he was the first to operate in the age of steam and he may have been the best of all time. Notwithstanding the unavailability of any home port, he managed to keep a wooden ship at sea for nearly two years without an overhaul and without losing either a crewman or a prisoner to disease. As a strategist, he demonstrated that a nation with a weak navy could nevertheless inflict great damage on any foe with a substantial merchant fleet. It is hardly surprising that Kaiser Wilhelm II made Semmes's postwar memoirs required reading for his admirals. In both world wars, German submarine and surface raiders would refine the qualities of speed, surprise, and endurance demonstrated by the *Alabama,* but with little of Semmes's regard for the lives of prisoners and crew.

In taking on the *Kearsarge,* however, Semmes had let his emotions control his judgment. His gun crews were insufficiently trained, he underestimated the enemy, and he committed a cardinal sin: He didn't keep his powder dry.

*Summer 1991*

---

John M. Taylor, who spent his early career with agencies of the United States government, is the author of *William Henry Seward: Lincoln's Right Hand* (1991). His most recent book is *Confederate Raider: Raphael Semmes of the Alabama* (1994).

# 15

# The Second Surrender

## By John M. Taylor

*On April 9, 1865, General Robert E. Lee surrendered his army to General Ulysses S. Grant at the McLean house in the Virginia town of Appomattox Court House. Although most Americans remember this surrender as the official end of the Civil War, it was not. Confederate president Jefferson Davis refused to surrender. Instead, he counseled continued resistance and proclaimed that the South would "meet the foe with fresh defiance." Nor was the Confederacy totally without arms, for other Confederate armies than Lee's still remained in the field, including the 30,000-man force under General Joseph E. Johnston in North Carolina. Johnston, however, refused to follow Davis's lead, arguing that surrender was imperative; further resistance would only destroy the South. Though not as well remembered as the events at Appomattox, Johnston's surrender to Sherman at the Bennitt farm, near the North Carolina town of Hillsboro, played an essential and healing role in concluding America's bloodiest war.*

On a spring day in 1865, an unscheduled train chuffed into the depot at Greensboro, North Carolina. The peaceful town of 2,000, all but ignored during four years of civil war, found itself a reluctant host to what remained of the government of the Confederacy. Aboard the train, which had left Danville, Virginia, twelve hours before, were President Jefferson Davis and most of his Cabinet. A second train carried a considerable cargo of Confederate gold.

Richmond had fallen on April 3. With Confederate currency now all but worthless, the ladies of the former capital were reduced to selling pastry to the Yankees in order to secure bread for their own tables. Six days later, on April 9, Robert E. Lee's Army of Northern Virginia had surrendered at Appomattox. Lee told a group of his soldiers, "I have done my best for you. My heart is too full to say more."

In the South as in the North, the fall of Richmond and the surrender by Lee were seen as signaling an end to a war that had killed more than 600,000 people and entailed total casualties of more than 1 million.

Suggestions that the war might not be over were unpopular, and the reception accorded the Davis party at Greensboro was cool. One young Confederate soldier, eyeing the decrepit train that had brought Davis south from Richmond, characterized the president and his retinue as "a government on wheels . . . the marvelous and incongruous debris of the wreck of the Confederate capital."

Spring had come to North Carolina, but there was war-weariness everywhere. In Greensboro there was also fear—fear of economic collapse, fear of the embittered parolees from Lee's army who were filtering into the town, and, most of all, fear of Sherman. Sherman's Yankee army was approaching, and nothing the South could do seemed even to slow his advance.

One person for whom the war was not over was Jefferson Davis. Four years of war had left the Confederate president pale and wan, afflicted with insomnia and a variety of other ailments. But the fifty-six-year-old Mississippian was no less convinced of the justice of his cause in 1865 than he had been four years before. From Danville he had issued yet another call to arms. "We have now entered upon a new phase of the struggle," he proclaimed. "Relieved from the necessity of guarding particular points, our army will be free to move from point to point to strike the enemy. . . .

"Let us not despond then, my countrymen; but, relying on God, meet the foe with fresh defiance and . . . unconquerable hearts."

Defiance was in short supply in the Confederacy, but had Davis chosen to do so, be might have cited some numbers. Joseph E. Johnston, commanding the only Confederate force of any size in the East, still had some 30,000 men. In Mississippi and Alabama, General Richard Taylor had perhaps 20,000 more. And across the Mississippi lay Davis's main hope, a scattered force of 40,000, mostly in Texas, commanded by General Edmund Kirby Smith. Any wishful thinking based on these numbers, however, overlooked several pertinent facts. One was that Federal forces included a million men under arms with whom to confront the remaining Confederates. Another was that Sherman's army, totaling about 80,000 effectives, was close by, threatening to end all meaningful resistance east of the Mississippi.

No other name struck such fear into Southern hearts as that of William Tecumseh Sherman. The wiry, red-bearded Ohioan had begun the war in obscurity. Whereas prominent Confederates like Robert E. Lee and Joseph E. Johnston had risen to senior ranks in the Old Army, Sherman was the ex-superintendent of a little-known military academy in Louisiana. In 1861 something resembling a nervous breakdown had almost ended his Civil War career before it began. But Sherman was then assigned to serve under General Ulysses S. Grant in Kentucky. Teamed with Grant, he contributed to the series of Federal triumphs along the Mississippi that cut the Confederacy in two.

Sherman eventually was given an independent command, the Army of the Tennessee. After his augmented force had captured Atlanta in November 1864, he asked for and received permission to cut loose from his supply lines and "march to the sea." In devastating Georgia's economy en route to Savannah, Sherman set the pattern for total war.

"Cump" Sherman was an American original. He made a virtue of simple dress and simple life in the field. His men affectionately called him "Uncle Billy"; he in turn would sometimes stop and talk to groups of soldiers, bantering with them in his gruff, staccato manner. Like Davis, Sherman was something of an insomniac. He could be found in the small hours of the morning pacing his camp, poking a dying fire, visiting pickets.

Sherman hated war but liked soldiers and soldiering. Even though his brother John was a senator from Ohio, Sherman's greatest ire was reserved for politicians and newspaper reporters. He had no strong views on slavery, but had given a great deal of thought to how the war should be prosecuted. He saw the destruction of the Confederate economy as a means of hastening the end of the war, and he had no apology for the devastation his army wreaked. His march to the sea contributed only indirectly to the defeat of Lee's army, but it sapped the morale of the entire Confederacy.

Sherman had done little to control looting while his army was in South Carolina, for he shared his soldiers' animosity toward the state that had for so long been identified with secession. Discipline was tightened somewhat as the army crossed into North Carolina, and personal property was spared in some instances. Nonetheless, army foragers—or "bummers," as they were called—continued to roam the countryside in advance of the regular troops, "requisitioning" supplies. And entire pine forests, tapped for turpentine, were burned by soldiers for sport. The conflagrations were tremendous.

Sherman, at his headquarters near Smithfield, knew that organized Confederate resistance was near an end. But he was eager to see a formal surrender, lest Johnston's army disperse into guerrilla bands that might prolong the fighting indefinitely. In late March, Sherman had attended a conference aboard the gunboat *River Queen*—a meeting that had included President Abraham Lincoln, Grant, and Rear Admiral David Dixon Porter—at which Lincoln had stated his desire to get the rebel armies "back to their homes, at work on their farms and in their shops." Sherman thought he knew the kind of peace that the president had in mind. From Raleigh he wired Secretary of War Edwin Stanton, "I will accept the same terms as General Grant gave General Lee, and be careful not to complicate any points of civil policy."

SHERMAN'S OUTNUMBERED opponent was the makeshift Confederate army of General Joseph E. Johnston. Although Johnston had been unable to obstruct Sherman's march through the Carolinas, he had kept an army in the field and had fought tenacious delaying actions where circumstances permitted. On March 19 at Bentonville, North Carolina, he had thrown his little army against one wing of Sherman's command and had managed to come within an ace of victory.

Joe Johnston was one of the enigmas of the Civil War. The dapper, courtly Virginian made no attempt to mingle with his soldiers, as Sherman did, yet he was perhaps as respected by his men as Robert E. Lee had been by the Army of Northern Virginia. His superiors, however, had difficulties with Johnston. At the outset of the war, Davis had named three other generals, Lee among them, senior to Johnston, despite the fact that Johnston had outranked them in the Old Army. Johnston protested the slight and never forgave Jefferson Davis.

It was Johnston who had confronted Sherman in the campaign for Atlanta, and although the Virginian directed a skillful delaying action, Davis had relieved him in July 1864 for failing to halt the Yankee advance. When Johnston's successors had even worse luck against the rampaging Sherman, the wily Johnston—always formidable in defense—was restored to command. From the time of Lee's surrender, however, Johnston believed that his duty lay in making a decent peace.

At Greensboro, Davis was met by General P.G.T. Beauregard, another senior officer with whom Davis had crossed swords. Beauregard, now second in command to Johnston, had opened the war with the capture of Fort Sumter and a subsequent victory at the First Battle of Manassas. Since then his reputation had been in eclipse. At Greensboro, however, Beauregard greeted Davis cordially. He advised Davis that Johnston would be arriving the following day, April 12, and moved his headquarters, located in a baggage car, to a railroad siding within sight of Davis's train.

At the Cabinet meeting on April 12, Davis proposed re-forming the Army of Virginia, apparently ignoring the fact that the paroles granted to Lee's soldiers were conditioned on their not bearing arms against the Union. Johnston heard the president out in disdainful silence, and when he spoke it was in a tone of rebuke. In Johnston's view, the South now lacked both money and munitions, and to protract the war would be a crime. "The effect of our keeping [to] the field," he said, "would be, not to harm the enemy, but to complete the devastation of our country and the ruin of its people."

Johnston counterproposed that peace negotiations be initiated with Sherman at once. He was supported in this idea by all the Cabinet members in attendance except for Secretary of State Judah P. Benjamin. But Johnston reckoned without Jefferson Davis. Writing his memoirs two decades later, Davis recalled, "I had reason to believe that the spirit of the army in North Carolina was unbroken, for, though surrounded by circumstances well calculated to depress and discourage them, I had learned that they earnestly protested to their officers against . . . surrender."

That afternoon, Confederate secretary of war John C. Breckinridge arrived at Greensboro. Breckinridge had been vice president of the United States under James Buchanan, and an opponent of secession until nearly three months after First Manassas. He had served the Confederacy as a major general and enjoyed a wide measure of respect among Confederate leaders. After meeting with Johnston and Beauregard, Breckinridge agreed that further resistance was useless.

He joined Davis's Cabinet meeting on April 13. Around a table in the drab railroad car, Davis once again expressed confidence in victory, and then asked Johnston for his views. Johnston reiterated his pessimistic assessment of the previous day—"My small force is melting away like snow before the sun"—and stated flatly that the South was tired of war. Of those present, only Benjamin again supported Davis in his view that the war should continue. Reluctantly, Davis authorized Johnston to open negotiations with Sherman. Johnston could offer to disband Confederate troops and to recognize Federal authority, but only on condition that state governments in the South would be preserved and that Southerners would not be penalized for their rebellion. The status of former slaves was not even mentioned.

While Davis and his colleagues drafted a letter for Johnston to send to Sherman, their world continued to collapse about them. Pillaging soldiers roamed the streets of Greensboro, undeterred by the presence of the Confederate Cabinet and much of the army high command. Navy captain John Taylor Wood, who was a member of Davis's party, wrote, "Troops greatly demoralized, breaking into and destroying the public stores."

Because Johnston's letter was delayed in reaching Sherman—who had just established headquarters at Raleigh—their first meeting was set for April 17, eight days after Lee's surrender. Sherman had boarded the train that would take him to the rendezvous when a telegrapher ran up to say that an important telegram, in cipher, had just arrived. Sherman delayed his departure, and thirty minutes later was reading a message from Stanton that told of the assassination of Lincoln and the assault on Secretary of State William H. Seaward. Swearing the telegrapher to secrecy, Sherman folded the telegram into his pocket and told the engineer to proceed.

At about 10:00 A.M. Sherman's train reached Durham, where a squadron of Union cavalry was waiting. Sherman and his entourage, under a white flag, rode for five miles along the Hillsboro road, where they met Johnston and his party. In Sherman's words:

> We shook hands, and introduced our respective attendants. I asked if there was a place convenient where we could be private, and General Johnston said he had passed a small farmhouse a short distance back. . . . We rode back to it together side by side, our staff officers and escorts following.

Sherman and Johnston had never met, but in the course of the previous months they had developed a healthy professional respect for one another. Alone in the parlor of a farmer named James Bennitt, Sherman passed Johnston the telegram from Stanton and watched his antagonist closely.

> The perspiration came out in large drops on his forehead, and he did not attempt to conceal his distress. He denounced the act as a disgrace to the age, and hoped I did not charge it to the Confederate Government. I told him I could not believe that he or General Lee, or the officers of the Confederate army, could possibly be privy to acts of assassination; but I would not say as much for Jeff. Davis.

The two soldiers quickly agreed that there should be no more fighting. But Sherman was bound by the terms that Grant had accorded Lee, and

Johnston in theory was bound by the instructions that Davis had given him. The Virginian, prompted by his contempt for Jefferson Davis, had an idea: Why not "make one job of it" and settle the fate of all Confederates still under arms? Sherman was tempted, but he was also realistic. Could Johnston in fact deliver "all armies to the Rio Grande"? Johnston pointed out that Secretary of War Breckinridge was close at hand, and that Breckinridge's orders would be obeyed anywhere. It was sunset when the two generals parted, to meet the following day.

Sherman's immediate task, on returning to his headquarters, was to break the news of Lincoln's assassination. He first ordered all soldiers to camp, then issued a bulletin announcing the death of the president but exonerating the Confederate army from complicity in the assassination. Sherman and his generals watched their men closely. Many wept, and some demanded a final battle to avenge Lincoln, but Sherman's handling of the announcement prevented any serious breakdown in discipline.

On the morning of April 18, Sherman set off to meet with Johnston again, determined, in Sherman's own words, "to manifest real respect for [Lincoln's] memory by following after his death that policy which, if living, I felt certain he would have approved." At the Bennitt farmhouse, the two men resumed their talks. Johnston asked Sherman about the status of whites in the South. Were they "the slaves of the people of the North"? Nonsense, Sherman replied; Southerners would be "equal to us in all respects" once they had submitted to Federal authority. Johnston was leading his conqueror into uncharted waters, but Sherman seemed oblivious to the danger. When Johnston suggested that they bring Breckinridge into their talks, Sherman at first refused, but when Johnston pointed out that Breckinridge might participate in his capacity as a Confederate general, Sherman assented.

Johnston and Breckinridge attempted to outline terms for Davis's personal surrender, but Sherman refused to deal on the basis of individuals. Then a courier arrived with surrender terms drafted by Confederate postmaster general John Reagan in Greensboro. Sherman looked them over, but set them aside as too general and verbose. He took pen in hand himself and began to write. At one point he rose, walked to his saddlebag, took out a bottle, and poured himself a long drink of whiskey. After sipping his drink at the window, he returned to his drafting. Shortly he passed a paper to Johnston with the remark "That's the best I can do."

Sherman's terms were sweeping. They called for all Confederate armies "now in existence" to be disbanded and all soldiers paroled. Existing state governments would continue, once their personnel had sworn allegiance to the Union. The inhabitants of all the Southern states were guaranteed their political rights, as defined by the Constitution. There was no mention of slavery, or of the status of former slaves. Sherman's only hedge was in the final paragraph, where the signatories pledged "to obtain the necessary authority . . . to carry out the above program."

Sherman and Johnston signed the document and parted on warm terms.

As Johnston and Breckinridge rode away, Johnston asked what Breckinridge thought of their antagonist. "Oh, he's bright enough and a man of force, but Sherman is a hog," the Kentuckian responded. "Did you see him take that drink by himself?" asked Breckinridge—who was himself well known for his hard drinking. Johnston replied that Sherman had only been absent-minded, but Breckinridge was unforgiving. "No Kentucky gentleman would ever have taken that bottle away. He knew how much we needed it."

President Andrew Johnson was meeting with his Cabinet when Grant, who was there by special invitation, outlined the terms agreed to by Sherman and Johnston. The Cabinet was shocked: The terms went far beyond those of Appomattox and constituted a virtual peace treaty. Particularly galling was the section that recognized the legality of the state governments of the Confederacy. When it became clear that the administration would not accept Sherman's agreement, Grant offered to go in person to Sherman and explain why his terms had been disapproved. The new president agreed to this suggestion and told Grant to order Sherman to annul the April 18 agreement and to draft new terms applicable only to Johnston's army.

Meanwhile, Sherman and Johnston awaited word from their respective superiors. Grant sent Sherman a telegram, then departed by oceangoing steamer to Beaufort, South Carolina. There he would have to find a train to take him north. He kept his mission a secret because he wanted to avoid publicly embarrassing Sherman. The Confederate Cabinet agreed to Sherman's terms on April 23, after Attorney General George Davis had noted cheerfully, "Taken as a whole the convention amounts to this: that the states of the Confederacy shall reenter the old Union upon the same footing on which they stood before seceding from it." Sherman received Grant's telegram that same day and took the rejection of his terms calmly. In the five days since the signing of the treaty, he may well have come to regret its scope, if not its spirit. He wrote Stanton on April 25 that "I admit my folly in embracing in a military convention any civil matters," but added that he had understood from Stanton that "the financial state of the country demanded military success and would warrant a little bending [as] to policy.

"I still believe that the General Government of the United States has made a mistake but that is none of my business."

Sherman called for a third meeting, and on April 26, seventeen days after Appomattox, he met Johnston again at Bennitt's farm; Grant, who had by then arrived in Raleigh, remained discreetly behind. Sherman explained the need for new terms of surrender, and he and Johnston quickly signed a five-point convention. It surrendered Johnston's army but took no account of other Confederate forces and avoided all political matters. As with Lee's army, officers and men were permitted to return to their homes. By establishing a rapport with Johnston, Sherman had effectively prevented any resort to guerrilla warfare on the part of Johnston's forces—the result that he had feared most.

Johnston, who may have anticipated a disavowal of Sherman's April 18 terms, issued a brief statement to his soldiers: Lee's surrender and the disintegration of the Confederacy's industrial base had "destroyed all hope of successful war." He had therefore surrendered, "to spare the blood of this gallant little army, [and] to prevent further sufferings."

So the war wound to a close. On May 4, at Mobile, Alabama, Confederate general Richard Taylor surrendered his Alabama-Mississippi command in accordance with the terms granted Lee and Johnston. Three weeks later, on May 26, the trans-Mississippi forces of General E. Kirby Smith—the last Confederate army of any size—stacked their arms. President Davis and his entourage had been captured in Georgia on May 10; the Confederate president would be incarcerated for two years before being released in 1867. Two important figures, however, broke off from the Davis group and set out on their own: Breckinridge and Benjamin eventually made it to Cuba. Breckinridge later returned with a presidential pardon; Benjamin lived out a prosperous life in England.

As THE CONFEDERACY collapsed, Sherman became further involved in the surrender imbroglio. The way in which the administration repudiated his original terms soured relations between Sherman and Stanton, the acerbic secretary of war. In the course of informing the press of the terms that Sherman had offered Johnston, Stanton had suppressed a letter in which Grant had characterized Sherman as believing that he was acting in accordance with Lincoln's wishes. Rather, Stanton announced that Sher-man had deliberately ignored Lincoln's instructions, as reiterated by Presi-dent Johnson. Not content with these allegations of insubordination, Stan-ton charged Sherman with having made troop dispositions that would facilitate Davis's escape with his supposed hoard of Confederate gold, and virtually accused Sherman of disloyalty. The *New York Herald* declared that "Sherman's splendid military career is ended; he will retire under a cloud. . . . With a few unlucky strokes of his pen, he has blurred all the triumphs of his sword."

Sherman had not protested the overruling of his terms, but word of Stanton's charges infuriated him. He wrote to Grant, saying that he had never in his life disobeyed an order, "though many and many a time I have risked my life, health and reputation in obeying orders." Toward the end of May, Sherman appeared before the Committee on the Conduct of the War; he said that his April 18 terms, although not specifically authorized by Lincoln, would have been authorized by him had he lived.

In Washington, Sherman took his revenge in the most public way possible. The capital celebrated the end of the war with a two-day military review. Sherman's army paraded on the second day, May 24, and after passing President Johnson in the reviewing stand set up in front of the White House, Sherman dismounted and joined the reviewing party. He saluted the president and shook hands. But when Stanton, standing next to the president, started to extend his hand, Sherman, flushing deeply, ignored him; instead, the general shook hands with Grant and turned to watch the parade. Such was Sherman's prestige that his discourtesy went without rebuke.

Sherman never forgave Stanton. In contrast, the negotiations at Bennitt's farmhouse began a lasting friendship between Sherman and Johnston. The Ohioan went on to become commanding general of the army, while Johnston served a term in Congress and was later appointed commissioner of railroads by President Grover Cleveland. When Sherman died in 1891—reviled in the South but widely admired in the North—one of the honorary pallbearers was Joseph E. Johnston. The day of the funeral was cold and rainy, and Johnston was by then eighty-two. "General, please put on your hat," a member of the party admonished. "You might get sick." Johnston replied, "If I were in his place, and he were standing here in mine, he would not put on his hat."

In ten days, Johnston, too, was dead.

*SPRING 1991*

---

John M. Taylor is the author of the previous article on the *Alabama*.

# 16

# Ulysses S. Grant's Final Victory

## By James M. McPherson

*Military historians—indeed, all historians—are wont to argue. It seems as natural as breathing. But they are in nearly universal agreement that* The Personal Memoirs of U.S. Grant *not only stands as the outstanding memoir of the Civil War, but ranks as one of the truly great memoirs by any general at any time in any war. That Grant completed it at all is a testament to his indomitable will, his determination to see a responsibility through, his refusal to backtrack from a path once started: As he wrote, the general was dying of throat cancer. As in his earlier essay on Lincoln, Professor James M. McPherson studies the words and character of this man and finds that the qualities Grant displayed in writing his memoir were the same qualities that made him the greatest general of a generation of generals.*

When I put my pen to paper I did not know the first word that I should make use of in writing the terms. I only knew what was in my mind, and I wished to express it clearly, so that there could be no mistaking it.

So wrote Ulysses S. Grant in the summer of 1885, a few weeks before he died of throat cancer. He was describing the scene in Wilmer McLean's parlor at Appomattox Court House twenty years earlier, when he had started to write the formal terms for the surrender of the Army of Northern Virginia. But he could have been describing his feelings in July 1884, as he sat down to write the first of three articles for *Century* magazine's "Battles and Leaders" series on the American Civil War.

These articles were subsequently incorporated into Grant's *Personal Memoirs*, two volumes totaling nearly 300,000 words written in a race against the painful death that the author knew would soon overtake him. The result was a military narrative that Mark Twain in 1885 and Edmund Wilson in 1962 judged to be the best work of its kind since Julius Caesar's

*Commentaries,* and that John Keegan in 1987 pronounced 'the most revelatory autobiography of high command to exist in any language."

Grant would have been astonished by this praise. He had resisted earlier attempts to persuade him to write his memoirs, declaring that he had little to say and less literary ability to say it. There is no reason to doubt his sincerity in this conviction. Grant had always been loath to speak in public and equally reluctant to consider writing for the public. As president of the United States from 1869 to 1877, he had confined his communications to formal messages, proclamations, and executive orders drafted mainly by subordinates.

In 1880, after a postpresidential trip around the world, Grant bought a brownstone in New York and settled down at age fifty-eight to a comfortable retirement. He invested his life's savings in a brokerage partnership of his son and Frederick Ward, a Wall Street high roller. Ward made a paper fortune in speculative ventures, some of them illegal. In 1884 this house of cards collapsed with a crash that sent Ward to jail and left Grant with $180 in cash and $150,000 in debts.

It was then that he overcame his literary shyness and accepted a commission to write three articles for the *Century.* They revealed a talent for lucid prose, and although the $3,000 he earned for them would not begin to pay his debts, it would at least pay the bills.

While working on the articles, however, Grant experienced growing pain in his throat. It was diagnosed in October 1884 as cancer, incurable and fatal. Grant accepted the verdict with the same outward calm and dignity that had marked his response to earlier misfortunes and triumphs alike. To earn more money for his family, he almost accepted an offer from the *Century* of the standard 10 percent royalty for his memoirs. But his friend Mark Twain, angry at being exploited by publishers, had formed his own publishing company, and he persuaded Grant to sign up with him for 70 percent of the net proceeds of sales by subscription. It was one of the few good financial decisions Grant ever made. The *Personal Memoirs* earned $450,000 for his family after his death, which came just days after he completed the final chapter.

Grant's indomitability in his battle against this grim deadline attracted almost as much attention and admiration as his victory over rebellion twenty years earlier. Both were triumphs of will and determination, of a clarity of conception and simplicity of execution that made a hard task look easy. To read Grant's memoirs with a knowledge of the circumstances in which he wrote them is to gain insight into the reasons for his military success.

In April 1885, when Grant had written a bit more than half the narrative—through the November 1863 battles of Chattanooga—he suffered a severe hemorrhage that left him apparently dying. But by an act of will, and with the help of cocaine for the pain, he recovered and returned to work. The chapters on the campaign from the Wilderness to Petersburg, written during periods of intense suffering and sleepless nights, bear witness to these conditions. The narrative becomes bogged down in details; digressions and repetition creep into the text. Just as the Union cause had reached a nadir in August 1864, with Grant blocked at Petersburg and Sherman seemingly stymied before Atlanta while war-weariness and defeatism in the North seemed sure to vanquish Lincoln in the presidential election, so did Grant's narrative flounder in these chapters.

As Grant's health temporarily improved in the late spring of 1885, so did the terse vigor of his prose. He led the reader through Sherman's capture of Atlanta and his marches through Georgia and the Carolinas, Sheridan's spectacular victories in the Shenandoah Valley, and the Army of the Potomac's campaign to Appomattox. These final chapters pulsate with the same energy that animated Union armies as they delivered their knockout blows in the winter and spring of 1864–65. Just as he had controlled the far-flung Union armies by telegraph during those final campaigns, Grant once again had the numerous threads of his narrative under control as he brought the story to its climax in Wilmer McLean's parlor.

Grant's strength of will, his determination to do the best he could with what he had, his refusal to give up or to complain about the cruelty of fate, help explain the success of both his generalship and his memoirs. These qualities were by no means common among Civil War generals. Many of them spent more time and energy clamoring for reinforcements or explaining why they could not do what they were ordered to do than they did in trying to carry out their orders. Their memoirs are full of self-serving excuses for failure, which was always somebody else's fault.

Early in his memoirs Grant described General Zachary Taylor, under whom he had served as a twenty-four-year-old lieutenant in the Mexican War. Taylor's little army won three battles against larger Mexican forces. Fearing that the general was becoming too popular and might win the Whig presidential nomination, Democratic president James Polk transferred most of Taylor's troops (including Grant's regiment) to General Winfield Scott's campaign against Mexico City. This left Taylor with only a handful of veterans and a few raw volunteer regiments. Nevertheless, he won the Battle of Buena Vista against an army three times larger than his own—and thereby ensured his election as the next president. Grant wrote nearly forty years later:

> General Taylor was not an officer to trouble the administration much with his demands, but was inclined to do the best he could with the means given him.
> . . . If he had thought that he was sent to perform an impossibility with the means given him, he would probably have informed the authorities of his opinion and . . . have gone on and done the best he could with the means at hand without parading his grievance before the public. No soldier could face either danger or responsibility more calmly than he. These are qualities more rarely found than genius or physical courage.

Whether subconsciously or not, with these words Grant described himself as much as he described Taylor. Old Zack became a role model for young Ulysses. "General Taylor never made any show or parade either of uniform or retinue." Neither did Grant when he was commanding general. "In dress he was possibly too plain, rarely wearing anything in the field to indicate his rank." Nor did Grant. "But he was known to every soldier in his army, and was respected by all." The same was true of Grant in the next war. "Taylor was not a conversationalist." Neither was Grant. "But on paper he could put his meaning so plainly that there could be no mistaking it. He knew how to express what he wanted to say in the fewest well-chosen words, but would not sacrifice meaning to the construction of high-sounding sentences." This describes Grant's prose perfectly, his memoirs as well as his wartime orders to subordinates.

This question of "plain meaning" is no small matter. There are many Civil War examples of vague, ambiguous, confusing orders that affected the outcome of a campaign or battle in unfortunate ways. Grant's orders, by contrast, were invariably clear and concise. Many of his wartime associates commented on this. George B. Meade's chief of staff wrote that

> there is one striking feature of Grant's orders; no matter how hurriedly he may write them on the field, no one ever has the slightest doubt as to their meaning, or even has to read them over a second time to understand them.

Unlike many other generals, Grant did not rely on staff officers to draft his orders and dispatches; he wrote them himself. Horace Porter of General George Thomas's staff first met Grant at Chattanooga in October 1863. After a daylong inspection of the besieged Army of the Cumberland, which was in dire condition, Grant returned to his headquarters and sat down to write. Porter was impressed

> by the manner in which he went to work at his correspondence. . . . His work was performed swiftly and uninterruptedly, but without any marked display of nervous energy. His thoughts flowed as freely from his mind as the ink from his pen; he was never at a loss for an expression, and seldom interlined a word or made a material correction.

After a couple of hours, Grant gathered up the dispatches and had them sent by telegraph or courier to every point on the compass from Vicksburg to Washington, giving orders, Porter said, "for the taking of vigorous and comprehensive steps in every direction throughout his new and extensive command." These orders launched the movements that opened a new supply line into Chattanooga, brought in reinforcements, and prepared the Union armies for the campaigns that lifted the sieges of Chattanooga and Knoxville and drove Braxton Bragg's demoralized Army of Tennessee into Georgia after the assault on Missionary Ridge.

Porter, amazed by Grant's "singular mental powers and his rare military qualities," joined Grant's staff and served with him from the Wilderness to Appomattox. His own version of those events, entitled *Campaigning with Grant,* is next in value only to Grant's memoirs as a firsthand account of command decisions in that campaign.

Porter had particularly noticed how Grant never hesitated but wrote steadily, as if the thoughts flowed directly from his mind to the paper. How can this be reconciled with Grant's recollection that when he sat down to write out the surrender terms for Lee's army, he had no idea how to start? How can it be reconciled with his initial reluctance to write his memoirs because he thought he had no literary ability? The truth is, as he admitted in his account of writing the surrender terms, "I only knew what was in my mind."

There lies the explanation of Grant's ability as a writer: He knew what was in his mind. That is a rare quality in a writer or a general, but a necessary one for literary or military success. Once unlocked by an act of will, the mind poured out the words smoothly.

Grant had another and probably related talent, which might be described as a "topographical memory." He could remember every feature of the terrain over which he traveled, and find his way over it again; he could also look at a map and visualize the features of terrain he had never seen. Horace Porter noted that any map "seemed to become photographed indelibly on his brain, and he could follow its features without referring to it again."

Grant could see in his mind the disposition of troops over thousands of square miles, visualize their relationships to roads and terrain, and know how and where to move them to take advantage of topography. Most important, he could transpose this image into words that could be understood by others—though the modern reader of his memoirs would be well advised to have a set of Civil War maps on hand to match the maps in Grant's head.

During the last stages of his illness, unable to speak, Grant penned a note to his physician: "A verb is anything that signifies to be; to do; to suffer; I signify all three." It is not surprising that he would think of verbs at such a time; they are what give his writing its terse, muscular quality. As agents to translate thought into action, verbs offer a clue to the secret of Grant's military success, which also consisted of translating thought into action. Consider these orders to Sherman early in the Vicksburg campaign:

> You will proceed . . . to Memphis, taking with you one division of your present command. On your arrival at Memphis you will assume command of all the troops there . . . and organize them into brigades and divisions in your own army. As soon as possible move with them down the river to the vicinity of Vicksburg, and with the cooperation of the gunboat fleet . . . proceed to the reduction of that place.

In the manner of Caesar's *Veni, vidi, vici,* these sentences bristle with verbs of decision: "Proceed . . . take . . . assume command . . . organize . . . move . . . proceed to the reduction. . . ." Note also the virtual absence of adverbs and of all but essential adjectives. Grant used these modifiers only when necessary to his meaning. Take, for example, his famous reply to General Simon B. Buckner's request to negotiate terms for the surrender of Fort Donelson: "No terms except an unconditional and immediate surrender can be accepted. I propose to move immediately on your works."

Not an excess word here; the adjectives and adverb strengthen and clarify the message; the words produce action—they become action.

The will to act, symbolized by the emphasis on active verbs in Grant's writing, illustrates another crucial facet of his generalship—what Grant himself called "moral courage." This was a quality different from and rarer than physical courage. Grant and many other men who became Civil War generals had demonstrated physical courage under fire in the Mexican War as junior officers carrying out the orders of their superiors. Moral courage involved a willingness to make decisions and initiate the orders. Some officers who were physically brave shrank from this responsibility, because decision risked error, and initiative risked failure.

This was George B. McClellan's defect as a commander: He was afraid to risk his army in an offensive because it might be defeated. He lacked the moral courage to act, to confront that terrible moment of truth, to decide and to risk. Grant, Lee, Jackson, Sheridan, and other victorious Civil War commanders had moral courage; they understood that without risking defeat they could never achieve victory.

Grant describes how he first confronted that moment of truth and learned the lesson of moral courage. His initial Civil War command was as colonel of the 21st Illinois. In July 1861 the regiment was ordered to find Tom Harris's rebel guerrilla outfit in Missouri and attack it. Grant says:

> My sensations as we approached what I supposed might be "a field of battle" were anything but agreeable. I had been in all the engagements in Mexico that it was possible for one person to be in: but not in command. If some one else had been colonel and I had been lieutenant-colonel I do not think I would have felt any trepidation. . . . As we approached the brow of the hill from which it was expected we could see Harris' camp, and possibly find his men formed ready to meet us, my heart kept getting higher and higher until it felt to me as though it was in my throat.

But when the 21st reached Harris's camp, they found it abandoned. Grant wrote:

> My heart resumed its place. It occurred to me at once that Harris had been as much afraid of me as I had been of him. This was a view of the question I had never taken before; but it was one I never forgot afterwards. From that event to the close of the war, I never experienced trepidation upon confronting an enemy, though I always felt more or less anxiety. I never forgot that he had as much reason to fear my forces as I had his. The lesson was valuable.

Grant may have taken that lesson too much to heart; he forgot that there were times when he *should* fear the enemy's intentions. This lesson he learned the hard way, at both Fort Donelson and Shiloh. After the failure of the Union gunboats to subdue the Donelson batteries on February 14, 1862, Grant went downriver several miles to consult with Flag Officer Andrew Foote of the gunboat fleet. Grant was therefore absent on the morning of February 15 when the Confederate garrison launched its breakout attack. He confessed that "when I left the National line to visit Flag-officer Foote, I had no idea that there would be any engagement on land unless I brought it on myself."

It took one more such experience to drive this lesson home. This time it was the Confederate attack at Shiloh on April 6, 1862, when Grant was again absent at his headquarters seven miles downriver. "The fact is," he admits in the memoirs, "I regarded the campaign we were engaged in as an offensive one and had no idea that the enemy would leave strong intrench-ments to take the initiative." Thereafter he had a healthier respect for the enemy's capabilities.

But this never paralyzed him or caused him to yield the initiative. At both Fort Donelson and Shiloh, Grant's recognition that the enemy still had as much reason to fear him as he to fear the enemy enabled him to wrest the initiative away and grasp victory. Upon returning to his troops at Donelson after a fast ride over icy roads, he calmly took charge and re-formed his broken lines. After hearing reports of the morning's fighting, he told a member of his staff: "Some of our men are pretty badly demoralized, but the enemy must be more so, for he has attempted to force his way out, but has fallen back: the one who attacks first now will be victorious and the enemy will have to be in a hurry if he gets ahead of me." Suiting action to words, he ordered a counterattack, drove back and penned in the Confed-erate forces, and compelled their surrender.

At Shiloh, Grant conducted a fighting fallback until dusk stopped the Confederate advance. His army was crippled, but he knew that the Confed-erates were just as badly hurt and that he would be reinforced during the night. Thus, he replied to one subordinate who advised retreat: "Retreat? No. I propose to attack at daylight and whip them." And he did.

One of Grant's superstitions, described in the memoirs, was a dread of turning back or retracing his steps once he had set forth on a journey. If he took the wrong road or made a wrong turn, he would go across country or forward to the next turn rather than go back. This superstition reinforced his risk-taking inclination as a military commander. Crucial decisions in the Vicksburg and Wilderness campaigns illustrate this trait.

During the winter of 1862–63, Grant's river-based campaign against Vicksburg bogged down in the Louisiana and Mississippi swamps. While criticism mounted to an angry crescendo in the North, Grant remained calm and carefully worked out a daring plan: to run the gunboats past Vicksburg; cross his army to the east bank; cut loose from his base and communications; and live off the land while operating in Vicksburg's rear.

This was the highest-risk operation imaginable. Grant's staff and his most trusted subordinates, especially Sherman, opposed the plan. Sherman "expressed his alarm at the move I had ordered," wrote Grant, "saying that I was putting myself in a position voluntarily which an enemy would be glad to manoeuvre a year—or a long time—to get me in." Go back to Memphis, advised Sherman, establish a secure base of supplies, and move against Vicksburg overland, keeping open your communications—in

185

other words, wage an orthodox campaign by the book.

But Grant threw away the book. He was confident his army could live off the land and substitute mobility for secure communications. "The country is already disheartened over the lack of success on the part of our armies," he told Sherman. He goes on to explain in the memoirs:

> If we went back as far as Memphis it would discourage the people so much that bases of supplies would be of no use: neither men to hold them nor supplies to put in them would be furnished. The problem for us was to move forward to a decisive victory, or our cause was lost. No progress was being made in any other field, and we had to go on.

Go on he did, to what military historians almost universally regard as the most brilliant and innovative campaign of the Civil War.

As Grant departed Washington a year later to set forth on what became the campaign from the Wilderness to Appomattox, he told President Lincoln that "whatever happens, there will be no turning back." What happened in the Wilderness, however, might have caused other Northern commanders to turn back; indeed, similar events in the same place had caused Joe Hooker to turn back exactly a year earlier.

On May 6, 1864, the second day of the Wilderness, Lee attacked and bent back both of Grant's flanks. That evening a distraught brigadier galloped up to Grant's headquarters to report disaster on the right. "I know Lee's methods well by past experience," panted the officer, in words recorded by Horace Porter. "He will throw his whole army between us and the Rapidan, and cut us off completely."

Grant slowly removed a cigar from his mouth and fixed the man with an icy stare. "Oh, I am heartily tired of hearing about what Lee is going to do. Some of you always seem to think he is suddenly going to turn a double somersault, and land in our rear and on both of our flanks at the same time. Go back to your command, and try to think what we are going to do ourselves, instead of what Lee is going to do."

Once again Grant suited action to words. He ordered preparations for a movement. Men in the ranks who had fought the Battle of Chancellorsville in these woods thought it was another retreat, but when they realized that this time they were moving south, the scales fell from their eyes. It was not "another Chancellorsville . . . another skedaddle" after all. "Our spirits rose," wrote a veteran who recalled this moment as a turning point of the war. "We marched free. The men began to sing." When Grant cantered by one corps, the soldiers recognized him and sent up a cheer. For the first time in a Virginia campaign, the Army of the Potomac was staying on the offensive after its initial battle. Nor did it turn back or retrace its steps until Appomattox eleven months later.

These incidents in the Wilderness do not come from the memoirs. Though Grant keeps himself at the center of the story, his memoirs exhibit less egotism than is typical of the genre. Grant is generous with praise of other officers (especially Sherman, Sheridan, and Meade) and sparing with criticism, carping, and backbiting. He is also willing to admit mistakes, most notably: "I have always regretted that the last assault at Cold Harbor was ever made. . . . No advantage whatever was gained to compensate for the heavy loss we sustained."

But Grant did not admit culpability for the heavy Union casualties in the whole campaign of May–June 1864. Nor should he have done so, despite the label of "butcher" and the subsequent analyses of his "campaign of attrition." It did turn out to be a campaign of attrition, but that was by Lee's choice. Grant's purpose was to maneuver Lee into an open field for a showdown; Lee's purpose was to prevent this by entrenching an impenetrable line to protect Richmond and his communications. Lee was hoping to hold out long enough and inflict enough casualties on attacking Union forces to discourage the people of the North and overturn the Lincoln administration in the 1864 election.

Lee's strategy of attrition almost worked; that it failed in the end was due mainly to Grant, who stayed the course and turned the attrition factor in his favor. Although the Confederates had the advantage of fighting on the defensive most of the time, Grant inflicted almost as high a percentage of casualties on Lee's army as vice versa. Indeed, for the war as a whole, Lee's armies suffered a higher casualty rate than Grant's. Neither commander was a "butcher," but measured by that statistic, Grant deserved the label less than Lee.

On one matter Grant's memoirs are silent: There is not a word about the rumors and speculations concerning his drinking. On this question there continues to be disagreement among historians and biographers. Most of the numerous stories about Grant's drunkenness at one time or another during the war are false. But drinking problems almost certainly underlay his resignation from the army in 1854, and he may have gone on a bender once or twice during the war—though never during active military operations. In any event, I think his silence on the subject reflects his sensitivity about it, not his indifference.

That sensitivity is indicated by Grant's curious failure to mention John A. Rawlins in the memoirs except twice in passing and once in a brief paragraph of opaque praise. Yet as his chief of staff, Rawlins was both Grant's alter ego and his conscience. So far as was possible, Rawlins kept him away from the temptations of the bottle. Grant may have been an alcoholic in the modern medical meaning of the term, but that meaning was unknown in his time. Excessive drinking was in those days regarded as a moral defect and was a matter of deep shame among respectable people. Grant himself doubtless so regarded it.

If Grant was an alcoholic, he should have felt pride rather than shame, because he overcame his illness to achieve success and fame without the support system of modern medicine and organizations like Alcoholics Anonymous. But lacking our knowledge and perspective, he could not see it that way. His support network consisted mainly of his wife, Julia, and John Rawlins. Grant, a happy family man, did not drink when his wife and family were with him. And when they were not, Rawlins guarded him zealously from temptation. Many contemporaries knew this, but to give Rawlins his due in the memoirs would perhaps have seemed a public confession of weakness and shame.

And, of course, the memoirs are about triumph and success—triumph in war, and success in writing the volumes in a race against death. They are military memoirs, which devote only a few pages to Grant's early years and to the years of peace between the Mexican War and the Civil War. Nor do they cover his less-than-triumphant career after the Civil War. But perhaps this is as it should be. Grant's great contribution to American history was as a Civil War general. In that capacity he did more to shape the future of America than anyone else except Abraham Lincoln. He earned a secure place as one of the great captains of history, an "unheroic" hero, in John Keegan's apt description. Both in their substance and in the circumstances of their writing, the personal memoirs of Ulysses S. Grant offer answers to that perennial question of Civil War historiography: Why did the North win?

*SUMMER 1990*

---

**James M. McPherson is the author of the earlier essay on President Lincoln.**

# 17

# Custer's Ghostherders

## By Neil Asher Silberman

*Neil Asher Silberman, who wrote the earlier article on the Pequot War, continues his examination of Anglo–Native American conflict in his discussion of battlefield archaeology and the clash at the Little Bighorn. Except for Gettysburg and Pearl Harbor, perhaps no confrontation in American military history is as well remembered as that fierce and bloody struggle between the 7th Cavalry and its Sioux and Cheyenne nemeses that hot day in June 1876. Yet well remembered does not mean well and accurately understood. As the example of the Little Bighorn instructs, the techniques of battlefield archaeology offer much to the historian: They can confirm or destroy older theories and accounts, add information and light to the previously unknown or unsuspected, and kindle a rethinking of our past.*

The desolate ridges and winding gullies above the Little Bighorn River in south-central Montana provide an eerie backdrop for a sanctified place on our national landscape. It was here on June 25, 1876, that Lieutenant Colonel George Armstrong Custer and more than 200 troopers of the 7th U.S. Cavalry were surrounded and wiped out by thousands of angry Sioux and Cheyenne warriors. Perhaps no other event in our history is more symbolic of the Indian-white conflict and of the vulnerability of American military might. And its final agonizing moments have been indelibly etched in the American psyche by the countless melodramatic paintings, dime novels, Wild West shows, and movie versions of "Custer's Last Stand."

Today, a dramatic new picture of that battle is emerging from the dry prairie soil of the Custer Battlefield. Since 1984, Dr. Douglas Scott, chief of the National Park Service's Rocky Mountain Research Division, Midwest Archaeological Center, has been directing a series of extensive excavations. Finds of human bone fragments, flattened bullets, spent cartridges, and discarded military equipment offer raw material for a new understanding of the Custer myth. Methodical sweeps by metal detectors and meticulous excavations have yielded thousands of battle-related artifacts, which have been carefully plotted on a master grid. Microscopic ballistic analysis of the recovered bullets and cartridge cases has led to the identification of dozens of individual Indian and cavalry weapons used in the battle. And because the location of each find has been registered with such precision, Scott and his colleagues have been able to generate an illuminating computer replay of the movements of the opposing forces that is quite different from the conventional interpretation of the events.

The unlikely juxtaposition of modern archaeological technology and the romantic Custer image has attracted enormous media attention. During the 1984 and 1985 excavation seasons, film crews and newspaper and magazine reporters converged on the site to convey breathless ac-counts of the archaeological discoveries. Yet, ironically, the publicity gained by the Custer Battlefield Archaeological Project aggravated long-standing tensions between Native Americans and whites. Even before the digging, in 1976 at the centennial of the Custer battle, a group of Native American activists appeared at the battlefield to express their contempt for the celebration. And in the summer of 1988, after the initial findings of the excavations had received widespread attention in the national media, another delegation of the American Indian Movement returned to the battlefield to gain some attention for their cause.

The demonstrators—from both the nearby Northern Cheyenne Reservation and the Sioux Pine Ridge Reservation in South Dakota—placed a hand-welded plaque on the base of the monument marking the mass grave of many of the 7th Cavalry soldiers. In the angry, heartfelt inscription, this plaque proclaimed an alternative understanding of the Battle of the Little Bighorn "in honor of our Indian patriots who fought and defeated the U.S. Cavalry. In order to save our women and children from mass murder. In doing so, preserving rights to our homeland, treaties, and sovereignty."

This graphic demonstration of Native American feelings offered an emotional counterpoint to the archaeological project, but it was not the main motivation for the recent continuation of the dig. The National Park Service staff at the battlefield had noted an alarming rise in reports of damage caused by visitors and, more ominous, illegal digging in the vicinity. Immediate steps had to be taken to protect the battlefield's endangered archaeological remains. So in the spring of 1989 the archaeologists returned to the site for three weeks of excavation. Their goals were to retrieve the remains of a cavalryman recently reported extruding from the earth at the end of one of the public trails; to search for the remains of twenty-eight missing soldiers; and to uncover a cache of military equipment that had been hastily destroyed and abandoned by a contingent of the 7th Cavalry about four miles south of Last Stand Hill.

Of course Scott and his staff recognized that they would have to deal with the modern repercussions of the Custer battle, as well as with the historical facts. At the Little Bighorn, archaeologists, Custer buffs, and Native Americans each have their own dearly held understandings of the significance of Custer's Last Stand. These historical understandings are closely linked to concerns of the present. And when I went to Montana to follow the progress of the recent excavations, it seemed quite clear that the scientific methods and unexpected discoveries of the Custer Battlefield Archaeological Project reflect far wider changes in our national consciousness.

Just a dozen yards beyond the visitors' center and its parking lot crowded with vans, flip-top campers, and huge RVs with out-of-state license plates, Last Stand Hill rises gently toward the enormous Montana sky. A squat obelisk of gray Vermont granite at the summit is inscribed with the names of the fallen cavalrymen, and at its foot is a mass grave that contains the remains of many of them. Although Custer himself is buried at West Point, the spot where he fell is marked by a white marble tablet—surrounded by forty-one others—within a black wrought-iron fence. More white tablets, marking the places where the bodies of other troopers were found, dot the nearby ridges and extend toward the valley below. They lend a spooky, frozen aspect to the last fatal moments of a battle that was closely connected to contemporary developments in American history.

THE BATTLE OF the Little Bighorn was the unexpected, if not unpredictable, outcome of a policy of westward expansion that had become irreversible as the United States reached its centennial year. The western frontier, that eternal Eden of seemingly inexhaustible resources and rich land for settlement, beckoned as a panacea for the severe depression that had gripped the country since the Panic of 1873. It seemed vital that this region now be opened for development—despite the explicit provisions of earlier treaties with the Northern Cheyenne and the Sioux.

The War Department's plan for the 1876 campaign was efficiently deadly. Three columns of cavalry and infantry would converge on a suspected concentration of Sioux and Cheyenne—followers of the charismatic Sioux chief Sitting Bull—somewhere between the Powder and Bighorn rivers in Montana Territory. Contingents of Crow and Arikara scouts (traditional enemies of the Sioux and Cheyenne) assisted in the search for the "hostiles," who were finally located in the Little Bighorn Valley in late June by the column spearheaded by Lieutenant Colonel George Armstrong Custer and the approximately 600 men of his famous 7th Cavalry.

Custer was clearly anxious to engage his enemies before they had a chance to scatter, and on the morning of June 25, when his scouts reported the sighting of the huge Indian village, he ordered an immediate attack. Dividing his troops into four battalions, he directed Captain Frederick Benteen to probe upstream with one battalion to make sure that no Indians were behind them. At the same time he ordered Major Marcus Reno and another battalion to attack the village from the south. Custer retained command of the remaining two battalions, promising to offer Reno immediate support.

As Reno and his 140 men charged toward the village, they quickly discovered that the Sioux and Cheyenne had no intention of retreating. The village in the Little Bighorn Valley, concealed by the cottonwoods and the bluffs on the eastern bank of the river, contained approximately 1,000 lodges and stretched northward for some three miles. When Reno and his men charged the southernmost circle of tepees, they were met with a fierce counterattack by hundreds of warriors. Suffering heavy casualties and unable to mount a defense, Reno led a panicky retreat across the river to the steep bluffs above.

Before Reno's precipitous retreat, Custer had ridden northward with his own battalions and had dismissed his Indian scouts from the imminent fighting, apparently planning to attack the village from the north. But the size, strength, and fearlessness of the Sioux and Cheyenne forces must have shocked him as they quickly poured out of the village to give battle and gradually encircle his men. The intensity of the gunfire, described by one of the fleeing Crow scouts as like "the snapping of the threads in the tearing of a blanket," took a murderous toll on Custer's men, who were forced into untenable, exposed positions. What happened then has remained something of a mystery.

While Reno's battalion, now joined by that of Benteen, fought for their lives on the high bluffs farther up the river, the Sioux and Cheyenne relentlessly pressed their attack on Custer. Custer's troopers could not hold back the Indian forces, who considerably outnumbered them. By late afternoon every man in his battalions was dead.

The beleaguered troops of the Reno-Benteen defense—four miles away—still maintained a desperate hope that Custer would return to help them (and their own failure to come to Custer's assistance would be the source of continuing controversy). But two days later, after the sudden dispersal of the Indian village, they finally discovered what had befallen their commander and comrades. Arriving at the Custer battlefield to face a "scene of sickening ghastly horror," they hastily buried 214 bloated, mutilated bodies and burned their excess equipment before they began their own retreat.

As the news flashed eastward on July 5 to a nation that had just celebrated its hundredth anniversary, politicians and military leaders scrambled for explanations. A simple defeat of the army's best and brightest by a horde of savages was too much for the nation to accept. Democrats hastened to blame the corrupt Grant administration; the Grant administration blamed Custer; and Custer's admirers found ample reason to blame Major Reno for his hasty retreat from the valley fight.

But in the years that followed, as the emotions of the moment subsided, the massacre of the 7th Cavalry gradually took on the trappings of a national myth. The image of a heroic commander fighting to the death with his soldiers against bloodthirsty savages in the far Montana wildness became a symbolic mandate for revenge against the Indians and for further conquest.

Of course, there are always two sides to every mythic image. As the decades passed, the lessons drawn from Custer's Last Stand gradually began to shift. By the 1950s, with the civil-rights struggle, and in the 1960s, with the Vietnam War and the rise of the Native American rights movement, the vivid symbolism of the Custer image was turned on its head. All that was once noble was now seen as evil, and Custer became the villain of a late-twentieth-century myth. In this version of the story, the ending was happy: He got what he deserved.

ALMOST ACCIDENTALLY, archaeology entered the picture. In 1958, some excavation of the Reno-Benteen defense site was begun. Then, in 1983, a prairie wildfire swept across the Custer battlefield and burned off the thick ground cover, revealing bullets, cartridges, buckles, and even human bone fragments left behind by the burial details and hidden under the sagebrush for more than a hundred years. The extensive archaeological excavations that followed opened a new era in the study of the Custer battle. As always, historical understandings of the Battle of the Little Bighorn had modern implications. And the resumption of the digging in 1989 would continue to play a role in separating fact from fantasy in our understanding of the Battle of the Little Bighorn.

From the very start of the excavations, the sensational appeal of digging at one of the most famous sites in American history brought a public outpouring of interest. Yet Doug Scott recognized that this project could have implications far wider than the study of Custer's Last Stand. Few systematic attempts had ever been made to study the archaeological remains on battlefields as anything more than isolated relics, valuable to collectors and students of military equipment perhaps, but still subservient to contemporary battle accounts. Scott, trained at the University of Colorado as an anthropologist, firmly believed that the buried bones and bullets might serve as a useful check on the vagaries of the memory of the participants, or on the carefully scripted memoirs of officers with specific axes to grind.

Scott recognized that in order to distinguish the patterns of battlefield action, it was important to utilize the most advanced technological tools. Metal detectors had been used before to locate relics at the Custer Battlefield, by both unauthorized diggers and the Park Service staff. But never before had they been used to establish an overall *pattern* of artifact areas. So beginning with the 1984 season, Scott recruited dozens of volunteers in a wide-ranging effort. After a master grid was established, a crew of metal-detector operators scanned the surface, followed by volunteers who placed small orange flags at the sites of all detected finds. Each artifact was then excavated and precisely plotted for both position and orientation. Since the majority of the finds were fired bullets and expended cartridges, ballistic analyses carried out later at the Nebraska State Patrol Criminalistic Laboratory provided the archaeologists with the raw material for an unprecedentedly detailed examination of the last stages of the Little Bighorn fight.

A distinctive pattern of artifacts did in fact begin to emerge from the plotted finds on the battlefield. The concentrations of spent army cartridges, discarded military equipment, and human bone fragments—representing the positions of cavalry troopers—were clustered in a large

V-shaped formation, with Last Stand Hill at its apex. This suggested a clear historical conclusion: Even though Custer's troops were substantially outnumbered, they had apparently attempted to mount an orderly defense. The Indian forces, for their part, showed themselves to be no less tactically minded, for the metal detector scans located seven clear Indian positions marked by expended cartridges of nonregulation weapons, impacted army bullets, and the split cartridges of captured army ammunition fired in the nonregulation guns.

Ballistic analysis identified 371 individual guns used at all the battle sites and thus provided the first detailed glimpse of the progressive stages of the fight. The picture that emerged proved to be a striking confirmation of Indian accounts: The initial assault on Custer's battalions apparently came from the south and southeast—an area that the fleeing Crow scouts and later testimony by Sioux chief Gall indicated was the location of the first Indian attack. From the two Indian positions in this area, the archaeological team identified almost eighty individual weapons, suggesting the intensity of the gunfire that rained down on the retiring Custer troops. But the most dramatic indication of the cavalry movements came from the evidence of its own expended cartridges: Several shells found at the first point of contact matched others scattered behind the retreating men, and still others farther back toward Last Stand Hill, suggesting that they fell back under fire.

The archaeological findings seemed to indicate that for the most part, the fighting took place at long distance, with the Sioux and Cheyenne forces directing intensive fire from their protected positions at the exposed concentrations of cavalrymen. The evidence also suggested that after overwhelming the southernmost group of soldiers, Gall's Sioux attackers shifted northwestward to support an advance from that direction led (according to later Indian accounts) by Crazy Horse and his Sioux warriors and by Lame White Man of the Cheyenne. Once again the patterns of the recovered cartridges were telling. Several individual Indian weapons could be traced as they moved from the initial point of contact on the south to intermediate positions to the west, finally centering on Last Stand Hill.

By the end of the 1984 and 1985 excavation seasons, it was therefore clear that the Sioux and Cheyenne forces were not undisciplined savages; the archaeological work supported the contention of earlier historians, such as Jerome Greene, that the Indian forces at the Battle of the Little Bighorn were well armed and ready to fight. Even more important, it now seemed likely that a series of opportune tactical movements by the Sioux and Cheyenne, rather than a simple imbalance of forces, were crucial factors in the Custer fight.

Now in 1989, with the groundwork laid by their earlier excavations, the archaeological team returned to the battlefield with more specific questions and objectives in mind. One task was to continue searching for the remains of Custer's troopers, for despite the reverence accorded the battlefield over the past century, the disposition of the fallen has been a source of continuing official embarrassment—and dispute. Nineteenth-century mythmakers were fond of evoking classical allusions in which Custer's troopers met their deaths "as grandly as Homer's demigods." But as it turned out, the fate of the mortal remains of those fallen soldiers was not nearly so grand.

On the morning of June 27, 1876, when the survivors of the Reno-Benteen defense arrived at the site of the Custer massacre, they faced the unpleasant task of burying badly mutilated bodies that had lain exposed in the summer heat for almost two days. The chore was made even more difficult by the lack of proper digging equipment and the hardness of the dry prairie soil. So while the bodies of Custer and the other officers were placed in shallow graves, the remains of most of the troopers were covered with only a thin layer of earth or with hastily gathered clumps of sagebrush.

In the years that followed the battle, disturbing reports of exposed human remains on the battlefield reached the War Department in Washington. In the summer of 1877 and again in 1879, new burial details were dispatched to disinter the bodies of the officers for reburial elsewhere and to dig proper graves for the rest of the troopers, each of which was marked by a cedar stake.

By 1881, after the declaration of the site as a national cemetery and with the erection of the granite monument on the summit of Last Stand Hill, it was decided that the cavalrymen's bodies should be buried together in a common grave. By that time, however, the original grave sites had become so overgrown that many could no longer be located, and in those that were found, the soldiers' remains consisted of jumbles of disarticulated bones. The reburial of 1881 was therefore something less than complete. Small bones, uniform buttons, and personal possessions remained scattered all over the battlefield—not to mention the considerable number of soldiers whose graves were not located at all.

The story became even more complicated with the placement of small marble memorial tablets in 1890. Those tablets, meant to mark the original grave sites, were placed wherever the original stakes could still be found—and at other locations where the soldiers initially might have been buried, judging by such indications as depressions in the ground or clumps of suspiciously luxuriant prairie grass.

That the positioning of these tablets was only approximate is evident from the fact that 252 were eventually placed on a battlefield where only 214 fell. Yet for decades the tablets were used by historians as an important source of information about the last stages of the Custer battle and were believed to mark the places where Custer's men were killed. One of the main objectives of the 1984 and 1985 excavations was therefore to dig around selected markers in search of bone fragments or personal possessions left behind by the reburial parties, in order to determine how closely the markers corresponded to the sites of the troopers' original graves.

Like investigators at a crime scene, the archaeologists have carefully dug beneath the grass around thirty-seven of the markers, recovering human bone fragments at almost all of them. While in some cases it appeared that pairs of closely set markers represented the grave of only a single soldier (and thus could explain the discrepancy in numbers), the excavations indicated that the placement of the majority coincided with the general location of the human remains, even if not all were precisely correct.

Even more intriguing were the conclusions drawn from detailed examination of the remains of more than twenty individuals uncovered in the digging. This analysis was undertaken by Dr. Clyde Snow, a nationally noted forensic anthropologist from Norman, Oklahoma, with the assistance of Dr. John Fitzpatrick of Cook County Hospital in Chicago, who reviewed the X-rays taken of all the recovered human bones. Their findings shed additional light on the progress of the battle and seemed to confirm the ballistic analyses. Snow's report in the published results of the excavations said that the

> available osteological evidence supports a scenario of the events as consisting of a brief firefight followed by the close-range dispatch of the wounded. It appears probable that the majority of the troopers were still alive but more or less helplessly wounded when resistance ceased and that many were finished off with massive crushing blows to the head.

Almost half of the human remains showed clear signs of slashing by knives, hacking by hatchets, or massive blunt force that resulted in the crushing of skulls. Early accounts of the battle had dealt at length with Indian brutality and had angrily argued for revenge. But now, in an age when enemies are never permanent and regional conflicts are matters of geopolitical strategy rather than colonial expansion, the archaeological team seeks to understand the meaning of the grisly mutilations as an expression of Indian culture rather than savagery.

Recognizing the rage that the Indian warriors must have felt as their village was attacked by the bluecoats, Scott suggests that "it is more appropriate to view mutilation from the cultural context of the Sioux and Cheyennes rather than the Victorians." That context, he argues, may even have included the idea of preventing one's enemies from enjoying the physical pleasures of the afterlife. Rather than seeing the cavalrymen as heroic martyrs to irredeemable savages, the modern investigators have tried to understand the cultural process by which "the mutilated dead at the Little Bighorn become symbols of victory to the culture that defeated them."

The archaeologists are therefore reluctant to express value judgments on the battle; they see their primary moral obligation in recovering, if possible identifying, and facilitating the proper burial of all human remains. Some notable successes in this quest have already been recorded. Through facial reconstruction and the photographic overlay of recovered skull fragments with faded nineteenth-century images, the team has identified the remains of Custer's scout Mitch Boyer and of Sergeant Miles O'Hara, who was killed in Reno's disastrous valley fight. And a complete skull discovered in 1989 on the banks of the Little Bighorn River will soon also undergo facial reconstruction and comparison with period photographs, in the hope that it too might be identified and reinterred in the mass grave on the summit of Last Stand Hill.

That is not to say that the recovery of human remains on the Custer Battlefield is devoid of modern emotional meaning. In 1987 a visitor to the site happened to notice with dismay what appeared to be a human vertebra poking out of the ground near one of the markers partially excavated in 1984. Since additional human remains might still be buried there, and be endangered by the constant tramping of tourists, the team returned in 1989 to complete the excavation of this marker—inscribed, like most others, with the simple words U.S. SOLDIER, 7TH CAVALRY, FELL HERE JUNE 25, 1876. That task was relatively simple from a technical standpoint, yet the archaeological remains found there provide a chilling reconstruction of the final moments of a 7th Cavalryman's life.

Scraping away the thin grass cover, the team exposed the human bone fragments left behind by the 1881 reburial detail: ankle bones, a vertebra, and splinters of a thoroughly smashed skull. Nearby were the instruments of destruction: an 1858 .44-caliber Remington civilian pistol ball (an outmoded but still deadly weapon of the Cheyenne and Sioux warriors); a .45–.55-caliber army regulation bullet (apparently fired from a captured army carbine); and most suggestive of all, a Colt .45 pistol bullet fired straight into the ground near the position of the body, possibly as a coup de grace. At the edge of the excavation were a few simple possessions that this young trooper carried at the moment of his death: a pocket comb of hard India rubber and a five-cent piece, dated 1876.

This was no demigod, just a young man, according to anthropological analysis, somewhere between eighteen and thirty-five years of age. Whatever his hopes may have been in joining up for a hitch in the 7th Cavalry, they were brutally dashed on that hot June day. The evidence of his wounds was clear in his excavated bones. The skull splinters represented a massive blunt-force injury to his face, which probably rendered him unrecognizable to the burial detail that arrived on the battlefield two days after his death. A cleanly cut cervical vertebra was evidence of even more horror—a clear sign that he had been decapitated with a single blow of an ax or tomahawk.

The shattered, partial remains of this trooper will be reburied in the mass grave beneath the monument, but twenty-eight of his comrades still await discovery. An intensive effort to find them was made in 1989 in a deep and winding gully called Deep Ravine. The question of the missing men in Deep Ravine has been in fact one of the Custer Battlefield's most intractable mysteries.

Two days after the battle, the original burial detail had found more than two dozen dead soldiers in Deep Ravine. Although they were identified by eyewitnesses as members of Company E of Custer's command, the circumstances of their deaths remained open to dispute. According to some, the bodies were discovered at regular intervals down the course of the gully, indicating that they had attempted to mount an orderly defense.

Others said the bodies were found heaped together at the head of the ravine—an indication that they had attempted to take cover or flee in panic from a battle that was nearly lost.

Whichever version was correct would color historical interpretations, but unfortunately the location of the bodies had been lost. By 1881 the site of the hasty 1876 burial was so completely obscured by the undergrowth in the ravine that no attempt to find and remove the bodies was apparently ever made. The few extra markers placed near the head of the ravine in 1890 were deemed a sufficient memorial to the missing detachment. But now, nearly a century later, the archaeologists were intent on finally solving the mystery.

The search, directed by Dr. Vance Haynes, Jr., of the University of Arizona, was ultimately unsuccessful, but the geological findings pointed to a logical hypothesis: The twenty-eight missing men had probably fled in panic from the battlefield and were cut down by the attacking Sioux and Cheyenne at the head of Deep Ravine. Analysis of the sediments in the ravine indicated that more than six feet of thick, wet silt had rapidly accumulated over the last century, obscuring all surface traces of the original grave. At the time of the reburial detail in 1881, the human remains already may have been deeply covered, and Haynes recognized that the disposition of the bodies themselves may have caused this geological change. If, as he suggested, they were slaughtered together in this death-trap—rather than being arranged in an orderly defensive line—their remains would have created a gruesome obstruction that would explain the abnormally rapid collection of silt.

Once again a modern image of brutal warfare emerges from the archaeological work. It was panic at their imminent death, not the orderly defensive plan of their commander, that had apparently led the twenty-eight missing soldiers to flee the battlefield into the deep and twisting ravine. Their attempted escape was unsuccessful and, in all probability, resulted in a last stand no less horrible than Custer's.

THE PATHOLOGY of death and the retrieval of the dead were not the only concerns of the new excavations. The team was anxious to uncover what might legitimately be considered one of the most fascinating concentrations of artifacts ever discovered in the history of frontier military archaeology. At the end of the 1985 season, Scott and his colleagues had found this cache almost accidentally, about four miles south of Last Stand Hill. After their intensive metal-detector scans and excavations at the Reno-Benteen defense site (which substantially confirmed the survivors' accounts of a desperate battle in which there was no practical possibility of rescuing Custer), the search was continued on the slopes below.

It was there on the battlefield that the metal-detector operators came upon an area that gave unusually intense indications of buried metal artifacts. A few trial probes uncovered a thick concentration of burnt leather, saddle fittings, personal possessions, and nails. But there were no human remains among them. This was clearly a dump of abandoned equipment, covered by a thin layer of soil that had washed down the slope in the intervening century. And a review of the memoirs of some of the survivors of the Reno-Benteen defense provided a suggestive account of its origin.

On June 27, 1876, after nearly two days of continuous fighting, Reno and Benteen's troops sensed that the attacks by the Sioux and Cheyenne had abated, at least temporarily. Hastily burying their own dead on the ridgetop, they moved their camp downslope to a small plateau away from the stench of the unburied horses that still lay where they fell. With the withdrawal of the Sioux and Cheyenne from the valley, most of the troopers were dispatched to the Custer battlefield for the distasteful task of burying the dead. Others remained at the campsite to prepare for an imminent retreat. Many of the wounded needed immediate attention, and it was crucial that the decimated regiment not be slowed by all the gear they had brought to the Little Bighorn in their packtrain. As a result, they destroyed and burned their excess equipment.

That dump, precisely dated to June 27, 1876, and presumably containing representative types of the 7th Cavalry's field equipment, offered invaluable information about the kinds and quality of equipment carried by the troopers under Major Marcus Reno's command. But unfortunately, the dump was discovered at the very end of the 1985 digging season, and a full excavation of its thousands of artifacts was impossible at that time. In the years that followed, Doug Scott and his colleagues, though fully occupied with the analyses of the other finds, still hoped to return. Meanwhile, they kept the location of the dump site a carefully guarded secret.

By the winter of 1988 it was clear that the secret had somehow gotten out. News of the discovery gradually spread among collectors of western military memorabilia, and Scott was alerted to disturbing rumors that professional relic hunters were planning to dig the dump secretly. Indeed, Park Service officials noted an alarming rise in illicit activities in the vicinity. In 1988 there were eight reports of unauthorized digging at the Reno-Benteen defense site, compared to only four at the Custer Battlefield. Thus, the renewed excavations were meant to uncover and preserve the valuable evidence before it was lost.

Even before the renewed excavations, Doug Scott suspected that the cavalry's equipment might provide an indirect insight into the political issues that lay in the background of Custer's Last Stand. Although largely ignored in the popular mythmaking that had swirled around Custer for more than a century, the policy of the U.S. government toward the Indians of the Northern Plains was a matter of intense debate in 1876. Public opinion wavered between a desire to "civilize" the Indians and the more expedient path of wiping them out.

The Grant administration tended to favor missionary work over killing, in order to transform the Indians of the region into productive farmers who would not object to the railroads and the settlement of the land. Opposing him and his Republican political allies was a coalition of eastern industrialists and southern Democrats who wanted the army in the West to be given a freer and more violent hand. Not unexpectedly, the debate manifested itself in the question of congressional appropriations. Scott hoped that the quality and type of equipment used by the 7th Cavalry might provide an indication of the practical effects of this national debate.

From the paved visitors' trail along the ridgetop, all that could be seen of this phase of the 1989 Reno-Benteen dump-site excavation were a small nylon tent for storing equipment, a few shallow squares and a few diggers, and a dappling of small orange flags where the metal detectors had pinpointed buried finds. But the finds from the dump site proved to be plentiful. By the end of the three weeks of digging, more than 2,000 individual artifacts had been found. Volunteer specialists were able to identify staples, rivets, and buckles as saddle and harness fittings. Nails of varying sizes were recognized as coming from boxes containing rations and ammunition. Personal items were also retrieved: a tin camp kettle, mother-of-pearl shirt buttons, and various gun parts.

None of the equipment recovered thus far seems to be the redesigned models that had been authorized for army use in 1875. Custer's famous 7th Cavalry, according to the initial archaeological findings, was equipped with refitted Civil War equipment that had already become obsolete. What role that may have played in the course of the battle is still uncertain, but months of detailed analysis still lie ahead. With the aid of computer plotting of the patterns of excavated nails, staples, and rivets, the team hopes to identify many more individual pieces of equipment that were burned or had rotted away. Scott and his colleagues are deeply intrigued by the question of whether the army's best and brightest—so bitterly mourned as fallen heroes after their deaths at the Little Bighorn—were provided with the army's most up-to-date equipment and arms. The antimythic implications of that question—even without its definitive answer—reflect a clear, late-twentieth-century perspective on the Battle of the Little Bighorn.

The myth of Custer has already been subtly altered by the new information gained in the digging—in attempting to understand the larger political context of frontier military operations, in offering a graphic description of the battlefield violence, and in underlining the tactical skill of the Indian forces. Yet few modern Native Americans have taken solace from the archaeological findings. In the midst of the chronic unemployment, alcoholism, and poverty that plague the reservations of the area, many of the Indians of the northern Great Plains are now looking back to the Battle of the Little Bighorn from their own embittered viewpoint.

Ernie Robinson, vice-chairman of the Northern Cheyenne tribe, put it succinctly when I spoke with him at his office at the tribal headquarters in Lame Deer, about twenty-five miles east of the Custer Battlefield. "At the Little Bighorn, we were pushed to the point where we had to make a statement. It was a turning point in our struggle for survival, but it wasn't only Custer's Last Stand, it was our last stand, too." And now, in the wake of the archaeological excavations and the attendant publicity, the Native

Americans of the Great Plains are intent on promoting their modern-day vision of that bitter chapter in Indian-white history.

As early as the 1930s, proposals had been put forth—mostly from white people—to erect a monument at the Custer Battlefield to acknowledge the victory and the later bitter sacrifices endured by the winning side. None, however, ever amounted to more than a passing suggestion, due to the continuing official veneration of Custer as a martyred hero and to a reticence by Native American authorities to bring up the issue at a time of more pressing modern concerns. For some Native Americans, the very idea of a historical monument is foreign; the mass grave of the 7th Cavalry soldiers on Last Stand Hill and the 252 white marble markers scattered across the battlefield seem to be the most eloquent commemoration of what took place there.

Yet the archaeological excavations at the site have refocused attention on the Custer battle at a time when Native American attitudes are changing. At this date, a new plan to memorialize the Indian viewpoint—and the estimated 100 Indian casualties in the battle—has moved far beyond the suggestion stage. On the official recommendation of the superintendent of the Custer Battlefield National Monument and the director of the National Park Service, a commission of historians, civic leaders, and Native American representatives has assembled to oversee the planning and construction of an Indian monument at the site. A design competition has formally opened under the aegis of the National Endowment for the Arts, and plans have been formulated for the erection of the monument on the Custer Battlefield by 1992.

Despite the long-standing tensions between the Crow tribe (who are still remembered as the scouts for the 7th Cavalry) and the Cheyenne and the Sioux (the primary Indian participants in the battle), the projected monument has become a unifying symbol for the current political and economic struggles of all Native Americans. Naturally, the old antagonisms among the various Northern Plains tribes will not be erased easily by this symbolic gesture, but the new historical emphasis at the Custer Battlefield may play a part in reshaping modern attitudes.

Many ghosts haunt the ridges and ravines of the Custer Battlefield; in fact, when the first superintendent was sent out by the War Department in 1893 to occupy the lonely stone house on the ridge above the river, the local Crows called him the "ghostherder." They believed that in raising the American flag every morning he was signaling to the spirits of the soldiers killed in battle to hasten back to their graves. Even today many Native Americans consider the archaeological search for human bones ghoulish and find it difficult to understand why the archaeologists would want to disturb the eternal rest of the dead. The recent discovery of the cavalryman's skull on the banks of the Little Bighorn River, on land still technically within the Crow Reservation, has brought angry criticism from Gilbert Birdingrand, a local Crow landowner, and from tribal authorities.

Yet for the archaeologists—the modern-day ghostherders—the recovery of bones, bullets, and abandoned military equipment has justified their faith in the importance of battlefield archaeology. Their methods may have profound implications for the study of battlefields all over the world. At the Little Bighorn, they have shown that the tangible remains of conflict may be invaluable in confirming or refuting conventional historical theories, participants' memories, and official battle accounts.

The Custer Battlefield National Monument—like the ancient sites of Troy in Turkey and Masada in Israel—remains the object of obsessive attraction, for it continues to offer a vivid backdrop to a still-potent myth. Though modern understandings may be changed by new facts about the battle, the event's symbolic significance remains. Custer's Last Stand did not end on that hot afternoon in June 1876. The struggle of whites to take over the West, and the struggle of Native Americans to resist it, is kept alive by the myth of George Armstrong Custer, whose troopers and Indian opponents, at least on a symbolic level, still stubbornly refuse to die.

*WINTER 1990*

Neil Asher Silberman is the author of the earlier essay on the Pequot War.

# 18

# Last Stand

## By Robert M. Utley

*Robert M. Utley's article provides a different perspective on the Little Bighorn than the previous essay by Neil Asher Silberman. In examining the battle, Utley asks why Custer lost. Was not Custer the best and boldest of the frontier army? And was not the 7th Cavalry just as famed as its commander? Was it Custer's folly that brought on the calamity? His misplaced daring? Or was it the fault of Custer's subordinates, Major Marcus Reno and Captain Frederick Benteen, who failed to support their brave commander at his critical moment of need? Or, just perhaps, did it have little to do with Custer and the 7th Cavalry at all?*

MASSACRED! screamed the headlines of newspapers all over the United States. An Indian fight in remote Montana stunned the entire nation in the centennial summer of 1876 and has stirred the popular imagination ever since. The Battle of the Little Bighorn—Custer's Last Stand—seems forever destined to command fascination, controversy, speculation, debate, and painstaking reconstruction.

In that year of 1876 the United States manufactured a war against the Sioux. Under the Treaty of 1868, most of these people had settled on a huge reservation in Dakota Territory. But some 3,000 tribesmen continued to roam the buffalo ranges in Wyoming and Montana, a right conceded by the treaty. They gave allegiance to the dynamic Sitting Bull, a political, military, and spiritual leader of commanding influence and rocklike opposition to all relations with the whites. At first these tribesmen, known as "nontreaties," were simply a nuisance, stirring up trouble and offering a summer haven for restless reservation Indians. But when they threatened violence to any chief who gave in to the Great Father's demand that the Sioux sell the gold-rich Black Hills, they had to be neutralized. Since the Sitting Bull bands had provided no recent pretext for war, the government simply labeled them "hostile" and ordered them to abandon the old free life and settle on the reservation. From this order, predictably ignored by the Sioux bands scattered over the winter landscape, sprang the Great Sioux War of 1876.

Lieutenant General Philip H. Sheridan, the Great Plains commander, ordered three strong columns to converge on the Indian country of the Powder and Yellowstone river basins. Their mission was to drive the "hostiles" to the reservation. Brigadier General George Crook marched north from Fort Fetterman in southern Wyoming, Colonel John Gibbon descended the Yellowstone River from Fort Ellis in western Montana, and Brigadier General Alfred H. Terry moved west from Fort Abraham Lincoln in Dakota. With Terry rode the entire 7th Cavalry Regiment under command of its lieutenant colonel, Brevet Major General George Armstrong Custer.

The personality of this flamboyant cavalier, now thirty-six, gave rise to much of the controversy that followed. A gloriously triumphant "boy general" in the Civil War, he had achieved new fame on the western frontier as Indian fighter, sportsman, plainsman, and author. Among acquaintances, he inspired veneration or loathing, never indifference. Some saw him as reckless, brutal, egotistical, unprincipled, and immature. Others looked on him as upright, sincere, compassionate, honorable, above all fearless in battle and brilliant in leading men to victory. And he was lucky.

In this campaign as in all others, Custer intended to win glory for himself and the 7th Cavalry. But besides his usual ambition, this time he had special incentive. As punishment for congressional testimony charging the administration of Ulysses S. Grant with frontier frauds, he had been publicly humiliated by the president himself, denied command of the Fort Lincoln column, and allowed to lead his own regiment only at the last moment. Whether he sacrificed 250 men in an attempt to wipe out the stain will be debated endlessly.

Although a veteran regiment, the 7th Cavalry was not a tightly knit fighting machine. The officer corps was severely faction-ridden. A "royal family" enjoyed Custer's favor, while those excluded suffered his discrimination and found constant fault with his leadership. Among other sins, they suspected him of a flagrant hypocrisy that concealed his own brand of frontier fraud as well as a supposedly idyllic marriage that nonetheless tolerated infidelity.

Aggravating the rift on this campaign, the "royal family" included no fewer than five Custers: the regimental commander himself; brother Tom, winner of two Civil War medals of honor and now captain of C Company; brother Boston, a civilian hired as a "guide"; a namesake nephew, Armstrong ("Autie") Reed, carried on the payroll as a herder; and brother-in-law James ("Jimmi") Calhoun, commander of L Company.

Moreover, Custer's two senior subordinates detested him and each other. Major Marcus A. Reno, socially inept, a weak man and weak officer, enjoyed little respect. Captain Frederick W. Benteen, a first-rate company commander but a sour, crotchety troublemaker, had led the opposition to Custer for ten years. That neither enjoyed a rapport with his commander held ominous tactical implications.

None of the column commanders did well. Colonel Gibbon found the main Indian encampment in March, but let it get away. More serious, on June 17 General Crook allowed himself to be surprised and routed at the

Battle of the Rosebud. He withdrew from the campaign altogether, with calamitous consequences. At last, in mid-June, Terry and Gibbon met on the Yellowstone and laid plans to corner the Sioux.

On the afternoon of June 21, Terry summoned Custer and the other senior officers to gather around a big map aboard the steamer *Far West,* moored to the bank of the Yellowstone at the mouth of Rosebud Creek. Terry laid out his plan. An Indian trail of about 400 lodges pointed up the Rosebud Valley, and the scouts guessed that it would lead over the mountains to the Little Bighorn River. The general envisioned a strong, swift-moving strike force searching out the Indians and driving them against a less mobile blocking force. Custer and his cavalry would attack, Gibbon and his infantry block.

Terry's plan called for Custer to push up the Rosebud on the Indian trail and Gibbon, with Terry accompanying, to march up the Yellowstone and Bighorn to a blocking position at the mouth of the Little Bighorn. If the Indians turned out to be on the Little Bighorn, Custer would attack from the south and Gibbon intercept any who tried to get away to the north.

Custer's movements, all understood, had to be governed by circumstances, for the Sioux might not be on the Little Bighorn. Therefore, Custer's written orders laid out his mission in discretionary terms. He was to follow the trail up the Rosebud. If it turned to the Little Bighorn, he was still to continue up the Rosebud before swinging west to the upper Little Bighorn—this to make certain that the Indians did not escape to the south or east and to give Gibbon, with his infantry, time to get to the Little Bighorn. Terry expected him to be there by June 26, but this date had no other significance. The notion that Terry meant Custer to attack on June 26 arose only after the offensive ended in disaster.

No one worried much about enemy strength. This reflected the usual military assumption that the Indians would scatter and run if given the chance. If only they could be caught, Custer often boasted, the 7th could whip any force of Indians on the Plains. Thus Terry's plan focused on how to catch the Indians, not how to defeat them.

The trail up the Rosebud was made by Sitting Bull's "nontreaties"— 3,000 people, 800 fighting men. The generals knew that each summer many Indians came from the reservations to join their brethren for the warm months, but how many there might be and when they might arrive did not enter into the planning.

At that time, Indian movements were taking place that would decisively affect the military plan. Sitting Bull's village had in fact turned from the Rosebud to the Little Bighorn. Here their brethren began to arrive from the reservation. In only six days, the encampment more than doubled, from 400 to 1,000 lodges, from 3,000 to 7,000 people, from 800 to 2,000 warriors.

There in the valley of the river the Sioux called the Greasy Grass lay a village of unusual size. Such numbers consumed immense quantities of game, forage, and firewood and so could not remain long in one place, or even together in one village. The coincidence of timing that brought the

7th Cavalry to the vicinity of this village during the few days of its peak strength was only the beginning of a run of ill fortune that ended in the utter collapse of "Custer's Luck."

For three days the 7th Cavalry marched in billowing dust up Rosebud Creek. The tree-lined stream snaked back and forth in the narrow valley, forcing frequent crossings. Ahead, the grassy ridges shouldering the valley merged into a low range of blue mountains dividing the Rosebud and the Little Bighorn.

"Passed several large camps," recorded Custer's itinerist on the afternoon of June 24. "The trail was now fresh, and the whole valley scratched up by the trailing lodge poles." Although the officers did not understand that additional reservation Indians were trampling the older trail made by Sitting Bull, they did perceive the meaning of the fresh pony droppings: Indians had to be just over the mountains, on the Little Bighorn.

Swiftly, Custer made a crucial decision. To continue up the Rosebud made no sense. It would force him to lose touch with an enemy that he had in his immediate front, to make a long detour through country that he knew could not harbor many Indians, and to risk the very possibility that everyone dreaded—the escape of the Indians.

Calling his officers together over a flickering candle, Custer outlined a new plan. Instead of continuing up the Rosebud, he would follow the Indian trail across the divide under cover of night, spend the next day resting the command and fixing the location of the Sioux, then hit with a dawn attack on June 26, the date Gibbon was to reach the mouth of the Little Bighorn.

Roused from their blankets at midnight, the troopers groped blindly forward in the darkness, marching about six miles up a rough, rocky valley. At 2:00 A.M., still short of the summit, they halted to await daylight.

At about 8:00 A.M. Custer received word that his scouts had spotted the Sioux village from a nearby mountain peak called the Crow's Nest. He rode to the top himself, but by this time the sun had risen and a haze had settled over the landscape. Nonetheless, he had no reason to doubt his scouts. His objective lay in the Little Bighorn Valley only fifteen miles to the west.

The scouts gave Custer other, and disquieting, information. From their perch high above the surrounding country, they had seen three separate parties of Sioux warriors. That at least one of these groups would discover the soldiers and rush to alert the village seemed probable.

Instantly, Custer made another crucial decision. All experience pointed to the certainty that he had been discovered. The gnawing fear that had ridden with the regiment all the way from Fort Lincoln was about to be realized: The village would break up and flee in all directions. In another stroke of bad luck, Custer could not know that the Sioux in his vicinity were on their way back to the reservations and in fact would not sound the alarm. From his perspective, there could be only one proper decision: Find the village and strike it as soon as possible.

An attack plan could not be formulated until the exact location of the village had been pinpointed and some impression gained of the surrounding terrain. So, instead of sending out the reconnoitering parties he had planned for this day, Custer advanced in a reconnaissance in force employing the entire regiment. The attack plan would have to take shape as events unfolded.

The noon sun shone torrid in a cloudless sky as the 7th Cavalry, 600 strong and trailing a mule train, crossed a low divide and paused at the head of a stream later named Reno Creek. Custer had shed his jacket and wore a dark blue shirt with buckskin trousers encased in boots. A broad-brimmed white hat shaded his bearded, sunburned face. Two holsters on his belt contained a brace of stubby English Webley "bulldog" pistols. His personal flag followed, but the regimental standard remained furled.

Custer had Adjutant William W. Cooke form the regiment into battalions, to reconnoiter or maneuver for combat as circumstances required. Major Reno commanded one, consisting of Companies M, A, and G—140 officers and enlisted men. Captain Benteen led another, Companies H, D, and K, about 125 strong. Companies E and F under Captain George W. Yates and C, I, and L under Captain Myles W. Keogh, about 225 horsemen, remained under Custer's direct control. Captain Thomas M. McDougall and B Company guarded the pack train and brought up the rear.

To Custer, the first task was to ensure that no Indians had found their way to the upper Little Bighorn. Since a ridge blocked the view to the south, he assigned Benteen to seek the needed intelligence. He was to oblique his battalion to the left and send a reconnaissance party to the crest of the ridge to scan the Little Bighorn Valley, then rejoin the rest of the command farther down Reno Creek.

The rest of the regiment took up the march down Reno Creek, Custer and his two battalions on the right side, Reno with his one on the left. The pack train and McDougall's B Company fell increasingly to the rear. They were half an hour behind when they met Benteen, returning to the main trail, at a spongy morass in the creek.

Benteen had accomplished his mission. The upper Little Bighorn Valley appeared to be empty of Indians. Doubtful that Custer knew what he was doing, Benteen neither sent a courier ahead with this information nor quickened the pace of his march to catch up.

Three miles ahead, Custer and Reno halted at an abandoned village site. From a nearby hill, Interpreter Fred Gerard began waving his hat and shouting. He had spotted a party of warriors down the creek valley in the distance racing their ponies toward the river. Custer ordered Reno to push forward at a trot. Following, Custer saw dust boiling up from behind high bluffs that hid the Little Bighorn Valley on his right front.

A trot of about three miles brought the two columns to within a mile of the Little Bighorn. Custer could defer decision no longer. The rising dust meant that he had at last found the village and, coupled with the warriors retreating in his front, that its occupants had taken alarm and were trying to get away. The situation demanded an immediate attack. Custer sent Cooke with orders for Reno: The village lay ahead two miles; the Indians were running away; move rapidly forward, "and charge afterward, and you will be supported by the whole outfit."

Instead of following Reno, however, Custer obliqued his five companies to the right, toward the crest of the bluffs. His subordinate expected support from the rear, but Custer had apparently decided to give support by falling on the Indians' rear as they fought Reno in front. This would have the added advantage, if the Sioux were running after all, of cutting off their escape route. In either event, hitting from more than one direction could be expected to strike panic in the enemy.

In parallel columns of twos, the five companies galloped up the long gentle slope toward the bluff tops. After a mile, they halted short of the brow. Custer, his orderly trumpeter for the day, John Martin, and several Crow scouts rode to the top and looked out over the valley. Just below, the river swung in a wide loop out over the valley. "Down the valley," recalled one of the Crow scouts, "were camps and camps and camps. There was a big camp in a circle near the west hills." Below also, related another of the Crows, "we could see Reno fighting. Everything was a scramble with lots of Sioux."

Battle had thus been joined, and Custer had to get the rest of the regiment into it as swiftly as possible. Back at the command he conferred briefly with Cooke and other officers, including his brother, Captain Tom Custer. As the march resumed, Tom rode to his company and, motioning to Sergeant Daniel Kanipe, told him to hurry back to Captain McDougall with orders from the general. "Tell McDougall," he instructed, "to bring the pack train straight across to high ground—if packs get loose don't stop to fix them, cut them off. Come quick. Big Indian camp."

As Kanipe turned aside, Custer signaled the advance. Some of the horses became excited and broke into a gallop, out in front even of Custer. "Boys, hold your horses," Custer shouted, "there are plenty of them down there for us all." The command swung to the right, down a long ravine falling away from the heights. It was narrow and forced the formation into a single column. After a mile, the ravine opened into a broad coulee now known as Medicine Tail, which ran toward the river and gave promise of ending in a ford. Custer signaled a left turn into the coulee.

Anxious to get Benteen into the fight and worried about ammunition, Custer decided to send another courier. He motioned for his orderly trumpeter, Martin, and barked instructions. Martin had immigrated from Italy, where his name had been Giovanni Martini. Adjutant Cooke, distrusting the trumpeter's mastery of English, scrawled a message on a page torn from his memorandum book and handed it to him: "Benteen. Come on. Big Village. Be Quick. Bring Packs. W. W. Cooke. P. bring pacs."

Spurring his horse up the back trail, Martin glanced over his shoulder. "The last I saw of the command they were going down into the ravine [Medicine Tail Coulee]. The gray horse troop was in the center and they were galloping."

Shortly after Martin's departure, Custer divided his command. He sent Yates's two-company battalion galloping down Medicine Tail Coulee toward the Little Bighorn, and he posted Captain Keogh's three-company battalion in dismounted positions on a ridge separating Medicine Tail from the next drainage to the north, Deep Coulee.

A plausible explanation is that Custer intended Yates to hold the ford and threaten the Indians, thus relieving the pressure on Reno, until Benteen could come up and join in a powerful thrust into the village itself. Keogh's mission was to cover Benteen's approach route, then accompany him to the attack position. Whether Custer went with Yates or remained with Keogh is unknown.

Whatever Custer's plans, two crucial developments elsewhere doomed them: First, Benteen dawdled on the back trail, falling farther and farther behind the rest of the regiment. Neither Sergeant Kanipe nor Trumpeter Martin stirred the cranky captain into more than a trot. Only a gallop would have been responsive to Custer's expectation and need. Second, Reno did not hold his position at the upper end of the village. Met by several hundred shouting warriors, he dismounted and formed a skirmish line. Flanked, he quickly withdrew into a grove of timber along the river. Then, pressed by Sioux for half an hour or more, he ordered a retreat, which turned into a demoralized rout back across the river to the bluff tops from which Custer had first looked over the valley. This "charge," as Reno termed it, cost forty dead and thirteen wounded.

The actions of his two subordinates left Custer to fend for himself. Reno's retreat freed all the Indians to concentrate on Custer. Benteen's languor brought him to Reno's hilltop position and thus under Reno's command. The demoralization of Reno's shattered battalion, combined with the indecision of the two ranking officers, kept seven companies and the pack train out of action at the most critical moment for the other five.

Yates's two companies reached the Little Bighorn opposite the center of the Indian camp. A hot fire greeted them from warriors posted in the brush on the other side. Sitting Bull, who remained in the village, later described this action succinctly: "Our young men rained lead across the river and drove the white braves back."

At first, only a handful of warriors, perhaps thirty, held the ford against Yates. But they quickly received help as men returned from the pony herd with their mounts, and others, freed by Reno's withdrawal, reached the new scene of action. Chief Gall, an inspiring leader, powerful in mind and body, led the forces across the river.

Yates's two companies retreated from the river, returning a ragged defensive fire as they rode, dismounting skirmishers to hold back the Indian advance. The soldiers "held their horses' reins on one arm while they were shooting," remembered Low Dog, "but the horses were so frightened that they pulled the men all around, and a great many of their shots went up in the air and did us no harm." The line of this fighting retreat lay up the northern slope of Deep Coulee toward a high ridge that offered the prospect of a better position.

Gall's warriors also hit Keogh. From dismounted skirmish lines, the troopers laid down a heavy fire that kept the Indians at bay. Although not seriously threatened, Keogh probably realized that Yates was in trouble and that the Indians gathering in Deep Coulee, to his rear, might isolate the two battalions from each other. Keogh withdrew northward toward a union with Yates.

Gall's warriors pressed closely. On the slope north of Deep Coulee. Keogh dismounted and formed a line. The Indians fired into the horse holders and dropped enough men to stampede the horses and put much of the battalion on foot. With the horses went the extra carbine ammunition. "After this," related Gall, "the soldiers threw aside their guns [carbines] and fought with little guns [pistols]." Dismounted, Keogh's men moved up the slope to join with Yates.

The union occurred on a flat hill, tilted toward the river and overlooking Deep Coulee, that is now named Calhoun Hill, for the L Company commander. Calhoun Hill formed the southern nose of a high ridge extending half a mile northward. This elevation came to be known as Battle Ridge. Commanding a sweeping vista of the river valley and the Bighorn Mountains beyond, Battle Ridge fell abruptly, amid tumbles of steep hills and deep ravines, to the valley below. On the east, a narrow ravine heading on Calhoun Hill bordered Battle Ridge and widened and deepened as it ran northward. On these slopes the final scenes of Custer's Last Stand unfolded.

What role Custer himself played can never be known. Almost certainly, no Indian recognized "Long Hair" in the smoke, dust, grime, and excitement of battle or, indeed, even knew they were fighting his soldiers. As hinted in some Indian account, he may even have fallen, dead or wounded, in the first fire at the mouth of Medicine Tail Coulee and been carried to the spot where his body was found. If he remained in the saddle on Calhoun Hill, he must by now have recognized how desperate was his plight. Faced with overwhelming numbers of well-armed warriors, caught in rough terrain unsuited to cavalry, partly dismounted, and with no trace of Benteen or the packs on the hills to the south, even Custer's robust self-confidence must have wavered.

If he still commanded, he saw more Indians to his left front, crossing the river at the mouth of a deep ravine draining the western slope of Battle Ridge. From this cover, they fired on the command's flank on Calhoun Hill. To counter this threat, one company advanced. "The Indians hidden there got back quickly," said a Cheyenne witness. The soldiers "stopped and got off their horses along another ridge, a low one just north of the deep gulch." Suddenly warriors led by Lame White Man, a Cheyenne, hit with an attack that overran the company and drove survivors back to Calhoun Hill.

Northward along Battle Ridge the fighting progressed with growing intensity. While Keogh held Calhoun Hill against the warriors streaming up Deep Coulee, Yates's two companies, possibly accompanied by Custer, fought their way along the ridge. From all directions, Indians converged in overpowering force.

The warriors made few if any grand mounted charges. Rather, they kept up a long-range fire, mostly from dismounted positions. They took advantage of hillocks, sagebrush clumps, tall grass, and folds and troughs of the terrain. From these hiding places, they struck down the cavalrymen with bullets and arrows. Loosed in high arcs, arrows fell with deadly effect on clusters of exposed troopers.

The fatal blow hit from the north. Crazy Horse, a magnetic leader and silent mystic, had led a large force of warriors down the Little Bighorn Valley to a crossing below the village, forded the river, and swept in a wide arc to climb Battle Ridge from the north. They struck the units with Custer and Yates and thrust up the ravine on the east leading to Calhoun Hill. Here they crushed Keogh's men against Gall's warriors beyond.

Although each of the companies made its "last stand," the last stand of history and legend occurred at the northern end of Battle Ridge, now known as Custer Hill. Here, most of F Company, part of E, and remnants of other companies gathered with the headquarters group. A large contingent of the cavalrymen broke toward the head of the deep ravine in the direction of the river. "We finished up this party right there in the ravine," said Red Horse.

On Custer Hill about forty survivors shot their horses for breastworks and fought until all died. Among the bodies found there were those of Custer, his brothers Tom and Boston, nephew Autie Reed, Yates, Cooke, and Lieutenants Algernon Smith and William Van W. Reily. Myles Keogh fell nearby, in the ravine east of Battle Ridge, with most of his company, I. Brother-in-law Jimmi and his company died defending Calhoun Hill, half a mile to the south.

The hot June sun hung low over the Bighorn Mountains when the last man fell, possibly two hours after Yates had opened the battle at the mouth of Medicine Tail Coulee. Exultant warriors raced their ponies around the battlefield, dispatching wounded men, firing their rifles in triumph, and raising great clouds of dust. Women and children made their way up the slopes from the village to rob, strip, and mutilate the bodies.

Four miles to the south, a trace of blue appeared atop a peaked hill beyond Medicine Tail Coulee. Hearing firing from the north, and irate over Reno's indecision, Captain Tom Weir had simply mounted his company, D, and moved to the sound of the guns. The rest of the command had followed hesitantly. Reaching the high hill later named Weir Point, the troops scanned the rugged terrain beyond. They discerned only a distant dust-clouded activity and, in the foreground, warriors galloping to head off their advance.

Falling back to their original hilltop position, the seven companies fought desperately until darkness brought relief. During the night they dug in, and next day, June 26, they held out as the emboldened Indians tried to carry their defenses. Reno displayed weak leadership. Benteen, fearlessly stalking the lines as enemy sharpshooters tried to drop him, inspired the troopers to valiant efforts. By midafternoon, the firing had tapered off.

Below, the Indians fired the valley's dry prairie grass. A wall of thick smoke screened the village. About 7:00 P.M., an immense procession of horsemen, women and children on foot, travois, ponies, and dogs emerged from behind the smoke. Slowly, it wound its way across the benchland to the southwest, toward the Bighorn Mountains.

Next morning, June 27, a blue column approaching up the valley explained the hasty withdrawal of the Indians. Two officers rode down to investigate. A short gallop brought them to the advance guard, General Terry in the van. Both general and lieutenants burst out with the same question: Where is Custer?

Lieutenant James H. Bradley and his Crow scouts brought the answer, and on the morning of June 28, Reno and his men rode down the river to see for themselves. "A scene of sickening ghastly horror," remembered one. The bodies, many of them stripped, scalped, and mutilated, all grotesquely bloated from the burning sun, lay scattered about the battlefield where they had dropped.

On Custer Hill, the knot of fallen men graphically portrayed the drama of the last stand. Although Cooke and Tom Custer had been badly butchered, most in this group escaped severe mutilation. "The bodies were as recognizable as if they were in life," Benteen wrote to his wife.

Although naked, "The General was not mutilated at all," a lieutenant remembered. "He laid on his back, his upper arms on the ground, the hands folded or so placed as to cross the body above the stomach: his position was natural and one that we had seen hundreds of times while [he was] taking cat naps during halts on the march. One hit was in the left temple, and one in the left breast at or near the heart."

A third wound may not have been visible to those who looked down on their former chief. The Cheyenne woman Kate Big Head related that two Southern Cheyenne women recognized Custer from his campaign in the Indian Territory in 1868–69, when he had been much admired by the women taken captive at the Battle of the Washita. Claiming that he was their relative, the two women prevented some Sioux men from mutilating the body. Continued Kate Big Head:

> The women then pushed the point of a sewing awl into each of his ears, into his head. This was done to improve his hearing, as it seemed he had not heard what our chiefs in the South said when he smoked the pipe with them. They told him then that if ever afterward he should break that peace promise and should fight the Cheyennes the Everywhere Spirit surely would cause him to be killed.

In their victory, the Sioux suffered defeat. After the Custer battle, they scattered. An outraged nation demanded retribution, and troops flooded the Indian country. Ultimately all the "hostiles" surrendered, even Sitting Bull—although only after four years of Canadian exile. Also, with soldiers now occupying the reservations, the chiefs had no choice but to sell the Black Hills. In fact, Custer's last stand had been theirs as well.

But the nagging questions remained: How could the massacre have happened? What flagrant blunders produced so awful a debacle? How could a commander and a regiment widely seen as the best on the frontier fall so spectacularly to a mob of untrained, unlettered natives?

Custer is usually branded the scapegoat. Given what he knew or could anticipate at each decision point, however, one is hard-pressed to say what he ought to have done differently. The failures of Reno and Benteen contributed to the disaster. But, more decisively, Custer's vaunted luck simply ran out on that day. Contrary to the popular interpretation, Custer died less the victim of bad judgment than of bad luck.

But to ascribe defeat entirely to military failings is an ethnocentric devaluation of Indian strength and leadership. The Sioux and Cheyennes were strong, confident, united, well led, well armed, outraged by the government's war aims, and ready to fight if pressed. Rarely had the army encountered such a mighty combination in an Indian adversary. Perhaps no strategy or tactics could have prevailed against the Indian power that day. Perhaps the truest explanation is that Custer lost because Sitting Bull won.

*AUTUMN 1988*

Robert M. Utley is a former chief historian of the National Park Service. He has written extensively on the American frontier, including his most recent work, *The Lance and the Shield: The Life and Times of Sitting Bull* (1993). At present, he is researching a book on the mountain men and the fur trade.

# 19

# Geronimo

## By Robert M. Utley

*Of all the Indians the United States Army faced on the western frontier, it considered the Apaches the toughest. The army viewed its opponent as wily, robust, and brutal, a foe who bedeviled the inhabitants on both sides of the American-Mexican border. Unlike the Sioux or Cheyenne to the north, the Apache warriors were even more effective on foot than on horse. They seemed to be as one with their harsh and unforgiving environment, appearing and then disappearing apparently at will, leaving their bloody work behind them. Arguably the greatest of the Apaches— and certainly the best known—was Geronimo. "No serpent," recalled one army officer, "can surpass him in cunning." The same could be said for lethality. But even the courage and determination of Geronimo could not stop the tide of westward expansion. His surrender to General Nelson A. Miles in 1886 effectively brought to an end the Indian wars that had for so long been a part of American history. As Geronimo faced General Miles that hot September day, he stood—Robert M. Utley reminds us—as America's last Indian warrior.*

The desert sun seared the rocky canyon as the Apache climbed from his horse and advanced cautiously to face the white general. Hard and wiry despite his more than sixty years, his countenance locked in a perpetual scowl, his dark leathery skin gnarled by a lifetime in the outdoors and scarred by the bullet and arrow wounds of countless battles, Geronimo confronted Brigadier General Nelson A. Miles. "He had the clearest, sharpest dark eye I think I have ever seen," Miles recalled. "Every movement indicated power, energy and determination."

For two days each rival took the measure of the other. Rarely had Geronimo trusted any American or Mexican, but now, failing to gain surrender terms, he sought some reassurance that the new soldier chief could be trusted not to hand him over to the vengeful citizens of Tucson who clamored for his execution. Geronimo's handful of followers, still armed, warily camped nearby, coiled to stampede on the slightest pretext. Suspicion had ruled the volatile Apache too long to succumb to a sudden impulse to trust, but the talks convinced him that his best course was to gamble that the white soldier would keep his word.

The next day, riding side by side across the shimmering flat expanse of the San Simon Valley, Geronimo and Miles scanned the dark mass of the Chiricahua Mountains on the horizon.

"This is the fourth time I have surrendered," mused the old Indian.

"And I think it is the last time you will ever have occasion to surrender," replied the veteran general.

Miles was right. On September 4, 1886, in Skeleton Canyon, a valley in a chain of mountains tracing the eastern boundary of the Arizona Territory, Geronimo's career as a warrior drew to a close. The Apache Wars ended. More than that, four centuries of war between Indian and European for mastery of North America ended. The Sioux ghost-dance troubles four years later cannot be dignified as war; they were not an outbreak or a rebellion but rather a spiritual movement that ended in violence. Geronimo, by contrast, rose in true revolt against the U.S. government, employing techniques of partisan warfare honed to perfection in half a century of nearly constant practice. When he yielded his rifle to General Miles on that scorching day in Skeleton Canyon, he laid claim to the distinction of being America's last Indian warrior.

Other Apaches enjoyed greater stature, but it was the squat, thickset Geronimo who emerged in the 1880s as the preeminent war leader. None of the others equaled him in mastery of the partisan fighting style that so confounded the U.S. Army. In cunning, stealth, endurance, perseverance, ruthlessness, fortitude, fighting skill, and command of the harsh conditions of his homeland, he excelled. Of all the Apache captains, recalled a warrior who rode with him, "Geronimo seemed to be the most intelligent and resourceful as well as the most vigorous and farsighted. In times of danger he was a man to be relied upon."

Although not a chief, and despised by many of his own people, Geronimo compiled a record of intransigence in peace and skill in war that made him the terror of two nations. Mexican peasants saw him as a devil sent to punish them for their sins. Americans looked on him as the personification of the merciless brutality of Apache warfare.

For citizens of both countries, it was surpassingly brutal. Nowhere else in the American West did residents work their spreads or travel their roads in more deadly peril. Children might be spared, to be reared as captive members of the tribe, but adults could expect no compassion. If not killed instantly, they were taken back to a *rancheria* to be dispatched by women who had lost a loved one. "They used to tie Mexicans with their hands behind their backs," remembered one Apache. "Then they turned the women loose with axes and knives to kill the Mexican prisoner. The man could hardly run, and the women would chase him around until they killed him."

Settlers on both sides of the boundary recounted dreadful tales of Apache butchery, mutilation, and torture. Doubtless some were true. But what made Apache warfare so brutal was the finality of nearly every encounter. Apache raids were economic in their purpose, centering more on plunder than homicide. But Apache warfare, undertaken only after intolerable provocation, centered on killing the enemy. Both Mexicans and, later, Americans furnished the provocation.

The essence of the Apache fighting qualities so perfectly embodied by Geronimo lay in consummate adaptation of man to environment. No region of North America presented more extreme environmental conditions than the Apache country in the southwestern United States and northern Mexico: vast expanses of sand and stone; islands of rocky peaks webbed by treacherous canyons; widely scattered and uncertain water holes; cactus, mesquite, prickly pear, and a profusion of other flora armed with thorns; snakes, scorpions, centipedes, tarantulas, and Gila monsters. Temperatures soared to 120° in the shade in summer and fell to chill depths at night in winter.

From infancy the Apache warrior was reared to master the environment and turn it to his advantage and the enemy's disadvantage. Powerful muscles, a barrel chest, and years of practice enabled him to run up to seventy-five miles a day on little or no water or food. He could function on horseback but preferred to move and fight on foot. With bow and arrows, lance, and knife, he was an imposing foe, but with repeating rifle he became the bravest, boldest, wiliest, most formidable fighter in North America. He excelled at ambush, sudden surprise, and hit-and-run tactics. He could appear out of nowhere and disappear without a trace. "No serpent can surpass him in cunning," marveled an army officer.

Apache warfare confronted the U.S. Army with three daunting challenges. First was the individual fighter himself, superior in every aspect of combat to the typical regular soldier. Second was the deftness of small parties of warriors in staging ambushes. "When you see Apache sign," cautioned an experienced frontiersman, "be *keerful;* n' when you don' see nary sign, be *more* keerful." Third was the Apache's ability to elude pursuit while wearing out his pursuers.

For the army, the third challenge proved the most baffling and most punishing—for it made the terrain and the weather, rather than the Apaches, the true enemy. Almost never could troops close with the foe. The recollection of one soldier typified most:

> For five or six nights we climbed the mountains on one side and slid down the other, leading our horses, battered and bruised ourselves among the boulders, pricked our flesh with the cactus spines we ran against in the dark, dodged the rolling stones sent crashing down by those above us on the trail, and suffered for want of water which was hardly to be had at all. We marched all night and lay during the day in the red hot cañons, their sides adding, by reflected heat, to the warmth of the sand on which we usually camped, without shade, and without having as much fire as would make a cup of coffee.

These endowments Geronimo possessed in full measure. More, he possessed the motivation to use them with ruthless tenacity. Within him lurked an abiding hatred of Mexicans, which powered a thirty-year vendetta without parallel even in Apache annals.

Geronimo's deadly malice had its origins in generations of hostility between his people and the Hispanic colonizers of the land. It was a relationship that was shaped by a strange alternation between raid and trade, by mutual enslavement, and by the bounty the Mexican government offered for Apache scalps. To this heritage Geronimo added his own personal vengeance.

Around 1850, when he was a young warrior approaching thirty, Geronimo had accompanied a trading party under the great chief Mangas Coloradas to the Chihuahuan town of Janos. While remaining in enmity with Sonorans west of the Sierra Madre Occidental, the Indians had patched up one of their periodic truces with the Chihuahuans east of the mountains. Late one night, returning from a drinking bout in Janos, the men discovered that a contingent of Sonoran provincials had fallen on their lodges, killed many of their families, and made off with their stock.

Goyahkla, not yet called Geronimo, lost all. "I found that my aged mother, my young wife, and my three small children were among the slain," he remembered many years later. "I was never again contented in our quiet home. I had vowed vengeance upon the Mexican troops . . . and whenever I . . . saw anything to remind me of former happy days my heart would ache for revenge upon Mexico." Over the next three decades, while acquiring more wives and more children, he carried out his resolve in a scourge that left no village, hacienda, or caravan in Chihuahua or Sonora secure from his pillage and butchery.

His personal tragedy added another dimension to Geronimo's makeup—the mystical virtue the Apaches called "Power." Grieving in wilderness solitude, he heard a voice call his name four times—a sacred counting for all Indians—and intone, "No gun can ever kill you." Indeed, although many bullets hit him, none ever killed him. Besides arming him with a reckless self-assurance in battle, Geronimo's special Power endowed him with extrasensory perception: Repeatedly he foresaw dangers or sensed distant happenings, astonishing his comrades and enhancing his stature.

In one of his first onslaughts, a well-organized revenge expedition for the Janos massacre, Goyahkla demonstrated his new Power and acquired the name by which his enemies knew him for the rest of his life. During a pitched battle with Sonoran troops near Arispe, according to tradition, Goyahkla fought with such conspicuous ferocity that the soldiers cried out, "*Cuidado!* Watch out! Geronimo!"—possibly a rough Spanish corruption of the guttural Apache rendering of Goyahkla. Admiring warriors picked up the shout as a battle cry, and thenceforth Goyahkla was Geronimo. (Another explanation is that the soldiers were invoking the name of Saint Jerome for help on the battlefield.)

The raids in Chihuahua and Sonora were an established element in the Apache subsistence pattern. Deer, small game, and edible desert vegetation afforded a scant and undependable source of food, especially after growing numbers of European invaders thinned the animal population. Plunder evolved as an essential supplement to the traditional diet and an important component of material culture.

The advent of Americans after the Mexican War of 1846–48 did not disturb Apache raiding habits. Except for a few isolated collisions, an uneasy accommodation reigned for more than a decade. The two most powerful chiefs, Mangas Coloradas of the Warm Springs and Cochise of the Chiricahuas, maintained generally friendly relations with Americans while continuing to devastate Mexico. By the early 1860s, however, official blundering and increasing encroachment by white settlers had turned the Apaches against the Americans.

As Geronimo grew in stature, especially after the death of Mangas Coloradas in 1863, he was more and more to be found with Chief Juh's Nednhis, a composite of offshoots from other Apache tribes, in the rugged, towering Sierra Madre of Mexico. But life was hard, with game scarce and raids on Mexicans dangerous and costly. The prospect of rations and security on American reservations enticed many to try the new life.

Geronimo was not immune to the lure. Joining in the peace concluded between General Oliver O. Howard and Cochise in 1872, he and his family settled down on the Chiricahua Reservation in Arizona. Here he and other warriors could leave their families in safety while conducting periodic forays south of the border. When the government broke up this reservation in 1876 and moved its people to the San Carlos Reservation, Geronimo bolted to New Mexico and joined the Warm Springs Apaches on their reservation at Ojo Caliente. From here he continued to strike at Mexico and also at American stockmen and farmers along the Rio Grande.

These indiscretions focused an official spotlight on Geronimo and his comrades and led to an event that raised Americans to the status of Mexicans in his gallery of personal demons. Ordered to arrest the "renegades," the brash young agent at San Carlos, John P. Clum, appeared at the New Mexico reservation in April 1877 with a contingent of Indian police. In a tense, face-to-face confrontation with Clum, Geronimo defiantly proclaimed: "We are not going to San Carlos with you, and unless you are very careful, you and your Apache police will not go back to San Carlos either. Your bodies will stay here at Ojo Caliente to make food for coyotes."

At Clum's signal, police reinforcements poured out of a nearby building and surrounded the rebellious Apaches. Geronimo's thumb sprang to the hammer of his rifle, then relaxed as he surveyed the odds.

Geronimo did go back to San Carlos, in irons. There he remained shackled for several months in the agency lockup while Clum prodded the sheriff at Tucson to come get Geronimo and have him tried in civil court for murder. But the sheriff did not come, Clum lost his position, and Geronimo went free. "It might easily have been death for me," he observed years later.

The humiliation of being taken without a fight, the indignity of the white man's shackles, and the brush with the hangman's noose left Geronimo with a deep hatred of Americans and a suspicion so intense it governed all his subsequent dealings with them.

Reservation life could not be expected to calm so fiercely independent a spirit as Geronimo's. His new home, moreover, was the most forbidding, corrupt, and tumultuous reservation in the West. The government wanted to concentrate all Apaches at San Carlos—the desolate, malarial, sun-blasted bottom of the Gila River. People with a history of intertribal animosity wallowed in boredom, feuded with one another, and longed for the free life of old in the cooler high country.

Geronimo did not remain long. As he later summed up in masterful understatement, although the irons were eventually removed, "I never felt at ease any longer. . . . All went well for a period of two years, but we were not satisfied." Actually, less than a year of life at San Carlos provoked a breakout—a sudden dash southward, bloody depredations on whites who strayed into his path, a futile scramble by the cavalry to cut him off, and sanctuary in the Sierra Madre.

After this breakout, in the autumn of 1881, the principal Apache leaders gathered in the Sierra Madre. A youth who was present remembered Geronimo as an "erect compact figure" but "blocky and muscular." Close by Geronimo, as he would be for the next five years, was Naiche, a "tall stately young man." Easygoing and pleasure-loving, Naiche nevertheless commanded respect as the only surviving son of the great Cochise. Geronimo always took pains to defer to Naiche but easily dominated him.

Conspicuously absent was Loco, a powerful Warm Springs chief who headed the peace faction of his tribe. Loco wanted no part of the fugitive life and kept his people tightly in hand at San Carlos. The determination of the Sierra Madre captains to add Loco and his formidable fighting force to their ranks led to fateful consequences.

At dawn on April 18, 1882, Geronimo and a party of warriors swept down on San Carlos, shot and killed the chief of police and one of his men, and forced Loco and his entire band to flee with them. A cavalry force gave chase and twice skirmished with the Apaches, once on Mexican soil, but failed to close in decisive combat.

More successful was a 250-man Mexican force under Colonel Lorenzo García that crept into position while the Indians were distracted by the Americans at their rear. "Almost immediately Mexicans were right among us all, shooting down women and children right and left," recalled one of the warriors. "People were falling and bleeding, and dying, on all sides of us." Geronimo rallied thirty-two warriors and stood off the Mexicans while the rest of the people escaped, but they left the battlefield littered with the bodies of seventy-eight Indians and twenty-two Mexicans. Thirty-three women and children had fallen captive to García.

The battle dealt the Apaches a shattering blow, but more portentous was an event prompted by the effrontery of Geronimo's raid on San Carlos. On September 4, 1882, Brigadier General George Crook assumed command of U.S. military forces in Arizona. A reticent, unpretentious man with forked beard, canvas suit, and durable mule, Crook had served in Arizona in 1871–73. Pioneering unorthodox techniques, Crook had scored a brilliant triumph. Packmules instead of wagons had given him unprecedented mobility, and Apache auxiliary units had turned their own people and their own methods of war against the Apache fugitives.

Now, in 1882, army leaders sent Crook back to Arizona to repeat the performance. Reverting to the tried techniques, he took the field himself. Unknown to the runaways in the Sierra Madre, he secured Mexico's permission to invade their stronghold.

The Apaches had spent the winter raiding Mexican settlements. A large base camp, containing the families of most of the marauding bands, hid in a pine grove high above the Bavispe River. Here the raiders returned periodically with herds of stolen cattle and other loot.

Raiding to the east, in Chihuahua, Geronimo once again displayed his uncanny Power. One evening in camp, recalled one of the band, "Geronimo was sitting next to me with a knife in one hand and a chunk of beef which I had cooked for him in the other. All at once he dropped the knife, saying, 'Men, our people whom we left at our base camp are now in the hands of U.S. troops! What shall we do?'"

It was true. On May 15, 1883, after days of toiling ever upward, Crook's scouts had burst upon the base camp. Nearly everyone escaped, but nine Indians were killed and five children fell captive to the scouts. Crook's command—193 Apache scouts, 47 regulars, and 76 civilian mulepackers—seized the camp and all its contents, including a horse herd.

Within three days Geronimo and his band took positions on a rocky slope overlooking the military camp, where the soldiers and scouts threw up defensive barricades. Already, discouraged by Crook's penetration of their mountain hideout, nearly fifty Apaches had drifted in and surrendered. By May 20 the number had risen to 121, chiefly women and children and old men.

The blow to the Indians' morale and the widespread sentiment favoring surrender affected Geronimo. Warily, he and some of his men ventured down for a talk with the soldier chief. "He and his warriors were certainly as fine-looking a lot of pirates as ever cut a throat or scuttled a ship," noted Crook's aide. "In muscular development, lung and heart power, they were, without exception, the finest body of human beings I had ever looked upon. Each was armed with a breech-loading Winchester; most had nickel-plated revolvers of the latest pattern, and a few had also bows and lances."

Several times in the next few days, Crook and Geronimo talked. The general professed complete indifference to whether the Indians surrendered. If they wanted to stay out, American and Mexican troops would hunt them down and kill them all. Despite his suspicions, Geronimo at length agreed to give up. Like his comrades, he was troubled by Crook's success in turning their own people against them and in penetrating their stronghold. Even so, he stalled; he needed time to collect his scattered people, he explained.

Crook had little choice but to agree. He had worked a huge bluff on the Indians, as they doubtless sensed. He lacked the men and supplies to enforce any measure to which they did not agree. He could not have campaigned longer in these forbidding mountains. When he emerged from

Mexico on June 10, he brought out 325 people, but not Geronimo—only his promise to follow.

He did, but only after long delay. Not until late February 1884 did he and his band cross the boundary to enroll once again at San Carlos.

He remained a little more than a year. Settled in the high country near Fort Apache, north of San Carlos, Geronimo and his fellow captains swiftly grew disgruntled. Impatient at all controls, they especially took offense at Crook's ban on two traditional practices: beating and disfiguring wives and manufacturing and drinking the potent brew *tiswin*. The inevitable breakout came on May 17, 1885, when Geronimo, Naiche, and others—42 warriors in all, with 92 women and children—dashed southward for the border. Once more the Sierra Madre harbored the deadly Apache menace.

Lightning Apache raids flashed across southern Arizona and New Mexico, leaving behind death and destruction. The army seemed powerless, although Crook's Indian scout units in Mexico scored a success by surprising Geronimo's camp and capturing his three wives and five children. Later, he slipped into the agency and recovered a wife and a daughter. The terror continued, and in November 1885 the army's commanding general, Philip H. Sheridan, hurried to Arizona to confer with Crook. They resolved once again to send Apache scout units into Mexico to root out the offenders in their camps.

Again Geronimo had cause to marvel at the ability of Crook's Apache scouts to find him. His main camp nestled among a tangle of mountains near the head of the Aros River, fully 200 miles south of the boundary. Shortly before dawn on January 10, 1886, braying mules sounded the alarm, and the inhabitants of the camp scrambled for safety just as bullets rattled through their wickiups. No one was hit, but Indian scouts quickly occupied the Apache camp.

Disconcerted by the near disaster and the loss of their horses and food supplies, Geronimo and Naiche decided to parley with the white officer. He was Captain Emmet Crawford—"Tall Chief" or "Captain Coffee." The Indians had known him on the reservation and respected him as a fair and humane man. They sent a woman to him to make arrangements. Crawford agreed to a conference the next morning.

In the misty dawn, full of the usual suspicion, Geronimo, Naiche, and all their people gathered on a stony hillside above the riverbank appointed for the meeting. Suddenly, below, a volley of rifle fire broke the silence. Mistakenly or not, Mexican militia had opened fire on Crawford's camp. "Tall Chief" sprang to a rock and waved a white handkerchief. A bullet struck him in the forehead and knocked him off the rock. Furious, his scouts fired back, cutting down the Mexican officers and hitting about ten of their men. From the slope, said one of the warriors, "Geronimo watched it and laughed."

On January 15, Geronimo, Naiche, Nana, and Chihuahua, with a squad of heavily armed warriors, met with Crawford's second-in-command, Lieutenant Marion P. Maus. Maus had come unarmed, as instructed, and the odds scared him.

Geronimo fixed the lieutenant with an icy gaze and demanded, "Why did you come down here?"

"I came to capture or destroy you and your band," Maus replied.

The brave honesty of the young officer impressed Geronimo, who walked over and shook hands with him. After pouring out a long list of grievances, the Apache agreed to meet personally with General Crook and discuss still another surrender. Bearing the wounded Crawford, who died several days later without regaining consciousness, Maus and his scouts made their way back to the border.

The conference took place on March 25, 1886, in a shady grove of the Canyon de Los Embudos, a short distance south of the border. The Apaches, wary of treachery, camped in an impregnable position atop a lava cone. They were "fierce as so many tigers," observed Crook, and "knowing what pitiless brutes they are themselves they mistrust everyone else."

Again Crook spoke bluntly, even insultingly, although again he lacked the force to back his hard words by storming the Apache defenses. He brusquely rejected Geronimo's labored explanation of the Apache grievances and delivered his ultimatum.

"You must make up your own mind whether you will stay out on the warpath or surrender unconditionally," the general warned. "If you stay out, I'll keep after you and kill the last one, if it takes fifty years."

As usual, factional disagreements sharply divided the Apache camp. Crook exploited the divisions and succeeded in isolating Geronimo. In the end, the general had his way.

"Once I moved about like the wind," declared Geronimo. "Now I surrender to you and that is all."

A handshake sealed the bargain.

Almost at once the bargain collapsed. Crook hastened to Fort Bowie to report the news to Washington, leaving Lieutenant Maus to escort the Indians. Just south of the border, however, Geronimo and Naiche fell in with a liquor peddler, got drunk, and on the night of March 28 took off to the mountains with families totaling nearly forty people. As Geronimo later explained, "I feared treachery and decided to remain in Mexico."

In fact, something resembling treachery was already taking shape. To persuade Geronimo to surrender, Crook had promised that he and his people could return to their reservation after a two-year exile in the East. Washington, however, balked at these terms. General Sheridan, backed by President Grover Cleveland, wanted no conditions at all. Crook therefore endured not only implied censure for letting Geronimo escape but the repudiation of his promises to those who had not bolted. Disheartened and tired, he asked to be relieved. At once Sheridan named a replacement— Brigadier General Nelson A. Miles.

The new general faced a daunting mission: to find and capture or kill eighteen Apache warriors and their families. Sheridan gave him 5,000 soldiers—one-fifth of the U.S. Army—but made clear his distrust of the Apache scouts on whom Crook had relied.

Five thousand regular soldiers could watch over the border, but they could not seal it off, nor root a handful of Apaches out of the Sierra Madre. In bold, destructive raids on both sides of the border. Geronimo and Naiche exposed the helplessness of the regular soldiery. Fourteen citizens fell victim to the raiders in New Mexico and Arizona, and many more Mexicans in Sonora and Chihuahua. "We were reckless of our lives," explained Geronimo, "because we felt that every man's hand was against us . . . so we gave no quarter to anyone and asked no favor."

As the hot summer of 1886 wore on with no progress, Miles made two decisive moves. First, he recruited two Chiricahuas to accompany an officer into Mexico and try to reopen talks with Geronimo. The officer was Lieutenant Charles B. Gatewood, a quietly competent protégé of Crook's who had earned the confidence of the Apaches and spoke their language. Second, Miles set in motion a sweeping plan to isolate Geronimo by moving all the reservation Chiricahuas, nearly 400 people, out of Arizona altogether.

In Mexico, Geronimo spent the late summer dodging a column of U.S. regulars under Captain Henry W. Lawton. In the middle of August, the elusive old warrior appeared in the neighborhood of Fronteras, only thirty miles south of the boundary. Asking for peace talks, he hoped to trick the Mexican authorities into giving him needed supplies. For their part, the Mexicans strove to lure the Apaches into town and massacre them. Into this tense maneuvering, while Lawton and his command hovered in the background, rode Lieutenant Gatewood and his two Chiricahua emissaries.

Sporting a white flag high on an agave stalk, Gatewood's little party tracked the Apaches into the rugged mountains. Sentinels reported their approach to Geronimo, who ordered them killed. Others, however, had recognized Gatewood's companions, Kayitah and Martine, as kinsmen and argued against this course. "Let them come," Geronimo conceded.

The parley, by now almost a set piece in Geronimo's relations with the United States, began on August 24, 1886, on the banks of the Bavispe River. The Apaches knew and liked the tall, thin officer with the big nose. "Bay-chen-daysen," they called him—"Beak" Gatewood. Badly hung over from a three-day drunk, Geronimo had little capacity for concentrating. But he understood the lieutenant's ultimatum: "Surrender, and you will be sent with your families to Florida, there to await the decision of the president as to your final disposition. Accept these terms or fight it out to the bitter end."

Even these terms, harsher than Crook had offered, would land Miles in trouble with the president himself, who wanted to dispose of Geronimo by handing him over to the Tucson civil authorities to be tried for murder. But Geronimo could not be conquered. He had to be coaxed in, and terms of some sort were imperative.

Fight it out was Geronimo's angry response to Gatewood's alternatives. The reservation was acceptable, but Florida, a far-off dumping ground for recalcitrant Indians for a decade, held the terrors of the unknown.

All day the talks continued as tension built. Breaking off for the night, Gatewood confided to Naiche the revelation that was to prove decisive: All the Chiricahuas—the family and kin of Geronimo, Naiche, and the others—had already been sent to Florida. Only antagonistic Indian groups now lived at San Carlos. (Although Gatewood did not know it, this was not yet true, but within two weeks it would be.)

The next day a chastened Geronimo began to waver. Over and over he quizzed Gatewood about General Miles—his appearance, his demeanor, his trustworthiness. Finally, near sundown, Geronimo broke. "We want your advice," he said. "Consider yourself not a white man but one of us. Remember all that has been said today and tell us what we should do."

"Trust General Miles and surrender to him," replied the lieutenant.

Although trust did not come readily, the Apaches took Gatewood's advice. Suspicion, doubt, uncertainty, and near stampedes dogged the slow movement north to Skeleton Canyon, Arizona, where the historic meeting between Miles and Geronimo occurred on September 4, 1886. It was, as the general predicted, the last time the Apache would ever have occasion to surrender.

Four days later, on the parade ground at Fort Bowie, Geronimo, Naiche, and the last little knot of Apache holdouts packed themselves into the wagons that would take them to the railroad and the long journey to Florida. A military band drew up at the flagpole to provide a parting serenade. The music meant more to the whites than to Geronimo, who could not have appreciated the irony of the selection: "Auld Lang Syne."

The Apache exile proved bitter—bitter for the Indians and bitter for the nation. The prisoners died of strange diseases and longed for their desert and mountain homeland. Controversy between East and West, and within the army between partisans of Crook and Miles, exposed the fate of the Indians to public scrutiny. The nation agonized over the emerging record of broken promises, bad faith, and rank injustices that marked the path of the Apaches from Skeleton Canyon to Florida, then to Alabama. In 1894 they were allowed to settle as far west as Fort Sill, in the Indian Territory (now Oklahoma), but never would these Apaches return to their Arizona homeland.

Geronimo accepted his fate and in the Fort Sill years came to enjoy growing stature as a celebrity. The Indian wars were now a nostalgic chapter in the nation's memory, and the ancient Apache became the embodiment of chilling scenes of atrocity out of the penny dreadfuls on the drugstore news racks. He rode in parades and was dragged around the country to be exhibited at expositions. Death finally came, as he approached his ninetieth year, on February 17, 1909.

The nation last glimpsed Geronimo as the incongruous caricature he had become—topped by a shiny stovepipe hat and perched at the steering wheel of a large touring sedan. The photograph drew a sharp contrast with the crafty, suspicious, powerfully muscled Apache captain who had surrendered to General Miles at Skeleton Canyon more than two decades earlier. On that hot desert day he was truly America's last Indian warrior.

*WINTER 1992*

Robert M. Utley authored the earlier essay on the Little Bighorn.

# 20

# "One Learns Fast in a Fight"

## By Michael Blow

*Although Americans vaguely associate the battleship* Maine, *the "Rough Riders," and San Juan Hill (in the San Juan Heights) with the Spanish-American War, they generally recall little else from this conflict. After all, the war was quick and relatively bloodless, with hostilities lasting only a few months and costing fewer than 200 American combat deaths. Michael Blow explores a little-remembered firefight from that war, the battle of Las Guásimas. Although comparatively small as contests go—U.S. dead numbered under 20—the battle served as something of a symbol for the way America fought the Spanish-American War: haphazardly but with great spirit. And, as with such earlier struggles as Yorktown, New Orleans, Tippecanoe, Buena Vista, and Vicksburg, it would produce a future president.*

Private Charles Johnson Post of the 71st New York Volunteers sat on the berm of his muddy trench on "Misery Hill," peered through the darkness at Santiago, and thought about mutton chops and ice-cold beer. His regiment had participated in the V Army Corps's costly assault on the San Juan Heights on July 1, 1898. Almost immediately, heavy rains had gridlocked the narrow supply trail from Siboney on the coast. Malarial fevers and dysentery had struck the army. There was little food, no medicine, and—worse yet—no tobacco. The troops were soaked by morning rains, boiled by the afternoon sun, haunted by the absence of dead comrades.

Post heard the clink of a glass bottle against a tin mess cup. Artillery Captain Allyn K. Capron's dog tent was pitched just behind him. Capron drank at night, murmuring to himself and sobbing. "I'll get 'em, Allyn, I'll get 'em, goddamn 'em." He would repeat himself, over and over, slurring the words, and then fade off to sleep.

Post and the other troops in the trench sympathized with the old man. Caprons had fought in every war since the Revolution. Now Allyn Capron, Jr., the captain's son, was dead, killed two weeks earlier at a little hamlet called Las Guásimas.

Named after the hognut trees that grew at the junction of two jungle trails, Las Guásimas is today an all but forgotten scrap, overshadowed by the battle for the San Juan Heights a week later and the destruction of the Spanish fleet along the shores west of Santiago on July 3. It probably involved no more than 3,000 men and lasted just over an hour. But it committed Major General William Rufus Shafter to a course of attack that brought near disaster to the V Army Corps; featured an all-star cast that included Leonard Wood, Theodore Roosevelt, John J. Pershing, Stephen Crane, and Richard Harding Davis; typified the rambunctious nature of the American fighting in the war with Spain; and almost killed the man who would become—thanks in part to the battle itself—the twenty-sixth president of the United States.

Roosevelt had reached Las Guásimas by a circuitous route. In April 1897, President William McKinley had appointed him assistant secretary of the navy. Lamenting Spain's "murderous oppression" of a Cuban uprising that had been going on for two years, he began to ready the navy for war. Then, on February 15, 1898, the battleship *Maine* blew up in Havana Harbor. A month later, a naval court of inquiry fixed the blame on a mine. In April, the United States declared war. Roosevelt, who had no intention of sitting out the conflict in Washington as an armchair jingo, immediately resigned his navy post, secured an army commission with the 1st United States Volunteer Cavalry Regiment, and ordered a lieutenant colonel's uniform from Brooks Brothers.

Secretary of the Navy John Long thought it an act of folly. He wrote in his diary that Roosevelt would end up on the Florida sands swatting mosquitoes. Still, "how absurd all this will sound if, by some turn of fortune, he should accomplish some great thing and strike a very high mark."

The commander of the regiment was Colonel Leonard Wood, recently White House physician to McKinley, and before that a dogged Indian fighter who had won the Medal of Honor campaigning against the Apache rebel leader Geronimo. For a while the press tabbed the regiment, largely composed of cowboys and marksmen from Texas and the Arizona, New Mexico, and Indian territories, "Wood's Wild Westerners." The name didn't stick. "Roosevelt's Rough Riders" soon became the favored sobriquet.

At the last minute, a number of what Roosevelt called "gentleman rankers," Ivy League graduates with formidable sports credentials, qualified for the regiment. As Stephen Crane, reporting for Joseph Pulitzer's *New York World,* wrote, "Lean slit-eyed plainsmen with names like Cherokee Bill and Rattlesnake Pete served beside men from Boston's Somerset Club and the Knickerbocker Club of New York."

Wood and Roosevelt assembled the frontiersmen and blue bloods in San Antonio for cavalry training. They were soon honed to a fighting edge. Roosevelt was confident they could have whipped Caesar's Tenth Legion. At the end of May, they entrained for Tampa, Florida, where General Shafter, at 300 pounds perhaps the most corpulent man in the army, struggled ineffectually amidst a bedlam of incoming troops and war matériel to ready the V Army Corps for embarkation.

There were inevitable delays, but on June 14 some 17,000 men finally departed for Cuba in a hastily improvised gaggle of army transports. At the last moment, Wood was advised there was room for only eight of his twelve troops, about 90 to 100 men each, and horses only for the officers. The Rough Riders would have to fight on foot.

The army, which had originally planned to assault Havana, instead went to Santiago on the southeastern coast, because Admiral Pascual Cervera y Topete's squadron of cruisers was there. The capture or destruction of his fleet was the key to a swift ending of the war; the city itself, four miles north of the harbor entrance, was of little military consequence. When Shafter arrived off Santiago on June 20, Rear Admiral William Thomas Sampson urged him to assault the poorly defended heights of Morro and Socapa, guarding Santiago Bay. That done, Sampson could remove the mines and the log and chain booms at the entrance, steam his ships in, and engage Cervera's fleet.

Shafter had seen the imposing heights guarding the harbor entrance. He had little stomach for a direct assault—even if, as reported, they were armed with eighteenth-century cannon. While he had been ordered to cooperate earnestly with Sampson "in destroying the Spanish fleet," he had also been given tactical latitude. He advised Sampson that he would land at Daiquirí, a town some eighteen miles southeast of Santiago. Sampson, confused, agreed to assist the landing but still assumed Shafter would move troops westward down the railway line that hugged the coast, under the protection of the fleet's guns, and hit the Morro bastion from the flank.

The landing at Daiquirí began on Wednesday morning, June 22. Lighters, lifeboats, and launches brought the troops through heavy swells and tried to land them on a single decrepit dock or on the beach through dangerous surf. Horses and mules were simply pushed overboard. "We disembarked," Roosevelt reported, "higgledy-piggledy." Fortunately, there was no Spanish resistance. By evening, Shafter had gotten 6,000 men ashore and Brigadier General Henry W. Lawton started two brigades of his 2nd Infantry Division westward along the seven-mile road to a town called Siboney.

Shafter, still headquartered offshore on the *Segurança,* had ordered Lawton, or the "senior officer at the front," to occupy Siboney, dig in, and cover subsequent landing operations. Lawton camped on the road for the night and took the undefended town around nine o'clock on Thursday morning. Brigadier General Jacob Ford Kent's 1st Infantry Division followed.

At the time, the Rough Riders and the other regiments in the Cavalry Division were still encamped at Daiquirí. The commander, Major General Joseph ("Fighting Joe") Wheeler, was not used to bringing up the rear—dismounted or otherwise. A frail, sixty-one-year-old Alabamian, barely over five feet tall, white-haired and white-bearded, Wheeler had achieved the rank of lieutenant general in the Confederate army at the age of twenty-eight. When McKinley, seeking to heal old wounds, asked him to serve, Wheeler agreed. He had no qualms about putting on a Union uniform; if he had to greet Robert E. Lee at the heavenly gates dressed in blue, so be it.

Fighting Joe finally got some of his cavalry going on Thursday, June 23, and the troopers reached Siboney early that afternoon. Wheeler promptly set up his headquarters, conferred with Cuban general Demetrio Castillo, whose insurgents had sparred with Spanish troops that day, and made a short reconnaissance up the trail that led to Las Guásimas. On his return, he met with his brigade commander, Brigadier General Samuel B. Young, who proposed a reconnaissance in force.

Without question, Wheeler was eager to steal a march on the infantry. The order to entrench along a miasmic coastal strip less than four miles from a large Spanish force struck him as unwise. He spotted a loophole in Shafter's order delegating command ashore to Lawton or the senior officer at the front. Almost certainly, that meant the senior officer in Lawton's absence. But Lawton was not absent; moreover, the intent of the directive clearly was to take up defensive positions. Major General Wheeler, however, outranked any officer ashore. He quickly approved Young's request.

The Rough Riders barely made the escapade. They had landed on Wednesday, helped to unload the transports, entrenched, then set out at a forced march down the grandly named Camino Real (Royal Road) to Siboney on Thursday in the murderous midafternoon heat. The narrow, tortuous, hilly trail took its toll; the regiment scrambled into the town long after nightfall, shuffled past Lawton's entrenched infantry, and camped at what Roosevelt called "the extreme front" of the American line. Soon afterward, a tropical downpour drenched the campsite. When the rain finally stopped, the troopers fired up hardtack and tried to dry out. By the flickering light, Roosevelt looked over at Captain Allyn K. Capron, Jr.—whose twenty-seventh birthday was only minutes away. Roosevelt thought him perhaps the best soldier in the regiment. Wood was telling Capron of Wheeler's plan. "Well," said Capron, "tomorrow at this time the long sleep will be on many of us."

It was after midnight when they finally turned in. Reveille was set for 3:15 A.M. Exhausted as they were, it was hard to sleep. Richard Harding Davis—"Richard the Lion-Harding," as fellow reporters and New York society called the impeccably dressed *New York Herald* correspondent, who had modeled for the escort to Charles Dana Gibson's "girl"—recorded the surrealistic nighttime scene as additional troops came ashore from transports off Siboney in the glare of searchlights: "It was a pandemonium of noises. . . . The men already on shore were dancing naked around the camp-fires on the beach . . . shouting with delight . . . and those in the launches as they were pitched headfirst at the soil of Cuba, signalized their arrival by howls of triumph." Three miles to the north, General Antero Rubin's Spanish troops felled trees in the jungle to improve the defenses on the ridge overlooking Las Guásimas.

Two paths led northward from Siboney to the crossroads at Las Guásimas. The Camino Real, the eastern route, led up a marshy valley between two ranges of hills. It was, for the most part, wide enough for wagons. The path to the west, little more than a trail, followed a ridgeline roughly parallel to the road. The two routes were never more than about a mile apart, but jungle vegetation made it impossible to see one from the other.

Wheeler's plan called for Young to lead four troops of the 1st Regular Cavalry and four more of the 10th Regular Cavalry (a regiment of black soldiers), with two Hotchkiss mountain guns, down the Royal Road. Wood would take his eight troops up the more difficult ridge trail. General Castillo had promised to support them with 800 insurgents; only a handful of scouts materialized. Half a dozen correspondents did, too, including Davis and Stephen Crane. Altogether, Wheeler's force numbered fewer than 1,000 men.

The early reveille on Friday, June 24, was particularly hard on the Rough Riders. Correspondent Edward Marshall of Hearst's *New York Journal* observed that even Wood looked haggard. Young got his better-rested troops down the valley road at 5:45 A.M. The Rough Riders started up the steep trail above Siboney promptly at 6:00. A regular army major looked at the casual volunteers with disdain. "Goddam it!—they haven't even got a point out!"

The regulars tramped easily down the valley road, but the hillside at Siboney took its toll on "Wood's Weary Walkers." Kennett Harris of the *Chicago Record* pictured "Capron's tall figure striding over the boulders in the steep ascent." For many of the dismounted cavalry, however, it was a tough scramble. Crane, who had landed at Siboney from a dispatch boat just as the troopers crested the hill, struggled to catch up. To him, the jungle "seemed almost upon the point of crackling into a blaze under the rays of the furious Cuban sun."

Davis, dressed in a blue jacket, white shirt, and felt hat banded with a white puggaree, had attached himself to the Rough Riders. Riding along with Roosevelt toward the front of the column, he took a casual view of the morning's expedition: "I doubted that there were any Spaniards nearer than Santiago." Roosevelt grumbled a bit at the pace Wood was setting but found the tropical forest beautiful and peaceful.

Crane confessed that he knew little about war—his 1895 novel *The Red Badge of Courage* was an imagined drama—but he had landed with the marines at Guantánamo on June 7 and endured the fierce fighting there for a week. Obviously, the Spanish had picked up elements of guerrilla warfare from the Cubans. As he pushed along the narrow path leading through the jungle, the jovial babbling of the volunteers terrified him.

By now Wood had established points: first, two Cuban scouts; behind them, five trailers under Sergeant Hamilton Fish; then young Allyn Capron's troop of sixty men. Wood and the rest of the regiment followed. But it was impossible to put out flankers; Davis observed that "the dense undergrowth and the tangle of vines that stretched from the branches of the trees to the bushes below made it a physical impossibility for man or beast to move forward except along the beaten trail."

To the east, shortly before 7:30, Young paused in an open glade to regroup. Captain A.L. Mills and two troopers advanced about 150 yards toward the ruins of an old building with a sundial on its side. There, several hundred yards to the north, they spotted breastworks. The Spanish line appeared to be in the shape of an obtuse triangle, with the salient jutting toward the space between the advancing American forces. Young, alerted to the situation, deployed the 1st Cavalry to both sides of the road while holding the 10th in reserve. General Wheeler joined him, and Young pointed to the straw hats jutting up from the breastworks.

Up on the ridge, Wood's advance scouts came across the body of a dead soldier—whether Spanish or Cuban was not clear—that Castillo had reported to be only a few hundred yards from the Spanish lines. Capron gave the news to Wood, who ordered silence in the ranks. Crane, still thinking that "this silly brave force was wandering placidly into a great deal of trouble," heard a sergeant bawling, "Ah say, can't ye stop talkin'?"

Wood ordered Roosevelt to deploy three troops to the right of the trail while Major Alexander Brodie took two more off to the left. Roosevelt later recalled that parade-ground etiquette called for the men to be deployed into a line of squads and then the order given: "As skirmishers, by the right and left flanks, at six yards, take intervals, march." What actually came out was "Scatter out to the right there, quick, you! Look alive!"

Across a ravine that ran northwest past the Spanish salient, Wheeler proposed to Young that they fire a round from one of the Hotchkiss one-pounders at the straw-hatted troops at their front. As the shell whined off, Captain William D. Beach, chief engineer of the Cavalry Division, pulled out his notebook and jotted down the time: 8:15 A.M. Then his hand jerked as a terrifying volley of rifle fire erupted from the breastworks. Wheeler, too, was staggered by the volume of fire—it seemed greater than anything he had experienced in the Civil War. Nearby, an enlisted man and several officers crumpled to the ground.

Over on the hill trail, as the Rough Riders deployed, a fusillade of bullets ripped through the air. Crane knew the sound of the Spanish rifles: "The Mauser says 'Pop!'"—plainly and frankly pop like a soda water bottle being opened close to the ear."

"Everyone went down in a lump without cries," Edward Marshall noted, but the *chug* "of bullets striking flesh is nearly always audible."

In the first minutes of the battle on the left, the point men went first. Sergeant Hamilton Fish, grandson of Ulysses S. Grant's secretary of state, was hit by a slug that entered his left side, tore out his right, and slammed into the chest of Private Ed Culver, a half-breed Cherokee. Fish had time only to gasp, "That bullet hit both of us," before he died. Culver gazed blankly at Fish, then crawled back along the trail. Private Tom Isbell, another Cherokee on point, thought he saw a Spaniard and fired at him. His shot triggered a vicious volley from the underbrush. Isbell was severely wounded by seven bullets, three in the neck. In just three minutes, Davis estimated, "nine men were lying on their backs helpless."

Wood had ordered Roosevelt to try to connect with the regulars. "In theory this was excellent, but as the jungle was very dense the first troop that deployed to the right vanished forthwith, and I never saw it again until the fight was over," Roosevelt later observed. "I managed to keep possession of the last platoon. One learns fast in a fight."

Roosevelt was astonished by the smokeless Mausers; the enemy was "entirely invisible." Fortunately, the Rough Riders were equipped with the .30-caliber Krag-Jorgensen carbine, which also fired a smokeless cartridge. Roosevelt had faced down an old-line supply corps officer in Washington who wanted to provide his men with black-powder Springfields, on the theory that the smoke would conceal them from the enemy.

Davis had followed Roosevelt into the underbrush to the right of the trail. He and Roosevelt came to an outcropping that jutted out over a ravine. Beyond was a ridge. Davis, on his stomach, was scanning the ridge with his binoculars when he suddenly spotted the conical hats of the Spanish troops. "There they are, Colonel. Look over there!"

In turn, Roosevelt pointed them out to the men around him, got more troopers up on the line, and ordered quick firing. Flushed from their cover, the Spanish retreated up the ridgeline. Apparently they were hurt, and the Rough Riders, dodging behind bushes and trees, went after them. As Roosevelt hunkered down behind a large palm and cautiously peered out to one side, "a bullet passed through the palm, filling my left eye and ear with the dust and splinters." Roosevelt later made light of his brush with death, noting only that it was "fortunate" his head was not behind the tree.

The firing was now less intense, and Roosevelt's troopers continued to deploy to the right. Soon they saw soldiers in the valley beyond the ravine. They appeared to be American, but their first action was to fire off a volley at the Rough Riders. Sergeant Joseph Jenkins Lee, one of Roosevelt's gentleman rankers, scrambled up a tree and flogged the air with his red-and-white banner. The guidon of the 10th waved back. Then skirmishers from both regiments fanned out to connect the line, securing Wood's right wing.

Feeling he was not doing enough fighting "to justify his existence," Roosevelt thought it time to rejoin the regiment near the trail where the firing was now heaviest. He began trotting back to the left. In the thick growth, his sword got between his legs and tripped him up. The refrain of an old fox-hunting song kept jingling through his head: "Here's to every friend who struggled to the end." Finally he found Wood, who told him to take command of the left wing, since Major Brodie had been wounded.

Davis followed, passing dead men, and came to a dressing station at the point where the cavalrymen had first stopped. He noticed "a tall, gaunt young man with a cross on his arm approaching . . . carrying a wounded man much heavier than himself across his shoulders." He realized he had seen the doctor before at "another time of excitement and rush and heat."

William Randolph Hearst had paid Davis richly to cover the Yale-Princeton football game in 1895, and suddenly Davis remembered: "He had been covered with blood and dirt and perspiration as he was now, only then he wore a canvas jacket and the man he carried was trying to hold him back from a whitewashed line. And I recognized the young doctor . . . as 'Bob' Church, of Princeton." Church had won the approval of his college peers that day; on this one, he would win something more—the Medal of Honor.

To Davis, it sounded as though the firing had moved half a mile forward; the Spaniards had been driven back. He trotted down the trail toward the front, despondently noting the horrors of war. "The rocks on either side were spattered with blood and the rank grass was matted with it." Through the whining of bullets he heard "the clatter of the land-crabs, those hideous orchid-colored monsters that haunt the places of the dead." Later he would see the corpse of a trooper whose eyes were torn out and lips ripped off.

He came across Lieutenant John R. Thomas, Jr., lying on a blanket, half-naked, soaked in blood from a wound in his leg. He was raving deliriously, ordering attending medics to carry him to the front. "You said you would! They've killed my captain—do you understand? They've killed Captain Capron. The — Mexicans! They've killed my captain."

Capron was lying only fifty feet away, a big black open spot on his chest. Davis plodded on, his boots slipping over loose stones and Mauser shell casings.

Edward Marshall, conspicuous in a white coat, was also hit. He carried a revolver and, correspondent or not, had been firing away "cheerfully." Suddenly there was a *chug,* and Marshall fell wounded in the long grass.

Crane was not far behind him. A passing soldier told him, "There's a correspondent up there all shot to hell." He led Crane to the spot where his friend and rival was lying. "Hello, Crane," Marshall said.

"Hello, Marshall. In hard luck, old man?"

"Yes, I'm done for." He asked if Crane would file his dispatches—not ahead of his own, "but just file 'em if you find it handy."

Crane got some soldiers to carry Marshall on tent canvas to a dressing station. Then he trudged wearily back toward Siboney to file his own dispatches for Pulitzer's *World* and Marshall's for Hearst's *Journal.* In the fierce battle for circulation between Hearst and Pulitzer, there was no room for compassion. Crane's act of perceived betrayal cost him his job when he returned to the United States in July. Hearst promptly offered him employment.

Meanwhile, down in the valley, Captain Beach listened nervously to the Spanish volleys. The advance had stalled, and casualties were piling up. All the troopers were now on the line; there were no reserves. He turned to Wheeler and reminded him there were nine regiments of infantry at Siboney, only a few miles back up the road. "Let me send to Lawton for some of them and close this action up."

Wheeler hesitated. The idea had been to steal a march on the infantry, not call on them for rescue. The vision of a Spanish counterattack rolling up his exhausted cavalry and surging down to the valley to strike the jumble of troops on the beachhead may have made up his mind. He nodded. "All right!" Beach called for an orderly and sent him off to Siboney at a gallop.

By the time Crane approached Siboney, bugles were sounding urgently. "The heroic rumor arose, soared, screamed above the bush," he wrote.

"Everybody was wounded. Everybody was dead." He watched the 9th Regular Cavalry and the 71st New York Volunteers dash into formation. There was no roll call, Private Post of the 71st remembered. Just "'Fall in—fall in! Count off! . . . Fours right!' And we were off."

At the field dressing station, surrounded by wounded troopers, Edward Marshall, his spine shattered by the Spanish bullet, heard a man quietly begin to sing:

> *My country 'tis of thee,*
> *Sweet land of liberty . . .*

Most of the men joined in. Marshall remembered that "the quivering, quavering chorus, punctuated by groans and made spasmodic by pain, trembled up from that little group of wounded Americans in the midst of the Cuban solitude." Shortly afterward, Marshall was carried to Siboney by other Hearst reporters and placed on a hospital ship. Though crippled by his wound, he survived.

At the front, Davis continued down the trail, carrying a carbine. He could see Roosevelt on a slight upward slope, rushing his men forward toward an old ranch house that anchored the Spanish right.

Roosevelt took a rifle from a wounded man and fired a few experimental shots at the red-tiled ranch buildings. "Then we heard cheering on the right, and I supposed this meant a charge on the part of Wood's men, so I sprang up and ordered the men to rush the buildings ahead of us."

The charge erupted all up and down the American line. On Wood's right, the black troopers of Young's 10th Cavalry surged up the hill. One of their white officers, Lieutenant John J. Pershing (known as "Black Jack" to white soldiers because of his admiration for the black troopers), noted that the 10th "opened a disastrous enfilading fire upon the Spanish . . . thus relieving the Rough Riders from the volleys that were being poured into them."

In amazement and admiration, Davis watched the exhausted Rough Riders scramble up the hill. "It was called 'Wood's bluff' afterwards," he wrote, "for he had nothing to back it up with. . . . The Spaniards naturally could not believe that this thin line . . . was the entire fighting force against it. . . . As we knew it was only a bluff, the first cheer was wavering, but the sound of our own voices was so comforting that the second cheer was a howl of triumph."

The Spanish fired a few volleys, then broke and ran. Without thinking, Joe Wheeler launched a cry he had not shouted in more than thirty years: "Come on, boys, we've got the damn Yankees on the run!"

"When we arrived at the buildings," Roosevelt recalled, "panting and out of breath, they contained nothing but heaps of empty cartridge-shells and two dead Spaniards, shot through the head." It was all over. On the right wing, the punctilious Captain Beach checked his watch. It showed 9:20. In disbelief, he put it to his ear. The timepiece was ticking. The battle had in fact lasted just over an hour.

The infantrymen coming up to support the Rough Riders were forming up for action, Post wrote, when "the popping grew fainter; then there were no shots at all. We realized that the fight was over." One of the 71st hailed a wounded Rough Rider along the trail. "'Yeah, we knocked hell out of them' was the response."

In fact, eight Rough Riders were dead and thirty-four wounded. Young's force had also suffered eight deaths, and eighteen had been wounded. (Spanish losses were officially recorded as ten killed and twenty-five wounded, but they were probably greater.) The first press accounts, written in Siboney by correspondents who had not made it to the front, reported that the Rough Riders had rushed blindly and recklessly into a trap. Crane's dispatch for the *World* called the foray "a gallant blunder."

Davis, who had thought the prospect of battle remote as he rode down the jungle trail, wrote to his family, "We were caught in a clear case of ambush." On reflection, he modified his stand: "There is a vast difference between blundering into an ambuscade and setting out with the full knowledge that you will find the enemy in ambush." Roosevelt asserted that "there was no surprise; we struck the Spaniards exactly where we had expected."

In fact, ambushed or not, and whether or not the Spanish had planned to withdraw all along, as one of their accounts later had it, the Rough Riders and Young's troopers had shown extraordinary courage in driving back a superior enemy force, variously estimated at from 1,200 to 4,000 men, well entrenched, well armed, and hidden from view on the jungle heights above the trails. A Spanish soldier later explained, "The Americans were beaten, but persisted in fighting."

As to Wheeler's precipitate advance, Roosevelt observed trenchantly that "war means fighting; and the soldier's cardinal sin is timidity." Wheeler was "a man with 'the fighting edge.'" The Rough Riders were "children of the dragon's blood."

Lawton reportedly wagged a finger at Wheeler and told him that he, Lawton, was in charge of the advance until Shafter came ashore, and that Wheeler should corral his venturesome cavalry. Shafter congratulated Wheeler but firmly warned him to hold his position "until all the troops are well in hand."

Later, Shafter claimed he had always intended to attack Santiago directly by way of the inland route rather than assault the Morro and Socapa fortifications at the harbor entrance, but this was not the impression he had given Admiral Sampson and others. Whatever his intent when he landed at Daiquirí, Shafter, with Las Guásimas in hand, was now committed to the perilous overland route that shattered the V Army Corps in the bungled, chaotic attack on El Caney and the San Juan Heights a week later.

By the time that was over, Shafter's army had taken 1,200 casualties in its blunt thrust toward Santiago, his men were strung out along the heights in vulnerable positions, and he still had not seized the Morro bastion or the Socapa batteries guarding the harbor entrance. Even Roosevelt felt, "We are within measurable distance of a terrible military disaster." Shafter strongly considered retreat and plaintively asked Admiral Sampson to force the heavily guarded harbor entrance. Sampson demurred.

Then, on July 3, Admiral Cervera made a courageous but doomed attempt to escape the American blockade. The total destruction of the Spanish squadron firmed up Shafter's resolve, and he demanded the surrender of Santiago and all the Spanish troops in the region. Two weeks later, even as malarial forces prostrated his V Corps, he got it.

As for Roosevelt, he thought the fight at Las Guásimas "really a capital thing for me, for practically all the men had served under my actual command, and thenceforth felt enthusiastic belief that I would lead them aright." And when the second batch of press reports, notably those of Davis and the dispatches Crane filed for Marshall, lauded the courage of "Roosevelt's" Rough Riders and the importance of their victory, a group of independent Republicans announced that it would run him for governor of New York in the fall.

Thus, with Las Guásimas, Roosevelt began his charge into history as the hero of Kettle and San Juan hills on the heights, governor, vice president, and, on McKinley's assassination, president. As historian Walter Millis noted, the "hurried hour in the bush above Siboney was largely instrumental in giving us our next President of the United States."

SUMMER *1995*

---

Michael Blow, a former editor of *American Heritage, Newsweek,* and *Reader's Digest,* is the author of *A Ship to Remember: The "Maine" and the Spanish American War* (1992).

# 21

# Iron General

## By Thomas Fleming

*If ever a general looked like a general, it was John J. Pershing, the commander of the American Expeditionary Force in World War I. Handsome, erect, and physically fit, this confident former cavalry commander was, in the words of one observer, "lean, clean, keen." As befitting a native of Missouri, Pershing was also stubborn. Combining an iron will and a bulldoglike determination, Pershing held true to two goals: to defeat the German army and to protect the integrity and identity of the AEF from the assault of his own allies. Together Pershing and the AEF would win both battles.*

On February 5, 1917, the rear guard of the 11,000-man Punitive Expedition to Mexico recrossed the Rio Grande to American soil. With them was John J. Pershing, the lean, grim-lipped, jut-jawed major general who had managed to pursue Pancho Villa around northern Mexico for nearly eleven months without starting a war. Although he had not captured the guerrilla chieftain, Pershing had scattered Villa's army and killed a number of his lieutenants—and silently swallowed his frustration when President Woodrow Wilson ordered a withdrawal. Within hours of his return to the United States, Pershing called a conference of the newspapermen who had followed him into Mexico. "We have broken diplomatic relations with Germany," he said. "That means we will send an expedition abroad. I'd like to command it. . . . Tell me how I can help you so that you can help me."

It was neither the first nor the last time Pershing would reveal the shrewd self-promotion that lay behind the image of the "Iron General." When he had invaded Mexico, he had obligingly posed on horseback fording the Rio Grande with his staff. Actually, he had traveled across the inhospitable Chihuahuan desert in a Dodge touring car. In many surprising ways, large and small, Pershing was a very modern major general. In other ways, he was a man of his own time.

Pershing had graduated from West Point in 1886 as first captain of the cadet corps, a coveted title that testified to an aptitude for things military. Scholastically he was in the middle of his seventy-seven-man class. Post–Civil War West Point was intellectually moribund, turning out men who learned by rote what little was taught. If they acquired anything from their four-year indoctrination, it was a ferocious dedication to discipline and military minutiae.

Robert Lee Bullard, who graduated a year ahead of Pershing and would later serve under him, admired his ability to give orders, which seemed to come naturally to him. The Alabama-born Bullard also noted that Pershing inspired admiration and respect, but not affection. There was something impersonal, almost detached, in his style of command. With women, on the other hand, a different man emerged, full of wit and charm. He was a "spoony" cadet, with a pretty girl on his arm for every hop. Later, as a cavalryman on the western frontier and a guerrilla fighter in the Philippines, he gravitated inevitably toward the prettiest woman in sight.

Another large factor in his life soon emerged—what some people called "Pershing luck." Others called it an uncanny ability to ingratiate himself with men in high places. Having watched Pershing in action during the last of the Indian Wars, Nelson Miles selected the young man as his aide after he became commanding general of the army. In 1896, Miles sent Pershing to New York to represent him at a National Guard tournament in Madison Square Garden. Avery Andrews, a classmate who had retired from the army to go into business, invited Pershing to share his box. Another guest was Theodore Roosevelt, on his way to becoming President William McKinley's assistant secretary of the navy. An avid western buff and admirer of soldiers, TR was fascinated by Pershing's skirmishes with Sioux who were part of the Ghost Dance cult, his knowledge of Indian dialects, his Missourian enthusiasm for the West's potential. A friendship was born that became a pivot of Pershing's career.

In the West, Pershing had served with the black troopers of the 10th Cavalry. Posted to West Point in 1897, he became the most unpopular tactical officer in recent memory—an accomplishment in itself. In retaliation for his uncompromising discipline, the cadets nicknamed him "Nigger Jack"—a reference to his service with the 10th and a sad commentary on the racism of the era. (It was later softened to "Black Jack"—a name that stuck, largely because most people thought it had something to do with the potentially deadly nature of the instrument of the same name.) When the Spanish-American War broke out in 1898, Pershing rejoined the regiment and went up San Juan Hill with the dismounted black regulars, proving himself "as cool as a bowl of cracked ice" against Spanish sharpshooters who killed or wounded 50 percent of the regiment's officers.

In 1902, while serving in the Philippines, Captain Pershing pacified much of Mindanao with 700 troops, cajoling Moro *dattus* out of their forts whenever possible, demolishing them in short, savage attacks when necessary. His exploits won headlines in many newspapers. His friend Theodore Roosevelt, now ensconced in the White House, tried to promote Pershing to brigadier general. But not even the president could alter the rigid, seniority-based promotion system.

A military celebrity, back in Washington for service on the General

Staff, Pershing in 1905 married a vivacious Wellesley graduate, Helen Frances Warren, the daughter of the wealthy Wyoming senator who headed the Military Affairs Committee. Confronted with subtle threats to their annual budgets, the army's higher ranks became more amenable to Pershing's promotion. In 1906, Roosevelt vaulted him over 862 senior officers to brigadier, making most of these gentlemen instant enemies. They retaliated with a smear campaign about his sex life in the Philippines, claiming he had had a series of native women as mistresses and had sired several children. He denied everything, but the scandal stained his reputation so badly that, six years later, newspapers howled when he was proposed as superintendent of West Point.

Marrying influential daughters was an old army custom. Nelson Miles had married the daughter of Senator John Sherman, who was the brother of General William Tecumseh Sherman and the most powerful senator of his day. In Pershing's case, surviving letters and diaries make it clear the marriage was loving. As his honeymoon ended, Pershing confided to his diary that he was "the happiest man in the world." Four children, three girls and a boy, were born to Jack and "Frankie."

On August 27, 1915, while Pershing was patrolling the restive Mexican border against guerrilla incursions, an excited reporter called headquarters and got the general himself. Without realizing to whom he was talking, the newsman blurted out that Pershing's wife and three daughters had been killed in a midnight fire at their quarters in the Presidio in San Francisco. Only his six-year-old son, Warren, had survived, saved by a courageous orderly. A devastated Pershing wrote a friend: "All the promotion in the world would make no difference now."

Pershing seemed to deal with his sorrow through work, responsibility, the grinding details of duty. That is one explanation of his pursuit of the command of the American Expeditionary Force (AEF). Another is the very strong probability that he thought he was the best man for the job. One of Pershing's characteristics was his matter-of-fact assumption of his ability.

He courted Woodrow Wilson with a fulsome letter praising the president's speech of April 2 before Congress, calling for a war to make the world safe for democracy. He wrote a similar letter to Secretary of War Newton D. Baker. Senator Warren worked hard on Pershing's behalf, telegraphing him at one point to ask about his knowledge of French. Pershing had barely passed the subject at West Point, but he replied that he could easily acquire "a satisfactory working knowledge" of the language.

There was only one other major general who could compete with Pershing for the job: Frederick Funston. He had won instant fame by capturing rebel leader Emilio Aguinaldo and crippling the Philippine insurrection in 1901. On February 19, 1917, Funston dropped dead in the lobby of a San Antonio hotel—perhaps another instance of Pershing luck.

In early May, Pershing got the job—leaping over five major generals senior to him. What he found in Washington, D.C., would have daunted a less confident man. The U.S. Army had little more than 11,000 combat-ready regulars. The 122,000-man National Guard was a joke. Fully half its members had never fired a rifle. Hugh Scott, the aging chief of staff, frequently fell asleep at meetings with his officers. The only plan Scott had on his desk was the brainchild of Wilson and Secretary Baker—to send Pershing at the head of a 12,000-man division to France as part of a "flexible" response to the war.

French and British missions swarmed to American shores to deluge the War Department and the president with frantic pleas for men. Instead of Wilson and Baker's symbolic 12,000, they wanted 500,000 men immediately—and they did not particularly want John J. Pershing, or any other American general. The British suggested that the half-million recruits be shipped directly to depots in England, to be trained there and sent to France in British uniforms, under British officers. The French were a bit more polite, but it came down to the same thing: They wanted American soldiers to become part of their army.

From the day he heard the idea, Pershing opposed amalgamation of forces. He had no intention of becoming superfluous in France. For the time being, Wilson, Baker, and General Tasker H. Bliss—the large, slow-moving military politician who soon succeeded Scott as chief of staff—agreed with him. Not without some conflict, Pershing also opposed a proposal by his friend Theodore Roosevelt to raise 50,000 volunteers and lead them himself to Europe to bolster the Allies' sagging morale. As an observer in Manchuria during the Russo-Japanese War in 1904, Pershing had seen a modern battlefield, and he did not think there was room on it for amateurs like TR. He may also have sensed, with his finely honed instinct for command, that there could be only one American leader in Europe.

Pershing saw himself not only as that American leader but as the general who could win the war. He thought he had the answer to breaking the bloody stalemate on the Western Front—"open warfare." This idea was a variation on the doctrine taught at West Point by Dennis Hart Mahan, the man who dominated the academy for much of the nineteenth century. Speed, fire, and movement were the essence of Mahan's ideas, along with seizing and holding the initiative. Pershing believed the American soldier's natural gifts as a marksman and wielder of the bayonet would shock the German army—and the Allies' armies—out of their trenches.

Three weeks after his appointment, Pershing sailed for Europe with a 191-man staff. In London, people liked what they saw. One American reporter, Heywood Broun, opined, "No man ever looked more like the ordained leader of fighting men." Another, Floyd Gibbons, called him "lean, clean, keen." But even as he was charming the newsmen, Pershing was requesting from Washington the power to impose rigid censorship on everything they wrote in France.

In Paris the population went berserk, chanting the "Marseillaise" and pelting Pershing and the staff with flowers as they rode to the Hotel Crillon. On the balcony overlooking the place de la Concorde, when the wind whipped a tricolor toward him, Pershing reverently kissed its folds. The crowd screamed its approval. Inside, he got a very different reception. The American ambassador, William Sharp, said: "I hope you have not arrived too late." The writer Dorothy Canfield Fisher, an old friend, told Pershing the French were beaten: They had had 2 million casualties, and "there is a limit to what flesh and blood . . . can stand."

Pershing learned even worse news from General Henri Pétain, the French commander in chief. In April, after a disastrous offensive on the Aisne River that cost 120,000 casualties, the French army had mutinied. Most of it was still in a state of "collective indiscipline," as Pétain put it. Russia, with its immense reservoir of manpower, was even closer to military collapse. The March revolution, which ousted the czar, had failed to add vigor or coherence to their army. More bad news soon arrived from the British front, where Field Marshal Sir Douglas Haig was in the process of squandering 300,000 men on futile attacks in the Ypres salient. An appalled Pershing told his military censor, Major Frederick Palmer, that he feared the worst: "Look at what is expected of us and what we have to start with! No army ready and no ships to bring over an army if we had one."

Pershing soon decided he could not rely on the General Staff in Washington for anything; it took weeks to get a reply from anyone. Tasker Bliss was still writing orders with the stub of a pencil and hiding urgent telegrams under his blotter while he made up his mind what to do about them. Pershing set up his own general staff in France—a far more efficient one than the fumbling team in Washington.

For his chief of staff, Pershing chose Major James Harbord. Neither a West Pointer nor a close friend, but extremely intelligent, Harbord had caught Pershing's eye in the Philippines. He was his commander's opposite in many ways—genial, warm, a man with first-class diplomatic instincts. Harbord kept a voluminous diary, from which we get a good picture of Pershing on the job.

> He thinks very clearly . . . and goes to his conclusions directly when matters call for decision. He can talk straighter to people when calling them down than anyone I have ever seen. . . . He loses his temper occasionally, and stupidity and vagueness irritate him more than anything else. . . . He develops great fondness for people whom he likes . . . but . . . is relentless when convinced of inefficiency. . . .
>
> He does not fear responsibility. . . . He decides big things much more quickly than he does trivial ones. Two weeks ago, without any authority from Washington, he placed an order . . . for $50,000,000 worth of airplanes . . . and did not cable the fact until too late for Washington to countermand it. . . . He did it without winking an eye, as easily as though ordering a postage stamp.

Alfred Thayer Mahan, Dennis Mahan's son, was fond of saying that war is business. As commander of the AEF, Pershing proved it. Until he took charge, each army bureau and department had its own supply officer with its own budget, a system that caused immense confusion and duplication of effort and expense. (For example, the various bureaus had ordered a total of 30 million pairs of shoes when 9 million were needed!) Pershing organized the AEF's purchases around a single man, an old friend and future vice president, Charles Dawes. A canny businessman, Dawes had absolute authority to buy anything and everything the army needed from the French and British at the best possible price.

The decisions Pershing and his staff made to prepare the AEF for battle were awesome. Along with French planes for their newly created independent air force, they bought French .75s for their artillery; the English Enfield rifle and steel helmet and the French light machine gun, the Chauchat, for their infantry; and the French light tank, the Renault, for George S. Patton's embryonic tank corps. Pershing also decided to make an AEF division, an entity that did not exist in the prewar American army, of 28,000 men, twice the size of an Allied or German division. He wanted an organization large enough to mount a sustained attack under the command of a single general. Unfortunately, he did not double the size of the new division's artillery, the first symptom of his inability to appreciate the lethal increase in firepower that had transformed warfare on the Western Front.

Pershing also strove to put his own stamp on the spirit of the AEF. In October 1917, he announced: "The standards for the American Army will be those of West Point. The . . . upright bearing, attention to detail, uncomplaining obedience to instruction required of the cadet will be required of every officer and soldier of our armies in France." To have every private behaving like a Pershing was an impossible dream, but the Iron General never wavered in his insistence. To improve the appearance of the officer corps, he ordered them to wear the British Sam Browne belt and authorized the use of canes. The first item was hated by many officers, the second mocked by enlisted men, but they became part of the dress code nonetheless.

Heywood Broun, who followed Pershing around France for a while, was bewildered by the general's appetite for details. He climbed into haylofts where soldiers were quartered and discussed onions with cooks, to make sure men were being billeted in reasonable health and comfort. Broun derided this attention to detail, sneering that Pershing thought he could read a man's soul "through his boots or his buttons." The reporter quoted a junior officer who thought Pershing's favorite biblical figure was Joshua, "because he made the sun and moon stand at attention." Broun's candor got him kicked out of France; Pershing's AEF censors had a low tolerance for such negative remarks. The rest of the press corps remained firmly in Pershing's corner.

One man who never succumbed to the system was Charles Dawes. Pershing made him a brigadier general to give him some weight with his French counterparts, but Dawes remained a civilian. His shoes went unshined, and his uniform was usually a rumpled mess. Pershing would frequently button Dawes's shirt or coat before they would appear together in public. Once, when he walked into a Dawes conference, everyone rose and saluted. But Dawes neglected to take a large cigar out of his mouth.

241

"Charlie," Pershing said, "the next time you salute, put the cigar on the other side of your mouth."

Although he could relax that way with close friends, and make visual gestures for photographers or admiring crowds, the one thing Pershing could not do was inspire soldiers or civilians with a ringing phrase. He was astute enough psychologically to trace this limitation to a boyhood episode, in which he forgot a speech during an elocution performance. A speech his staff wrote for him to make at Lafayette's tomb on July 4, 1917, ended with the oratorical high note, "Lafayette, we are here." Pershing crossed it out and wrote "not in character" beside it. He let one of his staff officers who spoke good French say it instead.

Another flaw, which drove Harbord and the rest of his staff to near distraction, was a complete lack of a sense of time. Pershing constantly arrived late to dinners or receptions, leaving kings, queens, prime ministers, and Allied generals impatiently tapping their VIP feet. The explanation was his appetite for detail. Devouring a report on weapons procurement or shipping schedules, Pershing would lose touch with the external world.

The euphoria of Pershing's arrival soon vanished: The promise of American aid remained unfulfilled. In the fall, the Germans and Austrians wrecked the Italian army at Caporetto. The Bolsheviks, having seized power in Moscow, took Russia out of the war, freeing an estimated seventy-seven German divisions for service on the Western Front. As a handful of American divisions trickled into Saint-Nazaire on their way to training areas in Lorraine, the Allies put more and more pressure on Pershing to give them control of his army.

The French and British generals summoned political reinforcements. Premier Paul Painlevé and Prime Minister David Lloyd George assailed Washington, D.C., with warnings of disaster and grave doubts about Pershing's capacity—simultaneously arranging for Pershing to be made aware of these fires being ignited in his rear. The only reinforcement Pershing got from Wilson was Bliss, an Anglophile who immediately sided with the British on amalgamation. Bliss said they should cable their opposing views to Washington and let the president decide. Pershing responded with some very straight talk. "Bliss," he said, "do you know what would happen if we did that? We would both be relieved from further duty in France and that is exactly what we should deserve." Bliss capitulated for the time being, a tribute not to the inferiority of his ideas but to the force of Pershing's personality.

The amalgamation pressure hardened Pershing's determination to make the AEF the best army in Europe. He was particularly tough on the 1st Division, which arrived in time to march through Paris on July 4—without the precision he expected. He took an instant dislike to the division's commander, Major General William Siebert, an engineering officer with little field experience. In October, inspecting the division, Pershing blasted Siebert in front of his officers. A young staff captain, George C. Marshall, stepped forward and launched a passionate defense of the general and the division, which was hampered by shortages of everything from motor transport to ammunition. The rest of the staff watched, wide-eyed, certain that Marshall and his military career were about to be obliterated. Instead, Pershing studied him for a long thoughtful moment and more or less apologized for his bad temper. It was the beginning of Marshall's rise to a colonel's rank and a dominant role on the AEF staff.

But Marshall did not change Pershing 's opinion of Siebert. "Slow of speech and of thought . . . slovenly in dress . . . utterly hopeless as an instructor or tactician" were among his comments. Within a month, Bullard had replaced Siebert as commander of the 1st Division. Pershing was equally unrelenting about most of the other generals who were shipped to Europe to survey the Western Front while their divisions were training in the United States. "Too old," "very fat and inactive," "could not begin to stand the strain" were some of the judgments he made of them. Washington ignored his criticisms and sent almost all of these losers back to France, giving Pershing the unwelcome job of relieving them—a task he performed with grim efficiency.

Ironically, one of the few who escaped Pershing's lash was the fattest general in the army, Hunter Liggett. Pershing kept him because Liggett, former head of the Army War College, had a brain. The Pershing within the Iron General had enough humor to like Liggett's defense of his bulk: There was nothing wrong with fat as long as it was not above the collar.

In the fall of 1917, Pershing moved AEF headquarters to Chaumont, a hilly town of 20,000, some 140 miles east of Paris. There, he and the staff were less exposed to the temptations of the *guerre de luxe,* as more cynical types called service in the City of Light. But Pershing had already succumbed. In September he had begun a liaison with a twenty-three-year-old Romanian artist, Micheline Resco, who had been commissioned by the French government to paint his portrait. He visited her by night in her apartment on the rue Descombes, sitting up front with his chauffeur on his way there and back, the windshield signs with the U.S. flag and his four stars flat on the dashboard, out of sight. Contrary to appearances, it was another love match, and it lasted, without benefit of clergy, for the rest of his life.

The Germans gave him other things to think about. In November they raided the 1st Division just after it entered the lines, killing three Americans, wounding five, and taking twelve prisoners. When Pershing heard the news he wept—not with grief for the dead, but with the humiliation of even a small defeat, which he knew would lead to more French and British condescension and demands for amalgamation. When the 1st Division planned a retaliatory raid of its own, the AEF commander supervised it personally. It was a humiliating flop. The infantry and the engineers failed to meet in no-man's-land and, without the latter's bangalore torpedoes, no one could get through the German barbed wire.

Eventually the division pulled off a successful raid, led by Theodore Roosevelt's oldest son, Ted, but these trivial skirmishes only intensified Allied disillusion with Pershing. The new French premier, Georges Clemenceau, locally known as the Tiger, bared his claws and remarked that Pershing's chief preoccupation seemed to be having dinner in Paris.

As 1918 began, Pershing had only four divisions in France, and three of them were short a total of 20,000 men. None but the 1st had fired a shot at the Germans. Wilson complicated Pershing's life by issuing his own peace terms, the Fourteen Points, infuriating the French and English with the president's blissful ignorance of political realities. The Germans ignored Wilson and continued to shift divisions to the Western Front—with new tactics designed to create their own version of open warfare.

The tactics had been developed by the German General Staff and first used in Italy and on the Eastern Front. They depended heavily on surprise. German artillerists had solved the problem of aiming guns accurately at night without registering fire, which had previously announced offensives on both sides. The key troops were elite *Sturmtruppen* with mission-oriented orders—rather than the detailed timetables that had hobbled earlier offensives. Instead of being assigned a particular objective, the storm troopers were told to penetrate as deeply as possible and disrupt the enemy rear areas. Commanders would commit additional infantry only at break-throughs, leaving enemy strongpoints isolated and eventually vulnerable to assault from the rear.

On March 21, 1918, the Germans unleashed these innovations on the British Fifth Army, guarding the hinge between the two Allied forces in Picardy. In three days, 90,000 Tommies surrendered, and another 90,000 became casualties. The Fifth Army ceased to exist, and the Germans men-aced Amiens, the key rail hub connecting the British and French armies. The frantic Allies convened a conference at Doullens, to which they did not even bother to invite Pershing or any other American. The only general who seemed interested in fighting was Ferdinand Foch, until recently in disgrace for squandering his men in suicidal attacks. The politicians per-suaded Haig and Pétain to accept Foch as the supreme commander, to coordinate the collapsing battle line.

Instead of sulking over being ignored, Pershing made his only grand gesture of the war. He drove to Foch's headquarters outside Paris and, in reasonably good French, declared: "I have come to tell you that the American people would consider it a great honor for our troops to be engaged in the present battle. I ask you for this in their name and my own." Everyone applauded the performance. It made headlines. But Pershing soon learned he had embraced a rattlesnake.

Instead of taking the four available American divisions and putting them into line as an army corps, which was what Pershing wanted, Foch assigned them to quiet sectors, piecemeal, after the battle for Amiens sub-sided. Next, behind Pershing's back, Foch dispatched a cable to Wilson telling him that unless 600,000 infantrymen were shipped to Europe in the next three months, unattached, for use as replacements in the French and British armies, the war was lost.

Pershing fought the Frenchman with his only weapon: an immense stubbornness and rocklike faith in his vision of an independent American army. Even when the secretary of war was cajoled into backing Foch by the devious Bliss, who seized the first opportunity to revoke his capitulation to Pershing, the Iron General clung to his determination. In May, soon after a second German offensive had come perilously close to smashing through the northern end of the British line and seizing the Channel ports, the Allies convened another conference at Abbeville. Pershing faced Lloyd George, Clemenceau, and Italian prime minister Vittorio Emanuele Orlando, plus Haig, Foch, and a half-dozen other generals and cabinet officers. Bliss said not a word in his support. The others raged, screamed, cursed, and pleaded—but Pershing would not change his mind. He absolutely refused to let the Americans fight in units smaller than a division—and he insisted that even this concession would be temporary, pending the formation of an American army.

"Are you willing to risk our being driven back to the Loire?" Foch shouted.

"Gentlemen," Pershing said after another forty minutes of wrangling, "I have thought this program over very deliberately and I will not be coerced."

Pershing was taking one of the greatest gambles in history. On May 27, the Germans struck again, this time at the French along the Chemin des Dames ridge northeast of Soissons. Once more, the German artillery's fiendish combination of high explosives and poison gas tore apart the front lines, and the storm troopers poured through the gaps. The French Sixth Army evaporated. In a week Soissons and Château-Thierry fell, and the Germans were on the Marne, only fifty miles from Paris.

This time, American divisions were not diverted to quiet sectors. The 2nd and 3rd divisions went into line around Château-Thierry as *poilus* streamed past them shouting, "La guerre finie." Except for some lively skirmishing, the Germans did not attack. Their infantry went on the defensive, while the generals brought up their artillery and tried to decide what to do with the huge salient they had carved in the French lines between Soissons and Reims.

The French commander of the sector, General Jean-Marie-Joseph Degoutte, was, like Foch, an apostle of the school of frontal attack—which had done little thus far but pile up Allied bodies in front of German machine-gun emplacements. Finding himself in possession of fresh American troops, he went on the offensive, ordering an attack on Belleau Wood. He found a willing collaborator in Colonel Preston Brown, the 2nd Division's chief of staff. Brown—who dominated the overage and incompetent division commander, Omar Bundy—was burning to demonstrate American prowess. He accepted at face value French reports that the Germans held only the northern corner of the wood. In fact, they occupied it to the last inch with infantry supported by machine guns set up for interlocking fields of fire.

On June 6, without sending out a single patrol to find more information, Brown and Harbord, recently reassigned to the division as commander of the 4th Marine Brigade, ordered their men forward in a frontal assault. The marines advanced in massed formations unseen on the Western Front since 1914. Incredulous German machine gunners mowed them down in windrows. The slaughter revealed the limitations of Pershing's doctrine of open warfare. As Liggett later mournfully remarked, no one, including Pershing, had thought it out.

The marines eventually captured Belleau Wood, after the French pulled them back and treated the Germans to a fourteen-hour artillery barrage that smashed the place flat. Pershing rewarded Harbord for his incompetence (there were 50 percent casualties) by making him commander of the 2nd Division in place of Bundy, who had stood around during the battle without saying a word while Harbord and Brown made their bloody blunders.

The desperate French trumpeted Belleau Wood as a major victory in their newspapers, and reporters around the world followed suit. Pershing went along because he was even more desperate for proof that his men could stand up to the Germans. The battering he had taken from Foch, Haig, and others had broadened his definition of what constituted a battlefield success. Henceforth, Pershing would countenance the pernicious idea that high casualties were proof of a commander's fighting ability.

Beginning on the night of July 14, seven American divisions (troops were starting to arrive in ever-greater numbers) played crucial roles in smashing the next German offensive, code-named Friedensturm—the "peace assault." Casualties were relatively light because the Allies, perhaps borrowing a bit of Pershing luck, discovered the exact day and hour of the attack from a captured German officer. Ignoring Foch's senseless order to hold every inch of sacred soil, General Pétain created an elastic defense that inflicted enormous losses on the *Sturmtruppen*. Pershing was only a spectator at this three-day clash, his divisions being temporarily under the orders of French generals.

Foch, an apostle of attack, at last became the right general in the right place at the right time. He threw the American 1st and 2nd divisions and a French colonial division into the soft left flank of the German Marne salient around Soissons. The first day, July 18, was a sensational success, but on the second day the Germans recovered from their surprise. Their machine guns sprouted everywhere, and casualties mounted. Again and again, Americans advanced across open ground without concealment or cover—with predictable results. The 1st and 2nd had 12,000 casualties. The 2nd, already bled by Belleau Wood, collapsed and was withdrawn after two days. The 1st, equally battered (the 26th Infantry Regiment lost 3,000 out of 3,200 men), was withdrawn the following day. This was hardly the staying power Pershing had envisioned for his double-sized divisions. But he ignored the danger signs and told Harbord that even if the two divisions never fired another shot, they had made their commanders "immortal."

Having seized the initiative, Foch was determined not to relinquish it. For the next six weeks, he ordered attacks all around the Marne salient. In the vanguard were American divisions, fighting under French generals. This little-studied Aisne-Marne offensive proved the courage of the American infantrymen—and the limitations of their open-warfare tactics. Before it ended in early September, over 90,000 Americans were dead or wounded.

Inept tactics were not the only problem. Too often, Americans found their flanks exposed by the failure of a French division to keep pace with their attack. Bullard, who by then was supposed to be supervising American operations as commander of the III Corps, fretted about the murderous casualties but did little else. There is no record of Pershing saying anything.

The climax of this messy operation was on August 27, when an isolated company of the 28th Division was annihilated in Fismette, on the north bank of the Vesle River. Bullard had tried to withdraw the soldiers—they were the only Americans on that side of the river, surrounded by some 200,000 Germans—but Degoutte, now commander of the Sixth Army, had revoked the order. When Bullard reported the episode a few days later, Pershing asked, "Why didn't you disobey the order?"

"I did not answer. It was not necessary to answer," Bullard wrote in his memoirs.

By this time, five other American divisions were training with the British army. On August 8, the British had made a successful attack on the western flank of the salient that the Germans had created when they routed the Fifth Army in Picardy. Pershing had permitted these divisions to go directly into British training areas when they arrived in Europe—an example of the partial surrenders of control extracted from him by Foch and Haig, with the help of the German army. But Pershing stubbornly discounted the possibility that perhaps this was the best way to use the Americans finally flooding into France—brigading them with British or French armies, who already had sophisticated staffs and supply systems in place.

Instead, the Iron General never stopped insisting on a totally independent army. On August 10, he opened First Army headquarters; five days later, he handed Foch a plan for an attack on the Saint-Mihiel salient, another huge bulge into the French lines, south of Verdun. He withdrew three of his five divisions from a choleric Haig, and all that were under French control.

On August 28, as the Americans moved into the lines, Foch descended on Pershing with one last attempt to utilize the AEF in—from the viewpoint of the supreme commander—a more rational way. He announced a master plan he had conceived while visiting Haig. The whole German battlefront, he said, was one huge salient that should be attacked from the north, the south, and the center. He therefore wanted Pershing more or less to abort the Saint-Mihiel operation, limiting it to a few divisions, and transfer the rest of his army back to French control for attacks in the Aisne and Argonne theaters.

A vehement argument ensued. At one point, both men were on their feet screaming curses at each other. "Do you wish to take part in the battle?" Foch shrilled, the ultimate insult one general could throw at another. For a moment, Pershing seriously thought of flattening the little Frenchman with a roundhouse right. "As an American army and in no other way!" he replied.

"I must insist on the arrangement!" Foch shouted.

Pershing squared his jaw. "Marshal Foch, you may insist all you please, but I decline absolutely to agree to your plan. While our army will fight wherever you decide, it will fight only as an independent American army."

After another week of wrangling, Pershing accepted a dangerous compromise. He would attack the Saint-Mihiel salient on September 12, as planned, then transfer the bulk of his 500,000-man army west of the Meuse to attack north through the Argonne as part of the overall Allied offensive on September 26. It was an ambitious assignment for a general who had never commanded more than 11,000 men in action and a staff that had yet to fight a single battle. Only a man with Pershing 's self-confidence would have tried it. To compound his potential woes, he accepted a battle plan from Foch that gave French generals command east of the Meuse and west of the Argonne Forest, violating a primary military maxim: An attacking army should be responsible for both sides of a natural obstacle such as a forest or a river.

On September 5, Pershing, disturbed by AEF casualties in the Aisne-Marne offensive, made a stab at defining open warfare. In a general order issued to the First Army, he contrasted it to trench warfare, which he claimed was "marked by uniform formations, the regulation of space and time by higher commands down to the smallest details and little initiative." Open warfare had "irregular . . . formations, comparatively little regulation of space and time . . . and the greatest possible use of the infantry's own firepower to enable it to get forward . . . [plus] brief orders and the greatest possible use of individual initiative." It was much too late for such complex ideas to filter down even to division staffs, much less to the captains and lieutenants leading companies. Nor did this inchoate rhetoric offer a clue to how to deal with the primary defensive weapon on the Western Front—the machine gun.

At first, Pershing luck seemed to hold. The Saint-Mihiel offensive was the walkover of the war. The Germans were in the process of withdrawing from the salient when the Americans attacked. Resistance was perfunctory. The bag of prisoners and captured guns was big enough to make headlines, although the take was not nearly as large as originally hoped. Pershing and his staff now tried to imitate the Germans and achieve surprise in the Argonne. He left most of his veteran divisions in Saint-Mihiel and shifted largely green units west. No significant snafus developed on the roads, thanks to the planning genius of George C. Marshall, who was nicknamed the Wizard for managing the sixty-mile transfer in wretched rainy weather.

On September 26, after a German-style, 4,000-gun artillery barrage, Pershing threw 250,000 men in three corps at an estimated 50,000 unprepared German defenders in the twenty-mile-wide Argonne valley. A massive hogback ran down the center, forcing the attackers into defiles on both sides. It was, Liggett said, a natural fortress that made the Virginia Wilderness seem like a park. Yet Pershing's plan called for no less than a ten-mile-abreast advance the first day to crack the Kriemhilde Stellung, the main German defensive line.

Five of Pershing's nine divisions had never been in action before. Even experienced divisions such as the 77th, which had been bloodied under the French, were full of green replacements. The 77th received 2,100 men who had never fired a rifle the day before they attacked. Everything imaginable proceeded to go wrong with Pershing's army. The Germans fell back to well-prepared defenses and began machine-gunning charging Americans. Massive amounts of enemy artillery on the heights east of the Meuse and along the edge of the Argonne Forest, which loomed a thousand feet above the valley floor, exacted an even heavier toll.

Rigid orders, issued by Pershing's own staff, held up whole divisions at crucial moments. The 4th Division could have captured the key height of Montfaucon the first day, but it stood still for four hours, waiting for the green 79th Division, assigned the objective, to come abreast of it. By the time Montfaucon fell the following day, the Germans had poured in five first-class divisions, and the American advance had stumbled to a bloody halt.

In the north, where the British and French were attacking, the Germans could give ground for sixty or a hundred miles before yielding anything vital. But only twenty-four miles from the American jumping-off point in the Argonne was the Sedan–Mézières four-track railroad, which supplied almost all the food and ammunition to the Germans' northern armies. They were fighting to protect their jugular in the Argonne. By October 4, they had elements of twenty-three divisions in line or local reserve.

Withdrawing his green divisions, Pershing replaced them with the veteran units he had left in Saint-Mihiel and tried to resume the attack. He was on the road constantly, visiting corps and division headquarters, urging generals and colonels to inject their men with more "drive" and "push." But Pershing was discovering that rhetoric could not silence a machine gun.

His men bled, and also began to starve. Food did not get forward, as monumental traffic jams developed on the few roads into the Argonne. Wounded lay unevacuated. Clemenceau, caught in a jam while visiting the front, lost half a day and departed vowing to get rid of Pershing. Stragglers were another problem. Liggett estimated that at the height of the battle, 100,000 fugitives were wandering around the First Army's rear areas. One division reported an effective frontline strength of only 1,600 men. Early in October, Pershing authorized officers to shoot down any man who ran away—proof of his growing desperation.

Worsening Pershing's woes, while the Americans were withdrawing the wreckage of the green divisions, was a visit from Foch's chief of staff, who informed Pershing that the generalissimo thought he had too many men in the Argonne. Foch proposed shifting six divisions to nearby French armies. Recent historians have been inclined to think Foch was probably right. The French on Pershing's right and left were making little progress and could have used some help. But by now, Pershing hated Foch too much to take his advice about anything. He told the supreme commander to go to hell. Foch retaliated with a formal on-the-record letter ordering him to attack continuously "without any [further] interruptions."

Killing fire from the guns east of the Meuse stopped the veteran divisions when they jumped off on October 4. German counterattacks drove them back again and again. Only the 1st Division, under the Cromwellian Charles Summerall, gained some ground, plunging up the left defile for a half-dozen miles—at a cost of 9,387 casualties. On October 8, Pershing sent two divisions east of the Meuse to join the French in an attempt to silence the artillery. The attack faltered and collapsed into a pocket on the banks of the Meuse, deluged by gas and shellfire.

Pershing drove himself as hard as he did his men. He sat up until three or four in the morning reading reports and pondering maps. Rumors drifted into headquarters that Foch and Clemenceau were urging Wilson to replace him with Bliss. One day, in his car with his favorite aide, Major James Collins, a played-out Pershing put his head in his hands and, speaking to his dead wife, moaned: "Frankie . . . Frankie . . . my God, sometimes I don't know how I can go on."

Outwardly, no one else saw anything but the Iron General, still in charge. "Things are going badly," he told Major General Henry Allen, commander of the 90th Division. "But by God, Allen, I was never so much in earnest in my life, and we are going to get through." Marshall thought this was Pershing's finest hour. More critical recent historians, pointing to the substantial gains being made, and the huge numbers of prisoners and guns being captured, by French and British armies on other fronts, suggest Pershing was hopelessly out of his depth but was refusing to admit it.

There may be some truth to this assertion—except for the last part. On October 12, tacitly admitting he did not have the answer to the Argonne, Pershing gave Liggett command of the First Army and created a Second Army, under Bullard, to operate east of the Meuse. Pershing became the commander of the army group—chairman of the board instead of chief executive officer. The First Army continued to attack for another seven days, finally breaching the Kriemhilde Stellung on October 19. It had taken three weeks and 100,000 casualties to achieve what Pershing and his staff had thought they could do in a single day.

At this point, the First Army was, in the opinion of one staff officer, "a disorganized and wrecked army." Liggett promptly went on the defensive. When Pershing persisted in hanging around headquarters, talking about launching another attack, Liggett told him to "go away and forget it." Pershing meekly obeyed.

It was just as well, because he soon had a more serious topic on his mind. Early in October, the Germans had announced they were willing to accept peace on the basis of Wilson's Fourteen Points. As Wilson began negotiating with them, Pershing came perilously close to making the president look foolish by issuing a public statement that he favored unconditional surrender.

The Wilson administration was infuriated. Many people assumed Pershing's statement was the opening salvo of a run for the presidency. On the contrary, Pershing was motivated by two things. His political mentor,

Theodore Roosevelt, was savaging Wilson back in the United States with a similar call for unconditional surrender. The Iron General was also seething because Haig, the British commander, had recommended an armistice, arguing that the British and French were close to exhaustion and the American army was too inept to bear any substantial share of another offensive. Pershing wanted more war to make Haig eat those words.

Under fierce pressure from Wilson, Pershing accepted the idea of armistice. But he remained convinced it was a mistake. When the First Army resumed the offensive on November 1, he urged it forward with ferocious intensity, hoping it could smash the Germans before negotiators agreed on terms. Rested and reorganized, imbued with new tactics that urged infiltration and flank attacks rather than piling men against enemy strongpoints, the Americans were sensationally successful. They stormed across the Meuse, cutting the Sedan–Mézières railroad and threatening the German armies in the north with imminent starvation and collapse. At Pershing's insistence, they kept attacking until the armistice went into effect at 11:00 A.M. on November 11. "If they had given us another ten days," Pershing said, "we would have rounded up the entire German army, captured it, humiliated it." There are strong reasons to doubt this postwar Pershing boast, however. In the final days, replacements had become a major AEF problem. The German army was still a formidable fighting force—and a policy of unconditional surrender might have inspired it to resist with desperate ferocity, as it demonstrated in World War II.

In these same final days, Pershing, still fuming over Foch's condescension and Clemenceau's sneers, attempted to retaliate with a ploy that seriously endangered the fragile alliance. He decided the Americans would capture Sedan, the city where the French had ingloriously surrendered to Bismarck's Germans in 1870. Ignoring a boundary drawn by Foch that placed Sedan in the zone of the French Fourth Army, he ordered the First Army to capture the city and deprive the French of this symbolic honor. The order—which directed the I Corps, spearheaded by the 42nd Division, to make the main thrust, "assisted on their right by the V Corps"—was so vague that it encouraged General Summerall, by then the commander of the V Corps, to march the 1st Division across the front of the 42nd Division to get there first. In the darkness and confusion, the 1st Division captured Douglas MacArthur, one of the 42nd's brigadiers, who looked like a German officer because of his unorthodox headgear. It was a miracle that the two divisions did not shoot each other to pieces. If the German army had been in any kind of fighting shape, a counterattack would have wreaked havoc. The episode suggests Pershing's limitations as a practitioner of coalition warfare. In the end, the French Fourth Army was permitted to capture Sedan. Liggett wanted to court-martial Summerall, but Pershing dismissed the whole affair.

When the bells rang out across France and the people erupted into mad joy, not even Pershing could resist the emotions of victory. In perhaps his most significant summary of the war, he said several times, "The men were willing to pay the price." Perhaps this was as close as the Iron General came to admitting he had made some mistakes.

For the rest of his long life—he did not die until 1948—Pershing spent a good deal of his time fostering the career of the man who would lead America's armies in World War II. Marshall served as his aide when he was chief of staff after the war, they became close friends, and Pershing was best man at Marshall's wedding in 1927. When MacArthur, then the army chief of staff, tried to short-circuit Marshall's advancement by appointing him senior instructor to the Illinois National Guard in 1933, Pershing visited him in Chicago, creating headlines for the obscure young colonel. The next chief of staff, a Pershing man, brought Marshall back to Washington as his assistant. In 1939, Pershing persuaded FDR to make Marshall the chief of staff.

In his private life, Pershing was a dutiful father to his only son, Warren. He made no objection when Warren chose a civilian rather than a military career. Pershing remained devoted to Micheline Resco, but he was frequently linked romantically to other women. He once remarked that if he married all the women he was reported to be romancing, he would have to start a harem.

Trying to sum up Pershing, almost everyone found him full of contradictions. Secretary of War Baker wondered how a man could combine such large views with an obsessive concern for buttons. "If he was not a great man," wrote the newsman Frank Simonds, "there were few stronger." The British military thinker B.H. Liddell Hart said no other man could have built the AEF, and "without that army the war could hardly have been saved and could not have been won." Perhaps his unmilitary friend Charles Dawes came closest to the Iron General's inner secret: "John Pershing, like Lincoln, recognized no superior on the face of the earth." Unquestionably, Pershing left something to be desired as a field commander. But without him, American doughboys might have become cannon fodder for French and British generals—a development that would have caused a huge political backlash on the home front. Meanwhile, he and his men learned the bitter lessons of how to fight on the Western Front. Fortunately for Pershing, the doughboys were willing to pay the price.

*WINTER 1995*

---

Thomas Fleming is the author of the earlier article on George Washington. His novel of World War I, *Over There,* was published in 1992.

# 22

# Belleau Wood: One Man's Initiation

## By Allan R. Millett

*In early June 1918, after four bloody and indecisive years of fighting, the German armies seemed on the verge of final victory. With just one more lunge, Paris seemed within their grasp. But the German advance would go through Belleau Wood, a dark tangled mass of brush and hardwood trees, far more hospitable to birds and small game than to man. In fact, in prewar days a Paris businessman used it as a hunting preserve. Now it would witness the initiation of the American 5th and 6th Marine regiments into the reality of World War I. Neither the Marine Corps nor the individual marines who fought there—including Sergeant Gerald C. Thomas of Illinois—would ever be quite the same.*

*E*ager to have U.S. Marines fight in World War I as part of General John J. Pershing's American Expeditionary Forces, the Marine Corps commandant, Major General George Barnett, successfully persuaded the War Department to accept a marine brigade as part of the token force sent to France in 1917. Eventually organized as the 4th Brigade of the U.S. 2nd Division, it consisted of a brigade headquarters, a machine-gun battalion, and two infantry regiments, the 5th and 6th Marines.

One member of the 1st Battalion, 6th Marines, was a twenty-one-year-old former football player from Bloomington, Illinois, named Gerald C. Thomas. Like most of his comrades, Thomas volunteered for the Marine Corps in the spring of 1917. Like many of the new marines he also expected to be an officer, since he had completed three years of college at Illinois Wesleyan University, and Commandant Barnett had announced that he wanted college men to be the lieutenants in the expanded corps. Barnett had more officer candidates than openings, however, so Jerry Thomas had to serve first as a corporal and then as *a sergeant in the 75th Company until German bullets created sufficient openings in 1918. Before he left the Marine Corps at the end of 1955, General Gerald C. Thomas had fought in three wars and served as assistant commandant and chief of staff of the Marine Corps. His own service reputation, which soared on Guadalcanal and in Korea, began at the Battle of Belleau Wood.*

*When the German army began its last desperate attempt to win the war on the Western Front in March 1918, it found no Americans except scattered soldiers training with the British. By the end of the spring, General Pershing had committed the four divisions he considered more or less combat ready to the French armies attempting to hold positions north and east of Paris. Late in May, the Germans shattered a mixed Anglo-French force along the Chemin des Dames ridge northeast of Paris, and the 2nd Division joined the French XXI Corps (under Général de Division Jean Degoutte), which was fighting a confused withdrawal north of the Marne River near the city of Château-Thierry.*

*Having had a taste of trench warfare in March, Thomas's battalion entered its first major battle with some combat experience, but as its officers and men left their camp near Paris by truck on May 30, none of them could have foreseen the ferocious battle that awaited. At the van of the 4th Brigade (under Brigadier General James G. Harbord, U.S. Army—no marine brigadier generals had been immediately available to fill that opening), the 6th Marines moved into an extemporized (and poorly chosen) defensive position anchored on the farming village of Lucy-le-Bocage. From their hastily dug rifle pits, the marines of the 75th Company, 1st Battalion, 6th Marines, looked across the pasture and wheat field in front of them and saw a thick wood. Sergeant Thomas, by now acting platoon sergeant of the 75th Company's Third Platoon, certainly had no idea that the wood to his front would prove historic to him and the entire United States Marine Corps.*

*The following account is adapted from the author's biography of Gerald C. Thomas,* In Many a Strife: General Gerald C. Thomas and the U.S. Marine Corps, 1917–1956, *just published by the Naval Institute Press.*

A DARK FORTRESS of tall hardwoods, Belleau Wood stretched for about a mile along the edge of a low plateau a few miles from the Marne River. It took its name from the farming village of Belleau, beyond the wood's northeast corner. Belleau's only noteworthy feature—a clear, cold spring—gave the town its name ("beautiful water"). Neither the wood nor the town had any importance except that both lay between two major roads that gave the attacking Germans, the IV Reserve Corps, a way to flank the Allied positions along the nearby Paris–Metz highway.

The wood provided an excellent place to assemble an attack force safe from Allied observers. Moreover, German spotters on its western edge could see the marine brigade's positions around Lucy-le-Bocage. The wood also made an excellent defensive position. Used by a rich Paris businessman as a hunting preserve, Belleau Wood deceived the Americans who watched it from a mile away. Inside the outer edge of trees, it was a tangle of brush and second growth, cut by deep ravines and studded with rock outcroppings and large boulders. Only narrow paths and rocky streams provided access through the wood. Little light penetrated the trees. A haven for game birds and animals, it was meant for hunting by men, not for the killing of men. In June 1918, however, the 4th Marine Brigade and the German 28th and 237th divisions made Belleau Wood a battlefield.

On the morning of June 3, 1918, General de Infanterie Richard von Conta, commander of the German IV Reserve Corps, ordered a three-division attack on the French forces screening the 2nd Division. As the fighting increased, German artillery, assisted by spotters in aircraft and balloons, crashed down upon the marines' defensive positions. The 1st Battalion, 6th Marines, did not occupy well-built trenches, only quickly dug foxholes. As the shells dropped, shovels and picks rose and fell. Jerry Thomas and the 75th Company soon learned that only a direct hit or a near miss would destroy a foxhole; the 75th pulled the ground around itself and endured. Nevertheless, it suffered casualties: a curious marine decapitated when he looked outside his hole, two men knocked senseless by a near miss, a carrying party destroyed on its way forward with water. French soldiers began to drift back through Lucy. To the north, small-arms fire swelled as the first German patrols made contact with a battalion of the 5th Marines defending the woods and high ground west of the Torcy–Lucy road. The 75th Company could hear the noise of troops moving in Belleau Wood.

Soon the French delaying action collapsed, and the only sign of French combativeness was the occasional group of *poilus* who stayed with the marines. In Jerry Thomas's position, the Third Platoon gained a Hotchkiss machine-gun crew, a welcome addition since marine machine-gun teams did not arrive until late in the day. The 6th Marines was spread thin, for its commander, Colonel Albertus W. Catlin, had committed three of his four reserve companies to his endangered left flank, where the 5th Marines had first met the Germans. In the late afternoon the 1st Battalion shifted positions to meet an expected attack to its left, which meant that Thomas's platoon moved from the edge of the village into an open field.

Hardly had the platoon scooped out shallow holes than a German battalion—probably between 400 and 500 men—emerged from Belleau Wood in lines of skirmishers and squad columns and started across the fields toward Lucy. At a range of 400 yards the 1st Battalion opened fire, savaging the German infantry with rapid, accurate rifle fire. The French Hotchkiss crew raked the Germans, and Thomas watched soldiers in baggy *feldgrau* uniforms spin and slump into the wheat and poppies. The attack collapsed, and the survivors scuttled back into Belleau Wood, where the rest of the 461st Infantry Regiment, 237th Division (about 1,200 officers and men), had concentrated for another attack.

Uncertain about the nature of the new resistance his corps had encountered, General von Conta halted the advance on the afternoon of

June 3 and instead continued his assault on the 4th Marine Brigade's lines with artillery fire. As the heavier German guns and trench mortars moved into range, the marines felt the increased weight of the bombardment. They especially disliked the heavy mortar shells, which they could see curling in on top of them and which detonated with both fearsome noise and destructiveness. Much of the artillery fire, in fact, was now falling on positions to the rear where the Germans guessed—incorrectly—the enemy might have its reserve infantry and artillery positions. The next day (June 4) the infantrymen on either side remained in their holes as German and Allied artillery swept the front with a desultory bombardment. On the left flank of the 6th Marines' position, a German patrol found a marine's corpse and identified its foe for the first time. Von Conta shifted to the defense while he awaited the German Seventh Army's decision on whether the IV Reserve Corps should make another extreme effort to reach the Paris–Metz highway from the north.

Meanwhile, the 6th Marines continued to improve its defensive position by building up its artillery and logistical support. Thomas and two companions were dispatched to map the battalion positions in the sector. The battalion commander, Major John A. ("Johnny the Hard") Hughes, liked their work—but not their findings. The entire 1st Battalion position had neither adequate cover nor concealment. In fact, Hughes told Colonel Catlin that the entire regiment was exposed and persuaded the colonel to order a withdrawal that night to a reverse-slope defense two miles to the rear.

However, General Degoutte, headmaster of the school of the unrelenting attack, had other plans for the 2nd Division, and a withdrawal was not part of his concept of operations. Degoutte's XXI Corps was, for all practical purposes, the French 167th Division, the U.S. 2nd Division, and some French artillery regiments, for his other two French divisions no longer existed as effective fighting organizations. At midafternoon on June 5, Degoutte ordered the 167th and 2nd divisions to attack the Germans the next day in order to disrupt the massing of German artillery and infantry reserves in the Clignon River valley north of Torcy. Hill 142, at the left of the line held by the marines, was their first objective. The 2nd Division received a second objective—Belleau Wood—which was to be attacked as soon as possible after the completion of the attack to the north.

The 1st Battalion, 6th Marines, was sent back to a reserve position. Hughes was not unhappy. He did not like the attack plan, a straight-ahead advance like Pickett's Charge. The 1st Battalion marched five miles to the rear into a protected, defiladed wood near Nanteuil, a village on the Marne. Arriving by daybreak, the marines stripped off their sodden equipment, ate their first hot meal in a week, and collapsed in sleep in the welcome haylofts. In the meantime, the roar of artillery at the front introduced a new phase in the battle for Belleau Wood.

THE 4TH BRIGADE attacks of June 6, 1918, produced a fury of heroism and sacrifice that remained fixed as a high point of valor in the history of the

American Expeditionary Forces and the Marine Corps in World War I. Although Degoutte's and Harbord's conduct of operations on that day showed little skill, no one then or now has faulted the marines for their efforts to turn bad plans into good victories. The first mistake was Degoutte's in insisting that the attacks begin on June 6 rather than a day later, after the attacking battalions had time to enter the front lines, to conduct some reconnaissance, and to make their own analyses of the situation. Artillery-fire support could certainly have profited by the delay. As it was, the battalions had to conduct a relief of frontline positions and also mount an attack within hours after a night movement, no ingredient for success. Moreover, a 6th Marines nighttime patrol had reported that Belleau Wood was strongly defended. This report reached brigade, but it made no difference. The attacks proceeded on the assumption that the German front was lightly held, reinforced by reports that French aerial observers saw little movement in the area.

The early-morning attack on Hill 142, mounted by only two 5th Marine companies, produced a costly victory that widened with the arrival of four more marine companies and supporting machine gunners, who beat back a series of German counterattacks. The action ended around 9:00 A.M. Afterward, General Harbord ordered the Belleau Wood attack to begin at 5:00 P.M. His order reflected an optimism unjustified by the stiffness of the German resistance that morning, for he expected Catlin to take Belleau Wood and the town of Bouresches with only three battalions—perhaps 2,000 men. (Two of these battalions had additional assignments that prevented them from using all four of their rifle companies.) Presumably the fire of thirteen Allied artillery battalions would clear the way of Germans. In any event, Catlin mounted the attack as ordered—although Harbord's concept of "infiltration" changed to a converging standard battalion advance of two companies up, two back—and saw the better part of three battalions shot to pieces by German machine-gun positions along the western and southern edges of Belleau Wood.

From the west, Major Benjamin S. Berry's 3rd Battalion, 5th Marines, barely entered the wood; so few, shocked, and exhausted were the survivors that they could advance no farther. Most of the battalion remained in a wheat field, dead or wounded. The southern attack by the 3rd Battalion, 6th Marines, penetrated the wood at sufficient depth to hold a position, but only at great cost. Casualties in these two battalions approached 60 percent, with losses among officers and NCOs even higher. The two-company attack on Bouresches, on the other hand, produced success, even though the two companies also took prohibitive losses. The Germans quickly recognized that the loss of Bouresches menaced their lines of communications, so they counterattacked heavily, thus drawing the rest of the 2nd Battalion, 6th Marines (under Major Thomas Holcomb), into the battle. Whatever its original tactical value, Belleau Wood had to be taken in order to protect the left flank of the Bouresches salient.

As he analyzed the scattered reports that arrived at his post of command (PC) during the evening of June 6, General Harbord began to understand that the marine brigade had not taken Belleau Wood and that it had lost more than a thousand officers and men—including Colonel Catlin, who was wounded by a sniper's bullet while observing the attack. More marines had become casualties in a few hours than the Marine Corps had suffered in its entire history. Although the attacks on Hill 142 and Bouresches had succeeded, the attack on the wood itself had not. Perhaps stung by his own shortcomings as a commander, Harbord lashed out at Catlin's replacement, Lieutenant Colonel Harry Lee, and demanded the attack be resumed. At that point, Belleau Wood basically remained German except for a corner of its southern edge held by the 3rd Battalion, 6th Marines.

As the situation cleared during June 7, Harbord assumed that the 6th Marines could hold Bouresches—with help from the U.S. 23rd Infantry Regiment to its right—so he ordered Lee to continue the attack within the wood itself. His marines fought alone in Belleau Wood, without making much progress. Neither side could mount overwhelming artillery support, since the opposing positions were imprecise and too close; the battle pitted German machine-gun and mortar crews, supported by infantry, against marine infantrymen, who depended primarily on rifles and grenades. Small groups of marines crawled up to the machine-gun positions, threw grenades, then rushed in with bayonets. Few German prisoners survived. The marines ran out of grenades, however, which increased their own casualties. By midmorning of June 8, the battalion had little fight left, and it withdrew from the wood. There were no marines there now.

Harbord let the 2nd Division artillery shell Belleau Wood for the rest of that day, while he organized his next attack. Degoutte had decided that he would not press the attack against Torcy, so Harbord could use his only two relatively unscathed battalions—2nd Battalion, 5th Marines (under Lieutenant Colonel Frederic M. Wise), and 1st Battalion, 6th Marines—for another attack on Belleau Wood. On the evening of the eighth, Harbord ordered Major Hughes to move his battalion into woods southeast of Lucy-le-Bocage. Although the general had not yet committed himself to a particular plan, Hughes believed that Harbord wanted him in position to move into Belleau Wood the following afternoon.

Hughes again sent Sergeant Jerry Thomas on a reconnoitering expedition, this time to locate the mouth of a sunken road that could lead the battalion to the front along a gulley, which would provide cover and concealment. Thomas found the mouth of the sunken road, then jogged back to the battalion. He reported to Captain George A. Stowell, the senior company commander and a veteran of three Caribbean operations, who would move the battalion while Hughes conferred with Harbord at the PC.

The battalion stepped out around 9:00 P.M.—and, in the dark, entered a nightmare of confusion and wrong turns. It did not reach the sunken road until midnight. There, the column met First Lieutenant Charles A. Etheridge, the new battalion intelligence officer. Thomas thought Etheridge knew the rest of the route, but Etheridge had not reconnoitered the trail because Hughes had not told him to do so. As dawn broke, the 1st Battalion strayed into the open fields west of Lucy-le-Bocage and into the view of German observation-balloon spotters. Stowell quickly ordered the men into a nearby wood, where they would have to stay until night came again. Furious, Hughes rejoined his battalion and relieved Stowell of command. (Stowell later returned to the battalion and had a distinguished career.)

Stowell's 76th Company went to First Lieutenant Macon C. Overton, a thin, handsome, laconic, twenty-six-year-old Georgian who had joined the corps as an enlisted man in 1914. Later in the day (June 9) Harbord ordered Hughes to resume his approach march and to be in position on June 10 to enter Belleau Wood behind a crushing barrage. After dark, the wandering 1st Battalion set off again for the front. This time it did not become lost. On the other hand, it also had nothing between it and the Germans but the outposts of one 2nd Battalion company. The attack on Belleau Wood would have to start again from scratch.

Despite the setback of June 6, Harbord did not change his concept of attack for the June 10 operation. The 1st Battalion would attack the southern part of the wood while the 2nd Battalion, 5th Marines, would later attack the northern part from the west. The two battalions would join one another at Belleau Wood's narrow, middle neck. It was a maneuver that looked good on a map, but it worked poorly on the battlefield because of the roughness of the terrain. Fortunately, the extra day of shelling had persuaded the German defenders—still battalions from the 237th and 28th divisions—to concede the wood's southern edge. But the German combat teams still manned a thick belt of defenses that covered the wheat fields to the west and faced the trails inside the southern woods. The Allied artillery bombardment had taken its toll, but had not crushed the defenders. The Germans endured the intense barrage at daybreak on the tenth and then manned their positions to wait for the next two marine battalions.

Disobeying Major Hughes's orders to remain near the phones at the battalion PC, Sergeant Thomas joined the waves of marines as they left the woods and started across the lower-lying wheat field for Belleau Wood. The moment had seized him: "The sight of those brave waves moving through the wheat with bayonets fixed and rifles carried at the high post in our first offensive was a little too much to bear." With two companies forward and two back in the standard French attack formation, the battalion marched steadily across the Lucy–Bouresches road. Rifles at the high port, bayonets fixed, unreliable Chauchat automatic rifles pointed to the front, the marines crossed the swale between the highway and the trees and entered the wood. During the advance, Thomas ran through the wheat until he caught up with the Third Platoon of the 75th Company, avoiding the bodies of marines killed in the June 6 attack. Much to the battalion's surprise, not a shot was fired at it. Instead of entering the wood, Thomas started back to the PC, for he recalled "that I had another job to do." He met Hughes, who was elated by the attack and wanted to report his success by phone. The battalion commander did not censure him for joining the attack, but told him to move the PC across the road to the raised bank at the edge of Belleau Wood. As Thomas helped reestablish the battalion PC, he heard the roar of gunfire within the wood. The 1st Battalion had discovered the Germans.

For the 1st Battalion, 6th Marines, the battle began around 6:00 A.M. on June 10 and did not end until it left the wood seven days later, an exhausted, smaller, but still combative group of veteran marines. Jerry Thomas fought with his battalion from start to finish. He learned to cope with stress, fear, hunger, thirst, exhaustion, and the death of friends over a protracted period of combat. The fighting on June 10 struck hard at Thomas's 75th Company, which moved through the wood with Lieutenant Overton's 76th Company on the left, in the center of the battalion front. When the company struck a strongpoint of three German machine guns, Thomas lost a dozen comrades from the Third Platoon. The marines crawled forward through "a great mass of rocks and boulders," Thomas later recalled, until they could throw grenades at the machine-gun nests.

Through most of the day, Thomas remained with Hughes at the battalion PC to manage scouting missions and analyze the vague company reports. During the afternoon the regimental intelligence officer, First Lieutenant William A. Eddy, came forward and told Hughes that Colonel Lee wanted an accurate report of the German positions. Taking Thomas with him to prepare sketch maps, Eddy crawled around the woods and quickly learned that no one could see much through the brush. Then, against Thomas's advice, he climbed a tree. Eddy immediately tumbled from the branches into Thomas's lap and said, "My God! I was looking square at a German in a machine-gun nest right down in front of us!" Eddy and Thomas returned to Hughes to report that the Germans still held Hill 181, a rocky rise that divided the western and southern wheat fields. Any attack across the western wheat field would still meet flanking fire from Belleau Wood. Having taken thirty-one casualties in the wood on June 10, Hughes agreed with Eddy's assessment that one battalion could not clear out the remaining Germans.

General Harbord then committed the 2nd Battalion, 5th Marines, to the battle, establishing its attack for 4:30 A.M. the next day. Hughes's left-flank company, Overton's 76th, was supposed to protect the right flank of Wise's battalion. Hughes assigned Thomas the job of ensuring that Overton contacted Wise's battalion as Harbord directed and "conformed to the progress of the attack," as noted in the brigade attack order. As the rolling barrage lifted, Thomas and one of his scouts left the wood and found Wise's battalion moving across the same deadly wheat field that had become the graveyard of Berry's battalion on June 6. Its passage was only slightly less disastrous. As the battalion neared Belleau Wood, German artillery fire crashed down upon it and machine-gun fire raked its front and flanks. Instead of pivoting to the north, the marines plunged straight ahead into the wood's narrow neck and across the front of the 1st Battalion, 6th Marines, which had joined the attack, too.

Pressured by his own company commanders for help, Wise asked Thomas where the 76th Company was and why it had not appeared on his right flank. Off Thomas went again, back into the wood. He found Overton, whose company was indeed in action and successfully so. Under Overton's inspired and intelligent direction, the 76th Company had destroyed the last German positions around Hill 181 and opened Belleau Wood for Wise's battalion. Overton found Wise's anger mildly amusing and wondered why the 5th Marines could not use the available cover. Certain that Overton had the situation under control, Thomas returned to Hughes's PC and told "Johnny the Hard" that the 76th Company had fulfilled its mission.

The two-battalion battle for Belleau Wood became a muddled slugfest, with Wise moving east when he should have been moving north. His battalion engaged the strongest German positions, and suffered accordingly. At one point, Wise, Lee, and Harbord all thought that the marines had seized Belleau Wood. Hughes knew better, but his battalion had its own problems as the Germans responded to the attack with intense artillery fire and reinforcing infantry.

Jerry Thomas continued his duties in Hughes's PC. Each morning and each evening for the next five days, he checked the company positions and discussed the enemy situation with the battalion's four company commanders. "On occasion enemy artillery made my journey a warm one." He helped draft situation reports as well as messages for the regiment, interrogated couriers and occasional POWs, and carried messages himself to the company commanders. Thomas and Lieutenant Etheridge were all the operational staff Hughes had, since the adjutant and supply officer had their hands full with administrative problems. Thomas and Etheridge watched the battalion's effectiveness wane from lack of sleep, water, and food, and they recognized their own limited capacity. Thirst accelerated fatigue, dulling everyone's judgment and ardor. "Food was not a problem— there just wasn't any during our first week in the wood," he recalled later. The marines stripped all casualties of water and food, then worried about ammunition. Everyone moved as if in a drunken stupor.

In the early morning of June 13, the Germans mounted heavy counterattacks on the marines, punishing positions on the 1st Battalion's left flank, still held by the 76th Company. Macon Overton asked battalion headquarters to investigate the fire to the rear, since he thought it might be coming from the disoriented 2nd Battalion, 5th Marines. Etheridge and Thomas, who were reconnoitering the lines, decided to check Overton's report. Working their way through the wood, which was now splintered and reeking of cordite smoke and souring corpses, they found an isolated 5th Marines company.

The company commander, a young lieutenant named L.Q.C.L. Lyle, told them that he was sure the firing came from bypassed Germans. He had no contact with the company to his left. Etheridge volunteered to scout the gap in the 5th Marines' lines, but before he and Thomas had moved very far, they saw some Germans who had just killed a group of Wise's marines and occupied their foxholes. Before the Germans could react with accurate rifle fire, the two marines sprinted back to Lyle's position and told him about the Germans. Lyle gave Etheridge a scratch squad armed with grenades, and Thomas and Etheridge led the group back through the wood until they again found the German position. In the short but intense fight that followed, the marines killed four Germans and captured a sergeant, who showed them another German stay-behind position, which the 6th Marines attacked and wiped out later the same day. Impressed with Thomas's performance in this action, Hughes had him cited in brigade orders for bravery in combat.

The German prisoner also provided Thomas with a temporary reprieve from battle, for brigade headquarters wanted to interrogate the POW immediately. Hughes ordered Thomas to escort the sergeant to the rear. When he arrived at the brigade PC, Thomas reported to Harbord's aide, Lieutenant R. Norris Williams (in civilian life, a nationally known tennis player). Williams asked him when he had last eaten a real meal. Thomas knew exactly: five days. The lieutenant sent him to the brigade mess, where a sergeant who had obviously not been missing his meals fixed Thomas a large plate of bacon, bread, and molasses, accompanied by hot coffee. Food had seldom tasted so good.

Jerry Thomas returned to a 1st Battalion that had reached the limit of its endurance. German shellfire had increased with intensity and accuracy on June 12, continuing through the night and the next day until around 5,000 rounds had fallen on the two marine battalions in the wood. Two company commanders were killed, and one 1st Battalion company, the 74th, was all but wiped out. By the end of June 13, the 1st Battalion had also lost its commander: Major Hughes, staggering with fatigue, his eyes swollen shut from gas, allowed himself to be evacuated. His own condition, however, did not prevent his telling Harbord that his battalion could defend itself, but could no longer advance: "Have had terrific bombardment and attack. I have every man, except a few odd ones, in line now. . . . Everything is OK now. Men digging in again. Trenches most obliterated by shellfire. . . . The conduct of everyone is magnificent. Can't you get hot coffee and water to me using prisoners?" Before Hughes could receive an answer, he had been replaced by Major Franklin B. Garrett, a forty-one-year-old Louisianan who had spent most of his fourteen years as a marine officer aboard ship, administering barracks detachments, and in Caribbean assignments that did not include combat operations. At the moment, however, the 1st Battalion, 6th Marines, did not need a heroic leader. It needed rest.

The effects of sleep deprivation, hunger, and thirst were severe, exacerbated now by gas attacks. The marines fought in their masks, but had to remove them often to clear condensed water and mucous, increasing the chances of inhaling gas. They simply endured burns over the rest of their bodies. The Germans tried no more infantry counterattacks, but they pummeled the battalion with heavy mortars and Austrian 77mm cannon, which fired a flat-trajectory, high-velocity shell dubbed a "whiz bang." In the meantime, Wise's battalion (or rather its remnants) and the 2nd Battalion, 6th Marines, had finally reached the northern section of Belleau Wood, but could advance no farther without help. The 1st Battalion, 6th Marines, completed the occupation and defense of the southern woods. On June 15 the battalion learned it would finally be replaced, by a battalion of the U.S. 7th Infantry. Two days later, at less than half their original strength, they shuffled out of Belleau Wood.

FOR ALL THEIR exhaustion, the 1st Battalion, 6th Marines, and Sergeant Jerry Thomas had proved themselves tough and skillful during their week in Belleau Wood. After the "lost march" of June 8–9, their performance had been exemplary. Largely because of "Johnny the Hard's" tactical skill and an extra day of artillery preparation and planning, theirs had been the only one of five marine battalions to enter Belleau Wood without suffering serious casualties. If the 74th Company had not been destroyed by gas and high-explosive shellfire on June 13, the battalion would have fought within the wood with fewer losses than the other marine battalions. Its men also captured their objectives, and never lost cohesion.

Although casualty statistics are difficult to assess then and now, the 1st Battalion, 6th Marines, appears to have suffered between 50 and 60 casualties a day on June 10, 11, and 12. On the night of June 12, Hughes reported that he had around 700 effectives. The shelling on June 13, however, cost the battalion over 200 casualties, many of them from gas. Casualties on June 13–15 numbered less than 50. By comparison, the 2nd Battalion, 5th Marines, reported that it had only 350 effectives by the night of June 12, after two days of fighting. Total losses for the two marine infantry regiments (May 31 to July 9, 1918) were 99 officers and 4,407 enlisted men. In the 4th Brigade overall, 112 officers and 4,598 enlisted men were casualties (including 933 killed), more than half the brigade's original strength.

Although no one could determine which of the infantry battalions killed the most Germans in Belleau Wood—from German accounts, Allied artillery probably inflicted the greatest casualties—the 1st Battalion at least shared with Wise's battalion the claim of destroying the German 461st Infantry Regiment, which had fallen from around 1,000 effectives on June 5 to only 9 officers and 149 men a week later. In addition, the battle of June 10–12 had cost the German 40th Infantry Regiment of the 28th Division almost 800 men killed, wounded, or missing. A battalion from the 5th Guards Division had also fallen to the marines. The 1st Battalion and Wise's battalion had captured ten heavy mortars, more than fifty heavy machine guns, and at least 400 prisoners. Within the wood, the 1st Battalion, 6th Marines, and 2nd Battalion, 5th Marines, broke the back of the German defense, even though the battle did not actually end for another two weeks.

The tactical effectiveness of the 1st Battalion, 6th Marines—to which Jerry Thomas had made an important contribution—became obscured by the valor of the entire 4th Brigade in the battles for Hill 142, Belleau Wood, and Bouresches. Paired with the performance of the U.S. 1st Division at

Cantigny (May 28–31), the 4th Brigade's fight proved to the Germans and Allies alike that the AEF would be a significant force in offensive combat on the Western Front. (The 2nd Division's 3rd Brigade reinforced this conclusion by seizing Vaux on July 1.) The intelligence section of the German IV Reserve Corps filed a major report praising the valor of the marines and predicting glumly that their tactical skill might soon match their heroism:

> The Second American Division must be considered a very good one and may even perhaps be considered as a storm troop. The different attacks on Belleau Wood were carried out with bravery and dash. The moral effect of our gunfire cannot seriously impede the advance of the American infantry. The Americans' nerves are not yet worn out.
>
> The qualities of the men individually may be described as remarkable. They are physically well set up, their attitude is good, and they range in age from eighteen to twenty-eight years. They lack at present only training and experience to make formidable adversaries. The men are in fine spirits and are filled with naive assurance; the words of a prisoner are characteristic—WE KILL OR WE GET KILLED!

French and American headquarters up to and including Pershing's staff and the French Grand Quartier Général (or Army General Staff) praised the 4th Brigade's performance. At the emotional level, however, their reactions varied. Pershing and his staff believed that the marines had received altogether too much newspaper coverage, especially for the attacks of June 6 and 11. (The AEF censor was at fault, not the marines.) The French, on the other hand, proved as always capable of the classic *beau geste:* They awarded the 4th Brigade a unit Croix de Guerre with Palm and renamed Belleau Wood the Bois de la Brigade de Marine. For marines of the twentieth century, Belleau Wood became the battle that established the corps's reputation for valor, and Jerry Thomas had been part of it all.

FOR THE 1ST Battalion, 6th Marines, the battle for Belleau Wood really ended when the battalion returned to the rest area at Nanteuil-sur-Marne on June 17, but it did not leave the sector until the entire division departed in early July. On the road to Nanteuil, the battalion found its kitchens and enjoyed hot stew ("slum") and *café au lait* that tasted like a five-star meal. For three days the battalion did little but sleep and eat. The Marne River became a welcome marine bathtub. Ten-day beards and dirt came off; thin faces and sunken eyes took longer to return to normal.

The battalion returned to the Belleau Wood sector on June 20–21 in order to give Harbord two fresh battalions in brigade reserve. The battle in the northern wood had grown as the Germans committed a fresh regiment, and Harbord had countered with an attack by the 7th Infantry and the 5th Marines. After the 5th Marines' attacks finally cleared the north woods on June 26—Harbord could report accurately, "Belleau Wood now U.S. Marine Corps entirely"—the battalion marched back into the wood, a doleful walk through the clumps of unburied German and American dead. Except for occasional harassing shellfire, the battalion did not have to deal with live Germans, although the smell of the dead ones was bad enough.

Jerry Thomas spent most of his time in the PC or checking the battalion observation posts. His last special duty in Belleau Wood was to help guide the U.S. 104th Infantry, 26th Division, into the sector. Learning that the relieving "Yankee Division" had already lost men to German artillery fire, he once again proved his intelligence and force by persuading an army lieutenant colonel to move the 104th Infantry into the wood by a longer but more protected route than the one the colonel intended to use. Thomas had no desire to add more Americans to the 800 or so dead who were scattered throughout the 6th Marines' sector.

JUST AS DAWN was breaking, the 1st Battalion left Belleau Wood for the last time. "Led by our chunky commander, Major Garrett, we traversed the three-quarters of a mile to Lucy at a ragged double time." Pushing along on his weary legs, Sergeant Jerry Thomas turned his back on Belleau Wood, at last certain that he would never see it again, at least in wartime. The battle, however, had made him a charter member of a Marine Corps elite, the veterans of the Battle of Belleau Wood. From this group the Marine Corps would eventually draw many of its leaders for the next forty years, including four commandants (Wendell C. Neville, Thomas Holcomb, Clifton B. Cates, and Lemuel C. Shepherd, Jr.). On June 10, 1918, Jerry Thomas had entered Belleau Wood a sergeant whose early performance in France had marked him as a courageous and conscientious noncommissioned officer. He left the wood a proven leader of marines in combat, a young man clearly capable of assuming greater responsibilities in the most desperate of battles.

*AUTUMN 1993*

Allan R. Millett is the Raymond E. Mason, Jr., Professor of Military History at Ohio State University. He is the author of the standard history of the Marine Corps, *Semper Fidelis* (1980; 1991), and coeditor of *Calculations: Net Assessment and the Coming of World War II* (1992). His most recent book is *In Many a Strife: General Gerald C. Thomas and the U.S. Marine Corps, 1917–1956* (1993). He is currently writing a history of the Korean War.

# 23

# Bywater's Pacific War Prophecy

## By William H. Honan

*Tom Clancy, the immensely successful American writer of military techno-thrillers, is not the first author to detail imagined future wars on the pages of a novel. In the 1920s the British journalist, self-appointed naval strategist, and occasional spy Hector Bywater penned* The Great Pacific War, *a novel describing a future Japanese-American naval confrontation across the vast chessboard of the Pacific. Beginning with a surprise Japanese attack on the American fleet and following with an invasion of Guam and the Philippines, Bywater's pen came close to predicting the events that would explode across the Pacific two decades later. And, William H. Honan argues, the close similarity of fact and fiction was no mere happenstance.*

Hector C. Bywater—a convivial, pub-crawling English journalist, author, spy, and raconteur who in the 1920s and 1930s knew more about the world's navies than a roomful of admirals—had an obsession: the possibility of war between Japan and the United States.

By 1925, sixteen years before Japanese forces struck at Pearl Harbor, he had accurately predicted the general course of the Pacific war. The fulfillment of his prophecies was no mere accident: What he wrote powerfully influenced Admiral Isoroku Yamamoto, the commander in chief of the Combined Fleet of the Imperial Navy, and a host of leaders of the U.S. Navy as well.

Bywater imagined that Japan would make a surprise attack against the American naval presence in the Pacific and launch simultaneous invasions of Guam and the Philippines. By taking such bold steps, Bywater calculated, Japan could build a nearly invulnerable empire in the western Pacific. He also surmised that, given time, the United States would counterattack. Immense distances would separate the adversaries after the fall of Guam and the Philippines, but ultimately, Bywater believed, the United States would be able to reach Japan by pursuing a novel campaign of amphibious island-hopping across the central Pacific. The result, he said, would be "ruinous" for the aggressor. With that outcome in mind, he advanced his ideas in the hope of deterring Japan from attempting any such adventure.

Bywater's two books and many articles on Pacific strategy attracted brief notice from the public and were soon forgotten. But for professional navy men on both sides of the Pacific, his work became required reading. Indeed, Bywater succeeded Admiral Alfred Thayer Mahan as the world's leading authority on naval theory and practice.

Until now, historians believed that Admiral Yamamoto, architect of the Pearl Harbor strike and many of Japan's subsequent moves in the war, conceived his war plans independently. But today it can be shown that Yamamoto, while serving as naval attaché in Washington in the late 1920s, reported to Tokyo about Bywater's war plan and then lectured on the subject, adopting Bywater's ideas as his own. Yamamoto followed Bywater's plans so assiduously in both overall strategy and specific tactics at Pearl Harbor, Guam, the Philippines, and even the Battle of Midway that it is no exaggeration to call Hector Bywater the man who "invented" the Pacific war.

Bywater's influence on the U.S. Navy was such that many officers at the highest level considered him "a prophet." He was the first analyst to publicly spell out the revolutionary concept of island-hopping across the Marshall and Caroline chains, a concept that became a fundamental of American strategy during the war. A year and a half after Bywater published this proposal, the navy drastically revised its top-secret War Plan Orange—the official contingency plan for war against Japan. The option of a reckless lunge across the Pacific, which Bywater said was doomed to failure, was replaced with his careful, step-by-step advance.

Bywater was a man of mystery and paradox. A tall, imposing figure, he could hold the rapt attention of a packed pub room when he recited poetry, sang, or told anecdotes, such as the one about how he mischievously persuaded Mussolini to invest a fortune in modernizing a couple of old rust buckets. But Bywater also had a hidden side: Between 1908 and 1918 he lived the double life of a spy—first as a British Secret Service agent and later as a naval intelligence agent. He deceived not only the Germans, from whom he extracted a bounty of naval secrets, but also his friends and neighbors in Britain and the United States.

He was nothing if not quintessentially British—coolly precise, wry, and steel-nerved. He used to say he was drawn to the navy by the accidents of his surname and his birthday—Trafalgar Day. Although he was renowned for his penetrating intellect and unaffected by the illusions that blinded so many in his generation, his private life was storm-tossed by emotion. He angrily resigned from the two daily newspapers he worked for the longest, the *Baltimore Sun* and the *London Daily Telegraph;* fought with and divorced two wives; excoriated the British Admiralty; and once indignantly rejected one of his country's highest decorations—the Order of the British Empire.

In the last analysis, however, one marvels at his daring, dazzling mastery of all things naval and at his remarkable but as yet unacknowledged influence on the history of our time.

IN THE YEARS after World War I, Bywater's imagination was captured by the naval rivalry developing in the Pacific between Japan and the United States. He began to write a series of articles on the subject for such publications as the British *Naval & Military Record and Royal Dockyards Gazette.* He soon expanded these ideas into a book, *Sea Power in the Pacific,* which was published in 1921—just in time to become a major topic of discussion at the International Conference on Naval Limitation, which convened in Washington later that year. Bywater covered it as a correspondent for the *Sun.*

Bywater was not the first Western thinker to focus on the strategic importance of the Pacific Ocean; nor was he alone in imagining that diminutive Japan might overcome the United States in a future Pacific war. In 1909, Homer Lea's *Valor of Ignorance* had gone so far as to forecast Japan's domination of the Pacific and capture of California, Oregon, Washington, and Alaska. Lea's book was followed by a score of imitations by American and Japanese authors. In 1911, even Mahan, while dismissing Homer Lea's nightmare vision as "improbable," observed that it was not inconceivable that the new Japanese navy might one day defeat the American navy in the Pacific.

What was new and different about Hector Bywater's analysis was, first, his clear-sighted recognition of exactly how far Japan could go in a war against the United States. Japan, he understood, could snatch U.S. territories in the western Pacific and thereby build a nearly unassailable ring of insular territories around herself, yet she did not have it within her power to seize Hawaii, let alone seriously menace the continental United States.

Second, he foresaw that such an aggressive move by Japan might well be in the cards, so to speak. He was the first journalist of his generation to grasp that the central arena in the struggle for naval supremacy had shifted from the North Sea and the Mediterranean, where Great Britain and Germany had vied with each other since the turn of the century, to the Pacific Ocean. The Pacific, as he saw it, was no longer an exotic backwater or even merely the scene of a possible future war, but the fateful setting in which the victorious allies of the First World War would test each other to determine who should be mistress of the seas in the twentieth century.

In 1924 Bywater realized that the treaties that had emerged from the Washington conference postponed but did not eliminate the possibility of war between the United States and Japan. So he started to work on a second book—a technically precise novel that played out the revolutionary ideas he had developed in *Sea Power in the Pacific.* He called this new book, published in 1925, *The Great Pacific War.*

Bywater had no desire to stir up enmity between Japan and the United States; a war between the two powers would be "a terrible and protracted struggle," he wrote in the preface. His object was "to bring to light certain facts concerning the strategical situation of the rival Powers the full significance of which does not appear to be realized either in Japan or the United States." Accordingly, he stated, "such modest influence" as his book might exert would be "in the direction of peace rather than of war."

The first question Bywater had to answer in writing *The Great Pacific War* was: What would prompt the fighting to begin? From his reading of Japanese history and current affairs, he had come to believe that the military caste in Japan would rise to power. Thus, he imagined that a group of "military chiefs" might gain control of the Japanese government. They then adopt a policy "aimed at the virtual enslavement of China," he wrote, and very quickly find themselves on a collision course with the United States. Diplomatic notes are exchanged—"bellicose" and "truculent" dispatches from the Japanese, "courteously worded" ones from the Americans, who are "determined to prevent the catastrophe of war." Amid these negotiations, Japan launches a surprise attack, rendering her declaration of war a few days later "a somewhat superfluous formality."

Such a surprise attack was by no means unprecedented. In 1904, prior to a declaration of war, a dozen Japanese torpedo boats had assaulted czarist Russia's Asiatic squadron at Port Arthur, sinking three capital ships. But at Port Arthur, Japan had risked no major units of the Imperial Navy and sought only the limited goal of throwing the enemy off-balance. In contrast, Bywater imagined that the Japanese commander would assemble a major fleet of capital ships so as to hurl an "overwhelming" force at the U.S. fleet in the Philippines—the fleet was not stationed at Pearl Harbor until 1940—aiming for its "annihilation" during the first hours of the war.

Accordingly, he described the Japanese surprise-attack fleet as a force that would include an aircraft carrier, the battleships *Hiei* and *Kirishima* (both of which were in fact in the Pearl Harbor strike force in 1941), and numerous auxiliaries. Commanded by an imaginary Vice Admiral Hiraga, this armada steams south hoping to catch the Americans napping at their base at Manila Bay, just as George Dewey found the Spanish fleet there in 1898. But at the eleventh hour Rear Admiral Ribley, the imaginary commander in chief of the U.S. squadron, takes his ships to sea because, as he puts it, "we do not know if war has been declared, but . . . there is something in the air which tells us the fight is about to begin."

In Bywater's drama, the first shots come from carrier-based aircraft. Japanese fighter-bombers are engaged by American planes, including a number from the aircraft carrier *Curtiss* (in fact, a seaplane tender *Curtiss* was in action at Pearl Harbor in 1941). But these skirmishes are indecisive, and soon the Americans spy on the horizon the pagodalike foremasts of Japanese men-of-war bearing down on them. Shortly, Japanese heavy-caliber guns find the range of their targets. Bywater describes the devastating rain of bombs and shells in the words of a U.S. naval officer, a Lieutenant Elkins:

> All around us the sea spouted and boiled; there were half a dozen terrific explosions in as many seconds; . . . then there was a blaze of light . . . and everything came to an end for me. When I recovered my senses, I was being dragged into a boat from the destroyer *Hulbert*. They told me the flagship had foundered at 11:30, having been practically blown to pieces. There were only six survivors

besides myself. [Admiral Ribleyl had gone down with the ship. . . .

From our boat, we could see the Japanese sweeping up the remnants of our squadron. Shortly before the flagship went down, the *Frederick* had blown up with all hands. We could see the *Denver* lying over on her beam ends, on fire from stem to stern. Nearby was the *Galveston* in action with Japanese light cruisers, which were absolutely pumping shells into her. Even as we watched she put her bows deep under, the stern came up, and she took her last dive. . . .

Concluding the narrative with a flash of seeming clairvoyance, Bywater has Lieutenant Elkins report: "Our squadron had been wiped out and upwards of 2,500 gallant comrades had fallen." At Pearl Harbor in 1941, the precise number of American casualties was 2,638.

Bywater was not writing a novel of the usual kind. Instead, by precisely describing the geographic and topographical features of contested areas, and by using the exact names, tonnages, fuel ranges, and arms and armor specifications of real warships and aircraft, he was staging a complex war game. The result, he hoped, would point to the way a war in the Pacific would *really* work itself out.

The Japanese surprise attack comes like a "bolt from the blue" to the American people. The United States is swept by "a wave of grief . . . thinking of those thousands of gallant seamen who had gone to their doom, fighting to the last against tremendous odds, with the old flag still flying as the waters closed above the torn and battered hulls of their ships." After the attack, the mood of the nation is not one of defeatism as the Japanese hope, but rather of "a stern resolve to see this struggle through to the bitter end."

Before the United States can respond to the destruction of its fleet, however, Japan follows up with simultaneous amphibious assaults against Guam and the Philippines. Although a highly publicized disaster at Gallipoli in World War I had given amphibious operations a bad name in the West, this was not the case in Japan. "Landings on supposed hostile coasts had been practiced year after year as a regular feature of Japanese Army maneuvers," Bywater wrote. "All necessary equipment—boats, barges, pontoons, and portable jetties—had been in readiness at the military depots for years."

With virtually all American warships destroyed, out of commission, or far away, the Japanese perceive that the chief danger would come from American aircraft. "Thirty machines of a new and powerful type," Bywater stated, had just arrived in the Philippines from the United States. (The parallel with the arrival of thirty-five new B-17 Flying Fortresses in early December 1941 is remarkable.) He also assumed that the Japanese had studied the Philippines closely. "Every yard of ground had been personally surveyed and mapped by Japanese officers," he wrote.

In the invasion plan, much of which would prove to be astonishingly prophetic, the Japanese first bombard Santa Cruz, on the west coast of Luzon, the principal island in the Philippines. This stratagem, however, is "so obviously a ruse to draw the Americans away from other parts of the coast that it failed in its purpose." Next come air strikes. Japanese interceptors attack American patrol craft on the east coast of Luzon, and then bombers hit the airport at Dagupan, on Lingayen Gulf, aiming to destroy those thirty American craft "of a new and powerful type."

Between dusk and the next morning, the main landings take place. They come in the shape of a three-pronged attack, simultaneously throwing ashore 40,000 troops at each of two sites on Luzon and another 50,000 at Sindangan Bay on Mindanao, the second-largest and southernmost of the major Philippine islands. Luzon is attacked from both east and west. On the west coast, Japanese troop transports assemble in Lingayen Gulf; their landing barges head for the gently sloping beaches that lead directly to the Pampanga Plain, which extends all the way to Manila.

On the east coast of Luzon, the transports make for Lamon Bay; here the terrain is mountainous, but the landing site is even closer to Manila. The western and eastern forces, equipped with tanks and heavy artillery, rapidly converge on the capital, obliging its defenders to divide their strength and fight on two fronts. Meanwhile, a Japanese expeditionary force overwhelms the garrisons at Zamboanga and Davao. In less than three weeks, Manila surrenders and the Philippines are in Japanese hands. So is Guam.

"A cordon had been established across every line of approach to the waters of the South-West Pacific," Bywater wrote, explaining Japan's formidable posture. "For a war with the United States, Japan's strategical position very closely approached the ideal."

This was a thesis Bywater had been propounding since his first articles on Pacific strategy in 1920, yet it was one that he doubted most U.S. authorities could accept. He knew that many top strategists believed the U.S. Navy could whip the Japanese navy regardless of the location of enemy bases and the length of American supply lines. To dramatize the foolhardiness of this belief, he described a reckless American stab at the Bonin Islands.

If successfully captured, a base so close to the Japanese home islands might lead to a speedy conclusion of the war. However, the Americans have underestimated the obstacles in their way. After suffering heavy losses, the U.S. fleet limps home ingloriously. There is a public outcry in the United States, followed by resignations in the high command of the navy. American leaders have now learned the hard way that the only practicable means of striking Japan is by hopping from island to island across the Pacific, carefully retrenching after each new conquest and pausing to bring up the rear.

The "guiding genius" of this island-hopping campaign, Bywater imagines, is an Admiral Joseph Harper, former commander of the U.S. garrison on Guam, who escapes from the island in a submarine—much as MacArthur would depart from the Philippines in 1942. Harper, whose knowledge of Pacific islands is extensive, plays the bluff-and-deception game craftily.

Bywater has Admiral Harper begin his campaign (as did U.S. forces in 1942) with noisy preparations in Alaska and the Aleutians to lure the

Japanese to the North. But his real attack is aimed at the central Pacific—from Hawaii to Tutuila in American Samoa. He next makes a long thrust to Truk in the Carolines, deep inside the Japanese defensive perimeter. Just when it seems that U.S. forces might be cut off from their line of supply, he whirls around and makes simultaneous thrusts to Ponape, also in the Carolines, and to Jaluit in the Marshalls; this maneuver opens a direct, and much shorter, line of communication with Hawaii. Then comes a feint at Guam and a leap to Angaur in the Palaus, followed by a feint at Yap in the westernmost Carolines. The Battle of Yap—which Yamamoto aped in his plan for the historic Battle of Midway—is a turning point in Bywater's war.

By this time, it is approximately a year and a half since the Japanese surprise attack that started the war. The Americans have managed to replace all naval losses, and, thanks to Admiral Harper's brilliant tactics in the central Pacific, American warships in the vicinity of Yap are within striking distance of the Philippines—the final link in the chain of islands reaching across the Pacific toward Japan. The tables have turned: The U.S. Navy is now the superior force in the Pacific. At this point in the narrative, Bywater spelled out the American strategy for compelling Admiral Hiraga, the fictional Japanese commander in chief, to accept battle.

The commander of the American fleet, an imaginary Admiral Templeton, concentrates at his base a prodigious force: seventeen aircraft carriers and battleships, numerous cruisers, destroyers, and other support ships. A vanguard of this force, including the battleship *Florida,* commences a bombardment of Yap while troop transports "so maneuver as if to suggest that a landing was about to be attempted." The Japanese commander, Admiral Hiraga, has no choice but to employ every weapon at his disposal to block this advance—which, if successful, would carry U.S. forces to Japan's door. The Japanese Grand Fleet (including a dozen battleships and aircraft carriers, twenty-one cruisers, and two immense destroyer flotillas) abandons its lair at Manila and strikes out for Yap.

First contact takes place when fifty torpedo planes from the carriers *Lexington* and *Saratoga* are met by an equal number of Japanese aircraft. After all of these planes—about a third of those available to either side—are brought down by "a hurricane of fire," Bywater argues that a decision must then "be achieved by weapons other than the air arm." Bywater goes on to describe a naval gunfight in the classic Jutland tradition.

Bywater's belief that the big naval gun would remain the supreme weapon of war was his most serious lapse in a otherwise stunningly far-sighted book. In 1925 he could not imagine the coming importance of air power. By the mid-1930s he sensed this defect in his forecasts; in subsequent editions of *Sea Power in the Pacific* and in articles, he declared that Japan's opening stroke in the war would be delivered by her new aircraft carriers. For now, however, he remained—in this respect—a prisoner of his times.

Of course, Bywater did not foresee the atomic bomb. Yet he did sense that the United States might attempt something out of the ordinary to spare both sides the horror of an invasion of the Japanese homeland. This coup de grace, he guessed, would be a "demonstration" air raid over Tokyo with bombs containing not TNT but leaflets urging the Japanese to petition their government to surrender, rather than "waste more lives."

Fictional characters always extricate themselves from predicaments better than real people do, and Bywater's Japanese are no exception. After the demonstration raid has made its point, Japan soberly accepts defeat. A surrender is arranged, and a peace treaty is signed, in which, among other things, the formerly German Pacific islands, mandated to Japan by the League of Nations, are turned over to the United States "for their future administration"—precisely as happened after the actual surrender of Japan in 1945.

A BOYISH-LOOKING Isoroku Yamamoto began serving as naval attaché at the Japanese Embassy in Washington soon after *The Great Pacific War* came out. Two years later, in 1928, Captain Yamamoto returned to Japan and delivered a lecture in which he presented Bywater's ideas as his own. Many years later, as commander in chief of the Combined Fleet of the Imperial Navy, Yamamoto put into practice a war plan astonishingly similar to that spelled out for Japan in *The Great Pacific War*.

Born in 1884—the year of Bywater's birth—Yamamoto was small and fine-boned, slightly built even by Japanese standards. His left hand was missing the first two fingers, the most obvious of many wounds received at the Battle of Tsushima in 1905. The injuries he sustained at Tsushima nearly disqualified him from continued service, but he nonetheless rose rapidly in the ranks.

Because the Imperial Navy regarded the United States as its most likely future opponent, the brightest young naval officers were sent there on various tours of duty. Yamamoto visited several ports on the West Coast aboard a training ship in 1909, studied English for a year at Harvard in 1919, returned for the Washington Conference on Naval Limitation in 1921, and finally took up his duties as naval attaché at the embassy in March 1926.

Yamamoto's chief duty was to keep a close watch on the U.S. Navy. According to former Japanese naval attachés in Washington before the war, he gathered most of his information by carefully reading U.S. newspapers, magazines, and books. A voracious reader, he was well chosen for his work. At Harvard he had raced through four or five biographies of Abraham Lincoln before pronouncing Carl Sandburg's the finest of the lot. At the Washington Conference, he scanned as many as forty newspapers and periodicals a day for references to Japan or to the Japanese proposals, such as one asking the United States not to fortify any naval bases west of Hawaii.

Thus, it would hardly be surprising if he seized upon *The Great Pacific War*. Bywater, after all, had written the important *Sea Power in the Pacific* and was the correspondent who during the Washington Conference had found out what Japan's delegates were going to announce about such matters as her refusal to scrap the battleship *Mutsu*.

273

Did Yamamoto in fact read and react to *The Great Pacific War?* The most solid evidence would be among the reports from the naval attachés. However, all attaché reports written after 1921, and most records of the navy general staff (Gunreibu), which kept copies of these documents, were destroyed either by the American bombing of Tokyo on May 25, 1945 (which burned out half of the Navy Ministry building), or by the Japanese themselves just before American occupation troops arrived at the war's end.

Fortunately, the Diplomatic Record Office in Tokyo holds a treasure of revealing documents from the 1920s. These files show that during the time Yamamoto served as naval attaché, quite a number of Japanese officials assigned to the United States sent reports home about newspaper and journal articles on *The Great Pacific War*. Two such officials were close friends of Yamamoto, and in the opinion of former members of the Japanese diplomatic corps, his friends would not have failed to mention the book to him. Then again, Yamamoto may have brought the book to *their* attention.

The most convincing documentary evidence linking Bywater and Yamamoto appears in two top-level Japanese military briefing papers that deal predominantly with *The Great Pacific War* and the controversy surrounding it. Found in the Diplomatic Record Office, these documents remove all reasonable doubt that Yamamoto followed the controversy over *The Great Pacific War* and reported extensively on it.

Shortly after returning to Japan, Yamamoto delivered a lecture at the Imperial Navy Torpedo School at Yokosuka about the course of a possible future war between Japan and the United States. No text of the lecture exists. But the postwar Compilation Committee on the History of the Japanese Naval Air Force, which published a four-volume history in 1970, found and interviewed a former naval officer, Ichitaro Oshima, who recalled attending Yamamoto's lecture at the Torpedo School.

"In the event of a future war between Japan and the United States," Oshima recalled Yamamoto saying, "Japan will lose if she adopts the traditional defensive strategy. Japan's only chance of victory would be to attack American forces at Hawaii." According to Oshima, Yamamoto then went on to predict that aircraft carriers would soon replace battleships as the supreme weapon of naval war, and that the attack on Hawaii should therefore be made by naval aircraft.

Those words require careful analysis. What did Yamamoto mean by "American forces at Hawaii"? He surely could not have meant the handful of U.S. troops stationed there. Nor is it likely that he was thinking of Pearl Harbor as it existed at the time; in 1928 Pearl Harbor was merely a navy yard and supply depot, and no commissioned warships were based there. It appears that Yamamoto was looking to the future. In December 1926—ten months after taking up residence in Washington—he had learned that the U.S. Navy was planning to dredge 9 million cubic yards of coral from the channel and anchorage at Pearl Harbor so that the base could accommodate a fleet of the largest warships. Thus, Yamamoto understood that in the not-too-distant future, a sizable American fleet would be stationed at Pearl Harbor.

But why attack an American fleet 3,374 miles from Tokyo? There can be only one explanation. Yamamoto envisioned Japan boldly extending the boundaries of her Pacific empire. A preemptive strike at Pearl Harbor would prevent American warships from interfering with highly vulnerable landing operations in the Philippines and perhaps on Guam. In short, Yamamoto was proposing the strategy for Japan that he had read about in *The Great Pacific War*.

Later, Yamamoto became acquainted with Bywater himself. In December 1934 the two spent an evening discussing Pacific strategy at a conference in London. It was one of several contacts between them.

Six years after this meeting, when war in the Pacific seemed inevitable and Yamamoto was concerned with contingency planning for the Imperial Navy, he fell back on Bywater's ideas. Yamamoto's strategy and tactics in launching war in the Pacific are strikingly similar to Bywater's hypothetical scenario—right down to the beaches where invading forces would land.

Yamamoto's grand strategy for the commencement of the Pacific war was twofold. First, he believed that Japanese forces must destroy the American Pacific Fleet outright. Second, they must quickly move into the resulting power vacuum and seize any territories that would expand the Japanese empire, so as to render it nearly invulnerable to attack. These objectives are spelled out in notes that Yamamoto gave to a Naval Academy classmate for safekeeping in January 1941, and in "Combined Fleet Top Secret Operation Order No. 1," which Yamamoto and his staff prepared aboard the flagship *Nagato* and issued on November 5, 1941.

In deciding on the Pearl Harbor attack, Yamamoto was not simply following historical precedent, as has been frequently suggested. On the contrary, in his notes Yamamoto criticized the tactics of the Port Arthur attack of 1904, stating that "lessons must be learned" from Tōgō's failures in that action. He went on to say that unlike Tōgō at Port Arthur, he would employ a massive strike force at Pearl Harbor—in order to *"thoroughly destroy* the main body of the enemy fleet in the first moments of the war" (italics added). Once the American fleet had been disposed of, Japan could "occupy strategic places in East Asia [Guam, the Philippines, British Malaya, and the Dutch East Indies] to secure an invincible position." Japan then "might be able to obtain her goals and secure the peace in the Greater East Asia Co-Prosperity Sphere." That, of course, was precisely Bywater's idea.

In mid-September 1941, Yamamoto attempted to demonstrate the feasibility of his plan at the annual Table Top Conference at the Imperial Naval War College—where Bywater's *Sea Power in the Pacific* and *The Great Pacific War* were still being read. So passionate was Yamamoto about his plan that when the navy general staff balked at accepting it, he sent an emissary to Tokyo to declare that he and his entire staff would resign if not permitted to carry it out. Osami Nagano, chief of the navy general staff, was dismayed but finally said that the navy had to trust Yamamoto, who after all had been living with the problem longer than anyone else—a truer statement than he realized. Authorization from the highest councils of the government and the emperor followed quickly.

To cite one instance of Bywater's profound influence, Yamamoto's plan for invading the Philippines, demonstrated at the September Table Top Conference, conformed in great detail to the tactics spelled out in *The Great Pacific War*. Bywater had imagined simultaneous main landings—at Lingayen Gulf, at Lamon Bay between Cabalete and Alabat islands, and at Sindangan Bay on Mindanao. Astonishingly, the plan demonstrated at Yamamoto's Table Top Conference consisted of roughly those same simultaneous landings in the Philippines—at Lingayen Gulf, at Lamon Bay between Cabalete and Alabat islands, and at Davao on Mindanao.

Yamamoto's plans, of course, departed from Bywater's scenario in certain respects. By the time Yamamoto folded into his master plan all the objectives of the Imperial Army, together with those of the navy general staff, he went far beyond Bywater, to include attacks on territories and forces of the United States, Great Britain, and the Netherlands. The other important difference between Bywater and Yamamoto concerned the use of air power: Although Bywater eventually recognized its coming importance, the collective use of aircraft carriers, awesomely demonstrated at Pearl Harbor, was Yamamoto's (and his air chief, Minoru Genda's) contribution to naval science.

It is tempting to wonder what course events might have taken if Bywater had never written about strategy in the Pacific—or if Yamamoto had not been affected by the British author's thinking. Quite possibly the war would have taken a very different course and left a much different mark on history. The military historian Louis Morton has written that if the Japanese had never conceived of the Pearl Harbor attack, had bypassed the Philippines and concentrated their territorial aggrandizement on the Dutch East Indies and British Malaya, "it is possible that the United States might not have gone to war, or, if it had, that the American people would have been more favorably disposed to a negotiated peace."

Although Roosevelt was prepared to ask Congress to declare war on Japan if Japan attacked Singapore, no one knew how Congress—or the American people—might respond to such a request. In February 1941 a Gallup poll found that although 56 percent of Americans favored efforts "to keep Japan from seizing the Dutch East Indies and Singapore," only 39 percent were willing to risk war to do so. Evidently, many were unwilling to commit American lives to help beleaguered European empires cling to their Asian colonies. After the Pearl Harbor attack, Secretary of State Cordell Hull said: "I don't know whether we would have been at war yet if Japan had not attacked us."

WHAT EFFECT DID BYWATER have on the American conduct of the war?

He apparently knocked some sense into navy heads in 1925. Possibly having been informed about the American contingency plan for war with Japan, he devoted two chapters of *The Great Pacific War* to dramatizing the folly of the reckless expedition, such as proposed in War Plan Orange.

He then described the humbled U.S. Navy carrying out a carefully planned, step-by-step advance to Manila across a bridge of islands in the Marshall and Caroline chains. The visionary U.S. Marine Earl ("Pete") Ellis and the air-power pioneer William ("Billy") Mitchell made somewhat similar proposals, but Bywater was the first naval expert to publicly spell out such a campaign.

If Bywater could not precisely claim paternity for U.S. Pacific strategy, his writings undoubtedly influenced overall planning. Once the war broke out, most of the naval strategists working for the Joint Chiefs of Staff in Washington, and for Chester W. Nimitz, the commander of the central Pacific theater, were familiar with *The Great Pacific War*—or one of its many imitations, such as Sutherland Denlinger's *War in the Pacific.* Bywater's ideas had become part of the naval culture.

Hector Bywater died in London on August 18, 1940, shortly after Yamamoto commenced secret preparations for carrying out the strategy he had conceived. The cause of death, according to the medical examiner's report, was heart failure consistent with alcoholism. But one former colleague suspected that the Japanese, fearing that Bywater might unmask their preparations for a surprise attack, murdered him. No hard evidence supports this suspicion. Thus, about all that can be said with assurance is that Bywater's sudden death in the summer of 1940 came as a gift for Isoroku Yamamoto—considering the course he was then embarked upon.

*Spring 1991*

William H. Honan is the chief cultural correspondent of the *New York Times.* He is the editor of *"Fire When Ready, Gridley!" Great Naval Stories from Manila Bay to Vietnam* (1993).

# 24

# "They Can't Realize the Change Aviation Has Made"

## By Richard M. Ketchum

*Although many Americans were slow to understand the danger present-ed by the rise of German air power, Franklin D. Roosevelt was not one of them. He understood the great diplomatic power the new Luftwaffe gave Adolf Hitler, as well as the military threat the Third Reich's air force pre-sented to Europe. The mere potential of air power in the hands of the German leader had molded the diplomacy of Europe in the late 1930s and cowed western Europe into near impotence. If France and Britain had only possessed more aircraft, Roosevelt avowed in January 1939, "there would not have been any Munich."*

*On the power of the Luftwaffe, Charles Lindbergh agreed. It was per-haps the only point of agreement between the President and this Ameri-can hero. Their personal and political differences were intense—in fact, Roosevelt considered Lindbergh an out-and-out fascist. Yet Lindbergh, while under intense criticism for his apparent pro-German sympathies, was actually providing the Roosevelt administration with invaluable mil-itary intelligence on the looming German aviation threat.*

On the same September day in 1938 that Neville Chamberlain returned in triumph to London from the Munich Conference wav-ing a scrap of paper before his countrymen and telling them it meant "peace for our time," Charles A. Lindbergh arrived at the U.S. Embassy in Paris. Ambassador William Bullitt had invited him to a con-ference and thoughtfully offered him the same room in which he had stayed on the momentous night of May 21, 1927. It seemed strange, Lindbergh thought, to see once again the familiar surroundings of the embassy—the court, the staircase, the corner parlor he remembered—and he noticed that there was now a brass plate on the bed he had slept in eleven years earlier.

Surely other memories flooded back: of a hundred thousand deliriously happy Frenchmen swarming onto the field at Le Bourget to greet him when he landed after the thirty-three-hour flight, some of them ripping pieces of fabric off the *Spirit of St. Louis,* others dragging him from the cockpit and carrying him away on their shoulders until he escaped to the pilots' quarters, identified himself self-consciously—"I am Charles A. Lindbergh"—and handed letters of introduction to then-Ambassador Myron Herrick. Then came the medals, the speeches, the crowds—always the crowds—and the trip home to the States aboard the cruiser *Memphis,* to be greeted with half a million letters, 75,000 telegrams, two railroad cars filled with press clippings, the engulfing admiration of his countrymen, and promotion from captain to colonel in the Air Corps Reserve. President Calvin Coolidge, awarding him the congressional Medal of Honor and the nation's first Distinguished Flying Cross, told throngs in Washington that the transatlantic flight was "the same story of valor and victory by a son of the people that shines through every page of American history." Then there was New York, a city gone berserk, with some 4 million ecstatic people cheering their hearts out during an incredible ticker-tape parade up Broadway.

Of all the public figures who captivated America in that decade of noise and hero worship, only Lindbergh retained his almost magical hold on the public through the thirties, perhaps because he embodied the youthful, unquenchable spirit Americans felt they had left behind, the national belief that the unattainable was somehow within reach. His achievement alone would have caught the imagination of the entire world—and did—but the fact that he was a boyish Galahad out of the West, a guileless, modern-day knight in aviator's helmet and goggles, with tousled blond hair and a smile that melted the heart, brought him such adoration as few men in history have known.

He maintained that he had no wish to be a celebrity, but America would not allow him *not* to be one, and in a perverse sort of way he abetted the process. He flew the *Spirit of St. Louis* to all forty-eight states after his transatlantic flight; he went to Mexico and South America; he wrote a book, *We,* about his famous adventure, and this plus a series of newspaper and magazine articles brought him wealth along with additional fame; he flew from coast to coast, setting a new speed record; he had a whirlwind romance with Anne, the lovely daughter of Dwight Morrow, a prominent lawyer, partner of J.P. Morgan, and ambassador to Mexico; and he and his bride flew off the next year to Canada, Alaska, Siberia, Japan, and China—a journey chronicled in Anne Morrow Lindbergh's best-selling *North to the Orient.* It seemed that he was never out of the news, was constitutionally unable to avoid being the public figure, all the while insisting that he wanted only privacy and to be let alone. The paradox was that he appeared to be sustained in a curious way by these frequent forays into the public eye, even as he denied that it was so and raged at reporters and photographers who considered it their job to document the doings of the famous man.

Then came the dark time, the hour of lead, as Anne Lindbergh would call it. On March 1, 1932, their firstborn child, Charles Augustus, Jr., was kidnapped from his nursery crib in their home near Hopewell, New Jersey. A $50,000 ransom payment was delivered to a cemetery in the Bronx, but the baby was not returned; on May 12 his body was found in a shallow grave not far from their house. To the Lindberghs it seemed that the newspaper and radio publicity, the reporters' morbid curiosity about every personal facet of the tragedy, would never end. And when Bruno Richard Hauptmann, a Bronx carpenter, was arrested and tried in 1934, their nightmare had to be relived in agonizing detail, imposing an almost unendurable strain on the family.

Believing that the only escape from the "tremendous public hysteria" surrounding him in the United States was to leave the land of his birth, Lindbergh took his wife and second son to England in December 1935 to seek sanctuary and peace. He found both, and during this self-imposed exile he probably had a better opportunity to see what was going on behind the scenes in Europe than any other American private citizen. The British and French treated him with respect, allowing him the privacy he so much desired, and because he was a distinguished aviator he was sought out by Europe's public figures and invited by government officials to inspect the aircraft, factories, and aviation facilities of the major nations on the Continent.

His trip to Paris on September 30, 1938, persuaded Lindbergh to make a personal study of Europe's general situation during the approaching winter. "I don't know how much I can do here," he wrote, "but I feel that if anything can be done to avoid European war, it must be based upon an intimate understanding of conditions in Europe."

Before going to France, Lindbergh had heard from Ambassador Bullitt about the parlous state of that nation's air force. France did not have enough modern military planes even to "put up a show in case of war," Bullitt told him, and in a conflict between France, England, and Russia on one side and Germany on the other, the Germans would have immediate air supremacy. Lindbergh had suspected as much. "Germany has developed a huge air force," he said, "while England has slept and France has deluded herself with a Russian alliance." From Guy La Chambre, the French minister of air, he learned how desperate the situation was. France was producing just forty-five or fifty warplanes a month, compared with Germany's five or six hundred.

When Lindbergh arrived in Paris, Bullitt said he hoped he would take part in a discussion with La Chambre and Jean Monnet, the French banker and economist, to consider the possibility of establishing factories in Canada to manufacture planes for France. The idea, of course, was to circumvent the terms of the U.S. Neutrality Act, which was designed to prohibit the shipment of arms to belligerents, and Monnet was talking about a production potential of 10,000 planes a year. (Bullitt's opinion was that it should be 50,000.)

In the course of that day and the next, Lindbergh discovered that French intelligence put the existing German air fleet at 6,000 modern planes, plus 2,000 to 3,000 older models, and estimated that the Reich had the capability of building 24,000 planes a year—versus France's existing potential of 540 and predicted capacity of 5,000 a year. It was believed further that Britain—which had 2,000 aircraft (only 700 of them modern types)—might be producing 10,000 planes annually in a year's time; but this left an immense gap of 10,000 aircraft a year between Germany's output and the combined expectations of Great Britain and France.

France had not a single modern pursuit plane available for the defense of Paris, and indeed no aircraft of any type as fast as the new German bombers. It would be impossible to obtain planes from the United States because, apart from the restrictions of the Neutrality Act, the U.S. Army, Navy, and commercial airlines were absorbing virtually all of America's productive capacity. Pondering these seemingly insurmountable problems, Lindbergh ventured an astonishing suggestion to the group: Why not purchase bombers from Germany?

At first the Frenchmen laughed, assuming he was joking, but he argued that such an arrangement might quickly smoke out Germany's military intentions and could be in the interest of both parties. While giving France the aircraft she needed, opening up some trade between the two countries, possibly decreasing tension, and reducing the arms disparity, it would also afford Germany a measure of relief from the staggering cost of constructing warplanes.

The meeting broke up without a decision, but in the months to come the French began taking Lindbergh's proposal ever more seriously. Several months later La Chambre asked him to ascertain whether or not the Germans would sell planes to France, and Lindbergh undertook this mission when he went to Berlin. In mid-January 1939, a surprised Lindbergh was informed by General Erhard Milch, who was responsible for Luftwaffe production, that Germany *would* be willing to sell 1,250-horsepower Daimler-Benz engines to France, provided absolute secrecy was observed while negotiations were taking place and provided further that France paid in cash, not goods.

When Charles and Anne took off from Le Bourget in Paris on October 10, 1938, headed for Berlin's Tempelhof Airport, it was their third trip to Nazi Germany in as many years. Thanks to Major Truman Smith, the U.S. military attaché in Berlin, the couple had been invited there in 1936 and 1937 by Hermann Göring, Reich minister for air and, after Hitler, the most powerful man in the nation. Smith, an infantryman by trade, was responsible for reporting to Washington on developments in aviation as well as those in land warfare, and he was not satisfied with the quality of intelligence he was receiving. At the breakfast table one morning, his wife read him a news story about Colonel Lindbergh inspecting an airplane factory in France, and it occurred to Smith that an official visit to Germany by the famous aviator might uncover information the United States wanted.

So the trips were arranged, resulting eventually in more than Smith ever dreamed of obtaining—a full and detailed "general estimate" of German air strength. Sent to Washington over Smith's signature, it was based entirely on Lindbergh's firsthand inspection, expert analysis, and experience of the factories, airplanes, personnel, research, and command structure that constituted Germany's air establishment. That nation, the report declared, had outdistanced France in all respects and was generally superior to Great Britain, except for aircraft engines. By 1941 or 1942, it was estimated, Germany's technical development would equal that of the United States—a "phenomenon of the first diplomatic importance." Lindbergh himself put the case even more strongly, writing to a family friend: "The growth of German military aviation is, I believe, without parallel in history. . . ."

When the Lindberghs first visited Berlin, correspondent William Shirer grumbled that "the Nazis, led by Göring, are making a great play for them," but that was nothing compared to the reception that greeted them on their return in 1938. During the course of a month, the American flier was given an opportunity to talk with all the principals of the aviation establishment—General Milch; General Ernst Udet, a World War ace who developed the dive-bombing technique first employed in Spain; Heinrich Focke, the aeronautical engineer; and Marshal Göring—not to mention scores of pilots and technicians. He met members of the diplomatic circle in the capital, visited aircraft factories, inspected bomb shelters and antiaircraft batteries, was permitted to fly many of the latest German planes—including the Junkers Ju 90 transport and the Messerschmitt 108 and 109 fighters—and was the first non-German to see the secret new Ju 88 bomber.

Neither Lindbergh nor the Americans to whom he was supplying information seem to have given much thought to the possibility that they were being used, but his seeming freedom of access to Germany's secrets was very carefully planned. Like Lindbergh, high-level visitors from other countries were taken on conducted tours to see the impressive Messerschmitt assembly lines, the performance of the latest planes, the exhibitions of precision bombing. Understandably, this thoroughly memorable experience was guaranteed to make visitors return home and speak with awe of what they had beheld.

On the night of October 18, a Tuesday, Ambassador Hugh Wilson gave a stag dinner at the embassy, and the occasion was the scene of an incident that was to plague Lindbergh for years to come. In addition to German officers and members of the U.S. Embassy staff, Wilson's guests included the Belgian and Italian ambassadors, Generals Milch and Udet, Heinkel and Messerschmitt, and Göring. As an aviator, Hermann Göring ranked at the top of Germany's pantheon: A World War ace, he had succeeded to the command of Baron Manfred von Richthofen's "Flying Circus" after the Red Baron was killed. Under his leadership, the Luftwaffe had become the most fearsome weapon of the Third Reich. Vain, arrogant, and complex, Göring was a diplomat, economic planner, art connoisseur, gourmand, dandy, morphine addict, and Hitler's most powerful associate in the high command.

Given the nature of the ulterior motive Ambassador Wilson had in mind, he could be forgiven for using Charles Lindbergh as bait to lure

Göring to this dinner. Wilson was eager to establish friendly relations with the number two Nazi in hopes that he would do something to ameliorate the financial plight of Jews who were being forced to emigrate from Germany in a penniless state. Göring was no humanitarian and he lacked the courage to stand up to Hitler, but at least his attitude toward the Jews was ambivalent, which was more than could be said of other top Nazis. It was known that he opposed the use of indiscriminate violence and had helped his actress wife get her Jewish friends away from the Gestapo on a number of occasions.

Lindbergh was standing at the back of the room when Göring arrived, and he noticed that the marshal was carrying a red box and some papers in his hand. Göring chatted briefly with several other guests and gradually made his way over to Lindbergh, handed him the box and the papers, and spoke a few sentences in German, which Lindbergh did not understand. Afterward, the American said, "I found that he had presented me with the German Eagle, one of the highest German decorations, 'by order of *der Führer.'*"

Perhaps a man accustomed to receiving medals does not give much thought to their political significance, but Lindbergh's wife did when he spoke to her about it later that night. She called it "the Albatross," and an albatross it would be, as he learned to his lasting discomfort.

In the journal he kept, Lindbergh described the encounter rather casually, but one gets the impression that he considered it an event of more than usual significance, which indeed it was. For when he and Anne left Germany at the end of October, he could say that he had a fairly clear picture of the overall situation in Europe. "I had seen the strength of Germany," he wrote, "and I knew the weakness of England and France." In his opinion the Germans were a great people whose welfare was inseparable from the rest of Europe, and he was certain that the only hope of avoiding war and preserving Western civilization was to establish a rapport between Britain and Germany. If that failed, and if war should come, America must stay out of it.

LESS THAN TWELVE months after the poor bargain of a truce that was Munich, when Czechoslovakia was abandoned by its allies, Britain and France, Europe was at war for the second time in twenty years, and most Americans—like Charles Lindbergh—wanted no part of it. In the wake of Hitler's brutal attack on Poland on September 1, 1939, a Roper public opinion poll revealed that 30 percent of Americans wanted nothing whatever to do with any warring nation, while another 37 percent wished to "take no sides and stay out of [any] war entirely" but would agree to sell arms to belligerents on cash-and-carry terms. These two groups represented two thirds of the American public. They were folk of just about every persuasion, and all of them felt intensely about an issue that might easily alter the lives of their families and the future of their country.

Their fervor was fueled by long-standing disillusionment and political consequences of the First World War, an ingrained suspicion of "foreigners," and an all but universal belief that the United States—secure behind two oceans—was big enough and powerful enough to go it alone and had no business bailing out the French and English, whose stupidity at Munich had produced what looked like 1914 all over again.

The great debate that was beginning to cut across all levels of American society was now to be governed by an entirely different set of premises. The question was no longer "What do we do if war comes?" War *had* come. It was here. The chessmen were on the board, and the first move had been made. This meant that arguments about intervention or nonintervention were no longer theoretical. On the outcome of the debate would hinge the nation's peace and security and the lives of all those who might be sent into battle in what still seemed to just about everyone to be Europe's, not America's, war.

Charles Lindbergh was acutely aware of this. On April 14, 1939, he had arrived in New York aboard the liner *Aquitania,* one of a passenger list that included numerous refugees. Because of his incisive knowledge of Europe's air fleets, he was immediately sought after by government officials, among them Congressman Sol Bloom, chairman of the House Committee on Foreign Affairs, who hoped Lindbergh would testify on the neutrality legislation then under consideration. Lindbergh declined that invitation, but accepted one to meet with General Henry H. Arnold, the popular chief of the U.S. Army Air Corps, to whom the flier had for months been supplying information on the present and potential air strength of the European nations, particularly Germany. (One of "Hap" Arnold's beliefs—which he said he had learned from the Wright brothers, who also taught him to fly in one of their twelve-horsepower planes—was that nothing was impossible. Fortunately for his country, he put that belief into practice by doing everything in his power to encourage the buildup of production facilities that would enable U.S. factories to turn out the planes so desperately needed in the war ahead.)

Just now, Arnold was eager to learn about the Luftwaffe, and the two aviators arranged to get together at the Thayer Hotel at West Point. They talked for several hours in the dining room, which was closed to the public to ensure their privacy, before strolling out to the military academy's baseball diamond. The Army team was playing Syracuse, and the two men continued their discussion while the game went on. What he obtained from Lindbergh, Arnold said later, was "the most accurate picture of the Luftwaffe, its equipment, leaders, apparent plans, training methods, and present defects" he had yet received. Not incidentally, it heightened his determination that the American air force must surpass and be capable of overpowering the Germans.

The two met again at Arnold's house in Washington, where Lindbergh was asked if he would be willing to make a study of American aeronautical research and manufacturing operations with an eye to improving their efficiency. He accepted, and went on active duty as a colonel almost immediately. On April 20 he met with Harry Woodring, the isolationist secretary of war whose resignation President Franklin D. Roosevelt would request a year later. Then—after pushing his way through a crowd of press photographers and "inane women screeching" at the door—he entered the White House to meet Roosevelt for the first time.

Lindbergh found both interviews disquieting: the one with Woodring because the secretary asked him not to testify before any congressional committees; the one with Roosevelt because he thought the president "a little too suave, too pleasant, too easy." He was predisposed to like Roosevelt, who was an accomplished, interesting conversationalist, but he believed that since the president was "mostly politician," the two of them "would never get along on many fundamentals." He also got the impression that the chief executive was a very tired man who seemed unaware of how fatigued he was.

In the months that followed, Lindbergh talked with the men who constituted the U.S. aviation establishment, he visited the drafting rooms and factories where aircraft were being designed and built, and he reported to Arnold and other Air Corps chiefs his conviction that only by instituting a significant research-and-development program could the nation catch up with the European countries, even in five years. As August wore on, his thoughts were continuously on Europe and the imminent likelihood of war: He was reminded of the tense hours before Munich, except that now, in the United States, he did not sense the same atmosphere of apprehension and depression he had felt in England a year earlier.

On August 28 he received a telegram from his friend Truman Smith, who was now in Washington after four years as military attaché for air with the U.S. Embassy in Berlin. The message read simply, "Yes, 80," which was Smith's estimate of the percentage probability of war. It started Lindbergh wondering if anything he might say in a radio broadcast would be constructive, perhaps helping in some way to halt Europe's rush to war. But then came Friday, September 1, and the huge headlines: GERMAN TROOPS ENTER POLAND.

Along with millions of people everywhere, Lindbergh speculated about what Britain and France would do. He concluded that if they tried to break through Germany's defensive Westwall in an effort to support Poland, they would surely lose the war unless America entered the fight. What in the world were the two allies thinking of? he wondered. Why, if they wanted to prevent the Germans from moving eastward, had they chosen this particular set of circumstances as an excuse to go to war? He had heard that Chamberlain had not even consulted his general staff before entering into an alliance with Poland, and now people everywhere were asking why the governments of Britain and France had not yet declared war. Lindbergh spoke about that to his wife, Anne, who replied, "Maybe they've talked to a general."

What stand should the United States take? Lindbergh kept asking himself. He and Anne listened to Roosevelt's radio talk on Sunday evening, September 3, and the next morning read in the paper that the Cunard liner *Athenia,* carrying 1,400 passengers, had been torpedoed off the Hebrides and that German troops were overrunning Poland. On September 7 Lindbergh made up his mind. "I do not intend to stand by and see this country pushed into war if it is not absolutely essential to the future welfare of the nation," he wrote in his journal. "Much as I dislike taking part in politics and public life, I intend to do so if necessary to stop the trend which is now going on in this country." On September 10 he made a brief entry: "Phoned Bill Castle and Fulton Lewis. Decided to go on the radio next week."

William R. Castle was a conservative Republican who had served in the State Department during the Harding and Coolidge administrations, to become undersecretary of state under Hoover. At Castle's home Lindbergh had met Fulton Lewis, Jr., a conservative (some thought reactionary) commentator who appeared nightly on the Mutual Broadcasting System, and had heard him describe an instance in which "Jewish advertising firms" threatened to remove their sponsorship if a certain feature were carried by Mutual. The network, Lewis added, had decided to drop the feature. "I do not blame the Jews so much for their attitude," Lindbergh observed, "although I think it unwise from their own standpoint." When Castle suggested that Lindbergh speak out against U.S. involvement in the European war, Lewis said he could make arrangements for a network broadcast, and it was later agreed that the address would be carried on Friday evening, September 15, by Mutual. When this news was released, NBC and CBS also decided to carry the speech.

The day before the broadcast, Lindbergh informed Hap Arnold of his plans, and the Air Corps chief suggested he go on inactive duty while actively involved in politics. Arnold read the speech Lindbergh was going to deliver, agreed that it contained nothing that could be considered unethical, and asked if he planned to show it to Woodring. The colonel replied that he had no confidence in the secretary of war, and as he said so he "could tell from Arnold's eyes that he was on my side." He decided not to let Woodring read the talk.

The following day Arnold reported this conversation to Woodring and let Lindbergh know that the secretary was "very much displeased." Woodring's reaction had been to state sourly that he "had hoped to make use of" Lindbergh in the future, whatever that might mean, but that any such plans were out of the question now. The next day Truman Smith told him that the administration was deeply troubled by his intention to take an active role in this touchy political matter, and Smith had been authorized to inform Lindbergh that if he did not make the broadcast, a cabinet post of secretary of air would be created and he would be appointed to the job.

Having sized up Roosevelt as a political animal, Lindbergh was not surprised that he would resort to such a ploy; what astonished him was that the president would think that he, Lindbergh, might be influenced by it. Since the offer had come from Woodring to Arnold to Smith, it was evident that word of it would get around, and Lindbergh thought it a great mistake for the president "to let the army know he deals in such a way." (When Arnold told Smith to take the offer to Lindbergh, Smith asked the general if he thought Lindbergh would accept it. "Of course not" was Arnold's immediate reply. Arnold knew his man.)

And so, at 9:45 on Friday evening, September 15, 1939, the only man in the United States who could rival Franklin Roosevelt for the public's attention stood before six microphones in the Carlton Hotel and made the first broadcast in what would become his crusade against American intervention in the war. In a clipped, slightly nasal tone, he declared that the war just begun was a continuation of "an age-old struggle between the nations of Europe." His voice sounded unnatural to Anne, even though it was "strong and even and clear." She was sitting in the hotel room with a group of friends and network technicians, praying that the American people might understand, that they might realize how difficult it was for her husband to give this speech, turning his back on France and England, two nations that had given their family sanctuary.

"Our safety does not lie in fighting European wars," he was saying. "It lies in our own internal strength, in the character of the American people and of American institutions." Western civilization itself was at risk, he went on, and if Europe was prostrated by war, then the only hope for the survival of those rich traditions and culture lay in America's hands. "By staying out of war," he said, "we may even bring peace to Europe more quickly. Let us look to our own defenses and our own character. . . ." Behind this view lay his certainty that Germany was far more powerful militarily than either France or Great Britain, and that the only way Hitler could possibly be defeated would be in a long, exhausting war. Lindbergh was by nature a questioner and a seeker, and when he asked himself whether the consequences of such a terrible struggle could be measured in terms of winning or losing, he was sure that victory could not be worth what it would cost the United States.

ELABORATING AGAIN and again on this basic theme during the course of the next year, Lindbergh would make a dozen major addresses, four of them on network radio; speak at major public rallies; write several magazine articles; testify before congressional committees; and devote countless hours to discussions with leaders of the noninterventionist movement (most of whom he considered hopelessly conservative and incapable of assuming positions of national leadership). Almost as important as the dedication he brought to his self-appointed task, according to a man who shared speakers' platforms with him, was the way in which he "evokes a fervor, a tension, such as an ambitious politician would give anything to arouse."

In September 1940, when a group of noninterventionists formed a national organization—the America First Committee—to oppose U.S. entry into World War II, they immediately turned to Charles Lindbergh for assistance. He became their most successful, most sought-after speaker, the very personification of the isolationist cause, capable of attracting more than 30,000 people to a rally.

As a result of his increasing involvement in the debate, he was soon to be one of the most controversial figures in American politics, feared and reviled by the administration, which perceived him—quite accurately—as the most forceful opponent of the president's foreign policy and the man most likely to appeal to and influence the public. Indeed, the immediate reaction to Lindbergh's first speech had been overwhelmingly favorable: It was front-page news in the New York and Washington papers; telegrams and letters from all over the country greeted the colonel and his wife when they returned home from Washington, including one from Herbert Hoover congratulating him on a "really great address" and a polite note from General Arnold saying that he and Secretary Woodring thought the speech "very well worded and very well delivered."

There were brickbats as well as roses: It was only a matter of days before the opposition was in full cry. Dorothy Thompson lashed out at Lindbergh in her column, calling him the "pro-Nazi recipient of a German medal." And that was just the beginning. As the wrangling over America's neutrality grew ever more passionate and strident, Lindbergh and his wife would discover that old friends dropped them, that streets honoring the hero of the first solo transatlantic flight had been renamed. To cap it all, the president of the United States would insult him publicly by likening him to Clement Vallandigham, the Ohio congressman who spoke, during the Civil War, for a group called the Copperheads and predicted the North would never win.

IN ONE OF THOSE remarkable coincidences that fate sometimes concocts, the great debate came to a head on the night of September 11, 1941, with the two chief protagonists confronting each other. Lindbergh had agreed to speak to an America First crowd in Des Moines, Iowa, that evening. President Roosevelt was to have addressed the nation after the U.S. destroyers *Greer* and *Kearny* were attacked by German submarines, but his mother died and the radio speech was rescheduled for September 11.

Rather than change plans, the America First Committee decided on the unusual approach of broadcasting the president's talk to the 8,000 Iowans attending the rally, with the scheduled speakers to follow. So what the crowd heard first was a stirring "shoot-on-sight" speech by Roosevelt, and when the America First speakers filed on stage they were greeted with a mixture of boos and applause, with hecklers shouting from the gallery.

When Lindbergh came to the lectern, he promised to speak "with the utmost frankness" about who was responsible for trying to force the United States into the war, and then named "the British, the Jewish, and the Roosevelt administration."

In the contest between isolationists and interventionists, the administration was fair game; so to a lesser degree was Britain. But even to name the Jews—whose danger to America, he said, lay in their dominant influence over the motion-picture industry, the press, radio, and government—and to segregate them *en bloc* from the rest of American society as "other peoples," was to introduce something altogether different into the equation. It was a reminder of the horrors perpetuated inside Nazi Germany, no matter how carefully Lindbergh tried to argue his case. It was, in short, the unmentionable topic, a sacred taboo, and no matter how he might explain his position, it was a political blunder from which America First never recovered.

While it would be improper to blame the demise of that organization on Charles Lindbergh—after all, the Japanese attacked Pearl Harbor less than three months after his speech—it was evident that the heart went out of the movement after the night of September 11. For one thing, the president struck a responsive chord with his "shoot-on-sight" message; events in Europe had made the public increasingly ready for tough talk, if not action. But Charles Lindbergh, a courageous man who never shied away from speaking the truth as he saw it, who had warned his country about the threat from Germany and had then become the noninterventionists' most powerful and persuasive voice, had an equal share in sending America First from the stage of history.

Until then, Lindbergh and the isolationists had profoundly affected Franklin Roosevelt's tactics concerning foreign policy As FDR's speechwriter Robert Sherwood put it, their campaign had so put the president on the defensive that "whatever the peril, he was not going to lead the country into war—he was going to wait to be pushed in."

*AUTUMN 1989*

---

Richard M. Ketchum is the author of *The Borrowed Years, 1938–1941: America on the Way to War* (1989), from which this article is adapted.

# 25

# Hard Liquor, Easy Duty

## By Elihu Rose

*Few soldiers would argue with General Sherman's famous dictum that "war is hell." One wonders what complementary dictum on the subject of peace the general would have declaimed had he served in the American colonial-style army in Tientsin, China, between the two world wars. For the 15th Infantry Regiment, the assignment was nearly perfect; easier duty could be neither imagined nor wished. Yet even this idyllic and exotic task had its moments of high drama and dangers for both the army and the nation it served.*

It was a glorious scene, like something out of an old movie—perhaps *Four Feathers* or *Gunga Din*. The date: March 2, 1938. The place: Tientsin, China. The setting: The 15th United States Infantry Regiment was going home after nearly twenty-six years in the Tientsin garrison. The road from the American Barracks to the railway station was lined with British police and British, French, and Italian troops. Flags were everywhere. As the Americans marched by, the foreign regimental bands in turn headed the procession. To add to the hullabaloo, the British municipality provided the traditional Chinese farewell firecrackers. The British civilians and military had already given valedictory receptions during the morning, and now the parade stopped at the French Club long enough for the presentation of a bouquet to the regimental commander's wife. By the time the 15th reached the station, all was pandemonium. Honor guards crashed out their salutes, and the three regimental bands were joined by the Chinese police band.

Years later, a retired colonel recalled that last day in Tientsin:

> Tears as big as cobblestones streamed down my cheeks as the troop train pulled out of East Station, with the bands playing "Auld Lang Syne." We were headed for the transport that was to carry us back to the States. Every day of my service with the 15th I was fully aware that not only had I never had it so good, I would probably never have it so good again.

The chronicle of the 15th Infantry in China really started with the

Boxer Rebellion of 1900, when the United States participated in an inter-national effort to relieve beleaguered foreign legations during the famous fifty-five-day siege at Peking. The subsequent treaty granted the major European powers the right to maintain garrisons in China, ostensibly to preserve rail communications between the capital at Peking and the sea. The United States did not avail itself of this privilege until 1912, when the turmoil attending the Chinese Revolution brought a renewed threat to local foreigners. The 15th Infantry, 850 strong, was sent out to Tientsin, and there it stayed until that tearful, noisy day twenty-six years later when the regiment made its farewell parade through the city.

Notwithstanding the delights of Tientsin, the more pragmatic U.S. Army planners questioned what national interest could possibly be served by so small and exposed a garrison. After all, China constituted a scant 1 percent of America's total foreign investment and less than 4 percent of her overseas trade. And there were only 9,000 to 10,000 Americans living in the entire country, of whom perhaps 2,000 lived anywhere near Tientsin. The town itself had only 600.

Mindful of the possibility of a Custer-like debacle, the army had been trying to extricate the Tientsin garrison since the mid-1920s. The requests for permission to withdraw were continually rebuffed by the State Department, which cited any number of imprecise political reasons for maintaining the garrison: the protection of American nationals in North China, the protection of the American legation in Peking, the protection of American business interests, the protection of American missionaries, the protection of rail communications between Peking and Tientsin, the demonstration of American political support for China in the face of Japanese expansionist tendencies, the maintenance of national prestige, and the general support of American policy in the Far East. All this was a tall order for 850 soldiers. The military means for the execution of these diverse and sometimes contradictory goals were left vague, but with no other choice, the 15th Infantry simply made the best of it. And the best of it was very good indeed.

The press liked to call them "America's Foreign Legion," or "the Forgotten Fifteenth." They themselves preferred "the Old China Hands" or "the Can Do Boys." The regimental motto was "Can Do," an adaptation from pidgin English. But however martial the label, the activities of the 15th were distinctly more boring than bellicose: no shots fired in anger, no blood, no thunder. Its most warlike activity consisted of setting up roadblocks or guarding bridges. It lived the day-to-day existence typical of any American infantry regiment of those years, from on-post ceremonial to off-post dissi-pation. But the locale was Tientsin; and that made all the difference.

Tientsin was China's second-greatest commercial city, after Shanghai, with about 1 million inhabitants in the 1920s. By 1992, Tientsin—now known as Tianjin—would be a megacity of 9.8 million, fourteenth largest in the world. In the days of the 15th Infantry it was already a thriving twentieth-century metropolis, having been virtually rebuilt following the devastation of the Boxer uprising. Like Shanghai, much of Tientsin was divided into foreign concessions—British, French, Japanese, and Italian—whose Western architecture gave it the ambience of a European city: sober office buildings, imposing hotels, wide boulevards, and manicured parks. Its cosmopolitan character was enhanced by a profusion of uniforms: Indian Sikh police in turbans, French Annamite troops in lampshade hats, Highlanders in kilts. An American officer recalled that "the mounting of the guard at Gordon Hall, the Headquarters of the British Concession, was a never-to-be-forgotten military spectacle, rivaling Buckingham Palace."

One veteran of the 15th described Tientsin as a complex, puzzling, and beautiful city. Yet its all-embracing Western milieu could be disconcerting to those who sought the essential sophistication and subtlety of Oriental life. Joseph Stilwell, then a major on his second China tour, felt that Tientsin lacked the charm of Peking and was dismayed to find Chinese-style housing unavailable. He had to "settle" for a home that could have been found on any upper-class American suburban street.

In one particular, even Major Stilwell might have longed for a touch of Western convenience. As the U.S. Army's 1927 intelligence summary noted: "There is no such thing as sanitation in China except in the modern hotels and office buildings in the big cities." Correspondence and recollections abound with references to the unbearable odor of sewage that pervaded the city; newly arrived soldiers found the smell literally overpowering. Tientsin's sanitary system, such as it was, consisted of open gutters and sewers that emptied directly into the Hai River bordering the city center. A hoary joke among 15th Infantrymen was the advice to take a bottle of Hai River water back home to the States and, when overcome by nostalgia for the attractions of Tientsin, simply take a whiff.

But one got used to the smell, and Major Stilwell's repugnance to colonial culture was atypical. Most American officers considered Tientsin the cream of foreign service; the word "fairyland" appears more than once in old letters and memoirs. Accustomed to the meager salaries of a depression-era army, officers found themselves living like kings in China. Lieutenants had household staffs of five or six; the commanding officer had as many as fifteen. Unlike their previous lives at such places as Fort Huachuca, Arizona, or Fort Missoula, Montana, junior officers and their wives, invariably addressed as "Master" and "Missy," now awoke to breakfast served in bed, with baths already drawn. Inexpensive food, combined with the extravagant size of household staffs, permitted entertaining on a scale unknown in their former existence. The favorable exchange rate also encouraged shopping, and it was unusual for an officer's wife not to return to America laden with rugs, silver, lingerie, brocades, carved chests, or screens that ordinarily would have been beyond her means. China duty meant the outfitting of one's home for a lifetime. One officer's diary noted his homeward shipment of nearly six tons of furniture and other effects. The wife of George C. Marshall regarded her husband's service with the 15th as a "three-years' shopping trip."

Officers, of course, were thoroughly at home with the parochial formalities of the typical American military post: the endless receptions, dinners, dances, receiving lines, and social calls. As one observer noted, "The leisure to do minutiae correctly, and the continuity to know what is right, form the essence of garrison life." But in China, the officers were now embraced by a much larger and more cosmopolitan community. In addition to the usual foreign colony—commercial representatives, diplomats, adventurers, White Russian refugees—were almost 200 fellow officers of foreign military units, making for a continual parade of welcome and farewell parties and regimental guest nights. For soldiers in Tientsin, the most essential weapon seems to have been the full-dress uniform. Reciprocity was the foundation of etiquette; every dinner party, every courtesy call, every invitation to drinks had to be repaid. One captain wrote his mother: "We have about cleared up our calls—something between fifty and sixty."

In the absence of a regular American officers club, officers became, as a matter of course, members of the downtown Tientsin club and—the epicenter of all social activity—the Country Club, with its full range of graceful and elegant amenities. No cash ever changed hands; everything was on credit. The chit, a British invention and the precursor of the modern credit card, efficiently and effortlessly took care of everything, for officers and enlisted men alike: A soldier just signed his name and unit for almost any service in almost any establishment, and bills were mysteriously rendered monthly. Settlement of these accounts was a matter of honor, and default was unthinkable.

These diversions did not exhaust all the recreational possibilities. The American army, like all others, had a soft spot for equine sport, and the racing club provided the occasion not only for racing but for riding, polo, and hunting. And when even these amusements palled or, in the words of one officer, the "frantic pace of enforced socialization back at the compound" became overwhelming, you could always travel throughout the exotic Orient.

Insularity from civilian society was a long-standing feature of garrison life in the American military. But in Tientsin, insularity had different roots and fostered a different behavior. It took its cue from the colonial racist attitudes of the small foreign community, which separated itself from the native Chinese residents by an unbridgeable gulf. The segregation was absolute. Other than with servants or shopkeepers, there was virtually no social intercourse between officers—or indeed any foreigners—and the local Chinese. Money was not the issue. Not even very rich Chinese were admitted to the clubs, and there were almost no other places where social contacts between the two groups could be cultivated. It was the perfect embodiment of Kipling's East-is-East-and-West-is-West dichotomy. For the American officers, the one million Chinese of Tientsin were nonpeople.

Given the many agreeable social activities and obligations, it is no small wonder that the officers ever found time to pursue the profession of arms that brought them to Tientsin in the first place. But the American army between the wars was hardly a demanding employer: Except for occasional tours as officer of the day or officer of the guard, or service on a court-martial, the duty day ended by noon. Although the ceremonial nature of the 15th Infantry's service probably encouraged an overemphasis on spit and polish—all officers and first sergeants wore sabers on duty—the daily routine was essentially indistinguishable from that of any other army post.

Because service in the 15th was so desirable, some commentators have concluded that officers either pulled strings to be assigned or were hand-picked because of especially fine records. The roster itself certainly lends credence to the latter hypothesis: In one five-year period (1925–30), no less than twenty-five future generals served with the regiment, among whom were such luminaries as Stilwell, Marshall, and Matthew B. Ridgway. But the army's assignment policies of those days make it unlikely that the War Department went out of its way to choose the crème de la crème as officers for the 15th, and the standard selection process probably yielded a reasonable cross section of the officer corps: good, fair, and poor.

The commanding officers also ran the gamut in quality from outstanding to outright eccentric. General William D. Connor, who commanded during the mid-1920s, was in the outstanding category. Number one in his West Point class, he was the first to recognize the tactical vulnerability of the 15th Infantry and to counsel its removal. He also appreciated the importance of language as the key to understanding a foreign culture, and he insisted that officers learn the rudiments of Chinese; the course was optional for the enlisted men. Language instruction continued until 1931, when Colonel Reynolds J. Burt terminated the program, referring to Chinese as a "fool language," useful to the troops only in their dealings with tradesmen.

Burt was something of a character. Described by one of his officers as "an old fuddy-duddy," he was typical of those martinets for whom punctilio, ceremony, and appearance were the sine qua non of the military profession. In a triumph of form over function, the troops were "armed" with dummy wooden pistols, thus preventing an unsightly sag at the belt. And, lest the blanket rolls on the backpacks appear the slightest bit wrinkled, stovepipes wrapped in blanket material were employed as an ideal substitute. As the troops stood for inspection, thus accoutred in their tidy if ersatz equipment, coolies would dash out to give a final dusting to their already spit-shined shoes. A careful observer would have noticed that the wood of the rifle stocks had a lustrous patina reminiscent of Old World gunsmithing. If the truth be told, each soldier had two stocks: one for field use and range firing, and one—carefully honed and stored in rags soaked with linseed oil—for parades and formal guard mounts. Even in their more bellicose combat garb, the Old China Hands were a sight to behold. Sacrificing the utility of camouflage for the sake of chic, their helmets were polished and shellacked, bearing the regimental crest stenciled on the front. And their bayonets—the most bloodthirsty of weaponry—were burnished until they gleamed. As the French general was reputed to have said while observing the Charge of the

Light Brigade, "C'est magnifique, mais ce n'est pas la guerre."

Colonel Burt was in his element in such a unit, so long as no untoward military exigencies interfered with the meticulously executed guard mounts and parades. He also fancied himself the 15th Infantry's John Philip Sousa. He had written a march entitled "Kings of the Highway," although there was certainly no thoroughfare worthy of that name in northern China. The bandmaster naturally acceded to his desire to have the march played at every possible regimental function. As Burt boarded the ship for his return home, the band struck up one final rendition in his honor. In a finale, unobserved by the colonel, the bandsman unceremoniously threw all copies of the song in the water.

Colonel Burt's antithesis was Brigadier General Joseph Castner, best described by such adjectives as choleric, overwrought, and unstable. Castner was not a West Pointer and possibly for that reason affected a one-of-the-boys demeanor. In a unit that prided itself on immaculate turnout, Castner enjoyed dressing in dirty, unpressed, enlisted men's fatigues. His slovenly and disheveled appearance was no doubt calculated to irritate his officers, whom he referred to as "tea-drinking SOBs." He is remembered riding around Tientsin in one of the city's few automobiles, a Cadillac no less. Woe betide the soldier—officer or enlisted man—who failed to salute; not seeing him was no excuse. Castner's consuming passion was marching, and on most days he could be seen walking or jogging around the race-course. His obsession reached its apotheosis in what came to be known forever after as the "blockbuster hike," a forced march of about thirty-six miles that he personally led at a blistering pace, covering the distance in thirteen hours. Some 120 men fell out of ranks, slumping and sprawling along the route in various attitudes of exhaustion. That evening the post hospital was literally overflowing with the walking wounded. Mercifully, a visiting inspector general insisted that the march, scheduled to be resumed the following day, be canceled forthwith.

The most famous regimental commander was, of course, George C. Marshall. Actually, he was acting commander for only a two-month period. However, his three-year tenure in the mid-1920s as executive officer to a phlegmatic, easy-come-easy-go commanding officer encouraged the general observation that the maxim "Let George do it" must have been coined in the 15th Infantry. But Colonel Marshall was too straitlaced and persnickety to be beloved by his subordinates. Indeed, one of his officers found him "often irritable, capable of grotesquely unfair judgments." Incidentally, that same officer, in commenting upon his colleague, the illustrious General-to-be Matthew B. Ridgway, noted that he "didn't enter into the spirit of things over here." The word "spirit" was left without further interpretation.

CONCERNING ENLISTED MEN, the 15th Infantry must be seen in the context of the entire U.S. Army of those years. It was like all regiments, like some regiments, and like no other regiment. In its essence, however, it was more typical than unique. Its members led a pure version of American army life between the wars, a life so perfectly described by sometime Private First Class Victor Vogel in his charming memoir, *Soldiers of the Old Army,* as "a school, an athletic club, an orphans' home and a boys' camp all rolled together."

The 120,000 men who lived in this school-club-home-camp-army between the wars were a mixed bag. In the late 1920s the adjutant general observed that "the demand for labor in civilian activities" made it "necessary to accept every man who could be included under the most liberal interpretation of the regulations." True, the best recruiter remained the proverbial Sergeant Hardtimes, and during the Great Depression years the army could be more selective. But even then, it appeared to one historian as "a combination of Rudyard Kipling's British Army and the French Foreign Legion." Yet the characters in James Jones's *From Here to Eternity* or Richard McKenna's *The Sand Pebbles* who are perceived as stereotypical of that era—profane, alienated, dissipated, having enlisted at the behest of some local judge as an alternative to jail—may have been the basis for a misapprehension of the nature of that army. There were, of course, those types to be found, but certainly not a whole armyful. More typical were men who just needed a job; or believed the recruiting posters' promise of "Earn, Learn and Travel"; or sought a safe, predictable home with no responsibility; or hoped to mend recently broken hearts; or were genuinely motivated by patriotic zeal; or liked the macho atmosphere of military life; or were driven by any one of a hundred other reasons.

It was a single man's army. Marriage was possible, with the permission of one's commanding officer, but pay was so low for all but the top three enlisted grades that having a wife and family almost automatically consigned a soldier to near poverty. So being mostly single, healthy young men, they behaved the way single, healthy young men did. Although neither chastity nor temperance was thought to be a cardinal virtue, the army was puritanical in the matter of venereal disease and on-duty drinking. Women and liquor, or more specifically, venereal disease and alcoholism, have been the twin nemeses of every army since Alexander the Great—probably before. They were major concerns for the American army in both its continental and foreign garrisons.

It was not what could be called a stressful life. Military duties customarily ended by noon, and unless one were enrolled in educational or vocational classes, most afternoons were free for organized sports. Thursday afternoon was parade; Saturday morning, inspection. And that was all. Every evening after 5:00, Wednesday and Saturday afternoons, and all day Sunday, a man's time was his own. Victor Vogel, that most perceptive chronicler of life in the Old Army, quotes an adage of the period: "Every day in the army is like Sunday on the farm." And like the farm, the main occupational hazard was not tension but boredom.

The army's twin institutional fetishes were athletics and individual marksmanship. Interunit athletic competition had a hard edge, with the definition of "sportsmanship" pushed to its farthest limit. The preoccupation with boxing, featured in *From Here to Eternity*, was mirrored in other sports as well: soccer, basketball, volleyball, cross-country, hockey, football, baseball, wrestling, track, you name it.

The obsession with marksmanship was based not only on the notion of military competence or unit esprit, but also on simple economic incentive: A "marksman" rating was worth an extra $2 a month; an "expert," $5. As a percentage of a private's monthly pay of $21, that amounted to a considerable premium, well worth the endless hours of painstaking drill. Months of grueling practice with the classic '03 Springfield rifle—both indoors and on the range—led each year to the final event, firing for record. But the Springfield was an unforgiving master; according to Vogel, "Hardly a man left the firing line without a black eye, a bloody nose, a bruised cheek, a fractured jaw or busted teeth."

The social parameters of an enlisted man's world were exceedingly narrow. Civilians regarded all enlisted men as pariahs, as if leprosy automatically came with the uniform. Noncommissioned officers had considerable prestige, at least on the post, and consorted with the lower ranks only in the line of duty. Commissioned officers barely recognized the existence of privates; officers were addressed only by rank and in the third person, as if they themselves were not present: "Begging the captain's pardon, will the captain be riding today?"

This, then, was the life in virtually every regiment in the army, the 15th Infantry included. But the 15th was in foreign service, and that lent it an aura shared by only a few other units. Compared with England or France, the United States had only a handful of overseas stations. Today one certainly doesn't think of Puerto Rico, Hawaii, or Alaska as "foreign," but the between-the-wars army thought them foreign enough to earn a soldier a pay supplement. And besides China, there were garrisons in Panama and the Philippines. In those days soldiers enlisted directly into the unit of their choice. Vogel recalled the foreign-service privates as "a different breed . . . with restless feet and a faraway look in their eyes . . . (who) seldom served out an enlistment in the States and who were not concerned about being reduced in rank to get a transfer."

For this rolling-stone kind of soldier, Tientsin was just the place. Statistics confirmed Vogel's observations: In 1929, reportedly, "at least 18 percent of the men had either purchased their discharges in order to enlist for duty [in China] or had voluntarily taken a reduction in rank in order to serve with the Fifteenth Infantry." As noted, much of its day-to-day military life was similar to that of all other army units, but there was an undeniable fascination in the exotic, Oriental hustle and bustle just outside the barracks gate. And for many, there was emotional comfort in the simple geographic fact that Tientsin was about as far away from home as a man could get.

There were more down-to-earth benefits as well. Even American privates in China were well paid compared to soldiers in the other foreign garrisons, or to the European clerks in the foreign concessions. And off the post, the universal acceptance of the chit—implicitly underwritten by the signer's American uniform—insured the availability of enough credit to tide a soldier over until payday. An extremely favorable exchange rate, combined with a limitless availability of inexpensive labor, meant that local Chinese performed all routine military chores. There was none of the traditional peeling of potatoes on KP; in fact, there was virtually no fatigue duty of any kind. The lowliest private had his bed made, his shoes shined, his buttons polished, his canteen filled. He was even shaved. (The troops did, however, have to clean their own weapons.) Nor did the Old China Hands have to undergo the indignity of a cafeteria-style mess; they were served by Chinese attendants, on china plates set on tablecloths. A veteran of the 15th recalled years later that the cuisine one particular mess sergeant prepared would have graced the dining room of a French ocean liner. All in all, not a bad life.

In 1925, Lieutenant Colonel George C. Marshall summed up some of the other attractions of China service in a letter to his old commander, General John Pershing: "Today is payday and we are up against the problem of cheap liquor and cheaper women." This reflection was seconded by the mercurial General Joe Castner, who complained to the War Department that "women, intoxicants and narcotics can be obtained in their vilest forms for a few cents. The men seek long tours in order to continue cohabitation with low-caste Chinese, Japanese, Korean and Russian women." Hardly a soldier in the 850-man garrison would have disagreed—or, indeed, would have wished it any other way.

The opportunities for dissipation reached mythic dimensions in China. Because enlisted men had to pay the considerable costs of bringing their wives out to China, there was a greater proportion of unmarried men than usual. That, and the ready availability of prostitutes, led to a venereal-disease rate that was three times higher than the army average. One officer estimated that 50 percent of the regiment was infected—an exaggeration, maybe, but one that indicated the general perception of the extent of the problem. According to a report to the adjutant general, perhaps 12 percent of the command had "syphilitic infection."

As pervasive as it was, venereal disease might have been even more prevalent had not semipermanent living arrangements with local women been so accessible. The influx of White Russians into North China in the wake of the Russian Revolution provided an entirely new and attractive source of companionship, the 15th Infantryman's version of safe sex. These liaisons were mutually beneficial: In the words of one officer, "The soldiers of the 15th (were), as the Chinese say, 'their food, clothes, and parents.' " Most of the White Russians lived in abject and degrading poverty. For many of the women, prostitution, or the next thing to it, was all that stood between them and actual starvation. So many of the young White Russian women claimed to have been former Czarist princesses that "princess" became the generic name given to them by the troops. It was easy to manage these alternative accommodations. Soldiers were not required to sleep in the barracks but could stay out all night, returning only for reveille roll call. One officer reminisced that "80 percent of my company . . . at one time or another were what they called shacked up."

Notwithstanding the relative hygienic benefits of cohabiting with real or imagined White Russian princesses, the army tried every possible means of limiting venereal disease, from humiliating personal inspections to free rickshaw rides to bring the men back from the bars at closing time. Contracting venereal disease was even made a court-martial offense. In desperation, the War Department retained the services of a social worker from the American Social Hygiene Association especially trained in the arts of venereal-disease control. The results of this initiative are lost to history. The redoubtable General Castner tried, via his "blockbuster hike," to sweat the troops into a state of celibacy and temperance; but he devised other programs as well. Back in Washington, the adjutant general applauded his efforts: "I am especially gratified to know that you have interested yourself so much in protecting the men from the degrading influences that prevail at that place. The surest remedy is what you have adopted of athletics, physical activity, and sport that will occupy the time and the interests of the men instead of having them seek harmful recreation." Yet one can be reasonably sure that the troops preferred both the "degrading influences" and the "harmful recreation."

For the record, it must be stated that Tientsin offered wholesome entertainment as well. There was an enlisted men's club, a YMCA, and a Knights of Columbus, establishments where the less dissolute could while away their off-duty hours in more benign surroundings than the ubiquitous bars with their ritual, just-for-the-hell-of-it brawling. The YMCA ran tours, and there were the usual band concerts, amateur theatricals, and lending libraries. However, Tientsin is fondly remembered by veterans more for the princesses on Woodrow Wilson Street than for the coffee at the Y.

Such minimal military duties as were necessary were performed with an éclat that befitted the unit, one of whose main purposes was to impress the natives. For example, the standard-issue dress uniforms, straight from the quartermaster, simply would not do for so fastidious and discriminating an organization. The 15th Infantry turned out in uniforms tailored in Hong Kong, with British-style buttons and spiral puttees, carefully wrapped around breeches as highly pegged as a motorcycle policeman's. The outsize collars and wide lapels of the greatcoats were patterned after those of the British Guards. And when a soldier strolled about the city, he did so in slacks creased to a razor sharpness; in a dress tunic whose brass buttons shone; in cap and belt whose leather his Chinese orderly had patiently buffed to a high gloss. The shirt was white, the tie black. The ensemble was completed with a swagger stick, an accessory long out of style in the rest of the army, but de rigueur in the 15th. In the words of one commentator, "It took a nice eye to discern that he was still (only) a private."

Indeed, the whole question surrounding the wearing of the uniform was fraught with social implications. In the continental United States, the military uniform conveyed so negative an image among the general public that most off-duty soldiers lost no time in changing into civvies at the first opportunity. In China, too, soldiers were at the bottom of the social scale, but that prejudice did not extend to foreign troops; these were foreigners first and soldiers second. The Old China Hands found their uniform not a stigma but a mark of distinction to be worn with pride, if not outright arrogance. In China between the wars, it was a not-so-subtle indication of who was boss.

The unbearable summer heat of Tientsin and the need for rifle-range exercises required the regiment to rotate by companies to its summer camp on the beach at Chinwangtao, a small port about eighty miles from Tientsin. There the troops enjoyed an idyllic life, interrupted only by the tensions of firing their weapons for qualification. Charles Finney, a writer who served with the 15th in the late 1920s, left an enchanting picture of the camp there:

> All we did was eat and swim and shoot on the target range, and drink beer at night at Jawbone Charlie's back of the camp. . . . Reveille was at four-thirty in the morning. Lights were out at night at 9 P.M. Camp activity usually stopped at noon. Almost every afternoon we took naps before going swimming. . . . "Maskee the uniform," the sergeants would say monotonously. *Maskee* is one of the most wonderful words in any language. It means, roughly, "just do as you please."

For those needing more relaxation than drinking beer at Jawbone Charlie's, there was a small brothel close at hand. In a reassuring display of New Deal–inspired patriotism, a sign in its window read: NRA, We Do Our Part.

THUS DID THE 15TH Infantry live comfortably within its cocoon, and only rarely did the harsh realities of the Chinese political-military world intrude into its otherwise carefree existence. The so-called Warlord Wars of the mid-1920s were such a time, and they provided the 15th with its few real harum-scarum military adventures. But, to use a modern rubric, they turned out to be more peacekeeping than war making.

The term *Warlord War* itself needs more precise definition. Warlords, or *tuchuns*, were provincial military governors who recruited personal mercenary armies. The *tuchuns* were a colorful lot, to say the least. Barbara Tuchman wrote that the fearsome Chang Tsung-chang was said

> to have "the physique of an elephant, the brain of a pig and the temperament of a tiger" and to be "dangerous even to look at." . . . A former wharf coolie in his youth, nearly seven feet tall, Chang bore the nickname "Three Things Not Known,"—how much money he had, how many soldiers and how many concubines. . . . He was also known as "Old Eighty-six" because the height of a pile of that number of silver dollars reputedly represented the length of the most valued portion of his anatomy in action.

Cut from similar cloth was Marshal Chang Tso-lin. Known as the "Mukden Tiger," he was first a common private, then an uncommon bandit, before becoming the master of Manchuria. At the other end of the spectrum was Marshal Wu Pei-fu, a highly cultivated mandarin who had even passed the classical examinations. Marshal Feng Yu-hsiang was in a league of his own; he was called the "Christian General," and he manifested his religious zeal by having his troops baptized wholesale with a fire hose. He had enlightened social views, and his troops marched to songs with such lyrics as "We must not drink or smoke," and "We must not gamble or visit whores."

The word *army,* when applied to the forces of the warlords, must be taken with a grain of salt. Hsi-Hseng Chi, a historian of the phenomenon, has written:

> Weapons were few and not standard. Sometimes there were more officers than soldiers, more soldiers than rifles, and more rifles than bullets. . . . [The armies themselves] were sarcastically dubbed "the two-gun armies," one gun being the regular military rifle, the other being the long opium pipe, also standard equipment. In times of military reverses, the soldiers would not hesitate to abandon the gun in order to keep the pipe.

The wars these armies fought are monuments of muddle, comprehensible only to the most diligent student. An unending square dance, the warlord alliances were in a continual state of constitution and dissolution, in which double-crossing one's confederate was as natural as breathing. It was even difficult to tell winners from losers, because the battles were rarely decisive. In fact, the battles themselves were frequently only illusory encounters, the outcome having been negotiated beforehand. In the euphemism of the time, they had been fought with "silver bullets."

This military hurly-burly with its attendant civil chaos was of little interest to the Can Do Boys, walled up in their pleasant *Mei kuo ying p'an,* as the American compound was called. But in late 1924, northern China was suddenly aswarm as three opposing warlord armies infested the area around Tientsin. As many as 100,000 troops a week streamed down upon the city and lapped at its gates. They came on foot and on horseback; they jammed troop trains, steamers, and barges. Within Tientsin, both Chinese and foreign inhabitants were panic-stricken, fearing—not without reason—the hell-raising that would likely occur should the warlords go on a rampage within the city. The Chinese regulars in Tientsin were confined to their barracks under the watchful eyes of their officers, lest they get out of hand or, worse, get into an unintentional scrap with the warlords. But the biggest threat to tranquillity came from the surrounding countryside. The plains west of the city teemed with the bedraggled flotsam of the contending armies, victors and vanquished alike, all drawn as if by some magnet toward fat, prosperous, tempting Tientsin. Keeping this leaderless, hungry rabble under control was the most pressing consideration.

The international troops, including the 15th Infantry, fanned out in a wide arc on the outskirts of Tientsin, setting up positions and barricades at every important access to the city: roads, railroads, dikes, canals, and bridges. At these stations, the warlord troops were to be fed, disarmed, and persuaded to give the foreign-concession areas of Tientsin a wide berth as they made their desperate way around the city. The 15th's sector was seven miles long and consisted of five large outposts, with three smaller ones in the intervals. Although these strongpoints looked menacing enough and bristled with arms, the weapons were unloaded. Rather than risk the danger of an accidental shootout, the American outpost commanders were ordered to dissuade the renegades by means of "bluff, entreaty and expostulation." However, should the bluffs, entreaties, and expostulations fall on deaf ears, the greater part of the regiment was back at the compound, helmets issued, guns loaded, packs on, ready to ride to the rescue at a moment's notice.

Happily, things never got that far, although there were plenty of close calls. The individual outpost commanders were granted wide latitude in the discharge of their delicate assignments, and they performed with admirable professionalism. George C. Marshall reported, "Many of the officers carried out their missions . . . with guns or knives pointed at their stomachs." In the 15th's most glorious episode, a single captain and nine men faced down 5,000 warlord troops. Fortunately, they were not a ragtag mob but an organized unit, advancing in open order with bayonets fixed. The captain and his opposite number parlayed in Chinese for what must have seemed like an eternity, after which—honor satisfied—the Chinese officer ordered his troops to withdraw. Matthew B. Ridgway reported a similar encounter in which he and two other mounted volunteers "accompanied" a 12,000-man force as it skirted the city. As always, the 15th was concerned with the proper way of doing things. As the regimental yearbook summed up this typical 15th Infantry problem: "To shoot or not to shoot; to salute or not to salute." For the Old China Hands, these questions were, no doubt, of equal importance.

By early 1926, things had returned to normal, or to what passed for normal, in China. The small rural villages that came under the protection of the 15th Infantry during the late unpleasantness, realizing that they had escaped plunder and pillage by a hairbreadth, expressed their appreciation by presenting the regiment with a stone monument. It remained in the compound until the 15th left China, and today it stands in front of the officers club at Fort Benning, Georgia. But however touching the sentiment expressed by the village elders, there was no denying that the brushes with the warlords were too close for comfort, an opinion that General Connor forthrightly expressed in his annual report: "We escaped conflict by as narrow a margin as I considered possible."

It took twelve more years and the danger of a real war—not a warlord war—to finally get the 15th Infantry brought home. In the mid-1930s Japan became ever more deeply embroiled in what was euphemistically referred to as the "China Incident"—actually, a full-scale invasion—and in December 1937 Japan came to blows with the U.S. Navy, when the American gunboat *Panay* was sunk on the Yangtze River. Apologies and crocodile tears notwithstanding, tempers were frayed. Both sides were acutely aware that the slightest barroom scuffle—a regular feature of garrison life at the best of times—might easily escalate into warfare. In March

1938, Japanese and American commands breathed a collective sigh of relief as the 15th packed up and marched into history.

Some years earlier, an American officer about to leave China wrote that he hated to be giving up his "front row seat in the midst of the performance." But in China, he noted, a "front row seat is only a step from the stage and this drama may easily involve the audience." After twenty-six years, it was definitely time for the 15th Infantry to exit, with fanfare.

*AUTUMN 1993*

---

**Elihu Rose teaches military history at New York University.**

# 26

# The Final Scrimmage

## By Thaddeus Holt

*When Germany invaded Poland on Friday, September 1, 1939, and thus triggered World War II, the United States was ill prepared for any war— large, small, or in between. Including reserves, the army numbered fewer than 200,000 men, which in size placed it in the category of the Portuguese and Bulgarian armies. In terms of the percent of its population serving in the military, the United States stood forty-fifth in the world. President Roosevelt, though approving substantial air and naval increases, proved reluctant to augment the size of the ground forces, and not until the establishment of the draft in the fall of 1940 did the army begin to receive recruits in essential numbers. A year later the army was ready for its first large-scale war games. Held in Louisiana and the Carolinas, these maneuvers would have a critical impact on the development of the army that would do so much to win the Second World War. The war games provided a vital test of leaders, tactics, and weapons, finding some wanting, others not. Although the voluminous writings on the war pay scant attention to these rehearsals, Thaddeus Holt rightly reminds us that they are the "stuff that wins or loses wars."*

Have you heard of the Battle of the Red River? The Battle of Shreveport? The Battle of the Pee Dee? The Second Battle of Camden? They were history's biggest battles in the Western Hemisphere, bigger than Gettysburg or Shiloh, Celaya or Tuyutí; yet not one bullet was fired in anger. They were the "battles" that were "fought" in Louisiana and the Carolinas in the great autumn maneuvers of 1941.

Through 1940 and 1941 General George C. Marshall, U.S. Army chief of staff, and Marshall's own chief of staff, Lieutenant General Lesley J. McNair, had been raising and training an army against the eventuality that the United States might be drawn into the Second World War. The design and building of this force were largely Whitey McNair's work. From disparate materials—national guardsmen, reservists, draftees from the country's first peacetime conscription—he had by the middle of 1941 created a force of

1.4 million men, and the great army-level maneuvers—following earlier division- and corps-level maneuvers—were its final test. They were the first army-versus-army maneuvers in U.S. history.

To some extent their purpose was to test the officers of the National Guard divisions. At least at the higher levels, very few of these passed; and Marshall weeded them out mercilessly. Heartlessly, too, in some eyes, for these were men whose weekends and vacations had been loyally sacrificed over two long dreary decades, and now that they had a chance to serve their country they were being shoved aside to make room for regular officers—or so it seemed to their supporters. Many victims were influential and well connected, and Marshall himself was far more politically attuned than is often realized; but he meant to have the best officer corps he could, and he let the chips fall where they might. To give just a few examples out of very many, Major General Ralph E. Truman of the Missouri National Guard was dropped from command of the 35th ("Santa Fe") Division even though the influential senator Harry Truman was his cousin; Major General Edward Martin of the Pennsylvania National Guard was dropped from command of the 28th ("Keystone") Division even though he was a political power and soon to be governor of his state; Major General Claude Birkenhead of the Texas National Guard was dropped from command of the 36th ("Texas") Division even though he was a prominent San Antonio lawyer with significant political connections; and so on.

As for regular officers, the maneuvers probably did not tell Marshall much that he did not already know. He had spent a lifetime filling his famous "little black book" with notes about officers he had observed. He kept it in his desk drawer. When he learned or observed something about a man, favorable or unfavorable, out the book would come and a note would be made. He may not really have needed it, for he had an elephant's memory for such matters. Once he formed an opinion about a man—which he might do on the basis of a single incident or personal trait—it was not easy to change it. (Injustices sometimes resulted. The best-known case is that of James A. Van Fleet, who was a corps commander by the end of the war and finished with four stars as the American commander in Korea, but who was still a colonel at D-Day because Marshall had him confused with an officer of similar name who was on his blacklist.)

So the 1941 maneuvers were primarily designed not to select people but to test training, organization, and technique. Dull stuff? Not at all; it is the stuff that wins or loses wars.

The most interesting test would be of the organizations and techniques McNair and his colleagues had designed for employing (and defending against) the weapon systems brought to the fore in the European campaigns of 1939–40—tanks, airplanes, paratroops.

Especially tanks. In July 1940, with the world bemused by the armored blitzkriegs in Poland and France after the fall of France, the U.S. Army created an Armored Force. This ended twenty years of dispute as to whether the tank was an independent weapon or merely infantry support, but it left open the key question whether tanks should be used in mass or integrated with other weapons. And was the tank as unstoppable as armor enthusiasts claimed? Or, as McNair suspected, would massed tanks be vulnerable to massed antitank guns—especially if they were rendered at least as mobile as the tanks themselves by being mounted on half-tracks or tank chassis? (Such "tank destroyers" were one of McNair's pet concepts. Most armor officers, on the other hand, thought that the best tank destroyer was another tank.)

Closely related was the question of tactical aviation. The German armored-warfare genius Heinz Guderian paced his panzer divisions to the speed of tanks rather than of foot soldiers, with his infantrymen riding trucks and half-tracks and the Luftwaffe's dive-bombers substituting for slow-moving towed artillery. It was easy to motorize infantry, but could the Air Corps, legally part of the army but de facto a separate and cantankerous service, be induced to set aside its obsession with strategic bombing and tactical interdiction and emulate the brilliantly coordinated close-air-support tactics of Göring's Luftwaffe?

And what about the traditional infantry divisions in this new mobile age? National Guard divisions still followed the old "square" design based on two infantry brigades of two regiments each—huge divisions, ponderous but immensely powerful. Should at least some divisions retain this structure? Or should they all be reorganized into the lighter but more flexible "triangular" three-regiment structure first introduced in the regular divisions in 1937?

Was there any future for horse cavalry? Though in the Great War it had taken a negligible part on the stalemated Western Front, it had played a major one on the Eastern Front and in the Middle East. Did it still have a role in the gasoline age, as the horse soldiers desperately insisted?

Finally, airborne troops. Did the German conquest of Crete portend whole airborne armies? Less extreme, did airborne forces now make true "vertical envelopment" possible, as if at Second Manassas Jackson had descended on Pope's rear from the sky? Or were airborne forces suited only for seizing initial lodgments in enemy territory—or perhaps only for commando-style raids?

For some of these questions McNair's 1941-model army offered at least provisional solutions; others remained open. On the most important question, the role of the tank, the Armored Force's initial structure reflected a fairly rigid concept of massed tank attacks. The armored division was built around an armored brigade of one medium and two light tank regiments; divisional infantry, artillery, and engineers were strictly auxiliaries. There would also be "motorized divisions," essentially regular infantry divisions whose men would ride rather than march, and "armored corps" made up entirely of armored and motorized divisions. All four of the autumn maneuvers would feature a full armored corps, testing whether this approach was sound, or whether the new American units should follow the design of Guderian's panzer divisions, composed of flexible all-arms *Kampfgruppen* (battle groups) that could be tailored to specific missions. And in Louisiana there would be three, in the Carolinas six, independent regiment-size antitank groups to test McNair's concept of mobile antitank guns controlled at corps or army level.

The maneuvers would test air-ground coordination, too. At the last minute the Air Corps—the Army Air Forces, rather, for in June 1941 it was renamed and granted even more autonomy—agreed to participate with substantial forces, forming an Air Task Force to operate with each of the armies. The AAF was so short of dive-bombers, though, that it had to ask the navy to help. Help the navy did, and generously, lending not only four squadrons of dive-bombers but three of fighters and one of torpedo planes. (This inspired Marshall to invite the 1st Marine Division to join the maneuvers, but Admiral Harold R. Stark, chief of naval operations, declined; the marines needed to spend their time on small-unit and amphibious training, he said.)

As for the other issues: Square and triangular divisions would be fighting side by side, enabling direct comparison of the two structures. Cavalry would get a full and fair trial, with at least a cavalry regiment, sometimes even a division, in every corps and at army level, and some of these would be "mechanized" with supplemental motor transport. Only the infant airborne arm would have less than a fair test, for only a single parachute battalion—in Louisiana, only one company—was yet available.

MCNAIR AND HIS operations deputy, Brigadier General Mark W. Clark, planned four big maneuvers in the eastern United States for the fall of 1941 (plus a separate, smaller maneuver for Fourth Army on the West Coast). The first two, in Louisiana in September, would pit Lieutenant General Ben Lear's "Red" Second Army against Lieutenant General Walter Krueger's "Blue" Third Army. The second two, in the Carolinas in November, would pit Lieutenant General Hugh A. Drum's "Blue" First Army against Major General Oscar W. Griswold's "Red" IV Corps—smaller, but armored and motorized.

Prominently featured in all four would be the 1st and 2nd Armored Divisions, commanded respectively by Major General Bruce Magruder and Major General George S. Patton, Jr. Magruder was an infantryman, not a particularly colorful character, whom the press hardly noticed at the time and whom history has largely forgotten. By contrast, the flamboyant Patton—"squeak-voiced Major-General George S. Patton, Jr.," said *Time*, "who hides much military culture behind the Army's best smoke screen of profanity"—was already a media favorite. Reporters had not yet thought up "Old Blood and Guts"; instead, in honor of his odd-looking green tank coveralls with matching helmet, they called him "The Green Hornet," after the hero of a popular radio program. Patton was a cavalryman, independently wealthy. (When assigned to Hawaii he had sailed there in his own yacht, shipping his string of polo ponies separately; his house in Washington is now the Australian embassy.) He had competed in the modern pentathlon in the 1912 Olympics, served as Pershing's aide in the pursuit of Pancho Villa, and been wounded in France. Patton was a tank enthusiast and one of the founders of the old Tank Corps in 1918, and his assignment to command one of the original armored divisions was a near-miraculous reprieve from the stagnation of the dreary interwar years. Many of his fellow officers wondered whether the ebullient "Georgie" was suited to high command. In a confidential memorandum to Marshall after the Louisiana maneuvers, McNair's dry comment about Patton was "Good; division possibly his ceiling."

Since people could not really be killed, shells really fired, bridges really blown up, tanks really burned, an elaborate set of umpires' rules was worked out. Firepower points were assigned (one point for a rifle, six for a .30-caliber machine gun, and so on), and when hostile units met, the umpires would decide who advanced and who fell back based on comparative firepower scores. Human "casualties" would not drop out; a unit's firepower would simply be reduced in proportion to them, while a "destroyed" tank was deemed "resurrected" and returned to its unit at midnight after its "destruction." The impact area of artillery fire would be marked with flags, and casualties would be assessed against a unit caught in the area. Engineers would simulate the laying of demolition charges and roadblocks, and if properly done the umpires would rule the bridge or road out of commission and units would have to work around the obstruction. (At least once, naturally, a commander reproved for marching his force across a theoretically destroyed bridge told the umpire his men were theoretically swimming.) There were casualty percentages for troops attacked by airplanes, and loss percentages for air units exposed to antiaircraft fire.

Most controversial—reflecting McNair's bias—were the tank and antitank rules. An antitank gun was scored as knocking out up to one tank a minute and was given an unrealistically long range; the .50-caliber machine gun was allowed as an antitank weapon; tanks could knock out antitank guns only by "overrunning" them; for the Carolina maneuvers GHQ added the rule that a tank could be knocked out by an infantryman hitting it with a flour-bag "hand grenade." ("If hand grenades could destroy tanks we would quit building them," groused Major General Charles L. Scott of I Armored Corps.) Inconsistently, infantry within 100 yards of an enemy tank was deemed immobilized.

Journalists swarmed to cover the shows and found they had to hustle. They were assigned to one side or the other and were subject to capture by the opponent, so they had to be careful; and they got few briefings, so they had to scramble around the countryside looking for stories in taxis rented for them by the government at ten dollars a day, or in the newfangled sassy little vehicle that the Armored Force called a "peep" (the infantry called it a "jeep," and that was the name that eventually stuck). Eric Sevareid, who covered the maneuvers for CBS as a twenty-eight-year-old reporter fresh from the European war, told a *Time* colleague: "War in Louisiana is rougher than war in Europe. Over there you sit around waiting for communiqués. Over here you go to the front or you don't find much to report." (Half a century later, Sevareid recalled that many of his colleagues were at least as interested in personal strategies as in military ones, notably how to get a drink amid the patchwork of wet, dry, and in-between counties that made up the 1941 South.)

For the average soldier the maneuvers, like real war, meant hard work and misery with little idea of the big picture. In Louisiana they meant mud and dust and bugs and sudden downpours; in the Carolinas they meant ice on the water buckets in the morning, and a scramble to find kerosene heaters. (Guns without bullets could still hurt, as Private Bill Mauldin of the 45th ("Thunderbird") Division recalled: "Blank cartridges use wads to hold their powder charges; at very close range the wads emerge as projectiles and hurt like hell." The chow, as always, was a prime complaint. It was mostly the primitive early version of the C ration, or prepared lunches consisting of "1 sandwich, ham; 1 sandwich, jam; 1 apple, eating." The chicory-laden coffee of Louisiana was startling to outlanders. ("You don't stir this stuff, you crank it," somebody said to Hanson W. Baldwin of the *New York Times*.) Thanksgiving fell during the first phase in the Carolina maneuvers, but there was to be no turkey till after the "battle"; a soldier who got a piece of fried chicken from a rolling field kitchen counted himself lucky.

At least the soldiers' physical condition was good, and they had some real equipment—a sharp improvement over the first maneuvers in the summer of 1940, when National Guard units armed with wooden artillery and trucks with TANK painted on their sides lumbered about the countryside, lawyers and bankers in colonel's and general's uniforms puffing to keep up. By 1941 the men were in shape, and while wooden guns and stovepipe mortars were still abundant, there was far more equipment than there had been a year before.

There was yet no talk of "GIs" or "dogfaces." The infantrymen were "doughboys" or "doughs" like their fathers in 1917. And they looked like their fathers. They still wore the doughboy's trademark, the flat British-style tin hat; the familiar pot-shaped M1 helmet had only been approved in June 1941, and in the maneuvers early production models were worn by only a handful of officers. (To distinguish friend from foe, only one side in each maneuver wore helmets.) And many of the doughs still carried the old reliable bolt-action Springfield, though the War Department promised in late September that all frontline troops would have the new semiautomatic Garand by the end of October.

They got into the swing of things, and the adrenalin flowed as if the battle were real—sometimes tragically so, as when two soldiers drowned after they volunteered to swim a flooded river, and another was blinded when an overenthusiastic opponent hurled a smoke bomb into his tank. There were any number of fistfights between members of opposing armies and plenty of rage at umpires' alleged bad calls. And there were some imaginative efforts to lend a touch of realism. Signal Corps sound trucks roved about playing loud records of bullets, artillery, airplanes, and tank sirens. As Red columns fell back toward Shreveport in the second Louisiana maneuver, Blue planes showered them with leaflets: "Your commanders are withholding from you the terrible fact of your impending defeat. . . . Your food stores have been captured. No one is going to bring up any of the steaks that the men of the Third Army are going to have tonight. Rout, disaster, hunger, sleepless nights in the forest are ahead of you. Surrender while there is still time." Civilians joined in the enthusiasm: The citizens of Shreveport, sporting red armbands to show their solidarity with their Red "defenders," rang church bells to celebrate deliverance from Krueger's invaders and cheered, "We're for Lear."

Still, you could not get entirely away from normal life. The umpires stopped the Battle of Shreveport partly because street fighting would disrupt rush hour. At a lull in the savage struggle for Mount Carmel, Louisiana, newsboys and soda-pop vendors promptly appeared as if by magic. Lieutenant F.I. Fox, the Sergeant York of the Louisiana maneuvers, put twenty Blue officers and thirty-five enlisted men out of action in a daring foray behind enemy lines but was captured when held up by a red light. And when in his swing around Shreveport Patton was cut off from supplies, he cheated a bit by buying gasoline for his tanks from civilian filling stations.

The horse soldiers knew what they had at stake; Lieutenant Guy Chipman of the 1st Armored Division recalls running into an old pal, Lieutenant Booth Thomas of the cavalry, somewhere in Louisiana, who reported that he and his friends were "working their tails off trying to prove that horse cavalry was still OK."

LIEUTENANT GENERAL WALTER KRUEGER, the Blue commander in Louisiana, was known as a friend to enlisted men and to the National Guard—reflecting his own career, for he had started as a private and worked his way up to three stars the hard way. German-born, he had translated a number of German military texts and was a recognized expert on the German army. In his later wartime command Krueger would be famous for his slowness, but his Louisiana performance was notable for speed and flexibility. (The credit for this is doubtless due in great measure to his chief of staff, Colonel Dwight D. Eisenhower. Ike Eisenhower was universally recognized as a comer. Though his academic career at West Point had been undistinguished and he had missed going to France in 1918, he had graduated at the head of his class in all the army schools thereafter; MacArthur, with whom he had worked closely, had thought him the best officer in the army; and Pershing had specifically recommended him to Marshall.)

By contrast, the Red commander, Lieutenant General Ben Lear, was a by-the-book soldier who got off to a bad start in the public eye when he disciplined soldiers for whistling at shorts-clad female golfers, and he was derided as "Yoo-Hoo Lear" by the press.

The theater of operations was a substantial chunk of the middle of Louisiana and a sliver of adjoining Texas. Its dominant terrain features were the Red River, slicing diagonally northwest to southeast from Shreveport to Alexandria, thence east to the Mississippi, and Peason Ridge, an east–west range of high ground in Kisatchie National Forest. American soldiers had long known this region well and unfavorably. A century before, Lieutenant U.S. Grant, stationed in the area when it was the U.S. borderland with the independent Republic of Texas, had recorded that "the troublesome insects of creation . . . abound here. The swamps are full of alligators and the woods full of redbugs and ticks." It was the scene of Banks's disastrous Red River campaign in 1864. Colonel Eisenhower wrote to a friend that "All the old-timers say we are going into a God-awful spot, to live with mud, malaria, mosquitoes and misery." (He might have added "monsoons": It was hurricane season, and the maneuvers opened in a subtropical downpour.)

The first Louisiana maneuver was designed to test whether numbers—Krueger's Blue army of 270,000, concentrated north of Lake Charles—could be offset by mobility—Lear's 130,000-man Red army, concentrated north of the Red River. The centerpiece of the Red army was I Armored Corps, built around Magruder's and Patton's two armored divisions. The two sides' orders were in effect simply to have at one another. D day was September 15.

Lear planned to cross the Red River and launch an armored attack from the west end of Peason Ridge into Krueger's left flank and rear. Patton's tanks got a toehold on Peason Ridge by nightfall the first day, September 15, but Lear's infantry moved more clumsily. Krueger swept forward, reorienting overnight his axis of advance toward the northwest, and by nightfall on the 16th had almost pushed Patton off Peason Ridge. Lear wasted the 17th while Krueger pressed on. Lear's attack on the 18th met with disaster. Magruder's main force bogged down in swamps and densely wooded hills; the Blues hit it hard, surrounded it, and captured its gasoline train. Meanwhile, Patton, in the bitterest fighting of the maneuver, failed to break through at Mount Carmel. (Mount Carmel was a tiny clearing in the woods with three frame buildings and a cemetery, but five roads met there, and even though three of these were impassable to civilian automobiles, it was to the Kisatchie National Forest what Bastogne would be to the Ardennes three years later.)

Sure that Lear's armor was pinned down, Krueger released his reserves. The Reds nearly panicked as cavalry and armor were entangled in a traffic jam while Blue cavalrymen infiltrated among them and Blue aircraft pounded them. The Red armor stabilized the front, though with heavy losses, but Lear's left wing continued to crumble. By the afternoon of the 19th Krueger's men had fought their way to the eastern and southern approaches to Natchitoches when headquarters halted the maneuver, and the Battle of the Red River was over.

There was only a five days' pause for logistical regrouping, and then began the second Louisiana maneuver. This one was designed to test the defensive ability of a smaller army, Lear's Reds, against a greatly superior attacker, Krueger's Blues. Headquarters, I Armored Corps, and Patton's 2nd Armored Division were transferred to Krueger. His orders were to capture Shreveport and destroy the Red forces; Lear's were to defend Shreveport till the arrival of imaginary reinforcements. Krueger planned an advance straight for Shreveport, with his armor to be unleashed once the Red forces were engaged and fixed. Lear's strategy was delay, falling back to a succession of defensive lines while destroying every bridge and culvert left behind. D day was September 24.

Lear's strategy worked, slowing Krueger to a crawl. So Colonel Eisenhower devised a drastic plan to bring Lear to battle through a sweeping armored and motorized envelopment of the Red western flank. Patton himself took a small force on a wide outer sweep while the bulk of his forces swung around on an inner arc. Swinging wide through Texas, Patton covered nearly 200 miles in twenty-four hours. Lear took no aggressive countermeasures, and on the 27th Patton veered around behind Shreveport and closed in on the town. Meanwhile, on the main front Krueger continued struggling through the demolitions the Reds had left behind. By the 28th Red and Blue main forces were at last locked in battle at Mansfield. Patton split his already small command, driving into the western edge of Shreveport with one column while the other ferried the Red River north of town, swung around to the east, and captured the airport. Lear finally reacted to Patton's drives by sending elements of Magruder's 1st Armored Division to oppose him north of Shreveport—when GHQ terminated the Battle of Shreveport.

THE SCENE SHIFTED now to the more hospitable terrain of the Carolinas, where Lieutenant General Hugh Drum's 195,000-man Blue First Army would face the 100,000-man Red IV Corps (augmented by I Armored Corps), under Major General Oscar W. Griswold. The object was to explore an offensive contest between Drum's big force, largely infantry, and Griswold's smaller, highly mechanized force.

Griswold was new to corps command but knowledgeable in mobile warfare. Drum was a self-important stuffed shirt who had expected to be made chief of staff instead of Marshall; except for a surprising airmindedness, his thinking had not advanced much beyond 1918, when he had headed the staff that planned the Saint-Mihiel offensive. He detested Patton: At a polo match in Hawaii a few years before, when Drum had rebuked Patton for his strong language, the civilian players—drawn from Honolulu's moneyed elite, with whom the wealthy Colonel and Mrs. Patton (but not General and Mrs. Drum) hobnobbed on terms of easy equality—had humiliated Drum by standing up for Patton. This had not prevented his asking Patton to intercede with Patton's old mentor Pershing on Drum's behalf when Drum was campaigning to be appointed chief of staff. Indeed, during the maneuvers Drum seems not to have been inhibited by any very punctilious sense of honor; at least three times he blatantly cheated on the rules, twice by stationing troops in advance of the restraining line before H hour, and once by moving men in trucks that, under the rules, were to be used only for carrying rations and were thus immune from capture.

The theater of war was an area some 90 miles by 150 miles, lying south and east of Charlotte and extending to the Columbia–Camden–Cheraw–Fort Bragg line. Its dominant terrain features were the big southerly-flowing river systems that cut it roughly into thirds: in the west the Catawba-Wateree River running from near Charlotte down past Camden, and in the east the Pee Dee flowing down past Cheraw. The key to the middle ground between the rivers was the town of Monroe, from which paved roads radiated in six directions.

For the first maneuver the "international boundary" was the Pee Dee, though Griswold was directed to stay behind the Catawba till H hour. The two sides' orders were mirror images of each other: Drum was to cross the Pee Dee into Red country and keep the Reds from crossing the Catawba in force; Griswold was to cross the Catawba and drive to the Pee Dee to prevent the Blue invasion. Drum's plan was methodical and conventional, crossing the Pee Dee on a seventy-five-mile front. Griswold planned to race his three mobile divisions to the Pee Dee to contain the Blue bridgeheads while his infantry divisions secured Monroe; these would then take over the job of bridgehead containment, freeing the armor for a concentrated stroke.

The maneuver had a gratifying curtain raiser for George Patton. At 6:30 A.M. on D day, November 16, the Reds began crossing the Catawba, reconnaissance units racing for the Pee Dee; some of Patton's men actually crossed it—and captured General Drum. He was soon released, and the maneuver went on. Red air and armor slowed Drum's buildup in the center and south, but the Red mobile force lost coherence as the day wore on. By sunrise on the 17th, Drum had six divisions across and opened his attack, bending the north of Griswold's line back at right angles and seizing Cheraw in the south until an end run by Patton drove the Blues out of the town. On the 18th Drum returned to the attack, recaptured Cheraw, and thrust on to Chesterfield in the south, while pushing forward against stubborn resistance in the center and pounding away in the north with a threatened envelopment of Griswold's whole command. On the 19th and 20th Magruder's 1st Armored, seeking to make a flank and rear attack, was battered into hopeless shape by Blue antitank units. Drum closed in for the kill, while Griswold ordered a general retreat to a new V-shaped line with its point at Monroe and its flank refused toward the Catawba. At dawn on the 21st Drum assaulted this line across the whole front. By 8:30 A.M. Monroe had fallen. Patton opened a counterattack, but at 8:40 A.M. headquarters terminated the maneuver, and the Battle of the Pee Dee was ended.

For the second Carolina maneuver the "international boundary" ran east–west, along the Monroe–Wadesboro highway. Griswold's orders were to organize and defend a bridgehead covering the crossing of the Wateree at Camden. Drum was not told Griswold's mission; he was informed only that strong Red forces advancing from the southeast were reported crossing the Wateree near Camden and was ordered to destroy hostile forces east of the Catawba-Wateree line.

On D day, November 25, Drum advanced cautiously while his aviation bombed the Pee Dee bridges from Cheraw south. Griswold readied two concentric defensive lines covering Camden, while combined-arms columns from his three mechanized divisions conducted spoiling attacks. These were successful: Patton found and turned the Blue line west of Monroe, while the Red 4th Motorized Division struck Monroe itself. Thinking that the Reds planned to make the Monroe front their main defensive line, Drum ordered Monroe held while his left struck westward from Cheraw against the Red rear, ejecting the Reds from Monroe and Cheraw on the 26th.

Then Drum had a stroke of McClellan's luck: A Blue reconnaissance detachment captured a full set of Red plans. Drum quickly issued new orders focused on Camden. Aided by a snafu that left the Red front between Monroe and the Catawba thinly held, he had victory in his grasp by the 27th. But the Reds mounted an armored attack toward Pageland south of Monroe, and, though Patton had to fend off counterattacks, Magruder's tanks pierced deep into Blue territory. Instead of driving home his own attack, Drum threw away his victory by sending forces to contain Magruder and diverting others to attack the Reds in the rear. But Griswold had no intention of overextending his breakthrough; in the afternoon he ordered his whole force back into the Camden perimeter. Drum issued a triumphant end-of-the-day message to his troops announcing that the Reds east of the Catawba were encircled.

He learned differently on the morning of the 28th, when he found himself defending against vigorous armored attacks. He ordered a reinforced attack toward Camden, but it accomplished little against Red mechanized forces. Griswold had ordered his armored divisions back into the Camden perimeter for more counterattacks the next day, when GHQ ended the Second Battle of Camden.

And the big shows were over.

IN ONE RESPECT the maneuvers were an unqualified success: They gave American officers priceless hands-on experience in moving large units. Until the Battle of the Red River, no American since Grant and Sherman had maneuvered as many as 100,000 men in the open field, for the handful of officers with large-scale experience had gained it in the positional warfare of 1918. Years later, Mark Clark recalled how in the scramble of activity after Pearl Harbor he had thought to himself: " 'How lucky we are that we just had maneuvers.' We'd moved a corps. Two or three months before that you would say, 'How do you move a corps?' "

The maneuvers were only partially successful in their second major purpose, to test organization and doctrine. The conclusions Marshall and McNair drew from them defined many aspects of the U.S. Army of World War II. Events proved some of these right, and some wrong.

As to the preeminent issue, the tank, they were partly right and partly wrong. Still fixed on the notion of mass tank attacks (and disregarding the view of the chief of the Armored Force that "We were licked by a set of umpires' rules"), McNair pointed to the success of more than 700 antitank guns in holding back an equal number of tanks in the Carolinas as showing that "the tank could be stopped." This meant full speed ahead on McNair's "tank-destroyer" program—scores of battalions of specially designed antitank vehicles, to be controlled at division and higher levels. This program— unique to the U.S. Army—never worked out as expected and was quietly abandoned soon after the Second World War was over.

In a parallel (and infinitely more successful) development, experiences like Magruder's disaster in the Battle of the Pee Dee and his and Patton's troubles in the Kisatchie National Forest confirmed the view that the massed-tanks approach was misguided and that tanks must have support from the traditional arms. In 1942 the armored division received more infantry and artillery and fewer tanks, and a version of Guderian's *Kampfgruppen* design was adopted: The division was built around "combat commands"—brigade-level commanders and their headquarters staffs, to which the division commander would assign the mix of tanks, infantry, and artillery needed to perform a specific task. Thereafter, the idea of entire armored corps was dropped (as well as the "motorized-division" concept); instead, the prototypical American corps was to consist of one armored and two infantry divisions. And in a parallel recognition that ordinary infantry often needed tank support, independent tank battalions were formed for attachment to infantry divisions. These were happy changes, for thus were born the formations that raced across France in August 1944, punched through to Bastogne that Christmas, and swarmed over the Reich in the spring of 1945.

As for the infantry, the maneuvers convinced many officers that there was, as General Griswold said, "a distinct need for both the triangular and the square division." But during 1942 all infantry divisions were "triangularized." This defiance of the maneuver experience was a less happy decision than was the armored division reorganization. It broke up many effective and experienced formations, and there would be times—in the Normandy hedgerows, in the Hürtgen Forest, at the Gustav and Gothic lines—when American generals would yearn for the brute might and staying power of the square division.

The maneuvers provided but half a loaf with respect to air-ground cooperation; the whole loaf was not to come for three years. The aviators finally accepted ground support. But they insisted that the maneuvers had shown that it could effectively be controlled by army-level air-support groups subordinate to the theater air commander. This meant that a frontline ground unit might or might not get the air support it requested, depending on the views of an air officer in a faraway air headquarters. (The air task force supporting Krueger's Third Army had far outperformed its opposition. Its commander, Major General Herbert A. Dargue, had allowed air liaison officers attached to particular corps or divisions to deal directly with operations officers at the air bases supporting their units. But Dargue died in the opening days of the war.) Not till France in 1944 would permanent air-support groups attached to individual armies be fielded, and air officers be found who wholeheartedly accepted the ground-support role—officers like the legendary Major General Elwood ("Pete") Quesada of IX Tactical Air Command, who permanently assigned a flight of fighter-bombers to each combat command of the armored divisions he supported, together with an aircraft radio and air liaison officer in each combat command headquarters.

The 1941 maneuvers saw one lasting innovation in the air. The Piper, Taylor, and Aeronca firms had lent the army eleven light "cub" planes. These proved so useful for both spotting and general liaison that such "grasshoppers" became established in the army's inventory—the forebears of modern army aviation.

For the horse cavalry the Carolina maneuvers were the last ride. They had made every effort, and they simply had not measured up. All-horse units had been tried. "Horse-portee" units, in which the horses were loaded onto trailer trucks for long-distance movements, and then unloaded and ridden into action, had been tried. The results were uniformly unsatisfactory in comparison with the performance of motorized units. McNair concluded that horse cavalry was no longer viable, and by the end of 1942 all its steeds were gone. The 1st Cavalry Division kept the name for sentimental reasons, but fought in the Southwest Pacific as an infantry division.

Airborne doctrine might have suffered a comparable setback. The tiny airborne units available had been used only for small-scale commando-type operations, and the maneuvers suggested to some officers that the airborne role should be limited to these—and, for good measure, that drops should be made at a distance from the target. Fortunately—perhaps because he was so intently focused on the tank-versus-antitank problem—McNair did not draw this conclusion, and five full-size airborne divisions would see action in Europe and the Philippines.

Finally, the maneuvers served well their third and major purpose: They tested the quality of essential training—and found it wanting. Many small-unit commanders had failed to show a grasp of basic tactics. Communications, liaison, and reconnaissance had often been poor. Too many orders had been slow in preparation and vague or ambiguous. Colonel J. Lawton Collins, chief of staff of VII Corps in Lear's army, thought that at the lowest level the maneuvers might have done more harm than good, by developing bad habits. "It is almost impossible to get American soldiers to take seriously attacks from planes that simply fly overhead," he wrote in later years. "Troops tend to stick to the roads instead of moving in deployed formations across country, and they fail to take cover from theoretical bombardment, artillery or machine-gun fire." Worst, perhaps, was this lack of air discipline. Troops had stood in the open to gawk at hostile aircraft, and McNair had growled, "There can be no excuse for another Guadalajara," referring to the savaging of Italian troops by Soviet aircraft in Spain in March 1937. (But there were to be near-Guadalajaras in North Africa nevertheless.)

ON DECEMBER 3 the topmost brass—Secretary of War Stimson and his under and assistant secretaries, Generals Marshall, McNair, and Clark, and Marshall's three deputy chiefs of staff—assembled in Washington for a postmortem. They were not wholly happy with what they had learned. Though McNair opined that the maneuvers had settled the "outstanding question" about whether the tank could be stopped, nobody was pleased with the results of a year's training at the individual and small-unit levels. And there were other questions. The future size of the army was itself an unknown. President Roosevelt had decided to augment the navy and the army air forces at the ground forces' expense. The national guardsmen would begin going home in February. A program of remedial small-unit training for the remaining regulars and draftees had already been decreed for 1942. But to what end?

On the other side of the world, Vice Admiral Chuichi Nagumo's carrier task force was plodding through the harsh gray seas of the North Pacific. In four days it would be off the coast of Oahu.

*Of the four Red and Blue top commanders only Krueger held wartime army command, heading Sixth Army under MacArthur. Drum, expecting to be the second Pershing, scorned Marshall's offer to make him chief of staff to Chiang Kai-shek—and that was the end of his career. Lear held Pentagon posts and in 1945 went to Europe as Eisenhower's manpower deputy.*

*Griswold commanded a corps in Guadalcanal and the Philippines and was unsuccessfully proposed by MacArthur to take over Tenth Army when its commander was killed on Okinawa. Of the other corps commanders in the maneuvers, only Major General Robert C. Richardson, who led VII Corps under Lear, and Major General Lloyd R. Fredendall, who led II Corps under Drum, held major wartime commands. Richardson was commanding general of army forces in the central Pacific—essentially an administrative post; Fredendall commanded II Corps in North Africa, and was shipped home after his disastrous failure at Kasserine Pass in 1943.*

*Division commanders fared little better. Of thirteen National Guard generals who commanded divisions in the maneuvers, only Major General John C. Persons of the 31st ("Dixie") Division, in civilian life a Birmingham banker, and Major General Robert S. Beightler of the 37th ("Buckeye") Division, in civilian life Ohio's director of highways, showed the military talent to lead their divisions in war (as both did, with distinction, in the southwest Pacific and the Philippines). Five more held rear-echelon jobs during the war, and six were let go entirely. Of sixteen regular army division commanders, one, Patton, went on to army command in Europe; two, Sultan of the 38th ("Cyclone") and Hartle of the 35th ("Santa Fe"), became theater commanders or deputy theater commanders; two, Swift of the 1st Cavalry and Millikin of the 2nd Cavalry, led corps in Luzon and Europe; two more, Hester of the 43rd and Walker of the 36th ("Texas") Division, led their divisions in combat; most of the remaining nine saw only training, garrison, or other special duty, and some were simply retired.*

*The four air-group commanders fared better at wartime assignments, but most had bad personal luck. Major General Millard F. Harmon, Lear's air-group commander, became the top air commander in the South, and then the central, Pacific; he was lost in flight in 1945. Colonel William E. Kepner, Drum's air-group commander, headed the great fighter command of Eighth Air Force in Europe. Major General Herbert A. Dargue, Krueger's highly effective air-group commander, crashed and died five days after Pearl Harbor, on his way to take over the Hawaiian Department. And Colonel Asa N. Duncan, Griswold's air-group commander, died in Europe in 1943 after serving as temporary commander of Eighth Air Force.*

*A number of staff officers and junior commanders went on from the 1941 maneuvers to wartime success. Aside from those who eventually led divisions, Colonel J. Lawton Collins, chief of staff of Lear's VII Corps; Brigadier General Willis Crittenberger, commander of Patton's armored brigade; and Colonel Manton S. Eddy, commander of Drum's "anti-airborne detachment," all had commanded corps in action by the end of the war.*

*And then, of course, there was Lieutenant General Krueger's chief of staff, Colonel Dwight D. Eisenhower.*

*WINTER 1992*

Thaddeus Holt is the author of the earlier article on the Mexican War.

# 27

# Why Weren't We Warned?

## By David Kahn

*For America, the greatest single controversy of the Second World War has always been the attack on Pearl Harbor. The success of the Japanese assault seared the psyche of the nation. How, with the United States reading the highest-level Japanese diplomatic codes, could the country be caught by surprise? How, despite a November 27, 1941, warning of imminent war with Japan, could the Pacific Fleet be found at anchor? How, despite the brilliant and heroic efforts of its gnomelike cryptanalysts, could the nation have been so unprepared? Some historians have argued that the answer lies with human failure, others that it rests with criminal conspiracy. In its fixation on self-flagellation, however, America has usually ignored another possibility: The answer may center not on what the Americans did wrong, but on what the Japanese did right.*

Fifty years later, Americans still wonder how Japan's surprise attack on the pride of the Pacific Fleet could have succeeded. The joint congressional committee that in 1945 and 1946 investigated the attack put the question sharply:

Why, with some of the finest intelligence available in our history, with the almost certain knowledge that war was at hand, with plans that contemplated the precise type of attack that was executed by Japan on the morning of December 7—Why was it possible for a Pearl Harbor to occur?

The "finest intelligence" came from code breaking. Solving the secret messages of a hostile power is like putting a mirror behind the cards a player is holding, like eavesdropping on the huddles of a football team. It is nearly always the best form of intelligence. It is faster and more trustworthy than spies, who have to write up and transmit their reports and who are always suspected of setting up or falling for a deception. It sees farther into the future than aerial reconnaissance, which detects only what is present. It is broader in scope than the interrogations of prisoners, who know little more than what they have experienced. And it is usually cheaper and less obtrusive, hence more secret, than all of these. But it has a serious double-barreled failing: It cannot provide information that a nation has not put onto the airwaves, and its apparent omniscience and its immediacy seduce its recipients into thinking they are getting all the other nation's secrets.

This is one of the lessons of Pearl Harbor. American code breakers performed prodigies, giving remarkable insight into Japanese thinking. But that insight was not total, and so even the extraordinary U.S. cryptanalysis could not warn policymakers of Japan's secret intentions.

The nations of the world learned the value of code breaking during World War I. Radio—used extensively in that conflict for the first time—gave them their opportunity. Messages were easily intercepted, so armies and navies sheathed them in codes and ciphers. But linguists and mathematicians on both sides learned to crack them, and the information thereby obtained provided victory after victory to generals, admirals, and political leaders. Cryptanalysis substantially helped France to block a supreme German offensive in 1918, Germany to defeat Russia, Britain to bring the United States into the war, the United States to convict a German spy. When hostilities ended, the powers refounded these agencies to retain in peace the benefits won in war.

The United States was one of these nations, and its main target was Japan. Before World War I, Japan had defeated China and then Russia to become mistress of the western Pacific. Now it was building a fleet to match that of the United States and, under a League of Nations mandate, had occupied islands that enabled it to menace the ocean routes to the Philippines. It was generally felt that Japan constituted the greatest danger to the United States.

The State and War departments jointly set up the Cipher Bureau in 1919 under the inspiring leadership of Herbert O. Yardley, a thirty-year-old who had created and run a code-breaking unit for military intelligence in World War I. The Cipher Bureau scored the first great achievement of American code breaking while working out of a narrow brownstone at 141 East Thirty-seventh Street in Manhattan. Despite only a rudimentary knowledge of Japanese, Yardley and his associates cracked Japanese diplomatic codes. A bewhiskered missionary then turned the messages into English. Sent to the State Department, they informed American negotiators at the Washington naval disarmament conference of 1921–22 about Japan's fallback position on capital ships. Armed with this knowledge, the negotiators drove Japan to promise to build such ships in a U.S.–Japan tonnage ratio not of ten to seven, as Japan had wanted, but of ten to six—the equivalent of three fewer battleships.

Although the navy was more concerned about Japan than was any other element of government, it had no code-breaking unit. Then, early in 1923, naval intelligence came upon a 1918 Japanese naval codebook while rifling the steamer trunk of a Japanese naval officer visiting New York. This impelled the navy to create a code-breaking agency—called, for security reasons, the Research Desk—within the Division of Naval Communications. Its first head was Laurance F. Safford, a lieutenant with a flair for mechanics and mathematics. He set up shop with four civilians in Room 1621 of Main Navy, a temporary wooden building on Constitution Avenue near the Lincoln Memorial. One of the first things he did was to set up radio intercept stations in the Pacific, to furnish more material for code breaking than was obtainable through haphazard monitoring by ships and the naval radio station in Shanghai.

In August, Safford took one of his most important strides forward when he hired Agnes Meyer Driscoll, thirty-two, as a cryptanalyst. A onetime mathematics teacher and a former employee of the Code and Signal Section, under which the Research Desk came, she soon proved to be an outstanding code breaker. Among her first assignments was to work on the photographed code from the rifled steamer trunk. The Research Desk had found that not only was the "plaintext," or the original message, encoded; its code groups were themselves enciphered. "Miss Aggie," as she was called, had to remove that encipherment. Incessantly turning the pages of the reproduced codebook with the rubber tip of her eraser, she completed that job after two to three years of work. A husband-and-wife team of translators turned the Japanese into English. By then, in 1926, Safford had returned to sea. He was succeeded by Lieutenant Joseph J. Rochefort, one of the first American naval officers to have studied Japanese in Japan. He was a "mustang"—a former enlisted man who had won a commission. This had made him tough and independent in a world dominated by Annapolis graduates; he neutralized his caustic speech with a conciliatory smile. Rochefort became one of the very few Americans with aptitude both in the Japanese language and in code breaking.

A subordinate, probably solving one of the Imperial Japanese Navy's subsidiary codes, described the work:

> Hours went by without any of us saying a word, just sitting in front of piles of indexed sheets on which a mumbo jumbo of figures or letters was displayed in chaotic disorder. . . . [We] gave ourselves to cryptography with the same ascetic devotion with which young men enter a monastery.

The hardest part of breaking a code is the beginning. Rochefort explained it in colorful terms:

> It first off involved what I call the staring process. You look at all of these messages that you have, you line them up in various ways, you write them one below the other, and you'd write them in various forms and you'd stare at them. Pretty soon you'd notice a pattern; you'd notice a definite pattern between these messages. This was the first clue. . . . You notice a pattern that when you follow through, you say this means so-and-so; you'd run that through, and it doesn't work out. Then you'd proceed on some other effort and eventually, if you're lucky and the other fellow makes mistakes, which he invariably will, then you come up with a solution that will stand up under test, and this gives your first lead-in.

Rochefort said he felt good while doing this work "because you have defied these people who have attempted to use a system they thought was secure, that is, it was unreadable. It was always somewhat of a pleasure to defeat them or challenge them." But the work took its toll. While engaged in the actual cryptanalysis, he said, he generally felt frustrated. The tension was so great that after work he had to lie down for two or three hours before he could eat anything; he developed ulcers anyway, and this, together with the fact that duty in communications intelligence hurt a man's career, drove him to get out of the work when his tour at the Research Desk ended in 1927.

The translation of the photographed Code No. 1 originally had been put together in ten "volumes" with metal-strip Acco office binders. When Safford returned from sea duty to the Research Desk in June 1929, he had the material retyped in four copies on huge twelve-by-eighteen-inch forms and bound in two volumes in red buckram McBee binders, far more convenient to use. This gave the code its more common name, the Red Code.

On December 1, 1930, the Japanese replaced it with a new code. But Miss Aggie by then had learned the ships, communications patterns, and frequently used phrases of the Japanese fleet, and she solved its transposition encipherment and then reconstructed the entire 85,000-group, two-part code. It was later called, from the color of its binding, the Blue Code. Her work was a remarkable feat of cryptanalysis, and for years it gave the U.S. Navy insight into Japanese forces and tactics.

Two events in 1929 led the army to expand its own code-breaking activities. In May, after giving the new secretary of state a little time to understand the realities of the job, Yardley passed him some solved messages. Henry L. Stimson was shocked at what he regarded as a dishonorable and counterproductive activity—"Gentlemen do not read each other's mail," he said later, maintaining that "the way to make men trustworthy is to trust them." He withdrew State Department support from the Cipher Bureau. In the meantime the army decided that Yardley was not doing what it needed most: training cryptanalysts for immediate use in case of war. These events doomed the unit, which was dissolved on October 31, 1929—two days after the great stock-market crash. Its papers went to the army's Signal Corps.

This body had set up a small cryptologic group of its own in 1921, hiring a twenty-nine-year-old who was on his way to becoming the world's greatest cryptologist. William F. Friedman—natty, uptight, brilliant—had written some theoretical treatises of landmark importance and had solved German codes in France during World War I. His new job was nominally to improve the army's own codes and ciphers, but doing this properly required him to test cryptographic systems offered to it. This gave him experience in cryptanalysis and expanded the army's knowledge of it. With the closing of Yardley's agency, it was logical for the Signal Corps to add code breaking to its responsibilities, and Friedman became the head of a new Signal Intelligence Service (SIS). He hired three young men who knew languages and mathematics to be junior cryptanalysts. The first to report was Frank B. Rowlett, twenty-one, a former teacher from Virginia with an all-American look to him. At 8:00 A.M. on April 1, 1930, Rowlett found himself entering Room 3406 of the Munitions Building—next door to the main

Navy Department building, which housed the navy code breakers—on Constitution Avenue near the Lincoln Memorial.

Two months later Rowlett and his colleagues were excitedly combing through the secret files of Yardley's defunct organization. This most clandestine and most valuable form of intelligence thrilled them. They went on to study basic cryptography and the solution of machine ciphers, clearly the wave of the future. In 1932, their training completed at last, they attacked Japanese diplomatic cryptographic systems, working on messages provided by the army's new intercept service.

They first cracked a simple code, the LA. That code did little more than replace the syllables of the plaintext with pairs of code letters listed in a codebook. In fact, the system resembled simple cryptograms found in Sunday newspapers. First the Japanese words of the message were transliterated into romanized letters (so that Western telegraphic systems could be used in sending them). This was done by using the *katakana* (literally, "borrowed words"), a syllabary that expresses Japanese words phonetically. The cryptographer then took the phonetically spelled words and encoded them, syllable by syllable, looking each of them up in the code list.

When the young cryptanalysts discovered that LA encrypted only insignificant messages, such as expense or vacation reports, and when they had gained experience and knowledge of Japanese diplomatic language and communications practices, they turned their attention to the more important messages. These were protected by electromechanical machines that enciphered messages at one end and deciphered them at the other. The machines rendered more complicated codes than a codebook did because they constantly changed the enciphered letters as the cipher clerk typed the message. Only a counterpart machine, properly set and advancing at the same pace as the sender's, could decipher the message. This system served two main Japanese diplomatic communication networks—one covering the Far East, the other linking Tokyo with major world capitals.

As difficult as machine systems are, however, study of the cryptograms did yield clues. Vowels, for instance, had a remarkably higher frequency than consonants. It appeared that the machine divided the romanized alphabet (used in the *katakana* transliteration) into two subsets, the six vowels and the twenty consonants. Working with one of the less garbled intercepts, and perhaps with some help from the navy's solution of another Japanese cipher machine, Rowlett and Solomon Kullback, one of the other original junior cryptanalysts, struck gold one day: Among their tentative recoveries of plaintext were three letters followed by an unknown and then another letter: *oyo?i*. They knew then that they had cracked the system, because *oyobi* is romanized Japanese for *and*. They named this machine system RED (not related to the Red Code).

By 1937, for the first time in American history, solutions of foreign messages began going to the White House, probably to President Franklin D. Roosevelt. The gentlemen were once again reading someone else's mail. It revealed, for instance, advance information about Italy's possible adherence to the German-Japanese Anti-Comintern Pact. This was in March 1937, six months before American diplomats began reporting on it. Later it provided part of the text of the treaty.

The next year, messages began to appear suggesting that a new machine would supplement and probably eventually replace the older one, which was physically wearing out. On February 20, 1939, three messages in the new system were intercepted, and over the next three months messages in RED gradually disappeared. Japan's major diplomatic messages had become unreadable. Faced with the loss of the nation's paramount intelligence, the SIS mounted a concentrated attack to solve the new machine. Friedman put Rowlett in charge and exercised overall supervision himself. The Americans called the new machine PURPLE, perhaps in part because its deeper hue fit its deeper mystery.

In the absence of American spies almost anywhere in the world, these half-dozen cryptanalysts were providing the United States with its best secret intelligence on Japan as relations with that nation, which was persisting in its aggression against China, deteriorated. The cryptanalysts plunged into their work in Rooms 3416 and 3418 in the Munitions Building. Room 3418, about twenty-five feet square with a steel door secured by a combination lock and with barred windows, was known as the vault. As additional cryptanalysts were assigned to the PURPLE problem, the group moved into larger quarters, finally occupying about eight rooms.

Rowlett worked in Room 3416. His desk was usually neat, for he spread out his worksheets on a nearby table. He was extremely focused on the work, arriving at 7:00 A.M., an hour early, and leaving at 5:00 P.M., an hour late. He never hummed or chewed his pencil or muttered to himself; he looked out the window only when something distracted him; he never drank coffee at work, though he did puff on a pipe. His mind didn't dwell on the cryptanalytic problems during the fifteen-minute drive to work from Arlington County, but he would awaken each night after a few hours of sleep and, lying there in the dark, review the day's work and think of ways of improving it. In the morning, at work, he would exchange ideas with the other cryptanalysts—Robert O. Ferner, Albert W. Small, Genevieve Grotjan, and Mary Jo Dunning, assisted by Leo Rosen, Sam Snyder, Kenneth D. Miller, Glen S. Landig, and Cyrus C. Sturis, Jr. (their names deserve to be remembered). After the conference, they all would return to their desks. Quiet reigned as they pored over the intercepts, most of which had been teletyped in from the monitoring stations; sometimes they puzzled over statistical and alphabetical tables compiled by hand from the intercepts. Only the rustling of papers and the scratching of pencils disturbed the brooding silence, although for a time the banging and hammering of workmen on another floor proved frustrating.

Reconstructing a cipher system is like solving an immensely complicated scientific problem, with this difference: Nature does not deliberately conceal her secrets. The researchers concoct hypotheses and test them. If x stands for *e*, will the other cipher-to-plain equivalents that it entails make sense? Or will they merely yield gibberish, or lead to a self-contradiction? Can one recovered alphabet be linked with another? There's no clear way to the answer, as there is in the algebra problems posed in math classes. Particularly in the early stages of a difficult cryptanalysis, the work is one of the most excruciating, agonizing, tantalizing, compelling mental processes known to humans—and, when successful, one of the most satisfying.

PURPLE had carried over from RED the division of letters into groups of six and twenty letters. But this time the six were not exclusively vowels. Nevertheless, within a few weeks the cryptanalysts ascertained how they were enciphered. This enabled the team to recover the plaintext for those letters. The process was slow and painstaking. Assigned to devise a way to mechanize this pencil-and-paper method, Leo Rosen hit upon the idea of using telephone selector switches, employed in dialing. They worked like a dream, and the solution process was considerably speeded up.

Despite Rosen's remarkable advance, the totality of PURPLE still resisted the Americans. Friedman, who had been supervising the work rather loosely, was asked by his bosses—all extremely supportive, financially as well as psychologically—to participate personally. His genius helped considerably. The navy also lent a hand temporarily, organizing its files the same way as the army's to facilitate cooperation. After about four months, however, the navy returned to its main effort, Japanese naval codes. The Signal Intelligence Service pushed ahead. Within Rowlett's group, teamwork was extremely close; determination was pervasive. No one complained that a task was too menial. Rowlett was confident from the start that they would reconstruct the PURPLE mechanism the way he and others had reconstructed the RED. He never got depressed, even as months went by without a solution.

As they sought a breakthrough, the cryptanalysts spent much of their time trying to match possible plaintext—guesses, often educated, as to the text of the original message—to the cipher text, or encoded language and numbers. Early in the effort, for example, many identical Japanese telegrams were sent to multiple addresses; some of the telegrams were composed using the RED machine, some the PURPLE. The cryptanalysts could read RED, which then gave them the text of the same PURPLE messages. They knew, too, that many diplomatic dispatches began "I have the honor to inform Your Excellency that . . ." and they often tried that as the start of the plaintext. In a very few cases, the State Department gave them the text of notes to or from the Japanese ambassadors, which the code breakers used as cribs.

The code breakers had to make all sorts of guesses. They theorized that the PURPLE machine would have to advance in some regular fashion, that its mechanism would have to click forward at some prescribed rate. Suppose, for example, that the probable plaintext word *Japan* was guessed. If the probable $a$'s were represented in the ciphertext by, say, x and z, then the cryptographers could hypothesize that the encoding machine had simply moved forward one space with each new letter: x for $a$, something for $p$, and z for the next $a$.

More than a year of painstaking trial-and-error work passed. Then, about 2:00 P.M. on a warm Friday, September 20, 1940—in the middle of Roosevelt's campaign for an unprecedented third term, as Britain anxiously awaited a German invasion from occupied France—Albert Small noticed that Genevieve Grotjan, a dignified, twenty-six-year-old statistician, seemed to be concentrating extremely intently. When he asked, she told him that she had just discovered a couple of the needed intervals and was looking hard for others. He took her in to see Rowlett, who was conferring with Bob Ferner. Grotjan showed the men her discoveries; then a third interval leaped out at the code breakers. They saw at once that these intervals proved that their concept of PURPLE was correct. The ebullient Small dashed around the room, hands clasped above his head. Ferner, normally phlegmatic, shouted, "Hooray!" Rowlett jumped up and down. "That's it! That's it!" Everybody crowded around. Friedman came in. "What's all the noise about?" he asked. Rowlett showed him Grotjan's findings. He understood immediately. Grotjan's discovery constituted the decisive breakthrough in the solution of PURPLE—it was the greatest moment in the history of American code breaking. And what did the egghead cryptanalysts do? They sent out for Coca-Colas!

When the euphoria and the effects of the colas had worn off, the cryptanalysts drifted back to work. Grotjan, who seems to have gotten excited about the breakthrough mainly because everybody else did, soberly regarded it as just one step in a series of steps. A week later—the day after Japan started to occupy French Indochina and the very day the Tripartite Pact establishing the Rome-Berlin-Tokyo axis was signed—the Signal Intelligence Service handed in its first two solutions of PURPLE messages. This did not mean its work was done. The settings for the machine changed each day, and the cryptanalysts had to recover these. But this work was facilitated by Rosen's construction of two American analogues of the Japanese PURPLE machine, at a cost of $684.65. Later, additional copies of the machine were built, several at the Washington Navy Yard; some of them were given to the navy, which had rejoined the PURPLE work to help with the heavy volume of solutions, and some to the British, so they could read the messages without having to wait for American solutions to be forwarded to them.

Soon navy lieutenant Francis A. Raven discovered a pattern to the daily setting changes. With this knowledge the Americans were able to read reports from and instructions to Japan's ambassadors on average within a day or so, sometimes within hours. They had gained access to the most secret diplomatic dispatches of the empire of Japan as relations continued to worsen, with an American embargo on the export of iron and steel scrap and, later, with the movement of Japanese forces toward Thailand.

The beginning of wisdom was to know that there was no such thing as "the" Japanese code. For PURPLE was not the only cryptographic system of Japan's Foreign Ministry, much less of the empire. The Foreign Ministry employed a hierarchy of systems, of which PURPLE was the apex. Under it came several codes that—unlike PURPLE, which served embassies exclusively—were used at both embassies and consulates. LA, the simplest, lay at the bottom. Above it rested a two-part system, PA-K2. More complex still was the Foreign Ministry's J series of codes. The K transposition key for these codes changed daily; the code breakers had to undertake a fresh analysis with each day's messages. Some 10 to 15 percent were not solved at all, and those that were took an average of a week from interception through translation to distribution.

By contrast, most PURPLE messages were solved within hours, and all but 2 to 3 percent of the keys were recovered. Did the Japanese err in assessing the security of their cryptographic systems? Yes and no. PURPLE was a much more difficult system to solve in the first place, but once solved it was easier to keep up with.

While the army was concentrating on Japan's diplomatic systems, the navy's code-breaking agency—except for its occasional help to the army—focused on Japan's naval systems. This agency, again under Safford, now a commander, was called OP-20-G. During the 1930s it continued to read messages in what it called the Blue Code, gaining considerable knowledge about Japan's naval maneuvers. This code was replaced on November 1, 1938. But the paucity of intercepts in the new code, which the Americans called the flag officers' code, meant that almost no progress was made in reading it.

On June 1, 1939, the Japanese introduced yet another code. Called JN25 by the Americans, as it was the twenty-fifth Japanese naval code they attacked, it encoded messages dealing with naval operations. Miss Aggie, greatly helped by Lieutenant Prescott Currier, attacked the new code. About a year and a half later, in almost the very week that the army was producing its first PURPLE solutions, the first JN25 solutions emerged. But the navy's satisfaction did not last long. On December 1, 1940, the Imperial Navy substituted a new version, which the Americans called JN25b. But the Japanese foolishly kept the prior version's latest encipherment in force for the first two months of JN25b's service. This bared the underlying code and permitted the quick determination of the meaning of 2,000 code groups. When the new encipherment went into effect, OP-20-G's IBM tabulators were able to strip it off, enabling the Americans to read bits and pieces of the coded messages. But progress continued to be slow.

So in March 1941, OP-20-G requested that the radio intelligence unit on Corregidor Island in the Philippines help with its search for a solution. A British code-breaking unit in Singapore exchanged recoveries of JN25b code groupings with Corregidor. Despite all these efforts, the code remained readable only to a very small degree. By December 1941, only 10 to 15 percent of each message could be understood.

This, then, was the cryptanalytic situation with Japan on December 6, 1941: The main diplomatic system could be read rapidly and completely; other diplomatic and consular systems could be read with a few days' delay; the main naval system could be read only slightly.

Nearly all intercepts came from army or navy stations listening to commercial frequencies such as RCA's that radioed messages from Japan. The intercepts were sent to the SIS or OP-20-G by teleprinter, airmail, courier, or radio, re-enciphered in an American system. Translation was a bottle-neck because of the difficulty of finding enough qualified people who understood Japanese. On the other hand, not all of the PURPLE messages were in Japanese: Some of the notes, intended to be handed to the State Department, were in English.

Fifty to seventy-five intercepts were solved and translated each day. The most important of these were selected for distribution to a handful of high-level officials: the president; the secretaries of state, war, and the navy; the chief of staff and the chief of naval operations, the war plans chiefs of the two services; and some intelligence officers. Fourteen copies of each were typed up, some for the files, and intelligence officers carried them in locked briefcases to these officials, calling attention to some of the more critical dispatches and explaining obscure references. Then they took the papers back with them and burned them. As a cover, this intelligence was called MAGIC.

What did these messages say? Many revealed the empire's reaction to world events and American policies. They included the reports of and the instructions to the Japanese emissaries. "If the United States expresses too many points of disagreement to Proposal A," Tokyo cabled its ambassadors in Washington on November 5, in a PURPLE message that the navy solved the same day, "and if it becomes apparent that an agreement cannot be reached, we intend to submit our absolutely final proposal, Proposal B (contained in my message #727)." That other message had been inter-cepted and solved the day before. Messages to and from the consulates fre-quently dealt with the movement of U.S. Navy warships into and out of har-bor. On November 15 Tokyo told Honolulu in the J19 code, "As relations between Japan and the United States are most critical, make your 'ships in harbor' report irregular, but at a rate of twice a week." The navy cracked that message on December 3.

By the fall of 1941, high levels in the U.S. government had become almost addicted to MAGIC. Secretary of State Cordell Hull, who looked upon MAGIC "as I would a witness who is giving evidence against his own side of the case," was "at all times intensely interested in the contents of the intercepts." The chief of army intelligence regarded MAGIC as the most reliable and authentic information that the War Department was receiving on Japanese intentions and activities. General George C. Marshall, the army chief of staff, called it a "priceless asset." And when the president was not given MAGIC for a few days in November, through a bureaucratic mix-up, he specifically asked for it. This was the situation as the Pearl Harbor strike force slipped out of Japan's naval bases to assemble in the foggy Kuril Islands north of the main islands of Japan, far from any prying eyes, thence to sail in utter silence across the empty wastes of the North Pacific toward its unsuspecting target: a palm-fringed inlet in Hawaii.

SOME PEOPLE HAVE conjectured that this fabulous decoded information made it clear to Roosevelt and his advisers that Pearl Harbor was going to be attacked. They say the president, wanting to bring the United States into the war on the side of Great Britain, traitorously suppressed this information and sacrificed American ships and American lives to achieve his goal. Various theories have been put forth to support this notion.

Safford himself, by then a captain, agreed. He based his argument upon the so-called winds code. Japan had notified its diplomatic posts in a J19-K10 circular telegram on November 19 that if diplomatic relations and international communications were likely to be cut off, it would warn these posts with a fake weather forecast in the middle of the Japanese shortwave news broadcast. If Japanese-American relations were in danger, the forecast would predict "east wind rain." American code breakers solved this message on November 28. Immediately a frantic effort was made to pick up this broadcast. Safford insisted that the "winds execute"—the forecast—was heard on December 4 and that the intercept was subsequently removed from the files as part of a cover-up. Virtually no one has supported this contention. But even assuming that an execute had been transmitted, it would at best confirm that relations were strained. In no way could it point to Pearl Harbor.

Rear Admiral Edwin T. Layton has argued that the lack of a PURPLE machine in Hawaii prevented Admiral Husband Kimmel and General Walter Short, the commanders there, from using MAGIC-provided information on international affairs to illuminate their situation. This would have enabled them to predict the attack, Layton has claimed. But this is speculation, supported only by hindsight. Moreover, the presence of a PURPLE machine in the Philippines did not prevent the American forces there from being surprised.

Author John Toland found several former radio operators who had been listening in San Francisco or at sea. They said that in the week before December 7, they had heard a cacophony of radio signals from northwest of Hawaii—presumably the strike force heading for Pearl Harbor. They said they reported this, to no effect. But this story founders because, according to the Japanese, the strike force maintained absolute radio silence throughout its voyage. And American naval intercept units, straining to pick up whatever they could on the Japanese naval circuits, heard nothing. (U.S. radio-intelligence operators knew that several carriers had dropped out of the traffic picture. They thought that the ships were in home waters, covering a movement to the south—the Philippines or the oil- and rubber-rich Dutch East Indies. Carrier communications had likewise vanished in February and July 1941, and naval radio-intelligence operators hypothesized then that the carriers had been held near Japan—a hypothesis later determined to be factual. But what happened then was not what was happening in December.)

Several writers have suggested that the solution of the many messages dealing with ship movements in and out of Pearl Harbor should have alerted the authorities to the impending attack. But similar messages were transmitted about the Philippines, the Panama Canal, San Francisco, San Diego, and Seattle. In fact, from August 1 to December 6, fifty-nine such intercepts dealt with the Philippines and only twenty with Hawaii. The writers have pointed to one intercept, instructing the consulate in Hawaii to divide the Pearl Harbor anchorage into smaller areas for more precise reporting of ship locations, as a clear indication of a forthcoming attack. This is hindsight. At the time, the authorities viewed it merely as evidence of the thoroughness of Japanese intelligence or of the need to abbreviate communications.

James Rusbridger, in his recent book *Betrayal at Pearl Harbor*, claims that the British code-breaking unit at Singapore solved enough of JN25 to reveal the plan to attack Pearl Harbor and that this information was passed on to Prime Minister Winston Churchill, who withheld it from Roosevelt to ensure American entry into the war, thereby enabling the attack to succeed. Citing the Official Secrets Act, British authorities have denied Rusbridger any access to the records of the unit, and the U.S. Navy reports that it cannot find any of these JN25b solutions, partial or complete, from before December 7. His thesis rests on the memory of an Australian code breaker working in Singapore. This is a slender reed upon which to base so heavy a charge. Moreover, Rusbridger does not distinguish between the *a* and *b* editions of JN25—and does not make clear why Churchill would try to get the Americans to fight Japan instead of Germany.

A retired communications intelligence analyst, Fred Parker, has dredged through the files of Japanese messages intercepted before Pearl Harbor but not solved until afterward. Though he has found no smoking gun, no message referring specifically to an attack on Pearl Harbor, he believes that the messages he has found point clearly to an impending attack there. He cites, for example, the presence of an oiler on what became the strike force's homeward route and the broadcast of the message "Climb Mount Niitaka 1208." The oiler obviously was put there, he says, to refuel the returning ships. The 1208 in the message meant December 8, the attack date on the Tokyo side of the International Date Line. Mount Niitaka (Hsin-kao, in Taiwan) was the highest peak in what was then the Japanese Empire. Parker contends that a solution of these messages would have suggested an attack on Pearl Harbor. Like the other theories, however, this is hindsight.

Some historians have contended that if only the army and navy intelligence officers, and perhaps State Department officials as well, had found the time to analyze all the intercepts as a group, they would have discerned a pattern that pointed to Pearl Harbor. This argument resembles one that Roberta Wohlstetter made in her book *Pearl Harbor: Warning and Decision*, in which she holds that the noise of the false evidence drowned out the indications of the true signals: "We failed to anticipate Pearl Harbor not for want of the relevant materials, but because of a plethora of irrelevant ones." This is wrong. There were no true signals, no clear indications of the attack.

The fact is that code-breaking intelligence did not prevent and could not have prevented Pearl Harbor, because Japan never sent any message to anybody saying anything like "We shall attack Pearl Harbor." The ambassadors in Washington were never told of the plan. Nor were any other

Japanese diplomats or consular officials. The ships of the strike force were never radioed any message mentioning Pearl Harbor. It was therefore impossible for the cryptanalysts to have discovered the plan.

What then is the answer to the joint congressional committee's question? What about that "finest intelligence"? The simple answer is that fine though it was, it was not fine enough. Perhaps if the United States had established intercept operators in the U.S. Embassy in Tokyo to obtain enough messages to make a solution of JN25b more likely, or had been able to buy a spy in the top circles of the Japanese government, or had been able somehow to fly aerial reconnaissance regularly above the island empire—then perhaps there might have been a chance that the Pearl Harbor attack would be detected in advance. None of these things could have been easily done. Even if they had, discovery of the plan would not have been certain. Japan had successfully closed all openings through which foreigners might gain information about its intentions. The real reason for the success of the Pearl Harbor attack lies in the island empire's hermetic security. Despite the American code breakers, Japan kept her secret. For Americans, the Rising Sun rose in eclipse.

*AUTUMN 1991*

An authority on cryptology, David Kahn is the author of *The Codebreakers: The Story of Secret Writing* (1967) and *Seizing the Enigma: The Race to Break the German U-Boat Codes, 1939–1943* (1991).

# 28

# Kimmel's Hidden Agenda

## By Edward S. Miller

*Edward S. Miller provides additional insight into the Pearl Harbor disaster. Admiral Husband Kimmel, commander of the Pacific Fleet and an officer known for his aggressive spirit, had his mind set on offensive— not defensive—action in those uneasy days before December 7, 1941. He planned for nothing less than a major engagement with the Japanese Combined Fleet and its commander, Admiral Isoroku Yamamoto. Anticipating that the American fleet could ambush the Japanese forces in the waters west of Midway, the American plan bore a striking resemblance to the Japanese effort six months later that would result in the decisive American victory off that same island. If successful, Kimmel's blueprint would have produced a Pacific Trafalgar, and Kimmel would have become an American Nelson. But fate held another role for Kimmel and his Pacific Fleet.*

At Pearl Harbor on Saturday, December 6, 1941, the war plans officer of the U.S. Pacific Fleet noted the whereabouts of the large American warships at sea and in port. He then updated a vigorous plan of battle that the fleet was ready to execute when the widely expected war with Japan broke out. But no American knew that six Japanese aircraft carriers were bearing down on Hawaii for a surprise attack the following morning.

The true story of this battle plan is totally new, one of those rare finds that illustrates the asymmetry of historical perception. The scheme of Admiral Isoroku Yamamoto to strike the fleet at Pearl Harbor has become one of the most thoroughly studied plans in military annals. Yet the equally daring strategy of his American counterpart, Admiral Husband E. Kimmel, embodied in a 113-page document approved by the highest officer of the U.S. Navy, has remained unknown for five decades. The commander in chief of the Pacific Fleet, Kimmel became the scapegoat for the American defeat. He was undone by his defensive failures while his mind was absorbed in dreams of a Trafalgar in the Pacific.

It is curious that Kimmel's intentions have been so long overlooked. I pieced them together during twenty years of research for a book about American war planning against Japan before World War II. I had become intrigued as formerly secret information was declassified. I found plans and orders in the Operational Archives, tucked away in a converted factory at the Washington Navy Yard. In another repository in Maryland, I discovered in boxes encrusted with dust drafts of similar plans, and spirited memos among fleet chieftains, that were ignored by investigators zealously combing through messages between Washington and Hawaii. There was also an intriguing chart maneuver, or war game, of the plan, played at Pearl Harbor from August to November 26, 1941, with task force commanders like Vice Admiral William F. Halsey, Jr., representing themselves, the war planners playing the enemy, and Kimmel umpiring. The fleet plan itself had been published for all the world to see, during headline-making congressional investigations in 1946.

The real mystery is why scholars of a hundred books about Pearl Harbor have gullibly accepted the self-serving testimony of nervous officers who said that, on the eve of the Japanese attack, the Pacific Fleet was merely contemplating a raid on minor Japanese outposts. None has bothered to analyze the real portent of the 1941 blueprint.

In fact, Kimmel's plan contemplated nothing less than a titanic clash of up to twenty battleships, perhaps as early as Christmas of 1941. Kimmel's nine battleships, the most potent element of the Pacific Fleet, constituted the only Allied force in 1941 that could match Yamamoto's awesome Combined Fleet. Kimmel cherished the same goal as his opponent: destruction of the enemy navy at the outset. He planned to achieve this by luring the Imperial Fleet to the central Pacific and then destroying it in an ambush by his powerful dreadnoughts.

The secret strategy was embodied—but not spelled out openly—in Navy Plan O-1, also called Pacific Fleet Plan WPPac-46. It was an attachment to Rainbow Five, the global plan that governed U.S. strategy throughout World War II. If Japan had opened hostilities elsewhere than Pearl Harbor—not so unlikely a possibility, considering the extreme distaste of Yamamoto's peers for the risky operation—the Pacific war might well have unfolded in accordance with Kimmel's scenario.

Plan O-1 took shape when the admiral raised his flag as CinCPac (commander in chief, Pacific Fleet) on February 1, 1941. The United States had just abandoned the hoary admonition of the guru of sea power, Alfred Thayer Mahan, never to divide the fleet. Aggression by dictatorships across both oceans had forced it to split its fighting strength into separate Atlantic and Pacific fleets. President Franklin Roosevelt, according to navy gossip, wanted "the two toughest sons of bitches" to run them. He had been disappointed by Admiral J.C. Richardson, the commander in chief of the entire fleet before it was divided, who complained endlessly that the navy was not ready to fight and should withdraw from the inadequate base at Pearl Harbor, where FDR had placed it as a deterrent to Japanese adventurism. Admiral Harold R. Stark, chief of naval operations, proposed Kimmel and Admiral Ernest King. King was already commanding units in the Atlantic, and Kimmel in the Pacific, so Stark assigned each to command the nearer fleet, an act of simple convenience that was to cast a long shadow on history.

At fifty-eight, Kimmel was a proud and handsome man who had climbed an impressive career ladder both afloat and ashore. Plucked from command of the cruiser flotillas in the Pacific, he had been promoted by Stark over the heads of many senior admirals. He was obsessive about detail and efficiency. He was also a warrior full of fight and ready to tangle with the Japanese. Although he had studied and taught at the Naval War College and would pore over war plans aboard his flagship at night, his grasp of strategy was mundane. To translate his zeal for combat into a systematic plan, Kimmel needed an innovative war plans officer who shared his pugnacious attitude.

He chose Captain Charles Horatio McMorris, known in the navy as "Soc" for a philosophical bent that his peers deemed a bit Socratic. McMorris was shrewd, tough, and in appearance regarded as "the ugliest man in the navy," yet with a delightful turn of personality that helped him sell ideas. His naval experience was wide, but his planning background was rather unimpressive. Nevertheless, Kimmel had the highest confidence in this "very able, outspoken officer." Aided by four junior officers, McMorris set about to shape the admiral's instinctive ferocity into vivid plans of maneuver, ignoring the gripes of some commanders that he went too far, that, as historian Gordon Prange writes, he "let his imagination and enthusiasm carry him out to sea."

The brain center at Pearl Harbor inherited a strategic dilemma. For more than three decades the navy had honed War Plan Orange, a program for total war against Japan. (Orange was the code name for Japan in the U.S. "color" plans; Great Britain was called Red; and the United States, Blue.) Reliance on offense had characterized the plan since its inception in 1906. To satisfy army commanders intent on rescuing American troops who would be cut off in the Philippines, naval planners had originally envisioned a charge of the Blue fleet across the Pacific. But by 1934, modern weapons of attrition such as planes and submarines would doom this "Through Ticket to Manila."

Instead it adopted a more cautious advance across the Japanese mandated islands of the central Pacific (the Marshall, Caroline, and Marianas groups), one by one. It wrote off the troops that General Douglas MacArthur would eventually command in the Philippines. By the end of 1940 the attack timetable had been stretched out. The first amphibious landing in the Marshall Islands was expected in the sixth month of war—not far off the first actual landing date on Guadalcanal—followed by occupation of the Japanese naval base at Truk at the end of a year.

In Washington, Admiral Stark fretted throughout the autumn of 1940 that Great Britain would succumb to the Nazi onslaught. If the Royal Navy fell into Hitler's hands, America would face immense peril before it could rearm. After Roosevelt's election to a third term in November, Stark convinced the president to scrap War Plan Orange and focus on new plans for fighting a war in alliance with the British Empire against the three Axis powers: Germany, Italy, and Japan. The chief of naval operations assigned priority to defeating Germany first. His thesis evolved into Plan Rainbow Five.

A British military delegation arrived in Washington early in 1941 to commence joint planning. Prime Minister Winston Churchill was delighted at the beat-Germany-first decision. He was deeply concerned, however, about the fate of Singapore, the British naval bastion of the Far East. The Royal Navy had suffered in the Atlantic, and it had little to spare for Singapore. His delegates pleaded for an American fleet to defend the base and to deny Japan the oil fields of the Dutch East Indies. Loss of Singapore, they declared melodramatically, would mean the loss of Australia and India and "a disaster of the first magnitude, second only to the loss of the British Isles."

U.S. planners had been toying with Rainbows Two and Three, scenarios of defending the Malay Barrier, as the Singapore-Indies-Australia line was known. (They had shelved Rainbows One and Four, narrow plans for defense of the western hemisphere.) They concluded that Singapore was neither defensible nor crucial to victory. Their trepidations were well-founded; the smashup at Pearl Harbor would have been child's play compared to the catastrophe awaiting a fleet at Singapore.

The two most influential strategists in Washington opposed sending major forces to the Far East at all. Major General Stanley Embick had long been a vigorous opponent of offensive war in the Pacific. (He had called the Orange Plan "literally an act of madness.") Rear Admiral Richmond Kelly Turner, director of the Navy War Plans Division, was coauthor of Stark's Germany-first strategy. "Terrible Turner," a man of violent fits of temper, was actually timid about Pacific ventures. Worrying that the gung-ho Kimmel might get his fleet so entangled in fighting far from his base that it could not return to reinforce the Atlantic Fleet if Britain collapsed, Turner decreed that it must not operate west of longitude 155° east, just beyond the Marshall Islands but well short of Truk, far from Japan's vital sea arteries.

The British yielded ungraciously. However, their appeals to Roosevelt induced Turner to offer a sop. The minuscule Asiatic Fleet would desert Manila and help defend the Indies. King would steam to Gibraltar at the outbreak of war and relieve British ships for a rescue mission to Singapore. His Atlantic Fleet was reinforced by the transfer of many ships from Hawaii (depleting Kimmel of more strength than the attack on Pearl Harbor did!).

The rub was that the Royal Navy's rescue mission wouldn't arrive for seventy days, during which time Singapore and probably all other Allied bases in the Far East would fall. To prevent this, the U.S. Pacific Fleet was to support the Malay Barrier indirectly, acting offensively elsewhere to induce Yamamoto to withhold his capital ships from the drive toward Singapore and the Indies. Stark and Turner believed that poising the fleet in Hawaii had persuaded the Japanese to keep their Combined Fleet at home, and that naval demonstrations against ocean outposts would keep it there in a defensive position. They ordered the Pacific Fleet to design what they called a vigorous offensive, specifically to raid the air and light naval bases that Japan was hurriedly building in the Marshall Islands. They felt such operations might even give it a crack at an important section of the enemy fleet; Turner told the British that the Japanese main body would fight for the Marshalls. He and Stark then turned their attention to the U-boats in the Atlantic.

Kimmel, a fighting man aware that his predecessor had been fired for squeamishness, asked if "bold aggressive action" were expected of him. If so, leashing him to seas within 2,000 miles of Hawaii was not helpful. Stark told him that he could risk severe losses to accomplish his mission. "Light and ineffective blows," he advised, would merely "reduce respect for our power."

The CinCPac got the message. Soc McMorris went to work on a program to distract the Japanese navy. But how? And where? The fleet couldn't hurt vital enemy interests in its backwater cruising zone. Kimmel thought that raids on Japan by its "woefully deficient" carrier force were inconceivable. Submarine harassment from Hawaii would scarcely trouble the foe. American battleships would be ineffective until advance bases were acquired. Yamamoto could afford to play a waiting game.

Other officers agreed that fleabite raids on Japanese atolls would be ineffective. The commander of the puny Asiatic Fleet, Admiral Thomas C. Hart, begged for forceful action. Even Stark admitted in a moment of candor that if the Japanese main body hung about in home waters anyway, the raids could distract only minor enemy warships and planes from the Malay Barrier. Soc McMorris was "extremely doubtful" that battering the Marshalls would accomplish much. The Pacific Fleet would fail in its strategic mission unless it invented a daring plan.

Kimmel's eye fell on his most forward outpost, Wake Island. The little atoll, uninhabited until 1935, had recently become the scene of lackadaisical efforts to dredge a harbor and erect a minor sea-air base. It began to loom in his mind as the key to "offensive operations to the westward." A secure American base on Wake would do more than bolster raids on the Marshalls: It would, if fortified, generate an opportunity for sea combat, by luring the Japanese naval force to an area where the Americans could get at it.

Kimmel moved swiftly. By the summer of 1941, his prodding had gotten 1,200 civilian workmen onto Wake to erect shore facilities. Reconnaissance operations from the lagoon became feasible, although lack of gasoline storage was expected to inhibit flying until a channel through the rock-hard coral reef was opened for seaplane tenders in mid-1942. He also posted a marine defense battalion at Wake. On December 4 a squadron of fighter planes arrived. General George C. Marshall thought that the army ought to take control of Wake, which was being readied for the operation of heavy bombers. Kimmel retorted, "Over my dead body."

Nevertheless, Kimmel and McMorris did not truly believe the Pacific Fleet could accomplish its strategic mission by a stakeout at Wake any more than by a raid against the Marshalls. Only one circumstance would prove decisive beyond doubt: defeating Yamamoto's Combined Fleet. To induce Yamamoto to engage, they were apparently willing to offer an irresistible lure—the American aircraft carriers. McMorris drafted the concept into a preliminary Plan O-1 in March 1941. He refined it after the promulgation of Rainbow Five and submitted the final version to the Navy Department on July 25, 1941.

The intentions underlying Plan O-1 are found in its elaborate offensive deployments. The initial steps consisted of sorties of submarines, flying boats, and cruisers from Pearl Harbor, primarily for reconnaissance. The bulk of the fleet's undersea force of thirty-two vessels was to sortie on J Day—the first day of war—"or earlier, if so directed." Sweeping ahead on a broad front, they would advance to the sea gates of the Combined Fleet at Yokohama and the outlets from the Inland Sea of Japan. They were instructed to radio word of "important enemy movements" and to damage "important enemy units." Since Japan was thought to have few long-range planes, the submarines would cruise most of the way on the surface. They could arrive at their stations as early as 8J (the eighth day of war). Even if delayed, the submarines could form a scouting line across the path of a Japanese sortie.

U.S. naval doctrine stipulated that capital ships in enemy waters were to be covered by long-range Catalina flying boats, the eyes of the fleet. McMorris's plan allocated five of the nine fleet squadrons, each with twelve planes, to fly to advance bases west of Hawaii (Wake, Midway, and Johnston islands) for "the earliest possible information of advancing enemy forces." By late 1941 every fuel drum in Hawaii was commandeered to support flights from primitive bases on the atolls for three or four weeks, the limit of their endurance.

The final scouting element, comprising two heavy cruisers, was to sortie immediately—possibly even before the war began, depending on warnings—and race into the Philippine Sea. The cruisers' eight float planes could form a scouting line hundreds of miles wide to observe if Yamamoto's fleet were steaming that way.

The initial deployment of scouting forces does not in itself reveal Kimmel's battle plan, since they would have been launched anyway to support a raid on the Marshalls. Seaplane scouting was needed to protect the raiders, and the submarines might have found profitable quarry other than the Combined Fleet. Yet the particulars of the wide dragnet fit best with a battle scenario.

The most profound evidence of a battle plan lay in Kimmel's extraordinary casting of American capital ships. Under the plan, Vice Admiral Halsey was to thrust the three aircraft carriers—the *Lexington, Saratoga,* and *Enterprise*—toward the Marshall Islands in a most unusual manner. Streaking out of Pearl on 1J, the day after J Day, his fast task force would rendezvous with an oiler standing by at a spot of ocean dubbed Point Tare that lay safely within the scouting envelopes of the U.S. atolls. From 6J to 9J—about the time submarines were reaching the Japanese coast—the task force would reconnoiter the Marshalls in search of targets, especially sea and air forces. It was then to withdraw and link up with battleships chugging toward Point Tare. At that midocean rendezvous, the entire Pacific Fleet would spend two days refueling while the admirals studied photographs and chose targets. Only then would Halsey's carriers, shielded by three dozen fast escorts, hasten back to the northern Marshalls to blast the Japanese. He was told, however, to expend no more than 25 percent of his bombs or shells against fixed targets.

The double cruise through the Marshalls was a bizarre stratagem. Even in 1941, waiting a week to strike after a reconnaissance had alerted the foe would have been an unorthodox gambit. Mock rehearsals against the Panama Canal and Hawaii had proven the clout of unannounced strikes. Yet Halsey's first cruise would have wasted the element of surprise; the second would have courted disaster, because the Japanese would have poured in air reinforcements. The chart maneuvers at Pearl Harbor in late 1941 showed the probability of high losses. Stark urged Kimmel to combine the two forays, or at least shorten the interval between them. The CinCPac retorted that his need of information was so great that he was willing to expose his carriers to "grave risks."

The fleet strategists were reacting to an information vacuum, but their risk–reward analysis cannot be taken at face value. To expose his three carriers solely for news about Japan's outermost picket line would have been a grossly disproportionate gamble. Still, McMorris refused to revise the plan, which in fact best fits a prebattle maneuver. The first cruise apparently was to signal a forthcoming raid and set Yamamoto in motion toward the central Pacific—Halsey was going to show a bit of garter. The second, the full attack, would destroy Japanese air power lured to the region, neutralize its bases within range of Wake, and thus assure Wake's operability during a major engagement.

The capstone of Plan O-1's combat disposition was a battleship ambush. The United States and its allies in the Pacific were outnumbered in every category of weapon save the biggest-gun vessels. Kimmel had nine battleships. Japan had six battleships and four battle cruisers, but it would need to employ some against two British capital ships coming to Singapore and others, the planners supposed, to operate in the Dutch East Indies. Japanese dreadnoughts were faster and their crews better adapted to night fighting; the American vessels had longer steaming range and thicker armor. Kimmel also held a three-to-two advantage in sixteen-inch guns, the most potent batteries then afloat. It was plausible to think that the Pacific Fleet could achieve momentary superiority in a gun battle.

Husband E. Kimmel had served aboard seven battlewagons and as chief of staff of the big-gun force. He had instructed in shot and shell and had supervised production at the naval gun factory. Although a battleship orientation was not uncommon in the U.S. Navy of 1941, Kimmel's case was extreme. The CinCPac frequently mourned the transfers of three battleships to the Atlantic, and he begged fruitlessly for the *North Carolina* and *Washington*—fast, heavily gunned new dreadnoughts. During a meeting on June 9, 1941, FDR casually suggested detaching three more battleships, leaving just three to defend Hawaii and three for raiding. "That's crazy!" Kimmel exploded. The president backed down.

Plan O-1 called for the battleships to set forth from Pearl Harbor in two waves. The first, the *Pennsylvania, Nevada,* and *Arizona,* would hover at Point Tare as a support force, to which Halsey would retire after the reconnaissance. Their mission was to fend off night torpedo attacks by enemy destroyers and cruisers that might pursue the carriers, as well as to shepherd wounded vessels home. These tasks were unworthy of their power. There was probably another reason for their presence in waters likely to be infested by Japanese submarines. Kimmel was very reluctant to remain ashore when the shooting began. He probably wanted to be on the bridge of his flagship, the *Pennsylvania,* as his armada assembled. "The Fleet will be kept informed of the location of the Commander-in-Chief," the plan said laconically.

The other six battlewagons, organized with screening units as another task force under Vice Admiral William S. Pye, were to put to sea on 5J and reach Point Tare on 11J. There, in the middle of the Pacific Ocean, would occur a magnificent rendezvous. All sixty-seven of the fleet's surface men-of-war would gather to drink from fresh oilers while the admirals conferred, Kimmel himself probably in tactical command.

On 12J, as Halsey raced back to pummel the Marshalls, the dreadnoughts were to steam toward a new position north of the island group. Again, their stated mission was curious. Nobody imagined that the ponderous sluggers could raid Japanese outposts or lumber up to a swift Japanese detachment sacking Wake. They were merely supposed to offer "such support . . . as developments require," to "cover" Halsey and stand by as a force for him to retire to. Their presence would have been most unwelcome to that carrier admiral, who despised the aging leviathans but was obliged to "furnish security" to them.

Why was the CinCPac so keen to take his proud dreadnoughts to sea? The stakeout made sense only as a battle disposition.

The nine battleships of the reconstituted second task force, screened by eighteen light cruisers and destroyers, would reach their waiting position in two or three days while the carriers beat up the Marshalls. Halsey's flattops would then steam north to join them and pass under command of the senior gunnery admiral present, no doubt Kimmel. The exact rendezvous "northward of the Marshalls" was not identified. The fleet would have sought a place under friendly air cover and far from prying eyes in the sky. (The planners in Washington, nervous that the wild men of Hawaii might probe for battle near Japan, advised that if an engagement were sought, it should occur where flying boats could cover it.) But after two weeks of war, Wake Island's squadrons would have suffered grievously from breakdowns and combat.

Midway, on the other hand, lay 1,000 miles to the east and appeared immune to serious danger. As many as forty-eight flying boats could mass there for long-distance patrols. Kimmel would probably have massed his ships along the Wake-Midway line, although not near either atoll, since he had a phobia about submarine dangers within 200 miles of bases and Wake might still be subject to spy flights from the Marshalls or from Marcus Island. Nearer to Midway would have been safer. Midway's dense reconnaissance pattern of 1,000-mile-radius planes would be sure to spot an enemy fleet at a distance greater than it could close during a long winter night. No U.S. admiral would have wished to blunder into Japanese battleships in the dark, because few American ships had radar and they were ill prepared to match the foe with rapid, sustained night fire.

The fleet's waiting position would have eerily resembled the ambush site at Point Luck before the Battle of Midway in June 1942: northeast of a "bait" island, on the flank of an unsuspecting Japanese armada, under the wing of its best advance base, and beyond the eyes of shore-based aerial prowlers. Wherever its precise locale, the entire Pacific Fleet would be concentrated and ready about 15J or 16J.

The authors of Plan O-1 didn't spell out Yamamoto's expected reaction, but the deployments made clear what they thought he would do. At anchor in Japan as war erupted in the Far East, Yamamoto would learn from spies and submarines that task forces were sortieing from Pearl Harbor. On 6J he would also learn tht Halsey was scanning the Marshalls, presumably preparatory to a raid. He would grasp the opportunity for a fight (as Japan's First Carrier Air Fleet did in February 1942, when it futilely raced after American carriers raiding the Marshalls). U.S. planners might have assumed he could weigh anchor as quickly as their fleet, say after two days' alert, on 8J. Kimmel would probably hear of its emergence from his submarine cordon, the two cruisers in the Philippine Sea, or perhaps from arcane sources such as code breaking, to judge from McMorris's promise of juicy intelligence.

Where would Yamamoto head? He could not hope, while burdened with slow oilers, to cut off Halsey by a sweep through the North Pacific. He would want to avoid the search arcs of Wake and Midway as long as possible. His soundest course would be to put in at Truk for fuel and then approach the Marshalls from the west-southwest. Assuming a movement at fifteen knots—the customary assumption for the American battle line—the Combined Fleet, goaded on by Halsey's reappearance to scorch the northern Marshalls on 14J, would be spotted in the vicinity of Eniwetok by air scouts from Wake about 15J to 17J. The Japanese carriers might sprint ahead to bash Wake or hunt for the U.S. carriers, but Kimmel would have expected Yamamoto to keep them close to his battle line, just as he would have done. The two fleets, 1,000 miles apart, would then close rapidly near Wake Island.

What might have been the outcome of a sea battle in 1941? Japan's navy outnumbered the Pacific Fleet in carriers, ten to three. American carrier wings were larger, but Japan's 500 planes would still constitute a two-tone edge (perhaps more if Halsey suffered losses while raiding). The Japanese planes also had a distinct edge in performance. To modern readers knowing the superiority of carriers over battleships, Kimmel's scheme might appear suicidal, but in 1941 this was far from clear. Kimmel's appreciation of air power, except for reconnaissance, was rather primitive. He thought of carriers as auxiliaries: They could sally forth on raids, but their place in a fleet engagement was with the battle line. The CinCPac didn't understand, and sometimes irritated, his aviators. "Fly-boys," he called them. McMorris, too, was somewhat contemptuous of airmen.

The situation of the American battle line might have been a good one. It would be assembled in toto, whereas some enemy dreadnoughts might be occupied elsewhere and others might already have been torpedoed by submarines as they emerged from their home bases. The United States also would enjoy the exclusive benefit of distant air scouting. (By November 1941 plans were afoot to place army heavy bombers on the atolls too.) Kimmel might well have had the advantage of surprise. Years later he mused that a clash would have been "a nice mix-up" and not at all one-sided in favor of Japan. He might have played some of the same cards used by the outnumbered American navy at the Battle of Midway: use of the sole air base, a clever ambush strategy, and of course intelligence. (Conversely, some elements of the Plan O-1 deployment resembled Yamamoto's disposition for that battle, such as task forces scattered about the ocean and the battle line poised for the coup de grace after air preliminaries.)

It may be argued that the battle projected by Plan O-1 could never have been implemented because of deficiencies of the Pacific Fleet. In hindsight after the Pearl Harbor disaster, Kimmel said his dreadnoughts were slower than believed, and Turner scoffed that they were suited only for sinking slow landing convoys off Hawaii. Normal overhauls and a shortage of oilers would also have reduced fleet capabilities.

However, a supposition that the plan would not have been executed denies certain facts. On September 9, 1941, the chief of naval operations approved it without significant comment. McMorris's updatings, the last on the morning of December 6, confirmed that if war had broken out the next day where expected—in the Orient—the plan would have been activated, with certain adjustments for current ship locations. Many witnesses testified in the various hearings on Pearl Harbor held between 1941 and 1946 that Kimmel unquestionably intended to send out every ship, including the battleships. McMorris recalled his boss fretting about the risks, yet confident and determined to go forth. The hawkish strategist considered the fleet virtually mobilized, ready to sortie within one to four days. McMorris "knew the power" the fleet had and expected it to prevail. The CinCPac himself believed to the end that his duty was to act aggressively. Halsey, who was anxious to go, was sure that Kimmel would not have split his command and let it be taken in detail.

An early battle might have had a profound effect on the course of World War II. An American victory might have unnerved Japan and slowed its southward thrust, perhaps allowing British and U.S. forces to retain a toehold in the East Indies, deny oil to Japan, and eventually launch an offensive from that quarter. On the other hand, an American defeat more punishing than Pearl Harbor might have caused the United States to divert its energies from the Germany-first strategy and focus on Japan. Such a choice would have boded ill for the fate of Europe—although without the galvanizing shock of Pearl Harbor, the United States might have negotiated a settlement after a short war in the Pacific and redeployed against Hitler before all was lost.

More mysterious than the outcome of the hypothetical battle is its absence of notice by historians. Eight official investigations and the many books about Pearl Harbor have failed to catch the real implications of Plan O-1. They have noted only what was stated, not what was implied. Rainbow Five instructed the fleet to divert the Imperial Navy, not engage it. Plan O-1 spelled out the raiding strategy, but only hinted at a combat. Battle as the true grail emerges from careful assessment of its extraordinary details.

Why was the true nature of the plan so covert, even to other Americans with access to it? Kimmel and McMorris were known to play their cards close to the chest. They probably didn't share all their ideas with cautious fleet colleagues and the worriers in Washington. Pye, for example, testified that he knew his battleships were supposed to be ready "for the conduct of a major action," but he didn't say how soon he expected it. After the Pearl Harbor debacle, it would not have been in anybody's interest to admit to a swashbuckling scheme that was not explicitly written down, one that bordered on insubordination unless it was blessed by a nod and wink from headquarters. To acknowledge its existence after the frailty of battleships was demonstrated at Hawaii and Malaya would have cast the naval leaders as even greater fools. By the time the higher-ups of the Navy Department were called to the witness stand, they had heroic wartime reputations to preserve. This does not imply a conspiracy or a cover-up, simply that they might have preferred to forget a vague, unrecorded, and in hindsight bizarre intention. Besides, the interrogators never asked about it.

Kimmel was cashiered in disgrace nine days after the attack on Pearl Harbor. Bitter at being made the scapegoat of defeat, he reproached his superiors for failing to warn him adequately by sharing code-breaking intelligence. It would hardly have been wise to bring up a sensationally aggressive scheme. On the contrary, the admiral played down the planned concentration at sea and claimed that the battleships had been better off in the shallow harbor, where most were salvaged, than on what he called the "dangerous course" of cruising without carrier cover—the very course that his plan dictated.

Soc McMorris remained faithful to the rationality of his plan. "It was intended to have the entire available strength in easy supporting distance" of each other, he said. While hedging about encountering the main part of the Japanese fleet, his true feelings shone through when he rose to the bait of a hypothetical question during 1944 army and navy inquiries. What would he have advised had he known that Vice Admiral Chuichi Nagumo's flattops were bearing down on Pearl Harbor? The battleships, he replied, certainly shouldn't have been at their moorings; they should have been massed at sea for contact. Given Nagumo's six-to-two carrier dominance in the central Pacific that day (the *Saratoga* being on the West Coast), the dreadnoughts would have "suffered quite severely," he admitted. But hope lay in bringing the foe to bay with gunfire, he testified, no matter how improbable the odds.

Historians have scribbled barrels of ink debating whether Kimmel and the army chief in Hawaii, Lieutenant General Walter C. Short, understood the import of the famous "war warning" from Washington on November 27, 1941. It stated that hostilities were imminent but didn't specify a threat to Pearl Harbor. It contained the fateful words, "Execute an appropriate defensive deployment preparatory to carrying out the tasks assigned to WPL 46" (the navy's version of Rainbow Five to which Fleet Plan O-1 was appended). The chief of naval operations and his staff later argued that the Pacific Fleet should have adopted a defensive posture despite that plan's stipulation of offensive action. Kelly Turner, a bona fide war hero when he was interrogated, denied all personal blame but in fairness reaffirmed that "it would be a grave error for anyone to get the idea that the war in the Central Pacific was to be purely defensive. Far from it."

The fleet's two foremost advocates of offensive action differed in their postmortems. Kimmel, furious at having been denied inside information, decided that he had honored the warning by taking defensive measures, all of which proved to be in vain. None of those measures involved the forty-nine flying boats sitting on Oahu the morning of December 7. The admiral declared that, having been ordered to slam the Marshalls, he needed the planes in tip-top condition, not worn out by patrols around Hawaii. In hindsight he grimly acknowledged that if he had known what was coming, he would have sent them out to scout. McMorris, his reputation redeemed by wartime successes in planning and command, was unrepentant. He had taken the war warning to mean that national leaders worried that "in our enthusiasm to strike as promptly as possible," the fleet might sail to the Marshalls prematurely "and thus destroy any remote chance of retaining peace." This seemed so evident, he said, that neither he nor Kimmel had sought clarification. The fleet's job, McMorris believed, was to lunge forward immediately.

By 1941 American leaders had diluted the swift revenge of War Plan Orange to trivial demonstrations in the ocean. The hawks in Hawaii had been fenced in and left with only one weapon of dominance. Never ordered to seek a gunnery Trafalgar, neither were they told to avoid one. The brilliant young lawyer who drafted the congressional report that condemned the commander in chief for the disaster—but who also admired Kimmel's nerve—later summed it up: "The admiral," he mused in 1976, "appeared consumed with the idea of becoming himself 'the American Nelson.'"

*AUTUMN 1991*

---

Edward S. Miller is the author of *War Plan Orange: The U.S. Strategy to Defeat Japan, 1897–1945* (1991), published by the Naval Institute Press. His current research centers on the economic struggle between the United States and Japan prior to World War II.

# 29

# Why Hitler Declared War on the United States

## By Gerhard L. Weinberg

*One of the continuing puzzles of the Second World War is why Hitler, on December 11, 1941, declared war on the United States. Up to that point in World War II, the führer had assiduously avoided war with America. This evasion was in spite of repeated American actions—the Atlantic Fleet's escorting of British convoys from Canada to Iceland, the clash between the USS Greer and U-652, and FDR's "shoot on sight" declaration—that easily could have served the Third Reich as a casus belli. In addition, Hitler had ignored the pleas of his submarine captains for more permissive rules of engagement against American warships in the Atlantic. Yet upon word that the Japanese had attacked the American fleet at Pearl Harbor—the location of which neither Hitler nor any of his immediate military staff even knew (!)—Hitler rushed to embrace war with the United States. Why? Gerhard L. Weinberg provides insights into the mysteries of Hitler's action.*

When news of the Japanese attack on Pearl Harbor reached Germany, its leadership was absorbed by the crisis in its war with the Soviet Union. On December 1, 1941, after the serious defeat the Red Army administered to the German forces at the southern end of the Eastern Front, Adolf Hitler had relieved Field Marshal Gerd von Rundstedt, the commander in chief of the army group fighting there; the next day Hitler flew to the army group headquarters in the southern Ukraine. Late on December 3 he flew back to his headquarters in East Prussia, only to be greeted by more bad news: The German army group at the northern end of the Russian front was also being pushed back by Red Army counterattacks. Most ominous of all, the German offensive in the center, toward Moscow, not only had exhausted itself but was in danger of being overwhelmed by a Soviet counteroffensive. Not yet recognizing the extent of the defeat all along the front, Hitler and his generals saw their reverses merely as a temporary halt in German offensive operations.

The reality was just beginning to sink in when the German leaders got news of Japan's attack on Pearl Harbor. On the evening of December 8, within hours of hearing about the previous day's attack, Hitler ordered that at any opportunity the German navy should sink American ships and those of Central and South American countries that had declared their solidarity with the United States. That evening, too, he left East Prussia by train for Berlin, but not before sending out a summons to the members of the German parliament, the Reichstag, to meet on December 11 and, in a formal session that would be broadcast to the whole country, declare war on the United States.

Why this eagerness to go to war with yet another great power, and at a time when Germany already faced a serious situation on the Eastern Front? Some have argued that it was an irrational reaction by Hitler to his failure to take Moscow; some have attributed the delay of a few days to reluctance on Hitler's part, when it had more to do with the fact that Japan's initiative had caught the Germans by surprise; still others imagine that Germany had finally reacted to America's policy of aiding Britain, even though in all his prior declarations of war Hitler had paid scant heed to the policies, for or against Germany, of the countries invaded. Ideological considerations and strategic priorities as Germany saw them were always more important. The most recent case was that of the Soviet Union, which had been providing critical supplies to Germany until minutes before the German attack of June 22, 1941.

The reality is that war with the United States had been included in Hitler's agenda for years, that he had deferred hostilities only because he wanted to begin them at a time, and under circumstances, of his own choosing, and that the Japanese attack fitted his requirements precisely. It had been an assumption of Hitler's since the 1920s that Germany would at some point fight the United States. Already in the summer of 1928 he had asserted in his second book (not published until I did it for him in 1961, as *Hitlers zweites Buch*) that strengthening and preparing Germany for war with the United States was one of the tasks of the National Socialist movement. Because his aims for Germany's future entailed an unlimited expansion and because he thought the United States might at some time constitute a challenge to German domination of the globe, a war with the United States had long been a part of the future he envisioned. It would come either during his own rule or during that of his successors.

During the years of his chancellorship before 1939, German policies designed to implement the project of a war with the United States had been conditioned by two factors: belief in the truth of the stab-in-the-back legend on the one hand and the practical problems of engaging American military power on the other. The former, the widespread belief that Germany had lost the First World War because of the collapse at home rather than defeat at the front, automatically carried with it a converse of enormous significance, and one that has generally been ignored. The more credence one gave to the stab in the back, the more negligible the military role of the

United States in that conflict seemed. To Hitler and to many others in Germany, the idea that American participation had enabled the Western powers to hold on in 1918 and then move toward victory was not a reasonable explanation of the events of that year but a legend instead.

Only those Germans who remained unenlightened by nationalist euphoria could believe that American forces had played any significant role in the past or would do so in the future. A solid German home front, which National Socialism would ensure, could preclude defeat next time. The problem of fighting the United States was not that the inherently weak and divided Americans could create, field, and support effective fighting forces. Rather it was that the intervening ocean could be blocked by a large American fleet.

Unlike the German navy of the pre-1914 era, in which discussions were really debates about the relative merits of landing on Cape Cod versus landing on Long Island, the German government of the 1930s took a more practical approach. In line with its emphasis on building up the air force, specifications were issued in 1937 and 1938 for what became the Me 264 and was soon referred to inside the government as the "America bomber" or the "New York bomber." The "America bomber" would be capable of carrying a five-ton load of bombs to New York or a smaller load to the Midwest, or of flying reconnaissance missions over the West Coast and then returning to Germany without refueling at intermediate bases. Several types and models were experimented with, the first prototype flying in December 1940, but none of them advanced beyond preliminary models.

Instead, Hitler and his advisers came to concentrate ever more on the concept of acquiring bases for the German air force on the coast of northwest Africa, as well as on the Spanish and Portuguese islands off the African coast, to shorten the distance to the western hemisphere. Hitler also held discussions with his naval advisers and with Japanese diplomats about bombing the United States from the Azores; but those consultations did not take place until 1940 and 1941. In the meantime, prewar planning had shifted its focus to naval matters.

Like the Japanese, the Germans in the 1930s faced the question of how to cope with the American navy in the furtherance of their expansionist ambitions; without the slightest consultation, and in complete and deliberate ignorance of each other's projects, the two governments came to exactly the same conclusion. In both countries the decision was to trump American quantity with quality, to build super-battleships, which by their vastly greater size could carry far heavier armament that could fire over greater distances and thus would be able to destroy the American battleships at ranges the enemy's guns could not match.

The Japanese began constructing four such super-battleships in great secrecy. The Germans hoped to construct six super-battleships; their plans were worked out early in 1939 and the keels laid in April and May. These 56,200-ton monsters would outclass not only the new U.S. battleships of the *North Carolina* class then beginning to be built but even the successor *Iowa* class.

The precise details of how a war with the United States would actually be conducted was not a subject to which Hitler or his associates devoted a great deal of attention. When the time came, something could always be worked out; it was more important to prepare the prerequisites for success.

When World War II began in September 1939, work ceased on those portions of the blue-water navy not already near completion; that included the super-battleships. The immediate exigencies of the war took precedence over projects that could not be finished in the near future. Almost immediately, however, the German navy urged steps that would bring the United States into the war. Admiral Erich Raeder, the navy's commander in chief, could hardly wait to go to war with the United States. He hoped that the increase in sinkings of merchant shipping, including American, that would result from a completely unrestricted submarine campaign would have a major impact on Britain, whose surface navy Germany could not yet defeat. But Hitler held back. As he saw it, what was the point of marginally increasing U-boat sinkings when Germany had neither a major surface navy yet nor bases for it to operate from?

The spring of 1940 appeared to provide the opportunity to remedy both deficiencies. The conquest of Norway in April immediately produced two relevant decisions: First, Norway would be incorporated into the Third Reich, and second, a major permanent base for Germany's new navy would be built on the Norwegian—now German—coast at Trondheim. In addition, a large, entirely German city would be built there, with the whole complex to be connected directly to mainland Germany by special roads, bridges, and railways. Work on this colossal project continued until the spring of 1943.

The conquest of the Low Countries and France, soon after that of Norway, appeared to open further prospects. In the eyes of Hitler and his associates, the war in the West was over; they could turn to their next objectives. On land that meant an invasion of the Soviet Union, a simple task that Hitler originally hoped to complete in the fall of 1940. At sea, it meant that the problem of making war on the United States could be tackled.

On July 11, 1940, Hitler ordered the resumption of the naval construction program. The super-battleships, together with hundreds of other warships, could now be built. While that program went forward, the Germans not only would construct the naval base at Trondheim and take over the French naval bases on the Atlantic coast, but would push a land connection to the Strait of Gibraltar—if Germany could control Spain as it did France. It would then be easy to acquire and develop air and sea bases in French and Spanish northwest Africa, as well as on the Spanish and Portuguese islands in the Atlantic. In a war with the United States, they would be the perfect advance bases for the new fleet and for airplanes that did not yet meet the earlier extravagant specifications for long-range flight.

These rosy prospects did not work out. Whatever Francisco Franco's enthusiasm for joining the war on the side of Germany, and whatever his willingness to assist his friend in Berlin, the Spanish dictator was a nationalist who was not about to yield Spanish sovereignty to anyone else—neither in territory now held by Spain nor in French and British holdings that he expected to pick up as a reward for joining the Axis. The fact that the German leadership in 1940 was willing to sacrifice the participation of Spain as an equal fighting partner rather than give up on their hopes for German-controlled bases on and off the coast of northwest Africa is an excellent indication of the priority that they assigned to their concept of war with the United States. Franco's offer of the use of Spanish bases was not enough for them: German sovereignty was what they believed their schemes required. When the Spanish foreign minister went to Berlin in September 1940, and when Hitler and Franco met on the French-Spanish border in October, it was the sovereignty issue that caused a fundamental rift between the prospective partners in war.

But it was not only the bases that proved elusive. As the preparations for war with the Soviet Union made another reallocation of armament resources necessary in the late fall of 1940, the construction of the blue-water navy was again halted. Once more Hitler had to restrain the enthusiasm of the German navy for war with the United States. The navy believed that in World War II, as in World War I, the way to defeat Great Britain lay in unrestricted submarine warfare, even if that meant bringing the United States into the conflict. But Hitler was doubtful whether what had failed the last time would work now; he had other ideas for coping with Britain, such as bombing and possibly invading it. When it came to taking on the United States, he recognized that he could not do so without a large surface navy. It was at this point that Japan came into the picture.

Since the Germans had long regarded a war with the Western powers as the major and most difficult prerequisite for an easy conquest of the Soviet Union, and since it appeared to them that Japan's ambitions in East Asia clashed with British, French, and American interests, Berlin had tried for years to achieve Japanese participation in an alliance directed against the West. The authorities in Tokyo had been happy to work with Germany in general, but major elements in the Japanese government had been reluctant to fight Britain and France. Some preferred a war with the Soviet Union; others were worried about a war with the United States, which they saw as a likely result of war with Britain and France; still others thought that it would be best to settle the war with China first; and some held a combination of these views.

In any case, all German efforts to rope Japan into an alliance actively opposing the West had failed. The German reaction to this failure—their signing of a nonaggression pact with the Soviet Union in 1939—had only served to alienate some of their best friends in a Japan that was then engaged in open hostilities with the Soviet Union on the border between their respective East Asian puppet states of Manchukuo and Mongolia.

In Tokyo's view, the defeat of the Netherlands and France the following year, and the need of the British to concentrate on defense of the home islands, appeared to open the colonial empires of Southeast Asia to easy conquest. From the perspective of Berlin, the same lovely prospects lay in front of the Japanese—but there was no reason to let them have all this without some military contribution to the common cause of maximum looting. That contribution would lie in pouncing on the British Empire in Southeast Asia, especially Singapore, before Britain had followed France and Holland into defeat, not after. It would, moreover, at one stroke solve the problem of how to deal with the United States.

In the short run, Japanese participation in the war would divert American attention and resources from the Atlantic to the Pacific. In the long run, and of even greater importance, the Axis would acquire a huge and effective navy. At a time when the United States had a navy barely adequate for one ocean, the Panama Canal made it possible to move that navy from the Pacific to the Atlantic, and back. This was the basic concern behind the American desire for a two-ocean navy, authorized by Congress in July 1940. Since it would be years before that two-ocean navy was completed, there would be a lengthy interval when any major American involvement in a Pacific conflict would make substantial support of Britain in the Atlantic impossible. Furthermore, it obviously made no difference in which ocean American warships were sunk.

For Germany in the meantime, the obvious alternative to building its own navy was to find an ally who already had one. The Germans believed that Japan's navy in 1940–41 was the strongest and best in the world (and it is quite possible that this assessment was correct). It is in this framework of expectations that one can perhaps more easily understand the curious, apparently self-contradictory policy toward the United States that the Germans followed in 1941.

On the one hand, Hitler repeatedly ordered restraint on the German navy to avoid incidents in the Atlantic that might prematurely bring the United States into the war against Germany. Whatever steps the Americans might take in their policy of aiding Great Britain, Hitler would not take these as a pretext to go to war with the United States until he thought the time proper: American lend-lease legislation no more affected his policy toward the United States than the simultaneous vast increase in Soviet assistance to Germany influenced his decision to go to war with that country.

On the other hand, he repeatedly promised the Japanese that if they believed war with the United States was an essential part of a war against Britain, Germany would join them in such a conflict. Hitler personally made this pledge to Foreign Minister Matsuoka Yosuke when the latter visited Germany early in April 1941; it was repeated on various occasions thereafter. The apparent contradiction is easily resolved if one keeps in mind what was central in the thinking of the German leader and soon became generally understood in the German government: As long as Germany had to face the United States by itself, it needed time to build its own blue-water navy; it therefore made sense to postpone hostilities with the Americans. If, however, Japan came into the war on Germany's side, that problem would be automatically solved.

This approach also makes it easier to understand why the Germans were not particular about the sequence: If Japan decided to go to war in the spring or summer of 1941, even before the German invasion of the Soviet Union, that would be fine, and Germany would immediately join in. When it appeared, however, that Japanese-American negotiations in the spring and summer might lead to some agreement, the Germans tried hard to torpedo those talks. One way was by drawing Japan into the war through the back door, as it were. At a time when the Germans were still certain that the eastern campaign was headed for a quick and victorious resolution, they attempted—unsuccessfully—to persuade the Japanese to attack the Soviet Union.

During the summer of 1941, while the Japanese seemed to the Germans to be hesitating, the German campaign in the Soviet Union appeared to be going perfectly. The first and most immediate German reaction was a return to its program of naval construction. In the weapons technology of the 1930s and 1940s, big warships were the system with the longest lead time from orders to completion. The German leaders were entirely aware of this and highly sensitive to its implications. Whenever the opportunity appeared to be there, they turned first to the naval construction program. Once again, however, in 1941 as in 1940, the prospect of prompt victory over the immediate foe faded from view, and once again work on the big warships had to be halted. (But the Germans, despite their much-vaunted organization, failed to cancel an engine contract; in June 1944 they were offered four useless battleship engines.) Stopping the battleship construction only accented the hope that Japan would move, as well as the enthusiasm with which such an action would be greeted.

Just as the Germans had not kept the Japanese informed of their plans to attack other countries, so the Japanese kept the Germans in the dark. When Tokyo was ready to move, it had only to check with the Germans (and Italians) to make sure that they remained as willing to go to war against the United States as they had repeatedly asserted they were. In late November and again at the beginning of December, the Germans reassured the Japanese that they had nothing to worry about. Germany, like Italy, was eager to go to war with the United States—provided Japan took the plunge.

There were two ways in which the German declaration of war on the United States would differ from her procedure in going to war with other countries: the timing and the absence of internal opposition. In all other cases, the timing of war had been essentially in Germany's own hands. Now the date would be selected by an ally that moved when it was ready and without previously notifying the Germans. When Hitler met with the Japanese foreign minister back in April, he had not known that Japan would dither for months; he also did not know, the last time Tokyo checked with him, that on this occasion the Japanese intended to move immediately.

As a result, Hitler was caught out of town at the time of Pearl Harbor and had to get back to Berlin and summon the Reichstag to declare war. His great worry, and that of his foreign minister, Joachim von Ribbentrop, was that the Americans might get their declaration of war in ahead of his own. As Ribbentrop explained it, "A great power does not allow itself to be declared war upon; it declares war on others."

Just to make sure that hostilities started immediately, however, Hitler had already issued orders to his navy, straining at the leash since October 1939, to begin sinking American ships forthwith, even before the formalities of a declaration. Now that Germany had a big navy on its side, there was no need to wait even an hour. The very fact that the Japanese had started hostilities the way Germany had begun its attack on Yugoslavia earlier that year, with a Sunday morning attack in peacetime, showed what a delightfully appropriate ally Japan would be. The American navy would now be smashed in the Pacific and thus incapable of aiding Britain, while American troops and supplies would be diverted to that theater as well.

The second way in which this German declaration of war differed from most that had preceded it was in the absence of opposition at home. For once the frenetic applause of the unanimous Reichstag, the German parliament last elected in 1938, reflected a unanimous government and military leadership. In World War I, it was agreed, Germany had not been defeated at the front but had succumbed to the collapse of a home front deluded by Woodrow Wilson's siren songs from across the Atlantic; now there was to be no danger of a new stab in the back. The opponents of the regime at home had been silenced. Its imagined Jewish enemies were already being slaughtered, with hundreds of thousands killed by the time of Hitler's speech of December 11, 1941. Now that Germany had a strong Japanese navy at its side, victory was considered certain.

From the perspective of half a century, one can see an additional unintended consequence of Pearl Harbor for the Germans. It not only meant that they would most certainly be defeated. It also meant that the active coalition against them would include the United States as well as Great Britain, its dominions, the Free French, various governments-in-exile, and the Soviet Union. And without U.S. participation, there could have been no massive invasion of northwest Europe; the Red Army eventually might have reached the English Channel and the Atlantic, overrunning all Germany in the process. If the Germans today enjoy both their freedom and their unity in a country aligned and allied with what their leaders of 1941 considered the degenerate Western democracies, they owe it in part to the disastrous cupidity and stupidity of the Japanese attack on Pearl Harbor.

*SPRING 1992*

Gerhard L. Weinberg is the William Rand Kenan, Jr., Professor of History at the University of North Carolina at Chapel Hill and author of *A World at Arms: A Global History of World War II* (1994). His book *Germany, Hitler, and World War II* will be published in 1995.

# 30

# Women, Combat, and the Gender Line

## By D'Ann Campbell

*Until recently, women have been the ignored or forgotten warriors of World War II. Except for an occasional mention of Soviet women performing combat roles in the Great Patriotic War against Germany, the pages of combat history exclusively chronicle the affairs of men. To a large degree, that coverage reflects reality: A very small number of women served in combat units between 1939 and 1945. But, given the need, they did serve. The Japanese had their all-female "Lilly Brigade," while Hitler organized his Blitzmädchen. Among the western Allies, Great Britain led the way toward breaking the gender line, successfully using women in antiaircraft crews as early as 1941. Eisenhower reported positively on the British experience. In late 1942, the United States Army emulated its British partner, forming experimental antiaircraft units crewed by women and finding the units to be an outstanding success. And then the army quickly dropped the whole notion. D'Ann Campbell explores the reasons why.*

Women were the invisible combatants of World War II. Hundreds of thousands fought—not as partisans or guerrillas but as regular soldiers in uniform. They served on both sides and every front. German women soldiers helped inflict casualties on American and British forces, and in turn they were killed, wounded, or captured. Likewise, Soviet and British women fought bravely. American women, however, did not fight. The questions are: Why not? And what does that fact tell us about gender roles in America?

The U.S. War Department was well aware of the British experience with women soldiers. In 1940–41, the Luftwaffe had lost the Battle of Britain, but it remained a powerful force to be reckoned with. The preferred solution to the problem was strong antiaircraft (AA) units. By 1941, as more and more men were needed in frontline infantry units, the British began using their female Auxiliary Territorial Service (ATS) soldiers in "protected" AA units—protected because these home-front soldiers were immune from capture, and their living conditions could be closely monitored. To help emphasize the importance of women in AA units to free more men, Winston Churchill's daughter Mary served in one such brigade.

In August 1942, U.S. Army Chief of Staff George C. Marshall asked General Dwight Eisenhower, who was in England, to investigate the effectiveness of the British mixed-gender AA units. When Eisenhower gave a positive report, Marshall decided to conduct his own experiment to see if American women could serve the same function. Security was tight— there were no leaks whatever until long after the war.

For his experiment, Marshall wanted to recruit women who had already volunteered for military service. He turned to the only official American women's organization at that time, the Women's Auxiliary Army Corps (WAAC). A total of 21 officers and 374 enrollees were selected for this experiment. From December 15, 1942, to April 15, 1943, these "Waacs," as they were called, were trained in what had been designated the Military District of Washington, D.C., on two composite antiaircraft gun batteries and the nearby searchlight units. They served with the 36th Coast Artillery Brigade AA.

Colonel Edward W. Timberlake, the immediate commander of these experimental units, had nothing but praise for them: "The experiences . . . indicate that all WAAC personnel exhibited an outstanding devotion to duty, willingness and ability to absorb and grasp technical information concerning the problems, maintenance and tactical disposition to all types of equipment." Indeed, the Waacs learned their duties much more quickly than the men in such units, most of whom had been classified for "limited-duty service." Timberlake recommended that in the future, the training periods for women recruits could be shortened. When evaluating the searchlight units, he reported that "the same willingness to learn and devotion to duty has been manifested in these units as in the gun batteries."

Contrary to generally existing stereotypes of women being physically too weak to perform combat jobs, Timberlake concluded that women met the physical, intellectual, and psychological standards for this mission. In an echo of a widespread belief at the time, he reported, "WAAC personnel were found to be superior in efficiency to men in all functions involving delicacy of manual dexterity." He specifically listed their operation at the director, height finder, radar, and searchlight stations, and concluded that "their performance of repetitious routine duties is considered superior to that of men." Indeed, he judged that WAAC personnel could be substituted for men in 60 percent of all AA positions.

Because men and women were going to be working in close proximity, Timberlake was concerned about any possible scandals that might occur. Promiscuity, or even rumors of impropriety, could undermine a unit's combat effectiveness. He was relieved to find that "the relationship between the Army personnel and WAAC personnel, both enlisted and commissioned, has been highly satisfactory." No sexual harassment was noted; instead, he found, "a mutual understanding and appreciation appears to exist."

Timberlake asked his superior, Major General John T. Lewis of the Military District of Washington, to judge the experiment for himself. Soon Lewis was as enthusiastic as Timberlake. Lewis wrote that Waacs could "efficiently perform many duties in the antiaircraft artillery unit." Their high morale and a paucity of disciplinary problems "increases materially the relative value of WAAC personnel in antiaircraft artillery in fixed positions." Lewis was so proud of his Waacs that in May 1943 he asked Marshall for authority to continue the experiment, increase the number of Waacs to 103 officers and 2,315 enrollees, and replace half the 3,630 men in his AA Defense Command with these more efficient soldiers.

Marshall now had to make a choice. If he let Lewis have the women, the whole country could immediately hear that women were being sent into combat. What would that do to proposals to draft women? What would conservative southern congressmen, who never liked the WAAC in the first place, do to Marshall's plans to expand it? Would the general public disapprove? Would women stop volunteering? Would the male soldiers react unfavorably? The Judge Advocate General's Office said Congress would have to change the existing legislation, and it provided the wording for a suitable amendment: The new Section 20 would read, "Nothing in this act shall prevent any member of the Women's Army Auxiliary Corps from service with any combatant organization with her own consent."

Marshall asked his staff for advice. They recommended that he terminate the experiment immediately. General Miller White of the General Staff's personnel division acknowledged that "the War Department believes the experiment . . . has demonstrated conclusively the practicability of using members of the Corps in this role." However, since the strength of the WAAC was far below total requirements, he argued that the Waacs could "be more efficiently employed in many other positions for which requisitions are already in hand, and that their use in antiaircraft artillery to release limited service personnel is not justified under present circumstances."

In other words, the experiment was a success, but the army needed these women for higher-priority—as well as lower-risk—positions. If Germany or Japan had been able to pose a practical threat from the air to the continental United States, then putting women in AA positions might have become a high priority. However, given the relative safety of both coasts by 1943, Waacs were most needed to serve in clerical and administrative positions. The AA units had been using men available only for limited-duty service, and there were more than enough of these men to fill the units' current needs. Meanwhile, clerical and administrative positions normally filled by women in the civilian world were held by able-bodied men with football fingers who could be in combat instead.

In 1942, Marshall had discovered that some congressmen were so concerned about protecting the female sailors that they amended the law to forbid the naval women's reserve—Women Accepted for Volunteer Emergency Service, or WAVES—from serving overseas. Marshall had been lobbying Congress to upgrade the WAAC from auxiliary to full military status (the Women's Army Corps, or WAC). He wanted the "Wacs" to serve overseas. The War Department withdrew the WAC bill in April 1943, because of the flak over the navy bill. The department resubmitted it in May, and Congress passed it on June 28, with authority for overseas service. However, had Congress learned that Marshall wanted the Wacs to serve in combat units, the WAC bill might have been lost forever or many new restrictions placed on the ability of the army to utilize its women soldiers. General Russell Reynolds, director of the military personnel division, summarized the army staff's consensus to eliminate the AA experiment before Congress got wind of it: "It is not believed that national policy or public opinion is yet ready to accept the use of women in field force units."

Marshall made his decision: He terminated the experiment, reassigned the Wacs, ordered the results kept confidential, and never thought of using women in combat again. America had drawn the gender line. If the decision had been made exclusively on the grounds of efficiency and performance, women would have been assigned to AA batteries. Instead, it was based on the army's need for female office workers, on the state of public opinion, and on the general hostility toward women in nontraditional gender roles in 1943.

TO EVALUATE THE full implications of Marshall's decision—to explore what might have happened—it is essential to study the British model the United States had been watching closely. Before the war, in 1938, a prominent British engineer, Caroline Haslett, was asked to visit the AA batteries at practice and advise Major General Frederick Pile, the newly appointed commander of the 1st AA Division, if any of these jobs could be held by women. Except for the heavy work of loading ammunition, Haslett reported, women could perform all functions. As the British military began reassigning the most able-bodied antiaircraft men to the field army, Pile decided to experiment with integrated, or mixed, batteries.

The National Service Act of December 1941 drafted 125,000 women into the military over the next three years; 430,000 more volunteered. The largest of the women's units, Auxiliary Territorial Service (ATS), began as a woman's auxiliary to the military in 1938; in 1941 it was granted military status (with pay two-thirds that of men of equal rank). Pile went to the ATS to find women soldiers to serve alongside his men, who were battling the Luftwaffe bombers day and night. Sir James Grigg, under-secretary of state for war, declared Pile's proposal "breath-taking and revolutionary." Prime Minister Winston Churchill was enthusiastic. He argued that any general who saved him 40,000 fighting men had gained the equivalent of a victory.

By August 1941, women were operating the fire-control instruments, and men the actual guns, in Richmond Park, near the headquarters of AA

Command. By September 1943, over 56,000 women were working for AA Command, most in units close to London. The first mixed regiment to fire in action was the 132nd, on November 21, 1941, and the first "kill" came in April 1942. As Pile observed, "Beyond a little natural excitement and a tendency to chatter when there was a lull, they behaved like a veteran party, and shot an enemy plane into the sea."

The mixed batteries were commanded by men from AA regiments. Women officers from ATS served as "gender commissars," whose only official function was to supervise the military bearing of the enlisted women. ATS officers were given a brief course in the general principles of anti-aircraft work, but the only women allowed to participate in the actual fighting were the ATS enlistees. The male chain of command handled all instruction and supervision of both men and women in the technical areas.

In practice, the women officers soon took over some of the fire-control operations—a practice condoned by the AA Command and ATS leadership. As one woman explained, "When we arrived at our site we had all been trained for particular jobs, but since then we have learned to do every job in camp except fire the guns—and I bet we could do that too if we were allowed." Soon women skilled in fire-control operations also learned to set the range and bearing dials on the gun itself a few yards away and to adjust the fuses on the shells. Indeed, they could even take over the complete operation of a light 40mm AA gun. But regulations strictly prohibited women from engaging the firing mechanism. They could not pull the trigger on a man, even a Luftwaffe pilot.

ATS women were soon assigned to searchlight units. Operators were scattered around the gun complex, and therefore each searchlight was some distance from the next. Each unit had to be supplemented with a male soldier firing a tripod-mounted light machine gun to deter any raider who attacked down the beam; the women called him the "Lister Twister" since his other job was to crank the Lister generator providing the power for the light. Some AA officers fretted about what the British public (or the Luftwaffe) might think about these one-man/many-women searchlight units. The Germans seem never to have commented on the matter.

The much-feared sex scandals never materialized in the searchlight or battery units. While this was the official version, and no scandal embarrassed the mixed units, some mixing of the sexes did take place. "One of the girls cheerfully admitted to having been a prostitute before she joined up," an ATS woman recalled. "There were nights when she returned to the hut with her tunic and shirt in disarray and her bra slung somewhere around her neck."

At first, middle-aged men (presumably more prudent than younger men) were sent to the mixed batteries. This policy was not a success in creating close-knit units, because "the girls regarded the older men as grandfathers, and they for their part found the girls a bit tiresome." According to ATS volunteer Muriel I.D. Barker, "There was an absolutely monastic segregation when it came to living quarters." One mixed-battery commander noted, "When a couple of girls walk out of a hut in dressing gowns to go to the ablution huts for a bath, nobody takes the slightest notice. This matter of fact atmosphere is what strikes every first time visitor."

When younger men did arrive, both sexes segregated themselves at work and were not encouraged to mix off-duty. Soon, however, they developed close working relationships, a form of bonding that was vital when the batteries came under fire. As one British battery commander suggested, "Loyalty means loyalty in a mixed battery and 'devotion to duty' has a more definite meaning than it has had. Isn't a woman's devotion more sincere and lasting than a man's?" The women developed bonds with fellow AA workers, male and female, which they did not share with former workers and friends. "After experiencing just a couple of months of communal life, I found that the girls (civilians) with whom I had worked before I enlisted were self-interested," one woman recalled. "We no longer spoke the same language even and there seemed to be a barrier between us. It was even worse with the boys." Pile observed, "The girls lived like men, fought their fights like men, and alas, some of them died like men."

The first woman killed in action, Private J. Caveney (148th Regiment), was hit by a bomb splinter while working at the predictor—the device that predicted where the enemy plane would be when the shell finally arrived at the proper altitude. As had been practiced many times in the casualty drills, the woman spotter "stepped in so promptly that firing was not interrupted." In another attack, Privates Clements and Dunsmore stuck to their posts despite suffering injuries, caused "by being blown over by a stick of bombs dropped across the troop position." Total ATS battle casualties were 389 killed or wounded.

Morale was high in the mixed batteries; soon the women were allowed to wear the AA Command formation sign on their sleeves and to be called bombardiers and gunners (but only on duty). As one recruit explained, "I don't know what it was about Ack girls but we always seemed to be smarter than the rest of the service"—and they "acted accordingly." In 1944, morale in the mixed batteries soared when news came that some were to serve throughout England, not just around London, and even on the Continent. One woman volunteer described the command-post situation at the Great Yarmouth Gun Defended Area during and just after a raid:

> The atmosphere in the post was calm, almost subdued and little different from that which had prevailed during our many exercises in the past. This changed as soon as stand-down was given and, although we still had work to do, there was at least a buzz of excitement about the place and cigarettes were freely handed around. Somehow it seemed the thing to do for me to take one and light up as well—even though I didn't smoke, until then that is.

The living conditions for both sexes were often primitive; the ATS women boasted how harsh it was out on the hilltops at night. Nervous uncles were appalled. Pressure soon mounted to provide better conditions for the women. Before such facilities could be built, one commander assembled the thousand women of his brigade and offered to have any of them moved to another location within twenty-four hours. Only nine women asked for a change, and all of these were clerks who were not involved with the fire-control equipment. One male leader of a mixed unit confessed that he had initially hated the idea of commanding a mixed battery; "but now that I have joined this battery, raised it, watched it grow up and shared in its sorrows and joys, I can say I have never been happier than I am now."

After six months an AA corps commander told Pile, "It has been an unqualified success." He suggested that what immediately impressed observers was "the tremendous keenness and enthusiasm displayed by the ATS in assimilating their operational duties. They learn quickly, and once having mastered the subject very seldom make mistakes." He added, "Contrary once again to expectations, their voices carry well and can be clearly heard in the din of gunfire." Not surprisingly, Pile concluded that "the experiment had exceeded even my more sanguine hopes." The mixed unit had achieved a standard of drill and turnout "better than in any male unit; for when the girls took to polishing their predictors, how could the men have dirty guns?"

How did women compare with men doing identical jobs? British AA leaders concluded that women were inferior as spotters, comparable as predictors, and superior as height finders. Perhaps women's poor records as spotters were due to their previous lack of experience in distinguishing aircraft. Few women came to AA positions having memorized the British and German models. In a similar sense, women sailors often took longer to memorize the differences in ships than did men who may have grown up "playing" sailors or pilots as young boys. Also, women typically took longer to learn a military-rank system and to "spot" a senior officer approaching whom they must salute.

The British experience was more complete than the American four-month experiment, but there were no major differences in the findings. The women excelled in several areas, were comparable in others, and were inferior in a few. But phrasing the question in terms of men versus women is highly misleading. The British were not interested in setting up all-female units in order to promote feminism. Rather, they set up mixed units so they could shoot down more enemy planes and buzz bombs, while making the most efficient use of the limited human resources available. The effectiveness of a military unit depends on the team performance; team members who are better at lugging heavy shells can be assigned to that task, while those who are better at reading the dials can be doing that. The effectiveness of a team is not the average of each person measured as a Jack or Jill of all trades. Instead, it is a composite of how well each specialized task is performed, along with the synergy that comes from leadership, morale, and unit cohesion. The mixed units did very well indeed.

Britain had to balance public doubts and ingrained gender norms against pressing needs. When Pile and Churchill first assigned women to AA jobs, they encountered resistance from public opinion. It was not so much that the women were in danger—every woman in every British city was in danger of death from German bombs, and tens of thousands did die. But the public would not support a proposal to allow women to fire the AA guns.

Still, the British are a practical people, especially when bombs are falling. They soon decided, "A successful air defence was an even stronger political imperative than the possible moral and physical dangers to the daughters of the nation." The government did concede some details to public opinion by not formally classifying these AA jobs as combat and by symbolically prohibiting the women from pulling the lanyard. Nevertheless, the mixed AA crews were as much combat teams as were the airplane crews they shot down.

One factor in whether nations employed women in combat roles was the urgency of the need for combat soldiers. The "tail-to-teeth" ratio (rear to frontline distribution of personnel) was very high in the United States, because Marshall felt that only ninety combat divisions would be needed, and that the war would be largely won by the efficiency of the supply and support mechanism. Women were not needed in AA units (actually, few men were needed), but they were urgently needed to handle clerical and administrative jobs. Marshall thought caution the better part of valor when he decided not to risk a confrontation with Congress and public opinion on the matter of gender roles.

IN THE MEANTIME, how were other armies reacting to shortages in manpower? Hitler had always insisted that women remain at home and be full-time wives and mothers; Nazi women were to guarantee the survival of the Aryan race in the labor room, not on the battlefield. Even single women were not recruited for jobs in industry at the beginning of the war. By 1941, however, women were holding jobs in industry and serving in female auxiliary units, doing administrative work for the military. After the invasion of Russia, German auxiliaries increasingly began replacing men who had been sent to the Eastern Front. Berlin did monitor its Finnish ally, which successfully used "Lottas" as auxiliaries to the army, freeing up men for the front lines. But it was not until January 1943, when the war had clearly begun to turn sour and Albert Speer became the economic czar, that Germany began full mobilization of its human resources. Even so, measures to conscript women into industry were introduced "only with extreme reluctance, and were never efficiently implemented." Not surprisingly, then, measures to draft women into the military— including Goebbels's 1944 Second Order for the Implementation of Total War—were even less well enforced.

German women, however, did serve in the military; in all, 450,000 joined the women's auxiliaries, in addition to the units of nurses. By 1945, women were holding approximately 85 percent of the once all-male billets as clerical workers, accountants, interpreters, laboratory workers, and administrators, together with half of the clerks and junior administrators in high-level field headquarters. (*The Guidelines for Emergency Employment of Women* commented, "No work is to be given to women that requires particular presence of mind, determination, and fast action.") These German women, in uniform and under military discipline, were not officially referred to as female soldiers. They were unofficially nicknamed *Blitzmädchen*. While it may seem surprising that the Nazis ever allowed women to serve in the military in any capacity, to test our hypothesis we must examine the German model to see if women held more than combat-support or combat-service-support positions.

Antiaircraft units became increasingly central to Germany's war effort, so on July 17, 1943, at the urging of Speer, Hitler decided to have women trained for searchlight and AA positions. Basic training was to take four weeks. These AA auxiliaries were placed as follows: three to operate the instrument to measure distances, seven to operate the radio measuring instrument, three to operate the command instrument, and occasionally one woman to serve as a telephone platoon leader. By the end of the war, between 65,000 and 100,000 women were serving in eleven units with the Luftwaffe. Some searchlight units were eventually 90 percent female.

Similar to the British experience, German women who joined AA units became "proud to be serving as AA-Auxiliaries" and were "burning soon to be trained well enough to be able flawlessly to stand our ground at the equipment." These women developed the unit cohesion that had been evident in the British AA units. As one veteran recalled, "We have been raised with the same kind of spirit, we had the same ideals, and the most important was the good comradeship, the 'one for all.'" Here again, these AA-Auxiliaries emphasized their continued femininity. Another, Lotte Vogt, explained, "In spite of all the soldier's duties we had to do, we did not forget that we were girls. We did not want to adopt uncouth manners. We certainly were no rough warriors—always simply women."

As in Britain, although the German women serving with AA units learned all aspects of the guns, they were forbidden to fire them. Hitler and his advisers firmly believed that public opinion would never tolerate these auxiliaries firing weapons. Indeed, German propaganda warned all women in the auxiliaries not to become "gun women" (*flintenweiber*). In February 1944, one of the naval auxiliaries wrote to a friend who had been captured:

> I've been sent to the Naval Auxiliary Service. I am now a soldier who replaces you in the country. The service is not difficult as we are not raised to be gun women. What is good about it is that one is also treated as a woman. Obviously we must conduct ourselves honorably as women. . . . We are amongst sailors but we have nothing to do with them.

"Gun women" was the contemptuous German term for Soviet women who carried or fired weapons. Many Soviet women were without uniforms and thus considered de facto partisans. The Germans looked upon armed

Soviet women as "unnatural" and consequently had no compunction about shooting such "vermin" as soon as they were captured. The verbal degradation of enemy females made it easier for German soldiers to overcome any inhibitions about harming women. Nazi propaganda also mocked American Wacs as traitors to their sex because they performed functions in the army under the pretense of emancipation.

In November 1944, Hitler issued an official order that no woman was to be trained in the use of weapons. The only exception was for women in the remote areas of the Reich that could be easily overrun by the Soviets. According to German propaganda, in one such area, a twenty-two-year-old Pomeranian woman, "Erna," was awarded the Iron Cross (second class) when she, together with a male sergeant and private, destroyed three tanks with bazookas. Indeed, the propaganda suggested that the bazooka was the most feminine of weapons. (Bazookas were lightweight and did not have the heavy recoil that only a large body could absorb.)

The Freikorps Adolf Hitler was formed in 1945 and trained in the use of bazookas, hand grenades, and automatic rifles. Lore Ley, daughter of a leading Nazi, once knocked out a Soviet armored scout car and took military documents and money from its commander. In all, thirty-nine German women received the Iron Cross (second class) for their duty near the front. The majority of these women, however, were nurses. Hitler's test pilots Hanna Reitsch and Melitta Schilla-Stauffenberg were the only women to receive the Iron Cross (first class).

Nazis resisted weapons training for women auxiliaries serving with the army or Luftwaffe until the final stages of the war. As Reichsleiter Martin Bormann sputtered to Reichsminister Joseph Goebbels, as late as November 1944, "As long as there is still one single man employed at a work place in the Wehrmacht that could as well be occupied by a woman, the employment of armed women must be rejected." But, more and more desperate every day, Hitler capitulated in February 1945 and created an experimental women's infantry battalion. Ironically, this unit's mission was in part to shame cowardly men who were evading their natural gender role of dying for their country—thousands of men were deserting in 1945. In any event, the war ended before the women's battalion could be raised and trained.

IN CONTRAST TO the Germans, the Soviets mobilized their women early, bypassing the auxiliary stage entirely. About 800,000 women served in the Red Army during World War II, and over half of these were on the front lines. Many were trained in all-female units. About a third of the total number of women serving were given additional instruction in mortars, light and heavy machine guns, or automatic rifles. Another 300,000 served in AA units and performed all functions in the batteries—including firing the guns.

When asked why she had volunteered for such dangerous and "unwomanly" work, AA gunner K.S. Tikhonovich explained, " 'We' and 'Motherland' meant the same thing for us." Sergeant Valentina Pavlovna

Chuayeva from Siberia said she had wanted to settle the score and avenge the death of her father: "I wanted to fight, to take revenge, to shoot." Her request was denied, with the explanation that being a telephone operator was the most vital work she could do. She retorted that telephone receivers did not shoot. Finally, a colonel gave her the chance to train for the AA. "At first my nose and ears bled and my stomach was completely upset. . . . It wasn't so terrible at night, but in the day time it was simply awful." She recalled the terror of battle: "The planes seemed to be heading straight for you, right for your gun. In a second they would make mincemeat of you. . . . It was not really a young girl's job." Eventually she became commander of an AA gun crew.

Private Nonna Alexandrovna Smirnova, AA gunner from the Georgian village of Obcha, did not like the training program, in which men with little education, often mispronouncing words, served as instructors. In addition, the uniforms they received had been designed for men. Smirnova, the smallest person in her company, usually wore a size 34 shoe but was issued an American-made boot that was size 42. "They were so heavy that I shuffled instead of marching." (In every nation the women's services had trouble with the quartermaster's notion of what a shoe should be.)

The noncombat-combat classification that preoccupied the Americans, British, and Germans proved an unaffordable luxury to the Soviets. In a nation totally controlled by the Kremlin, organized public opinion was hardly a factor. Implicit public opinion regarding the primacy of traditional gender roles was another matter, but the available evidence does not speak to that. (The Kremlin controlled the media and the historiography—and even the memories of World War II; perhaps someday *glusnost,* if it continues, will loosen more tongues.) Article 13 of the universal-military-duty law, ratified by the Fourth Session of the Supreme Soviet on September 1, 1939, enabled the military to accept women who had training in critical medical or technical areas. Women could also register as part of a training group, and after they were trained they could be called up for active duty by the armed forces.

Once war broke out, these Soviet women—together with their fathers, brothers, and husbands—went to the military commissariats and to party and Komsomol organizations to help fight. They served as partisans, snipers, and tank drivers. Women constituted three regiments of pilots: one of fighter pilots, the 586th Fighter Regiment; and two of bomber pilots, the 587th and the most famous of the three, the 588th Night Bombers, who proved so effective at hitting their targets that the Germans nicknamed them the "night witches." According to one veteran German pilot, "I would rather fly ten times over the skies of Tobruk [over all-male British ack-ack] than to pass once through [Russia where] the fire of Russian flak [was] sent up by female gunners." In all, Soviet women made up about 8 percent of all combatants. Between 100,000 and 150,000 women were decorated during the war, including 91 who received the Hero of the Soviet Union medal, the highest award for valor.

The Soviets boasted of their women in combat, and even sent some abroad on publicity tours. (When Junior Lieutenant Liudmila Pavlichenko met with reporters in Washington, she was dumbfounded to be asked about lingerie instead of how she had killed 309 Germans.) But Germany, Britain, and the United States did not publicize the fact that women were serving in combat roles anywhere, although the generals realized that the women soldiers who were in AA units had combat missions after all. They were simply shooting at the enemy, and he—or she—was shooting back. The British discovered that Luftwaffe gunners fired at everyone around the searchlights or the guns, not just at the men there.

As Shelford Bidwell, the distinguished historian of artillery and of the ATS, concluded, "There is not much essential difference between manning a G.L. set or a predictor and firing a gun: both are means of destroying an enemy aircraft." He added, "The situation became more absurd when the advance of automation was such that the guns were fired by remote control when on target, from the command post." After June 1944, most of the targets were V-1 robots, but the women still were not permitted to shoot. What stopped the British, Americans, and Germans from allowing AA women to pull the trigger was their sense of gender roles—a sensibility that had not yet adjusted to the necessity of women in combat.

Apart from cartoons, I have never seen an American reference to fighting enemy women. In 1945 the Bill Mauldin character Willie tipped his hat to a *Blitzmädchen* he was taking, at gunpoint, to a POW compound. She wore a helmet, a Luftwaffe jacket, and a civilian skirt; a hand grenade was still tucked in her belt, probably because he was too much of a gentleman to search her. The cartoon succinctly captured the uncertainty of an unexpected change in sex role.

Certainly, many Japanese women soldiers died in hand-to-hand fighting on Okinawa. The Japanese drafted high-school students, male and female, into militia units that were hurled into combat, and killed to the last person. The saga of the all-female "Lilly Brigade" is now part of Japanese folklore. If MacArthur had invaded Kyushu, he probably would have encountered thousands of women infantry.

Understanding the reaction of servicemen to women in combat involves study of the structure of gender roles in society at large and the military in particular, and it calls for a comparative framework. In the United States, most male soldiers were strongly opposed to the WAC and urgently advised their sisters and friends not to join. Scurrilous rumors to the effect that Wacs were sexual extremists (either promiscuous or lesbian) chilled recruitment and froze the WAC far below its intended size. The rumors were generated almost entirely by word-of-mouth among servicemen. In point of fact, such rumors were false: The servicewomen were much less sexually active than servicemen, and rather less active than comparable civilian women. The rumors therefore reflected a strong hostility—but to what?

Many senior officers originally had been opposed to the WAC, but they almost unanimously reversed their position when they realized how effective the women were and how many men could thus be freed for combat. Most senior officers had been trained as engineers (especially at the military academies) and perhaps were more sensitive to efficiency than to human sensibilities.

Some enlisted men with noncombat jobs were aghast at the idea (explicit in recruiting posters) that women who enlisted would send a man to the front. As one officer in the Pacific explained:

> They [Wacs] are good workers and much more so than many of our regular men. You perhaps have heard many wild stories about them but I wouldn't believe everything that I hear. In comparison, our men are a lot worse. So many men talk about them and it seems they are the ones who haven't seen a Wac, or doesn't know anything about them, or even is a little jealous. Then again some of the girls take over easy jobs that some of the men hold and they don't like it when they have to get out and work.

Furthermore, young men saw military service as a validation of their own virility and as a certificate of manhood. If women could do it, then it was not very manly. The exhilaration of combat can be like an aphrodisiac, if not a sexual experience in its own right. Perhaps like the "Tailhookers" of recent days, they felt this should be forbidden territory to females.

The question of women in combat has generated a vast literature that draws from law, biology, and psychology, but seldom from history. The restrictions against women in combat that have persisted for decades in the United States have not been based on experimental research (quite the reverse), or on consideration of the effectiveness of women in combat in other armies. They have been primarily political decisions made in response to the public opinion of the day, and to the climate of opinion in Congress.

Still horrified by memories of Belleau Wood, Okinawa, and Ia Drang, many Americans to this day visualize "combat" as vicious hand-to-hand knife fighting. Major Everett S. Hughes displayed a keen insight into the issue in a report to the General Staff:

> We have handicapped ourselves by numerous man-made technical definitions of such things as Combat Zone. . . . Some of us conclude that women have no place in the Theater of Operations, others that women have no place in the combat zone. We fail to consider that the next war is never the last one. We forget, for example, that what was the Combat Zone during the World War may be something else during the next war. We use technical terms that are susceptible to individual interpretation, and that change with the art of war, to express the idea that women should not participate here, there, or yonder. We are further handicapped by man-made barriers of custom, prejudice and politics, and fail to appreciate how rapidly and thoroughly these barriers are being demolished.

Hughes's report was made in 1928, and it was not rediscovered until after the war. It was not feminism but fear of the lack of sufficient manpower to fight World War II that served as the catalyst for Marshall's experiment, Pile's mixed batteries, the Nazi *Blitzmädchen,* and the Soviet "night witches." Necessity, once it was dire enough, could overcome culture. "If the need for women's service be great enough they may go any place, live anywhere, under any conditions," concluded Major Hughes.

Success in combat is a matter of skill, intelligence, coordination, training, morale, and teamwork. The military is a product of history and is bound by the lessons it has "learned" from history. The problem is that the history everyone has learned about the biggest war of all times has airbrushed out the combat roles of women.

*AUTUMN 1993*

D'Ann Campbell is dean of arts and sciences at Austin Peay State University. This article was published in a somewhat different form in the *Journal of Military History* (April 1993).

# 31

# The Secrets of Overlord

## By Stephen E. Ambrose

*Spectacular surprises marked the Second World War. The German thrusts through the Ardennes Forest in 1940 and 1944, the Japanese attack on Pearl Harbor in 1941, the American naval ambush at Midway and invasion of Guadalcanal in 1942, all caught opponents unprepared. For the forces of the Third Reich, the Allied invasion at Normandy held its own surprises. While overall strategic surprise was impossible—the Germans knew the invasion was coming—other questions remained unanswered. Where would the Anglo-American-Canadian armies land? When? And with what forces? If the answers to those questions could be hidden from the enemy, the invasion had the chance to free Europe. If Germany successfully discovered the answers, the invasion was doomed. To mask their forces and intentions, the Allies executed Operation Fortitude. Stephen E. Ambrose's essay explores the many facets of this pivotal deception.*

On June 6, 1944, the United States, Britain, and Canada launched the largest force of warships in history across the English Channel. It escorted the largest concentration of troop transport vessels ever assembled, covered by the largest force of fighter and bomber aircraft ever brought together, preceded by a fleet of air transports that had carried tens of thousands of paratroopers and glider-borne troops to Normandy.

Not one German submarine, not one small boat, not one airplane, not one radar set, not one German anywhere detected this movement. As General Walter Warlimont, deputy head of operations of the German Supreme Headquarters, later confessed, on the eve of Overlord the Wehrmacht leaders "had not the slightest idea that the decisive event of the war was upon them."

IN WORLD WAR I, surprise on a grand scale was seldom attempted and rarely achieved. In World War II, it was always sought and sometimes achieved—as with the Japanese attack on Pearl Harbor and the German invasion of Russia, both in 1941, and the German attack in the Ardennes in 1940 and again in 1944. One reason for this difference between the wars was that World War II commanders judged surprise to be more critical to victory than a preattack artillery bombardment. In the age of machine guns, other rapid-fire artillery, and land mines, the defenders could make almost any position virtually impregnable, no matter how heavy the pre-attack bombardment. Another reason for the increased emphasis on sur-prise was that the much greater mobility of World War II armed forces made surprise more feasible and more effective. Because of improvements in and more imaginative use of the internal-combustion engine (especially in tanks and trucks), the geographic area in which the conflict was fought was much larger in World War II. The preinvasion bombardment for Overlord, carried out by aircraft, was spread all across France and Belgium. It may have wasted a lot of bombs, but it also kept the Germans from discerning a pattern that would indicate the invasion site.

None of the surprises achieved in World War II was more complex, more difficult, more important, or more successful than Overlord. To fool Hitler and his generals in the battle of wits that preceded the attack, the Allies had to convince them not only that it was coming where it was not, but also that the real thing was a feint. The first objective could be achieved by attacking in an unexpected, indeed illogical, place, and by maintaining total security about the plan. The second required convincing Hitler that the Allied invasion force was about twice as powerful as it actually was.

That there would be landings in France in the late spring of 1944 was universally known. Exactly where and when were the questions. To learn those secrets, the Germans maintained a huge intelligence organization that included spies inside Britain, air reconnaissance, monitoring of the British press and BBC, radio intercept stations, decoding experts, interro-gation of Allied airmen shot down in Germany, research on Allied economies, and more.

The importance of surprise was obvious. In World War I it was judged that to have any chance at success, the attacking force had to outnumber the defenders by at least three to one. But in Overlord the attacking force of 175,000 men would he outnumbered by the Wehrmacht, even at the point of attack, and the overall figures (German troops in Western Europe versus Allied troops in the United Kingdom) showed a two-to-one German advantage. Doctrine in the German army was to meet an attack with an immediate counterattack. In this case, the Germans could move re-inforcements to the battle much faster than the Allies, because they could bring them in by train, by truck, and on foot, while the Allies had to bring them in by ship. The Germans had storage and supply dumps all over France; the Allies had to bring every shell, every bullet, every drop of gaso-line, every bandage across the Channel.

Allied intelligence worked up precise tables on the Germans' ability to move reinforcements into the battle area. The conclusion was that if the Germans correctly gauged Overlord as the main assault and marched immediately, within a month they could concentrate thirty-one divisions in the battle area, including nine panzer divisions. The Allies could not match that buildup rate.

In the face of these obstacles, the Allies managed to maintain a deception about their true intentions even after the battle began. How they did so is a remarkable story.

Thousands of men and women were involved, but perhaps the most important, and certainly the most dramatic, were the dozen or so members of BI(a), the counterespionage arm of MI-5, the British internal-security agency. Using a variety of sources, such as code breaking and interrogation of captured agents, the British caught German spies as they parachuted into England or Scotland. Sir John Masterman, head of BI(a), evaluated each spy. Those he considered unsuitable were executed or imprisoned. The others were "turned"—that is, made into double agents, who sent messages to German intelligence, the Abwehr, via radio, using Morse code. (Each spy had his own distinctive "signature" in the way he used the code's dots and dashes, which was immediately recognizable by the German spy master receiving the message.) The British kept the double agents tap-tap-tapping, but only what they were told to send out.

This so-called Double-Cross operation, which had come into being in the dark days of 1940, managed to locate and turn every German spy in the United Kingdom, some two dozen in all. From the beginning the British had decided to aim it exclusively toward the moment when the Allies returned to France. Building up this asset over the years required feeding the Abwehr information through the spies that was authentic, new, and interesting, but either relatively valueless or something the Germans were bound to learn anyway. The idea was to make the agents trustworthy and valuable in the eyes of the Germans, then spring the trap on D-Day, when the double agents would flood the Abwehr with false information.

The first part of the trap was to make the Germans think the attack was coming at the Pas-de-Calais. Since the Germans already anticipated that this was where the Allies would come ashore, it was necessary only to reinforce their preconceptions. The Pas-de-Calais was indeed the obvious choice. It was on the direct London–Ruhr–Berlin line. It was close to Antwerp, Europe's best port. Inland the terrain was flat, with few natural obstacles. At the Pas-de-Calais the Channel was at its narrowest, giving ships the shortest trip and British-based fighter aircraft much more time over the invasion area.

Because the Pas-de-Calais was the obvious choice, the Germans had their strongest fixed defenses there, backed up by the Fifteenth Army and a majority of the panzer divisions in France. Whether or not they succeeded in making the position impregnable we will never know, because the supreme Allied commander, Dwight D. Eisenhower, decided not to find out. He chose Normandy instead. Normandy had certain advantages, including the port of Cherbourg, the narrowness of the Cotentin Peninsula, access to the major road network at Caen, and proximity to the English ports of Southampton and Portsmouth. Normandy's greatest advantage, however, was that the Germans were certain to consider an attack there highly unlikely, because it would be an attack in the wrong direction: Instead of heading east, toward the German heartland, the Allies would be heading south into central France.

The second part of the trap was to make the Germans think, even after the attack began, that Normandy was a feint. Geography reinforced Eisenhower's choice of Normandy in meeting this requirement, too: If there were major Allied landings at the Pas-de-Calais, Hitler would not keep troops in Normandy for fear of their being cut off from Germany—but he might be persuaded to keep troops in the Pas-de-Calais following a landing in Normandy, as they would still stand between the Allied forces and Germany.

The deception plan, code-named Fortitude, was a joint venture, with British and American teams working together; it made full use of the Double-Cross system, dummy armies, fake radio traffic, and elaborate security precautions. In terms of the time, resources, and energy devoted to it, Fortitude was a tremendous undertaking. It had many elements, designed to make the Germans think the attack might come at the Biscay coast or in the Marseilles region or even in the Balkans. Most important were Fortitude North, which set up Norway as a target (the site of Hitler's U-boat bases, essential to his offensive operations), and Fortitude South, with the Pas-de-Calais as the target.

To get the Germans to look toward Norway, the Allies first had to convince them that Eisenhower had enough resources for a diversion or secondary attack. This was doubly difficult because of Ike's acute shortage of landing craft—it was touch and go as to whether there would be enough craft to carry five divisions ashore at Normandy as planned, much less spares for another attack. To make the Germans believe otherwise, the Allies had to create fictitious divisions and landing craft on a grand scale. This was done chiefly with the Double-Cross system and through Allied radio signals.

The British Fourth Army, for example, stationed in Scotland and scheduled to invade Norway in mid-July, existed only on the airwaves. Early in 1944 some two dozen overage British officers were sent to northernmost Scotland, where they spent the next months exchanging radio messages. They filled the air with an exact duplicate of the wireless traffic that accompanies the assembly of a real army, communicating in low-level and thus easily broken cipher. Together the messages created an impression of corps and division headquarters scattered all across Scotland: "80 Div. request 1,800 pairs of crampons, 1,800 pairs of ski bindings," they read, or "7 Corps requests the promised demonstrators in the Bilgeri method of climbing rock faces." There was no 80th Division, no VII Corps.

The turned German spies meanwhile sent encoded radio messages to Hamburg and Berlin describing heavy train traffic in Scotland, new division patches seen on the streets of Edinburgh, and rumors among the troops about going to Norway. Wooden twin-engine "bombers" began to appear on Scottish airfields. British commandos made some raids on the coast of Norway, pinpointing radar sites, picking up soil samples (ostensibly to test the suitability of beaches to support a landing), and in general trying to look like a preinvasion force.

The payoff was spectacular. By late spring Hitler had thirteen army divisions in Norway (about 130,000 men under the German military system) along with 90,000 naval and 60,000 Luftwaffe personnel. In late May, Field Marshal Erwin Rommel finally persuaded Hitler to move five infantry divisions from Norway to France. They had started to load up and move out when the Abwehr passed on to Hitler another set of "intercepted" messages about the threat to Norway. He canceled the movement order.

To paraphrase Winston Churchill, never in the history of warfare have so many been immobilized by so few.

Fortitude South was larger and more elaborate. It was based on the First U.S. Army Group (FUSAG), stationed in and around Dover and threatening the Pas-de-Calais. It included radio traffic; inadequately camouflaged dummy landing craft in the ports of Ramsgate, Dover, and Hastings; fields packed with papier-mâché tanks; and full use of the Double-Cross setup. The spies reported intense activity in and around Dover, including construction, troop movements, increased train traffic, and the like. They said that the phony oil dock at Dover, built by stagehands from Hollywood and the British film industry, was open and operating.

The capstone to Fortitude South was Ike's selection of General George S. Patton to command FUSAG. The Germans thought Patton the best commander in the Allied camp (a judgment with which Patton fully agreed, but which Eisenhower, unbeknownst to the Germans, did not) and expected him to lead the assault. Eisenhower, who was saving Patton for the exploitation phase of the campaign, used Patton's reputation and visibility to strengthen Fortitude South. The spies reported his arrival in England and his movements. FUSAG radio signals told the Germans of Patton's comings and goings and showed that he had taken a firm grip on his new command.

FUSAG contained real as well as notional divisions, corps, and armies. The FUSAG order of battle included the U.S. Third Army, which was real but still in the United States; the British Fourth Army, which was imaginary; and the Canadian First Army, which was real and based in England. There were, in addition, supposedly fifty follow-up divisions in the United States, organized as the U.S. Fourteenth Army—which was notional—awaiting shipment to the Pas-de-Calais after FUSAG established its beachhead. Many of the divisions in the Fourteenth Army were real and were actually assigned to General Omar Bradley's U.S. First Army in southwest England.

Fortitude's success was measured by the German estimate of Allied strength. By June 1, the Germans believed that Eisenhower's entire command included eighty-nine divisions (of about 15,000 men each), when in fact he had forty-seven. They also thought he had sufficient landing craft to bring twenty divisions ashore in the first wave, when he would be lucky to manage five. Partly because they credited Ike with so much strength, and partly because it made such good military sense, the Germans believed that the real invasion would be preceded or followed by diversionary attacks and feints.

Security for Overlord was as important as deception. As Ike declared, "Success or failure of coming operations depends upon whether the enemy can obtain advance information of an accurate nature." To maintain security, in February he asked Churchill to move all civilians out of southernmost England. He feared there might be an undiscovered spy who could report the truth to the Abwehr. Churchill refused; he felt it was too much to ask of a war-weary population. A British officer on Ike's staff said it was all politics, and growled, "If we fail, there won't be any more politics."

Ike sent Churchill an eloquent plea, warning that it "would go hard with our consciences if we were to feel, in later years, that by neglecting any security precaution we had compromised the success of these vital operations." In late March, Churchill gave in; the civilians were put out of all coastal and training areas and kept out until months after D-Day.

Eisenhower also persuaded a reluctant Churchill to impose a ban on privileged diplomatic communications from the United Kingdom. Ike said he regarded diplomatic pouches as "the gravest risk to the security of our operations and to the lives of our sailors, soldiers, and airmen." When Churchill imposed the ban, on April 17, foreign governments protested vigorously. This gave Hitler a useful clue to the timing of Overlord. He remarked in early May that "the English have taken measures that they can sustain for only six to eight weeks." When a West Point classmate of Ike's declared at the bar in Claridge's Hotel that D-Day would be before June 15, and offered to take bets when challenged, Ike reduced him in rank and sent him home in disgrace. There was another flap a week later when a U.S. Navy officer got drunk and revealed details of impending operations, including areas, strength, and dates. Ike wrote Chief of Staff George C. Marshall, "I get so angry at the occurrence of such needless and additional hazards that I could cheerfully shoot the offender myself." Instead, Ike sent the officer back to the States.

To check on how well security and deception were working, SHAEF (Supreme Headquarters Allied Expeditionary Force) had another asset, the Ultra system. This involved breaking the German code, Enigma, enabling SHAEF to read German radio signals. Thanks to Ultra, the British Joint Intelligence Committee was able to put together weekly summaries of "German Appreciation of Allied Intentions in the West," one- or two-page overviews of where, when, and in what strength the Germans expected the attack. Week after week, the summaries gave Ike exactly the news he wanted to read: that the Germans were anticipating an attack on Norway, diversions in the south of France and in Normandy or the Bay of Biscay, and the main assault, with twenty or more divisions, against the Pas-de-Calais.

But Fortitude was an edifice built so delicately, precisely, and intricately that the removal of just one supporting column would bring the whole thing crashing down. On May 29, with D-Day only about a week away, the summary included a chilling sentence: "The recent trend of movement of German land forces towards the Cherbourg area tends to support the view that the Le Havre–Cherbourg area is regarded as a likely, and perhaps even the main, point of assault."

Had there been a slip? Had the Germans somehow penetrated Fortitude?

The news got worse. The Germans, in fact, were increasing their defenses everywhere along the French coast. In mid-May the mighty Panzer Lehr Division began moving toward the Cotentin Peninsula, while the 21st Panzer Division, which had been with Rommel in North Africa and was his favorite, moved from Brittany to the Caen area—exactly the site where the British Second Army would be landing. More alarming, Ultra revealed that the German 91st Division, specialists in fighting paratroopers, and the German 6th Parachute Regiment had moved on May 29 into exactly the areas where the American airborne divisions were to land. And the German 352nd Division moved forward from Saint-Lô to the coast, taking up a position overlooking Omaha Beach, where the U.S. 1st Division was going to land.

Ike's air commander, British Air Chief Marshal Sir Trafford Leigh-Mallory, was so upset by this news that he recommended to Ike that the airdrops be canceled. Ike refused, but the German movements and Leigh-Mallory's reaction badly stretched his nerves.

Eisenhower did not, however, give up on Fortitude. At about midnight on June 5–6, even as Allied transport planes and ships began crossing the Channel for Normandy, the supreme commander played the ultimate note in the Fortitude concert: He had the spy the Germans trusted most, code-named Garbo—actually a resourceful spy for the British from the start—send a message in Morse code to the Abwehr giving away the secret. Garbo reported that Overlord was on the way, named some of the divisions involved, indicated when they had left Portsmouth, and predicted they would come ashore in Normandy at dawn.

The report had to be deciphered, read, evaluated, reenciphered, and transmitted to Hitler. Then Hitler's lackeys had to decide whether to wake him with the news. They did, but then the whole encoding and deciphering operation had to be reversed to get the word to the German forces in Normandy. By the time it arrived, the defenders could see for themselves— there were 6,000 planes overhead and 5,000 ships off the coast, and the first wave of troops was coming ashore.

In short, Garbo's report, the most accurate and important of the entire war, arrived too late to help the Germans. But it surely raised their opinion of Garbo—and this was vital. For now that Fortitude had helped the Allies get ashore, the question was, could the deception be kept alive long enough to let the Allies win the battle of the buildup that would follow?

Garbo was the key. On June 9 he sent a message to his spy master in Hamburg with a request that it be submitted urgently to the German high command. "The present operation, though a large-scale assault, is diversionary in character," Garbo stated flatly. "Its object is to establish a strong bridgehead in order to draw the maximum of our [German] reserves into the area of the assault and to retain them there so as to leave another area exposed where the enemy could then attack with some prospect of success." Citing the Allied order of battle as the Germans understood it, Garbo pointed out that Eisenhower had committed only a small number of his divisions and landing craft. He added that no FUSAG unit had taken part in the Normandy attack, nor was Patton there. Furthermore, "the constant aerial bombardment which the sector of the Pas-de-Calais has been undergoing and the disposition of the enemy forces would indicate the imminence of the assault in this region which offers the shortest route to the final objective of the Anglo-Americans, Berlin."

Within half a day, Garbo's message was in Hitler's hands. On the basis of it, the führer made a momentous decision, possibly the most important of the war. Rommel had persuaded Hitler to sent two Fifteenth Army panzer divisions to Normandy. The tanks had started their engines, the men were ready to go, when Hitler canceled the order. He wanted the armored units held in the Pas-de-Calais to defend against the main invasion. He also awarded the Iron Cross (second class) to Garbo. (Garbo, a young Spaniard whom the British, secretly, also honored, ended a long silence about his elaborate and risky activities only in 1985, with the book *Operation Garbo.*)

The deception went on. On June 13 another spy warned that an attack would take place in two or three days at Dieppe or Abbeville. A third spy reported that airborne divisions (wholly fictitious) would soon drop around Amiens. In late June a fourth agent, code-named Tate, said he had obtained the railway schedule for moving the FUSAG forces from their concentration areas to the embarkation ports, thus reinforcing from a new angle the imminence of the threat to the Pas-de-Calais. One Abwehr officer considered Tate's report so important that he said it "could even decide the outcome of the war." He was not far wrong.

The weekly intelligence summary on June 19 read: "The Germans still believe the Allies capable of launching another amphibious operation. The Pas-de-Calais remains the expected area of attack. Fears of landings in Norway have been maintained."

July 10: "The enemy's fear of large-scale landings between the Seine and the Pas-de-Calais has not diminished. The second half of July is given as the probable time for this operation."

July 24: "There has been no considerable transfer of German forces from the Pas-de-Calais, which remains strongly garrisoned."

By August 3, when Patton came onto the Continent with his U.S. Third Army, most German officers realized that Normandy was the real thing. By then, of course, it was too late. The Germans had kept hundreds of their best tanks and thousands of their finest fighting men (a total of fifteen divisions in France) out of this crucial battle in order to meet a threat that had always been imaginary.

THERE WERE DELICIOUS ironies at the heart of Fortitude's success. Surprise in war often depends on the defenders underestimating the strength of the attacking force, but in Overlord that was reversed: Fortitude made the Germans overestimate Eisenhower's strength. Surprise also usually depends on exploiting the defenders' weaknesses, but this, too, got turned around: As in jujitsu, Eisenhower employed German strength to German disadvantage.

The Germans in 1944 held three major conceits as articles of faith. The first was that their spies in the United Kingdom were the best in the world. The second was that their Enigma was the best encoding machine ever developed, literally unbreakable. The third was that their own code breakers were the best available. Fortitude used these German conceits to do the Germans in.

Twenty-two years after the event, in 1966, when the author was interviewing Eisenhower on the subject of Fortitude, the supreme commander explained various parts of the operation, then gave one of his big, gutsy laughs, slapped his knee, and exclaimed, "By God, we really fooled them, didn't we?"

*SUMMER 1989*

---

Stephen E. Ambrose, Alumni Distinguished Professor at the University of New Orleans, is the author of numerous works on military history, including a two-volume biography of Eisenhower. His most recent book is *D-Day, June 6, 1944: The Climactic Battle of World War II* (1994).

---

# 32

# Overlord

## By Williamson Murray

*No single feat of the Second World War surpasses the Allied effort and achievement of the Normandy landings. In a single day, more than 150,000 men in a beachhead stretching some fifty miles long battered their way onto a hostile shore. Supporting their effort were approximately 600 warships, 4,000 transports and invasion craft, and almost 11,000 aircraft. The logistics struggle alone was the equivalent of moving the entire population of modern Little Rock, Arkansas, or Knoxville, Tennessee, across the English Channel in a single day. Professor Williamson Murray asks and then answers a series of questions that clarifies those events and decisions of 1944 that decided the fate of Europe.*

In a radio speech to the French in October 1940, Winston Churchill promised: "Good night then: Sleep to gather strength for the morning. For the morning will come. Brightly will it shine on the brave and the true, kindly upon all who suffer for the cause, glorious upon the tombs of heroes. Thus, will shine the dawn." Dawn came on June 6, 1944, four long years after the Germans had expelled the British army from the Continent.

In terms of its postwar implications, the return to the Continent—Operation Overlord—represented the most important effort of the war that Anglo-American military forces executed. The Battle of the Atlantic was the most crucial battle for the winning of the war that the British and Americans waged. Without control of the North Atlantic, neither strategic bombing nor Overlord would have been possible. But victory in the Atlantic only established the preconditions on which the continuance of aid to the Soviet Union, the strategic bombing of Germany, and the launching of Overlord could take place. Similarly, the combined bomber offensive achieved air supremacy over Europe and battered the German economy severely. But neither of these great efforts gained the political goals for which the United States and Britain waged World War II: namely, the projection of military and political power on the ground into the heart of Europe, where that power secured Anglo-American political and economic interests for the next forty-five years, until the collapse of the Soviet Union.

In examining this great undertaking, the historian must face a number of important questions: Could the Germans have won? Could the Americans have recovered from a defeat on Omaha beach? What opportunities did the Allies miss in the Normandy campaign? And finally, with the advantage of forty years of historical research, how does Allied leadership stack up in its conduct of the Normandy battle?

UNTIL THE ILL-fated raid on Dieppe in August 1942, Allied planners thought in terms of seizing a French port at the outset to build up forces faster than the Germans. But the defenders of Dieppe, mostly third-rate infantry, used the port's built-up areas to prevent the Canadian raiders from even crossing the beach wall—except as prisoners. Consequently, the planners had to alter their conceptions: Invasion forces not only would have to cross open beaches, but then would have to rely during the buildup phase on a supply system that lacked a port. That second problem, how to support a massive battle with a logistical system that ran over beaches, raised a nightmare of technical and engineering problems never before addressed.

Dieppe raised a third problem: German air power. The Luftwaffe, which had been holding its strength in the Reich, quickly deployed its formidable forces to forward operating locations in France. Its fighters then shot down 106 Allied aircraft, with the loss of only twenty-one fighters and twenty-seven bombers; German bombers did considerable damage to the Allied fleet and even sank a destroyer. It was clear that Allied air forces would have to achieve general air superiority over the whole continent before a successful landing could occur. Dieppe, however, did have one unexpected benefit: The Germans concluded that a major port would be the focus of any landing, and this would greatly aid the deception plans in 1944.

By 1943, Allied planners had selected Normandy as the invasion target. Pas-de-Calais was closer to England and provided a more direct route to the Reich, but those very advantages guaranteed that the Germans would concentrate their defensive buildup in that area. As late as the end of the year, the concept for the invasion called for landing only three infantry divisions at the beaches, with a drop of one airborne division. To the supreme commander, General Dwight D. Eisenhower, and the commander of land forces, General Bernard Montgomery, that was the recipe for military disaster: They demanded and got from the Combined Chiefs of Staff an increase to five infantry divisions and three airborne. Air commanders objected to the airdrop, but even when Sir Trafford Leigh-Mallory, commanding the Allied air forces, estimated the paratroops would suffer 90 percent losses, Eisenhower backed Montgomery in his request for a massive airborne operation.

The buildup phase was a daunting obstacle to planners. If the Germans successfully utilized the road and rail networks of western France, they could reinforce their units in Normandy faster than the Allies. As a result, Eisenhower's chief deputy, the renowned Air Chief Marshal Sir Arthur Tedder, developed a plan to use Allied air power, including the "strategic" bombers, to destroy the French transportation network before the landings occurred.

To achieve that objective, Tedder and Eisenhower had to fight a considerable battle with the bomber barons. Sir Arthur Harris, chief of the British Bomber Command, agreed that his planes could hit such targets as marshaling yards in France, but he argued that they might kill tens of thousands of Frenchmen in the process. Churchill, desperately worried about the political implications of such losses in the postwar world, came close to forbidding the attacks. But Harris was being completely disingenuous: As he admitted after the war, he had no compunction about blasting the "French who had run away in 1940." More to the point, Bomber Command's estimates of so-called collateral damage were based on the massive raids of 700 bombers it was launching against Germany rather than on the smaller raids that Tedder was proposing. Bomber Command then executed several small-scale test raids, which more than confirmed Tedder's estimate that relatively little collateral damage would occur.

In the end, the Combined Chiefs of Staff placed all the strategic-bombing forces of both nations under Eisenhower and Tedder's command. With Eisenhower's permission, Lieutenant General Carl Spaatz ordered his American bombers to attack German synthetic oil facilities in May. Meanwhile, other Allied air power focused on all of France's transportation system, since the planners did not wish to give away the invasion target. The interdiction campaign ranged across the length and breadth of France, and for the most part it achieved its goals. The combination of Bomber Command's heavy night attacks against marshaling yards, the Eighth Air Force's daylight bombing of other rail targets, and tactical strikes against locomotives and freight cars, as well as bridges, caused a collapse of the French rail system. By late May, when Allied air forces began an intensive campaign to destroy the bridges over the Seine, rail traffic had declined to 55 percent of January's levels. The wrecking of the Seine bridges reduced that level to 30 percent by June 6, and by early July rail traffic had fallen to 10 percent of what it had been at the beginning of the year. The attacks in western France were particularly effective; by mid-June, the trains that might have supplied the defenders in Normandy no longer operated. By shutting down the railroads, the air campaign forced the Germans to rely on the roads, where Allied tactical air strikes prevented movement by day. Destruction of bridges and attacks on roads made it extremely difficult for panzer divisions to reach the battlefield.

But American strategic bombing had rendered an even more important contribution to Overlord. The massive air offensive by the Eighth and Fifteenth air forces compelled the Luftwaffe to defend the factories on which its continued survival depended. Unlike the costly air offensive of 1943, U.S. strategic bombers received cover from long-range fighters; by March, P-51s were accompanying bombers all the way to Berlin. In February, the Luftwaffe lost 18 percent of its fighter pilots on active duty at the beginning of the month; in March, 22 percent; in April, 20 percent (but fighter units in the Reich lost no less than 38 percent of their pilots); and in May, 25 percent. The Luftwaffe collapsed as an effective defensive force even over the Reich. On June 6, Allied air forces would fly no fewer than 14,000 missions to support the invasion. On the other hand, Luftflotte 3, in charge of the air battle in France, could not get even 100 sorties over Normandy, of which 70 were by single-engine fighters.

In the crucial matter of logistics, the Allied air campaign had exacerbated one of the great weaknesses of the Germans throughout the war. The Germans paid minimal attention to their logistical arrangements, while the Allies possessed a resilient and deep supply system. And in the end, the battle for Normandy and France would turn on the ability of the contending sides to reinforce and supply the frontline troops locked in combat. Previous operations had solved most of the problems of amphibious warfare by June 1944; the Allies had a wealth of experience on which to draw from the Pacific and Atlantic theaters—including four major landings in the European theater of operations (ETO)—while the great industrial establishments of Britain and the United States had provided some unique solutions, including the creation of two great artificial harbors.

On the ground, however, the German soldier remained the best in Europe. His training, his officers, the coherent combat doctrine of his units, and the brutal, ruthless ideology that motivated him ensured that he would be extraordinarily effective in battle. Moreover, the topography of Normandy, with its *bocage* (hedgerow) country and its small villages and sturdy farmhouses, all of which were wonderful strongpoints for the defender, maximized the inherent strength of the German soldier and his tactical system.

Through late 1943 the Germans used France as a place to rebuild units that fighting on the Eastern Front had shattered. Moreover, German engineers had only begun preparatory work on the fortifications along the beaches. The Germans gambled that the Allies could not take advantage of their weak position in the West. It was a reasonable assessment; intelligence from Britain indicated that an invasion buildup had not yet begun. But by early 1944, the Germans recognized that an invasion was coming soon. Consequently, the buildup of the Wehrmacht in the West received highest priority; German forces in France underwent an impressive improvement. Hitler appointed Field Marshal Erwin Rommel to command Army Group B, across the north of France, and the coastal defenses that would most likely receive the assault. Rommel brought with him a restless energy that galvanized the preparations. By the time the Allies invaded, the Desert Fox hoped to have 12 million to 15 million mines sown along the beaches of France, to emplace tens of thousands of poles ("Rommel's asparagus") in fields behind potential landing areas to interfere with glider landings, and to erect a huge number of obstacles in the water and on the beaches to hinder landings.

Rommel recognized the overwhelming air and logistical superiority that the Allies would bring to the battle. He aimed, therefore, to defeat the invaders on the beaches before they could bring their logistical capabilities to bear. He recognized that if the Germans did not defeat the invasion in the first days of the fighting, they would lose the war. On the other hand, the supreme commander in the West, Field Marshal Gerd von Rundstedt, believed that the German army should fight a mobile battle in which its tactical and operational strengths would come into play. But neither Rommel nor Rundstedt possessed the freedom needed to fight the battle. Hitler and the OKW (the armed forces high command) controlled the placement of German reserves, and only they had the authority to release panzer divisions and other reserves for counterattacks and reinforcements. This arrangement was one of the greatest weaknesses on the German side. As usual there was no clear chain of command, and Hitler's directives, to say the least, could be bizarre. His desire to control everything deprived Rommel of the opportunity to place the bulk of his army in position to intervene immediately in the battle. Without that capability, the Germans stood less chance of preventing the Allies from gaining a beachhead.

But Allied commanders had considerable problems of their own. At the operational level, few understood how best to utilize the mobility of their forces or, among senior officers, how much the face of battle had changed in the last few years. As Sir Alan Brooke (later Lord Alanbrooke), chief of the Imperial General Staff and one of the most overrated officers in the war, announced to American generals in April, the war of movement was over and the fight in France would not see the lightning advances that had characterized the German campaign in 1940. Not surprisingly in view of such attitudes in the high command, logistical planners prepared for a slow methodical advance to the German frontier, a campaign that would have closely resembled that of autumn 1918.

In one sense, Brooke was right: The Allied forces that came ashore possessed considerable weaknesses. Even much of their equipment was inferior to that of the Wehrmacht. The most egregious example lay in Allied armor, which, as it had been throughout the war, remained undergunned and not so well protected. The Allies did possess great numerical superiority in tanks, which would eventually tell in the battle of attrition. That was small comfort to crews whose main weapons could not pierce the frontal armor of Panther and Tiger tanks at point-blank range.

But no defect was greater than the tactical preparation of ground troops. The British and Canadian armies had had four years to prepare for the landing in France. They had focused, however, too much on the landing phase and not enough on preparations for the fighting that would follow. Far too many of Brooke's friends found continuing employment in senior positions after failing in command assignments. The British corps commander whose troops could not seal off Falaise in August was General Sir Neal Ritchie, responsible for the May 1942 debacle at El Gazala, where Rommel had come close to destroying the Eighth Army.

At lower levels, the British possessed no common doctrine for the combined-arms employment of its various branches. As a result, British army training rarely reached the same high level of consistency and effectiveness that the German system managed. Hard, tough, realistic training seems to have been entirely a hit-or-miss affair. The afteraction reports by German military units engaged in fighting the British in Normandy suggest problems that reached well beyond explanations attributing such flaws to prewar funding or the army's social position in British society. Even the basic building block, infantry tactics, showed weaknesses; the British seemed to rely on little more than a straightforward rush and the hope that the artillery had smashed the Germans to bits. As one division commander noted to Basil Liddell Hart after the war:

> I have already told you how shocked I was at the meagre results of training in the United Kingdom when I met the 44 Div, 51 Div, 56 Div (not to speak of 50 Div which learnt nothing, ever, even after years in the desert. . . . If I told you what I had seen among those divisions, you'd not believe it.) It was nothing to leave the tanks to hold a position at night and retire the infantry—for a rest? too dangerous?—and let the [enemy] infantry infiltrate back and take the position.

The Canadians had most of the weaknesses of their British comrades. In World War I, they and the Australians had held the justifiable reputation of being the elite troops among Commonwealth forces. But extended exposure to the British way of war seems to have worn away the qualities of initiative and flexibility that had characterized their operations in the previous war. And except for the Dieppe disaster, those who went ashore at Normandy had been denied the leavening experience of combat.

The Americans, coming into the war last, had their own problems. The Germans had had six years, from 1933 to 1939, to prepare and then five years of terrible combat to hone their skills. But at the outbreak of war in 1939, the U.S. Army had ranked seventeenth in size among the armies of the world. Not surprisingly, many of the units that fought in Normandy displayed a depressing greenness and lack of tactical preparation, which resulted in the deaths of large numbers of young men. Moreover, the sudden expansion of air, naval, and ground forces, combined with the rapid mobilization of the American economy and the huge logistical infrastructure required to fight *two* separate wars—one in Europe, one in Asia—placed severe pressures on the manpower pool available to U.S. ground forces. After other services and the army's administration had grabbed their portion of recruits, the infantry often got what was left.

But the Americans displayed a greater capacity to adapt to combat than their British counterparts. From first contact, the Americans steadily improved. Such improvement owed much to the ruthlessness that American senior commanders displayed in sacking officers who did not measure up. When the battle finally went mobile at the end of July, the Americans displayed a capacity to exploit that no British army possessed, with the possible exception of General William Slim's in Burma.

Allied conceptions for the campaign were clear and straightforward. The initial landing force would seize the lodgment that would allow the logistical buildup to take place. Five attacking divisions, each with its own beachhead—code-named, from west to east, Utah, Omaha, Gold, Juno, and Sword—would seize the bridgehead. A massive paratroop drop by the U.S. 82nd and 101st airborne divisions west of Utah would prevent German counterattacks on that beach and take German defenses in the rear. Similarly, on the eastern side of Normandy, the British 6th Airborne Division would seize the bridges over the Orne River and the Caen Canal, blocking any counterattack from that direction. The airborne divisions would play the crucial role of protecting the invasion beaches from enemy interference in the first hours.

Montgomery, once he had sizable forces ashore, aimed to fight a mobile battle in the open country east of Caen with the bulk of his British armor. Meanwhile, the Americans would secure the logistical base by seizing Cherbourg and eventually Brest. As he had done in Sicily, Montgomery assigned a subordinate role to the Americans. But the British general, as arrogant as he was unimaginative, would not get to fight his battle; perhaps that was lucky, because his British troops were hardly trained to fight in mobile conditions.

Throughout May, in glorious weather, Allied forces concentrated in southern England. The target date for Overlord was June 5, but conditions failed to cooperate: Atrocious weather arrived with the new month of June. It appeared that a break in the storms would finally occur late on the fifth, so that conditions might be tolerable on the sixth. Eisenhower took the risk and ordered the invasion. This break was crucial because there was only a relatively small window in early June when the low tides around dawn would allow the attackers to escape the full impact of the beach obstacles that the Germans had implanted.

AS DUSK SETTLED over the English airfields on June 5, paratroops from three airborne divisions clambered aboard their aircraft. The first pathfinders were down before midnight. Most of the British paratroops in the east landed within their drop zones. But to the west, the Americans were less successful in achieving a tight concentration. To avoid both the bad weather and flak, U.S. aircrews flew higher and faster than normal, so that paratroops of the 82nd and 101st Airborne were blown all over the Cotentin Peninsula and elsewhere in Normandy. Fortunately, this worked somewhat to the advantage of the invaders: The presence of American paratroops everywhere completely muddied the picture for German commanders in the first hours of D-Day.

The launching of the invasion during a period of bad weather actually contributed to its success. As usual, most of German intelligence missed the indicators that suggested something big was in the offing, while the German weather service added to the illusion of calm by reporting that conditions would not be suitable for an invasion. Rommel journeyed home to visit his wife on her birthday; meanwhile, the commander of the Seventh Army, charged with defending Normandy, ordered his corps and division commanders to participate in a war game at his headquarters in Rennes.

The result was that there was little direction or coherence to the German moves throughout June 6.

As reports of major paratroop landings began to come in, Rundstedt gave two reserve panzer divisions near Paris—Panzer Lehr and the 12th SS Panzer Division, Hitler Jugend—the preparatory order to move to Caen, two hours before the seaborne landings began. But neither division could begin its actual movement until Hitler confirmed the order. Colonel General Alfred Jodl, the OKW chief of operations, informed a disgruntled Rundstedt that the führer was sleeping and would make the decision later in the morning when the situation was clearer. Thus, the German defenders in Normandy had to fight the battle of the first day with whatever troops they had in the immediate area, and that proved insufficient to counter the invasion.

For the most part, the British and Canadians overcame the opposition on their beaches with relative ease. British paratroops formed a successful blocking force over the Orne River and the Caen Canal, and after several hours they were reinforced by infantry. The largest problem that Commonwealth troops found in moving south out of the beachhead was not German opposition but the confusion of the beachhead itself. One appalled officer watched a Scots battalion under artillery fire march up the road in peacetime formation.

Even if there had been less confusion on the beaches, it is unlikely the British and Canadians could have captured Caen on the first day, as Montgomery had hoped, because the 21st Panzer Division had much of its forces deployed around Caen. The lead battalion of the Canadian 3rd Infantry Division did have a clear road into Caen, but its brigade commander twice ordered it to remain where it was, since any such move was not in the plans. Whether the Canadians could have held Caen is another question. That night the 12th SS Panzer Division arrived in the city, while the 21st lay to the north.

Late in the day, the 21st attacked the gap remaining between Sword and Juno. Running into the heavy guns of the Sherman Firefly tanks—which underline that the Sherman was not a bad tank if equipped with a decent weapon—the Germans immediately lost thirteen tanks. In the end, the 21st failed to achieve anything and lost 70 tanks of the 124 they had begun with that day.

At Utah, the beach farthest west, the Americans achieved an easy landing. The paratroop drops undoubtedly helped the tactical situation. Numerous small actions by paratroops disturbed, confused, and at times crushed German resistance. In one case, Lieutenant Richard Winters of the 101st and twelve paratroopers, later reinforced by a few soldiers, took out a battery of four 105mm guns looking directly down onto Utah beach. The German artillerymen also had the protection of a platoon of approximately fifty paratroopers; but Winters and his men took out the artillerymen, the paratroopers, and the guns. Such intervention by the American paratroops in innumerable other locations smoothed the going at Utah.

But American difficulties at Omaha imperiled the success of the entire invasion. Of all the beaches, Omaha was the most exposed to Channel weather, and the Americans paid a heavy price. Out of thirty-two amphibious tanks that were supposed to swim ashore to support the infantry, only five reached the beaches; the rest foundered, and most of their crews drowned. The story was equally depressing for the artillery; virtually no howitzers in the first wave made it through the roiling surf. The infantry had to fight their way ashore in the face of heavy resistance by the whole 352nd Infantry Division, instead of a weak infantry brigade as intelligence had reported. Not surprisingly, the initial landing waves suffered heavy casualties, and the Germans pinned the survivors down on the beaches. To a German officer commanding fortifications overlooking Omaha in the first hours, it looked as if the defenses had stopped the attack. He reported, after noting that the Americans lay huddled on the shoreline, that many vehicles were burning and German artillery fire was inflicting heavy casualties.

Reports to American commanders indicated much the same situation; for a short period, Lieutenant General Omar Bradley considered putting subsequent waves scheduled for Omaha into Utah. But gradually the situation improved. American infantry moved inland; heavy naval gunfire took an increasing toll on the 352nd; and after receiving optimistic reports from that sector, German commanders channeled reinforcements to deal with the more serious situation in front of the British. By the end of June 6, despite considerable confusion, the Americans at Omaha had fought their way far enough inland that reinforcements could flow into the beachhead. But it had been a close-run thing.

What might have happened if the Americans had not succeeded in making a lodgment is a difficult question. Could the Germans have won? The Allies would have had a difficult time linking up the American and British bridgeheads, and with two isolated positions, the Germans might have launched a more successful series of counterattacks. On the other hand, the continuing confusion of German commanders in the face of the onslaught makes it doubtful whether even so favorable a circumstance would have mattered in the end. As Rommel had warned, once the Allies were ashore, the Wehrmacht's position grew more and more desperate. It is possible that if the Germans had stationed virtually all of their reserves close to the coast as Rommel had wished, they might have defeated the landing at Omaha and perhaps bottled up one of the British landings. But it is worth noting that even Rommel felt the main landing would come at Pas-de-Calais, to the east; as a result, even he would have pushed most additional reserves to the Fifteenth Army. But this was Germany in 1944, and Hitler was not about to remove his influence from the conduct of operations. Under such circumstances, the Germans had no chance to keep the invasion from succeeding.

As the sun set on June 6, the Allies had gained a successful lodgment in western Europe. By the end of the day, they had gotten about 156,000 men ashore by aircraft and ship—75,215 across the beaches in British sectors, 57,500 in the American sectors, and 23,000 paratroopers and gliderborne infantry. In all, eight divisions were ashore. In the west, the Americans had established a solid beachhead for the VII Corps, into which vast numbers of men and a mountain of supplies were pouring. Though the British and Canadians had not captured Caen, at least they had established a solid lodgment with their three beaches already linked together. On the other side, the Germans were in general disarray, with most of their high command convinced—as they would remain for much of June and July—that a second and greater invasion would come in Pas-de-Calais. And that belief tied up a substantial portion of German forces in France, waiting for an invasion that never came.

At this point the Luftwaffe executed its plan to deploy its battered fighter squadrons to France to attack the invaders. Through Ultra—intelligence material derived from the decryption of German military radio traffic—the Allies knew the German plans and even the locations of the forward operating bases. Within thirty-six hours of the invasion, the Luftwaffe had moved over 200 fighters to France; an additional 100 followed over the next three days. But the movement only swelled Allied victory claims; in the first week the Germans lost 362 aircraft and the next week 232. Allied fighter aircraft continued to enjoy complete air superiority over northern France; by day nothing moved by road.

Not until midnight on June 6–7 did the first troopers from the SS division Hitler Jugend arrive in Caen, focusing the battle on that city for the next month and a half. Created from the elite of the Hitler Youth, it represented as ideologically fanatic a formation as the Germans fielded in the war. The next day Hitler Jugend's panzer brigade under the baleful Kurt Meyer piled into the Canadians. In ferocious fighting, the Canadians came off second best against the well-trained, juvenile murderers; but supported by naval gunfire and artillery already ashore, they held.

Several hundred Canadians surrendered to the SS, but many failed to reach prisoner-of-war cages. There is one testimonial in the Canadian archives to an incident in which the teenagers machine-gunned Canadian prisoners and then drove their tanks over the bodies. There is extensive evidence that the troops of Hitler Jugend followed a policy of executing large numbers of prisoners. About the best that can be said for justice is that most of the perpetrators were killed or mutilated in the fighting that followed. On the other side, Allied intelligence officers in some cases got wounded SS troopers who fell into their hands to talk by threatening that if they did not they would receive transfusions of Jewish blood.

But the German effort to batter the British and Canadians at the gates of Caen allowed the Allies to consolidate the beachheads. Hitler still hoped for a counterattack that would push the Allies into the sea. But Rommel found himself desperately trying to plug holes in a bulging dike. As German reinforcements flowed—or crept—into Normandy, they had to be immediately broken up and rushed to a number of different sectors.

German signal breakdowns exacerbated the situation. Ultra intercepts on June 9 and 10 indicated the precise location of the headquarters of

Panzer Group West. Obligingly the Germans placed their tents and supporting vehicles in an open field, where Allied fighter bombers wrecked the entire site and killed seventeen officers, including the chief of staff. This air attack effectively removed Panzer Group West as an operating headquarters and robbed the Germans of their only command organization in the West capable of handling mobile divisions.

Increasing French resistance and sabotage added to German difficulties. The SS panzer division Das Reich took nearly two weeks to arrive in Normandy from Limoges, a journey that should have taken only two days. Air attacks and ambushes made the move a nightmare. Along the way, members of the division instigated a number of atrocities that confirm that Hitler Jugend's behavior was symptomatic of the criminal nature of the Waffen SS as a whole. The worst occurred at Oradour-sur-Glâne, where SS troopers murdered 600 French civilians: They machine-gunned the men in open fields and burned the women and children to death in the village church.

Throughout the Normandy battles, outnumbered and outgunned German infantry held out against their superior opponents. But they were being gradually worn down in spite of the tactical carelessness and lack of initiative of U.S. and British troops. The British reported that they found it disconcerting to come over the tops of ridges to discover the Germans dug in on the reverse slope, "something that we had never envisaged," as one lieutenant put it— an extraordinary admission, because reverse-slope positions had been the basic principle of German defensive doctrine since 1917.

The British were often their own worst enemy. On June 12, their commanders recognized that the German positions west of Caen, between Villers-Bocage and Caumont, were up in the air; they thereupon switched the axis of the 7th Armored Division's advance to the west to take advantage of the situation. They were right; the Germans had little in the area, because the fighting around Caen was soaking up most of their strength. The lead brigade of the 7th Armored Division was soon through the German lines and reached Villers-Bocage without hindrance. But the British advanced as if on a peacetime maneuver: There were no reconnaissance units in front or on the flanks.

One of the few Germans in the area, however, happened to be Captain Michael Wittman, a great tank ace of the Eastern Front, with five Tiger tanks. Wittman and his tank crews blasted the head of the column and then rolled up the British formation. By the time the fighting in Villers-Bocage was over, the British had lost twenty-five tanks and twenty-eight other armored vehicles. Wittman's action plugged the dike long enough for the 2nd SS Panzer Division to arrive and reinforce him. In effect, this action prevented the British from rolling up the German position west of Caen. For over a month Montgomery attacked, but British and Canadian battlefield skills were not up to the task of creating a breakthrough.

The Canadians did not finally secure Caen until July 13. The Germans were well prepared, and from beginning to end British infantry and tanks failed to cooperate. But one must give the British their due; whatever their tactical and operational weaknesses, they fought the best formations in the German army in the West to exhaustion. The fighting around Caen served a larger purpose: It pinned the German armor on the eastern battlefield in Normandy and prevented them from concentrating their forces for a powerful counterthrust. Again and again Rundstedt and Rommel stabilized a collapsing line and prevented breakthroughs toward the east. But the price they paid was an attrition of their best units.

Ironically, the very failure to achieve a breakthrough to more open ground east of Caen worked to the Allied advantage. Battles of attrition played to Allied strengths—firepower and manpower—and wore away outnumbered German frontline units. Any breakthrough in June or July would have resulted in a mobile battle in central France—one in which the Germans would have fallen back on their supply dumps, extracted their forces from western France in less damaged fashion, and inflicted heavier casualties on Allied forces.

The area into which the Allied forces moved in early June was less open to German reinforcement and supply; at least for the short run it was also of less significance, because advances in the *bocage* country led only to more of the tall, thick hedgerows around each patch of field. The Germans could form one defensive line after another, making the *bocage* ideal defensive terrain. Not surprisingly, commanders had concentrated more on making the initial landings a success than on thinking through the implications of the terrain beyond which they would have to fight after the invasion occurred.

By June 18, the Americans had cut the base of the Cotentin Peninsula by reaching the Atlantic Ocean at Barneville. Major General J. Lawton ("Lightning Joe") Collins, the VII Corps commander, who had led a division at Guadalcanal, now drove north toward Cherbourg. The Americans fought their way into the city against third-rate troops; by June 27, enemy resistance had ended—but the Germans had wrecked the port facilities. Despite massive efforts to repair the damage, the Americans failed to open the port fully until September; by then the battlefield had moved far from Normandy. In retrospect, however, the clearing of the Cotentin Peninsula proved a wise decision, because it placed the American flank firmly on the Atlantic and meant operational freedom.

Worrisome for the American commanders was the weak performance of many units. That weakness forced Bradley to keep the airborne divisions in the front lines longer than planned and to rely on a small group of better-trained infantry divisions, such as the 1st and 9th. But Eisenhower and Bradley embarked on a ruthless program to weed out incompetents at all levels. The Americans were also paying a price in the *bocage* country for their emphasis on mobility over weight of weaponry. In the conditions of Normandy, mobility made little difference—though that changed once the breakout occurred. But, as Rommel noted, the Americans generally learned from experience, while all too often the British did not.

On July 3, the VII Corps launched a drive on Saint-Lô that Bradley hoped would carry all the way to Avranches. Such a success would end the stalemate that was rapidly increasing frustration among commanders and politicians alike. The American advance did no better than British attacks, and in this case against weaker forces. Nevertheless, though suffering heavy casualties, the Americans slowly pushed the Germans back to Saint-Lô, a wearing-down process that would eventually crack German defenses.

Meanwhile, by the end of the month, the Americans had solved the hedgerow problem: They designed a device with steel teeth attached to the front of a tank to cut through the roots. Code-named Rhino, it allowed American tanks to support infantry attacks directly. What made the device particularly noteworthy—and American—was the fact that noncommissioned officers developed it, mostly using the steel obstacles the Germans had scattered on the beaches of Normandy. It is almost inconceivable that NCOs in the British army would have invented such a device, and even more doubtful that senior officers would have embraced something invented by "other ranks." The hundreds of tanks equipped with Rhino gave the Americans cross-country mobility, while German tanks remained road-bound.

By late July, the Germans confronted a rapidly deteriorating situation. Their logistical position, particularly on the western side of the battlefield, was in shambles. Moreover, they were running out of reinforcements to rebuild the collapsing line, and Allied strength in Normandy had now reached over a million men. To add to German woes, their high command collapsed in July. Rundstedt, who had snapped that Field Marshal Wilhelm Keitel should "make peace," was replaced by Field Marshal Hans Günther von Kluge, a general officer notable for his malleability. Kluge arrived sure of himself and the tactical skills of the German army. Like most who had served in the East, he underestimated Allied air power. Kluge's first comment to Rommel was that he had better start obeying orders; but before relations between the two field marshals reached an explosive level, Allied fighter bombers caught Rommel's staff car in the open on July 17, severely wounding the Desert Fox.

Kluge refused to appoint a replacement for Rommel, but instead assumed command of Army Group B along with the overall command of the West. By the end of the month, he had recognized how desperate the situation had become. The explosion of a bomb in the führer's headquarters, on July 20, only added to the burdens besetting the German high command. Since Kluge had extensive connections with those who had launched the assassination plot—his own former headquarters in the Soviet Union was one of the most active centers of resistance—he was now desperately looking over his shoulder as the plot unraveled. His political problems were an important influence on the decisions he took as the front collapsed, and he would soon commit suicide.

AT THE END of July, Bradley unleashed the decisive offensive of the Normandy battle. Operation Cobra broke the deadlock. Crucial to American success was the contribution of British and Canadian attacks in the east:

Fourteen German divisions, including six of the Wehrmacht's best panzer divisions, faced the Commonwealth soldiers. Only eleven divisions confronted American attacks in the west—two of them panzers, and both in dreadful shape. Instead of attacking across a broad front, the VII Corps launched its offensive on just a 7,000-yard front. To prepare the way, Bradley asked for a carpet bombardment by strategic bombers. However, air commanders refused requests that their bombers make runs parallel to the front. Instead, the airmen came in perpendicular to U.S. lines; they believed that there was little chance of a "creep back"—friendly fire, as it were—after bombing began.

Bad weather delayed the start. On July 24, the bombers took off from bases in England, but by the time they reached the target the weather was again unsuitable. However, a number of aircraft bombed anyway, and the American infantry suffered casualties, twenty-five killed and 131 wounded. The results the next day were even worse for U.S. troops in the area. No fewer than 1,800 bombers from the Eighth Air Force struck the German positions, but even though the weather was nearly perfect, the last bomber waves dumped a substantial number of bombs on U.S. positions. This time the Eighth Air Force killed 111 American soldiers, including Lieutenant General Lesley McNair, and wounded 490 others.

The air attack did not completely break German resistance, but shaken American attackers discovered that enemy defenses now contained holes through which they could press forward. For the Germans, the fighting that followed destroyed what was left of many units. After receiving an order from Kluge that his division, the Panzer Lehr, must hold to the last, General Fritz Bayerlein replied: "Out in front everyone is holding out. Everyone. My grenadiers and my engineers, and my tank crews—they're all holding their ground. Not a single one is leaving his post. They are lying silently in their foxholes for they are dead."

The Americans failed to achieve a clear breakthrough. They did, however, eventually lever German defenders away from the coast. Mobile at last, they forced the Germans back, pushing them east rather than south. The German flank was soon up in the air, and the Americans pushed through to Avranches on July 30, liberating it the next day.

At this point, exploitation could take place. With activation of the Third Army and the arrival of General George S. Patton, Jr., the Americans rolled into high gear. But the Third Army's actions displayed the weaknesses as well as the strengths of the U.S. Army. The first units to move through Avranches headed west and not east, where the greatest opportunity for exploitation lay. Patton's instincts were to move rapidly forward, but since the plans called for him to go west into Brittany toward Brest, he obeyed his orders. Only when the Allied high command recognized that it had made a mistake did Patton turn the remainder of the Third Army to the east. What makes the move so inexplicable was the fact that whatever the logistical needs for more port capacity, the Germans had indicated by the destruction of Cherbourg that the Breton ports would not be a help. Brest would hold out until mid-September. Nevertheless, in slavish devotion to the plans and over the protests of one of the better American division commanders, Major General John Wood, the initial move went entirely in the wrong direction.

Luckily for the Allies, Hitler made a serious situation desperate. Instead of authorizing a withdrawal to save as much of his manpower and equipment as possible, the führer ordered Kluge to concentrate his armor, recapture Avranches, and cut off Patton's rampaging forces. As a result, he stuck German forces deeper into the sack. Ultra alerted Bradley, and with the Americans ready and waiting, the German counterattack, at Mortain, had no chance. At this point Patton's forces began their drive into central France, and a gigantic encirclement formed around German forces in Normandy.

Nevertheless, the Allies failed to reap full benefit from the German collapse. Patton's encircling spearheads stopped at Argentan to wait for the slower British and Canadian forces moving southward. Patton jokingly suggested to Bradley that the Third Army could continue north and push the British into the ocean for a second Dunkirk. But one senses that neither Bradley nor Patton nor their troops had much desire to close the Falaise gap: They knew that if they actually encircled the Germans, they would confront a battle even costlier to both sides. Nor did they understand how crucial such an action could prove to achieving victory in 1944. Without an American focus on Falaise, British and Canadian efforts from the north faced a tough road. Unfortunately, the efforts from the north were less than effective. The resulting failure of American, British, and Canadian forces allowed substantial numbers of the toughest German troops to make their escape from Falaise. Upon their return to the Reich, they found sufficient weapons and equipment from Albert Speer's economic efforts to prolong the war into 1945.

IN THE LARGEST SENSE, the Normandy campaign achieved its goals. The armies of the Western powers returned to the European continent. In an enormous battle of attrition, they fought the Germans to exhaustion and inevitable collapse. The Allied armies did not fight the battle according to the wishes of their commander—the historical evidence makes clear that Montgomery aimed to achieve a breakout from Caen in which his Commonwealth troops would fight a mobile battle to destroy the Germans, while the Americans mopped up rear areas and provided logistical support. Ironically, the opposite took place: It was the Americans who fought the mobile battle and the British who mopped up. In the end, the battle that took place emphasized the strengths and superiority of the Allies.

It is tragic that the Allies were not able to translate their success into the defeat of Nazi Germany in 1944. Their failure was partially the result of weaknesses in command. And yet that command failure was inevitable. The very qualities that made it possible for Eisenhower to persuade and cajole a collection of raging egos into the team that made the invasion possible could not provide the driving, ruthless push that might have tumbled Germany in August and September. Moreover, one can doubt whether any such commanding personality could have made the disparate coalition work in harness in the fashion that Eisenhower's combination of personal tact and toughness did. A supreme Allied commander with the personality of a King, a MacArthur, or a Brooke could well have fractured the coalition structure on which victory in war and peace depended. The campaign did mark many of the commanders who directed the Allied side. Eisenhower and Tedder look particularly good. And the campaign, at least until the breakout, did play to Montgomery's strengths; Normandy was one of his finer moments. Bradley also showed the stolid, steady performance that made him a soldier's soldier. The first team had passed its test.

For those who walk in the silent cemeteries of Normandy, the cost of that victory can seem excessive. That especially seems true when one looks at the ages of those who died and considers the deficiencies of the armies of the democracies on the field of battle. The price of prewar neglect was paid for in the blood of youth and lies in those long, silent rows of crosses and stars of David. Yet one must remember that the Anglo-Americans confronted enormous problems in dealing with the pernicious tyrannies that had arisen in the world during the 1930s. In the end they won, and they created the basis for a stable peace that led to the re-creation of Europe. The Normandy campaign brought the armed power and political ideals of the democracies back onto the Continent. That was a triumph of enormous political significance. It was not pretty, but it served the purpose.

*SPRING 1994*

---

**Williamson Murray authored the earlier article on why the North took so long to win the Civil War.**

---

# 33

# D-Day Revisited

## By Stephen E. Ambrose

*While the previous essay by Professor Williamson Murray deals with the broad picture of the Normandy campaign, this essay by Professor Stephen E. Ambrose illuminates the potentially lethal problems that confronted individual soldiers. To comprehend the sweep and hazard of these challenges, Ambrose combines the oral-history memoirs of participants with his own experiences in exploring the battlefield. He walked the invasion beaches, struggled in the grip of the surf and tides, looked out from the German gun positions, and cursed the sharp and impenetrable mass of the hedgerows. His words and the accounts of survivors detail the special hell that Allied soldiers faced that momentous sixth of June.*

As part of the research for a book I am writing about D-Day, timed for the fiftieth anniversary (June 16, 1994), my wife, Moira, and I spent a summer in Normandy. Staying in small hotels in the seaside villages, we walked along the beaches and swam in the surf. I've been studying this battle since I first went to work for General Eisenhower as editor and biographer in 1964. I have visited Normandy at least a dozen times, for periods ranging from a couple of days to a week or two. I am always startled to find out how much I don't know, and delighted at how much I learn.

One reason for our trip was new source material I had with me, transcripts of oral histories from the men of D-Day. For the past ten years, the Eisenhower Center at the University of New Orleans has been collecting tape-recorded memories from Normandy veterans; to date, we have about 1,000 from Americans and another 300 from German, French, Canadian, and British veterans. In most cases they are detailed enough to make accurate guides.

For example, on Omaha beach, on the shoulder of the bluff looking down on the Colleville draw, there is a series of German emplacements that impressed themselves forever on the minds of a dozen or so of my U.S. 1st Division informants. The Germans built a miniature Gibraltar to defend that draw. There are a dozen or so "Tobruks" of various sizes. Some are cement silos sunk into the ground, with openings that a mortar crew inside could fire from with all but perfect immunity. Others held machine guns or flamethrowers; some even had tank turrets on top. Climbing down into them, getting into the tunnel system that connected them, I marveled at how well situated they were to cover that draw, and was appalled at the thought of how much fire they could hurl down on it.

Even more impressive are the twin casemates built to hold 75mm cannon. Made of six-foot-thick, steel-reinforced concrete and big enough to hold the cannon and a five-man crew, they are tucked into the bluff, perfectly sited. Through the aperture of the higher casemates, there is a magnificent view of Omaha beach stretching out to the west, about four miles long: The sand is golden; the sky is blue; the Channel is gray; the surf is white; the bluff is green; the bathers' swimsuits add splashes of color. Altogether, it is a subject befitting an impressionist painting.

For the Germans firing those 75mm cannon on June 6, however, the scene was terrifying—thousands of young Americans coming ashore to kill them. To prevent that, they fired down on the invaders as rapidly as they could load. An American combat engineer who had been down on the beach told me that those two guns probably killed more Americans than any others in Normandy—he estimated more than 200.

The casemates took a pounding in return. I could locate damage from a 5-inch naval gun, or from a rocket—not much damage, just a pockmark in the concrete. Inside the upper casemate, I spotted the hole where an American 75mm shell had scored a direct hit. It had been fired from a Sherman tank on the beach. Following the angle of the hole, I could trace the exact position of the tank when it fired. A French employee at the Omaha cemetery told me that in 1984 the German battery commander met with the commander of the American tank to discuss their duel of forty years past—each had put the other man's weapon out of action.

That tank got ashore thanks to Lieutenant Dean Rockwell, who made a decision to bring his LCT group all the way in, rather than launch them, "swimming," offshore as planned. A crew member on Rockwell's LCT, Martin Waarvick, told me the story. Rockwell mistrusted the rubber inflatable skirts that guided the tanks and had thought the sea too rough for the tanks to swim, so he brought his four right on in. Of the thirty-three tanks launched at sea, only two others made it to shore; the rest sank.

For three decades, those tanks sat on the bottom of the Channel. Local fishermen knew their location; the wrecks were prime fishing areas. The fishermen refused to divulge the spots until embarrassed into doing so by the local mayors, who pointed out to them that the men whose bones were inside had come over to France to liberate them and deserved a proper burial. In the past ten years, all the tanks have been pulled out, the bones buried.

Lieutenant Rockwell saved the day at Omaha. Until he got his four tanks ashore, the Germans in the casemates at the Colleville draw could and did kill everything on that beach. The descending shells from the navy could not put those cannon out of action, but the flat-trajectory shells fired upward by the tanks directly into the aperture did.

What it was like for the first wave, before the tanks came in support, is best described by S.L.A. Marshall. He has come under considerable criticism lately, some of it justified, but I carried his writings with me all summer and found them to be vivid, moving, and generally reliable.

As the first wave approached, the Germans held their fire. Survivors tell me they thought it was going to be an easy assault, that the naval and air bombardments had put the German defenders out of action. But Marshall writes (in *Atlantic Monthly,* November 1960) that at the dropping of the ramps, the beach "is instantly swept by crossing machine-gun fire from both ends." The first men out

> are ripped apart before they can make five yards. Even the lightly wounded die by drowning, doomed by the waterlogging of their overloaded packs. . . . Half of the people [in Boat No. 4] are lost to the fire or tide before anyone gets ashore. All order has vanished from Able Company before it has fired a shot.

The company is part of the 116th Infantry, 29th Division. Within minutes of its landing, "the sea runs red." Wounded men who drag themselves ashore "lie quiet from total exhaustion, only to be overtaken and killed by the onrushing tide." The few who make it to the beach untouched cannot hold, and they return to the water for cover. "Faces turned upward, so that their nostrils are out of water, they creep toward the land at the same rate as the tide."

To get a better idea of what happened, I spent a dozen afternoons swimming off Omaha beach. In June the water is still cold, although not bitterly so; by July it is pleasant. The tide is spectacular, alternately covering and uncovering a 1,500-foot-wide beach.

This enormous tide created all kinds of problems for the invaders, the full extent of which can be appreciated only by swimming. When the sea was running at all high—say, two- or three-foot waves—it was virtually impossible for me to stand up, even in waist-deep water, or rather what would have been waist-deep water if the sea were calm. When the waves were up, the surf would be ankle-deep as one wave washed out, over my head when the next one came on. Even on a calm day, I found it difficult to swim because of the powerful current that runs parallel to Omaha just beyond the breakers.

Another difficulty—one that nearly every survivor mentions—is the sharp drop-offs. I would swim out a couple of dozen yards, then start in. My feet would hit bottom and I'd start walking. Suddenly, I'd be over my head again. At least three of the men who have given oral histories to the Eisenhower Center swear that the Germans dug antitank trenches when the tide was out, and that the invaders fell into them. Nothing of the kind was attempted, for the obvious reason that the next incoming tide would have caved in a man-made trench. These depressions are natural, created by the tidal action, and they shift with every tide.

In short, I found it difficult to get ashore from even a short distance out, in a calm sea and wearing only a swimsuit. The men of D-Day had a moderately rough sea to deal with. In addition, their clothing had been treated with an antigas chemical that stiffened the fabric, and they were loaded down with helmets, heavy boots, rifles or mortars, grenades, ammunition, radios, and other tools of war. I now understand better why drowning was a major cause of death at Omaha beach.

Once ashore, the invaders entered the killing zone. For the first wave, landing at dawn at low tide, it was pure hell. The Germans concentrated their fire on the GIs trying to struggle their way through the thousands of obstacles Rommel had placed on the beach. With rifle and machine-gun fire kicking up the sand, the Americans tried to crouch and run, but the weight of their waterlogged uniforms and equipment plus the wet sand made running impossible. A dozen veterans have used the same image to describe what it was like: the nightmare in which a demon is chasing you but your legs are so heavy you can't run.

Many tried to hide behind Rommel's obstacles. They were of all different types and descriptions, but the most common were six-foot sections of steel rails welded together as a tetrahedron. These only gave the illusion of protection—they were in fact often more dangerous than the open sand because they were topped with land mines. The Germans would wait until a group of GIs were behind such an obstacle, then fire at the mine to set it off.

Combat engineers coming ashore in the first waves had the job of blowing those obstacles before the tide covered them. Sergeant Vince DeNiccio of New York City told me that his toughest job was getting the men away from a tetrahedron so he could blow it up. As I made various runs across the beach, I could hear the surf and the laughter of children playing on the beach, but I had in mind what Vince had told me: The noise on the beach on June 6 was so great that he had to go up to an individual, cup his hands around the man's ear, and shout as loud as he could, "Get the hell out of here—I'm going to blow this thing!"

Shingle runs parallel to and at the edge of the sand dunes. It consists of small round stones piled up about three feet high and fifteen feet wide. Many of the GIs hit the ground on the edge of the shingle, trying to use it for protection. It didn't work: although they were then relatively safe from rifle fire, the Germans hit them with mortars. They clung there anyway, because a swamp lies between the dunes and the base of the bluff, and that swamp was full of barbed wire and land mines—and exposed to rifle fire.

I walked through the swamp with ease—today a raised, all-weather path leads through it. But when I thought of the men who decided that lying on their bellies behind the shingle, their noses in the sand, was only going to get them killed, and who then crossed the dunes, cut through the barbed wire, and started up the bluff—my admiration soared.

Looking up the bluff, I reminded myself that the brush and small trees that today make it such a lovely sight were all cut down in 1944. The bluff was crisscrossed with rifle pits and trenches, machine-gun pillboxes, and Tobruks. Barbed wire was everywhere.

The men who moved up the bluff were charging a replica of a World War I trench system: The rifle fire was intense; the machine-gun fire was interlocking; the mortars were presighted and active; the mines (which were not a feature of World War I) were everywhere. In the face of this, infantry worked their way up the bluff, got into and through the German trenches, and began pitching grenades into the pillboxes or picking off German soldiers in the Tobruks with their rifles.

Taking that bluff was one of the greatest feats in the history of the U.S. Army. The D-Day plan had been to move forward by going up the draws, at Colleville, Vierville, and Saint-Laurent. And in Darryl Zanuck's movie version of Cornelius Ryan's *The Longest Day,* that is the way it was done. In the climactic scene, a bangalore torpedo blows a gap in the barbed wire protecting the cement wall that blocks the draw. Men rush forward to place dynamite at the base of the wall. A plunger sets the explosive off; it blows a hole in the wall; GIs rush forward and up the draw. As Robert Mitchum, playing General Norman Cota, climbs into his jeep and drives up the hill, the music swells.

But climbing the bluff myself, and listening to the veterans' words on the tapes, I made a discovery: That wasn't the way it happened. The victory was won by individuals and small groups struggling up the bluff. German defenses at the draws were too strong to be breached, and had to be out-flanked.

In his oral history, Lieutenant John Spaulding told how. He was leading Privates Richard Gallagher and Bruce Buck.

As we climbed, we bypassed a pillbox, from which MG fire was coming and mowing down F Company people a few hundred yards to our left. There was nothing we could do to help them. We could still see no one to the right. We didn't know what had become of the rest of our company. Back in the water, boats were in flames. After a couple of looks back, we decided we wouldn't look back anymore.

About this time Gallagher said to follow him up the defilade, which was about four hundred yards to the right of the pillbox. We were getting terrific small-arms fire. We returned fire but couldn't hit them.

When Gallagher found the way up, I sent Buck back to bring up my men. [Buck returned with four men from the section.] I couldn't take my eye off the machine gun above us, so Sergeant Bisco kept saying, "Lieutenant, watch out for the damn mines." These were a little box-type mine, and it seems that the place was infested with them, but I didn't see them. We lost no men coming through them, although H Company coming along the same trail a few hours later lost several men. The Lord was with us and we had an angel on each shoulder on that trip.

Trying to get the machine gun above us, Sergeant Blades fired his bazooka and missed. He was shot in the left arm almost immediately. Sergeant Phelps with his BAR [Browning automatic rifle] moved into position to fire and was hit in both legs. By this time practically all my section had moved up. We decided to rush the machine gun about fifteen yards away. As we rushed it, the lone German operating the gun threw up his hands and yelled, "Kamerad!"

Coming up along the crest of the hill, Sergeant Clarence Colson, who had picked up a BAR on the beach, began to give assault fire as he walked along, firing the weapon from his hip. He opened up on the machine gun to our right, firing so rapidly that his ammunition carrier had difficulty getting ammo to him fast enough.

With the strength of the German defenses at Omaha, and the enemy's natural advantage due to the lay of the land, the question arises: Why on earth did Ike land there? The answer is, because he had to. Between the British right flank at Arromanches and the Carentan estuary, Omaha is the only beach available. Everywhere else, the Channel runs right up to the bluffs and cliffs, most spectacularly at Pointe du Hoc. Had the U.S. 1st and 29th divisions not gone ashore at Omaha, there would have been a twenty-five-mile gap between the British right flank and the American left flank on Utah beach. I walked on the edge of the bluff the entire twenty-five miles and can testify that there is not a single spot, other than Omaha, where an ordinary soldier could possibly get to the top.

I say "ordinary" because at Pointe du Hoc soldiers did make it from the base of the cliff to the top, but they were Rangers, elite troops specially trained and especially brave. The men of Colonel James Earl Rudder's 2nd Ranger Battalion scaled the cliffs using one of the oldest implements of war, the grappling hook. Looking at the vertical cliff today, with the sea dashing against the base, it just seems impossible that men could get up it under the best of conditions. Indeed, I had the best of conditions: I was determined to experience as much of the physical challenge of D-Day as I could. I wanted to secure a rope at the top of the cliff, then descend and climb back up it. But I didn't make it. I chickened out. Rudder's men did make it, carrying 60 to 100 pounds of equipment on their backs, despite German defenders firing down on them, dropping grenades over the edge, and cutting the climbing ropes attached to the grappling hooks.

For me, Pointe du Hoc is one of the premier World War II battlefields, not because it was the most important but because there is no better place in Normandy to see the scars and destruction of battle. The German fortifications rival the great World War I fortress at Douaumont north of Verdun. The steel-reinforced concrete casemates protecting the 155mm cannon are at least six feet thick. The casemates are connected by extensive tunnels that contain an underground railroad.

These casemates were pounded by 500-pound blockbusters dropped by the bombers and by huge shells from the fourteen-inch guns on British and American battleships. They were hit by thousands of tons of high explosive, equal to two or three tactical atomic weapons. The results were devastating. The place reminded me of Stonehenge on the Salisbury Plain, except that these stones are fortifications blasted apart, lying at all angles. The bomb craters are huge.

The D-Day veterans are careful to tell me that in many cases the German defenders were inferior troops. That was not so at Pointe du Hoc, where the

Germans in the ruins kept fighting for two and a half days, inflicting nearly 75 percent casualties on Rudder's Rangers. In other areas, however, and especially at Utah beach, the German soldiers surrendered at the first opportunity. In most cases, this was because they were not Germans but Poles, Russians, French, Belgians, and others forced into the Wehrmacht after capture in 1940 or 1941. There were thousands of such conscripts.

Some German units did fight effectively. Some fought magnificently. At Saint-Marcouf, about six miles north of Utah beach, I found a tremendous German emplacement—four enormous casemates, each housing a 205mm cannon. I had read about the emplacement but had not previously been able to locate it. Those guns got into a duel with American battleships on D-Day and sank one destroyer. American infantry surrounded them on D-Day plus one. To hold the Americans off, the German commander called down fire from another battery some nine miles to the north, right on top of his own position. That, plus the pounding from American ships, kept the Americans at bay for more than a week while the German cannon continued to fire on Utah beach. The Germans surrendered when they ran out of ammunition.

Walking on top of the fortresses, I could see innumerable direct hits, all from big shells. They made little more than dents in the concrete. Crawling around inside, I marveled at the fortitude of the German gunners: the noise, the vibrations, the dust shaking loose, the terror they must have felt, along with bad water, stale bread, and no separate place to relieve themselves—and for nine days they kept firing.

Sainte-Mère-Eglise, a small village about six miles inland from Utah beach, rivals Pointe du Hoc for fame, thanks in large part to Zanuck's movie. The director took considerable liberties with the truth here, too, making the firefight in the square at Sainte-Mère-Eglise into a much bigger thing than it was. His most memorable scene, however—the one in which trooper John Steele (Red Buttons in the movie) caught his chute on the church steeple and hung there for hours playing dead—Zanuck underplayed. I know, because I got the full story from trooper Ken Russell of the 82nd Airborne.

Ken was a seventeen-year-old then. As he was coming down, he saw three buddies land on telephone poles around the square: "It was like they were crucified there." Next to him, another trooper had his grenades on his hip. A tracer bullet hit the grenades "and instantaneously there was just an empty parachute coming down."

Standing in the square years later, I listened to Ken on the tape describe what happened next. There was a fire in the hay barn across the street, caused by tracers.

> The heat drew the nylon chutes toward the fire. The air to feed the fire was actually drawing us towards the fire. One guy, I heard him scream, I saw him land in the fire. I heard him scream one more time before he hit the fire, and he didn't scream anymore.

In the middle of the square is a Norman church. Ken jerked his suspension lines to avoid the fire, and as a result came down on the church's steep slate roof. He slid. His chute caught on a steeple. He was hanging there when "John Steele came down, and his chute caught too." Sergeant John Ray floated down past them. Ken says:

> He hit in front of the church. A Nazi soldier, billeted on the next street behind the church, came around from behind, a red-haired German soldier. He came to shoot Steele and myself, hanging there. As he came around, he shot Ray in the stomach. John being a sergeant, he had a forty-five pistol and while he was dying in agony, he got his forty-five out and when this German soldier turned around to kill us, John shot the German in the back of the head and killed him.

Where the barn burned down, there is today the Parachute Museum, run by Phil Jutras, a World War II veteran who was a politician in Maine until 1972, when he decided to leave what he calls the "American rat race" and retire to this quiet Norman village. He married a local widow and began helping out at the small museum. Soon he became director. He has expanded it to include a C-47, a Waco glider, a tank, some artillery, a movie (in French and English), and, at the entrance, a full-scale model of a paratrooper.

Phil introduced me to locals who have filled me in on the events of 1944 at Sainte-Mère-Eglise. Over the years he has also passed on other stories he has heard from the veterans who come to see him and has guided me to many sites, such as General Matthew Ridgway's command post and General James Gavin's foxhole. For this portion of the story, I have also relied heavily on S.L.A. Marshall's *Night Drop*. It is a book full of marvelous maps. A bit fanciful, it has been criticized by paratroopers and scholars. Nevertheless, I recommend it as the best and most vivid account of the action.

Confusion and chaos marked the night drop, and thus the after-action reports and later oral histories are contradictory. I have great sympathy for Marshall in his attempt to put together an authoritative account of a complex series of small actions.

At La Fière, Captain Ben Schwartzwalder (later famous as the football coach at Syracuse) of the 507th Parachute Infantry Regiment led forty-four men on a maneuver to capture a manor house next to a bridge over the Merderet River. Using football analogies, Marshall details the action minute-by-minute. Following step-by-step, I held my breath—figuratively—as I moved along beside a hedge and turned a corner. The manor loomed before me, the barns and house joined by connecting stone walls higher than a man.

"Held for downs, Schwartzwalder took time out," Marshall relates. On the other side of the road, "Slim Jim Gavin arrived on the scene, in the van of his band of 300." Unable to see through the hedgerow, Gavin was unaware of Schwartzwalder's party, and he moved on.

I was trying to penetrate the hedge, to get a better fix on the positions of the American units, when I got hit by a foe that made further movement impossible. That foe is present in all the hedgerows and is mentioned by nearly all airborne veterans, but it is so commonplace that it makes almost none of the books. Nettles—they sting like fury. They cause a rash that lasts, a burning that is painful and maddening, and there is no remedy but time. In this one instance I had it worse than the men of D-Day, because their bodies were covered except for hands and faces, whereas I was wearing only a T-shirt and Bermuda shorts.

Everyone knows how the GIs cursed those hedgerows, even beyond the nettles, and what a barrier they were to offensive action, but you cannot appreciate why until you have seen them and tried to crawl through one. They dominate the terrain, making each tiny field a miniature fortress. They are anywhere from four to ten feet high and have only one gate, too narrow for a tank. The Germans set up their heavy machine guns in the two corners away from the gate, and pre-positioned mortar and artillery fire on the middle of the field. In the first days of the Battle of Normandy, the Germans would let unsuspecting GIs get into the field, then hit them with interlocking machine-gun, mortar, and artillery fire.

One solution was to use dynamite to blast a hole in the hedge, then ram a tank into the hole and fire white phosphorous shells point-blank at the machine-gun positions. Another was to weld short sections of steel rails onto the front of a tank, then drive it into the hedge. The rails kept the Shermans from going belly-up. Here and there I thought I could see where a Sherman tank had penetrated a hedge, but after forty-five years I couldn't be positive.

All along the French coast from Brest to Belgium and beyond, there are extensive German permanent emplacements. They range from small field fortifications to massive blockhouses that brought to my mind the Great Wall of China or the Maginot line. Built by millions of French slave laborers, they are unpleasant to look at, squat, gray, forbidding, in many cases their cannon still pointed out at the Channel.

The juxtaposition of these fortifications with the lovely Norman seaside—the villages, the cathedrals, the châteaus, the cattle and horses, and the friendly people—struck us hard. It is a sad and futile thing that the Germans spent four years putting prodigious effort into building projects that are now only symbols of ugliness, fear, and hate.

They paid for their offenses against the French people. We saw the consequences at Longues-sur-Mer, just outside Port-en-Bessin, where the Germans built a four-gun battery, set back about three-fifths of a mile from an observation on the edge of the bluff. Each 155mm cannon had its own casemate, built of steel-reinforced concrete about nine feet thick. The guns had a range of more than twelve miles and were thus capable of firing on both Omaha beach to the west and the British Gold beach to the east. On D-Day, however, they were mainly involved in fighting duels with cruisers and battleships offshore. HMS *Ajax,* already famous for sinking the *Graf Spee* in December 1939 off the River Plate, put three of the guns out of action.

The Royal Navy scored many direct hits on the casemates, but as at Pointe du Hoc and elsewhere, the damage was relatively slight. Even the biggest naval shells could not penetrate the concrete. To do any effective damage, the shells had to come right through the relatively narrow—ten feet at most—aperture, almost impossible with high-trajectory shells. Still, the *Ajax* did it. How?

I got the answer from André Heintz, one of the founders of the new D-Day museum in Caen. At age seventeen in 1944, he was a member of the French resistance. André told me that when the Germans built the battery, they took away a farmer's best field. The farmer wanted to fight back, and figured out a way to do so.

He had a teenage son who was blind. Like many blind people, the boy had a fabulous memory. The farmer filled his mind with details about the location of the guns—so many meters back from the bluff, so many meters from the crossroads, so many meters between the casemates, and much more. Because the boy was blind, the Germans paid little attention to him, hardly glancing at his papers, allowing him to travel more or less freely.

The boy journeyed to Bayeux, where he relayed the information to André Heintz. With his primitive, handmade radio set (now on display in the Caen museum), André sent the information on to England. From air reconnaissance and local resistance informants, the Allies already knew that there were emplacements on the bluff at Longues-sur-Mer, but they did not have the exact coordinates. Thanks to the farmer and his son, on D-Day they did.

But even with perfect intelligence and brilliant shooting, there was luck involved in the Ajax's victory. Two of the guns were put out of action by shells that burst on the edge of the aperture, damaging the mounting and making the cannon immobile. With the third gun, the shell came right through the aperture and burst inside.

The Germans were great at conquering, terrible at occupying. They had an opportunity in France to play on traditional anti-British feelings, heightened by the British withdrawal from the Battle of France in June 1940, and on French fears of communism, to bring the French in on the new German order in Europe. Instead, they acted like beasts. The result was the French resistance, without which victory on D-Day would scarcely have been possible. That, at least, was Eisenhower's judgment: He once told me the resistance was worth five divisions on D-Day.

The British and Canadian beaches—Gold, Sword, and Juno—are not so evocative of D-Day as Omaha and Utah, except at Arromanches, where the cement breakwaters for the artificial harbors can still be seen, and where the museum displays models that show how the system worked. The coast from Arromanches to Ouistreham at the mouth of the Orne River is a traditional vacation spot for the French middle class. Small cottages and shops now cover what was the battlefield. But by staying in small hotels or bed-and-breakfast places, we got to meet people who were there forty-five years earlier, and each of them had a story to tell.

On the morning of D-Day, Jacqueline Noel, seventeen years old, pedaled her bike down to the beach at Ouistreham. She wanted to help. Because she was a nurse wearing a red-cross armband, the Germans did not stop her. On the beach, she worked with the medics. She told me a story that made the sheer scope of D-Day vivid for me in a way that little else could.

About midmorning an Allied bomber was hit. Burning, it began descending in circles. "Everybody started watching," she said, "Germans and British alike. It was obvious that the pilot was trying to find some open piece of water where he could safely ditch his plane. I looked at that armada of landing craft, LSTs, and all the rest, and could not see how he could ever find a place to land. The beach was so jammed with men, guns, and vehicles that it, too, was impossible." Sure enough, the bomber crashed into an LCT.

We were sitting on the beach as she told me the story. The Channel was all but covered with French kids windsurfing, hundreds of them. Jacqueline said there were more landing craft on D-Day than windsurfers that day.

On the beach, she had met Lieutenant John Thornton. She got to know him better in the days that followed. After the war, they married; he took a job as a shipping clerk for a British steamship line, and they lived in Ouistreham. I discovered five other couples who met on D-Day, three British and two American, all still married.

John Thornton told a story that gave me a sense of the ferocity of the battle. He was an artilleryman. On D-Day plus five, he was riding a bike past an artillery park in an open field, a few miles inland. The guns had been firing constantly for three days. Suddenly, on signal, they all ceased firing at once. He was so stunned by the quiet—the first he had experienced since June 6—that he fell off his bike into a ditch, where he lay looking up at a clear blue sky. A lark flew over his head and sang.

*Praise the Lord,* he thought to himself. *Life goes on.*

And so it does. Normandy endures. Except for the military cemeteries and the German fortifications, it is not much different from the way it was a half century ago. The cream, the cheese, the seafood, the cider remain the best in the world. You sense the presence of William the Conqueror and the Normans in every church, in every village square, in every 1,000-year-old farmhouse or manor. Standing on the bluff looking down on Omaha beach, or among the sand dunes behind Utah beach, or among the hedgerows around Sainte-Mère-Eglise, you can also sense the ghosts of the men who died there on D-Day.

*WINTER 1993*

---

**Stephen E. Ambrose is the author of the earlier essay on Operation Fortitude.**

# 34

# The American Rommel

## By Caleb Carr

*Anyone with even a cursory knowledge of World War II remembers George S. Patton, with his ivory-handled pistols, his swagger, his ego, and his reputation for bold advances. Only the most serious students of the war might remember Major General John S. Wood. Commander of the 4th Armored Division in its 1944 breakout through Saint-Lô and its dazzling thrust across France, he became known to his men as "Tiger Jack." His continual stress on speed, maneuver, and concentration of force, Caleb Carr argues, marks him as America's greatest World War II tank commander. Yet his devotion to the concept of deep armored strikes rather than linear attritional warfare served only to have him relieved of command—by George S. Patton—and forgotten.*

The historic French town of Troyes controlled an important stretch of the upper Seine River, so it was a likely spot for the armies of Nazi Germany and the Allies to clash during their struggle for control of Europe. Troyes had once been a celebrated meeting place for European nobility—King Henry V of England and Princess Catherine of France had been married there in 1420—and the distant rumble of 460-horsepower engines may not have seemed wholly congruous when the defenders of the town first heard it.

The plains of the surrounding Seine valley offered a good five miles of open ground that the approaching machines would have to cover before reaching their objective. This gave the defenders some cause for hope, and when the distant silhouettes of enemy tanks finally did appear, the two to three thousand soldiers in Troyes dug in determinedly.

Atop a gently sloping rise that grew out of the valley plains, the company of medium tanks spread out into "desert formation," about a hundred yards apart. Supported by infantry in half-tracks and by self-propelled assault howitzers, the attack group numbered some 800 troops in all. They did not pause when enemy artillery fire began to burst around them; rather, they picked up speed, and were soon traveling at full throttle.

The infantry half-tracks veered sharply, attempting to throw the defending gun crews off their marks by deliberately heading for spots where enemy shells had already burst. Meanwhile the tanks' guns fired continuously, the crews having been rigorously trained in the practice of what their divisional commander called "violent execution of fire and maneuver." Accounting for the pitch and roll of their speeding vehicles, the gunners required no pause to hit their targets.

As they neared the town, the roaring thirty-ton monsters jumped a seven-foot-wide antitank ditch. At the same time, they disposed of the first enemy enfilades. The tanks then sped on through the streets of Troyes to cut the defenders' lines of supply and communication. The armored infantry and mobile artillery meanwhile moved in to engage in street fighting.

By dawn of the next day, the battle was over. A superior defending force had been first stunned and then crushed by the audacity and speed of the attackers. This was mobile armored warfare at its best. But the tank crews did not stop to congratulate themselves. Securing a Seine crossing, they continued their dramatic sweep through the French countryside.

The open plains and historic towns of France had seen many such engagements during the war, but the battle for Troyes had a twist: The date was August 25–26, 1944, and the defending troops were German. The blitzing attackers were moving east, not west, and they were Americans. Yet in the quality of their tactics and leadership, they could easily have been mistaken for the best of the 1940 German panzer crews.

The credit for this achievement belongs to the man who had trained and was in command of the tanks that hit Troyes: Major General John S. Wood, of the American 4th Armored Division. Britain's great military theorist Basil Liddell Hart would later call Wood "the Rommel of the American armoured forces" and "one of the most dynamic commanders of armour in World War II." Wood was all this and more. For while his tactical acumen accounted for dozens of victories such as that at Troyes, his strategic insight was perhaps even more profound.

During the summer and fall of 1944, Wood perceived more clearly than any other Allied commander the opportunity for an early defeat of Germany. By employing the same bold strategic method—blitzkrieg—that had brought Hitler himself to within a hairbreadth of European rule, Wood believed that the Allied armies could deal the fatal blow to the Nazi Reich within mere weeks of their breakout from the Normandy beachhead on July 25. Personally irrepressible and outspoken, Wood made these opinions known—first to his various corps commanders, then to his Third Army leader, General George S. Patton, and finally to the high command. Wood's recommendations consistently fell on deaf—or, more often, annoyed—ears, and his suggestions turned to protests. In December 1944 he was dismissed by General Patton and sent home.

But Wood's efforts were not in vain. By spearheading the conquest of France, he dramatically demonstrated the validity of employing bold armored strategy; and despite his dismissal, the ultimate conquest of the

Reich would come only after the Allied high command realized that Wood had in fact been right, and adopted his methods on a grand scale.

THE ATHLETIC and high-spirited son of an Arkansas judge, Wood had not as a youth aspired to soldiering. At the age of sixteen, he was admitted as a sophomore to the University of Arkansas to study chemistry. His characteristic prankishness was demonstrated in his junior year, when he was almost expelled because of, as he later put it, "certain laboratory experiments which led to a series of minor explosions on the steps of the women's library." A football star and an exceptional student, Wood readied himself for a career as a chemist upon graduation from the university. Then a teammate suggested that he come along to West Point—the military academy would offer them a chance to get in a couple of extra years of football. (In the early years of the century, colleges were not fussy about sports eligibility.)

At the Point, Wood quickly made a strong impression. Repelled by the plebe system, he undertook the tutoring of less academically gifted cadets and soon earned the sobriquet *Professor* (also shortened to just *P*). This sympathy for his fellow soldiers would grow with time, as would his impatience with unenlightened army traditions. "Individual hazing has no place in the formation of true military character," he wrote; nor did he think that the mentality such behavior bred would be useful in the army, "where sensitive, intense natures are needed as well as the thicker-skinned, hard boiled types."

While at West Point, Wood became acquainted with many of the men who would go on to become leaders of the American effort in the Second World War—Dwight Eisenhower, Omar Bradley, Carl Spaatz, and Jacob Devers, to name only a few. But the most portentous acquaintance he made was that of George Patton. Wood graduated after Patton, but the two shared common interests—primarily an intense preoccupation with military history—and their paths were destined to cross many times.

Following his graduation, Wood was posted to coastal artillery, then to ordnance, and finally to field artillery. He served in France during the First World War, seeing action in such battles as Château-Thierry, and was sent to the staff college at Langres, where he was a classmate of Patton's. Wood was deeply disturbed by the static carnage of the 1917–18 experience, and when tanks made their debut, he, like Patton, was enthusiastic. But on their return to the United States, the two men began to display different approaches to the new weapons of movement, and it was these differences that would later cast them into separate camps.

Armor's brief moment in the sun during the First World War was enough to convince progressive officers the world over that the future of land warfare lay with this new military arm. At the Battle of Amiens on August 8, 1918, British tanks not only broke the seemingly unbreakable trench lines but also created a panic among the German troops even more demoralizing than the Allied guns.

The implications of this development were dramatic, and the first theorists to fully comprehend them were a pair of Englishmen: Basil Liddell Hart and J.F.C. Fuller. During the decade of the 1920s, Liddell Hart and Fuller called with increasing insistence for the adoption of innovative armored techniques that had as their goal not merely tactical successes such as Amiens but spectacular strategic achievements. While Liddell Hart and Fuller's own British army did not, as a whole, subscribe to these radical theories, several influential German officers did; and it was in later describing the style of warfare that burst on the world in 1939 that Fuller gave perhaps the best short summary to date of the secret of blitzkrieg:

> It was to employ mobility as a psychological weapon: not to kill but to move; not to move to kill but to move to terrify, to bewilder, to perplex, to cause consternation, doubt and confusion in the rear of the enemy, which rumour would magnify until panic became monstrous. In short, its aim was to paralyse not only the enemy's command but also his government, and paralysation would be in direct proportion to velocity.

This effect could be heightened, Liddell Hart emphasized, by adopting the strategy of the "indirect approach," whereby armored divisions would avoid striking along a broad front or attempting to move an enemy's front line backward. Instead of such "linear" strategy, the tanks should adopt the practice of concentrating at unexpected points on the line with devastating strength, thereafter roaring into the enemy's rear areas.

In the United States (as in Great Britain), these theories were dismissed from the beginning by the army's senior officers. Fuller's pronounced emphasis on the political paralysis (rather than the physical destruction) of the enemy as the primary goal of armored warfare conflicted sharply with the dominant American military tradition. As established by Ulysses S. Grant, that tradition was based on the steady, brutal grinding down of the enemy army along a linear front by overwhelming numbers of troops (primarily infantry) sustained by superior amounts of supplies. That this attitude remained preeminent in America during the interwar years was demonstrated in 1925, when the American general-services schools dismissed one of Liddell Hart's most important works as "of negative value to the instructors of these schools."

Certainly there were advocates of armor in the United States Army during the 1920s and 1930s—but the goals of these advocates were not in all cases similar or even consistent. The examples of Wood and Patton provide a case in point. The National Defense Act of 1920 placed America's tank forces—blindly but predictably—under the command of the infantry. For those officers who, like Wood and Patton, had already begun to explore the possibilities of armored divisions, the question now became how to proceed. Patton elected to return to his old arm and first love, the horse cavalry. Wood, too, returned to his roots: artillery. But while Patton dreamed of finding ways to breathe new life into traditional cavalry tactics by replacing his horses with tanks and armored cars, Wood soon became involved with mobile artillery, opening his mind far more fully to the strategic possibilities of armor.

A gifted linguist, Wood went beyond Fuller and Liddell Hart to read France's outspoken armor advocate, Charles de Gaulle, and Germany's Heinz Guderian, father of the panzer division. By the early 1930s Wood was reporting to the War Department that the next war would "be one of rapid movement, of motors, tanks and aviation, of indirect approach and deep penetrations, regardless of flank protection and linear formations." In 1936 Wood was scoffed at by fellow officers for turning down an assignment at the Army War College and instead seizing the chance to command the army's only independent truck-drawn howitzer organization in Des Moines, Iowa.

The list of Wood's unusual tendencies did not end with accepting what seemed to others obscure postings—he soon gained a reputation for readily voiced intolerance of narrow thinking in both subordinates and superiors. This in turn led to his being branded, in the words of General Ben Lear (later commander of U.S. Army ground forces in Europe), "obstreperous, hard to handle, a difficult subordinate." In the close-knit world of the interwar American army, professional criticism of—and intellectual condescension to—superiors was a dangerous path to follow.

But Wood's attraction to radical armored doctrine (and hence his disagreements with his colleagues) was not purely strategic in origin. It also centered on one of Liddell Hart and Fuller's incidental goals: greatly reduced casualty lists. For beneath Wood's buttoned-up exterior beat the heart of a man who, though a stickler for details of dress and deportment, cared for the average soldier to a degree not often found in the U.S. officer corps. A speech he later gave to his officers and noncoms on the eve of the 4th Armored Division's departure for Europe summarized this attitude:

> You may have only eight, or even thousands of men in your unit, but always remember—each one has a Mother, Father, perhaps a wife and children. They want that soldier home, after this war ends! So you *invest* them carefully—*lead* them, don't just order them! Reconnoiter, see, estimate, *what* you are taking them into, weigh every advantage and disadvantage of your plan, attack fast and hard, pound out a win and come out of it with 90 percent of your people and equipment! Less than that—you are only a brass-buttoned figurehead!

Such an approach was clearly at variance with the haughty posturing of men like Patton, who would be well remembered for his physical and verbal abuse of soldiers suffering from battle fatigue during the Sicilian campaign. Indeed, the differences in style between the two men were marked on every level. Patton, ever the flamboyant prima donna, enjoyed showy displays of decorations and ivory-handled revolvers, and spent his idle moments practicing his "war face" in the mirror. Wood, while always correct in appearance, disdained the wearing of ribbons as well as any more flashy display of military etiquette than the simple salute (which he insisted on). Patton was tall and fair, a California aristocrat. Wood was stocky, heavy-browed, and pugnacious. Patton's principal nonmilitary activity was womanizing. Wood was a devoted fancier of roses. Given such contrasts, it is perhaps a surprise, then, that they should have been friends.

Throughout the 1920s and 1930s, Wood often found himself posted to the same location as Patton, and the two spent much time together. Patton, Wood later recalled, "possessed a splendid library of military works, and we read everything from the maxims of Sun Tsu and Confucius to the latest articles in our own and foreign military publications. We often sat, glass in hand, arguing loud and long on war, ancient and modern, with its battles and commanders."

By 1941 Wood had been made artillery commander of Patton's 2nd Armored Division, but he didn't stay at the post long enough for any differences in strategic thought or style of command to become pronounced.

That same year he was promoted to brigadier general and transferred to Combat Command A of the 5th Armored Division. (American armored divisions were divided into three combat commands, or battalion task forces, two labeled "A" and "B" and one held in reserve, or "R.") In June 1942 Wood was given the twin stars of a major general, along with the task of training the 4th Armored Division for combat abroad.

It was in Europe that Wood was to test his theories in the field and under fire for the first time. The job of leading his young division across France involved many important discoveries for him, none more critical than the realization that the arguments he had enjoyed with Patton could have far more than merely intellectual repercussions.

Shortly before the Normandy landings of June 6, 1944, Basil Liddell Hart spent some time discussing the upcoming European campaign with various Allied leaders. The experience was a distressing one for Liddell Hart, who discovered that the "prevailing mood" among the Allied high command was that the campaign would be all too reminiscent of the nightmare of the First World War. Even Patton—who had already earned a reputation for tactical boldness in North Africa and Sicily—believed that in Normandy the Allies would be forced, as Liddell Hart recalled the conversation, to "'go back to 1918 methods' and could not repeat the kind of deep and swift armoured drives that the Germans, especially Guderian and Rommel, had carried out in 1940" in France.

Discouraged that such a linear mentality should be dominant in Allied thinking, Liddell Hart was happily surprised by his discussions with General Wood—so surprised that he spent a full two days with the 4th Armored's commander. Liddell Hart found Wood "more conscious of the possibilities of a deep exploitation and the importance of speed than anyone else." Such consciousness, however, did not change the fact that Wood was only a divisional commander, and that his 4th Armored had yet to receive its baptism by fire. Whether the rigidly traditional strategic approaches of Eisenhower, Bradley, and even Patton could be overcome by field commanders such as Wood remained to be seen.

For Wood, the first great test came during the American army's Cobra operation of July 25, more than a month and a half after D-Day. For weeks the Allied troops had been penned up in Normandy and on the Cotentin

Peninsula—Patton's prediction about "1918 methods" was turning out to be grimly accurate. The high command was as much to blame for this fact as was the vicious *bocage,* or "hedgerow," countryside of northwestern France. In both the eastern sector of the bridgehead (controlled by Bernard Law Montgomery's British and Canadian Twenty-first Army Group) and the western (under the supervision of Omar Bradley's American Twelfth Army Group), a startling inability to exploit successes became apparent.

The simple fact that every attempt to break out of the beachhead had failed miserably finally drove Bradley to accept one of Liddell Hart and Fuller's prime directives—that armored attacks not be launched along broad fronts but concentrated at key points. The Cobra plan called for massive air bombardment of a strip of road 7,000 yards long, followed by infantry attacks to open a corridor. Armored exploitation by the 2nd, 3rd, 4th, and 6th armored divisions would ensue. These units were to move south and seize the vital town of Avranches, gateway to the Brittany Peninsula.

From the moment Cobra struck, Wood demonstrated the hallmarks of his command style. Straying from the letter of the plan, the 4th Armored Division was first to seize vital road centers and strategic towns, including Avranches. Racing with dramatic speed, Wood concerned himself far less with the destruction of German units in his area than with disrupting the enemy rear and securing avenues of attack.

Wood covered the fifty miles to Avranches in just five days, and he was soon joined by the 6th Armored Division under the immensely capable General Robert Grow. On August 1 both divisions were placed under the operational control of the newly formed American Third Army, commanded by Patton. With Avranches secure, Patton—in accordance with the pre-invasion plan drawn up by the high command—ordered Wood to continue south and then southwest into Brittany, while Grow was sent due west to execute a bold, lightning-fast move to the port of Brest.

The Third Army's wild rampage through Brittany obscured one central fact—west was precisely the *wrong* direction for American armor to be moving. Patton described this part of the campaign delightedly as "a typical cavalry action in which, to quote the words of the old story, 'The soldier went out and charged in all directions at the same time, with a pistol in each hand, and a saber in the other.'" This description amply displays Patton's greatest deficiency as a tank commander: his tendency to think as a traditional cavalry tactician and to care little what direction he was attacking in, so long as he was attacking.

No one saw this problem more clearly or felt its effects more severely than Wood. On the first day of his advance south from Avranches, Wood traveled thirty miles and almost reached the vital crossroads of Rennes. Bypassing its strong defenses, he raced on to the bottom of the peninsula—and came to the realization that he was only slightly closer to Brest than he was to Paris. His commanders claimed that they needed Brest's port facilities, as well as those of the southern Brittanic ports of Vannes and Lorient. But Wood believed that the Germans would be well dug in at these ports (they were), that they would be likely to destroy the port facilities before they surrendered (they did), and that there were not many German troops blocking his path to the Seine (there were not).

If he now could induce Patton, Bradley, and Eisenhower to change their plan and consent to an immediate turn eastward, a long encirclement of the German armies in France could be achieved with a speed and decisiveness that would match the Germans' own 1940 campaign. Assuming that approval for this idea would be forthcoming, Wood turned away from Brittany and ordered his lead units to advance southeast to Angers.

"When General Patton found out about this, he exploded," a member of Patton's staff later recalled. But Wood was never one to shy away from confrontations with his superiors when strategic questions that affected the lives of his men were involved. When his corps commander demanded to know why Wood was moving in a direction diametrically opposed to that indicated in his orders, Wood angrily protested, "They [the high command] are winning this war the wrong way!" But Patton persisted, and Wood was forced to turn west to Vannes on August 5. After reaching that town, he wired a message to Patton: "Trust we can turn around and get headed in the right direction soon." But it was to be ten days before Patton would allow Wood to proceed east—ten days, as much time as it had taken for the Germans to defeat the French and British in the field in 1940.

Meanwhile Wood's popularity among his own troops was growing. They dubbed him "Tiger Jack," both because of his habit of pacing angrily when perturbed and because of his ability to roar back at Patton. Also growing was the fearful respect accorded his division by the Germans. One German general, who was captured in a surprise raid by Wood's men, announced that he "would like to meet that general who commands Fourth Armored Division—he is outstanding among generals of American divisions."

But none of this assuaged Wood's bitterness over Patton's restraining order. "I could have been there," Wood later recalled, "in the enemy vitals, in two days. But no! We were forced to adhere to the original plan—with the only armor available, and ready to cut the enemy to pieces. It was one of the colossally stupid decisions of the war." As always, Wood was more than willing to express such opinions to his superiors. He encountered Patton soon after the Brittany fiasco, and that general, referring to Wood's conduct during that episode, remarked, "You almost got tried for that." To which Wood replied, "Someone should have been tried but it certainly was not I."

Hitler's own unwillingness to pull back to a coherent line of defense mitigated the possibly disastrous effects of the Brittany sideshow—but the Allied high command soon gave the Germans yet another opportunity to escape disaster. Instead of dashing straight for the Seine and destroying both the German lines of supply and the Wehrmacht's only avenue of retreat (at minimal cost to their own forces), Patton, Bradley, Montgomery, and Eisenhower all became attracted to the idea of enveloping the Germans in a small pocket centered around the Falaise plain south of Caen. If they could achieve this encirclement, they could engage in as battle of annihilation.

The plan that led to the Battle of the Falaise Pocket would have been merely backward and brutal had it worked. But having decided on a "short envelopment" (as opposed to the "long envelopment" that could have been achieved to the east), the Allied commanders next demonstrated that they lacked the steadiness of purpose to execute even this flawed maneuver. On August 13, Bradley—fearful of running headlong into the British and the Canadians—halted the southern American pincer at Argentan. To the north, Montgomery proved too cautious to break through to the Americans with a decisive stroke. This left a wide gap between the two Allied spearheads, which was not sealed until August 20. Some 50,000 Germans were taken prisoner and 10,000 were killed inside the Falaise Pocket, but another 40,000 had already escaped to harry the Allied attempt at a long envelopment at the Seine.

That such an envelopment was still possible had been apparent since August 15, when the American tanks had finally resumed their eastward advance. Wood's 4th Armored Division led the way: Before the end of August 16, Combat Command A had reached Orléans, south of Paris.

Making their presence felt during this drive were the daring pilots of the 19th Tactical Air Command, screaming out of the sky in their P-47 Thunderbolts. Directed by air liaison officers who actually rode with the armored columns, the pilots became an integral part of the American drive, in the best blitzkrieg style. The 4th Armored Division soon became the 19th TAC's favorite ground unit, and not simply because of the cases of captured cognac that Wood periodically sent to the pilots. Wood's troops, 19th TAC commander General O.P. Weyland later recalled, "took immediate and full advantage of friendly air power and didn't whimper if they got a bloody nose in an engagement. Air-Ground teamwork was terrific."

Because of the success of this mid-August drive, the American spearhead units were still in a position to undo the damage of Falaise and complete the long envelopment at the Seine. But astoundingly, Patton—backed up by the high command—again halted his troops, for a crucial forty-eight-hour period on August 16. The official explanation was supply difficulties. But as much trouble as the Allied high command was having supplying its forward units, it was having more trouble comprehending the breathtaking speed of the American drive and the extent of the Wehrmacht's collapse in the face of it. This was precisely the kind of war that the American senior commanders had thought it would be impossible to wage—and if there was one quality that the high command lacked, it was the ability to adapt and improvise quickly.

Wood's handling of supply questions belied the high command's repeated supply concerns—and because supply would continue to be used as the main rationale for slowing the American advance, it is worth noting how the 4th Armored Division dealt with the problem. A high priority was placed on the capture of enemy gasoline stores, and gas was also flown in from the Allied rear. Supply trucks carried at least double their usual loads, and instead of riding to the rear of the column, they stayed close to the advance combat units. Serviceable vehicles were seized wherever they were found. American kitchen trucks were stripped and packed with gas and ammunition—rations were loaded onto the combat vehicles. Wood's grasp of every detail of mobile armored warfare was instinctive and uncanny.

By the time the American troops were finally unleashed once more, it was too late to prevent a large-scale German retreat across the Seine. The tanks of the 4th Armored Division nonetheless pursued the German troops across the open ground between the Seine and the German frontier—and as they did, the high command made another colossal blunder. In early August, Eisenhower began openly promulgating his plan for the conquest of Germany: "the broad front strategy." All of the Allied armies were to close on the German frontier simultaneously. The front would be steadily rolled up at all points, as had been attempted during the First World War.

The plan was classically American, sheer linear thinking that had comparatively little relevance to mobile armored warfare. Instead of outmaneuvering the enemy, you overwhelmed him. Many American field commanders were enraged, none more so than Wood. "There was no conception of far-reaching directions for armor in the minds of our top people" was his terse and (considering the circumstances) charitable postwar assessment. By August 31, with a dramatic victory at Troyes under its belt, the 4th Armored Division had crossed the Meuse River at Verdun, and was faced by a completely disorganized and demoralized enemy. Yet Eisenhower was still talking about abandoning this dramatic undertaking to ensure that some measure of success would be achieved by all Allied units, including the British and Canadians to the north, who were a full hundred miles behind Wood's spearheads.

The cost of this decision was to prove dramatic, and the explanations offered for it utterly inadequate. Eisenhower continued to claim that he worried about the dangers of supplying armored columns that were traveling farther and farther from their supply sources. Yet as Wood had already demonstrated, America's armored units, by scrounging, innovating, and economizing, could survive far longer in the field than the extravagant Allied supply estimates believed possible. (The average Allied division in Europe was scheduled by the high command to consume 700 tons of supplies a day—the Germans were fighting on 200.)

Given the remarkable performance of America's armored divisions generally—and Wood's 4th Armored in particular—there seems no credible way to dispute Liddell Hart's claim that if the American tankers had been allowed to continue their advance, and to slice through Germany by way of the southern "indirect" route, the war against Hitler could well have ended in the fall of 1944. Instead, the Germans pulled together a tenacious defense and another two seasons of brutal fighting were ensured.

During September and November 1944, the Germans not only rallied for a determined defense of their frontier but even, in some areas of the Western Front, managed to stage counterattacks. The most ambitious of these were a series of spoiling raids. Designed to keep the Americans so off-balance they would be unable to maintain the offensive, the attacks were opened by the Fifth Panzer Army under Hasso von Manteuffel against the 4th Armored Division at Arracourt, just east of Nancy, on September 19. Wood called this "the greatest tank battle of the war on the Allied front," a justifiable claim if judged by the ferocity with which the division fought against superior German numbers and tanks. Over four days of fighting, Wood crippled two new panzer brigades, knocking out 150 increasingly precious German tanks and killing hundreds of enemy soldiers. The cost to his own division was twenty-one tanks destroyed and twenty-five men killed.

Stung by this unexpected display of brilliant armored defense, Manteuffel was forced to withdraw. But that such attacks could be staged at all indicated that the Wehrmacht was far from beaten. Wood recognized this, and he began to protest ever more vehemently against being held back. His protests led not only to violent disagreements with his corps commanders but also to increasing friction with Patton's Third Army headquarters.

Much of the fame that Patton had enjoyed as a result of his Third Army's advance across France belonged rightfully to Wood and the 4th Armored Division. To Patton's credit, he acknowledged this debt throughout the summer and early fall. But by November the situation seems to have changed. By now Patton's irritation at Eisenhower's restraining orders was—like Wood's—considerable, and he consistently found ways to circumvent those orders and go on the offensive. But his plans of attack in the month of November, when he faced a reconstituted German defense, again began to display the strategic shortcomings that had periodically plagued his actions.

Both Patton and his Twelfth Army Group commander, Omar Bradley, conducted their initial attempts to break through the German frontier without any apparent indication that they had learned the lesson of Cobra: that armored attacks must be concentrated. With Bradley's approval, Patton once again indulged his taste for attacking in all directions, stringing his forces out along the entire Third Army front between the Moselle and Saar rivers. This allowed the Germans, under General Hermann Balck, to parry each attack skillfully with inferior forces. As the autumn rains turned the ground to mud, Patton's ill-conceived assault bogged down.

The only unit to achieve any meaningful advance was Wood's 4th Armored Division. Forgoing Thanksgiving turkey, Wood had by November 25 pushed most of his unit across the Saar River into the area just south of what would become, in a matter of weeks, the launching of Hitler's Ardennes offensive—the Battle of the Bulge. His division's progress in late November surprised Wood himself, for, as he later said, "there was no opportunity for the maneuver of armor at which we were adept." The enemies now were many—Wood cited the "fanatical resistance of the enemy, bad weather, soft terrain, [and] heavy artillery fire." That Wood nonetheless made progress was fully appreciated by the Germans—by now they, too, had taken to calling him "Tiger Jack," and in his radio addresses Joseph Goebbels had launched a series of tirades about the "butchers" of the American 4th Armored Division.

Wood, however, remained dissatisfied with both the general disposition of forces in his area and the strategic directives of his superiors, and he continued to say so. By early December, Patton had had enough. With a suddenness that stunned the men of the 4th Armored Division (some broke down in tears), Patton relieved Wood of his command for reasons of "health," and Wood was sent back to the United States for "a rest."

Patton's explanation for this move seems, even today, more than a little disingenuous: "Unquestionably, in a rapid moving advance, [Wood] is the greatest division commander I have ever seen, but when things get sticky he is inclined to worry too much, which keeps him from sleeping and wears him down, and makes it difficult to control his operations."

Things had certainly gotten "sticky" in November—and the fault had been largely Patton's. That stickiness translated into casualties for Wood's division, without any sufficiently dramatic advance—something that Wood had always found infuriating. As to Wood's being "worn down," it is certainly true that both he and his division had been continuously involved in some of the most exhausting action of the European campaign ever since the Cobra breakout; but other commanders had been involved for as long or longer, and some of these were to stay on for many months to come.

Wood's own explanation for his relief seems far more credible than Patton's: "Perhaps I had been too outspoken in my criticism of the static minds and rigid conceptions of the high command in Brittany. . . . And perhaps I had been too emphatic in my protests against linear employment of our forces, particularly armor, in frontal attacks all along the front instead of in deep thrusts in decisive directions." Patton and Eisenhower told Wood that he was being sent back to the States to be prepared for a higher command, but on his return Wood was appointed to the Armored Replacement Center at Fort Knox. Safely tucked away at this post, he would not again challenge the decisions of his superiors.

Although he did not return to Europe before the end of the war, Wood saw his theories of armored warfare validated by other commanders during the German campaign. Hobbled by the high command's linear strategy until early spring of 1945, the Americans finally did break out along the Rhine River, sending large armored formations into Germany to execute a series of deep, bold penetrations and encirclements. These culminated in the dramatic sweep to the Elbe River, a campaign after Wood's own heart: American armored columns reached the river just three weeks after the breakout and soon linked up with the Russians, finally shattering the Nazi Reich.

Remarkably but typically, Wood never gave voice to recrimination during the two decades between the end of the war and his death in 1966. He stayed in the army until the late 1950s, and after his retirement kept up an active interest in national and international affairs. In an "autobituary" that he left behind, he wrote of himself: "[He] hated nothing except meanness and cruelty. His friendships and loyalties were deep and abiding and he could not understand nor condone disloyalty."

It was perhaps this inability to understand disloyalty that kept Wood from ever delving too deeply into the circumstances surrounding his relief. "George Patton," Wood recalled, "I loved like a brother, and Eisenhower I had liked since my first sight of him when he reported . . . as a new cadet [to West Point]."

With that, Wood let the controversies surrounding the strategic prosecution of the European campaign and his own dismissal simply fade away; and the cults of personality that grew to surround both Eisenhower and Patton have long kept Wood in relative and unjustified obscurity. But with time, he may once again receive the recognition accorded him during the war—by other Allied officers, by the men who served under him, and by the Germans he fought against—as America's finest commander of armor.

*SUMMER 1992*

Caleb Carr is the author of *The Devil Soldier: The Story of Frederick Townsend Ward* (1992) and coauthor of *America Invulnerable: The Quest for Absolute Security from 1812 to Star Wars* (1988). His most recent book is a novel, *The Alienist* (1994).

# 35

# The Bulge

## By Stephen E. Ambrose

*The Battle of the Bulge remains the United States Army's largest engagement ever. Fought in the cold, fog, and snow of December 1944–January 1945, the battle wrecked Hitler's last offensive of World War II and ended any vestige of hope for the Third Reich. It was, however, a costly and difficult victory, with 80,000 American casualties. Yet, as Stephen E. Ambrose asserts, the clash could have been Eisenhower's most spectacular victory at much less cost. The German offensive had caught the supreme Allied commander by surprise, but Eisenhower quickly realized that the enemy's forces, pulled out from behind their Westwall fortifications and composed of their last reserves, presented a superb opportunity. The German attack had produced a bulge that looked like a large nose protruding into the American lines. If an Allied counterthrust from the north and south could cut off the Bulge at its bridge and base, it could annihilate the entire German force. It was not to be, Ambrose contends, because of the ego and caution of General Bernard Montgomery. Temporarily in command of Allied forces north of the Bulge, the British general refused to move quickly, and when he did move he insisted on attacking the tip of the nose rather than its bridge and base. As a result, the Allies lost a superb opportunity, and—as at the earlier Falaise Gap in August 1944— German soldiers escaped to fight another day.*

It was the biggest single battle on the Western Front in World War II and the largest engagement ever fought by the United States Army. The human losses were staggering: Of the 600,000 GIs involved, almost 20,000 were killed, another 20,000 were captured, and 40,000 were wounded. This was almost as many casualties as in Vietnam over the four-year period from 1965 to 1969 and more than the total number of men in the Army of Northern Virginia at Gettysburg. Two U.S. infantry divisions were annihilated; in one of them, the 106th, some 7,500 men surrendered, the largest mass surrender in the war against Germany. Nearly 800 American tanks were destroyed.

Beyond human and material losses, the U.S. intelligence officers were embarrassed, indeed humiliated, for the attack had come as a complete surprise. From the supreme commander in Paris, through the army group, army corps, and division commanders, down to the lowliest private dozing in a foxhole in the Ardennes at midnight of December 15–16, 1944, not a single soldier in the entire U.S. Army dreamed that it was possible for the Wehrmacht to launch an offensive. Yet in the Eifel—the rough, mountainous country in westernmost Germany—at the spot where Belgium, Luxembourg, and Germany meet, the Wehrmacht had gathered more than 200,000 troops and almost 2,000 tanks. That no Americans were aware of anything suspicious going on in the Eifel was an intelligence blunder as bad as Pearl Harbor.

How could Germany, a nation of only 85 million people that had already lost nearly 2 million fighting men in five years of war, hard pressed on three fronts, produce two new armies of nearly a quarter of a million troops? How could Germany, after two years of intensive bombardment by British and American heavy bombers, produce tanks in such numbers? How could the Wehrmacht, after spending 1943 and 1944 in retreat, manage so soon to regain the initiative and the offensive spirit? And finally, why would Germany decide to launch a major attack, one that would surely be its last, into an area devoid of strategic importance?

The answers to these questions help explain why American intelligence was so badly fooled. They illustrate the resourcefulness and strength of the Germans, their great skill in making war, their desperation in 1944, and the fundamental principle that the easiest way to surprise is to do something that makes no sense (e.g., for the Japanese to attack the United States, or for the Germans to attack the Soviet Union).

"The German army has had it," said a late-September intelligence report from the U.S. First Army. When the Wehrmacht nevertheless managed to create a new defensive line, along the prepared positions of the Westwall, it was assumed that this was a temporary, stopgap achievement. A Third Army officer dismissed the German defenders as "nothing but Poles with ulcers." In fact, however, the new formations already gathering in the Eifel for the counteroffensive were composed of highly motivated German teenagers. In the German cemetery in Luxembourg, where the Wehrmacht dead from the Battle of the Bulge are buried four to a grave, the headstones tell the stark facts: name, date of birth, date of death. The most common year of birth is 1928; next is 1929. In the American cemetery just across the road, nearly all the dead were born between 1918 and 1925. In short, Hitler's last offensive was a children's crusade.

Those young Germans were four or five years old when the Nazis seized power, and they had been deliberately raised for this critical moment. Fanatics who were ready, even eager, to die for Hitler and the Third Reich, they made courageous, if not always very skillful or prudent, soldiers. And they were well armed. Although the American .30-caliber M1 was superior to any German rifle, the German light and heavy machine guns were better than the U.S. models, as were German tanks and hand-held antitank rockets. The German Panther tank carried a long-barreled, high-muzzle-velocity, 75mm cannon, while the Tiger fired an 88mm dual-purpose gun that was the terror of the World War II battlefield. Both were also very heavily armored (113 millimeters thick in the turret for the Panther). Against these demons, the American bazooka was little more than a peashooter, and the short-barreled cannon on the standard U.S. tank, the Sherman, was not much better. It took heavy artillery, accurate and well laid on, to stop the Panthers and Tigers. Fortunately, U.S. artillery was at least equal in quality, and superior in quantity, to that of the Germans.

To gain such weight of armor and to carry such a heavy cannon, the German tanks had to be enormous. The thirty-three-ton Sherman was a lightweight compared to the forty-seven-ton Panther and sixty-three-ton Tiger. These new German tanks (the Panther was a 1943 model; the Tiger appeared in August 1944) sacrificed range and mobility for size and were better designed for defense than offense, especially in terrain like the Ardennes, where the roadnet was limited and the sharp turns and steep climbs numerous. The maximum range of the Panther, cross-country, was sixty-two miles; of the Tiger, fifty-three miles. (They got about one-third of a mile to a gallon of gas.)

The absolutely critical German shortage, and the place where the Americans had the advantage, was in the mundane but crucial area of motor transport. The Germans simply did not have sufficient numbers of trucks to bring forward the ammunition, gasoline, and other matériel necessary to sustain an offensive; indeed, for all the technological sophistication of the German armament industry, in jet aircraft, in tanks, in rockets, and in other areas, most German matériel was still brought to the front by horse-drawn transport. The Americans, by contrast, were by far the most mobile army in the world. The truck was their secret weapon. (It is worth noting that the truck drivers were black soldiers who, forbidden by the War Department to join fighting outfits, made their contribution to the war effort in strictly segregated, noncombat units.)

Hitler himself devised the plan of attack. He realized that it was a desperate gamble, but recalled Clausewitz's principle: "He who is hard pressed will regard the greatest daring as the greatest wisdom." Gerd von Rundstedt, called out of retirement by Hitler to serve as titular commander on the Western Front, was opposed to using up Germany's last resources in a reckless gamble, as were most high-ranking German officers, but Hitler wanted to win the war, not just prolong it. His plan was to strike in the Ardennes, where the Americans were badly stretched out (four divisions on an eighty-mile front), achieve a breakthrough, cross the Meuse River with armor, capture fuel stocks from the Allies, and drive on to Antwerp. In the process he would split the British and American forces and capture the port on which the Allies depended for most of their supplies. After that, who knew? He would be free to reinforce his Eastern Front. Perhaps then the Russians would drop out of the war, forcing the British and Americans to sue for peace.

Success depended on six factors: surprise; the strength of the blow; the speed of the advance; a slow American response; poor performance by the GIs; and bad weather, which would neutralize U.S. air superiority.

Through superhuman effort, Hitler was able to gather together in the Eifel a force big enough to achieve the objective. He gained surprise through a combination of skill, secretiveness, incredibly tight security, and audacity. Using many of the same techniques the Allies had used to fool the Germans about the time and place of the cross-Channel attack in June—the creation of fictitious units, false radio traffic, and playing on preconceptions—Hitler gave the Americans a false sense of security about the Ardennes, heightened by the fact that there were no cities, supply dumps, headquarters, railroad lines, or highways of strategic importance in that region.

Speed of advance depended on the commitment of the field commanders to Hitler's concept; for that reason, he put Josef ("Sepp") Dietrich, a former butcher and SS bullyboy, in command of the Sixth Panzer Army. Dietrich had commanded an SS division in Russia but had no experience of command at army level. His qualifications for this crucial assignment were fanaticism and unquestioned personal bravery.

Hitler assumed a slow U.S. response. He believed that Prime Minister Churchill and President Roosevelt controlled the U.S. supreme commander, Dwight D. Eisenhower, as tightly as he, Hitler, controlled German field commanders. He therefore figured that before Eisenhower could call off the major attacks to the north and south to build a defense in the Ardennes, he would have to get approval from Churchill and Roosevelt. Hitler told the Wehrmacht High Command that it would take Eisenhower at least two days to comprehend the seriousness of the situation, then two or three more days of wrangling with his bosses before he could react. By that time, the Germans would be across the Meuse River, if not already in Antwerp.

Even when Eisenhower was free to react, Hitler believed, his forces would be slow to move. For one thing, Americans were unaccustomed to fighting on the defensive—the last time they had done so was almost two years earlier, at Kasserine Pass in Tunisia—and would find it difficult to adjust their thinking and operations. Further, in spite of the terrible pounding the Wehrmacht had taken in France, Hitler was contemptuous of the American army. He thought the Allies had won in France only because of overwhelming air and matériel superiority. He believed the average GI was soft, poorly trained, badly led, and liable to panic.

As for the final factor—bad weather was simply a question of waiting. It was certain to come sometime in the fall in northwest Europe.

THE ATTACK BEGAN at dawn on December 16, without artillery preparation. It was cold and foggy. The Americans did not occupy a continuous defensive line but were strung out in isolated groups; thus many German units advanced westward encountering no opposition. Taken completely by surprise, American units, many of them in unfortified villages, were cut off, overwhelmed, and annihilated or forced to surrender. Often the biggest obstacles to the German advance were traffic jams due to the inadequate roadnet.

But where the Wehrmacht ran into American strongpoints, villages that had been fortified, it was a different story. Units as small as squads poured out deadly fire from farmhouses, barns, and crossroad taverns, from behind hedges, trees, and bends in the road. The inexperienced German infantry just kept coming, to be mowed down in waves. It was almost as if it were the First Battle of Ypres and the year 1914. Eventually, by sheer weight of numbers, the Germans eliminated these pockets of resistance, but in every case the Americans managed to slow the advance—so that by nightfall on December 16, the Wehrmacht was already badly behind schedule.

To the north, between Monschau and Losheim, the U.S. 99th Infantry Division, newly arrived in Europe, and the 2nd Infantry Division, which had come ashore at Utah beach on D-Day plus one and had been fighting ever since, did not simply delay the German advance but stopped it along the critical point of the whole battle, Elsenborn Ridge. This low ridge lay across the direct line from the Eifel to Antwerp and was the main objective of Sepp Dietrich's Sixth Panzer Army.

Elsenborn was the Little Round Top of the battle. Dietrich drove his units mercilessly, but he could not take it. In the vast literature on the Battle of the Bulge, Elsenborn Ridge always yields pride of place to the far more famous action to the south, at Bastogne. Everyone knows about the 101st Airborne at Bastogne; almost no one knows even the names of the 99th and 2nd infantries. Yet it was along the Elsenborn Ridge, on the first and second days, that these two ordinary infantry divisions, largely out of touch with their commands, outnumbered five to one and, worse, outgunned and surprised, managed to stop the Germans on their main line of advance. The Germans never did take the ridge.

The practical effect of the Elsenborn resistance was to force the German thrust southward. Instead of moving out on a northwest line through Namur to Antwerp, Dietrich was now squeezed southwest, toward the Meuse at Dinant. In essence this meant that the offensive no longer had a strategic objective. Rundstedt, and even Dietrich, recognized that immediately. From December 17 on, they wanted to go for the "small solution"—that is, an offensive whose obejctive was to gain some ground and capture some prisoners while inflicting heavy casualties, rather than to attempt to reverse the entire course of the war. Hitler insisted on continuing to try for the Meuse, then Antwerp. But without Elsenborn, he was never going to get there.

Thus did a bunch of junior officers, noncoms, and privates, many of them new to battle, some of them exhausted by six months of continuous warfare, prove that Hitler was wrong in thinking the American GI could not fight.

In the center, Hasso von Manteuffel's Fifth Panzer Army did achieve a clean breakthrough. To the south, the Seventh Army made some penetrations. All along the line, meanwhile, the Americans were in a state of confusion, and in some cases panic. In Belgium and northern France, American flags hanging from windows were discreetly pulled inside and hidden. In Paris the whores put away their English-language phrase books and retrieved their German versions. In New York the stock market, which had tumbled after the German retreat from France indicated that peace was at hand, became bullish again.

General Omar Bradley, commanding the Twelfth Army Group, which consisted of the U.S. First Army (Courtney Hodges) and the U.S. Third Army (George S. Patton, Jr.), was in Luxembourg City the evening of December 15. The next morning, unaware of an attack approximately twenty miles away, he drove to Versailles; he was out of touch for almost an entire day. He arrived at the Trianon Palace Hotel, Eisenhower's headquarters, to find his boss in a good mood. Ike had just received word of his promotion to the rank of five-star general of the army.

At dusk, an intelligence officer arrived with news. There had been an enemy attack that morning in the Ardennes. Bradley dismissed it as of little consequence, just a local spoiling attack designed to throw the First Army off-balance. But an hour or so later, another report came in—there were at least twelve German divisions involved, eight of them not previously identified as being on the Ardennes front.

Bradley still thought it merely an irritant, nothing major. Eisenhower disagreed. The absence of any objective of strategic importance in the Ardennes led him to believe that Rundstedt had launched a counteroffensive, not a counterattack. He studied his situation map. Noting that the 7th and 12th armored divisions were out of the line (they were preparing to spearhead the offensives scheduled to begin in a couple of days), Ike ordered Bradley to send the 7th to Saint-Vith on the northern flank, and the 12th to Echternach in the south. Bradley protested that Patton would be furious at losing one of his armored divisions and having to call off his offensive.

"Tell him," Eisenhower replied, "that Ike is running this damn war."

To indulge in a bit of hyperbole—with that sentence, Eisenhower won the battle. First of all, because he was absolutely correct in his judgment that getting the 7th Armored into Saint-Vith was critical to the effort to prevent Dietrich from breaking through on the northern flank in the direction of Antwerp. Second, Hodges was preparing a major offensive against the Ruhr River dams, and Patton was about to launch a major offensive in the Saar. Before night fell on the first day of the Battle of the Bulge, Eisenhower decided to switch both armies from offensive missions outside the Ardennes to defensive missions in the forest area. He thus undercut Hitler's most basic assumption: that the Allied response would be slow and hesitant because Eisenhower would not dare to act until he had cleared his decisions with Churchill and Roosevelt.

In reporting the Ardennes offensive to the War Department, Eisenhower accepted the blame for the surprise. He was right to do so, as he had failed to correctly read the enemy's mind and had failed to realize that Hitler would take desperate chances. Eisenhower was responsible for the weakness in the line in the Ardennes, because he was the one who had insisted on maintaining general offensives north and south of that area. But despite his mistakes, Ike was the first to grasp the full import of the attack, the first to be able to readjust his thinking, the first to realize that although the surprise and the initial Allied losses were painful, Hitler had in fact given the Allies a great opportunity. On the morning of December 17, Eisenhower wrote the War Department that "if things go well we should not only stop the thrust but be able to profit from it."

After dictating that letter, he went over the maps and reports with his aides, then handed down a series of orders. He sent half the 10th Armored to Bastogne, which he had identified as a key road junction in the southern half of the Bulge. He ordered the U.S. 101st and 82nd airborne, then resting and refitting after their battles in Holland in September, into the battle, directing the 101st to Bastogne and the 82nd to the northern flank. Since the weather precluded an airdrop, he used his secret weapon, the 2.5-ton trucks, to move the paratroopers to the battle.

On December 19, as Manteuffel's forces approached Bastogne, where the 101st was arriving to set up its defenses, Eisenhower met with his senior commanders in a cold, damp squad room in a barracks at Verdun, the site of the greatest battle ever fought. There was but one lone potbelly stove to ease the bitter cold. Ike's lieutenants entered the room glum, depressed, embarrassed. They kept their faces bent over their coffee cups. Eisenhower walked in, looked disapprovingly at the downcast generals, and boldly declared, "The present situation is to be regarded as one of opportunity for us and not of disaster. There will be only cheerful faces at this conference table."

Patton quickly picked up the theme. "Hell, let's have the guts to let the bastards go all the way to Paris," he said. "Then we'll really cut 'em off and chew 'em up."

Ike said he would not let the Germans get away with emerging from the Westwall without punishing them. He told Patton to switch the direction of his offensive from east to north, to get started in three days, and to make his attack a major blow toward Bastogne.

Within three days after the beginning of the battle, even as Manteuffel's men circled Bastogne, Eisenhower had sealed off the penetration on both flanks and was rushing troops into the Bulge much more speedily than the Germans had estimated. On December 17 alone, 11,000 trucks carried 60,000 men, plus ammunition, gasoline, medical supplies, and other matériel, into the Ardennes. In the first week of the battle, Eisenhower was able to move 250,000 men and 50,000 vehicles into the fray. This was mobility with a vengeance. It was also an achievement unprecedented in the history of war. Not even in Vietnam was the U.S. Army capable of moving so many men and so much equipment as quickly.

Thus were Hitler's assumptions about the ability of the Allied high command to respond, and of the Allied armies to move, proved wrong.

GERMAN MOVEMENT, meanwhile, was slow at best. Icy roads, snow, and a shortage of gasoline, combined with American resistance, made a shambles of Hitler's timetable. The Germans did not have the trucks to bring forward the necessary gasoline. Near Stavelot, however, an American major poured thousands of gallons of gas into a deep road and set it afire to stop German tanks; the German spearhead was stranded for lack of fuel within one-half mile of the U.S. Army's largest gas dump in Europe.

On December 22, Patton hammered away at Bastogne, without success. Inside Bastogne, General Anthony C. McAuliffe and the 101st beat off German attacks. To the north, the U.S. 106th Infantry Division had surrendered when surrounded, but the 101st never flinched. Some of its members explained later that paratroopers are accustomed to fighting while surrounded—"Hell, we are always surrounded," one said. When the German commander demanded they surrender, McAuliffe gave him that famous one-word reply: "Nuts."

The night of December 22, a hard freeze set in; the next day the weather was bright and clear. The Americans got every fighter-bomber, fighter, and bomber they had into the air, blasting away at panzers and dropping badly needed ammunition, medical supplies, and food to the men in Bastogne.

On Christmas Eve the 2nd Panzer Division of Manteuffel's Fifth Panzer Army got to within a few miles of Dinant on the Meuse River. This was the deepest German penetration in the battle. The American 2nd Armored Division of Hodges's First Army counterattacked and stopped the advance, and on Christmas Day the Americans all but destroyed the 2nd Panzers. On the 26th, Patton's 4th Armored Division broke the siege of Bastogne.

Could the Allies now punish the Germans for emerging from the Westwall? Eisenhower was desperately eager to do so. His plan was to attack at the northern and southern base of the Bulge, pinch off the German salient, and destroy the enemy tanks in the Ardennes before Rundstedt could withdraw them in favor of infantry.

Ike was to be bitterly disappointed, as the counterattack failed to take full advantage of the opportunity. The fault, ironically, was his, stemming from his decision on December 20 to divide command of the battle between Field Marshal Bernard Law Montgomery, commanding the British Twenty-first Army Group, and Bradley. Ike reasoned that the German advance into the Bulge had split the U.S. First and Third armies and cut Bradley's communications with Hodges. Since Bradley's headquarters were on the southern flank, Ike decided it would be best to put Monty in charge of the forces north of the Bulge while Bradley retained command of those to the south. In practice, this meant giving Monty the U.S. First Army.

Bradley was furious. He protested that such a move would discredit the American command. Eisenhower insisted that nevertheless it must be done. Over the telephone, Bradley shouted, "By God, Ike, I cannot be responsible to the American people if you do this. I resign."

Eisenhower, who had known Bradley since they played baseball together at West Point thirty years earlier, was first shocked, then angry. "Brad," he said, slowly and coldly, "I—not you—am responsible to the American people. Your resignation therefore means absolutely nothing." Bradley protested again, this time without any resignation threats, but to no avail.

In the end, the command shift turned out to be a great mistake. Although it made sense on paper, it created an impossible situation. Montgomery was supercilious, haughty, sneering, and much too cautious. Given the command, he strode into Hodges's headquarters, according to a British officer who accompanied him, "like Christ coming to cleanse the temple." Monty later claimed that Hodges "seemed delighted to have someone to give him firm orders." Actually, however, Monty observed rather than directed Hodges's efforts, the main features of which were already set up by Ike: to hold firm along Elsenborn Ridge, stop the Germans short of the Meuse, and prepare a counterattack along the base of the Bulge.

When Monty did intervene, the result was a near disaster. By December 27, Ike was pushing hard to get the counterattack started. Patton was ready to go in the south. But Montgomery argued that the Germans would make one last assault themselves; he wanted to wait, stop it, and then counterattack. Even worse, he wanted to hit the Germans in the nose of the Bulge, driving them back to their original starting point, rather than along the base, to cut them off and then destroy them.

Eisenhower was almost frantic. When finally informed that Monty had a new plan and that he would launch his attack by New Year's Eve, Eisenhower cried, "Praise God from whom all blessings flow!"

But Montgomery never meant it. On December 30 he told Ike he could not attack until January 3 or later, and once again demanded—as he had been doing since August—that Eisenhower give him sole command of the Allied land armies. He said Eisenhower's policies had failed and that he must now give way to the more experienced commander. Once in command, he would attack with a single thrust by the Twenty-first Army Group toward Berlin, leaving Patton where he was—something that should have been done months ago, Monty added.

Eisenhower turned Montgomery down on every point. And to enforce his will, he used his ultimate weapon: If Monty kept demanding sole command and insisting on a single thrust, Ike would ask the Combined Chiefs of Staff to choose between them.

Monty initially thought Ike was bluffing. "Who could replace me?" he asked his chief of staff, Freddie de Guingand. To his consternation, de Guingand replied that it was all set—it would be Field Marshal Harold Alexander. Monty went pale. He had forgotten Alex was available. "My God," he said. "What shall I do, Freddie? What shall I do?" "Sign this," de Guingand replied, pulling out the draft of a message to Eisenhower he had already prepared. It pledged undying loyalty to Eisenhower and concluded, "You can rely on me to go all out one hundred percent to implement your plan." Montgomery read it and signed.

But he still did not mean it. He did not start his counterattack until January 3, as he initially had insisted, and then he concentrated on pushing the Germans back from the Meuse rather than on cutting them off along the Our River line. He made matters worse on January 7 when he held a press conference to explain how he had won the Battle of the Bulge. He said that on the first day, "as soon as I saw what was happening, I took certain steps to ensure that if the Germans got to the Meuse they would certainly not get over the river. And I carried out certain movements so as to provide balanced dispositions to meet the threatened danger, i.e., I was thinking ahead."

He had made no such dispositions, taken no such steps.

Worse followed. After Ike put him in command of the northern flank, Monty later claimed, he brought the British into the fight and thus saved the Americans. (Almost no British troops took part in the battle.) He went on to say that it had been a "most interesting" battle for him, rather like El Alamein—indeed, "I think possibly one of the most interesting and tricky battles I have ever handled." What he said next all but destroyed Allied unity—that GIs made great fighting men, when given proper leadership.

But most galling about Montgomery's version of the Battle of the Bulge was his immense satisfaction with the outcome. Patton ranted and raved. If not for Montgomery, he said, "we could have bagged the whole German army. I wish Ike were more of a gambler, but he is certainly a lion compared to Monty, and Bradley is better than Ike as far as nerve is concerned. Monty is a tired little fart. War requires taking risks, and he won't take them."

So the victory in the Battle of the Bulge was not complete, and the aftertaste was sour. Nevertheless it was a victory, one of the greatest in the long and proud annals of the U.S. Army. The GIs managed to kill nearly 30,000 Germans, wound 40,000, and take 30,000 prisoner. They destroyed 800 or more German tanks. And they completley frustrated Hitler's strategic aim.

Montgomery's boastful nonsense notwithstanding, the credit belongs to the American officer corps, from Eisenhower on down, and to the GIs who fought with magnificent skill, stubbornness, and bravery.

*SPRING 1989*

Stephen E. Ambrose authored two of the previous essays on D-Day.

# 36

# Bill, Willie, and Joe

## By David Lamb

*For many American veterans, the mention of the Italian campaign recalls
such bloody places as Salerno, Anzio, and Cassino, and a war where the
enemy always seemed to hold the high ground. For others, the memory is
of near-constant rain, quicksandlike mud, and wet feet. Or there remains
the frustration of fighting in a campaign that increasingly became a
"sideshow" to the main events in western Europe. But no remembrance
of Italy would be complete without mention of Willie and Joe. These cartoon figures, created by the pen and brush of twenty-two-year-old Bill
Mauldin and published in* Stars and Stripes, *became the embodiment of
the GIs in Italy. Battle-weary yet battle-wise, sardonic and irreverent,
simultaneously heroic and tragic, Willie and Joe became the most famous
American soldiers of World War II.*

It's hard to imagine Willie and Joe being old. But if they were alive
today—and mind you, Bill Mauldin has never announced their deaths
even though he hasn't drawn them in years—they would be pushing
seventy, like Mauldin himself, and I suspect they wouldn't have led very
eventful lives since coming home from Europe at the end of World War II.

The Willie and Joe I remember—bearded, sunken-eyed, unsmiling, and
somehow both heroic and tragic—looked older and sadder than the GIs I
encountered in Vietnam in the late 1960s, and in fact the GIs in both Korea
and Vietnam were much younger on the average. Perhaps that's why
Mauldin had the good sense not to bring America's two most famous privates
back into the army in those wars. By leaving Willie and Joe undisturbed, he
succeeded in making them ageless.

"You know, I had planned to kill Willie and Joe on the last day of the
war," Mauldin recalled when I visited him at his home in Santa Fe, New
Mexico. "That's the one thing every soldier dreads, getting killed on the
last day. I wasn't sure how I was going to do it. Most likely I would have
had a shell land in their foxhole or had them cut down by a machine gun.
I wouldn't have drawn their corpses. I'd just have shown their gear with

their names on it, or something like that."

Mauldin figured he had better warn Bob Neville, the *Stars and Stripes* editor, of their impending death. Neville had never rejected one of Mauldin's drawings, but this time he said, "Don't do it. We won't print it." Neville may have been the only person—editor or general—who ever got Mauldin to back down. "In the end I guess it worked out about right," he said, "but there are still times I wish I had done it. It would have been a very dramatic thing."

When the war was over, Mauldin brought Willie and Joe home with him. He gave them a shave, put them in civvies, and found them jobs in a gas station. "That lasted three or four weeks," he recalls. "Then I said, 'Screw it.'" Mauldin didn't feel comfortable drawing them without beards. He didn't even know who they really were anymore. And much to the horror of his syndicate, Willie (who had appeared on the cover of *Time* magazine in June 1945) and Joe vanished into obscurity. Except for appearing at the funerals of General George Marshall in 1959 and General Omar Bradley in 1981, the two dogfaces who had made Mauldin rich and famous before his twenty-third birthday haven't been seen since in a Mauldin cartoon.

To find Bill Mauldin today, you drive out of Santa Fe a few miles on the Old Santa Fe Trail, and head up the hill to the turnoff near the Anthropological Museum. It is 10:00 A.M., and Mauldin, shoeless and laughing, is out back, trying to prove to his newest batch of kids—eleven-year-old Kaja and two-year-old Sam—that he can get airborne on a Pogo Ball—a jumping ball with a ring. "If you break it, Dad, you owe me twenty bucks," Kaja says. Over the years Mauldin has raised eight children in three marriages, and Kaja refers to herself, with proud glee, as "Kid Number One, Litter Three."

Every nook of Mauldin's ranch home bears his stamp. The dining room is lined with books on World War II. The sewing room has been turned into a studio, where he still draws three political cartoons a week that are syndicated by King Features. The garage has been turned into a machine shop, and a spare bedroom is now a darkroom. A master tinkerer, he has put in new bellows and fixed the gears on his old eight-by-ten-inch Saltzman enlarger—"Crank it and see how smooth it turns," he challenges—and plans to take a look soon at a kitchen door, which swings shut with the help of a weighted Clorox container on a piece of rope. The walls of the breakfast alcove display many framed drawings, among them the only Willie and Joe original Mauldin has left and a Rube Goldberg strip, dated 1942 and signed, "To Bill Mauldin. Good luck in the Service."

Out in the backyard are a snowblower, a lawn mower older than his wife, a mobile home rigged into a darkroom for desert trips, a worn Chevy pickup, and a 1946 Willys jeep that Mauldin bought new in a Manhattan showroom for $1,180. Except for the spark plugs and points, every part is original, and as he clambers into the jeep's front seat and turns the key, a bottle of beer balanced beside him, I see in my mind's eye, like a black-and-white photograph, the young Bill Mauldin of three wars past. In this photo he wears an impish grin and his eyes speak of mischief. He looks no older than a teenager. His left hand—his drawing hand—holds a cigarette and his right arm is draped over the steering wheel of a muddy jeep named for his then wife, "Jeanie." He is on the Anzio beachhead bound for Cassino. It is the winter of 1943–44.

Willie and Joe took on their final identities in the Italian campaign. Mauldin gave them beards, put bullet holes in their helmets, and began working with a brush instead of a pen, producing stark, bold lines that captured the grimness of the mountain war and the fatalistic exhaustion of the men who fought it. Willie and Joe weren't gung-ho heroes and weren't really very funny. They were simply two undistinguished GIs, inseparable only because of their shared experience, who told us what it was like to live in foxholes, get hassled by officers and MPs in the rear, and fight for survival, not ideology. They were smelly and bored and they wanted to go home.

"War humor is very bitter, very sardonic," Mauldin says. "It's not ha-ha humor. I asked Tad Foster, a cartoonist I admired a lot from the Vietnam War, if people came up to him and said, 'I loved your stuff from the war—it kept me laughing all the time.' Foster said, 'Yup, the sons of bitches.' I feel the same way. When someone says Willie and Joe made them laugh, I get pissed off every time. I tell them, 'You're not supposed to laugh.' Maybe you grin or nod, but it's not ha-ha humor.

"My shtick was this. I never drew dead soldiers, but I always implied that they were lying just offstage. You felt their presence. Another thing, I didn't treat the Germans as monsters. I drew the German soldier as a poor unfortunate who didn't want to be there which could be said of our boys, too.

"Psychological warfare didn't interest me. I don't ever remember hearing a soldier in Europe or anyplace like Sicily refer to the Germans as Nazis or fascists or anything like that. They were krauts. It was the same in Korea and Vietnam. They weren't commie rats or any of that shit. They were gooks. They were slopes. But they weren't mentioned in political terms."

We had moved inside and were sitting on the sofa in his living room. I had brought along a copy of his book *Bill Mauldin's Army*—which has sold 20,000 copies since being reissued in 1983 by Presidio Press—and he was thumbing through the pages, critiquing himself. "This is Anzio. It's a great drawing. I wish I knew where the original was. . . . I did this one the day I got hit. . . . Here's Willie. I think it's the first time I drew him with a beard." Willie and Joe are climbing a cliff, holding on for dear life, and the sergeant yells, "Hit th' dirt, boys!"

"The main thing about Willie and Joe was that I always felt they were like two cops operating together as partners," Mauldin points out. "They don't particularly like each other. They aren't cut from the same cloth. They don't have the same friends. But they're damned good at what they do together, and each is the other guy's life-insurance policy. They're not devoted to each other, but they need each other. And that makes for a damned good relationship."

Mauldin was on the fast track by the time Willie and Joe were climbing those Cassino hills together. He had once written: "My drawing had become my Rock of Gibraltar. With it, I was still convinced the world might be mine.

Without it, I felt like an insignificant jerk." Now the war was bringing that world within his reach. He was talented, dedicated, ambitious, and his earthy depiction of the war was earning him wide recognition—even from General George Patton, who threatened to "throw his ass in jail" if Mauldin showed up in the Third Army area.

Just before Christmas in 1943, in the high mountains above Venafro, Mauldin was wounded by a German mortar while visiting the 179th Regiment of the 45th Division. It was a minor injury, to the shoulder, but it changed both him and his drawings. On the way back to Naples one of the corpsmen, who had a stack of green leatherette boxes, handed Mauldin a Purple Heart. He accepted it, but with considerable guilt, even anger, knowing that most of his friends in the unit he had shipped over with—K Company of the 45th Division's 180th Infantry—were already dead. The next day Mauldin drew Willie at an aid station telling a medic, "Just gimme th' aspirin. I already got a Purple Heart."

"I was hit very lightly, but it was a shock," Mauldin says. "It's always a shock to anyone who gets hit. It's like kids with automobiles: It can't happen to you. But something *did* happen to me. It was something about these guys I knew really getting killed, me really getting hit, and suddenly the war became very real to me.

"So I would say that it was in the fall of 'forty-three that I really sobered up and started realizing there were some things bigger than me and my ambition. Suddenly the drawings grew up, too. Southern Italy became sort of a Valley Forge scene for me. I was privileged to watch it as a guy who could visit a foxhole and not have to stay. I could watch a patrol take off and not have to go with it. And this fills you with—maybe not guilt but a great sense of respect for these guys and what they were going through.

"I remember Humphrey Bogart came over on a USO tour about that time and laid the biggest egg I'd ever seen. He came out on the stage of the San Carlo Opera House [in Naples] and there was this whole goddamned crowd of guys who'd come down off the mountain for four days' R-and-R. I think he was a little bit in the bag, and he got up on the stage and said something dumb like, 'I'm going back to the States to put my mob back together. Any of you guys want to go with me?'

"He was greeted with stony silence. He went on with his tough-guy act and they gave him a nice hand, but they just didn't think he was very funny. Because not one of those guys had a prayer of going home. They knew they were going to stay right there on that mountain until they died. It was a pretty gruesome proposition, and here's Bogart out there trying to make jokes. I got to know him later and he was really a good guy—I liked him. You know, years afterward he told me, 'I'll never forget all those eyes looking at me. I really put my foot in it.'"

Although Mauldin and his colleagues at *Stars and Stripes* were in the army, they lived a privileged existence: They moved with the freedom of civilian correspondents, and their newspaper enjoyed a remarkable degree of editorial independence. Mauldin, a nocturnal worker by choice and habit, lived and worked in a third-floor room overlooking the Galleria shopping arcade in Naples. His room had a chair, a large table against which he leaned his drawing board, and a canvas cot.

The title of his cartoon was "Up Front . . . with Mauldin," a name he was never quite comfortable with because it implied that he was always on the fighting lines, which he wasn't. "Anyone who can draw in a foxhole has my hat off," he told *Time* magazine in 1945. Just after he was hit by the mortar fragment, *Stars and Stripes* received a letter from a soldier in the headquarters of the 179th Infantry. Mauldin still remembers his name—Blankenship. What did Mauldin know about being "up front" anyway? the soldier asked. The editors printed the letter and added a note saying Mauldin had recently received a Purple Heart for a wound received while visiting I Company of the soldier's own regiment. Mauldin's wound was among the first the *Stripes* staff suffered, and it did the paper's image no harm.

"I have very strong ethics about taking things or getting things you don't deserve," Mauldin says "It's one of the things my parents did for me. I was pissed off when the medic gave me the Purple Heart. My bandage wasn't much bigger than a Band-Aid. But getting hit was probably the most fortuitous thing that could have happened to me. It established me as a guy who went out and got his material the hard way."

Ernie Pyle (later killed in the war) caught up with Mauldin and wrote a column mentioning Blankenship's letter and stating, "Sergeant Bill Mauldin seemed to us . . . the finest cartoonist the war had produced. And that's not merely because his cartoons are funny, but because they are also terribly grim and real. Mauldin's cartoons . . . are about the men in the line—the tiny percentage of our vast army who are actually up there doing the dying. His cartoons are about the war."

It was the exposure from Pyle—not the Pulitzer Prize or his highly publicized confrontation with Patton—that really put him in business, Mauldin says. Soon, syndicates were after him, and in a few months he signed with Pyle's syndicate, United Feature. *Stars and Stripes* printed Mauldin's cartoons first but let him own the copyright. His monthly wages as a sergeant were $66; his weekly income as a syndicated cartoonist, about $250.

"All of a sudden Bill was a blazing success," recalls Jack Foisie, a *Stripes* writer who went on to a distinguished career as a foreign correspondent for the *Los Angeles Times*. "I mean, he was making all this money. But he never lorded it over us. He was droll in his success. Most of us, if not in awe of him, were jealous of his success, in a good-natured way. But he was always popular, sort of one of the boys."

Mauldin's growing fame increasingly enabled him to throw barbs at the top brass and the military police. Patton wondered aloud if Mauldin wasn't an unpatriotic anarchist. In one of Mauldin's most famous drawings, two officers are admiring the Italian mountains, and one says, "Beautiful view! Is there one for the enlisted men?" Another drawing shows an officer in a freshly pressed uniform writing up the slovenly looking Willie and Joe. Willie tells him, "Them buttons was shot off when we took this town, sir."

That one still makes Mauldin grin. "No matter what Patton thought, I never disliked officers. If I'd had my druthers, I'd probably have been a smart-ass little lieutenant. I'd have gone to OCS or something, because I liked the army. I never objected to the concept of discipline, but if you're a leader, you don't push wet spaghetti, you pull it. The U.S. Army still has to learn that. The British understand it. Patton understood it. I always admired Patton.

"Oh, sure, the stupid bastard was crazy. He was insane. He thought he was living in the Dark Ages. Soldiers were peasants to him. I didn't like that attitude, but I certainly respected his theories and the techniques he used to get his men out of their foxholes. You wait around in a foxhole and you're going to get killed. We had a lot of good officers who understood that, who knew how to lead in combat. They didn't say, 'Go here, go there.' They said, 'Come here.'"

While Mauldin's dogfaces were scruffy and disheveled, Patton's clean-shaven troops wore neckties and polished boots (at least Patton tried to keep them that way). Why, Patton asked the Supreme Command, should *Stars and Stripes* make heroes of Willie and Joe? At the "suggestion" of his superiors, Mauldin headed up to the Third Army headquarters in Luxembourg one day early in 1945 to discuss the matter with the general who wore ivory-handled pistols. Patton threw down a drawing of Willie and Joe tossing tomatoes at their officers during a liberation parade. What was Mauldin trying to do, incite a goddamn mutiny? Patton's dog, a bull terrier named Willie, glowered at the young sergeant as the general ranted on.

"The whole thing was just so funny, really hilarious," Mauldin recalls. "The only guy who failed to see the humor was Patton. I didn't even try to give him any lip. I knew it was going to be an embarrassment for him. I think he died without any idea that he'd lost that little battle."

The meeting lasted forty-five minutes, of which Mauldin had been given a minute or so to lay out his artistic response. "All right, sergeant," Patton said, cutting him short, "I guess we understand each other now."

Six months later, the man who made the cover of *Time* magazine was Mauldin's Willie, not Patton, and a reporter asked the general what he thought of Mauldin's cartoons. "I've only seen two of them and I thought they were lousy," he said.

Few Americans agreed. By the time Mauldin came home in the summer of 1945—with a Purple Heart, a Pulitzer Prize, and a Legion of Merit—his drawings were appearing in hundreds of papers and his Willie-and-Joe book *Up Front* was a best-seller. "I haven't tried to picture this war in a big, broad-minded way," he wrote in the text. "I'm not old enough to understand what it's all about." He was twenty-three. *Up Front* sold 3 million copies and was number one on the *New York Times* best-seller list for eighteen months.

"You know, Willie and Joe weren't really based on anyone," Mauldin says. "They just evolved as prototypes. But once, about fifteen years after the war, a shrink came up to me at a party in Rockland County, where I was living in New York. He was sort of practicing without permission and he said, 'Do you know who Willie and Joe were?'

"I said, 'Who?' He said, 'Have you looked recently at a picture of your father?' And, my God, he was right. Willie was a caricature of my father, and Joe was a caricature of me—the round-faced, jug-eared kid. I had never thought of it. I'm not sure I appreciate the guy pointing it out to me, but who knows what family things I worked out through those cartoons?"

Mauldin had grown up poor in the hills of southern New Mexico. His father had been an artilleryman in France during World War I, and his grandfather had served as a civilian cavalry scout during the Apache Wars, so Mauldin was raised on war stories, many of them embellished over the years. He joined ROTC in high school and, as a ninety-seven-pound weakling, marched with a 1903 Springfield rifle, unloaded. "I took to ROTC like a duck to water," he once recalled. He also was a natural artist and a feisty needler who knew early on that he wanted to be a political cartoonist. "I was a born troublemaker and might as well earn a living at it," he wrote in his informal 1971 autobiography, *The Brass Ring*.

But after the war and the disappearance of Willie and Joe, Mauldin's career stalled. His drawings became erratic and bellicose. He took on the Ku Klux Klan, the House Committee on Un-American Activities, and conservative veterans' organizations. (In 1971 he suggested publicly that militant veterans' organizations be drafted to finish the Vietnam War.) His syndicate started censoring him, and newspapers started dropping his cartoon.

"Military service is one of those things you do as a duty," Mauldin says. "If you get wounded, crippled, or lose your life, the government owes it to your family to take care of you, but otherwise I don't think anyone's entitled to a goddamn thing. Some guy counts socks for three months at a quartermaster depot and then he's looking for a ride on the gravy train for the rest of his life. He's nothing but a professional sponger. At one point I joined the American Veterans Committee, which was considered very leftish. It no longer exists, but I liked its motto: Citizens first, veterans second."

Mauldin's old buddy Jack Foisie remembers seeing Mauldin at a *Stars and Stripes* reunion in New York in 1947. "There seemed to be some deflation for Bill," Foisie recalls. "He was very high during the war, and now he had other factors to face besides generals. He had a lot of irons in the fire, but Bill looked a little frustrated."

Foisie was right, and at the age of twenty-seven Mauldin retired to pursue other interests. He learned to fly a plane, went hunting, free-lanced for *Life* magazine, and published four more books. He also went out to California and acted in a couple of Hollywood movies, including *The Red Badge of Courage* with war hero Audie Murphy, and then moved back to New York, where in 1956 he became the Democratic candidate for Congress from the Twenty-eighth District. He was trounced by the incumbent—"a rather formidable broad"—in a campaign that personally cost him $50,000. His decade of drifting left him broke, but not washed up. He loved riding the career roller coaster.

He jumped at the chance to join the *St. Louis Post-Dispatch* in 1958, won another Pulitzer, and was the subject of a second *Time* magazine cover piece.

He briefly covered the Korean War (as a writer, not an artist) for *Collier's;* then spent a few weeks in Vietnam (where a mortar attack on his son's base in the Highlands made him a hawk for a few months), and reported on the Six-Day Arab-Israeli War for the *Chicago Sun-Times.* But none of these wars was *his* war as World War II had been, and in 1973 he wrote an article for the *New Republic* entitled "Ain't Gonna' Cover Wars No More." He had lost his emotional perspective and objectivity. "One of the startling things you learn in wars," he wrote, "is how much blood can come from a human body."

So Bill Mauldin came home, home to his roots in the peaceful silence of New Mexico. It is night now and we are mixing martinis in the kitchen. His wife, Chris, twenty-seven years his junior, has sent out for Mexican food. Mauldin seems a contented man in a young family full of love. He passes a bottle of vermouth over the chilling gin and marvels at his creation. He is, he says, "playing out the string" on his career, and that doesn't bother him a bit. The number of papers taking his cartoon has fallen to about seventy-five, and he has not tried to renew his expired contract with the *Chicago Sun-Times.* The arthritis in his hands is troublesome, so he no longer answers his fan letters. In growing old he has found that he is no longer in a hurry.

"I never felt I was all that talented or all that good at what I did," he says, "but I exploited whatever talent I had and gave it a good ride. That's the important thing. I think that's probably the reason I'm getting mellower. I don't have that desperate feeling of *What the hell have I been doing all my life? How can I make up for all this time I've been wasting?* I don't have any of that anymore."

He tells me about returning to the Anzio mountains in 1967. He set up his camera on a tripod in Cassino, on the very spot where the German artillery had been, and his lens swept over the distant American positions where Willie and Joe and thousands of other GIs fought their toughest battles. "What a position the Germans had!" he recalls. "Standing up there at the abbey, you could see why nobody in history ever took Rome from the south."

He also tells me about his return to Rome in 1984, at the invitation of the American ambassador to Italy, for the fortieth anniversary of Rome's fall to the Allies. He flew from Andrews Air Force Base outside Washington as a guest of the Pentagon in a "brass-hat" special—a red-white-and-blue Boeing 707 emblazoned with the words *United States of America* on the fuselage. The plane carried only four passengers, one of whom was the chairman of the Joint Chiefs of Staff, Jack Vessey.

Flying through the darkness high above the Atlantic, meal finished and drink in hand, Bill Mauldin settled back in his upholstered seat and said to himself on that night of memories, "Soldier, you sure have come a long way."

SUMMER *1989*

---

David Lamb, a *Los Angeles Times* national correspondent, covered the Vietnam War for United Press International. He is the author of *The Africans* (1983) and *The Arabs: Journeys Beyond the Mirage* (1987).

---

# 37

# The Price of Valor

## By Roger J. Spiller

*What makes a hero? Although long pondered, the answer to that question remains elusive. It defies quantification or predictability. America's most decorated hero of the Second World War, indeed of its military history, was Audie Leon Murphy of Hunt County, Texas. In his twenty-three months of combat, he won every award for valor that his army had to give. If the question of causation remains uncertain, the ultimate cost of heroism seems less so. The mundane world of peacetime is too often a curse rather than a reward for the brave. Asked once whether men ever get over war, Murphy replied honestly, "I don't think they ever do." As Roger J. Spiller demonstrates in this study of Murphy, the same can be said for being a hero.*

The woods were infested with German soldiers, and the men knew it. On the day before, their sister unit, the 30th Infantry Regiment, 3rd Infantry Division, had entered the Alsatian forest known as the Bois de Riedwihr and—having gone too far too fast, outrunning their artillery supports—been blown to pieces. The remnants of the 30th took refuge beyond the Ill River, in the direction of Holtzwihr, and awaited reinforcements. That was why, on January 24, 1945, the men of Company B, 115th Infantry Regiment, took up the approach march.

As Company B entered the woods, they encountered extremely heavy resistance in the form of sniper nests, artillery bursts fused for treetop detonation, mines, booby traps, mortars, and machine guns sited for cross fire. The company had to fight their way tree to tree, and by the end of the day they had little ammunition left. When the company commander was seriously wounded by a mortar round, a fresh-faced second lieutenant, who looked more like one of Norman Rockwell's newspaper boys than someone you'd trust your life to, was ordered to take command and resume the advance at first light.

The life of a second lieutenant in command of an infantry company during World War II was usually very short. The chances of surviving to become a first lieutenant were slim; of surviving the war, slimmer still; and of emerging physically unhurt, almost nil. In one fifty-day period as this particular division fought its way through the hills of Italy, line units reported a 152 percent loss in second lieutenants. The greatest likelihood of casualty occurred during a combat infantryman's first ten days in battle, but that of course did not mean that if he kept whole bones for ten days he would not be killed or wounded on the eleventh, or even that his experience would somehow shield him from what lay ahead in the days afterward.

The new commander of Company B was, as Bill Mauldin's Willie and Joe—and even he—would later say, "a fugitive from the law of averages." The lieutenant had joined the 3rd Infantry Division as a private in North Africa. After serving for a time as a battalion runner because he was considered too frail for line duty (his friends called him "Baby"), he was eventually permitted to join the line as a combat rifleman with Company B in July 1943, during the Sicilian campaign. For nineteen months he had been pushing his luck, a quality that he appeared to possess in abundance. Only the day before he assumed command, his right leg had been sprayed with fragments from a mortar burst. But compared to the mayhem he had already witnessed, his wound seemed so slight to him that he simply pulled out what fragments he could, applied his own field dressing, and continued his duties. Two officers who had been commissioned with him were killed in the same barrage.

Now, on January 26, the lieutenant moved his company through the Bois de Riedwihr. By early afternoon they had made their way to the edge of an open field, and as they walked into the clearing, the Germans opened fire with their usual murderous precision. In the barrage, an American tank destroyer operating in support of the company was set afire, and abandoned by its crew. Company B had gone to ground with the opening shot, and the lieutenant called for artillery counterfire. In the meantime, large numbers of German infantrymen and six tanks advanced across the open ground, making for the American position. The lieutenant ordered his men to withdraw to the relative safety of the woods, while he remained to direct the artillery fire. The Germans were not to be dissuaded, however, and they pressed their advantage. Despairing of any more help from artillery, the lieutenant crossed ground swept by enemy fire, leaped aboard the burning tank destroyer, and turned its .50-caliber machine gun against the advancing Germans. As he worked the fearsome weapon, those of his comrades who could see him from the woods were sure that the lieutenant would soon be killed by ammunition exploding in the tank destroyer. By this time, enemy tanks were actually abreast of his position, and he was under attack from three sides.

For the better part of an hour, an estimated 250 German infantrymen— two reinforced rifle companies—devoted themselves to killing the lieutenant, the only American then in their sights. As many as fifty of them paid for their devotions with their lives. Finally the Germans broke off the attack, and the lieutenant, unscathed, left the still-burning tank destroyer to rejoin his men.

Four months later, in Salzburg, Germany, First Lieutenant Audie Leon Murphy of Hunt County, Texas, stood nervously as Lieutenant General Alexander Patch draped the Congressional Medal of Honor around his neck. On that day, Murphy became the most highly decorated American fighting man not just in World War II, but in all of U.S. military history. The Medal of Honor was Murphy's twenty-eighth decoration. He had been awarded every other medal for valor in battle that the army had to offer, and several twice. He was alive, more or less in one piece, and he was not yet old enough to vote.

Extraordinary valor in mortal combat has been celebrated in verse and rhetoric since Troy. The hero's deeds are commemorated and held up as examples of manly behavior worthy of imitation. A man who models his life on the hero, so the reasoning goes, prepares himself for the moment when his own finely schooled qualities will be called on. At the moment of decision, the hero-aspirant must risk the possibility of annihilation, and in that moment his self-knowledge is pitted against forces beyond his control. No wonder men who have performed in these uncertain regions of behavior have long had an air of mystery, as if their valorous acts were beyond reason or understanding.

The institutionalization of valor—the elevation of the soldierly hero as a publicly honored figure—originated about 200 years ago, when, in an age of enlightened reason, there evolved an attitude in the military that a soldier deserves something more than minimal pay, death, or crippling wounds in return for the honor of serving his country. Napoleon, for example, although he thought little about marching his soldiers into the ground or wantonly spending their lives if doing so fit his plans, nonetheless was aware of the practical need to reward his men for heroic service. But in this, as in so many other matters, Napoleon was precocious.

The British occasionally struck a medal to commemorate this great battle or that. The Waterloo Medal allowed its bearer two years' credit toward his pension. No doubt the ranks applauded even the smallest emolument for especially hard service. When, during the Indian Mutiny, Sir Colin Campbell—a very conservative commander when it came to handing out awards—implored his old regiment to make a special effort to break through enemy lines to rescue the British Residency at Lucknow, one soldier cried out, "Will we get a medal for this, Sir Colin?" But it was not until the Crimean War that Britain established the fabled Victoria Cross. The Americans adopted a similar practice later still, creating the Medal of Honor in 1862. In the early days the medal was relatively easy to win: One Federal regiment was given the award en masse (later revoked) simply for extending its Civil War enlistment.

The institutionalization of valor also served ulterior purposes. Medals were given to foster morale among the troops and support for the war back home. Partly for this reason, with the proliferation of medals, their credibility became suspect among combat veterans. When pressed, modern soldiers will admit that it is better to have a medal for valor than not, but the medal mongering of the Vietnam War, for example, has created a cynical attitude toward battle decorations. Most soldiers today do not feel that, with the exception of the Medal of Honor itself, awards mean very much. One highly decorated officer said recently that during his own experience in Vietnam, "the Silver Star was essentially a company commander's good-conduct medal."

What can heroes tell us about themselves, other than that they are brave? By revealing the details of their own behavior, they can tell us something about all soldiers in battle and about the phenomenon of battle itself. Since their lives are documented more than others', they offer us a window not only on themselves, but on the hidden lives of ordinary soldiers as well. The difference between the two is not as great as we used to think.

Throughout history the most notable feature of the heroic act is that it transcends its military objective. Commanders experienced in leading men into battle, for instance, are not at all certain that heroes are militarily useful. Most, given a choice between leading a battalion full of heroes and one of ordinary soldiers, would prefer the latter. Successful military action depends on the commander's ability to impose order on the chaos of battle, to turn his tactical ambitions into reality. This requires discipline and regularity of behavior, and neither quality seems to be common among heroes.

Clearly, it is not the lure of a medal that drives a man headlong into combat, risking death or dismemberment. Profounder motivations are required. The great puzzle is that most soldiers already possess these motivations and have acted on them through centuries of hard campaigning.

"THE MEN KNOW who deserve the medals and who don't," wrote S.L.A. Marshall in *Colliers* during the Korean War. Marshall remembered one commander from the North African campaign of World War II who altogether stopped recommending his men for decorations, because invariably those least deserving awards received them, while true heroes did not. Marshall claimed that during World War II, an unwritten rule prevented combat medics—the one class of soldier whose life expectancy was actually shorter than the combat rifleman—from receiving any award higher than the Silver Star. Thus, the awarding of medals was too erratic to be just. There could be little assurance among the men that the ribbons over a man's pocket told the real tale, and most men were a little bashful about wearing them at all.

A hero's immediate comrades tend to know the truth about him, but among other soldiers, he is naturally somewhat distrusted. An officer who served in the 3rd Infantry Division admitted that Murphy "was not the most admired guy in the world." There are good and practical reasons for the ordinary soldier—whose first ambition is to survive the day, the next day, and perhaps even the war—to cock an eye at the consistent hero. Even though his actions are public, the hero is often a solitary soul who depends chiefly on his own passions, skills, and luck. It is his aloneness that singles him out. He tends to get killed, and his comrades with him. Worse, he sometimes survives while his comrades do not. Of course, this may be only luck—the bullet or shell just did not have his name on it that day—but you can easily sympathize with the suspicions of the ordinary soldier.

The bonds among the men in the smallest fighting units of World War II were extremely strong. The great wartime cartoonist Bill Mauldin, a perceptive observer of men in combat, believed that "you will seldom find a misfit who has been in an outfit more than a few months." (Those who could not fit in usually ended up dead or invalided to the rear.) And as for those occasions when someone in a unit is a candidate for an award, Mauldin added that "his friends are so willing to be witnesses that sometimes they have to be cross-examined to make sure they are not crediting him with three knocked-out machine guns instead of one."

After Murphy's action in the Bois de Riedwihr, he was pulled out of the line. Witnesses provided affidavits, and, within the month, the division had begun processing his award. By taking Murphy away from his unit—infantrymen were in very short supply in those days—the division signaled its view that the award would probably be the Medal of Honor. None other was sufficient to warrant relief from combat. Murphy was, after all, a rare commodity—a living and relatively undamaged candidate—and the authorities very likely did not want to risk losing him. (Captain Maurice Britt, also of the 3rd Division, had been recommended for the Medal of Honor during the Italian campaign, but he had stayed on the line, only to lose an arm in a subsequent action.) Murphy was promoted to first lieutenant, given a leave to Paris, and, upon his return, reassigned as a liaison officer to his regiment. This change of duty improved by a large margin his chances of surviving the war. There is no evidence that he complained.

In his letters home about this time, Murphy frequently mentioned his medals, especially the Purple Hearts. But he seems to have regarded them more as war souvenirs, booty to be sent home, than as badges of soldierly courage. He understood that a Medal of Honor would get him out of the line, and that was the main reason for his enthusiasm when he learned he might get one. On April 1, 1945, he wrote to friends that he had been given the Distinguished Service Cross, a Silver Star, and a Bronze Star, and then was waiting at regimental headquarters for the Medal of Honor to be awarded, "so I can come home." That, along with the Legion of Merit he was about to receive, meant that "since that is all the Medals they have to offer i'll [sic] have to take it easy for a while."

Eleven days after receiving the medal, Murphy stepped off a plane at San Antonio and, in company with other military notables from Texas, began a round of parades, toasts, speeches, and interviews, slowly working his way north to Hunt County. To the crowds that gathered around him that summer, Murphy was no doubt befuddling and endearing. He was not the iron-eyed, athletic, self-contained warrior Americans seem to expect their military heroes to be. He was not tall and muscular, and he did not swagger. He was very slight, soft-spoken, and wearily uncomfortable with all the attention. But for the tan officer's uniform, bristling with ribbons, he could have been the kid next door. The actor James Cagney, soon to be instrumental in helping Murphy get his start in motion pictures, said that what was appealing about Murphy was his "assurance and poise without aggressiveness."

Murphy certainly did not look like the kind of man who might have spent nearly two years fighting his way from the hills of Sicily to the German frontier in the worst kind of infantry combat. In the story that accompanied his cover photo in *Life* magazine in July, there is a picture of the lieutenant getting a haircut at Mrs. Greer's barbershop in Farmersville, Texas, near his home. Outside the big plate-glass window there stands a crowd of more than a dozen men, simply staring at him. There is an expectant air about the crowd, as if Murphy might suddenly bolt from the chair and do something herolike. His head is bowed and the barber's bib drapes across his knees. He looks very young and mortally tired.

What Murphy was about to discover is that the hero's deed is only the down payment on the price he must pay for acclaim. Frequently the medal becomes a curse for the man who wears it. Some 111 men won the Victoria Cross during Britain's nineteenth-century campaigns. Seven of these subsequently took their own lives, a horrendous rate for a time when in the general population there were only 8 suicides per 100,000. Still more had utterly disastrous postwar lives, finding that they were unequal to the more pacific rhythms of life beyond the battlefield. We know of the sad fate of the popular marine hero Ira Hayes, who assisted in the raising of the flag on Iwo Jima's Mount Suribachi; but no complete study of the postwar fates of medal winners has ever been done. Of course, you need not be a certified war hero to suffer problems after a war, but the hero may carry a heavier burden than the ordinary soldier. As it was put by Captain Ian Fraser of the Royal Navy, a Victoria Cross winner in World War II, "A man is trained for the task that might win him a VC. He is not trained to cope with what follows."

It is when you consider Murphy's record in context that his valor becomes truly impressive. During World War II, 433 Medals of Honor were awarded, 293 of them to soldiers. Thirty-four, or 11.6 percent, went to men in Murphy's own 3rd Infantry Division, the most remarkable fighting organization in that war, during campaigns from North Africa to Germany. Fourteen were awarded to Murphy's 115th Infantry Regiment alone. The 30th and the 7th also had an unusually high record of Medal of Honor awards, making the 3rd Infantry Division the most highly decorated American unit in the war.

The division's record naturally poses questions: Compared to others, was the 3rd somehow a better fighting organization? Did it have a more difficult, longer war? Were its leaders especially sensitive to the benefits of soldierly morale, and therefore did they apply more often for awards? And did Murphy's membership in the 3rd somehow encourage him to perform valorous deeds repeatedly?

Unquestionably, the 3rd Infantry Division was a fine fighting organization. It was a "heavy" infantry division as it entered the war during the North African campaign, carrying more than 15,000 troops on its rolls. During the war, it participated in four amphibious landings, fought in ten separate campaigns, and was in contact with the enemy on more than 500 days, with few opportunities to rest and refit. According to the testimony of one of its wartime commanders, Lucian K. Truscott, Jr., "few divisions have ever entered action in a higher state of combat efficiency." Truscott was a very plainspoken cavalryman, not given to hyperbole, and he was one of the very best division commanders of the war. But the appraisal of one's enemies always carries more weight. After Field Marshal Albert Kesselring, the German theater commander in Italy, was captured, he was asked to rate the quality of the units his armies had fought. He replied that the 3rd "was the best division we faced and never gave us a rest."

And then there are the numbers. Recently, when an officer who served with the division early in the war was asked about the official view of the awards, he agreed that the 3rd had more than its share; then he added, "Have you looked at the casualty figures?" Essentially, the division's membership turned over five times during the course of its campaigns. Battle and non-battle casualties amounted to a staggering 74,044 soldiers by the division's own count. Of these losses, Truscott reported during the fighting in Italy, 86 percent were in the infantry battalions. After the first thirty days of fighting, the infantry companies were at half strength, "although," recalled Truscott, "it had not seemed from day to day that losses were excessive."

Unfortunately, divisional battle streamers and casualty figures tell us very little about what the soldiering—the ordinary soldiering—was like. Well after the war, one army psychiatrist attempted to profile "normal" combat reactions; the result was a picture of a bedraggled, haggard, near neurotic, suffering from vague physical complaints, inability to concentrate on the task at hand, constant irritability, and, in general, uselessness for any sort of strenuous activity—certainly not combat. During the war, both Bill Mauldin and Ernie Pyle tried to describe for the public back home what the front was really like. In the end, both would have agreed with the British army's Captain Athol Stewart: "Do *you* know what it's like? Of course you don't."

In their reminiscences, veterans often despair of recalling the details of actual combat. Threading throughout their attempts at memory are references to "dreamlike states" and "floating," and in the more modern language of Vietnam, "out-of-body experiences." The novelist John Steinbeck, working as a war correspondent in Italy during some of the campaigns Murphy fought in, believed that combat is beyond the powers of memory to reproduce. "You try to remember what it was like, and you can't quite manage it," he wrote. "The outlines in your memory are vague. The next day the memory slips farther, until very little is left at all. . . . Men in prolonged battle are not normal men."

So combat riflemen like Murphy stood at the farthest and most dangerous end of grand military enterprises, where elegant strategies and refined tactics count for little. Those matters belong to a world bounded by traditional military science. When a soldier moves forward against fire, he steps beyond the boundaries of anything we understand. Then, centuries of military science are at the mercy of one bullet, and if reason is at play it must expend its power in forms so different that they have eluded us thus far.

For Murphy and his comrades in Company B, the authors of all their miseries were, of course, the Germans. From the time Murphy entered the line until his last day in combat, his enemies were on the strategic defensive and largely on the tactical defensive as well. In the terrain he had to cross, the advantage naturally rested with the defense, and at this the Germans were very, very good. After the fighting around Mount Fratello, Murphy wrote, "I acquired a healthy respect for the Germans as fighters" and "an insight into the furies of mass combat." That action, he recorded, had "taken the vinegar out of my spirit."

The Italian campaign was the worst yet for the 3rd Division. Casualties between the Allied landings at Salerno and Anzio amounted to more than the authorized strength of the division; as usual, the line units suffered the most. Because of the atrocious weather and the limitations it imposed on motorized tactical movement in monotonously hilly terrain, troops were often stranded in the lines for several days without food or water. Mules were pressed into service to carry needed supplies when enemy fire subsided. The enemy gave ground grudgingly. Murphy participated in several attacks during this time, attacks that succeeded less because of the power of assault than because of shrewd maneuvering. Often, the enemy seemed impervious to anything the Americans tried. "If the suffering of men could do the job, the German lines would be split wide open. But not one real dent do we make," Murphy wrote later of the fighting around Monte Lungo. When the enemy did give ground and the Americans occupied it, the Germans routinely shelled their old positions.

Murphy survived the Italian campaigns as a staff sergeant, with two Bronze Stars for valor, in command of a platoon—a position normally held by a second lieutenant. He had not been wounded, although he had been one of his division's 12,000 "nonbattle casualties." Meanwhile, he had come to the attention of his commanders as a canny soldier who possessed extraordinary combat sense. Insofar as a soldier could be battlewise, Murphy was.

The wisdom of battle exacts its price, however. During the war, researchers found that after the initial fear of combat passed, the ordinary soldier was likely to relax somewhat, take more chances, and in some cases harbor a feeling of indestructibility. That feeling would be challenged eventually by the grind of daily action, or more promptly by two dramatic events: a wound or a near miss, or the death of a close friend. Both were about to happen to Murphy.

On the morning of August 15, 1944, Allied troops invaded southern France, coming ashore south of Saint-Tropez. Military historians would later debate how relatively light the German defenses were compared to those at Normandy, and how easily the Sixth Army Group moved northward along the Rhone against a rapidly retreating German army. But invasion day was a very bad one for Murphy. Near the town of Ramantuelle, his best friend was killed when enemy troops played a false surrender. After his friend died in his arms, Murphy embarked upon a frenzied and single-handed assault, eventually killing or wounding thirteen German soldiers. "I remember the experience as I do a nightmare," he wrote; "the men . . . tell me that I shout pleas and curses at them, because they do not come up and join me." Murphy won the Distinguished Service Cross for his mad spree at Ramantuelle; no doubt he would have preferred the survival of his friend.

After a quick and cheering advance along the Rhone, the Sixth Army Group entered the Vosges Mountains, and all of a sudden the fighting seemed reminiscent of Italy. By this time, nearly all of the original members of Company B were gone—killed or wounded. Murphy began to withdraw into a fatalistic alienation from his fellow soldiers. The comradeship that had originally sustained him had been gradually shot away and could not, would not, be regenerated. Although still in the midst of his fighting company, Audie Murphy was essentially alone.

Remembering this bleak time, in his autobiography, *To Hell and Back,* Murphy wrote:

> So many men have come and gone that I can no longer keep track of them. Since Kerrigan got his, I have isolated myself as much as possible, desiring only to do my work and be left alone. I feel burnt out, emotionally and physically exhausted. Let the hill be strewn with corpses as long as I do not have to turn over the bodies and find the familiar face of a friend. It is with the living that I must concern myself, juggling them as numbers to fit the mathematics of battle.

As remarkable as his survival was the fact that Murphy had not by then succumbed to combat fatigue. Among the frontline troops, the conventional wisdom was that everyone had his "breaking point" if he stayed in the line too long. Nor did respite from battle, such as Murphy had had while training for the landing in southern France, particularly help in warding off that breaking point. Paul Fussell, the author of the acclaimed book *The Great War and Modern Memory,* but earlier a company commander with the 45th Division in the spring of 1945, recalls his experience after he returned from the hospital to the combat lines. His convalescence "helped me survive for four weeks more but it broke the rhythm and, never badly scared before . . . I found for the first time that I was terrified, unwilling to take the chances that before had seemed rather sporting."

By October 1944, both of the opposing armies were wearing down. Generalmajor Wolf Ewart, the commander of the German 338th Infantry Division then opposing the Sixth Army's advance, reported losses as high as 60 percent in the battles for Alsace. The casualties among the officers and noncommissioned officers were especially high. On the American side of the lines, infantrymen were at a premium, and as the winter approached, manpower shortages became severe. Having earlier refused a battlefield commission because it would separate him from his men—newly commissioned officers were routinely transferred to another unit—Murphy accepted his commission on October 15, with the understanding that he could stay with Company B. His regimental commander, Colonel Hallett D. Edson, pinned the gold bars on Murphy's shirt and told him to get a shave, take a bath, "and get the hell back to the front lines."

Twelve days later, Murphy was seriously wounded by a sniper. Getting to the field hospital took too long; Murphy's infected wound became gangrenous. He remained hospitalized for the rest of the year. When he finally returned to Company B, the unit was getting ready to penetrate the Colmar Pocket in the direction of Holtzwihr. However, the Bois de Riedwihr lay across their line of march, and it was within these woods that Murphy's fame awaited.

During World War II, battles often took place inside what the Germans knew as *der Kessel,* "the caldron." The phrase evokes the stuff of close combat in confined spaces, the abiding and numbing fear of the next step that grinds down the swift movement of armies. To a degree perhaps not appreciated by modern military historians, World War II was one of places and lines. The rapier's thrust, typified by the dash across France, was an exception in this war. Eventually, the men who did Murphy's kind of work had to take the ground away from their counterparts on the other side of the main line of resistance. For the better part of two years, Murphy lived inside *der Kessel.* As we shall see, he went to some lengths to get there, believing, as many do, that within war were mysteries of self to be discovered, and of worlds beyond the life of a Texas sharecropper.

In Stephen Crane's classic story of the soldier's rite of passage, *The Red Badge of Courage,* the young hero, Henry Fleming, is overtaken by a desire to see war. He frets that war might be too modern to permit the attainment of real glory. He wonders if "he might be a man heretofore doomed to peace and obscurity, but, in reality, made to shine in war." Remarkably—all the more so since Murphy later played Henry Fleming in the movie version of Crane's book—Murphy seems to have been "made to shine in war."

No one tried harder than Murphy to see, as Henry Fleming did, "the great Red God of War." Whether Murphy had a predisposition for war is a problematic question, but there is little doubt that he saw the war, as innocents often do, as a way of escaping the grinding poverty that had so far dominated his young life. He was drawn to the elite units: The marines were first on his list. Rejected twice, he tried to enlist for duty with the new airborne units, but he stood five-foot-six and weighed only 112 pounds— less than the battle gear the troops were often obliged to carry. Finally, he was made to settle for the infantry—unhappily, as "the infantry was too commonplace for my ambitions," he wrote later. Caught up in the great mobilization, Murphy was shifted from one post to another; at each place well-meaning superiors attempted to protect him from a combat assignment. "Fuming," he recalled, "I stuck to my guns." He was still just a child, really, when "Finally the great news came. We were going into action. . . ."

Audie Murphy was so adept at infantry combat that we are compelled to look for reasons. He was certainly willing, even earnest, to join the rush to the colors, but most recruits are willing in the first flush of war. Reality quickly cools the new soldier's ardor. Murphy did not cool quite so quickly. Despite his small size, he had the stamina that comes from years of farm work, but it cannot be said that he was any better prepared for the physical rigors of combat than anyone else. After a few weeks on the battle lines, infantrymen are usually in terrible physical shape. Long before he was wounded, Murphy spent several days in hospitals, suffering from respiratory ailments acquired in Sicily and Italy. He had plenty of company.

Murphy appears to have believed, and his home state was quick to claim, that having been born and reared in Texas had something to do with his military success. But pride in origins should not be confused with some sort of predestination. He was a rural boy, of course, accustomed to hunting in the hills and valleys of North Texas. The countryside and its forms held no mysteries for him. But these advantages, if advantages they were, can be noted only as indecipherable factors. Most Americans who fought well in the war were not from Texas and had been no closer to the country than the city park before they enlisted. How they performed in combat had more to do with what the great German military historian Hans Delbrück would have called "the material possibilities of the moment." And despite a great deal of official interest by the U.S. Army since World War II, a psycho-physical profile of "the natural fighter" has never been done.

Whether Murphy's behavior predisposed others to think of him as valorous is another question. It is true that even the most ordinary rifleman took terrifying risks day after day, but Murphy's practices were not typical. During his war, Murphy developed certain habits that automatically brought him to the approving notice of his superiors. Before the war he had been pugnacious, and this temperament served him well during his campaigns. And although he was as comfortable with his comrades as any combat soldier might be, he was given to independent action. He often volunteered for patrols to gather information or to take prisoners. Frequently, he would "go hunting," and, when he did, enemy snipers were in danger. As he gradually acquired command responsibilities, he usually would see his men safely placed, then go forward alone or with a couple of others to reconnoiter the ground ahead. For Murphy, then, the sequence of events during his action at the Bois de Riedwihr was not so unusual.

Nor was his endurance of notorious stresses unusual. One officer of the 1st Scots Guards who fought in Tunisia recalled seeing "strong, courageous men reduced to whimpering wrecks, crying like children." Murphy never seems to have had such a breakdown, although he had more than his share of reasons to do so. He seems, on the contrary, to have been able to redirect his reaction to stress against the military objective at hand. Obviously, stress was at play during the incident at Ramantuelle. Since the last century, military theorists have recognized that one of the many ways to escape immediate danger in combat is to move forward; Murphy did that more than once.

All of which is not to say that Murphy escaped suffering, either in the war or after it. After the sniper's bullet in Alsace proved he was not, after all, invulnerable, he adopted the fatalistic attitude common to soldiers long at war. From his hospital bed, he wrote home that "these Krauts are getting to be better shots than they used to be or else my lucks [sic] playing out on me. I guess some day they will tag me for keeps."

After he was recommended for the Medal of Honor and reassigned to his regimental headquarters, Murphy's luck was tested less often; but there was plenty of war left, and on several occasions he was drawn into combat, despite the army's desire to preserve the life of a Medal of Honor winner. And then, finally, the war ended. But Murphy's private war did not.

In ages past, once the colors were furled, soldiers gratefully went home. The signing of the peace was a signal for nation and individual alike that normal life could be resumed. But during this century there have been disturbing signs that the psychological effects of war are rather more persistent than anyone wants to think. The medical world has devised increasingly sophisticated interpretations of the spiritual lassitude, and worse, that seems to affect so many veterans. What was "shell shock" in World War I was gradually redescribed as "combat fatigue," or "neuropsychiatric casualty," in World War II, and finally as "post-traumatic stress" in the Vietnam War. So, too, did the supposed causes of the malaise change. Whereas shell shock was thought to be the result of concussions and gas from high explosives, combat fatigue was believed to be a pernicious mixture of the soldier's personality and the immediate stresses of combat. In the years since Vietnam, interpretations have tended to emphasize the stresses of combat alone as the cause of postwar emotional suffering.

Of course, there were vast differences among all these wars—the circumstances under which men fought, as well as the conditions they found at home upon their return. Students of the Vietnam era have noted that Vietnam veterans did not have the advantage of returning World War II soldiers, who came home in troopships, where they could "decompress" for at least several days. The flight from Saigon to San Francisco took only about eighteen hours; afterward, soldiers were discharged and left to their own readjustment—or lack thereof. Murphy's experience more nearly matched that of the Vietnam vet. Even with his own generation's opportunity to relax before discharge, Murphy thought, returning vets were poorly handled. He told an interviewer in 1960 that "they took army dogs and rehabilitated them for civilian life. But they turned soldiers into civilians immediately and let 'em sink or swim."

To be sure, Murphy's own postwar experience was unusual. Few other vets became national institutions. As his fame spread, one Dallas newspaper sought to tell the public "what Murphy is like—a swell kid, absolutely modest, sincere and genuine and unaltered by terrible experiences." Well, not quite, because while other veterans were allowed to contend with their personal demons in private, every event in Murphy's life after the war was played out in public. His skills did not easily translate into civilian life, and he clearly was unsure what to do when the cheering stopped.

Fortunately, before too long he was recruited by Hollywood, much as sports heroes are today. His photograph on the cover of *Life* had inspired James Cagney to invite him west. Originally intending to register Murphy at a hotel, Cagney was so startled by Murphy's fatigued appearance that he offered the young man the use of his pool house instead. Murphy was

Cagney's guest briefly, went home for a visit, and then returned to spend nearly a year at the actor's home. Within five years Murphy had parlayed his wartime fame into a peacetime career.

The movie career has been depicted as modest. Film histories do not mention his work—perhaps wrongly, for he was cast perfectly in John Huston's *The Red Badge of Courage* and Joseph L. Mankiewicz's *The Quiet American*. Murphy himself took a dim view of his acting ability and did not seem to think of his career as more than a way to make a decent living. "I didn't want to be an actor. It was simply the best offer that came along," he recalled long after the war. But he certainly did well enough: By the early 1950s, Audie Murphy had enough box-office power to demand script and director approval (as well as the lead role) for any movie he was in.

Yet the two years he spent in the caldron of war dominated his life and, to an extent that could be known only by himself, determined its course. His wartime heroism overshadowed everything he did, although by most standards he made a greater postwar success of himself than his early history would have suggested. Without that vital identity as a military hero, Murphy might well have returned to a quiet life in rural Texas, never to be touched by fame. Ironically, perhaps, it was that fame that kept the war too much alive for him. Decades after the war, he still could not relax. He had chronic stomach complaints, sensitivity to loud noises, and frequent nightmares. He always kept the bedroom lights on at night and a loaded pistol by his bed. Sometimes he carried the pistol.

Murphy's fortune declined in the 1960s: He had always gambled, but the habit began to get the best of him then. As bankruptcy threatened, he grasped at dubious business schemes and acquaintances. His political outlook, always on the conservative side, verged on the extreme. But none of these difficulties strike us today as particularly the effect of trauma. Indeed, we are so accustomed to heroic figures who fall from public grace that the concept of heroism itself has devolved. When Murphy was killed in a plane crash near Roanoke, Virginia, in 1971, he still seemed incomplete, searching for something elusive. Once asked whether men get over a war, he had replied reflectively, "I don't think they ever do."

*SPRING 1993*

---

Roger J. Spiller is George C. Marshall Professor of Military History at the United States Army Command and General Staff College, Fort Leavenworth, Kansas.

# 38

# Death and Life at Three-Pagoda Pass

## By John Stewart

*Allied prisoners of the Japanese faced a multitude of horrors during the Second World War, but few confronted such a combination of terrors as those POWs who labored on the infamous "Death Railway," made famous in the movie* The Bridge on the River Kwai. *Meant to connect Thailand and Burma, this rail link struggled through or over mountains, rivers, and jungles and, in the process of construction, consumed its conscripted laborers at a draconian rate. Of the 1,600 prisoners who arrived in May 1943 at Sonkurai camp near Three-Pagoda Pass (the highest point on the railroad), John Stewart was one of only 182 who were alive when the war ended. In this essay he wrestles with the question that so often haunts survivors: Why did some live while so many others died?*

> When you visit our comrades'
>     honored graves
> (Mists crowding in, quietly comes
>     dawn in the forest)
> The railbed grows chilly and mists
>     penetrate your body.
>                    —A SONG OF THE JAPANESE ENGINEERS

S ometime in the 1920s the British had envisaged linking the Thai and Burmese rail systems. The idea was never pursued. The terrain was mountainous. Numerous rivers and streams would require bridging. And in a jungle whose impenetrability is second only to the Brazilian rain forest, the maintenance of a large work force was problematic: The region is host not only to the usual tropical diseases, but to cholera and a fatal strain of cerebral malaria.

In 1939 the Japanese, too, looked at the feasibility of a similar rail link. They understood that in the event of war, if ever they failed to control the Bay of Bengal and were denied access to the port of Rangoon, they would have to convey troops and matériel overland from Bangkok. The civilian engineer appointed by Army General Headquarters in Tokyo reported that two years were needed to complete the *project. This estimate was confirmed by a clandestine reconnaissance party sent in August 1941, five months before the Japanese invasion of Thailand and Burma.*

*The destruction of the Japanese carriers at Midway brought about the dreaded eventuality: the loss of the Indian Ocean to the Royal Navy's Far East Squadron. The building of the Thai-Burma railway link had suddenly become an imperative. Unless it was operative in a year, the invasion of India would have to be scrapped.*

*In April 1943, 7,000 British and Australian POWs, designated as F Force, shipped out of Changi, the vast prewar barrack compound at the tip of Singapore Island, where the Imperial Japanese Army (IJA) had herded the defeated Allied troops after the capture of the city. Group after group had been shipped north to the railway, and F Force was one of the last to leave. It was earmarked for the work camps beyond the upper reaches of the Mae Nam Kwae Noi (or, as the movie popularized it, the River Kwai), south of the Three-Pagoda Pass, where three Buddhist structures marked the highest point of the Thai rail line near the border with Burma.*

*F Force suffered greater losses than any other group for two main reasons: the remoteness of the camps, which made access to food supplies problematic soon after the monsoon's onset; and the composition of the force itself, a third of which was made up of prisoners officially designated sick by the Japanese themselves.*

*A less obvious factor was that F Force was "loaned" by the Malaya POW Administration to the two IJA engineer regiments responsible for the "Death Railway," as it came to be known. Since F Force, unlike other groups, was not officially incorporated into their work units, they neither "owned" it nor felt responsible for its welfare. The engineers treated F Force as if it were expendable, as expendable in fact as the coolies.*                                                    —J.S.

I WAS DETAILED to accompany F Force as an interpreter. I was bilingual in French, had been taught bazaar Arabic, and was due to serve in counter-intelligence in the Middle East. The randomness of war, however, landed me in Singapore in January 1942, and a month later I'd become, as we used to put it, a guest of His Imperial Majesty. My commanding officer encouraged me to learn Japanese. It took six months of tutoring and study to become proficient enough to be included in the tiny roster of official interpreters, most of them sons of missionaries once stationed in Japan.

With the survivors of F Force, I was shipped back to Singapore when the "loan" to the engineers came to an end, nine months after our departure. But during that terrible year of 1943, to the cry of "Speedo!" 150,000 men—prisoners and Asiatic levies—perished building 350 miles of railway line that never served its intended purpose. No sooner was it completed than the Royal Air Force and the U.S. Air Force reduced its operational capabilities by two-thirds.

In Kranji, the POW hospital camp where I was posted as interpreter after the return from "up-country," the survivors seldom spoke about their year at the Three-Pagoda Pass. A sense of propriety held us back from closely investigating the factors that had kept us alive while many fitter and worthier men had gone under.

"It's all a matter of luck," we said.

It was indeed luck, or the accident of birth, if you were the right size. Everyone received the same quantity of food—except the sick, who were allotted no food at all by the engineers. ("No work, no rice" was their rule. Consequently, the healthy shared their scanty rations with the sick.) When, with the monsoon rains, neither bullock carts nor even elephants could negotiate the track, which had been transformed into a flowing stream of mud, we sent small parties of men to pick up what they could carry from camps on the other side of the pass. We all teetered at the edge of survival, but the tall men, needing more calories than their smaller comrades, were more vulnerable. The Military Police, all of them six-footers, were the first to go under. On the other hand, a smaller man might find the work imposed by the Japanese a lot harder than a big one. The most obvious, the most visible, causes of death—malaria, cholera, dysentery, and tropical ulcers—were enormously aggravated by starvation.

Curiously, a man's height might also influence his treatment at the hands of guards and engineers. A tall man, regardless of the respect accorded to stature in all societies, might present a challenge to an undersized private who passed on to the prisoner the slaps and blows that were part of the IJA routine, administered from higher to lower rank. As he might find it awkward to deliver a sharp upward swing to his victim's face, he'd concentrate on chest, belly, and limbs—more damaging than conventional slaps. Conversely, harsh punishment might harm the small and weak more than the large and strong. Luck, then, was to be below six feet and above five eight. I happen to be five eight.

Luck, too, if you had received proper food in your youth. There was a difference in the survival rate if your family had been poor or well off, if you had been brought up on a diet of sweet tea, biscuits, and occasional fish-and-chips, or on vegetables, fruit, and proteins. Because of their general state of health at the start of their three-and-a-half-year imprisonment, officers fared better than other ranks, as everyone not holding the king's commission was then called, and men from country-recruited regiments better than those born and bred in large cities and industrial areas.

Age mattered. On the Death Railway, the very young, who lacked endurance, and the older men, who lacked quick powers of recuperation, lost out. Colonel Julian Taylor, a celebrated London surgeon and yachtsman (to whom I was teaching French in return for a course in celestial navigation), thought that twenty-seven was the optimum for an infantryman, the age when endurance and recuperative powers are ideally balanced.

Both the strength and the weakness of youth were illustrated by an incident that took place a few days after the February 15, 1942, surrender of Singapore. In the middle of the night, Taylor was called out to operate on a man whose head had been partly severed by a sword blow. He was a sailor in his teens who had been captured a few hours before the cease-fire. Exceptionally, his life was spared. The officer in command of the unit that had captured him ordered a car and driver to deliver the young sailor to Changi. By evening, however, prisoner and driver were back, having failed to find the POW camp. The officer, estimating that he accomplished his humanitarian duty, decided to behead the prisoner. It must have been a perfunctory blow, for some hours later the boy came to, covered by a thin and loose layer of earth. As he tried to crawl out of his grave, he noticed that the muscles of the neck had been partially severed. Holding his head between his hands, he stumbled into a *kampong*, a native village, from which he was led by two Chinese to the edge of Changi and the POW camp. He was discovered and rushed to the hospital. His youth and vitality allowed him to survive the shock and the loss of blood. A year later, however, he died of disease and privation in the Burmese jungle.

Not much could be done to control or influence the existential aspects of our lives. Where you landed on the Death Railway was entirely a matter of chance. Parts of the line were preferable to others, especially if they were close to a base with food supplies or in open rather than hilly country. Certain work assignments, such as rock-blasting, were hazardous; working immersed in the river day after day was invariably fatal. Some guards and engineers showed compassion, while others were sadists who drove their working parties with barbed-wire whips. If your blanket was stolen while you were away at work, your chances of survival precipitously diminished.

Camps, of course, differed. Sonkurai, where I was sent as interpreter after a forced march of two weeks, acquired the worst reputation of any camp on the railway. Cholera had broken out and the Japanese had ordered the sick to be removed to a hill, without shelter, to die under the monsoon rains. Men worked sixteen hours a day, and rations were down to a few ounces of rice daily. The engineers were so ferocious that even our own guards, Koreans under the command of a Japanese regular sergeant, were terrified of them. The prisoners—or what was left of them—were set first to building the road, then laying down a railway track, and lastly erecting a bridge over a river. Discipline, social cohesion, and the esprit de corps that is the fundamental glue of the regimental system in the British army all vanished. Men hunted for food and basics in tiny groups. Only one man in ten survived Sonkurai.

Yet only three miles away, the Australian camp, Shimo-Sonkurai, also part of F Force and subject to the same conditions, was utterly different. As a rule, the Australians fared better than the British, who in turn were better off than the Dutch. Worst of all, way behind the Dutch, came the Asiatic coolies.

The few Americans, airmen and survivors of the USS *Houston*, sunk off Indonesia in early 1942, made out well. They all appeared to possess a remarkable ability for commerce, even in the jungle. Perhaps because they owned objects the Japanese found highly desirable, such as Rolex watches and Parker Pens (the national passion for the proper label was even then evident), they started off with a substantial capital. Freewheeling and un-hampered by the British class system, they were more nimble and more resourceful than the other prisoners, with perhaps the exception of the Australians.

Most Australians came from the bush. They were hardened by outdoor life and resourceful in the wilds—characteristics that under the circum-stances were far more valuable than being streetwise. Above all, solidarity between officers and men was maintained; and among the men, mutual help was the rule. The contrast between the two camps was dismally vis-ible every time I went over to help out the Australians, who didn't have a Japanese speaker among them.

The Dutch, among whom were found a high proportion of Indonesians familiar with life in the tropical forest, should have fared better than anyone else. They, too, suffered from social disintegration, however, and were un-able to maintain an effective internal organization. The British found them "selfish": Without a collective framework, everyone had to fend for himself.

As for the miserable Asiatic levies from Malaya, Thailand, and Burma, they were beaten to death if too sick to work, their scant rations were stolen from them, and they died by the tens of thousands. When the rail link was completed, the Japanese told them they had no use for them any-more, and let them starve to death in jungle clearings. They lacked what our captors admired most: a strong social cohesion whose natural con-comitants are discipline and devotion to duty.

BUT IT WASN'T ALL a matter of luck.

Like everyone else in F Force, I had my own explanation for making it back to the POW camps of Singapore, which to the survivors appeared like holiday resorts. At this great remove, however, I can't vouch whether these ideas came to me when I was on the railway, in Kranji after my return, or since the end of the war. What is certain is that, at the time, I had no doubt that I owed my life to being an interpreter.

Obviously, the scant rations held me up better than if, day after day, I'd been engaged in excruciatingly hard manual labor. But equally important was the nature of the work itself. Unlike the figure of Colonel Nicholson in *The Bridge on the River Kwai*, clearing the jungle and building a bridge for the benefit of the IJA gave us neither a feeling of pride nor one of achievement. On the contrary, our efforts clearly served the enemy. As a form of morale builder, we collected termites and released them into the pilings. The gesture was meant to give our lives a semblance of purpose, but the bridges were destroyed by aerial bombing long before the insects could prove their worth.

Deprivation of a meaningful activity induced such a sense of worthless-ness that on two separate occasions a prisoner approached me with a request to enroll in the Japanese armed forces. I produced lurid accounts of the trials of serving as "one-star" private in the IJA, and worse, of the horrors inflicted on the *heihos*, the foreign auxiliaries such as our Korean guards. One measure of their low status was a singular restriction: They were not thought worthy of receiving the standard Japanese rifle, supposedly entrusted by the emperor to each recruit, as attested by the crest of the Imperial Chrysanthemum embedded in the stock. The Koreans had to make do with captured British Lee-Enfields. If I failed to deter my would-be recruit, I turned him over to one of the better padres.

Because of its direct bearing on our relations with the Japanese, my work could affect, positively or otherwise, the welfare of the camp as a whole. My duties went beyond mere translation. In many situations the interpreter, with a better understanding of Japanese mentality than his superiors, might advise them to adopt a different approach; and if the confrontation took an ugly turn, he might be able to protect the officer for whom he was translating by blaming his own inadequacy with the language. No two situations were ever alike. In every confrontation there was always the possibility of winning, and this prevented me from the dumb and passive acceptance of orders. Alas, there was an unpleasant price to pay for this. Being frequently around the Japanese, I was often the recipient of slaps and blows.

A signal privilege of my work was the exposure it gave me to a culture utterly different from the one I had been brought up in. Much had been imparted by the two British interpreters who had been my teachers, but nothing matched those insights I received on the job. One remains uppermost.

It occurred when I was the interpreter at Tambaya, a camp at the edge of the jungle, on the Burmese side of the Three-Pagoda Pass. There the engineers had dumped about 2,000 F Force prisoners who were expected to die within a few weeks—throwaways, irremediably sick men from whom no more work could be expected. It was also a way, they imagined, to stop disease from spreading.

The commandant was a Lieutenant Eraiwa, a stern combatant officer who, by and large, treated us fairly. His quarters were at the extremity of a long and narrow hut that also housed his men. When I called on him, Eraiwa was seated on his bamboo sleeping platform. I entered, bowed, and, as I did so, noticed a surprising sight through the opening of the partition that separated the lieutenant's section from that of his men. A tree branch, pale gray, four or five feet in length, was hanging like a painting on one of the bamboo walls. It instantly evoked an ideogram written by a master. It incarnated both perfect equilibrium and dynamic strength. Neither leaves nor shoots impaired its linearity. Finally, its placement on the wall had been perfectly chosen.

A devil sprang in me, a fit of jealousy. Another tribe, an enemy tribe at that, had produced what I perceived as an extraordinary work of art, objet trouvé though it was. The emotion transformed itself into an acceptable form—disdain for such tomfoolery. Yet when I asked Eraiwa the meaning of "that thing on the wall," I could hear the bitterness in my voice.

"This morning," he answered slowly, "two of my men went for a walk in the forest. They found this branch, brought it back, and hung it in their part of the hut in order to refresh the spirit of their comrades."

I bowed once more when I left. Because I had to, and also in acknowledgment of Eraiwa's lesson.

UNDER THE EXTREME conditions of Sonkurai, I came to understand advice I'd been given in Singapore during the early days of our captivity. Its role in my survival may have been even greater than my position as interpreter.

The words were those of a captain in his late forties. One evening, after a game of bridge, he reminisced about his experiences in the First World War and warned us of the days to come.

"Who knows where we'll be sent to," he said, "or what's going to happen to us. We'll be in the bag for a long time. I was taken prisoner by the Germans in '17, and I'm sure of one thing: It was a picnic compared to what's awaiting us. But remember: Whatever happens, however dreadful the times you'll be going through, you've got to be able to say, 'This is something I never would have had the chance to see otherwise.'"

We looked at each other, the three young men who'd been playing cards with the captain. No doubt each of us was thinking, What's he talking about? It's bad enough here in Changi.

It was necessary, said the captain, to draw nourishment from the circumstances. Even though they seemed unbearable, they were exceptional. At the end of each day it should be possible to look back and say, "Today I have seen this, I have learned that."

"This is what will keep you going," he continued. "Just now your heads are filled with hopes of home. But that won't last forever. Memories of home will fade, become distant and unreal. Hope will thin out and won't sustain you anymore."

He was right. Deficiency didn't apply only to calories and vitamins. Pain and overwork drained a prisoner's psychic reserves. His will to live was whittled away. Despair set in. The threads that tied him to life, both his past life and the present one, slackened. As his attention failed he became vulnerable to the stresses of a harsh and dangerous existence. "Give-up-itis" set in, in most cases irreversible.

I'm thinking of L., a charming and cultivated friend. He was physically strong (he had rowed for his college at Oxford); his mind was incisive and his speech elegant. It was also obvious that he was ill-equipped to deal with *les détails matériels de la vie,* but there were always friends to take care of him and ensure his well-being. He was a life enhancer; we didn't want to lose him.

A disaster befell him during the early stages of the long and dreadful trek to the Three-Pagoda Pass, when the columns were traveling through semi-populated regions: The whole of his kit, loaded at considerable expense onto a bullock cart, was stolen. Even though there was always someone ready to share with him blanket and messtin, inevitably it made life much harder. L. arrived in Sonkurai suffering like everyone else from malaria and dysentery, but also profoundly discouraged. Much of his self-respect had disappeared; he no longer bothered to shave or wash. We managed to keep him off road and rail duties, finding him an easy job inside the camp, boiling water all day. But he failed at that and was sent off to work with a particularly murderous gang of engineers. His health and morale declined further. Once more, with the proper approach to the British senior NCO responsible for selecting the work parties (an approach backed by a twist of native tobacco and a spoonful of *shindegar*, or palm sugar), we kept him in camp for a few days. By that time all he owned were a grubby singlet, a shirt in shreds, and a few rags around his middle. His health declined and he was moved to the so-called hospital hut. Friends brought him rarities that had been hoarded since Singapore or bought from the coolies—an egg, tinned milk, a scrap of dried fish. He gave everything away, and died quietly two and a half months after his arrival in Sonkurai.

Death was part of the day's events. For many teetering at the edge of the decision whether to fight or to give up, death was the escape from hopelessness. Men died without fuss or struggle to hang on. They didn't call for someone to hold their hand, to be present at the extinction of life. It was a private and natural affair. The rites of passage were faced alone. Often, there was a smile on the face of the moribund: He was about to find deliverance.

Everyone was aware of death's closeness, but few consciously acted on the obvious questions: Will I really do anything to survive? What means shall I use? What compromises will I accept?

Those who said yes to the first mostly went under. The mere will to live apparently didn't suffice. Even when efforts to find more food and avoid the more strenuous work gangs were successful, the time came when you found the rewards wanting and solace nonexistent. You abandoned the struggle.

The other two questions were answered by a friend, Olaf Moore, a rubber planter before the war, who, when he saw the breakup of moral law in Sonkurai, said to me: "I don't know how to make my own rules. I won't start on that. All I think I can do is live like a Christian." I understood him. But I also feared for his life, and I was right, for within a month he died. Unwilling to engage in black-market transactions, to accept favors, to try to be assigned to light duties, or even to scrounge for food, he found himself among the most dispossessed. He became one of the prisoners who worked hardest and longest and received least.

Between the two groups, those who would stop at nothing and those who could never compromise, came the men who feathered their own nests as best they could, without, if possible, raiding their neighbors'. They were the pragmatists, and some of them survived.

In Sonkurai, not many. Of the 1,600 men who had arrived in May, only 400 returned to Singapore when the camp was evacuated eight months later. And of those 400, only 182 were still alive by the war's end.

A proper understanding of the Japanese attitude toward prisoners inevitably had a bearing on our welfare. It was a mistake to lump all Japanese into one mold; yet their common view was that, because we had permitted ourselves to be captured, we had forfeited all honor. Still, we existed within the military structure of the IJA, and the image that we projected was important, because the Japanese were sensitive to signs. In a rigidly structured hierarchical society, it was necessary to signal one's proper place in the structure. Two signs were expected of us: one to denote the prisoner's acceptance of his place, the other to confirm his understanding of his duties—namely, obeisance, observance of the rules, and devotion to work. If, over and above these signs, the Japanese detected indications that evoked "the way of the warrior," the virtues found in Bushido, they were susceptible to a change in attitude. The possibility then existed of overcoming to a small degree the shame and degradation of our status as prisoners.

As we embodied the virtues of Bushido in varying ways, so were we treated. The senior medical officer at Tambaya, Major Bruce Hunt, a fearless Australian whose unorthodox and vigorous measures were admired by the prisoners, was detested by the Japanese. They didn't deny his courage, but they found him lacking in that primordial samurai characteristic—loyalty. To them, loyalty meant respect for the IJA, and Hunt never hid his contempt for our captors. Ironically, the very source of his popularity with us rendered Hunt ineffectual in his dealings with the Japanese.

On the other hand, Lieutenant Colonel F.J. Dillon, an Indian army regular, understood the Japanese game and played it well. He dressed as neatly as possible, maintained at all times the Sandhurst posture (feet apart, spine slightly arched backward), and projected the picture of the perfect soldier. Among the prisoners his moral courage was famous up and down the line. Once, however, in his military zeal he overstepped the limits of the possible. In the jungle, after work, he instituted parade-ground drill. The sight of emaciated men, barefoot and in rags, square-bashing in the mud under the dripping jungle canopy, to the bark of the NCOs' "Mark time! Eyes right!" was bewildering even to the Japanese. The exercise lasted only a couple of days.

Dillon's axiomatic pronouncement was that without their officers, men perished. The truth was that survival depended more on the military framework itself than on the personal ability of most of the prisoner officers, who often were found wanting when it came to saving lives in the extreme conditions that were the norm on the Death Railway.

Yet such was the gap between officers and other ranks in the British army of that period that a corporal once remarked to me, "You know, there's really more in common between the Jap lieutenant and our officers than there is between them and us." This was at Tambaya, where relations between Lieutenant Eraiwa and our officers were based on mutual respect. The corporal was right, and I sensed his secret humiliation. He had correctly perceived the common imprint that codes and manners leave on the different strata of society, leaping over national and cultural differences, and bridging classes. This was the theme of the Jean Renoir film about French POWs during World War I, *La Grande Illusion,* and nothing much in that sphere seemed to have changed. Nor in fact since James Boswell hung on Samuel Johnson's every word: "Gentlemen of education [Dr. Johnson observed] were pretty much the same in all countries."

For myself and for many others, it was easier to seek solace in nature than in human society. We never failed to crane our necks when the greater toucans flew above the canopy. If we couldn't see them, we could hear the slow and powerful stroke of their wings.

I'd always had an affinity for elephants, and now I observed the intelligence and the delicacy these large animals would apply to moving a log that had become jammed in a gully, or to disentangling a towing chain wrapped around one of their legs. I learned much elephant lore from a Burma teak planter, an elephant wallah. These observations became part of the day's "nourishment," a glimpse also into a world both normal and harmonious.

Orchids and butterflies exploding into evanescent bursts of color brought poignancy, even tenderness, into our lives. In Tambaya I once observed a butterfly hovering above the bare foot of a corpse that had been laid out at the entrance to a hut. The insect's wings were shimmering with gold, yellow, and Prussian blue. Exceptionally large, it was looking for a suitable landing place. It chose the corpse's big toe. The two polarities, the brilliant, quivering insect and the pale, inert flesh, dissolved into one perception, in an instant as ephemeral as the flutter of gold on the butterfly's wings. I glimpsed the wholeness of everything around me, but at the same time I understood that I was seeing a reflection of my own mind.

Searching for quietude, I'd walk off into the jungle and sit in a small clearing. On rare occasions mind and body, kneaded by an involuntary asceticism, produced a tiny anthropomorphic experience. The boundaries of self appeared to fuse with nonself, and I entered into a brief but primal communion with my surroundings. In these moments of aloneness, I felt neither separateness nor threat nor hostility.

The captain had been right. When starved and worked to death in jungle camps, thoughts of home and freedom widened the gap between the reality and the hope. Only the present counted, not the past or future. He had been right when he spoke of "nourishment," when, at day's end, it was still possible to say, "This I have seen, that I have heard."

Everything around us was utterly new and unexpected. We had been prepared for none of it. Not for our extraordinary habitat, the rain forest; nor for our association with another people, another culture, the Japanese; and certainly not for the breakdown of our own group structure.

With its societal skin flayed, human nature became visible as never before. Greed, cowardice, and vanity; perseverance, altruism, and generosity—in brief, the wide panoply of vice and virtue was there to be observed in the open, without pretense, with no place to hide.

The captain, I later found out, died in Nikki, the base camp of F Force. So, after all, if your luck had run out neither "philosophy" nor help from your friends, nor even your own determination never to give up, was of much help. Your "number was up," as we used to say. Or *shikata ga nai,* to put it the Japanese way: "There is nothing to be done."

*SPRING 1993*

---

John Stewart is the author of *To the River Kwai: Two Journeys—1943, 1979* (1988). He served as a technical adviser to David Lean's 1957 Academy Award–winning movie *The Bridge on the River Kwai.*

# 39

# Fertile Blood

## By Margaret B. Wheeler

*War is the benefactor of medicine. Although historians have rarely explored this symbiotic relationship, it exists nonetheless. War has provided a vast laboratory for the theory and practice of healing, and no period has underscored this connection so clearly as the twentieth century. Medical progress can be and has been miraculous, but, as Margaret B. Wheeler relates in this discussion of battlefield wounds, blood loss, and shock, it has not come without its errors and false promises.*

"I am badly injured, Doctor; I fear I am dying. . . . I think the wound in my shoulder is still bleeding." . . . His clothes were saturated with blood, and hemorrhage was still going on from the wound. . . . His suffering at this time was intense; his hands were cold, his skin clammy, his face pale, and his lips compressed and bloodless; not a groan escaped him—not a sign of suffering, except the slight corrugation of his brow, the fixed rigid face, and the thin lips so tightly compressed, that the impression of the teeth could be seen through them. Except these, he controlled by his iron will, all evidence of emotion, and more difficult than this even, he controlled that disposition to restlessness, which many of us have observed upon the field of battle, attending great loss of blood.

D r. Hunter McGuire, Stonewall Jackson's physician, gives a textbook-perfect description of the shock the general suffered after his fatal wounding in 1863. It was a condition long familiar to military surgeons. The pallid, sweaty restlessness that often precedes the death of the severely wounded was first called "shock," in 1743, by those who had treated gunshot wounds, and who thought that these symptoms were caused by the violent, jarring impact of the bullet. They described shock eloquently as "the rude unhinging of the machinery of life" or "a momentary pause in the act of death," but they were unable to treat it.

Even Dr. McGuire, who seems to have understood that blood loss is the cause of shock, misunderstood the condition so gravely that he thought it had certain restorative qualities, and he actually bled the general. In fact, this belief in the restorative effects of shock led some of McGuire's colleagues to amputate without anesthesia, because they believed that the anesthesia would counteract the strengthening effects of shock.

We now understand that anesthesia, by causing the blood vessels to relax and thus the blood to pool, can reduce the circulating volume enough to cause shock. McGuire's colleagues, therefore, made the accurate observation that men already in shock tolerate anesthesia poorly. However, their interpretation that shock has some "strengthening" effect was clearly wrong. Modern-day anesthesiologists transfuse patients with fluid or blood, depending on the circumstances, to counteract the effects of blood pooling.

It has been only since World War II that we have finally understood shock. We now know that this condition is caused by a loss of circulating blood, leading to a lack of oxygen in the tissues and eventual death. States of disease that cause failure of the circulation, such as heart failure, or loss of fluid volume, such as dehydration, can also result in shock; nevertheless, hemorrhage, particularly in wounded men like Stonewall Jackson, is the most common cause. If we are able to replace lost blood, we can perform virtual miracles. We can reverse that "momentary pause" and heal people wounded even more severely than Jackson was.

The history of the understanding of shock and development of blood transfusion is, like the history of medicine itself, intertwined with the history of war. From the earliest days of medicine, war not only has forced physicians to develop techniques for repairing bodies mutilated by ever more ingenious weapons, but also has provided great numbers of patients for the trial-and-error advancement of science. The military hospital has been like some grim laboratory where physicians, often desperately understaffed and underequipped, must modify procedures or, because of either the novelty of the injury or the lack of standard equipment, invent new ones. They also see so many men suffering from similar injuries and diseases that they can closely monitor trends in the course of an illness and the success or failure of a particular treatment.

The catalogue of medical advances stimulated by the exigencies of war is a long one. Much of the understanding of how the human body works has been discovered in observing and trying to repair the injured. Indeed, wounded men have afforded the only opportunity to study the workings of a living human body; caring for them is the only legitimate form of human vivisection. Doctors from Galen (the second-century physician often called the "father of modern medicine," because he insisted that an understanding of human anatomy was the necessary foundation of medicine) to the surgeons of the Vietnam War have learned invaluable lessons by observing and treating wounded soldiers.

Surgery has advanced more on the battlefield than perhaps any other medical specialty. A military surgeon is likely to treat more cases of severe trauma in the course of a single engagement than he would in years of civilian practice. A review of twentieth-century surgery underscores how indebted we are to the war-wounded. Every surgical specialty has benefited from the experiences gained in war (the use of blood transfusions is a prime example), and some fields—surgery of the intestine, chest, head, and blood vessels—have been virtually transformed by them. Other disciplines, such as plastic surgery, needed the urgency of war and the plight of its survivors to catapult them into the position of full-fledged, modern specialties. Still other branches of medicine were actually born in the military field hospital—emergency-room medicine and the science of artificial-limb technology, for example. Even the modern urban trauma center, with its rapidly responding medic units providing early intervention, is an outgrowth of war. Physicians and medics with experience in Vietnam have been invaluable in organizing and staffing our large, regionally centralized emergency systems.

Significant advances have been made in other areas of medicine as well. Progress in combating infection and disease made World War II the first conflict in which an American soldier was more likely to die from his battlefield injuries than from infectious disease. Preventing and treating infectious disease, therefore, have had tremendous strategic importance: Typhus, typhoid, syphilis, bubonic plague, and influenza have all played roles in the history of war by sometimes obliterating the advantages of superior force, weapons, or leadership. Military-supported studies of everything from sanitation to drugs and vaccines have benefited not only soldiers but peacetime civilians as well, especially children and pregnant women.

Penicillin, the first potent antibiotic drug, was discovered by Sir Alexander Fleming, who, distressed by the numbers of men he had seen die of infected wounds during World War I, devoted his career to research on antibacterial substances. Although he discovered penicillin before the outbreak of World War II, it was the war's pressing need for antibacterial remedies that inspired the enormous and cooperative effort required to produce the drug. In 1941 there was only enough penicillin to treat a few patients (and it was so precious that it was recovered from the patients' urine and reused), but by the invasion of Normandy in 1944, ample penicillin was being produced to supply the Allied armed forces. Indeed, penicillin was considered of such potential strategic importance that in the early 1940s the scientists working on its development not only made plans to destroy all documents pertaining to their research if the Germans were to invade Britain, but even spread the mold that produces penicillin into the lining of their clothes, where it could be preserved and transported undetected. Today penicillin is an indispensable part of the clinician's armory against disease—another weapon that has made medicine in the latter half of the twentieth century so powerful.

Even the language of war has infiltrated and influenced medical theory. Nineteenth-century theories on disease and the body's defenses were couched in the bombastic rhetoric of imperialistic military strategists: Bacteria were described as rapacious invaders and the immune system as a valiant defending army. Today's understanding of those same bodily forces incorporates the contemporary realization that excessive emphasis on military might has the capacity to be destructive: We now believe that it is the body's own defensive actions that cause the most significant damage in some types of disease.

THE SPECIFIC HISTORY of blood transfusion clearly demonstrates the many ways in which war can stimulate medical progress. War's influence was fundamental to the development of transfusion: It stimulated changes in medical theory, technology, and practice. These changes radically transformed the capacity and scope of medicine. Blood transfusion was a technique almost never used before World War I and infrequently resorted to between the wars, but now it is commonplace. It has made operations ranging from face-lifts to heart transplants possible and safe. How revolutionary the ability to transfuse a patient and the understanding of shock have been to the practice of medicine is hard to overestimate. Resuscitation of trauma victims and advances in anesthesiology, in virtually every type of surgery, and in the treatment of burns, diarrhea, renal failure, anemia, and complications of childbirth are all based, practically and theoretically, on the capacity to transfuse.

Although it seems almost incomprehensible to us now, for thousands of years blood was not regarded as a remedy for hemorrhage. It has, however, been part of the medical and mystical pharmacopoeia from time immemorial. Almost every culture has invested blood with mysterious and powerful properties. It was the food reserved for the angry biblical god, and the bath given to Egyptian pharaohs afflicted with leprosy. Blood was long thought to determine both the physical and mental attributes of a person. Drinks and baths of blood were prescribed for centuries as treatments for madness and the infirmities of old age. To rejuvenate themselves, Romans drank the blood of bulls and gladiators slain in the arena. In 1492 an attempt was made to restore the health of Pope Innocent VIII, sapped by years of debauchery, by giving him the blood of three sacrificed young boys. Blood was also used in the rituals of war and state. The Scythians sealed oaths and treaties by mixing the blood of both parties in a cup of wine and drinking. The Roman devotees of Mithra anointed themselves with bull's blood to give them strength and prowess on the battlefield. And Herodotus describes how the Neurii tribes of central Africa drank the blood of their vanquished enemies to celebrate their victory and honor the victims.

The belief that blood might determine what were deemed to be some of a person's intangible qualities survived to modern times. Until the Korean War, the U.S. Army blood banks classified blood by the race of the donor, and the German blood-banking program established in 1940 permitted only "Aryans" to be blood donors. It is not surprising, then, that when people did begin to consider the possibility of transfusion, it was with the aim of curing madness and decrepitude.

In 1628 William Harvey, physician to James I and Charles I, published his revolutionary book that described the heart's connections to arteries and veins to form a circulatory system. Prior to his work, blood was thought to ebb and flow through the body like the tide, while the heart mixed the blood with a spiritual essence inhaled through the lungs. Harvey's work established the minimum knowledge required to perform a transfusion and inspired a spate of experiments on the circulatory system.

Christopher Wren, the famous English architect and a founder and fellow of the Royal Society of London, and his friend Robert Boyle, the chemist, performed the first well-documented intravenous infusion experiments, injecting opium, wine, and beer into the veins of dogs. Their experiments caught the attention of an Oxford physician, Richard Lower, who became the first person to attempt a direct blood transfusion. In 1665 he transferred the blood from the artery of one dog into the vein of another. He describes the experiment:

> The dog first set up a wailing but soon its strength was exhausted and convulsive twitchings began. In order to resuscitate this animal from such a great loss of its own blood with the blood of another, I securely bound a large hound along the smaller dog and allowed its blood to flow from the cervical artery into [the smaller dog, whose] . . . jugular was again [sewn up] and its chains unleashed. The animal immediately leapt down from the table and apparently forgetful of its injuries, fawned upon its master. It then cleansed itself of blood, rolled in the grass, and apparently was no more inconvenienced than if it had been thrown into a flowing stream. . . .

Lower was so encouraged by his success with dogs that he decided to attempt a human transfusion. (He had no way of knowing that his initial success was due in part to the fact that, unlike humans, canine blood does not naturally contain factors that might make one dog's blood incompatible with another's.) Despite his observation of the marked effects of exsanguination and subsequent replacement of the blood, Lower did not consider transfusion a treatment for blood loss. Transfusion, he wrote, should be used "in arthritic patients and lunatics" who would find "perhaps as much benefit from the infusion of fresh blood as from withdrawl of the old"; exchanging the blood of "Old and Young, Sick and Healthy, Hot and Cold, Fierce and Fearful, Tame and Wild Animals" would also give fruitful results. Samuel Pepys, the chronicler of seventeenth-century English life, echoed Lower's theories on the nature of blood when he commented in his diaries that these experiments "did give occasion to many pretty wishes, as of the blood of a Quaker to be let into an Archbishop."

Accordingly, Lower's first transfusion was undertaken with the aim of calming the "too warm" brain of a "poor" and "debauched" Cambridge cleric (who was paid twenty shillings) by transfusing him with the blood of a docile lamb. The transfusion appeared to be partially successful: The cleric survived and six days later was able to report, in Latin, that he was feeling much better; but he still seemed, at least to Pepys, who heard him give his address, "cracked a little in the head."

Lamentably, other animal-to-human transfusions did not meet with similar success; in fact, they often proved to be fatal. These early patients no doubt died from immune reactions to the foreign blood, infections, complications arising from infusing clotting blood, or from hemorrhage itself. A French physician who claimed to have preceded Lower in conducting the first animal-to-human transfusions was charged with murder when one of his patients died. He was acquitted, but transfusions were soon outlawed throughout Europe.

BLOOD TRANSFUSION was used to treat hemorrhage for the first time during the nineteenth century. Nevertheless, because nothing was understood about the incompatibility of different blood groups or blood coagulation, and aseptic medical technique was still in its infancy, the procedure was rarely successful and therefore used only in the most desperate of cases—above all in obstetrics, and occasionally, during the American Civil War and the Franco-Prussian War, to treat trauma. In these military settings transfusion was used only where there was direct, external evidence of bleeding, because, as we saw with Dr. McGuire, the connection between blood loss and shock was not understood. In *The Medical and Surgical History of the War of Rebellion (1861–65),* a heroic effort at compiling the medical records and experiences of the Civil War, shock is described as "a general perturbation of the nervous system. . . . the person affected turns suddenly pallid. . . . the surface of the body is cooled and bathed in profuse perspiration. . . . the circulation is feeble. . . . the mental condition is one of agitation. . . . this is independent of any loss of blood." The description of men dying of hemorrhage a few pages later in the same tome comments upon their "blanched" appearance, but does not associate this with the pallor of the men in shock.

Despite the observation of one Union physician—who studied the death of men on the battlefield and performed autopsies on many of them—that blood loss was a major, if often unrecognized, cause of death in those who perished, only three cases of transfusion from that war are recorded. It is curious that only three apparently were performed: Two were clearly successful. Private G.P. Cross, a nineteen-year-old wounded in the right leg before Petersburg on June 16, 1864, was transfused with blood by Surgeon E. Bentley, who noted that "immediately after the injection a marked difference was noticed in the patient's pulse, which became stronger. . . ." Private Cross survived his wound and the war. Private J. Mott, thirty-seven years old, also responded well: "The man's general condition was greatly improved. His pulse became fuller and slower, he slept well. . . . altogether the prognosis became more favorable. . . ." Unfortunately for Private Mott, when he hemorrhaged again a week later, he was not transfused again and died the following day. The third man died of his wounds, and no comment is made on the effects of the transfusion.

In 1900 it was discovered that not all human blood is identical, but rather can be classified into groups. Indeed, if the blood from two different groups is mixed, a reaction ensues, causing the blood cells to clump together or burst. This reaction, which was the basis for the discovery of blood incompatibilities, contributed to the failure of many early transfusions. By matching the blood type of donor and recipient, then, the problem of incompatibility is circumvented. Interestingly, the importance of this discovery was not recognized until the increased use of blood transfusions, prompted by the two world wars, made it relevant to most practitioners.

World War I dramatically increased the number of "desperate" cases and so spurred the development of blood-transfusion technology. Three main problems confronted the military surgeon performing a transfusion: blood incompatibilities, blood coagulation, and the lack of an orthodox theory of shock that justified transfusion as a rational treatment. The first two problems were overcome during World War I; the third was to have a devastating effect on how the Americans treated their war-wounded in World War II.

Minimizing the coagulation of blood as it was transferred from donor to recipient allowed blood transfusion to be useful in a military setting. Before this occurred, only direct transfusions were performed, and even these could be complicated by coagulation. Direct transfusions therefore not only could be dangerous, but also were enormously cumbersome. The procedure was not unlike that described by Lower for his dogs, with blood of the donor being transferred immediately into a vein of the recipient. In 1914 and 1915 three different researchers discovered that sodium citrate could act as an anticoagulant without dangerous side effects. Sodium citrate thus made indirect transfusion, and consequently the storage and typing of blood, possible. With stored blood more men could be transfused, and so resuscitation could begin closer to the front. In November 1917, during the Battle of Cambrai, preserved blood was first introduced into a casualty clearing station; by 1918 transfusions performed in advanced dressing stations were keeping men alive until they reached the clearing stations, where they could be operated upon.

Sir Geoffrey Keynes, brother of the famous economist, invented early standard transfusion equipment and wrote the first English-language text on blood transfusions. He described his experience in World War I:

> The donors were chosen by preliminary blood grouping of both patient and prospective donor, a procedure which was still a novelty. Official encouragement took the form of allowing a fortnight's extra leave in "Blighty" (England) to the donors chosen from among the lightly wounded men. Potential donors lined up eagerly for the test—rejection was regarded almost as a slur on their integrity. . . . Transfusion naturally provided an incomparable extension of . . . life-saving surgery. . . . A preliminary transfusion . . . enabled me to do a major amputation single-handed. A second transfusion then established the patient so firmly on the road to recovery that he could be dismissed to the ward without further anxiety. At other times I was greatly distressed by the state of affairs in one large tent known as the "moribund ward." This contained all the patients regarded by a responsible officer as being probably past surgical aid, since it was our duty to operate where there was reasonable hope of recovery, rather than to waste effort where there seemed to be none. The possibility of blood transfusion now raised hopes where formerly there had not been any, and I made it my business during any lull in the work to steal into the moribund ward, choose a patient . . . transfuse him, and carry out the necessary operation. Most of them were suffering primarily from shock and loss of blood, and in this way I had the satisfaction of pulling many men back from the jaws of death.

Despite the dramatic results achieved by transfusions and the technical advances that helped facilitate them, not all the wounded who might have benefited from a transfusion received one. The procedure was unwieldy and blood in short supply. World War I physicians thus began transfusing the wounded with fluids other than blood. This had already been shown to be a successful treatment for those in shock due to the severe dehydration caused by cholera. In an attempt, therefore, to maintain the circulation and to use a solution with bloodlike qualities, they tried infusing a number of solutions, including saline and gum acacia. These solutions were variously successful; nevertheless, it became abundantly clear that the replacement of fluid or volume alone was a remarkable, if temporary, step forward in the treatment of wounded men in shock.

In an article published in 1920, Major W. Richard Ohler argued that hemorrhage is the single most important factor in shock. It was his contention, supported by extensive wartime experience with transfusions, that restoring red blood cells, with their oxygen-carrying capacity, is at least as crucial in the treatment of shock as the replacement of fluid volume. In this view, however, he was not in the majority. This was partly because, in the words of another physician, E.G.C. Bywatters, "'shock' [is] a mysterious condition with as many definitions as there are writers on it." As the symptoms of shock can be caused by things other than hemorrhage, and the amount of blood lost is hard to calculate in the wounded, the importance of red blood cells was not often recognized. It was widely held that a toxin released by damaged tissue caused the lowered blood pressure, the feeble pulse, and the sweaty restlessness of shock. This theory, combined with the effectiveness of fluid replacement and the difficulty of using blood, concentrated much of the interwar research on finding a solution that would be easy to administer and store and that could treat the symptoms of shock. Plasma, the fluid part of blood with the blood cells removed, emerged from this research as the ideal substance. It does not need to be typed, can be frozen and dried, and maintains circulating volume well.

Whatever their views on shock and hemorrhage, Ohler, Keynes, and physicians like them were convinced by their military experience that blood transfusion was an invaluable medical tool. This conviction inspired them to introduce the technique to their skeptical civilian colleagues, who were afraid that transfusion might "get in the way" of surgeons. But now, emboldened by wartime successes, they attempted longer, more complicated operations, and they were pleased with the results.

During this same period, shock continued to be a subject of intense laboratory research. Evidence began accumulating, much of it from the laboratory of Alfred Blalock, that fluid loss at the site of injury was the most important factor in producing circulatory collapse in shock. This began changing the concept of shock, but more firmly entrenched the idea that plasma was an adequate treatment for every type of shock. Although Blalock notes in one of his seminal papers on the subject that following severe trauma it is mostly blood that is lost, he adds that with less severe trauma the escaping fluid is roughly equivalent to plasma. Laboratory animals that had been bled responded nicely to plasma replacement. Therefore, the loss of fluid, not of blood, was considered the main cause of shock. These facts, and the cumbersomeness of using blood, convinced many American physicians, even some of the most learned and astute, that plasma was an adequate treatment for men with traumatic shock.

The Spanish Civil War was the first war in which blood and plasma secured from a civilian population were used to supply medical installations on the front. From August 1936 to January 1939, the Barcelona Blood Transfusion Service collected over 9,000 liters of blood for the Republican army. They maintained a roster of about 28,900 donors, aged eighteen to fifty, whose blood type, syphilis titers, and even psychological profiles were known. The blood was preserved with sodium citrate and glucose in sterile containers and kept under refrigeration. Refrigerated trucks and coolers were used to transport it to the field. The medical staff all had their blood types tested in case stored blood was not available.

The strict protocol for the administration of blood and plasma indicated that the distinction between hemorrhage and traumatic shock was still being made. Men with severe hemorrhage were to get only blood; those with hemorrhage and shock, both blood and plasma; those with shock alone, only plasma. But by the end of the Spanish Civil War, some Republican surgeons were not making this distinction; they realized that hemorrhage could be the cause of shock and that blood was the treatment for it. Joseph Trueta, a renowned Republican surgeon who pioneered and perfected several new surgical techniques during this engagement, wrote that "transfusion with plasma . . . is only a temporary measure, however: the patient needs hemaglobin to combat his anoxemia [lack of oxygen] and for this purpose the presence of red blood corpuscles . . . is essential."

The evangelical zeal of British surgeons like Keynes and the success of the whole-blood service operating on the Republican side during the Spanish Civil War prompted the establishment of a British whole-blood program six months before Great Britain entered World War II. Despite this foresightedness, the British supply-and-distribution system was initially inadequate. At El Alamein, the first major battle in which all medical units, even the most advanced, were supplied with blood, the demand for blood outstripped available resources. In order to augment the blood supply, an enterprising officer, Major G.A. Buttle, sent his men to pick up old beer bottles in the streets of Cairo; these were sterilized, converted into containers for blood, and shipped, refrigerated, to the front. Edward Churchill, a Harvard surgeon who joined the army at the American declaration of war and was sent to North Africa in March 1943, describes visiting this transfusion unit:

> I saw Egyptian civilians sitting on the floor, placing bottles of blood into containers and packing straw around them. It seemed unbelievably primitive and yet, in the opinion of the doctors who needed this blood, Buttle's accomplishments warranted the Victoria Cross. To supply an army with a large quantity of blood in such a manner invited difficulties with putrefaction and infection.

The American preparation for war was far worse in this respect than the British. The development of an American blood service was first considered in May 1940, but not implemented. When the United States entered the war a year and a half later, only a program to collect blood for processing into plasma had begun operation. As the nation was plunged into the war, it became increasingly apparent, at least to those field surgeons who were treating the wounded, that whole blood, not plasma, was crucial to the survival of their patients. The army and the surgeon general, however, were less impressed with the reports they were getting from the North African front than with the fact that plasma was considerably less difficult to preserve, transport, and administer than whole blood. Moreover, although many military surgeons had concluded that shock resulted from loss of blood, theories abounded among civilian and laboratory practitioners supporting the view of plasma as a suitable substitute for whole blood. The use of plasma did save lives; but the use of whole blood would have saved many more. The entries in the diary of Major Kenneth Lowry dated February 2 and 3, 1943, are instructive:

> To date we have lost only one case here, a lower one-third thigh amputation with multiple wounds of the left leg and thigh. He was in profound shock in spite of 1,500cc of plasma, 500cc of blood and lots of glucose. The operation did not increase his shock, but neither did he improve. *Blood is so precious! so urgently needed!* What we do give is being obtained from our own personnel who are most willing, but they really need it themselves after putting in long hours without rest or sleep.
>
> We could not find a donor for a splendid chap from Maine last night. He was in severe shock and needed something in addition to plasma and glucose, so Frosty [a fellow surgeon] gave his blood, took a short rest and went back to operating again. . . . I cannot help but add one remark which I have observed in our work. Dried human plasma is saving hundreds of lives that would surely otherwise be lost. Of course whole blood is better but is more difficult to obtain.

Within two and a half weeks after arriving in North Africa to serve as a consultant in surgery for the U.S. Fifth Army, Edward Churchill sent a memorandum to the army surgeon of the Fifth declaring that blood was the agent of choice in the resuscitation of most casualties, and that the continued dearth of blood and reliance on plasma alone would increase the morbidity and mortality of the wounded. This memorandum was the first of many; he continued to send reports, drawn from meticulous study of British and American casualties, and grew frustrated when his repeated pleas for whole blood and the equipment to procure and store it safely were ignored. His superiors further asked him not to send any personal communications to Washington, but instead allow his information to be transmitted by the appropriate channels. Churchill describes the reception of his reports:

> I was not popular when I said that wound shock is blood volume loss. It is identical with hemorrhage. The wounded require replacement of blood loss. . . . The Theatre Surgeon General, Frederick Blesse, was placed in a difficult situation. I was a new consultant whom he had never seen before and who said: "We must have blood." The Surgeon General had said that we must fight the war on plasma.

Churchill began to feel that a "huge vested interest . . . starting up from assumptions and erroneous thinking" surrounded the program providing plasma to the army. Impressed only by the need for blood and not by military hierarchy or standard procedure, Churchill felt his only recourse was to ask the *New York Times* to report how urgently whole blood was needed and how inadequate plasma was as a substitute. An article appeared on August 26, 1943. "The initial breakthrough," writes Churchill, "thus came with upsetting the balance of power in Washington through the *New York Times* and making people in the States begin to think reasonably about the need to transfuse the wounded and realize that World War II could not be fought on plasma. . . . Soon we were able to get refrigerators for the mobile hospitals. For a long time they had to draw their own blood, but they could draw it in advance of pressing need."

Yet the response elicited by the *Times* article was insufficient. It did not fuel immediate or large-scale reform. The surgeon general, therefore, did not implement plans made in 1943 for the overseas provision of blood to the Mediterranean and European theaters, until the casualties of the Normandy invasion in June 1944, and a personal visit to the Mediterranean theater, convinced him of the urgent need for whole blood. Finally, in August 1944, the 1943 plan was implemented to supply the European theater from the United States, and in November a similar airlift supplied the Pacific. Until then the Americans had had to rely on local blood supplies, often begged from the British. During the invasion of Anzio in 1944, for example, the Fifth Army's surgeon complained to his superiors: "In this tactical situation we must have blood shipped in large quantities to the beachhead. If you don't get it to us, we'll get it from the British." But the British had little or no blood to spare.

At the 1944 meeting of the Southern Surgical Association, Colonel F.S. Gillespie, a British surgeon, commented on the American "borrowing" of blood, aiming his remarks at the "whole blood battlefront":

> I have often wondered at the physiological differences between the British and American soldier. The former, when badly shocked, needs plenty of whole blood, but the American soldier, until recently, has got by with plasma. However, I seemed to observe a change of heart when I was in Normandy recently and found American surgical units borrowing 200–300 pints of blood daily from British Transfusion Units, and I'm sure they were temporarily and perhaps even permanently benefited by having some good British blood in their veins.

Indeed, surgeons were at times so desperate for blood and even plasma with which to treat the wounded that they tried to expand their stores by using bovine serum albumin. By so doing they saved the lives of some, but risked the lives of others. Like Lower and his fellow pioneering blood transfusionists had found before them, World War II physicians encountered some patients who reacted violently to the injection of the blood products of another species. Detailed observations of this phenomenon were made, leading to a greater understanding of human immunological responses.

It was only late in the war that whole blood was readily available to American surgeons. Once implemented, the American blood program was very successful. On Okinawa the treatment of 40,000 casualties involved the use of approximately 40,000 pints of blood, all flown in from the United States. New American equipment also allowed for safer and less complicated blood-banking and was soon adopted by the British. Despite this success, at the end of World War II the Americans disbanded their blood program. They then repeated the mistakes of World War II at the outbreak of the Korean War, when it took six months to establish an adequate and constant supply of blood to U.S. troops.

It is hard to understand why the United States, ignoring the advice of its own field surgeons and of the National Research Council, an organization of scientists established to advise the government on national-security issues, was so slow to establish a whole-blood program in World War II. Perhaps the biggest stumbling block to the establishment of the program was theoretical. Before World War II the concept of shock was still very vague and erroneous in many respects. The absence of a cogent theory explaining the need for blood, combined with the expense of shipping whole blood and provisioning the army with blood-collecting equipment, prompted military administrators to ignore the reports received from their doctors at the front.

In addition, the surgeon general's office harbored the misguided, yet typical, notion that the medical research it supported in U.S. laboratories would provide answers to the problems faced by the surgeons in field hospitals, not the other way around. And although laboratory research was enormously important to the war effort, controlled conditions obtaining in the laboratory yielded results that were not always applicable to the hurly-burly of a field hospital. There is a big difference, for example, between a rabbit that has had 75 percent of its blood volume removed with a syringe in the quiet of its cage and a soldier shot in the gut far from the field station. Thus, the blood-transfusion story can be seen as yet another example of a problem fundamental to military operations: the gap between the front and the rear, which often makes the rear-based bureaucracies unresponsive to the needs of those engaged in combat.

Why the United States, unlike the British, had not learned from the experiences of World War I and the Spanish Civil War is less explicable, particularly when one remembers that Americans developed many of the innovations in transfusion equipment during the earlier war. American medical experience during World War I was limited compared to the British, and for some reason the British medical literature, but not the American, was full of discussion about the successful transfusion techniques used during the Spanish Civil War. Americans were reluctant to become engaged in another European conflict and thus delayed anticipating the needs of war, both medical and military. Furthermore, once it became clear that American involvement in World War II was inevitable, the American government regarded data derived from British medical experiences early in World War II as important military intelligence and so made it unavailable to the people for whom it could have proved invaluable. Edward Churchill, who was a member of the National Research

Council before the United States entered the war, complained: "Any written document, any report regarding the care of the British wounded was a carefully guarded secret. The Office of the Surgeon General of the Army would not allow even the N.R.C. to see such records. All information was filed away under lock and key."

The medical profession was also at fault. No concerted attempt had been made to evaluate the conviction that many World War I surgeons had concerning the importance of red blood cells in the treatment of hemorrhagic shock. No clinical studies comparing the virtues of plasma with those of whole blood were undertaken. And the U.S. Armed Forces embarked on their plans to provide only plasma to the troops with no evidence of protest from the ranks of their own surgeons or those convened by the NRC to advise them. One can only speculate on why it took so long for doctors to endorse the need for whole blood. It is clear that many thought that providing blood, with its need for refrigeration and typing, was impractical. Transfusion with plasma did constitute an improvement over the past in the treatment of shock; and in patients less severely wounded than a soldier—that is, most civilian patients—it must have seemed adequate. Even human error contributed to the initial lack of medical support for instituting a program for the procurement, distribution, and use of blood: In 1941 the NRC's Committee on Transfusions agreed that the U.S. Armed Forces should use whole blood in the treatment of shock; but somehow this opinion was omitted from the minutes of the meeting. Two years later the omission was recognized.

Given the limited number of American surgeons participating in World War I, the discontinuous nature of military surgery as a specialty, and the difficulty of keeping good medical records in the midst of war, it is perhaps understandable that the conviction of those World War I surgeons was not widely appreciated. Nevertheless, the reluctance to accommodate new sources of information or challenge prevailing dogma can be as devastating medically as militarily. During World War II, good medical studies on shock proved, once and for all, that whole blood is the best treatment for hemorrhagic shock. In conducting these studies, the American medical profession finally acknowledged, in the words of medical historian Sir Clifford Allbut, "how fertile the blood of warriors to rearing good surgeons."

WAR AND MEDICINE have had a complex relationship. Medical progress has been stimulated both directly and indirectly by war. Because medical advances can be so crucial to military campaigns, medical research has found a good patron in the armed forces. But perhaps more significantly, medical progress has been a by-product of war. This progress, bought at the enormous cost in human lives that only war would afford, has been the most lasting and vital benefit of war.

*SUMMER 1993*

Margaret B. Wheeler has published numerous articles on scientific matters. She is completing a residency in internal medicine at the University of California at San Francisco.

# 40

# Truman Fires MacArthur

## By David McCullough

*The most famous test of American civil-military relations came in April 1951 when President Harry S. Truman fired General Douglas MacArthur. The tradition of civilian control over military affairs is sacrosanct to American constitutionalism and democracy. It is at the core of the nation's political values. But as the Korean War moved toward its second year, an increasingly unpopular president presiding over an increasingly unpopular war found that his immensely prestigious and popular commander in the Far East would not accept White House control. David McCullough, in an excerpt from his prizewinning biography of Truman, recalls those pivotal personalities and events and the meaning they held for the future of the Republic.*

In the history of American arms, few personal showdowns have been quite so freighted with consequence as the confrontation between Harry S. Truman and Douglas MacArthur. How often do two such major figures find themselves on a collision course, from which neither is willing to veer? On the one hand, there was Truman, the artillery captain of World War I, the accidental president, the surprise election victor of 1948, whose decisions at the start of the Cold War would define the West's diplomatic and military policies for forty years. On the other, there was MacArthur, twice a Medal of Honor winner, the supreme commander of Allied forces in the southwest Pacific during World War II, the sometimes brilliant strategist turned benevolent autocrat who had presided over the reconstruction—and democratization—of Japan. This American Kitchener was a genuine hero; but then (although people did not recognize it at the time), so was Truman. The two men distrusted each other at long distance—they would meet only once. "Mr. Prima Donna, Brass Hat, Five Star MacArthur," Truman had once noted in his diary. "Don't see how a country can produce such men as Robert E. Lee, John J. Pershing, Eisenhower, and Bradley and at the same time produce Custers, Pattons, and MacArthurs." The feeling was mutual.

*It was the crisis of the Korean War that brought on the confrontation. On June 24, 1950, North Korean tanks had crossed the 38th parallel into the Republic of South Korea, in a blitzkrieglike attack. The United States had persuaded the United Nations to intervene, and MacArthur was given overall command. Meanwhile, the outnumbered and outgunned South Korean forces, along with contingents of American troops airlifted from Japan, tried vainly to delay the onslaught of the North Korean "People's Army." In the next months, as disaster changed to triumph and then disaster again, and a third world war loomed, Truman would come to one of the most difficult decisions of his presidency. What follows is excerpted from a book that is already being recognized as one of the signal American biographies of recent years, David McCullough's* Truman, *just published by Simon & Schuster.*

IT WAS, IN MANY RESPECTS, one of the darkest chapters in American military history. But MacArthur, now in overall command of the U.N. forces, was trading space for time—time to pour in men and supplies at the port of Pusan—and the wonder was the North Koreans had been kept from overrunning South Korea straightaway. Despite their suffering and humiliation, the brutal odds against them, the American and Republic of Korea units had done what they were supposed to, almost miraculously. They had held back the landslide, said Truman, who would rightly call it one of the most heroic rearguard actions on record.

In the first week of July, MacArthur requested 30,000 American ground troops, to bring the four divisions of his Eighth Army to full strength. Just days later, on July 9, the situation had become so "critical" that he called for a doubling of his forces. Four more divisions were urgently needed, he said in a cable that jolted Washington.

The hard reality was that the army had only ten divisions. In Western Europe there was but one, and as former British prime minister Winston Churchill noted in a speech in London, the full allied force of twelve divisions in Western Europe faced a Soviet threat of eighty divisions. The NATO allies were exceedingly concerned lest the United States become too involved in distant Korea. Years of slashing defense expenditures, as a means to balance the budget, had taken a heavy toll. For all its vaunted nuclear supremacy, the nation was quite unprepared for war. But now, in these "weeks of slaughter and heartbreak," that was to change dramatically and with immense, far-reaching consequences.

On Wednesday, July 19, first in a special message to Congress, then in an address to the nation, Truman said the attack on Korea demanded that the United States send more men, equipment, and supplies. Beyond that, the realities of the "world situation" required still greater American military strength. He called for an emergency appropriation of $10 billion—the final sum submitted would be $11.6 billion, or nearly as much as the entire $13 billion military budget originally planned for the fiscal year—and announced he was both stepping up the draft and calling up certain National Guard units.

"Korea is a small country thousands of miles away, but what is happening there is important to every American," he told the nation, standing stone-faced in the heat of the television lights, a tangle of wires and cables at his feet. By their "act of raw aggression . . . I repeat, it was raw aggression," the North Koreans had violated the U.N. Charter, and though American forces were making the "principal effort" to save the Republic of South Korea, they were fighting under a U.N. command and a U.N. flag, and this was a "landmark in mankind's long search for a rule of law among nations."

As a call to arms it was not especially inspirational. Nor did he once use the word *war* to describe what was happening in Korea. But then neither was there any question about his sincerity, nor was he the least evasive about what would be asked of the country. The "job" was long and difficult. It meant increased taxes, rationing if necessary, "stern days ahead." In another televised address at summer's end, he would announce plans to double the armed forces to nearly 3 million men. Congress appropriated the money—$48.2 billion for military spending in fiscal 1950–51, then $60 billion for fiscal 1951–52.

Was he considering use of the atomic bomb in Korea, Truman was asked at a press conference the last week of July. No, he said. Did he plan to get out of Washington anytime soon? No. He would stay on the job.

THAT TRUMAN WAS LESS than fond or admiring of his Far Eastern commander, Douglas MacArthur, was well known to his staff and a cause of concern at the Pentagon. Truman's opinion in 1950 seems to have been no different from what it had been in 1945, at the peak of MacArthur's renown, when, in his journal, Truman had described the general as "Mr. Prima Donna, Brass Hat," a "play actor and bunco man." The president, noted his press aide Eben Ayers, expressed "little regard or respect" for MacArthur, calling him a "supreme egotist" who thought himself "something of a god." But working with people whom one did not like or admire was part of life— particularly the politician's life. Firing the five-star Far Eastern commander would have been very nearly unthinkable. John Foster Dulles told Truman confidentially that MacArthur should be dispensed with as soon as possible. Dulles, the most prominent Republican spokesman on foreign policy and a special adviser to the State Department, had returned from a series of meetings with MacArthur in Tokyo convinced the seventy-year-old general was well past his prime and a potential liability. Dulles advised Truman to bring MacArthur home and retire him before he caused trouble. But that, replied Truman, was easier said than done. He reminded Dulles of the reaction there would be in the country, so great was MacArthur's "heroic standing." Nonetheless, at this stage Truman expressed no doubt about MacArthur's ability. If anything, he seems to have been banking on it.

BY THE FIRST WEEK IN AUGUST, American and ROK forces, dug in behind the Naktong River, had set up the final defense line to be known as the Pusan Perimeter, a thinly held front forming an arc of 130 miles around the port of Pusan. On the map it looked like a bare toehold on the peninsula. On the ground the fighting went on as savagely as before. But the retreat was over. At his briefing for the president on Saturday, August 12, in his customary, dry, cautious way, Omar Bradley, the chairman of the Joint Chiefs of Staff, described the situation, for the first time, as "fluid but improving."

Truman's special assistant Averell Harriman, meanwhile, had returned from a hurried mission to Tokyo, bringing the details of a daring new MacArthur plan. Harriman had been dispatched to tell the general of Truman's determination to see that he had everything he needed, but also to impress upon him Truman's urgent desire to avoid any move that might provoke a third world war. This was Truman's uppermost concern, and there must be no misunderstanding. In particular, MacArthur was to "stay clear" of Chiang Kai-shek. Truman had instructed Harriman to tell MacArthur that the Chinese Nationalist leader, now on Formosa, must not become the catalyst for a war with the Chinese Communists.

MacArthur had no reservations about the decision to fight in Korea, "absolutely none," Harriman reported to Truman at Blair House. MacArthur was certain neither the Chinese Communists nor the Soviets would intervene. MacArthur had assured Harriman that of course, as a soldier, he would do as the president ordered concerning Chiang Kai-shek, though something about his tone as he said this had left Harriman wondering.

Of greater urgency and importance was what Harriman had to report of a plan to win the war with one bold stroke. For weeks there had been talk at the Pentagon of a MacArthur strategy to outflank the enemy, to hit from behind, by amphibious landing on the western shore of Korea at the port of Inchon, 200 miles northwest of Pusan. Inchon had tremendous tides— 30 feet or more—and no beaches on which to land, only seawalls. Thus an assault would have to strike directly into the city itself, and only a full tide would carry the landing craft clear to the seawall. In two hours after high tide, the landing craft would be stuck in the mud.

To Bradley it was the riskiest military proposal he had ever heard. But as MacArthur stressed, the Japanese had landed successfully at Inchon in 1904 and the very "impracticabilities" would help ensure the all-important element of surprise. As Wolfe had astonished and defeated Montcalm at Quebec in 1759 by scaling the impossible cliffs near the Plains of Abraham, so, MacArthur said, he would astonish and defeat the North Koreans by landing at the impossible port of Inchon. But there was little time. The attack had to come before the onset of the Korean winter exacted more casualties than the battlefield. The tides at Inchon would be right on September 15. Truman made no commitment one way or the other, but Harriman left Blair House convinced that Truman approved the plan.

BY EARLY AUGUST, GENERAL BRADLEY could tell the president that American strength at Pusan was up to 50,000, which, with another 45,000 ROKs and small contingents of U.N. allies, made a total U.N. ground force of nearly 100,000. Still, the prospect of diverting additional American forces for

MacArthur's Inchon scheme pleased the Joint Chiefs not at all. Bradley continued to view it as "the wildest kind" of plan.

Then, on Saturday, August 26, the Associated Press broke a statement from MacArthur to the Veterans of Foreign Wars, in which he strongly defended Chiang Kai-shek and the importance of Chiang's control of Formosa: "Nothing could be more fallacious than the threadbare argument by those who advocate appeasement and defeatism in the Pacific that if we defend Formosa we alienate continental Asia." It was exactly the sort of dabbling in policy that MacArthur had assured Harriman he would, as a good soldier, refrain from.

Truman was livid. He would later say he considered but rejected the idea of relieving MacArthur of field command then and there and replacing him with Bradley. "It would have been difficult to avoid the appearance of demotion, and I had no desire to hurt General MacArthur personally."

But whatever his anger at MacArthur, to whatever degree the incident had increased his dislike—or distrust—of the general, Truman decided to give MacArthur his backing. "The JCS inclined toward postponing Inchon until such time that we were certain Pusan could hold," remembered Bradley. "But Truman was now committed." On August 28, the Joint Chiefs sent MacArthur their tentative approval.

In time to come, little would be said or written about Truman's part in the matter—that as commander in chief he, and he alone, was the one with the final say on Inchon. He could have said no, and certainly the weight of opinion among his military advisers would have been on his side. But he did not. He took the chance, made the decision for which he was neither to ask nor to receive anything like the credit he deserved.

In the early hours of September 15—it was afternoon in Washington, September 14—the amphibious landing at Inchon began. As promised by MacArthur, the attack took the enemy by total surprise; and as also promised by MacArthur, the operation was an overwhelming success that completely turned the tables on the enemy.

The invasion force numbered 262 ships and 70,000 men of the X Corps, with the 1st Marine Division leading the assault. Inchon fell in little more than a day. In eleven days Seoul was retaken. Meantime, as planned, General Walton Walker's Eighth Army broke out of the Pusan Perimeter and started north. Seldom in military history had there been such a dramatic turn in fortune. By September 27 more than half the North Korean army had been trapped in a huge pincer movement. By October 1, U.N. forces were at the 38th parallel and South Korea was under U.N. control. In two weeks it had become an entirely different war.

In Washington the news was almost unbelievable, far more than anyone had dared hope for. The country was exultant. It was a "military miracle." A jubilant Truman cabled MacArthur: "I salute you all, and say to all of you from all of us at home, 'Well and nobly done.'"

For nearly three months, since the war began, the question had been whether U.N. forces could possibly hang on and survive in Korea. Now, suddenly, the question was whether to carry the war across the 38th parallel and destroy the Communist army and the Communist regime of the north and thereby unify the country. MacArthur favored "hot pursuit" of the enemy. So did the Joint Chiefs, the press, politicians in both parties, and the great majority of the American people. And understandably. It was a heady time; the excitement of victory was in the air. Virtually no one was urging a halt at the 38th parallel. "Troops could not be expected . . . to march up to a surveyor's line and stop," said Secretary of State Dean Acheson.

Truman appears to have been as caught up in the spirit of the moment as anyone. To pursue and destroy the enemy's army was basic military doctrine. If he hesitated or agonized over the decision—one of the most fateful of his presidency—there is no record of it.

The decision was made on Wednesday, September 27. MacArthur's military objective now was "the destruction of the North Korean Armed Forces"—a very different objective from before. He was authorized to cross the 38th parallel, providing there was no sign of major intervention in North Korea by Soviet or Chinese forces. Also, he was not to carry the fight beyond the Chinese or Soviet borders of North Korea. Overall, he was free to do what had to be done to wind up the war as swiftly as possible. George Marshall, now secretary of defense, told him to "feel unhampered tactically and strategically," and when MacArthur cabled, "I regard all of Korea open for military operations," no one objected. Carrying the war north involved two enormous risks—intervention by the Chinese, and winter. But MacArthur was ready to move, and after Inchon, MacArthur was regarded with "almost superstitious awe."

At the end of the first week of October, at Lake Success, New York, the United Nations recommended that all "appropriate steps be taken to ensure conditions of stability throughout Korea," which meant U.N. approval for proceeding with the war. On October 9, MacArthur sent the Eighth Army across the 38th parallel near Kaesong, and on the following day, Truman made a surprise announcement: He was flying to an unspecified point in the Pacific to confer with General MacArthur on "the final phase" in Korea.

IT WAS THE KIND OF GRAND, high-level theater irresistible to the press and the American public. Truman and MacArthur were to rendezvous, as was said, like the sovereign rulers of separate realms journeying to a neutral field attended by their various retainers. The two men had never met. MacArthur had been out of the country since 1937. Truman had never been closer to the Far East than San Francisco.

The meeting place was a pinpoint in the Pacific—Wake Island, a minuscule coral way station beyond the international date line. The presidential expedition was made up of three planes: the *Independence* with Truman and his staff, physician, and Secret Service detail; an Air Force Constellation carrying Harriman, Dean Rusk, and Philip Jessup from the State Department, Army Secretary Frank Pace, Jr., and General Bradley, plus all their aides and secretaries, as well as Admiral Arthur Radford, commander of the Pacific Fleet, who came on board at Honolulu; and a Pan American Stratocruiser with thirty-five correspondents and photographers. General MacArthur flew with several of his staff, a physician, and John Muccio, the American ambassador to South Korea.

As a courtesy, Truman had let MacArthur choose the place for the meeting, and for the president, Wake Island meant a flight across seven time zones, a full round trip from Washington of 14,425 miles, while MacArthur had only to travel 4,000 miles from Tokyo and back. Events were moving rapidly in Korea, Truman would explain, "and I did not feel that he [MacArthur] should be away from his post too long."

To many the whole affair looked like a political grandstand play to capitalize on the sudden, unexpected success of the war and share in MacArthur's Inchon glory on the eve of the off-year elections in November. The president had been out of the headlines for some time, it was noted. Now he was back, and for those Democrats in Congress who were up for reelection, it was "the perfect answer to prayer and fasting." MacArthur himself, en route to Wake Island, appeared disgusted that he had been "summoned for political reasons." In fact, the idea for the meeting had originated with the White House staff as "good election year stuff," Charlie Murphy remembered, and at first Truman had rejected it for that very reason, for being "too political, too much showmanship." Apparently it was only after being reminded that Franklin Roosevelt had made just such a trip to meet with MacArthur at Hawaii in 1944 that Truman changed his mind. He appears to have had second thoughts, even as he flew the Pacific. "I've a whale of a job before me," he wrote on the plane. "Have to talk to God's right-hand man tomorrow. . . ."

The importance of the occasion, like its drama, centered on the human equation, the vital factor of personality. For the first time the two upon whom so much depended, and who were so strikingly different in nature, would be able to appraise one another not at vast distance, or through official communiqué or the views of advisers only, but by looking each other over. As Admiral Radford commented at the time, "Two men can sometimes learn more of each other's minds in two hours, face to face, than in years of correct correspondence." Truman, after returning, would remark simply, "I don't care what they say. I wanted to see General MacArthur, so I went to see him."

Also what would be largely forgotten, or misrepresented by both sides in time to come, after things turned sour, was how the meetings at Wake Island actually went, and what the president and the general actually concluded then, once having met.

TRUMAN'S PLANE PUT down at 6:30 A.M. on Sunday, October 15, just as the sun rose from the sea with spectacular brilliance, backlighting ranks of towering clouds. The single airstrip stretched the length of the island.

MacArthur was there waiting. Later, MacArthur would be pictured deliberately trying to upstage Truman by circling the airstrip, waiting for Truman to land first, thus putting the president in the position of having to wait for the general. But it did not happen that way. MacArthur was not only on the ground, he had arrived the night before and was at the field half an hour early.

As Truman stepped from the plane and came down the ramp, MacArthur stood waiting at the bottom, with "every appearance of warmth and friendliness." And while onlookers noted also that the general failed to salute the president, and though Truman seems to have been somewhat put out by MacArthur's attire—his open-neck shirt and "greasy ham and eggs cap" (MacArthur's famed, gold-braided World War II garrison cap)—the greeting between them was extremely cordial.

MacArthur held out his hand. "Mr. President," he said, seizing Truman's right arm while pumping his hand, which experienced MacArthur watchers knew to be the number one treatment.

"I've been waiting a long time meeting you, General," Truman said with a broad smile.

"I hope it won't be so long next time, Mr. President," MacArthur said warmly.

Truman was dressed in a dark blue, double-breasted suit and gray Stetson. In Honolulu, he had outfitted his whole staff in Hawaiian shirts, but now he looked conspicuously formal, entirely presidential, and well rested, having slept during most of the last leg of the flight.

For the benefit of the photographers, he and MacArthur shook hands several times again, as a small crowd applauded. Then the two men climbed into the back seat of a well-worn black two-door Chevrolet, the best car available on the island, and drove a short distance to a Quonset hut by the ocean, where, alone, they talked for half an hour.

According to Secret Service Agent Henry Nicholson, who rode in the front seat beside Floyd Boring, the driver, Truman began talking almost immediately about his concern over possible Chinese intervention in Korea. Nicholson would distinctly recall Truman saying, "I have been worried about that."

At the Quonset hut, according to Truman's own account in his *Memoirs,* MacArthur assured him that victory was won in Korea and that the Chinese Communists would not attack. When MacArthur apologized for what he had said in his Veterans of Foreign Wars statement, Truman told him to think no more of it, he considered the matter closed—a gesture that so impressed MacArthur that he later made a point of telling Harriman. What more was said in the Quonset hut is not known, since no notes were taken and no one else was present. But clearly the time served to put both men at ease. Each, to judge by his later comments, concluded that the other was not as he had supposed.

About 7:30 they reemerged in the brilliant morning sunshine and again drove off, now to a flat-roofed, one-story, pink cinderblock shack, a Civil Aeronautics administration building close to the beach where the Japanese had stormed ashore in 1941. Beyond the beach, blue Pacific rollers crashed over the dark hulks of two Japanese landing boats.

Some seventeen advisers and aides were waiting in a large, plain room. Truman, setting a tone of informality, said it was no weather for coats, they should all get comfortable. He sat in his shirtsleeves at the head of a long pine table, MacArthur on his right, Harriman on the left, the rest finding places down the table or aginst the walls. MacArthur, taking out a briar pipe, asked if the president minded if he smoked. Everyone laughed. No, Truman said, he supposed he had had more smoke blown his way than any man alive.

The meeting proceeded without formal agenda, and MacArthur later wrote, no new policies or war strategies were proposed or discussed. But the discussion was broad-ranging, with MacArthur doing most of the talking, as Truman, referring only to a few handwritten notes, asked questions. As so often before, MacArthur's performance was masterful. He seemed in full command of every detail and absolutely confident. The time moved swiftly.

MacArthur had only good news to report. The situation in Korea was under control. The war, "the formal resistance," would end by Thanksgiving. The North Korean capital, Pyongyang, would fall in a week. By Christmas he would have the Eighth Army back in Japan. By the first of the year, the United Nations would be holding elections, he expected, and American troops could be withdrawn entirely very soon afterward. "Nothing is gained by military occupation. All occupations are failures," MacArthur declared, to which Truman nodded in agreement.

Truman's first concern was keeping it a "limited" war. What were the chances of Chinese or Soviet intervention, he asked. "Very little," MacArthur said.

> Had they interfered in the first or second months it would have been decisive. We are no longer fearful of their intervention. . . . The Chinese have 300,000 men in Manchuria. Of these probably not more than 100,000 to 125,000 are distributed along the Yalu River. They have no Air Force. Now that we have bases for our Air Force in Korea, if the Chinese tried to get down to Pyongyang there would be the greatest slaughter.

The Russians, MacArthur continued, were a different matter. The Russians had an air force in Siberia and could put a thousand planes in action. A combination of Chinese ground troops and Russian air power could pose a problem, he implied. But coordination of air support with operations on the ground was extremely difficult and he doubted they could manage it.

The support he had been given from Washington was surpassing, MacArthur stressed. "No commander in the history of war," he said, looking around the table, "has ever had more complete and adequate support from all agencies in Washington than I have." How soon could he release a division for duty in Europe, Bradley wished to know. By January, MacArthur assured him.

Dean Rusk, concerned that the discussion was moving too fast, passed Truman a note suggesting he slow down the pace. Too brief a meeting, Rusk felt, would only fuel the cynicism of a press already dubious about the meeting. Truman scribbled a reply: "Hell, no! I want to get out of here before we get into trouble."

As to the need for additional U.N. troops, MacArthur would leave that for Washington to decide. It was then, at about 9:05, that Truman called a halt. "No one who was not here would believe we have covered so much ground as we have been actually able to cover," he said. He suggested a break for lunch while a communiqué was prepared. But MacArthur declined, saying he was anxious to get back to Tokyo and would like to leave as soon as possible—which to some in the room seemed to border on rudeness. "Whether intended or not," wrote Bradley, "it was insulting to decline lunch with the President, and I think Truman was miffed, although he gave no sign."

"The communiqué should be submitted as soon as it is ready, and General MacArthur can return immediately," Truman said. The conference had lasted one hour, thirty-six minutes.

IN LATER STUDIES, some historians would write that Truman had traveled extremely far for not much. But to Truman, at the time, it had all been worth the effort. He was exuberant. He had never had a more satisfactory conference, he told the reporters present. Tony Leviero of the *New York Times* described him beaming "like an insurance salesman who had at last signed up an important prospect."

The communiqué, which MacArthur read and initialed, stressed "the very complete unanimity of view" that had made possible such rapid progress at the conference table and called MacArthur "one of America's great soldier-statesmen." At the airstrip, in a little ceremony just before boarding his plane, Truman said still more as he honored MacArthur with a Distinguished Service Medal. He praised MacArthur for "his vision, his judgment, his indomitable will and unshakable faith," his "gallantry and tenacity" and "audacity in attack matched by few operations in history."

The whole spirit of Wake Island was one of relief and exhilaration. The awful bloodshed in Korea, the suffering, was all but over; the war was won. If MacArthur said there was "very little" chance of the Chinese coming in, who, after Inchon, was to doubt his judgment, particularly if what he said confirmed what was thought in Washington? If Truman and MacArthur had disliked or distrusted one another before, they apparently did so no longer. If the conference had accomplished that alone, it had been a success.

They said good-bye in the glaring sunshine of midday at Wake Island, as Truman boarded the *Independence*.

"Good-bye, sir," MacArthur said. "Happy landing. It has been a real honor talking to you."

It was their first and their last meeting. They never saw each other again.

NOVEMBER THROUGH DECEMBER 1950 was a dreadful passage for Truman. Omar Bradley was to call these sixty days among the most trying of his own professional career, more so even than the Battle of the Bulge. For Truman it was the darkest, most difficult period of his presidency.

That Chinese troops had come into the war was by now an established fact, though how many there were remained in doubt. MacArthur estimated 30,000, and whatever the number, his inclination was to discount their importance. But in Washington concern mounted. To check the flow of Chinese troops coming across the Yalu, MacArthur requested authority to bomb the Korean ends of all bridges on the river, a decision Truman approved, after warning MacArthur against enlarging the war and specifically forbidding air strikes north of the Yalu, on Chinese territory.

Another cause of concern was MacArthur's decision, in the drive north, to divide his forces, sending the X Corps up the east side of the peninsula, the Eighth Army up the west—an immensely risky maneuver that the Joint Chiefs questioned. But MacArthur was adamant, and it had been just such audacity, after all, that had worked the miracle at Inchon.

With one powerful, "end-the-war" offensive, one "massive comprehensive envelopment," MacArthur insisted, the war would be quickly won. As always, he had absolute faith in his own infallibility, and while no such faith was to be found at the Pentagon or the White House, no one, including Truman, took steps to stop him.

Bitterly cold winds from Siberia swept over North Korea, as MacArthur flew to Eighth Army headquarters on the Chongchon River to see the attack begin. "If this operation is successful," he said within earshot of correspondents, "I hope we can get the boys home for Christmas."

The attack began Friday, November 24, the day after Thanksgiving. Four days later, on Tuesday, November 28, in Washington, at 6:15 in the morning, General Bradley telephoned the president at Blair House to say he had "a terrible message" from MacArthur.

"WE'VE GOT A TERRIFIC SITUATION on our hands," Truman told his staff a few hours later at the White House, having waited patiently through the routine of the morning meeting. The Chinese had launched a furious counterattack with a force of 260,000 men, Truman said. MacArthur was going over on the defensive. "The Chinese have come in with both feet."

Truman paused. The room was still. The shock of what he had said made everyone sit stiff and silent. Everything that had seemed to be going so well in Korea, all the heady prospects since Inchon, the soaring hopes of Wake Island were gone in an instant. But then Truman seemed to recover himself, sitting up squarely in his high-backed chair. "We have got to meet this thing," he said, his voice low and confident. "Let's go ahead now and do our jobs as best we can."

"WE FACE AN ENTIRELY NEW WAR," MacArthur declared. It had been all of three days since the launching of his "end-the-war" offensive, yet all hope of victory was gone. The Chinese were bent on the "complete destruction" of his army. "This command . . . is now faced with conditions beyond its control and its strength."

In further messages MacArthur called for reinforcements of the "greatest magnitude," including Chinese Nationalist troops from Formosa. His own troops were "mentally fatigued and physically battered." The directives he was operating under were "completely outmoded by events." He wanted a naval blockade of China. He called for bombing the Chinese mainland. He must have the authority to broaden the conflict, MacArthur insisted, or the administration would be faced with a disaster.

THAT SAME DAY, NOVEMBER 28, at three o'clock in the afternoon, a crucial meeting of the National Security Council took place in the Cabinet Room— one of the most important meetings of the Truman years. For it was there and then, in effect, with Truman presiding, that the decision was made not to let the crisis in Korea, however horrible, flare into a world war. It was a decision as fateful as the one to go into Korea in the first place, and stands among the triumphs of the Truman administration, considering how things might have gone otherwise.

General Bradley opened the discussion with a review of the bleak situation on the battlefield. Vice President Alben Barkley, who rarely spoke at such meetings, asked bitterly why MacArthur had promised to have "the boys home for Christmas"—how he could ever have said such a thing in good faith. Army Secretary Pace said that MacArthur was now denying he had made the statement. Truman warned that in any event they must do nothing to cause the commander in the field to lose face before the enemy.

When Marshall spoke, he sounded extremely grave. American involvement in Korea should continue as part of a U.N. effort, Marshall said. The United States must not get "sewed up" in Korea, but find a way to "get out with honor." There must be no war with China. That was clear. "To do this would be to fall into a carefully laid Russian trap. We should use all available political, economic and psychological action to limit the war."

"We can't defeat the Chinese in Korea," said Acheson. "They can put in more than we can." Concerned that MacArthur might overextend his operations, Acheson urged "very, very careful thought" regarding air strikes against Manchuria. If this became essential to save American troops, then it would have to be done, but if American attacks succeeded in Manchuria, the Soviets would probably come to the aid of their Chinese ally. The thing to do, the "imperative step," said Acheson, was to "find a line that we can hold, and hold it." Behind everything they faced was the Soviet Union, "a somber consideration." The threat of a larger war, wrote Bradley, was closer than ever, and it was this, the dread prospect of a global conflict with Russia erupting at any hour, that was on all their minds.

THE NEWS WAS SO TERRIBLE AND CAME WITH SUCH SUDDENNESS that it seemed almost impossible to believe. The last thing anyone had expected at this point was defeat in Korea. The evening papers of November 28 described "hordes of Chinese Reds" surging through a widening gap in the American Eighth Army's right flank, "as the failure of the Allied offensive turned into a dire threat for the entire United Nations line." The whole Eighth Army was falling back. "200,000 OF FOE ADVANCE UP TO 23 MILES IN KOREA" read the banner headline across the *New York Times* the following day. The two calamities most dreaded by military planners—the fierce Korean winter and massive intervention by the Chinese—had fallen on the allied forces at once.

What had begun was a tragic, epic retreat—some of the worst fighting of the war—in howling winds and snow and temperatures as much as 25 degrees below zero. The Chinese not only came in "hordes" but took advantage of MacArthur's divided forces, striking both on their flanks. The Eighth Army under General Walton Walker was reeling back from the Chongchon River, heading for Pyongyang. The choice was retreat or annihilation. In the northeast the ordeal of the X Corps was still worse. The retreat of the 1st Marine Division—from the Chosin Reservoir forty miles to the port of Hungnam and evacuation—would be compared to Xenophon's retreat of the immortal ten thousand or Napoleon's withdrawal from Moscow.

"A lot of hard work was put in," Truman would remember of his own days in Washington. And, as Acheson would write, all the president's advisers, civilian and military, knew something was badly wrong in Korea, other than just the onslaught of the Chinese. There were questions about MacArthur's morale, grave concern over his strategy and whether on the actual battlefield a "new hand" was needed to replace General Walker. It was quite clear, furthermore, that MacArthur, the Far Eastern commander, had indeed deliberately disobeyed a specific order from the Joint Chiefs to use no non-Korean forces close to the Manchurian border.

But no changes in strategy were ordered. No "new hand" replaced Walker. No voices were raised against MacArthur. Regrettably, the president was ill-advised, Bradley later observed. He, Marshall, the Joint Chiefs, had all "failed the president." Here, in a crucial few days, said Acheson afterward, they missed their chance to halt the march to disaster in Korea. Acheson was to lament their performance for the rest of his life. Truman would never put any blame on any of them, but Acheson would say Truman had deserved far better.

General Matthew Ridgway would "well remember" his mounting impatience "that dreary Sunday, December 3," as hour after hour in the War Room discussion continued over the ominous situation in Korea. Unable to contain himself any longer, Ridgway spoke up, saying immediate action must be taken. They owed it to the men in the field and "to the God to whom we must answer for those men's lives," to stop talking and do something. For the first time, Acheson later wrote, "someone had expressed what everyone thought—that the Emperor had no clothes on." But of the twenty men who sat at the table, including Acheson, and twenty more along the walls behind, no one else spoke. The meeting ended without a decision.

Why didn't the Joint Chiefs just send orders and tell MacArthur what to do, Ridgway asked the air force chief of staff, General Hoyt Vandenberg, afterward. Because MacArthur would not obey such orders, Vandenberg replied. Ridgway exploded. "You can relieve any commander who won't obey orders, can't you?" he said. But Vandenberg, with an expression Ridgway remembered as both puzzled and amazed, only walked away.

The next day, in another closed session, this time at the State Department, Dean Rusk would propose that MacArthur be relieved of command. But again, no one else commented.

MacArthur, meanwhile, was being taken to task by the press, as he had never been. *Time,* which had long glorified him, charged him with being responsible for one of the worst military disasters in history. An editorial in the *New York Herald-Tribune* referred to his "colossal military blunder." Unused to such criticism, his immense vanity wounded, MacArthur started issuing statements of his own to the press. He denied that his strategy had precipitated the Chinese invasion and said his inability to defeat the new enemy was due to restrictions imposed by Washington that were "without precedent."

Truman did not hold MacArthur accountable for the failure of the November offensive. But he deplored MacArthur's way of excusing the failure, and the damage his statements could do abroad, to the degree that they implied a change in American policy. "I should have relieved general MacArthur then and there," he would write much later.

As it was, he ordered that all military officers and diplomatic officials henceforth clear with the State Department all but routine statements before making them public, "and . . . refrain from direct communications on military or foreign policy with newspapers, magazines, and other publicity media." Dated December 6, the order was widely and correctly seen as directed to MacArthur.

Truman did not relieve the Far Eastern commander, he later explained, because he knew no general could be a winner every day and because he did not wish to have it appear that MacArthur was being fired for failing. What he might have done had Acheson, Marshall, Bradley, and the Joint Chiefs spoken up and insisted that MacArthur be relieved is another question and impossible to answer.

For now the tragedy in Korea overshadowed the rest. If MacArthur was in trouble, then everything possible must be done to help. "We must get him out of it if we can," Truman wrote in his diary late the night of December 2, following an intense session with Acheson, Marshall, and Bradley that had left him feeling desperately low. The talk had been of evacuating all American troops. Marshall was not even sure such an operation would succeed, should the Chinese bring in their own air power. "*It looks very bad,*" Truman wrote. Yet bad as it was, there was no mood of panic, and this, as those around him would later attest, was principally because of Truman's own unflinching response.

The bloody retreat in Korea continued. Pyongyang fell "to overwhelming masses of advancing Chinese," as the papers reported. General Walker's Eighth Army was heading for the 38th parallel. But Truman remained calm and steady. He wrote in his diary, "I've worked for peace for five years and six months and it looks like World War III is here. I hope not—but we must meet whatever comes—and we will."

IT WAS HARRY TRUMAN'S LONG-STANDING CONVICTION that if you did your best in life, did your "damndest" always, then whatever happened you would at least know it was not for lack of trying. But he was a great believer also in the parts played by luck and personality, forces quite beyond effort or determination. And though few presidents had ever worked so hard, or taken their responsibilities so to heart in time of crisis as Truman had since the start of the war in Korea, it was luck, good and bad, and the large influence of personality, that determined the course of events time and again, and never more so than in late December 1950, in the midst of his darkest passage.

Two days before Christmas, on an icy highway north of Seoul, General Walton Walker, commander of the Eighth Army, was killed when his jeep ran head-on into an ROK army truck. Walker's replacement—as requested by MacArthur and approved immediately by Truman—was Matthew Ridgway, who left Washington at once, arriving in Tokyo on Christmas Day. At his meeting with MacArthur the next morning, Ridgway was told to use his own judgment at the front. "The Eighth Army is yours, Matt. Do what you think best." MacArthur, wrote Dean Acheson later, "never uttered wiser words."

That afternoon, Ridgway landed at Taegu, and in the weeks following came a transformation no one had thought possible. Rarely has one individual made so marked a difference in so little time. With what Omar Bradley called "brilliant, driving, uncompromising leadership," Ridgway restored the fighting spirit of the Eighth Army and turned the tide of war as have few commanders in history.

Since the Chinese onslaught of November 28, the Eighth Army had fallen back nearly 300 miles, to a point just below the 38th parallel, and for a while Ridgway had no choice but to continue the retreat. Abandoning Seoul, Ridgway withdrew as far as Oswan, near the very point where the first green American troops had gone into action in July. Now, instead of the murderous heat of summer, they fought in murderous cold.

The mood in Washington remained bleak. MacArthur continued to urge a widening of the war—again he proposed bombing and blockading China and utilizing the troops of Chiang Kai-shek—and, as before, his proposals were rejected. Dire consequences would follow, he implied, unless policy were changed. He reported:

> The troops are tired from a long and difficult campaign, embittered by the shameful propaganda which has falsely condemned their courage and fighting qualities . . . and their morale will become a serious threat in their battlefield efficiency unless the political basis upon which they are being asked to trade life for time is clearly delineated. . . .

Truman found such messages "deeply disturbing." When a general complained about his troops' morale, observed Marshall, the time had come for the general to look to his own morale.

MacArthur called on the administration to recognize the "state of war" imposed by the Chinese, then to drop thirty to fifty atomic bombs on Manchuria and the mainland cities of China. The Joint Chiefs, too, told Truman that mass destruction of Chinese cities with nuclear weapons was the only way to affect the situation in Korea. But that choice was never seriously considered. Truman simply refused to "go down that trail," in Dean Rusk's words.

Truman also still refused to reprimand MacArthur. Rather he treated MacArthur with what Acheson considered "infinite patience"—too much infinite patience, Acheson thought, having by now concluded that the general was "incurably recalcitrant" and fundamentally disloyal to the purposes of his commander in chief.

TRUMAN HAD BY NOW declared a national emergency, announcing emergency controls on prices and wages, and still greater defense spending—to the amount of $50 billion, more than four times the defense budget at the start of the year. He had put Charles E. Wilson, head of the General Electric Company, in charge of a new Office of Defense Mobilization; appointed General Eisenhower as supreme commander of NATO; and, in a radio and television address to the nation on December 15, called on every citizen "to put aside his personal interests for the good of the country." So while doing all he could to avoid a wider war, he was clearly preparing for one. As Marshall later attested, "We were at our lowest point."

But then, on the morning of Wednesday, January 17, Marshall telephoned Truman to read an astonishing report just in from General Joe Collins, who had flown to Korea for talks with Ridgway. "Eighth Army in good shape and improving daily under Ridgway's leadership," Marshall read. "Morale very satisfactory. . . . Ridgway confident he can obtain two to three months' delay before having to initiate evacuation. . . . On the whole Eighth Army now in position and prepared to punish severely any mass attack."

Plainly MacArthur's bleak assessment of the situation, his forecasts of doom, had been wrong—and the effect of this realization was electrifying. As word spread through the upper levels of government that day, it would be remembered, one could almost hear the sighs of relief. The long retreat of the Eighth Army—the longest in American military history—had ended. On January 25, 1951, less than a month after Ridgway's arrival, the Eighth Army began "rolling forward," as he said.

By the end of March, having inflicted immense casualties on the Chinese, the Eighth Army was again at the 38th parallel. Yet Ridgway's progress seemed only to distress MacArthur further. Unless he was allowed to strike boldly at the enemy, he said, his dream of a unified Korea was impossible. He complained of a "policy void." He now proposed not only to massively attack Manchuria, but to "sever" Korea from Manchuria by laying down a field of radioactive wastes, "the by-products of atomic manufacture," all along the Yalu River. As so often before, his request was denied.

Talking to journalists on March 7, MacArthur lamented the "savage slaughter" of Americans inevitable in a war of attrition. When, by the middle of March, the tide of battle "began to turn in our favor," as Truman wrote, and Truman's advisers at both the State Department and the Pentagon thought it time to make a direct appeal to China for peace talks, MacArthur refused to respond to inquiries on the subject. Instead he decried any "further military restrictions" on his command. To MacArthur, as he later wrote, it appeared that Truman's nerves were at a breaking point—"not only his nerves, but what was far more menacing in the Chief Executive of a country at war—his nerve."

Truman ordered careful preparation of a cease-fire proposal. On March 21, the draft of a presidential statement was submitted for approval to the other seventeen U.N. nations with troops serving in Korea. On March 20 the Joint Chiefs had informed MacArthur of what was happening—sending him what Truman called the "meat paragraphs" of the statement in a message that seems to have impressed MacArthur as nothing else had that there was indeed to be no all-out war with Red China. His response so jarred Washington as to leave a number of people wondering if perhaps he had lost his mind. Years afterward Bradley would speculate that possibly MacArthur's realization that his war on China was not to be "snapped his brilliant but brittle mind."

On the morning of Saturday, March 24, in Korea (Friday the 23rd in Washington), MacArthur, without warning, tried to seize the initiative in a manner calculated only to inflame the situation. He issued his own florid proclamation to the Chinese Communists—in effect, an ultimatum. He began by taunting the Red Chinese for their lack of industrial power, their poor military showing in Korea against a U.N. force restricted by "inhibitions." More seriously, MacArthur threatened to expand the war.

> The enemy, therefore, must by now be painfully aware that a decision of the United States to depart from its tolerant effort to contain the war to the areas of Korea, through an expansion of our military operations to his coastal areas and interior bases, would doom Red China to the risk of imminent military collapse.

In conclusion, MacArthur said he personally "stood ready at any time" to meet with the Chinese commander to reach a settlement.

All Truman's careful preparations of a cease-fire proposal were now in vain. MacArthur had cut the ground out from under him. Later MacArthur would dismiss what he had said as a "routine communiqué." Yet his own devoted aide, General Courtney Whitney, would describe it as a bold effort to stop one of the most disgraceful plots in American history, meaning the administration's plan to appease China.

In his *Memoirs,* Truman would write that he now knew what he must do about MacArthur.

> This was a most extraordinary statement for a military commander of the United Nations to issue on his own responsibility. It was an act totally disregarding all directives to abstain from any declarations on foreign policy. It was in open defiance of my orders as President and as Commander in Chief. This was a challenge to the President under the Constitution. It also flouted the policy of the United Nations. . . .
>
> By this act MacArthur left me no choice—I could no longer tolerate his insubordination. . . .

And yet . . . MacArthur was not fired. Truman said not a word suggesting he had reached such a decision. He sent MacArthur only a restrained reprimand, a message he himself dictated to remind the general of the presidential order on December 6 forbidding public statements that had not been cleared with Washington.

Meantime, on March 14, the Gallup poll had reported the president's public approval at an all-time low of 26 percent. And soon there were appalling new statistics: U.N. forces had now suffered 228,941 casualties, mostly South Koreans but including 57,120 Americans.

TRUMAN WAS DWELLING on the relationship between President Abraham Lincoln and General George B. McClellan during the Civil War, in the autumn of 1862, when Lincoln had been forced to relieve McClellan of command of the Army of the Potomac. Truman had sent one of his staff to the Library of Congress to review the details of the Lincoln-McClellan crisis and give him a report. Lincoln's troubles with McClellan, as Truman knew, had been the reverse of his own with MacArthur: Lincoln had wanted McClellan to attack, and McClellan refused time and again. But then, when Lincoln issued orders, McClellan, like MacArthur, ignored them. Also like MacArthur, McClellan occasionally made political statements on matters outside the military field. Truman later wrote that

> Lincoln was patient, for that was his nature, but at long last he was compelled to relieve the Union Army's principal commander. And though I gave this difficulty with MacArthur much wearisome thought, I realized that I would have no other choice myself than to relieve the nation's top field commander. . . .
>
> I wrestled with the problem for several days, but my mind was made up before April 5, when the next incident occurred.

On Thursday, April 5, at the Capitol, House Minority Leader Joe Martin took the floor to read a letter from MacArthur that Martin said he felt duty-bound to withhold no longer. In February, speaking in Brooklyn, Martin had called for the use of Chiang Kai-shek's troops in Korea and accused the administration of a defeatist policy. "What are we in Korea for—to win or to lose? . . . If we are not in Korea to win, then this administration should be indicted for the murder of American boys." Martin had sent a copy of the speech to MacArthur, asking for his "views." On March 20, MacArthur had responded—and virtually all that he said was bound to provoke Truman, as Martin well knew. Since MacArthur's letter carried no stipulation of confidentiality, Martin decided to make it public.

The congressman was right in calling for victory, MacArthur wrote, right in wanting to see Chinese forces from Formosa join the battle against communism. The real war against communism was in Asia, not in Europe. "There is no substitute for victory."

The letter was on the wires at once. At the Pentagon, Bradley called a meeting of the Joint Chiefs. "I did not know that Truman had already made up his mind to relieve MacArthur," he remembered, "but I thought it was a strong possibility." The Joint Chiefs, however, reached no conclusion about MacArthur.

On Friday, April 6, official Cadillacs filled the White House driveway. Marshall, Bradley, Acheson, and Harriman met with the president for an hour. Saying nothing of his own views, Truman asked what should be done. When Marshall urged caution, Acheson agreed. To the latter it was not so much a problem of what should be done as how it should be done. He later remembered:

> The situation could be resolved only by relieving the General of all his commands and removing him from the Far East. Grave trouble would result, but it could be surmounted if the President acted upon the carefully considered advice and unshakable support of all his civilian and military advisers. If he should get ahead of them or appear to take them for granted or be impetuous, the harm would be incalculable.

"If you relieve MacArthur," Acheson told Truman, "you will have the biggest fight of your administration."

Harriman, reminding the president that MacArthur had been a problem for too long, said he should be dismissed at once. "I don't express any opinion or make known my decision," Truman wrote in his diary. "Direct the four to meet again Friday afternoon and go over all phases of the situation."

He was a model of self-control. For the next several days, an air of unnatural calm seemed to hang over the White House. "The wind died down," remembered Joe Martin. "The surface was placid . . . nothing happened."

On Saturday, Truman met again with Marshall, Acheson, Bradley, and Harriman, and again nothing was resolved. Marshall and Bradley were still uncertain what to do. They were hesitating in part, according to Bradley's later account, because they knew the kind of abuse that would be hurled at them personally—an understandable concern for two such men at the end of long, distinguished careers.

On Monday, April 9, the same foursome convened with the president once more, this time at Blair House. But now the situation had changed. The Joint Chiefs had met the afternoon before and concluded that from a military point of view, MacArthur should be relieved. Their opinion was unanimous. Truman, for the first time, said he was of the same opinion. He had made his decision. He told Bradley to prepare the necessary papers.

"RARELY HAD A MATTER been shrouded in such secrecy at the White House," reported the *Washington Post* on Tuesday, April 10. "The answer to every question about MacArthur was met with a 'no comment' reply." In Tokyo, according to a United Press dispatch, a member of MacArthur's staff said meetings between the general and Secretary of the Army Pace were "going forward with an air of cordiality"—thus seeming to refute dismissal rumors. A photograph on page 1 of the *Post* showed a smiling MacArthur welcoming an even more smiling Pace at the Tokyo airport.

AT THE END OF A ROUTINE MORNING STAFF MEETING, the president quietly announced—"So you won't have to read about it in the papers"—that he had decided to fire General MacArthur. He was sure, Truman added, that

MacArthur had wanted to be fired. He was sure also that he himself faced a political storm, "a great furor," unlike any in his political career. From beyond the office windows, the noise of construction going on in the White House was so great that several of the staff had to strain to hear Truman. At 3:15 that afternoon, Acheson, Marshall, Bradley, and Harriman reported to the Oval Office, bringing the drafted orders. Truman looked them over, borrowed a fountain pen, and signed his name.

The orders were to be sent by State Department channels to Ambassador Muccio in Korea, who was to turn them over to Secretary Pace, who by now was also in Korea, with Ridgway at Eighth Army headquarters. Pace was to return at once to Tokyo and personally hand the orders to MacArthur—this whole relay system having been devised to save the general from the embarrassment of direct transmission through regular army communications. All aspects of the issue thus far had been kept secret with marked success, but it was essential that there be no leaks in the last critical hours. Announcement of the sensational news about MacArthur was not to be made until the following morning.

The next several hours passed without incident, until early evening. Harriman, Bradley, Rusk, and six or seven of Truman's staff were working in the Cabinet Room, preparing material for release, when Press Secretary Joe Short received word that a Pentagon reporter for the *Chicago Tribune,* Lloyd Norman, was making inquiries about a supposed "major resignation" to take place in Tokyo—the implication being that somehow MacArthur had already learned of Truman's decision and was about to resign before Truman could fire him.

Bradley telephoned Truman at about nine o'clock to report there had been a leak. Truman, saying he wanted time to think, told Bradley to find Marshall and Acheson. Marshall, it was learned, had gone to a movie, but Acheson came to the White House immediately; he thought it would be a mistake to do anything rash because of one reporter's inquiry. As he had from the start, Acheson stressed the importance of the manner in which the general was dismissed. It was only fair and proper that he be informed before the story broke.

Meantime, something apparently had gone wrong with the transmission of the president's orders. Nothing had been heard from Muccio about their receipt. By 10:30, Truman had decided. Short telephoned the White House to have all the orders—those relieving MacArthur, as well as those naming Matthew Ridgway his successor—mimeographed as quickly as possible.

"He's not going to be allowed to quit on me," Truman reportedly said. "He's going to be fired!" In his diary Truman recorded dryly, "Discussed the situation and I ordered messages sent at once and directly to MacArthur."

From a small first-floor study in his Georgetown home, Dean Acheson began placing calls to various officials. At the State Department, Rusk spent a long night telephoning the ambassadors of all the countries with troops in Korea. "Well, the little man finally did it, didn't he," responded the ambassador from New Zealand.

At the White House, switchboard operators began calling reporters at their homes to say there would be an extraordinary press conference at 1:00 A.M. And at 1:00 A.M. on Wednesday, April 11, Press Secretary Joe Short handed out the mimeographed sheets in the White House pressroom. Truman, in his second-floor bedroom at Blair House, was by then fast asleep.

GENERAL MACARTHUR LEARNED OF HIS RECALL while at lunch in Tokyo, when his wife handed him a brown Signal Corps envelope. If Truman had only let him know how he felt, MacArthur would say privately a few hours later, he would have retired "without difficulty." Where the *Tribune* reporter got his tip was never revealed. MacArthur would later testify that he had never given any thought to resigning.

According to what MacArthur said he had been told by an unnamed but "eminent" medical authority, Truman's "mental instability" was the result of malignant hypertension, "characterized by bewilderment and confusion of thought." Truman, MacArthur predicted, would be dead in six months.

## TRUMAN FIRES MACARTHUR

The headline across the early edition of the *Washington Post* on April 11, 1951, was the headline everywhere in the country and throughout much of the world, with only minor variations. The reaction was stupendous, the outcry from the American people shattering. Truman had known he would have to face a storm, but however dark his premonitions he could not possibly have measured what was coming. No one did; no one could have.

The day on Capitol Hill was described as "one of the bitterest . . . in modern times." Prominent Republicans, including Senator Robert Taft, spoke angrily of impeaching the president. The full Republican leadership held an emergency meeting in Joe Martin's office at 9:30 in the morning, after which Martin talked to reporters of "impeachments," the accent on the plural. "We might want the impeachments of 1 or 50." A full-dress congressional investigation of the president's war policy was in order. General MacArthur, announced Martin, would be invited to air his views before a joint session of Congress.

In New York, 2,000 longshoremen walked off their jobs in protest over the firing of MacArthur. A Baltimore women's group announced plans for a march on Washington in support of the general. Elsewhere, enraged patriots flew flags at half-staff, or upside down. People signed petitions and fired off furious letters and telegrams to Washington. In Worcester, Massachusetts, and San Gabriel, California, Truman was burned in effigy. In Houston, a Protestant minister became so angry dictating a telegram to the White House that he died of a heart attack.

In the hallways of the Senate and House office buildings, Western Union messengers made their deliveries with bushel baskets. According to one tally, of the 44,358 telegrams received by Republicans in Congress during the first forty-eight hours following Truman's announcement, all but 334 condemned him or took the side of MacArthur, and the majority called for Truman's immediate removal from office.

A number of prominent liberals—Eleanor Roosevelt, Walter Reuther, Justice William O. Douglas—publicly supported Truman. Further, throughout Europe, MacArthur's dismissal was greeted as welcome news. But most impressive was the weight of editorial opinion at home in support of Truman—including some staunch Republican newspapers—despite vehement assaults in the McCormick, Hearst, and Scripps-Howard papers, as well as the renewed glorification of MacArthur in Henry Luce's *Time* and *Life*.

Nothing had so stirred the political passions of the country since the Civil War. At the heart of the tumult was anger and frustration over the war in Korea. Senator Kenneth Wherry had begun calling it "Truman's War," and the name caught on. People were sick of Truman's War, frustrated, and a bit baffled by talk of a "limited war." America didn't fight to achieve a stalemate, and the cost in blood had become appalling. The country wanted it over. MacArthur at least offered victory.

EXCEPT FOR A BRIEF BROADCAST from the White House the night after his dismissal of MacArthur, Truman maintained silence on the matter. General MacArthur was "one of our greatest military commanders," he told the nation, but the cause of world peace was far more important than any individual.

MacArthur landed at San Francisco on Tuesday, April 17, to a delirious reception. He had been away from the country for fourteen years. Until now, the American people had had no chance to see and cheer him, to welcome the hero home. Ten thousand were at the San Francisco airport. So great were the crowds on the way into the city, it took two hours for the motorcade to reach his hotel. "The only politics I have," MacArthur told a cheering throng, "is contained in a simple phrase known to all of you—God Bless America."

When Truman met with reporters the next day, at his first press conference since the start of the crisis, he dashed all their expectations by refusing to say anything on the subject. Scheduled to appear before the American Society of Newspaper Editors on Thursday, April 19, the day MacArthur was to go before Congress, Truman canceled his speech, because he felt it should be the general's day and did not wish anything to detract from it.

There would be "hell to pay" for perhaps six or seven weeks, he told his staff and the Cabinet. But eventually people would come to their senses, including more and more Republican politicians who would grow doubtful of all-out support for the general. Given some time, MacArthur would be reduced to human proportions. Meanwhile, Truman could withstand the bombardment, for in the long run, he knew, he would be judged to have made the right decision. He had absolutely no doubt of that. "The American people will come to understand that what I did had to be done."

AT 12:31 P.M., THURSDAY, APRIL 19, in a flood of television lights, Douglas MacArthur walked down the same aisle in the House of Representatives as had Harry Truman so often since 1945, and the wild ovation from the packed chamber, the intense, authentic drama of the moment, were such as few had ever beheld. Neither the president's Cabinet nor the Supreme Court nor any of the Joint Chiefs were present.

Wearing a short "Eisenhower" jacket, without decoration, the silvery circles of five-star rank glittering on his shoulders, MacArthur paused to shake hands with Vice President Barkley, then stepped to the rostrum, his face "an unreadable mask." Only after complete silence had fallen did he begin: "I address you with neither rancor nor bitterness in the fading twilight of life, with but one purpose in mind: to serve my country."

There was ringing applause and the low, vibrant voice went on, the speaker in full command of the moment. The decision to intervene in support of the Republic of Korea had been sound from a military standpoint, MacArthur affirmed. But when he had called for reinforcements, he was told they were not available. He had "made clear," he said, that if not permitted to destroy the enemy bases north of the Yalu, if not permitted to utilize the 800,000 Chinese troops on Formosa, if not permitted to blockade the China coast, then "the position of the command from a military standpoint forbade victory . . ." And war's "very object" was victory. How could it be otherwise? "In war, indeed," he said, repeating his favorite slogan, "there can be no substitute for victory. There were some who, for varying reasons, would appease Red China. They were blind to history's clear lesson, for history teaches, with unmistakable emphasis, that appeasement begets new and bloodier war."

He was provocative, and defiant. Resounding applause or cheers followed again and again—thirty times in thirty-four minutes. He said nothing of bombing China's industrial centers, as he had proposed. And though he said "every available means" should be applied to bring victory, he made no mention of his wish to use atomic bombs, or to lay down a belt of radioactivity along the Yalu. He had been severely criticized for his views, he said. Yet, he asserted, his views were "fully shared" by the Joint Chiefs—a claim that was altogether untrue but that brought a deafening ovation. Republicans and most spectators in the galleries leaped to their feet, cheering and stamping. It was nearly a minute before he could begin again.

To those who said American military strength was inadequate to face the enemy on more than one front, MacArthur said he could imagine no greater expression of defeatism. "You cannot appease or otherwise surrender to Communism in Asia without simultaneously undermining our efforts to halt its advance in Europe." To confine the war only to Chinese aggression in Korea was to follow a path of "prolonged indecision."

"Why, my soldiers asked of me, surrender military advantages to an enemy in the field?" He paused; then, softly, his voice almost a whisper, he said, "I could not answer."

A record 30 million people were watching on television, and the performance was masterful. The use of the rich voice, the timing, surpassed that of most actors. The oratorical style was of a kind not heard in Congress in a very long time. It recalled, as one television critic wrote, "a yesteryear of the theater," and it held the greater part of the huge audience wholly enraptured. Work had stopped in offices and plants across the country, so people could watch. Saloons and bars were jammed. Schoolchildren saw the "historic hour" in classrooms or were herded into assemblies or dining halls to listen by radio. Whether they had any idea what the excitement was about, they knew it was "important."

"When I joined the army, even before the turn of the century, it was the fulfillment of all my boyish hopes and dreams," MacArthur said, his voice dropping as he began the famous last lines, the stirring, sentimental, ambiguous peroration that the speech would be remembered for.

> The hopes and dreams have long since vanished. But I still remember the refrain of one of the most popular barracks ballads of that day which proclaimed most proudly that is "Old soldiers never die. They just fade away." And like the old soldier of the ballad, I now close my military career and just fade away—an old soldier who tried to do his duty as God gave him the light to see that duty.
> Good-bye.

A "HURRICANE OF EMOTION" swept the room. Hands reached out to him. Many in the audience were weeping. "We heard God speak here today, God in the flesh, the voice of God!" exclaimed Republican Representative Dewey Short of Missouri, a former preacher. To Joe Martin, it was "the climaxing" of the most emotional moment he had known in thirty-five years in Congress. Theatrics were a part of the congressional way of life, Martin knew, but nothing had ever equaled this.

It was MacArthur's finest hour, and the crescendo of public adulation that followed, beginning with a triumphal parade through Washington that afternoon, and climaxing the next day in New York with a thunderous ticker-tape parade, was unprecedented in U.S. history. Reportedly 7,500,000 people turned out in New York, more than had welcomed Eisenhower in 1945, more even than at the almost legendary welcome for Lindbergh in 1927.

In fact, not everybody cheered. There were places along the parade route in New York where, as MacArthur's open car passed, people stood silently, just watching and looking, anything but pleased. In Washington, one senator had confided to a reporter that he had never feared more for his country than during MacArthur's speech. "I honestly felt that if the speech had gone on much longer there might have been a march on the White House."

TRUMAN HAD NOT LISTENED to MacArthur's speech, or watched on television. He had spent the time at his desk in the Oval Office, meeting with Dean Acheson as was usual at that hour on Thursdays, after which he went back to Blair House for lunch and a nap. At some point, however, he did read what MacArthur had said. Speaking privately, he remarked that he thought it "a bunch of damn bullshit."

AS TRUMAN HAD ANTICIPATED, the tumult began to subside. For seven weeks in the late spring of 1951, the Senate Foreign Relations and Armed Services committees held joint hearings to investigate MacArthur's dismissal. Though the hearings were closed, authorized transcripts of each day's sessions, edited for military security reasons, were released hourly to the press.

MacArthur, the first witness, testified for three days, arguing that his way in Korea was the way to victory and an end to the slaughter. He had seen as much blood and disaster as any man alive, he told the senators, but never such devastation as during his last time in Korea. "After I looked at that wreckage and those thousands of women and children and everything, I vomited. Now are you going to let that go on . . . ?" The politicians in Washington had introduced a "new concept into military operations—the concept of appeasement," its purpose only "to go on indefinitely . . . indecisively, fighting with no mission. . . ."

But he also began to sound self-absorbed and oddly uninterested in global issues. He would admit to no mistakes, no errors of judgment. Failure to anticipate the size of the Chinese invasion, for example, had been the fault of the CIA. Any operation he commanded was crucial; other considerations were always of less importance. Certain that his strategy of war on China would not bring in the Soviets, he belittled the danger of a larger conflict. But what if he happened to be wrong, he was asked. What if another world war resulted? That, said MacArthur, was not his responsibility. "My responsibilities were in the Pacific, and the Joint Chiefs of Staff and various agencies of the Government are working night and day for an over-all solution to the global problem. Now I am not familiar with their studies. I haven't gone into it. . . ." To many, it seemed he had made the president's case.

The great turning point came with the testimony of Marshall, Bradley, and the Joint Chiefs, who refuted absolutely MacArthur's claim that they agreed with his strategy. Truman, from the start of the crisis, had known he needed the full support of his military advisers before declaring his decision about MacArthur. Now it was that full support, through nineteen days of testimony, that not only gave weight and validity to the decision, but discredited MacArthur in a way nothing else could have.

Never, said the Joint Chiefs, had they subscribed to MacArthur's plan for victory, however greatly they admired him. The dismissal of MacArthur, said all of them—Marshall, Bradley, the Joint Chiefs—was more than warranted; it was a necessity. Given the circumstances, given the seriousness of MacArthur's opposition to the policy of the president, his challenge to presidential authority, there had been no other course. The fidelity of the military high command to the principle of civilian control of the military was total and unequivocal.

Such unanimity of opinion on the part of the country's foremost and most respected military leaders seemed to leave Republican senators stunned. As James Reston wrote in the *New York Times,* "MacArthur, who had started as the prosecutor, had now become the defendant."

The hearings ground on and grew increasingly dull. The MacArthur hysteria was over; interest waned. When, in June, MacArthur set off on a speaking tour through Texas, insisting he had no presidential ambitions, he began to sound more and more shrill and vindictive, less and less like a hero. He attacked Truman, appeasement, high taxes, and "insidious forces working from within." His crowds grew steadily smaller. Nationwide, the polls showed a sharp decline in his popular appeal. The old soldier was truly beginning to fade away.

TRUMAN WOULD REGARD the decision to fire MacArthur as among the most important he made as president. He did not, however, agree with those who said it had shown what great courage he had. (Harriman, among others, would later speak of it as one of the most courageous steps ever taken by any president.) "Courage didn't have anything to do with it," Truman would say emphatically. "General MacArthur was insubordinate and I fired him. That's all there was to it."

But if the firing of MacArthur had taken a heavy toll politically, if Truman as president had been less than a master of persuasion, he had accomplished a very great deal and demonstrated extraordinary patience and strength of character in how he rode out the storm. His policy in Korea—his determined effort to keep the conflict in bounds—had not been scuttled, however great the aura of the hero-general, or his powers as a spellbinder. The principle of civilian control over the military, challenged as never before in the nation's history, had survived, and stronger than ever. The president had made his point and, with the backing of his generals, he had made it stick.

*AUTUMN 1992*

---

David McCullough is the author of *Path between the Seas: The Creation of the Panama Canal, 1870–1914* (1977) and *Mornings on Horseback* (1981). His biography *Truman* won the 1993 Pulitzer Prize.

# 41

# The Man Who Saved Korea

## By Thomas Fleming

*In the fall of 1950, the Korean War seemed over. United Nations troops, sparked by the American landing at Inchon, had destroyed much of the invading North Korean Army and scattered its remnants north of the 38th parallel. All that remained, it appeared, was an easy walk to the Yalu River to reunify Korea. But the massive Chinese intervention turned victory into defeat—indeed rout—as the Eighth Army reeled backward from the surprising onslaught from the north. Retreat dominated thought and action, morale disintegrated, and the U.N. troops faced the specter of a 1940-style Dunkirk. Into this debacle strode Lieutenant General Matthew B. Ridgway. With a rifle over his shoulder and hand grenades hanging from his chest (British troops would soon nickname him "tin tits"), Ridgway's battlefield leadership, style, and determination revitalized the Eighth Army and turned retreat into advance. His accomplishment, Thomas Fleming suggests, marks Ridgway as perhaps America's greatest twentieth-century general.*

If you asked a group of average Americans to name the greatest American general of the twentieth century, most would nominate Dwight Eisenhower, the master politician who organized the Allied invasion of Europe, or Douglas MacArthur, a leader in both world wars, or George C. Marshall, the architect of victory in World War II. John J. Pershing and George S. Patton would also get a fair number of votes. But if you ask professional soldiers that question, a surprising number of them will reply: "Ridgway."

When they pass this judgment, they are not thinking of the general who excelled as a division commander and an army corps commander in World War II. Many other men distinguished themselves in those roles. The soldiers are remembering the general who rallied a beaten Eighth Army from the brink of defeat in Korea in 1951.

THE SON OF A WEST POINTER who retired as a colonel of the artillery, Matthew Bunker Ridgway graduated from the U.S. Military Academy in 1917. Even there, although his scholastic record was mediocre, he was thinking about how to become a general. One trait he decided to cultivate was an ability to remember names. By his first-class year, he was able to identify the entire 750-man student body.

To his dismay, instead of being sent into combat in France, Ridgway was ordered to teach Spanish at West Point, an assignment that he was certain meant the death knell of his military career. (As it turned out, it was probably the first of many examples of Ridgway luck; like Eisenhower and Omar Bradley, he escaped the trench mentality that World War I experience inflicted on too many officers.) Typically, he mastered the language, becoming one of a handful of officers who were fluent in the second tongue of the western hemisphere. He stayed at West Point for six years—in the course of which he became acquainted with its controversial young superintendent, Brigadier General Douglas MacArthur, who was trying in vain to stop the academy from still preparing for the War of 1812.

In the twenties and thirties, Ridgway's skills as a writer and linguist brought him more staff assignments than he professed to want—troop leadership was the experience that counted on the promotion ladder. But Ridgway's passion for excellence and commitment to the army attracted the attention of a number of people, notably that of a rising star in the generation ahead of him, George Marshall. Ridgway served under Marshall in the 15th Infantry in China in the mid-1930s and was on his general staff in Washington when Pearl Harbor plunged the nation into World War II.

As the army expanded geometrically in the next year, Ridgway acquired two stars and the command of the 82nd Division. When Marshall decided to turn it into an airborne outfit, Ridgway strapped on a parachute and jumped out of a plane for the first time in his life. Returning to his division, he cheerfully reported there was nothing to the transition to paratrooper. He quieted a lot of apprehension in the division—although he privately admitted to a few friends that "nothing" was like jumping off the top of a moving freight train onto a hard roadbed.

Dropped into Sicily during the night of July 9, 1943, Ridgway's paratroopers survived a series of snafus. Navy gunners shot down twenty of their planes as they came over the Mediterranean from North Africa. In the darkness their confused pilots scattered them all over the island. Nevertheless, they rescued the invasion by preventing the crack Hermann Göring panzer division from attacking the fragile beachhead and throwing the first invaders of Hitler's Fortress Europe into the sea.

In this campaign, Ridgway displayed many traits that became hallmarks of his generalship. He scorned a rear-area command post. Battalion and even company commanders never knew when they would find Ridgway at their elbows, urging them forward, demanding to know why they were doing this and not that. His close calls with small- and large-caliber enemy fire swiftly acquired legendary proportions. Even Patton, who was not shy about moving forward, ordered Ridgway to stop trying to be the 82nd Division's point man. Ridgway pretty much ignored the order, calling it "a compliment."

From Patton, Ridgway acquired another command habit: the practice of stopping to tell lower ranks—military policemen, engineers building bridges—they were doing a good job. He noted the remarkable way this could energize an entire battalion, even a regiment. At the same time, Ridgway displayed a ruthless readiness to relieve any officer who did not meet his extremely high standards of battlefield performance. Celerity and aggressiveness were what he wanted. If an enemy force appeared on a unit's front, he wanted an immediate deployment for flank attacks. He did not tolerate commanders who sat down and thought things over for an hour or two.

In the heat of battle, Ridgway also revealed an unrivaled capacity to taunt the enemy. One of his favorite stunts was to stand in the middle of a road under heavy artillery fire and urinate to demonstrate his contempt for German accuracy. Aides and fellow generals repeatedly begged him to abandon this bravado. He ignored them.

Ridgway's experience as an airborne commander spurred the evolution of another trait that made him almost unique among American soldiers— a readiness to question, even to challenge, the policies of his superiors. After the snafus of the Sicily drop, Eisenhower and other generals concluded that division-size airborne operations were impractical. Ridgway fought ferociously to maintain the integrity of his division. Winning that argument, he found himself paradoxically menaced by the widespread conclusion that airborne assault could solve problems with miraculous ease.

General Harold Alexander, the British commander of the Allied invasion of Italy, decided Ridgway's paratroopers were a God-given instrument for disrupting German defense plans. Alexander ordered the 82nd Airborne to jump north of Rome, seize the city, and hold it while the main army drove from their Salerno beachhead to link up with them. Ridgway was appalled. His men would have to fly without escort—Rome was beyond the range of Allied fighters—risking annihilation before they got to the target.

There were at least six elite German divisions near the city, ready and willing to maul the relatively small 82nd Airborne. An airborne division at this point in the war had only 8,000 men. Their heaviest gun was a 75mm pack howitzer, "a peashooter," in Ridgway's words, against tanks. For food, ammunition, fuel, transportation, the Americans were depending on the Italians, who were planning to double-cross the Germans and abandon the war.

Ridgway wangled an interview with General Alexander, who listened to his doubts and airily dismissed them. "Don't give this another thought, Ridgway. Contact will be made with your division in three days—five at the most," he said.

Ridgway was in a quandary. He could not disobey the direct orders of his superior without destroying his career. He told his division to get ready for the drop, but he refused to abandon his opposition, even though the plan had the enthusiastic backing of Dwight Eisenhower, who was conducting negotiations with the Italians from his headquarters in Algiers. Eisenhower saw the paratroopers as a guarantee that the Americans could protect the Italians from German retribution.

Ridgway discussed the dilemma with Brigadier General Maxwell Taylor, his artillery officer, who volunteered to go to Rome incognito and confer with the Italians on the ground. Ridgway took this offer to General Walter Bedell Smith, Alexander's American chief of staff, along with more strenuous arguments against the operation.

Smith persuaded Alexander to approve Taylor's mission. Taylor and an air corps officer traveled to Rome disguised as captured airmen and met Field Marshal Pietro Badoglio, the acting prime minister, who was in charge of the negotiations. Meanwhile, plans for the drop proceeded at a dozen airfields in Sicily. If Taylor found the Italians unable to keep their promises of support, he was to send a radio message with the code word *innocuous* in it.

In Rome, Taylor met Badoglio and was appalled by what he heard. The Germans were wise to the Italians' scheme and had reinforced their divisions around Rome. The 3rd Panzer Grenadier Division alone now had 24,000 men and 200 tanks—enough firepower to annihilate the 82nd Airborne twice over. A frantic Taylor sent three separate messages over different channels to stop the operation, but word did not reach the 82nd until sixty-two planes loaded with paratroopers were on the runways warming their engines. Ridgway sat down with his chief of staff, shared a bottle of whiskey, and wept with relief.

Looking back years later, Ridgway declared that when the time came for him to meet his maker, his greatest source of pride would not be his accomplishments in battle but his decision to oppose the Rome drop. He also liked to point out that it took seven months for the Allied army to reach the Eternal City.

Repeatedly risking his career in this unprecedented fashion, Ridgway was trying to forge a different kind of battle leadership. He had studied the appalling slaughters of World War I and was determined that they should never happen again. He believed "the same dignity attaches to the mission given a single soldier as to the duties of the commanding general. . . . All lives are equal on the battlefield, and a dead rifleman is as great a loss in the sight of God as a dead general."

In the Normandy invasion, Ridgway had no difficulty accepting the 82nd's task. Once more, his men had to surmount a mismanaged airdrop in which paratroopers drowned at sea and in swamps and lost 60 percent of their equipment. Ridgway found himself alone in a pitch-dark field. He consoled himself with the thought that "at least if no friends were visible, neither were any foes." Ten miles away, his second-in-command, James Gavin, took charge of most of the fighting for the next twenty-four hours. The paratroopers captured only one of their assigned objectives, but it was a crucial one, the town of Sainte-Mère-Eglise, which blocked German armor from attacking Utah beach. Ridgway was given a third star and command of the XVIII Airborne Corps.

By this time he inspired passionate loyalty in the men around him. Often it came out in odd ways. One day he was visiting a wounded staff officer in an aid station. A paratrooper on the stretcher next to him said, "Still sticking your neck out, huh, General?" Ridgway never forgot the remark.

For him it represented the affection one combat soldier feels for another.

Less well known than his D-Day accomplishments was Ridgway's role in the Battle of the Bulge. When the Germans smashed into the Ardennes in late December 1944, routing American divisions along a seventy-five-mile front, Ridgway's airborne corps again became a fire brigade. The "battling bastards of Bastogne"—the 101st Airborne led by Brigadier General Anthony McAuliffe—got most of the publicity for foiling the German lunge toward Antwerp. But many historians credit Ridgway's defense of the key road junction of Saint-Vith as a far more significant contribution to the victory.

Ridgway acquired a visual trademark, a hand grenade attached to his paratrooper's shoulder harness on one side and a first-aid kit, often mistaken for another grenade, on the other strap. He insisted both were for practical use, not for picturesque effect like Patton's pearl-handled pistols. In his jeep he also carried an old .30-06 Springfield rifle, loaded with armor-piercing cartridges. On foot one day deep in the Ardennes forest, trying to find a battalion CP, he was carrying the gun when he heard a "tremendous clatter." Through the trees he saw what looked like a light tank with a large swastika on its side. He fired five quick shots at the Nazi symbol and crawled away on his belly through the snow. The vehicle turned out to be a self-propelled gun. Inside it, paratroopers who responded to the shots found five dead Germans.

THIS WAS THE MAN—now at the Pentagon, as deputy chief of staff for administration and training—whom the army chose to rescue the situation in Korea when the Chinese swarmed over the Yalu River in early December 1950 and sent EUSAK (the Eighth U.S. Army in Korea) reeling in headlong retreat. Capping the disarray was the death of the field commander, stumpy Major General Walton ("Johnnie") Walker, in a jeep accident. Ridgway's first stop was Tokyo, where he was briefed by the supreme commander, Douglas MacArthur. After listening to a pessimistic summary of the situation, Ridgway asked: "General, if I get over there and find the situation warrants it, do I have your permission to attack?"

"The Eighth Army is yours, Matt," MacArthur responded. "Do what you think best."

MacArthur was giving Ridgway freedom—and responsibility—he had never given Walker. The reason was soon obvious: MacArthur was trying to distance himself from a looming disaster. Morale in the Eighth Army had deteriorated alarmingly while they retreated before the oncoming Chinese. "Bugout fever" was endemic. Within hours of arriving to take command, Ridgway abandoned his hopes for an immediate offensive. His first job was to restore this beaten army's will to fight.

He went at it with incredible verve and energy. Strapping on his parachute harness with its hand grenade and first-aid kit, he toured the front for three days in an open jeep in bitter cold. "I held to the old-fashioned idea that it helped the spirits of the men to see the Old Man up there in the snow and sleet . . . sharing the same cold miserable existence they had to endure," he said. But Ridgway admitted that until a kindhearted major dug up a pile-lined cap and warm gloves for him, he "damn near froze."

Everywhere he went, Ridgway exercised his fabulous memory for faces. By this time he could recognize an estimated 5,000 men at a glance. He dazzled old sergeants and MPs on lonely roads by remembering not only their names but where they had met and what they had said to each other.

But this trick was not enough to revive EUSAK. Everywhere Ridgway found the men unresponsive, reluctant to answer his questions, even to air their gripes. The defeatism ran from privates through sergeants all the way up to the generals. He was particularly appalled by the atmosphere in the Eighth Army's main command post in Taegu. There they were talking about withdrawing from Korea, frantically planning how to avoid a Dunkirk.

In his first forty-eight hours, Ridgway had met with all his American corps and division commanders and all but one of the Republic of Korea division commanders. He told them—as he had told the staffers in Taegu—that he had no plans whatsoever to evacuate Korea. He reiterated what he had told South Korean president Syngman Rhee in their meeting: "I've come to stay."

But words could not restore the nerve of many top commanders. Ridgway's reaction to this defeatism was drastic: He cabled the Pentagon that he wanted to relieve almost every division commander and artillery commander in EUSAK. He also supplied his bosses with a list of younger fighting generals he wanted to replace the losers. This demand caused political palpitations in Washington, where MacArthur's growing quarrel with President Harry Truman's policy was becoming a nightmare. Ridgway eventually got rid of his losers—but not with one ferocious sweep. The ineffective generals were sent home singly over the next few months as part of a "rotation policy."

Meanwhile, in a perhaps calculated bit of shock treatment, Ridgway visited I Corps and asked the G-3 to brief him on their battle plans. The officer described plans to withdraw to "successive positions."

"What are your attack plans?" Ridgway growled. The officer floundered. "Sir—we are withdrawing." There were no attack plans. "Colonel, you are relieved," Ridgway said.

That is how the Eighth Army heard the story. Actually, Ridgway ordered the G-3's commanding officer to relieve him—which probably intensified the shock effect on the corps. Many officers felt, perhaps with some justice, that Ridgway was brutally unfair to the G-3, who was only carrying out the corps commander's orders. But Ridgway obviously felt the crisis justified brutality.

As for the lower ranks, Ridgway took immediate steps to satisfy some of their gripes. Warmer clothing was urgently demanded from the States. Stationery to write letters home, and to wounded buddies, was shipped to the front lines—and steak and chicken were added to the menu, with a ferocious insistence that meals be served hot.

Regimental, division, and corps commanders were told in language Ridgway admitted was "often impolite" that it was time to abandon creature comforts and slough off their timidity about getting off the roads and into the hills, where the enemy was holding the high ground. Again and again Ridgway repeated the ancient army slogan "Find them! Fix them! Fight them! Finish them!"

As he shuttled across the front in a light plane or a helicopter, Ridgway studied the terrain beneath him. He was convinced a massive Communist offense was imminent. He not only wanted to contain it, he wanted to inflict maximum punishment on the enemy. He knew that for the time being he would have to give some ground, but he wanted the price to be high. South of the Han River, he assigned Brigadier General Garrison Davidson, a talented engineer, to take charge of several thousand Korean laborers and create a "deep defensive zone" with a trench system, barbed wire, and artillery positions.

Ridgway also preached defense in depth to his division and regimental commanders in the lines they were holding north of the Han. Although they lacked the manpower to halt the Chinese night attacks, he said that by buttoning up tight, unit by unit, at night and counterattacking strongly with armor and infantry teams during the day, the U.N. army could inflict severe punishment on anyone who had come through the gaps in their line. At the same time, Ridgway ordered that no unit be abandoned if cut off. It was to be "fought for" and rescued unless a "major commander" after "personal appraisal" Ridgway-style—from the front lines—decided its relief would cost as many or more men.

Finally, in this race against the looming Chinese offensive, Ridgway tried to fill another void in the spirit of his men. He knew they were asking each other, "What the hell are we doing here in this God-forgotten spot?" One night he sat down at his desk in his room in Seoul and tried to answer that question.

His first reasons were soldierly: They had orders to fight from the president of the United States, and they were defending the freedom of South Korea. But the real issues were deeper—"whether the power of Western civilization, as God has permitted it to flower in our own beloved lands, shall defy and defeat Communism; whether the rule of men who shoot their prisoners, enslave their citizens and deride the dignity of man, shall displace the rule of those to whom the individual and his individual rights are sacred." In that context, Ridgway wrote, "the sacrifices we have made, and those we shall yet support, are not offered vicariously for others but in our own direct defense."

On New Year's Eve, the Chinese and North Koreans attacked with all-out fury. The Eighth Army, Ridgway wrote, "were killing them by the thousands," but they kept coming. They smashed huge holes in the center of Ridgway's battle line, where ROK divisions broke and ran. Ridgway was not surprised—having met their generals, he knew most had little more than a company commander's experience or expertise. Few armies in existence had taken a worse beating than the ROKs in the first six months of the war.

By January 2 it was evident that the Eighth Army would have to move south of the Han River and abandon Seoul. As he left his headquarters, Ridgway pulled from his musette bag a pair of striped flannel pajama pants "split beyond repair in the upper posterior region." He tacked them to the wall, the worn-out seat flapping. Above them, in block letters, he left a message:

TO THE COMMANDING GENERAL
CHINESE COMMUNIST FORCES
WITH THE COMPLIMENTS OF
THE COMMANDING GENERAL
EIGHTH ARMY

The story swept through the ranks with predictable effect.

The Eighth Army fell back fifteen miles south of the Han to the defensive line prepared by General Davidson and his Korean laborers. They retreated, in Ridgway's words, "as a fighting army, not as a running mob." They brought with them all their equipment and, most important, their pride. They settled into the elaborate defenses and waited for the Chinese to try again. The battered Communists chose to regroup. Ridgway decided it was time to come off the floor with some Sunday punches of his own.

He set up his advanced command post on a bare bluff at Yoju, about one-third of the way across the peninsula, equidistant from the I Corps and X Corps headquarters. For the first few weeks, he operated with possibly the smallest staff of any American commander of a major army. Although EUSAK's force of 350,000 men was in fact the largest field army ever led by an American general, Ridgway's staff consisted of just six people: two aides, one orderly, a driver for his jeep, and a driver and radio operator for the radio jeep that followed him everywhere. He lived in two tents, placed end-to-end to create a sort of two-room apartment and heated by a small gasoline stove. Isolated from the social and military formalities of the main CP at Taegu, Ridgway had time for "uninterrupted concentration" on his counteroffensive.

Nearby was a crudely leveled airstrip from which he took off repeatedly to study the terrain in front of him. He combined this personal reconnaissance with intensive study of relief maps provided by the Army Map Service—"a priceless asset." Soon his incredible memory had absorbed the terrain of the entire front, and "every road, every cart track, every hill, every stream, every ridge in that area . . . we hoped to control . . . became as familiar to me as . . . my own backyard," he later wrote. When he ordered an advance into a sector, he knew exactly what it might involve for his infantrymen.

On January 25, with a thunderous eruption of massed artillery, the Eighth Army went over to the attack in Operation Thunderbolt. The goal was the Han River, which would make the enemy's grip on Seoul untenable. The offensive was a series of carefully planned advances to designated "phase lines," beyond each of which no one advanced until every assigned unit reached it. Again and again Ridgway stressed the importance of having good coordination, inflicting maximum punishment, and keeping major units intact. He called it "good footwork combined with firepower." The men in the lines called it "the meat grinder."

To jaundiced observers in the press, the army's performance was miraculous. Rene Cutforth of the BBC wrote: "Exactly how and why the new army was transformed . . . from a mob of dispirited boobs . . . to a tough resilient force is still a matter for speculation and debate." A *Time* correspondent came closest to explaining it: "The boys aren't up there fighting for democracy now. They're fighting because the platoon leader is leading them and the platoon leader is fighting because of the command, and so on right up to the top."

By February 10 the Eighth Army had its left flank anchored on the Han and had captured Inchon and Seoul's Kimpo Airfield. After fighting off a ferocious Chinese counterattack on Lincoln's birthday, Ridgway launched offensives from his center and right flank with equal success. In one of these, paratroopers were used to trap a large number of Chinese between them and an armored column. Ridgway was sorely tempted to jump with them, but he realized it would be "a damn fool thing" for an army commander to do. Instead, he landed on a road in his light plane about a half hour after the paratroopers hit the ground.

M1s were barking all around him. At one point a dead Chinese came rolling down a hill and dangled from a bank above Ridgway's head. His pilot, an ex-infantryman, grabbed a carbine out of the plane and joined the shooting. Ridgway stood in the road, feeling "that lifting of the spirits, that sudden quickening of the breath and the sudden sharpening of all the senses that comes to a man in the midst of battle." None of his exploits in Korea better demonstrates why he was able to communicate a fierce appetite for combat to his men.

Still another incident dramatized Ridgway's instinctive sympathy for the lowliest private in his ranks. In early March he was on a hillside watching a battalion of the 1st Marine Division moving up for an attack. In the line was a gaunt boy with a heavy radio on his back. He kept stumbling over an untied shoelace. "Hey, how about one of you sonsabitches tying my shoe?" he howled to his buddies. Ridgway slid down the snowy bank, landed at his feet, and tied the laces.

Fifty-four days after Ridgway took command, the Eighth Army had driven the Communists across the 38th parallel, the line dividing North and South Korea, inflicting enormous losses with every mile they advanced. The reeling enemy began surrendering by the hundreds. Seoul was recaptured on March 14, a symbolic defeat of tremendous proportions to the Communists' political ambitions. Ridgway was now "supremely confident" his men could take "any objective" assigned to them. "The American flag never flew over a prouder, tougher, more spirited and more competent fighting force than was the Eighth Army as it drove north beyond the parallel," he declared. But he agreed with President Truman's decision to stop at the parallel and seek a negotiated truce.

In Tokyo his immediate superior General Douglas MacArthur, did not agree and let his opinion resound through the media. On April 11 Ridgway was at the front in a snowstorm supervising final plans for an attack on the Chinese stronghold of Ch'ŏrwŏn, when a correspondent said, "Well, General, I guess congratulations are in order." That was how he learned that Truman had fired MacArthur and given Ridgway his job as supreme commander in the Far East and as America's proconsul in Japan.

Ridgway was replaced as Eighth Army commander by Lieutenant General James Van Fleet, who continued Ridgway's policy of using coordinated firepower, rolling with Communist counterpunches, inflicting maximum casualties. Peace talks and occasionally bitter fighting dragged on for another twenty-eight months, but there was never any doubt that EUSAK was in Korea to stay. Ridgway and Van Fleet built the ROK Army into a formidable force during these months. They also successfully integrated black and white troops in EUSAK.

Later, Ridgway tried to combine his "profound respect" for Douglas MacArthur and his conviction that President Truman had done the right thing in relieving him. Ridgway maintained that MacArthur had every right to make his views heard in Washington, but not to disagree publicly with the president's decision to fight a limited war in Korea. Ridgway, with his deep concern for the individual soldier, accepted the concept of limited war fought for sharply defined goals as the only sensible doctrine in the nuclear age.

After leaving the Far East, Ridgway would go on to become head of NATO in Europe and chairman of the Joint Chiefs of Staff under President Eisenhower. Ironically, at the end of his career he would find himself in a MacArthuresque position. Secretary of Defense Charles E. ("Engine Charlie") Wilson had persuaded Ike to slash the defense budget—with 76 percent of the cuts falling on the army. Wilson latched on to Secretary of State John Foster Dulles's foreign policy, which relied on the threat of massive nuclear retaliation to intimidate the Communists. Wilson thought he could get more bang for the buck by giving almost half the funds in the budget to the air force.

Ridgway refused to go along with Eisenhower. In testimony before Congress, he strongly disagreed with the administration's policy. He insisted it was important that the United States be able to fight limited wars, without nuclear weapons. He said massive retaliation was "repugnant to the ideals of a Christian nation" and incompatible with the basic aim of the United States, "a just and durable peace."

Eisenhower was infuriated, but Ridgway stood his ground—and in fact proceeded to take yet another stand that angered top members of the administration. In early 1954 the French army was on the brink of collapse in Vietnam. Secretary of State Dulles and a number of other influential voices wanted the United States to intervene to rescue the situation. Alarmed, Ridgway sent a team of army experts to Vietnam to assess the situation. They came back with grim information.

Vietnam, they reported, was not a promising place to fight a modern war. It had almost nothing a modern army needed—good highways, port facilities, airfields, railways. Everything would have to be built from scratch. Moreover, the native population was politically unreliable, and the jungle terrain was made to order for guerrilla warfare. The experts estimated that to win the war the United States would have to commit more troops than it had sent to Korea.

Ridgway sent the report up through channels to Eisenhower. A few days later he was told to have one of his staff give a logistic briefing on Vietnam to the president. Ridgway gave it himself. Eisenhower listened impassively and asked only a few questions, but it was clear to Ridgway that he understood the full implications. With minimum fanfare, the president ruled against intervention.

For reasons that still puzzle historians, no one in the Kennedy administration ever displayed the slightest interest in the Ridgway report—not even Kennedy's secretary of state, Dean Rusk, who as assistant secretary of state for Far Eastern affairs in 1950–51 knew and admired what Ridgway had achieved in Korea. As Ridgway left office, Rusk wrote him a fulsome letter telling him he had "saved your country from the humiliation of defeat through the loss of morale in high places."

The report on Vietnam was almost the last act of Ridgway's long career as an American soldier. Determined to find a team player, Eisenhower did not invite him to spend a second term as chief of staff, as was customary. Nor was he offered another job elsewhere. Although Ridgway officially retired, his departure was clearly understood by Washington insiders as that rarest of things in the U.S. Army, a resignation in protest.

After leaving the army in 1955, Ridgway became chairman and chief executive officer of the Mellon Institute of Industrial Research, in Pittsburgh. He retired from this post in 1960 and has continued to live in a suburb of Pittsburgh. At this writing he is 97. [Editor's note: General Ridgway died on July 26, 1993.]

When Ridgway was leaving Japan to become commander of NATO, he told James Michener, "I cannot subscribe to the idea that civilian thought per se is any more valid than military thought." Without abandoning his traditional obedience to his civilian superiors, Ridgway insisted on his right to be a thinking man's soldier—the same soldier who talked back to his military superiors when he thought their plans were likely to lead to the "needless sacrifice of priceless lives."

David Halberstam is among those who believe that Ridgway's refusal to go along with intervention in Vietnam was his finest hour. Halberstam called him the "one hero" of his book on our involvement in Vietnam, *The Best and the Brightest.* But for the student of military history, the Ridgway of Korea towers higher. His achievement proved the doctrine of limited war can work, provided those fighting it are led by someone who knows how to ignite their pride and confidence as soldiers. Ridgway's revival of the Eighth Army is the stuff of legends, a paradigm of American generalship. Omar Bradley put it best: "His brilliant, driving uncompromising leadership [turned] the tide of battle like no other general's in our military history." Not long after Ridgway's arrival in Korea, one of the lower ranks summed up EUSAK's new spirit with a wisecrack: "From now on there's a right way, a wrong way, and a Ridgway."

*WINTER 1993*

---

Thomas Fleming is the author of the earlier essays on George Washington and John J. Pershing. His most recent book is *Loyalties: A Novel of World War II* (1994).

# 42

# "Murderers of Koje-do!"

## By Lawrence Malkin

*From its beginning to its end, the Korean War caught the United States and its allies unprepared. By June 1950, the victorious American army of World War II had nearly disappeared in the enthusiasm of postwar budget cuts, and it now held little semblance of combat readiness. No one had foreseen a North Korean attack, nor had the Truman administration believed that Korea was vital to American national interests. Yet suddenly American soldiers, beginning with Task Force Smith, found themselves in the middle of a war. Nor did the surprises stop there. After halting the North Korean Army at Pusan and then routing it at Inchon, the apparently victorious United Nations troops were staggered by the November 1950 Chinese assault that sent them tumbling back across the 38th parallel. Then, after finally driving the Communist forces back into North Korea, the United Nations stood unprepared for Communist stalling that would drag armistice talks along for two more years. And, as part of those frustrating negotiations, the United Nations faced one more surprise: the Communists' use of U.N.–held prisoners as political pawns.*

For forty years of the Cold War, whenever the American military actually fought a hot war of any importance, it was bedeviled by the dilemma of how to deal with prisoners of war. The truce ending the Korean War was delayed for well over a year by political posturing over the fate of tens of thousands of Chinese and Korean prisoners who refused to return to Communism in their homelands. The Communists adroitly turned this conundrum into a second front by harassing their captors at the Koje island prison camp off the peninsula's southern coast. American generalship was utterly confounded by a sharp political engagement in the midst of enervating military stalemate. The allied truce negotiators judged the additional 50,000 casualties that their side suffered during the protracted talks to be wildly disproportionate to what they regarded as a dubious principle of free choice, which after all was being accorded to soldiers who only recently had been trying to kill their own troops. The negotiators' political masters, whatever the righteousness of their original motives, seem to have insisted on continuing to fight for the principle in order to salvage some moral victory from the humiliating battlefield stalemate inflicted on them by what they contemptuously regarded as an uncivilized Asian horde.

The Nixon administration also converted the U.S. prisoners in Vietnam into a domestic political issue, enabling it to display some token of victory through a class of heroes who could be celebrated upon their return. It never seemed odd that their heroism was based on suffering and not conquest, and this may have eased the pain of the only major defeat the United States ever suffered against foreign arms. But it also helped delay for years the solution of our most domestically divisive war by extending and politicizing the insoluble problem of the missing in Vietnam. This only envenomed the tragedy. It still poisons our political debate; even as late as the 1992 political campaign, it became an issue through the history of H. Ross Perot's personal attempts to redeem missing Americans by a variety of methods including outright ransom.

Although the decline of Communism removes for the time being the threat of ideological empires that cannot bear the sting of mass defection, the problem is not going to go away. The use of human captives as political pawns has merely reemerged in an age-old form, hostage taking. It has been turned into a heartbreaking game of cat and mouse by cruel appeals through the international media. Politicians can no more disable this tactic than could the stalwart World War II generals in Korea, many of whom were endlessly befuddled by what one 1952 intelligence summary described as "a new area of total war."

But not entirely new. The Ur-event in this recurring drama took place at the end of World War II when Stalin demanded and received from the Allies the forceful repatriation of thousands of Soviet soldiers who had been taken prisoner by the Germans—some to fight alongside them. The sense of horror turned to personal revulsion and guilt after the worst fears of the officers who handed them over were confirmed and many Russians were exiled, imprisoned, or executed, sometimes all three. For years afterward, Soviet commanders reminded their men that this would be their eventual fate if they surrendered. This memory seemed to dominate American minds from President Harry Truman on down, when prisoners began falling into the hands of American troops fighting in Korea under the United Nations flag. More than 130,000 were in allied prison camps by January 1951, six months before the Communists asked for negotiations. To support allied insistence on voluntary repatriation, teams began screening the captives. To the amazement of the U.N. command and the embarrassment of the Communists, the ratio of those polled who refused repatriation ran at about four to one before the process was suspended under a combination of invective at the Panmunjom truce talks and obstruction by the Communist leadership inside the prison camps.

If the wise policies of World War II had been followed, the prisoners would have been transferred out of Korea to the United States, or at least to

Okinawa. That was what General Douglas MacArthur recommended to Washington, but he never got a reply. The principal arguments against it were cost, political sensitivity in Japan about the status of Okinawa, and the unspoken fact that a stateside transfer of prisoners would constitute an admission that the conflict was more than a temporary "police action." As the numbers became unmanageable and even threatening behind the wavering front lines, the prisoners were shifted south to holding camps near Pusan, where the South Korean civilians who had been impressed into North Korean service units were separated from the Korean and Chinese soldiers.

I have always felt that retaliation was the real reason the Communists did not treat our own prisoners better. The captured Asian troops, many of whom had fought with more discipline and determination than their American opponents, were regarded by most ordinary soldiers with whom I served in Korea, and by altogether too many officers, as subhuman "gooks," which is what they were usually called. They were therefore deemed unworthy of the civilized treatment accorded less than a decade earlier to white European prisoners. They were crowded into improvised prison space at four times the level prescribed in U.S. federal penitentiaries and given little to do except dig drainage ditches and organize parties for the removal of their own excrement. They were beaten by military police, although this occasional brutality nowhere approached the murderous barbarity the North Koreans practiced on allied captives in the north. In fact, that brutality was matched in the allied POW camps only by the North Korean prisoners' enforcement of their own internal discipline, which was essential to their high command's strategy of holding out against the principle of voluntary repatriation.

THE NOW-OBSCURE EPISODE that crystallized the incompatibility of the Communists' subtle political tactics with the classical American military strategy of victory by overwhelming firepower took place on the small fishing island of Koje off the southern coast of Korea. Koje-do (the Korean suffix signifies an island) is about half again as large as Martha's Vineyard. Two rock-strewn valleys on its northern coast were hastily converted into a tented outdoor Alcatraz for 70,000 Chinese and North Korean captives in January 1951.

"The first blunder was the camp design," wrote Edward Hymoff, an International News Service correspondent, after a visit. "Instead of small compounds, easily policed, it was decided for ease and economy to make them fewer and bigger. The result was a sprawling series of mammoth, 100-acre compounds enclosed by double fences of barbed wire with a single sally-port gate system and guard towers at the corners. With this incredibly bad planning, all pretense of prisoner control was foredoomed."

The compounds were originally designed to hold from 700 to 1,200 men each, but about 5,000 were soon jammed into each one. Space between them was later filled to confine more prisoners, saving on the number of guards but making their task more dangerous because thousands of prisoners could quickly be mobilized for protests, strikes, and riots by orders shouted across the barbed wire from one enclosure to another. The guards, green recruits led by officer misfits sent down from the front with no knowledge of Chinese or Korean, often left their posts to trade souvenirs, cigarettes, or sex with the camp-follower town of 8,000 that had sprung up around the perimeter. Several were murdered. At night the small guard force feared it could easily be overwhelmed, and so it largely retreated to barracks, in effect leaving the camp under control of the prisoners. Their Communist commanders imposed brutal discipline on recalcitrants. They would be found in the morning stomped to death, with rib fragments causing fatal internal bleeding; choked by cotton forced down their throats; or hanging from the barbed-wire fences. One nonlethal method of discipline was to tie a prisoner to a tent pole by his testicles and then dump his head in water.

In this idleness and overcrowding, rebellion would have festered even without an ideological spur. Each compound developed its own arsenal, which was described by Colonel William R. Robinette, one of the Koje commandants:

> In each GI shoe, there is an eight-inch sliver of steel. These had been sharpened into knives. Twenty lengths of barbed wire made a club, wired together and with a cloth handle. One of Koje's many stones, put into a sock, made a deadly black-jack. They made pikes out of Army tent poles, sharpening the pin at the end. They even made mock weapons out of wood—replicas of machine guns, automatic rifles, and M-1's painted black with soot from the camp incinerator, their bayonets covered with tinfoil from American chewing gum or cigarette wrappers.

As so often happens, local commanders on the ground were either unwilling or unable to understand the grand political strategy of both sides. Brigadier General Paul Yount, the commander in the port city of Pusan, was grandiosely engaged in constructing a courthouse that was to be its largest building; it was intended to be the site of military trials to punish the camp's prisoner leadership as war criminals, just as if the Koreans were Nazis and this was to be their Nuremberg.

Various people sent to Koje-do late in 1951 to investigate found what amounted to a scandal. One of them was John E. Murray, then a major and secretary to the general staff of the Pusan Logistical Command, who reported that the administration of the camp was slapstick and slipshod. He tried to alert Eighth Army Headquarters in Seoul of the explosive situation, but there he ran up against General James Van Fleet's chief of staff, who was partly deaf and never quite seemed to understand what they faced. As the ranking army commander in Korea, Van Fleet himself counseled patience lest any sharp reaction provoke a riot that might sabotage the truce talks, which he believed would soon end the war.

Early in 1952, Washington prohibited Koje-do commanders from judicial prosecution to enforce discipline; so much for Yount's mini-Nuremberg. But Truman and his advisers were divided on much more than that. The Joint Chiefs of Staff at first hungered for the propaganda victory that would come from public mass defections by the Communist prisoners, but they realized this posed a risk that the Communists might end the talks and hold onto the allied prisoners as pawns. Army Secretary James M. Lovett argued for a straight exchange to avoid spinning out the talks and threatening the welfare of U.S. prisoners. Secretary of State Dean Acheson also backed a straight exchange under the Geneva Convention, which would of course get the far smaller number of American GIs back sooner. But it was too late for mere legalism, and Truman himself recognized that. In 1951 he ordered General Matthew Ridgway, who had succeeded MacArthur as Far East commander, to demand "some major concessions" preventing the forced repatriation of prisoners. In a lengthy public statement defending the diplomatic behavior of the United Nations, he declared with Trumanesque forthrightness, "We will not buy an armistice by turning over human beings for slaughter or slavery."

On the ground, the Communists thought of victory more than honor and had their tactics well coordinated. They viewed the prison camps as a mere extension of the battlefield, which of course included the worldwide battle for public opinion. Charges of germ warfare were a principal weapon, and U.S. prisoners were threatened and tortured—"brainwashed" was then the popular term—to make statements admitting they had conducted it, mainly from the air. The most notorious confession came from a senior marine pilot, Colonel Frank H. Schwable, who had been put in a hole outdoors and left in his own filth for six months before he cracked.

On Koje-do, most compound commanders were North Korean intelligence officers who had been smuggled through the lines, surrendering as enlisted captives. The overall political commissar was Pak Sang Hyong, a Korean raised in the Soviet Union who had served as a staff officer and interpreter to Russian troops occupying North Korea after World War II. He was a close associate of Nam Il, the chief truce negotiator at the Panmunjom talks, and the two worked together, passing reports and instructions back and forth through underground channels, the existence of which American officers found hard to believe. Pak had made his way via the POW process to Koje-do disguised as a private soldier; he was equal in rank to Nam Il, but American intelligence never identified him. Another high-ranking North Korean officer was Colonel Lee Hak Koo, who had surrendered in the summer of 1950 in full uniform with red piping and Russian pistol, claiming to have lost his Communist faith. He became the military commander inside the barbed wire on Koje-do. Under the leadership of Pak and Lee, the die-hard compounds of the camp had acquired a terrible potential for embarrassing its hosts.

The prisoners provided ample warning of their commitment. Their ideological activity was shouted out in slogans and posters, including drawings of the Soviet and North Korean dictators, Stalin and Kim Il Sung. They demonstrated for better conditions, drilled with homemade rifles, and of course forcibly resisted United Nations screening, to the point of murdering those who wavered. In the compounds they controlled, riots on command slowed down the U.N. process of screening out anti-Communist prisoners from the hard core. When the leader of Compound 62 declared that screening was unnecessary because all 5,600 prisoners demanded to be returned to North Korea, the 3rd Battalion of the American 27th Infantry Regiment was sent to subdue them on February 18, 1952.

As more than a thousand prisoners in Compound 62 ran yelling from their tents brandishing improvised weapons and throwing rocks, the men of the 27th hurled grenades and finally opened fire. Fifty-five inmates were killed outright; twenty-two more died in hospitals. One GI was killed and thirty-eight wounded. When the infantrymen returned to the front line shortly afterward in a supposedly secret transfer, they were greeted by Communist loudspeakers blaring at them, "Welcome, murderers of Koje-do!" It was, to say the least, unnerving; I know, because I was in the 14th Infantry on the flank.

More to the point was the opening the incident created for Nam Il at the truce talks. At Panmunjom he railed at the U.N. negotiators: "The fact now placed before the people of the world is that in spite of your barbarous measures, you violated the will of the captured personnel of our side. Thousands of them would rather die than yield to your forcible retention." In fact, the allied command had begun to retreat quietly. In a message on April 29, Ridgway cautioned the Joint Chiefs of Staff that resumption of forced screening would demand "brutal" repression and asked them to assume that those who refused to be screened had in effect accepted repatriation. The parlous security at the camp was confirmed early in May by a visit from Colonel Robert T. Chaplin, provost marshal of the Far East command. Chaplin's report prompted Ridgway to warn Van Fleet of the need to tighten control. Van Fleet's response was to complain that Chaplin had been sent to inspect over his head without the protocol of first informing Eighth Army Headquarters.

The Koje uprising had resulted in the appointment of Brigadier General Francis T. Dodd as camp commander on February 20, but with conflicting orders. Ridgway told Van Fleet to maintain tight control, while Van Fleet told Dodd to "go easy" on the prisoners and keep them quiet because the armistice was near. This muddle had been a major factor in turning the camp into what Dodd's predecessor, Colonel Maurice J. Fitzgerald, called a "graveyard of commanders"—a new one almost every month even before Fitzgerald had taken over the previous September.

In May 1952, the political and military elements collided dramatically in a way that none of the principal actors could have foreseen—not just Dodd and Van Fleet, but Ridgway himself. At the precise moment of the climax, he was in the process of handing over his Far East command to another celebrated World War II leader, General Mark W. Clark, and trying to avoid the stain on his glittering reputation before he became commander of the North Atlantic Treaty Organization forces in Europe.

Dodd, an imposing West Pointer with a fine combat record, was anxious to decrease tensions in the camp. He circulated freely, talking to the Communist leaders and fatuously trying to win their cooperation. He went unarmed as a show of goodwill—and also to avoid having his weapon seized and used against him. But because the Communists had already gained such mastery over their own compounds that neither guards nor officers had been allowed to enter them for months, Dodd easily fell into their trap. In a prisoners' dry run, Lieutenant Colonel Wilbur Raven, the commanding officer of the camp's military police guards, had actually been seized and held briefly; but this did not alert either officer to a plot. Nam Il himself had set it up, through bamboo-telegraph orders, to strengthen his negotiating hand at Panmunjom.

On the evening of May 6, members of a work detail from the hard-core Compound 76 complained to Raven that they had been beaten by the guards, and they asked to see Dodd. As an inducement, they agreed to be fingerprinted, thus assisting him in his program of positively identifying all prisoners. Just after 2:00 P.M. on May 7, Dodd arrived and started talking, as was his custom, at the unlocked sally port of the compound. The subject moved from food to politics to the truce negotiations, but however amicable the discussion may have seemed, the two officers refused the prisoners' invitation to enter the compound. A work detail carrying tents for salvage approached the gate, which was opened for them. The prisoners drew closer to Dodd and Raven to continue the discussion—and then jumped them. As the prisoners pulled at him, Raven held fast to a post. But before any guards could reach Dodd, he was dragged into the compound and placed in a specially prepared tent divided into a two-room suite. The prisoners quickly raised a banner, also prepared in advance: "We capture Dodd. As long as our demand will be solved, his safety is secured. If there happen brutal act such as shooting, his life is in danger." Within hours, a field-telephone line from camp headquarters was connected to Dodd's quarters in the prison compound, and tortuous negotiations for his release commenced.

No more vulnerable moment could have been chosen, and it was impossible that the Communist planners did not know that Dodd's kidnap coincided with the transfer of command from Ridgway to Clark. The new commander arrived in Tokyo almost at the moment Dodd was being seized on Koje-do, thus making for confusion through equivocal responsibility. The memoirs of the two generals make it easy to imagine the almost farcical relationship between them as they juggled this international incident in the hope that the onus for it might land on the other.

At first, Ridgway writes, he "was determined to work out a solution to this prickly matter myself, along with Van Fleet, and not toss it, on such short notice, onto General Clark's dinner plate." Nevertheless, Ridgway took himself on a final inspection tour of Korea on May 8, four days before he was to hand over command to Clark, and he asked Clark to fly with him to Korea. Only when they were aloft did he let Clark in on what was happening. According to Clark's memoirs, Ridgway, addressing him by his middle name as intimates did, confided, "Wayne, we've got a little situation over in Korea where it's reported some prisoners have taken in one of the camp commanders, General Dodd, and are holding him as a hostage. We'll have to get into that situation when we arrive at Eighth Army

Headquarters [in Seoul] and find out what the score is."

Clark likened himself to someone who was "walking into something that felt remarkably like a swinging door." But what really astounded him was that the prisoner uprising was "something for which I had no preparation whatever. Although I had been briefed in Washington on every conceivable subject, this was the first time I had ever heard of Koje or the critical prisoner of war problems that existed behind our lines."

He was to hear more, much more. At Seoul, Ridgway directed Van Fleet, in writing, to establish order, using tanks if necessary to "shoot and to shoot with maximum effect." Ridgway was ready to sacrifice Dodd, who, he argued, had accepted mortal risks when he took up the profession of arms. "In wartime," he wrote later, "a general's life is no more precious than the life of a common soldier. If, in order to save an officer's life, we abandoned the cause for which enlisted men had died, we would be guilty of betraying the men whose lives had been placed in our care." Brave words, after the fact, especially when Ridgway, in later reports to Truman and testimony to Congress, could not bring himself to take any blame as supreme commander. "In my view," he later stated, "the whole situation had been ineptly handled by the responsible officers in Korea."

Van Fleet, when he arrived at Koje-do, delayed attacking the compound until heavy armor arrived from the mainland. Meanwhile, negotiations to save his comrade, Dodd, were under way through Brigadier General Charles F. Colson, a staff officer suddenly vaulted into command of the Koje camp. It was, of course, not the mere seizure of Dodd that was at issue, but what the Communists could make of it. Under the direction of Pak, the political commissar, a statement in fractured English was proposed in which the U.N. command would agree to stop using "poison gas, germ weapons, experiment object of A-Bomb"—and, of course, to stop screening prisoners for repatriation. After several days of exchanging drafts with the Communists to determine their price for Dodd's release, Colson signed a statement assuring that in the future "the prisoners of war can expect humane treatment" and promising that after Dodd's release "there will be no more forcible screening" of any prisoners. Dodd was released May 11. The next day Ridgway turned over his command to Clark.

Colson had no idea that his words would be used against the allies in negotiations or in press and propaganda the world over to undercut the last remaining principle for which the allied troops were fighting: the right of voluntary repatriation. Clark later overrode a court of inquiry that largely exonerated Dodd and Colson. He appointed his own court, which demoted each to colonel. They were then exiled to rear-echelon jobs in Japan, and their military careers were effectively ended. General Yount, the Pusan base commander, received a reprimand for not keeping closer surveillance over the negotiations, although it is hard to see why he was brought in except to increase the number of scapegoats for the omissions of higher headquarters. Clark wrote later that he would have "let them keep that dumb son of a bitch Dodd, and then go in and level the place."

In the denouement, that is more or less what happened, although happily for Dodd, he was well out of the way. On May 13, wasting no time, Clark sent in Brigadier General Haydon ("Bull") Boatner, assistant commander of the 2nd Division and an old China hand who had served in World War II under Vinegar Joe Stilwell. He spoke Chinese fluently, understood the Oriental sense of hierarchy and face, and was not an especially nice man. John E. Murray, whose warnings had gone for nothing, recalled years later in his own retirement as a major general that Boatner's large round face with its thin lips "always looked like he was ready to spit." Boatner was not very smart, either. As Major General Thomas Watlington later remarked in a letter to Murray, "I have known three 'Bulls' in the Army, and all were nicknamed not for their size but their brains. I cannot truthfully say that Boatner is the most stupid of the three, for comparison of superlatives is not easy."

But Boatner did not have to be particularly smart; he merely had to know precisely what his orders were and carry them out efficiently. Clark told him he was "to regain control of the rebellious prisoners on Koje and maintain control thereafter." His policy was sharply enunciated after he received a demanding message from one prisoner compound. "Prisoners of war do not negotiate," Clark shouted at a surprised subordinate. Boatner quickly set about building stronger, smaller prison enclosures, each holding between 500 and 1,000 men, as International Red Cross representatives had previously recommended in vain. To start the transfer, he baited the Chinese prisoners by expressing amazement that they would take orders from Koreans, who were descendants of their former slaves. Meanwhile, he received reinforcements in the form of paratroopers of the 187th Regimental Combat Team, one of the best battle-tested units in Korea. Clark later wrote, "Staff planning for this operation was done as carefully as for any orthodox military campaign. We knew by this time that the Communist POW's were active combatants and had to be dealt with as soldiers, not as prisoners in the traditional sense."

In an initial feint, Boatner sent infantrymen and tanks to pull down the Communist signs and banners in several compounds, demonstrating that he intended to regain control. On June 10, he massed his forces directly against the enemy command, ordering Colonel Lee to assemble the prisoners of his Compound 76 in groups of 150 for transfer to new quarters. They rallied with homemade barbed-wire clubs and flails, tent-pole pikes, and Molotov cocktails made from hoarded cooking gasoline. Half an hour after the first order, disciplined troops of the 187th advanced, using concussion grenades, tear gas, bayonets, and their fists, but not firing a shot. The first prisoners were dragged from the trenches, and hundreds more were moved out by riot tactics. After Patton tanks trained their guns on the last holdouts, they gave up; Colonel Lee was dragged away by the seat of his pants to solitary confinement for the remainder of the war. The remaining compounds were broken up, and little more was heard from Koje-do thereafter, although the issue of forced repatriation continued to the last.

A year later, when peace was finally imminent, South Korean president Syngman Rhee tried to block an armistice that would not give him the entire country. Once again, the prisoners were the markers in his gamble. Just after midnight on June 18, South Korean guards opened the gates of camps holding about 35,000 North Korean POWs. They vanished into the night with the help of South Korean soldiers, who led them to hiding places and fed them. Only about 9,000 hard-core Communist POWs refused to leave, insisting on repatriation. To Rhee's chagrin, the Communist side shrugged off his provocation. An armistice was signed on July 27, 1953, leaving north and south split along the battle line, which became a demilitarized zone.

The armistice provided for a complex process of what was called "explanation" by representatives of both sides to persuade prisoners to remain or go home. But inside the barbed wire, the prisoners had chosen up sides long before, and there was no going back. LSTs brought the North Korean prisoners from Koje to Inchon on August 13, where they boarded trains for the exchange point at the demilitarized zone. The windows had been covered with wire mesh, and the Communists were warned against revealing themselves along the route. They nevertheless pulled off the mesh protection, cut up their underwear, turned it into North Korean flags with dye hidden in their caps, and waved the improvised red-and-blue banners out the train windows—to an angry shower of stones thrown by schoolchildren along the route. North Korean female prisoners trashed their railroad car by smashing the windows, slashing the seat covers, urinating on the upholstery, and then, as they left, defecating in the aisle.

Defiance marked every moment of the North Koreans' return. At the demilitarized zone, Communist Red Cross officials urged the prisoners to get rid of the uniforms that their captors had provided. They stripped themselves naked except for their Communist caps, GI shoes, and breechclouts made from towels. Snake-dancing, singing, and yelling, they were loaded onto trucks for the exchange point, whereupon they began throwing away their shoes along the dusty road to the north and repatriation.

These antics simply proved the futility of the exercise to the man who had conducted it, Vice Admiral C. Turner Joy, the chief allied truce negotiator. One of his main objectives in holding out against forced repatriation had been the hope that Communist regimes would be so gravely embarrassed by mass defections that they would be undermined. "I regret to say this does not seem to have been a valid point," the admiral later remarked drily. "Whatever temporary loss of prestige in Asia Communism suffered from the results of 'voluntary repatriation' has long since been overtaken by Communism's subsequent victory in the area."

He spoke too soon. If there is any military lesson in all of this, and indeed in the Korean War itself, it comes from turning on its head General MacArthur's famous dictum: "There is no substitute for victory." The prosperity of South Korea today, the visible crumbling of the regime in the north, and China's fundamental turn toward a market economy prove that there *is* a substitute: constancy of purpose, patience, and avoiding the chimera of mistaking propaganda victories for real ones. Commanders win when they recognize that tactics and politics are simply different sides of the same strategic coin and then, as Clark did, take the political measure of their opponents. By applying just the right amount of force, to bluff and stiff his opponents and then wait them out, he proved a far better Cold War general than he ever was in World War II. It is a military lesson that holds good in any war, hot or cold.

SUMMER *1993*

Lawrence Malkin is the chief U.S. correspondent for the *International Herald Tribune*. He was an infantryman with the 25th Division during the Korean War.

# 43

# The Invasion
# of Cuba

## By Dino A. Brugioni

*In the multiple studies of the Cuban Missile Crisis of October 1962, most authors have concentrated on the role of leadership, the process of decision making, the give-and-take of diplomacy, and the imminence of nuclear war. Rarely has there been more than a cursory mention of the military invasion the United States frantically organized and then came within hours of launching against the shores of Cuba. In just under two weeks, the United States prepared a military operation that would have made a World War II D-Day planner proud. In the end—to the relief of all—the plans were not needed. But that fact takes nothing away from those days of frenzied effort and anxious waiting that saw the American military prepare for possible Armageddon in its own backyard.*

Most published accounts and studies of the Cuban Missile Crisis tend to concentrate, almost exclusively, on the debates and decisions of the Kennedy White House during those harrowing days of late October 1962. Major aspects of the crisis, strangely overlooked, are just beginning to come to light. One is the preparation for war, against both Cuba and the Soviet Union, that took place in a period just short of two weeks and turned much of southern Florida into a D-Day–like staging area. The result would prove to be the largest short-term mobilization of men and equipment since World War II—exceeded in size only by Desert Storm. Nor have the plans for the invasion of Cuba, which came so close to happening, been revealed until now; the exact tactical details of Operational Plans 312-, 314-, and 316-62 remain classified. Fortunately for the world, the trains (and planes) could be stopped, and were. This would not be another 1914.

The following account is adapted from Eyeball to Eyeball: The Inside Story of the Cuban Missile Crisis. *Its author, Dino A. Brugioni, a renowned expert in the analysis of aerial photography, was a key player in the crisis. Working at the time for the National Photographic Inter-*

*pretation Center (NPIC) of the Central Intelligence Agency, he was one
of the people who confirmed the presence of Soviet medium-range ballistic missiles in Cuba.*

*Brugioni tells the story, as it unfolded day by increasingly tense day,
of that mobilization and the preparations to invade Cuba and destroy
the missile sites if the Soviets refused to back down. If the operation was
unbelievably swift and for the most part efficient, remember that in
1962 the United States armed forces had reached a Cold War peak of
morale and readiness. But that extraordinary mobilization did not
come off without some typically American glitches.*

OCTOBER 15 AND 16, 1962. Throughout the summer of 1962 the CIA had
maintained close surveillance over the heavy volume of Russian shipping
exiting the Baltic and Black seas bound for Cuba. The dramatic increase in
Soviet cargoes and the arrival of numerous "technicians" at Cuban ports
became a paramount intelligence concern. A U-2 mission over the island
on August 29 revealed that the Soviets were constructing an islandwide
SA-2 surface-to-air-missile (SAM) defense network. Soon after, the discovery of Komar guided-missile patrol boats and coastal cruise-missile sites to
defend against an amphibious landing alerted the U.S. government to more
sinister possibilities.

The emerging picture of a Soviet military buildup in Cuba particularly
worried John McCone, director of the Central Intelligence Agency. Of the
SA-2 missiles he stated: "They're not putting them in to protect the cane
cutters. They're putting them in to blind our reconnaissance eye." McCone
insisted that the number of U-2 flights over Cuba be increased, and he expressed to top policymakers his concern that the Soviets might introduce
offensive missiles in Cuba. On September 4 and 13 President Kennedy
issued warnings to the Soviets that "the gravest issues" would arise if they
installed surface-to-surface missiles (SSMs) in Cuba. In official statements
and high-level meetings with U.S. officials, the Soviets stated emphatically
that they would not deploy offensive weapons in Cuba.

On Monday, October 15, interpreting a U-2 mission flown over Cuba the
day before, NPIC discovered two medium-range ballistic missile (MRBM) sites
under construction in the San Cristóbal area. When the president was briefed
on October 16, he ordered the island completely covered by U-2 missions.
Interpreting the photographs these flights brought back, the center found four
additional MRBM sites and three intermediate-range ballistic missile (IRBM)
sites under construction. (The MRBMs could reach just beyond Washington,
D.C., the IRBMs could hit all parts of the United States except the extreme
Northwest.) NPIC also spotted four mobile Soviet combat groups.

General Maxwell D. Taylor, chairman of the Joint Chiefs of Staff (JCS),
saw the secret Soviet move into Cuba with nuclear missiles as a major
effort to change the strategic balance of power. It was an attempt to erase
in one stroke the U.S. nuclear superiority to the Soviets. That superiority,
according to a top-secret estimate, was at least 7 to 1. (In meetings with

Americans in Moscow two years ago, Soviet officials stated that the ratio was closer to 15 to 1—or greater—in favor of the United States.) Taylor and the other members of the JCS recommended a preemptive air strike, an airborne assault, and an invasion to wipe out the missile bases. As Dean Acheson, then a senior adviser with the National Security Council (NSC), put it—and Taylor agreed—one does not plan a military operation of the magnitude of the Soviets' with the expectation that it will fail.

The NSC debated three courses of action: a "quarantine" (actually a blockade) of Cuba, air strikes against the missile sites, and an invasion. The president chose the quarantine. At the same time, preparations were set in motion for the alternatives. Acheson began to press for a declaration of war against Cuba. He wanted to make it plain to the Soviets that "their bayonets had struck steel instead of mush."

To the intelligence community, the Soviet-Cuban venture had the Khrushchev stamp: a gamble—bold, large, premeditated, but not carefully thought through. That gamble would become a colossal Soviet blunder. Militarily, as General Taylor would remark, the Soviets chose the wrong issue and the wrong battlefield.

JCS contingency plans for air strikes, a quarantine, and the invasion of Cuba had been completed by the summer and were known as Operational Plans 312, 314, and 316 respectively. Practice for these operations had already been scheduled to take place with an amphibious brigade landing exercise from October 15 to 20 on Vieques Island, off Puerto Rico. At the last moment the exercise had been canceled because of bad weather. But thousands of marines were still on their ships, ready for a real landing.

During the same period the U.S. Army and U.S. Air Force were engaged in exercises called "Three Pairs" and "Rapid Roads" in central Texas. Units of the 82nd Airborne Division, the attacking force, were waiting at the James Connally Air Force Base at Waco, Texas, when ordered to return to their home base, Fort Bragg, North Carolina. The Tactical Air Command (TAC) fighters that were to support the 82nd Airborne were sent to airfields in Florida. The 1st Armored Division, which was to be the aggressor force in the exercise, was told to return to base at nearby Fort Hood and await orders.

OCTOBER 17–19. The JCS, through Admiral Robert Lee Dennison, commander in chief, Atlantic (CINCLANT), began alerting naval Task Forces 135 and 136 to head for the Caribbean. Commanding officers were told to round up their men as inconspicuously as possible. Task Force 135 consisted of two attack carrier groups built around the nuclear-powered USS *Enterprise* and the USS *Independence,* along with fifteen screening destroyers. It was to proceed to positions off the southern coast of Cuba. Task Force 136, the blockading force, consisted of the aircraft carrier *Essex* and cruisers *Newport News* and *Canberra,* along with an underway replenishment group and nineteen destroyers. The quarantine line was marked by twelve destroyers on an arc 500 miles from Cape Maisí.

Lieutenant General Hamilton Howse, commanding general of the

Strategic Army Command (STRAC) and the XVIII Airborne Corps at Fort Bragg, ordered the commanders of the 101st Airborne Division, the 1st Infantry Division, the 2nd Infantry Division, the 1st Armored Division, and the 82nd Airborne Division to report to his headquarters immediately. He briefed them on October 19, a Friday, with aerial photos provided by NPIC and ordered them to bring their commands to full alert status.

The 82nd and 101st airborne divisions stationed at Fort Bragg and at Fort Campbell, Kentucky, were alerted for immediate movement to intermediate staging areas in southern Florida. The 1st Division at Fort Riley, Kansas, and the 4th Division at Fort Lewis, Washington, were also alerted to possible movement. The 2nd Division at Fort Benning, Georgia, would be moved to New Orleans for embarkation. The 1st Armored would be sent to Fort Stewart, Georgia. The commanders assembled their staffs and gave detailed instructions for the movement of men and matériel from their commands to Georgia or Florida.

One of the first priorities was to establish an impenetrable air-defense umbrella over forces gathering in Florida. Just ninety miles and five minutes of jet flying time from Havana, Key West would become one of the principal bases of the crisis. Rear Admiral Rhomad Y. McElroy, the Key West commander, cleared Key West International Airport and the nearby U.S. naval air station at Boca Chica of all utility and support aircraft in order to accommodate the navy and marine strike, reconnaissance, and defense aircraft that had already begun arriving from bases along the East Coast. Naval Squadron VF-41, transferred to Key West from Oceana, Virginia, on October 6, was already patrolling along the Florida Keys and the north shore of Cuba. All leaves were canceled at the base.

Meanwhile, military aircraft of all types, from fighters to reconnaissance planes packed with computers and sophisticated listening equipment, began to converge on other Florida air bases. By the evening of October 19, hundreds of fighters were lined up wingtip to wingtip, ready for action.

Army air-defense battalions, equipped with Hawk and Nike Hercules SAMs, were given the highest priority for rail, air, and truck movement. From as far away as Fort Lewis, equipment was moved southward to defend the Florida airfields that were most vulnerable to Cuban attack. The Hawk surface-to-air missiles battalion at Fort Meade, Maryland, was ordered to proceed posthaste by road to Key West. The loading was quickly accomplished, but it was evident that there had been little regard for weight or orderliness in the packing of the equipment. The unit selected U.S. Highway 1 as the fastest route to Florida. As the convoy moved through Virginia, a state highway patrolman noticed that a number of the trucks appeared to be overloaded. He signaled the convoy to follow him to the weighing station. There his suspicions were confirmed. The military officers protested vehemently that they had an important defense mission to perform in Florida—they couldn't yet say what it was—and that precious time was being wasted. The patrolman remarked that military convoys were always in a hurry. He calmly proceeded to write out a ticket—a warning to the U.S. Army to be more careful in future loading of convoys.

OCTOBER 20–21. The great mobilization was under way. Ammunition and supplies were moving by rail and road from all parts of the country. Truck after truck left the Letterkenny Ordnance Depot in Chambersburg, Pennsylvania, and began to roll to Florida loaded with ammunition. Several ordnance plants were placed on three-shift, seven-day weeks to produce 20mm strafing ammunition required for the fighter aircraft. The war plans called for the use of napalm as well as conventional ammunition. Hundreds of napalm drop tanks began arriving at the naval and tactical airfields, where they were stacked, according to one observer, like "mountains of cordwood." Ammunition for naval gunfire against Cuban installations was also shipped to bases in Florida. Food rations came from such inland storage depots as Bonner Springs, Kansas. Army boat units, which would be needed for an invasion, were ordered to go to Fort Lauderdale and Port Everglades in Florida.

Military hospitals, especially those along the East Coast, previously devoted primarily to treating service dependents, were prepared to receive war casualties. Blood supplies were monitored, and troops not involved in the movement to Florida were asked to give blood. One hospital unit was sent to Florida on chartered buses. Presuming that this movement was another exercise, the buses had stopped at several liquor stores along the way. When it arrived in Florida, the unit itself was a casualty.

Billeting of the troops arriving in Florida was already becoming a problem. At some airfields the bachelor officers and enlisted men's quarters were operated on the "hot bunk" principle: Three men would be assigned to each bunk, with someone sleeping in it at all hours. Mess halls remained open around the clock. Later, after the president announced that missiles were in place in Cuba, the owner of the Gulfstream Park at Hallandale, Florida, invited the army to bivouac some of the troops of the 1st Armored Division at the racecourse. The army accepted, and soon military police were placed at all entrances; parking lots became motor pools, and the infield was used for storage and mess. Troops were billeted on the first and second floors of the grandstand. Weapons and duffel bags were stacked next to the betting windows. Church services were held in the photo-finish developing rooms.

According to Contingency Plan 316, the 82nd and 101st airborne divisions would be the first to land on Cuba. Large numbers of transport aircraft would have to be diverted to support the operation; more than 800 Lockheed Hercules flights would be needed to execute the invasion plan. Plans for deployment of the airborne divisions had been rehearsed and tested again.

Drops would be made at altitudes of from 700 to 900 feet. Airborne commanders knew conducting military operations on Cuba in October would not be easy. It was the season of rain and hurricanes, clouds and high winds, certainly not the best jump weather. Some drop zones would be in valleys containing sugarcane fields and cattle ranches. By the end of October, the cane fields would reach their maximum heights of seven to ten feet. The cane stalks not only posed a landing hazard for the parachutists but also presented problems in rallying and maneuvering—and provided the Cubans with sites that were ready-made for conducting guerrilla operations and harassing the airborne troops.

Those troops were issued a number of instructions about the treatment of any prisoners. They were specifically told that "Sino-Soviet bloc personnel" were to be carefully handled and taken into protective custody. At this point the United States was still trying its utmost to avoid a direct confrontation with the Soviet Union.

To assure proper interrogation of prisoners of war, Spanish-speaking military intelligence personnel were assigned to both division and regimental headquarters. Crash courses on interrogation techniques were offered to the airborne divisions. Prisoners of war were one thing, but it soon developed that the State Department had no specific plan for the handling of Cuban refugees. Although there were generalized plans for the occupation and a military government, there was no detailed plan for the recruitment of indigenous Cuban administrators. Nor were there plans to prevent starvation, disease, or civil unrest. When asked whether it had the funds to deal with such likely calamities, the State Department replied that "none had been budgeted." This enormous potential for trouble would never really be solved—and other matters were more pressing.

One of the first issues President Kennedy raised during the crisis had been whether U.S. dependents at the Guantánamo Bay U.S. Naval Station on the southeastern end of Cuba should be evacuated. At the time there were over 2,800 women and children living on the base. The navy had strong feelings that the Soviets and Cubans might regard removal of the dependents as a sign of weakness rather than a matter of practicality. More to the point, it might also tip them off that the United States knew about the missiles, and the Soviets and Cubans might respond by upgrading their military and naval defenses. But Secretary of Defense Robert S. McNamara had insisted that the dependents be removed. It had not yet been established that McNamara was reflecting the president's views. In an attempt to convince McNamara of the value of keeping the dependents at Guantánamo, the assistant secretary of defense for international security affairs, Paul Nitze, and the Second Fleet commander, Admiral Alfred G. Ward, met with him. Ward was in charge of the blockade—and the navy's role in any invasion. Nitze pointed out various reasons why it would be inadvisable to pull out the American civilians. After listening patiently, McNamara stood up and said. "Mr. Secretary, you have your instructions to get the dependents out of Guantánamo Bay. Please carry out those instructions."

Shortly after 11:00 A.M. on October 21, the Sunday-morning routine at Guantánamo was interrupted by phone calls and messengers hurrying to the buildings where families were housed. Each family was told to pack one bag per person and be prepared to evacuate within fifteen minutes' notice. Loading on aircraft and naval vessels was completed before 4:00 P.M. At this point the Cuban military threat was spelled out to them only in the most general way.

If the Cubans thought the Americans were showing signs of weakness by evacuating service dependents from Guantánamo, they were soon to see an impressive display of strength as cargo aircraft began landing on the airfield. By the evening of the next day, 3,600 marines and 3,200 tons of equipment had been airlifted by the Material Air Transport Service. In a glaring overestimate of U.S. strength, Soviet intelligence reported that "the garrison had been increased from 8,000 to 18,000 personnel from the 2nd Marine Division, and reinforced by 150 tanks, 24 antiaircraft missile systems and 70 recoilless guns. The number of airplanes had been increased to 120." The actual U.S. defense force deployed to Guantánamo, including men and equipment already in place, comprised 5,750 marines, a Hawk missile battery, 155 tanks, several battalions of 105mm artillery pieces, three gunfire support ships, two marine air-attack squadrons, and a patrol squadron. Two aircraft carriers were in the area to render support.

The Guantánamo reinforcement was largely a deception, and it worked. While the United States regarded this as a defensive operation, the Soviets and Cubans saw the "uninterrupted intensive reconnaissance along Cuban shores and approaches" as proof that Guantánamo was "actively being prepared as a bridgehead for military operation." But for the moment, the marines' function was to secure the Guantánamo defensive perimeter; once fighting started, it was to take on the Cuban artillery dug in on the surrounding hills. Only when the main amphibious and airborne forces established themselves on the island would the marines consider moving out.

Kennedy had originally intended to make his speech to the nation that evening, but politics dictated that he inform Congress first, and it proved impossible on such short notice to round up everyone who was out campaigning.

OCTOBER 22. This was the day, a Monday, when the "Cuban Missile Crisis" became public. Planes had been dispatched to bring back ranking senators and congressmen. Even so, their briefing took place little more than an hour before the president's speech, and there was considerable anger that he had waited until the last minute to inform them. Just before Kennedy went on the air at 7 P.M., U.S. jet fighters scrambled into the sky from bases in Florida. The action was termed an airborne alert—a precautionary measure "in the event of a rash action by the Cubans." Not just the Cubans: As the president made clear, any offensive action by them would be considered an offensive action by the Soviet Union.

As Kennedy was speaking, the secretary of defense placed the entire U.S. military establishment on DefCon (defense condition) 3 status (DefCon 5 was all normal; DefCon 1 meant war). In accordance with JCS directives, Strategic Air Command (SAC) B-47 bombers were dispersed to more than thirty predesignated civilian airfields in the United States. At two SAC bases in Spain, three in Morocco, and three in England, B-47 bombers were loaded with nuclear weapons and prepared for takeoff. Simultaneously, a massive airborne alert was begun by U.S.–based B-52 bombers and KC-135 tankers. The B-52s were loaded with nuclear weapons and ordered to fly under continuous command control, either far out over the Pacific, deep into the Arctic, or across the Atlantic and the Mediterranean. There the planes would wait for instructions either to proceed to the Soviet Union or to return to their home bases. In addition, fighter-bombers at American bases in England, France, Italy, Germany, Turkey, South Korea, Japan, and the Philippines were placed on alert and armed with ordnance, including nuclear, for striking targets in the Soviet Union or in Eastern Europe.

There were three intercontinental ballistic missile (ICBM) systems in the SAC inventory at the time: Atlas, Titan I, and Titan II. A fourth system, the solid-fuel Minuteman, would enter the inventory during the later days of the crisis. There were also 60 Thor IRBMs in England, 30 Jupiter IRBMs in Italy, and 15 in Turkey. Late in the evening General Curtis LeMay, chief of staff of the air force, notified McNamara that 91 Atlases and 41 Titans were being readied for firing. Nine missile-carrying submarines capable of firing 144 Polaris missiles had left their bases and taken up stations in the North Atlantic. Matador and Mace cruise missiles deployed in tactical wings were brought to combat status in West Germany; they could strike strategic targets in Eastern Europe.

Fifteen minutes before the president's address, the nation's railroads were also put on alert. The Pentagon asked the Association of American Railroads for the immediate use of 375 flatcars to move air-defense and air-warning units to Florida. That evening the 1st Armored Division began the 1,100-mile trek from Texas to an intermediate staging base at Fort Stewart. This division alone would require 3,600 flatcars, 190 gondola cars, 40 boxcars, and 200 passenger cars. In all, over 5,000 men, 15,000 vehicles, and thousands of tons of supplies would be loaded on 38 trains, some up to 150 cars long. At the height of the crisis, normal rail movement in the Southeast practically came to a halt. Another 10,000 men would be airlifted in 135 commercial flights.

OCTOBER 23. The president authorized the use of low-level aerial photo-reconnaissance and of the navy's F8U Crusaders; later, air force RF-101 Voodoos began flying from Florida at treetop level over the Cuban missile sites. The low-altitude photography, transferred immediately to Washington for analysis, added a new dimension to NPIC's reporting. Each piece of missile equipment could be identified precisely and its function in the missile system determined. Rather than taking the interpreter's word as they had with the U-2 photography, policymakers now could see clearly what the interpreters had seen and were reporting.

OCTOBER 24. The JCS ordered DefCon 2—maximum alert before war with the optimum posture to strike either Cuba or the USSR or both. With this change of status, 1,436 U.S. bombers loaded with nuclear weapons and 134 ICBMs were now on constant alert: One-eighth of the bombers were in the air at all times, and air crews were waiting near the rest of the bombers, prepared for takeoff on a moment's notice.

Both the White House press secretary and the news desk at the Pentagon were being besieged by reporters demanding to know more about the reported buildup for an invasion of Cuba. Although the president felt that the Washington press would exercise control in reporting military information, he was appalled by reports that local television crews throughout the United States had stationed themselves near military bases and were making public the sort of details that would never have been leaked during World War II and the Korean War.

Kennedy decided that a nationwide reporting guideline had to be established for the news media, and he asked the Department of Defense to draft it. While he made it clear he was not imposing censorship, he did want to restrict information on the deployment of forces, degrees of alert, defenses, dispersal plans, vulnerabilities, and air- and sea-lift capabilities.

Late that evening, the president called McNamara to confirm when U.S. forces would be ready to invade Cuba. The secretary replied, "In seven days." When Kennedy pressed him on whether all the forces would be well prepared, McNamara replied that they would be "ready in every respect in seven days": Wednesday, October 31, Halloween.

OCTOBER 25–26. Photo interpreters at NPIC had identified four camps suspected of housing Soviet armored combat groups. All were in the vicinity of the missile sites, which would tend to indicate that their main function was to protect them. But other intelligence analysts had maintained that they were simply camps where Cubans were being trained to handle Soviet arms—or that they were temporary equipment transfer points, places where, as one U.S. general put it, "The Cosmoline was removed." NPIC kept insisting that these were more likely to be Soviet combat facilities, since the equipment observed was parked in neat formations, characteristic of the Soviet army, rather than in the haphazard ones typical of Cuban installations. That equipment, of the most sophisticated recent vintage, included T-54 tanks, assault guns, tactical rocket launchers, antitank weapons, and personnel carriers. It wasn't until October 24 that the intelligence community agreed with the photo interpreters that these were Soviet installations and that they did house combat troops, as many as 1,500 each.

The next day a low-altitude reconnaissance aircraft brought back absolute confirmation. At the Santiago de las Vegas installation, Soviet ground-force-unit symbols and insignias were seen implanted in the flagstone and flowers in front of garrison areas. One unit proudly displayed the Elite Guards Badge, the Soviet equivalent of the U.S. Presidential Unit Citation. These four camps were quickly targeted, and ordnance, including nuclear, was selected for their destruction in the event of an invasion.

That day, too, the continuing Soviet denial that offensive missiles were in Cuba was exposed as a lie when Adlai Stevenson, the U.S. ambassador to the United Nations, confronted the Soviet ambassador with aerial photographs of the missile sites during a Security Council meeting.

Throughout the crisis, President Kennedy was concerned that an American move on Cuba would provoke a countermove by the Soviets on Berlin. Close watch of Soviet forces was maintained in the Soviet Union and East Germany, but there was no indication of preparations for offensive action. The Soviets were obviously concerned that any such indication might provoke a first-strike response by alerted U.S. forces. Soviet U.N. ambassador Valerian Zorin told a group of neutral African and Asian U.N. delegates that "The Americans are thoroughly mistaken if they think we shall fall in their trap. We shall undertake nothing in Berlin, for action against Berlin is just what the Americans would wish."

Khrushchev's overall behavior during this week appeared unsure and erratic. He continued to lie about the missiles after their presence had been established beyond doubt. Even as he attempted to pacify the United States, his soldiers at Cuban bases were working frantically to bring the missiles to an operational status. After ordering his ships to turn around, he threatened to run the blockade using submarines. He threatened to fire missiles but took no overt offensive action that might cause the United States to further increase its alert status. U.S. military leaders knew that Khrushchev could be ruthless when desperate. The JCS was wary of what direction the crisis would take, determined, as Admiral Ward later put it, that they were not going to be "the Kimmels and Shorts of this generation"—a reference to Admiral Husband Kimmel and Major General Walter Short, who were relieved of their commands after Pearl Harbor.

To ensure the success of possible amphibious landings in Cuba, Ward decided that exercises should be conducted in Florida in as realistic a manner as possible. A number of projected landing areas in Cuba were at or near resort areas, so Hollywood Beach, near Fort Lauderdale, was selected to simulate the Havana beach area. In the predawn chill the sea off Fort Lauderdale was rough, and it was late morning before the marines climbed down nets from the ships offshore into the bobbing personnel landing craft. The bigger LSTs (landing ship tanks) prepared to move toward the shore to disgorge tanks and armored personnel carriers.

The littoral behind the landing zone, situated along the central portion of Hollywood Beach, was dense with hotels, motels, restaurants, and bars. By the time the men and equipment hit the beach, the sunbathers had already gathered under their umbrellas. The tanks, armored personnel carriers, and infantrymen soon joined the crowd on the narrow beach. Instead of obeying the instructions of a forward observer who was installed on the roof of a jai alai court, some of the marines began fraternizing with bikini-clad girls on the beach; others posed for tourists' cameras in their combat gear; while an even greater number headed for the bars. Admiral Ward later characterized the exercise as about the closest thing to the Keystone Kops that he had ever seen. He never reported the Hollywood Beach fiasco to his superiors but, instead, emphasized that the landing exercises the same day at Hutchinson Island, Fort Pierce, and near Fort

Everglades had gone as planned.

At 6:00 P.M. on October 26, the White House began to receive transmission of a long, rambling polemic from Khrushchev—which did, however, give a glimmer of hope. The Soviet premier hinted that he was prepared to withdraw his missiles if Kennedy would agree not to invade Cuba.

OCTOBER 27. This was the day that would be referred to as "Black Saturday" by both the president and members of the National Security Council. Khrushchev remarked that "a smell of burning hung in the air."

Just before 10:00 A.M., Soviet personnel fired an SA-2 surface-to-air missile and downed a U-2 reconnaissance plane flown by Major Rudolf Anderson, who was killed. The order to fire was apparently given by General Igor D. Statsenko, commander of the Soviet forces in Cuba. The intelligence community could come up with no reason why the Soviets, who had been tracking the U-2 flights, would select this moment to down one. Most feared that the Soviets were escalating the crisis.

JCS Contingency Plan No. 312 directed CINCLANT to be prepared to strike a single SA-2 SAM site, or all Cuban SAM sites, within two hours of a U-2 shootdown. The established policy, agreed to by the president, was that any SAM site that fired at a U-2 was to be immediately neutralized. Sixteen armed F-100 Super Sabre fighters stood by at Homestead Air Force Base in southern Florida on thirty-minute alert to attack any firing SAM site.

When word that Anderson had been shot down reached General LeMay, he ordered the F-100s readied to strike. The White House, realizing that there was a standing order for this operations procedure, frantically contacted LeMay and asked if the fighters had been launched. LeMay replied that they were being readied. He was admonished not to launch the fighters until he received direct orders from the president. Angered, LeMay hung up. "He chickened out again," he said. "How in the hell do you get men to risk their lives when the SAMs are not attacked?" When an aide said he would wait at the phone for the president's order, LeMay disgustedly replied, "It will never come!"

The crisis had entered a new phase. A fragile and volatile situation existed that could explode into a major conflict with little or no warning. The CIA now believed that all the MRBM sites in Cuba were operational. Pilots returning from low-altitude flights reported that antiaircraft weapons were firing on them. Analysis of the aerial photography revealed that antiaircraft weapons were being installed around the MRBM sites. There was also a desperate effort by the Soviets to camouflage and conceal those sites. And hundreds of trenches were being dug to protect them from ground assault.

That afternoon ExCom (the Executive Committee of the NSC) discussed what retaliatory action should be taken. It decided that, beginning the next morning, all low-flying reconnaissance aircrafts would have armed escorts. That afternoon, too, McNamara ordered twenty-four troop-carrier squadrons of the air force reserve, along with their associated support units, to active duty. Besides paratroopers, these squadrons would drop supplies to the ground units that would be placed ashore in an invasion of Cuba. And LeMay announced to McNamara that 1,576 bombers and 283 missiles stood poised to strike the seventy principal cities of the Soviet Union.

In the evening the CIA briefed the president in depth on the startling events of the day. He had already responded to Khrushchev's message of the previous evening with the suggestion that he would be willing to make a pledge not to invade Cuba if the Soviets met his conditions. But Kennedy decided it was time to deliver an ultimatum. The president's brother, Attorney General Robert Kennedy, was sent to meet with Soviet ambassador Anatoly Dobrynin, warning him that the United States had to have a commitment by the next day that the missiles would be removed, or the United States would remove them by force.

At that moment in Florida, 156 tactical aircraft were ready to strike Cuba. They were backed up by almost 700 more strike planes that were on the ground or at sea. The air force and the navy were prepared to conduct continuous air strikes until all the SAM, MRBM, and IRBM sites, as well as the Cuban air force, had been destroyed. If an invasion of Cuba were ordered, a total of 1,190 sorties could be flown the first day.

U.S. planning for the invasion of Cuba and possible war against the Soviet Union was now going so well that the date had been moved forward: It could come as early as Tuesday, October 30. Military leaders openly admitted, however, that an invasion of Cuba would be as bloody as Korea. The estimate of total U.S. casualties for the first few days of the combined airborne and amphibious operation was about 1,000 a day. The invasion would be opposed by 75,000 Cuban regular troops, 100,000 militia, and 100,000 home guards—not to mention Soviet personnel, then estimated at 22,000. (The Soviets later maintained that there were almost 40,000 in Cuba at the height of the crisis.)

The aerial and naval bombardment of the island would begin early Tuesday morning. The 82nd Airborne Division would be dropped farther inland than the 101st. The 82nd's objective was to seize the San Antonio de los Baños military airfield and the José Martí International Airfield just outside Havana. The 101st would also take the military airfields at Mariel and Baracoa, along with the port of Mariel. There would be airdrops of humanlike dummies to confuse the enemy. These, however, would not be ordinary dummies: They would be armed with recorded tapes to create the sounds of firefights.

There were a total of ten battalions of marines afloat in the vicinity of Cuba. They would come ashore at a number of famous beaches on Cuba's northern shore between Havana and Matanzas and link up with the 82nd Airborne Division. (The Soviets and Cubans suspected the invasion would come ashore at these beaches and had deployed cruise missiles along the coast; they also had dug defensive trenches along those beaches.) Once the beaches and the port of Mariel were secured, the 1st Armored Division would come ashore. They would move along the major highways and isolate Havana; then they would head for the missile sites. Other units of the 1st Armored would strike southward to cut the island in half.

OCTOBER 28. That morning at nine o'clock, Washington time, the U.S. Foreign Broadcast Intercept Service, while listening to Radio Moscow, began picking up an extraordinary message: It was an open letter from Khrushchev to Kennedy. The Soviets were clearly so alarmed by the speed with which events were moving that they elected to bypass the usual method of sending such a high-level message. Even in the time it would take to encode, decode, translate, and deliver the message, the crisis might have escalated out of control and the invasion might already have begun. So the Soviets decided to broadcast Khrushchev's letter to the president on the radio. "The Soviet government," the message read, "has ordered the dismantling of bases and the dispatch of equipment to the USSR. . . . I regard with respect and trust the statement you have made in your message . . . that there would be no attack or invasion against Cuba."

Less than forty-eight hours remained before the invasion was set to begin.

EPILOGUE. U.S. military leaders greeted the end of the crisis with relief. No one relished the prospect of heavy casualties—not to mention the threat of nuclear war. The main responsibility now fell on the intelligence community to monitor the dismantling of the missile sites and verify the removal of the missiles from the island. "The military posture of the United States," Admiral Ward noted in his diary a week later, on November 4, "continued to be one of increased readiness." Ships carrying 12,000 marines from the West Coast were on their way, while sizable units of the 2nd Marine Division remained at sea off Florida. Air force and army units were poised for an assault, as were the carriers *Enterprise* and *Independence*.

But by now only Fidel Castro remained belligerent. He threatened to fire on the U.S. reconnaissance planes. Anastas Mikoyan, the first deputy secretary, was dispatched from Moscow to pacify the Cuban leader. When Castro told him that the Cuban people were prepared to fight as they had at the Bay of Pigs, Mikoyan replied, "You won't have a ragtag brigade against you this time. You will have the full might of U.S. forces. If you want to fight, you can fight—but alone." Mikoyan tightened the screws. He threatened to return immediately to Moscow and cut off all economic aid to Cuba. Grumbling, Castro backed down.

After the Soviet missiles had been removed from Cuba, but before the troops assembled in the southeastern United States were disbanded, Maxwell Taylor wanted the president to see firsthand the military machine that had been assembled for the projected invasion. On November 26, accompanied by the JCS and the chairman of the House Armed Services Committee, Kennedy arrived at Fort Stewart and reviewed just one of the three brigades of the 1st Armored Division. He looked on, incredulous, at the armor arrayed before him. That incredulity only grew as he traveled south that day, ending up on a pier at the Key West naval base. At Fort Stewart he recited a poem, supposedly found in a British sentry box at Gibraltar:

> *God and the soldier all men adore,*
> *In time of danger and not before.*
> *When the danger is past,*
> *And all things righted,*
> *God is forgotten and the old*
> *Soldier slighted.*

The president added, "The United States forgets neither God nor the soldier upon which we now depend."

But three decades later we have almost forgotten the great invasion that never happened—forgotten it, perhaps, because we never really knew how awesome it would have been.

*Winter 1992*

---

During the time of the Missile Crisis, Dino A. Brugioni worked for the National Photographic Interpretation Center. He is the author of *Eyeball to Eyeball: The Inside Story of the Cuban Missile Crisis* (1991) and *From Balloons to Blackbirds: Reconnaissance, Surveillance, and Imagery Intelligence: How It Evolved* (1993). He is currently working on a book to be entitled *Photo Fakery and Photo Manipulation.*

# 44

# "Thats Ocay XX Time Is on Our Side"

## By Geoffrey Norman

*Few images of the Vietnam War were more emotionally intense and poignant than the return of American prisoners of war. As Geoffrey Norman demonstrates, the story of their endurance as POWs is even more compelling. Cut off from their country and comrades, physically and mentally abused, bereft of succor or support, these Americans could depend only on themselves, their personal ingenuity, and their private determination to keep mind and body together. That they succeeded remains a lasting testament to the human spirit.*

On March 31, 1968, President Lyndon Johnson told the American people that he was suspending bombing of North Vietnam above the 21st parallel. At the end of his speech, he also announced that he would not be running for reelection. Johnson had been defeated by the North Vietnamese; he was quitting and going home. It remained to be seen if the U.S. prisoners of war, mainly airmen who had been shot down, would be so lucky.

The news was broadcast over speakers in every prison camp. And when there was nothing said about their release, many of the POWs drew the darkest conclusion. In a camp called the Plantation, on the outskirts of Hanoi, Lieutenant Commander Richard Stratton, the senior ranking officer, said to the three other men in his cell, "If we weren't part of some deal—no more bombing in exchange for our release—then we are going to be here for a long time. Probably until they start bombing again." Stratton's prediction was accurate. He and the others would spend five more years in North Vietnam.

While Hanoi was no longer being bombed, the air war continued in the Panhandle of North Vietnam, and new shootdowns arrived with the un-welcome news that the war was still going on. There were no negotiations yet and no reason to believe that peace and repatriation were at hand.

A single rail line ran outside the Plantation, just beyond the back wall of the old building that the men called the Warehouse, which had been divided into cells. In his cell, designated Warehouse One, Stratton and his cellmates could lean a pallet bed against the wall, climb the ladderlike studs that held the boards together, and look through the gunports at the passing trains. Even after Johnson's decision to halt the bombing of Hanoi, the passing cattle cars were full of young men in uniform on their way to the fight. More than any information from recent shootdowns or the small seeds of truth amid the propaganda of the camp news, this was the most vivid proof that the war was not winding down.

Guards still came to take prisoners out for interrogations, but these increasingly became what the POWs called "temperature quizzes." Instead of being pumped for military information or pressed for propaganda, they were asked how they were getting along and how they felt about their captors and the war. Most of the POWs maneuvered to avoid head buttings. They answered vaguely and were eventually returned to their cells. They began to suspect that in many cases the quizzes were merely a pretext for interrogators to practice their English. Still, to see the door open and the guard point his finger at you was a frightening experience.

There was no way of knowing, when you left the cell for the walk up to headquarters, if you were in for a temperature quiz or something a lot more serious. Delegations were still coming into Vietnam for tours; prisoners in all the camps were still being pressured to make statements, sometimes with the promise of early release; punishments were still being inflicted on men caught violating camp rules. In short, the weeks and months that followed the Tet offensive of early 1968 were not better by any objective measure.

The POWs began psychologically digging in, adjusting to the long haul. Most were in their twenties or early thirties. A few were barely old enough to have voted in one election before they were shot down. Some were fathers of children they'd never seen; husbands of women they had lived with for only a few weeks. It seemed increasingly possible—even probable—that they would be middle-aged or old men before they left Vietnam. Their survival now included facing this hard reality. Somehow, they had to find ways to fill those years, to salvage something from their youth.

At all of the POW camps in North Vietnam, communication between prisoners was strictly forbidden. Roommates managed to communicate without being overheard, but a man could not shout through walls or windows, or leave messages, or try in any other way to make contact with the other prisoners in the camp. Men were thrown into solitary, locked in irons, hung by ropes, and beaten when they were caught trying to communicate.

Still, it was worth the risk, since communication was the foundation of any kind of resistance. The senior man had to get his orders out to everyone in the camp, and everyone had to be tied in; four men alone in a room were not part of a unified resistance. With something called the "tap code," prisoners were able to communicate and establish an organization. Working together helped them overcome feelings of isolation and boredom, and ultimately enabled them to resist.

The principle of the tap code is ancient, at least as old as Greek civilization. In modern dress, it appears in Arthur Koestler's descriptions of life in the Soviet gulag in his novel *Darkness at Noon*. POWs believed that it had been invented by an air force captain named Smitty Harris, who came up with it while he was in survival school and remembered it in Hoa Lo after he had been shot down. Although the POWs may have been wrong about the origins of the tap code, no group in history ever employed it more successfully or more enthusiastically. Learning the tap code was like getting a telephone: It opened a world.

The basis of the code is a grid that looks like this:

| | | | | |
|---|---|---|---|---|
| A | B | C | D | E |
| F | G | H | I | J |
| L | M | N | O | P |
| Q | R | S | T | U |
| V | W | X | Y | Z |

The letter *C* could be substituted for *K*, and the code was read like the coordinates on a map—down and right. For example, the letter *M* would be three down and two across. To transmit an *M* through the wall, a prisoner would tap three times, pause, then tap twice.

Most men learned the code from a roommate, but it was possible to teach it through a wall to a man who was all alone and needed it worse than anyone. A man who knew the code would simply tap on the wall until he got a response. He might tap out the familiar rhythm of "Shave and a Haircut" until the man on the other side came back with "Two Bits." Once that happened, they were in communication. Then the tedious business of teaching a language began, first using a more primitive system. The first man would tap once, pause, tap twice, pause, tap three times, pause . . . and so on, until he reached twenty-six. Then he would do it again. Eventually the other man would understand that the twenty-six taps represented the alphabet. *A* was one, *B* was two, and so on.

When this had been established, a few messages could be transmitted. The men would exchange names, perhaps, and shootdown dates. It was exceedingly slow and tedious, but it established the link and the rudiments of the method. The next step was to tap out the message "Make a matrix." That done, the newcomer was instructed to fill in the alphabet. In this way the first code was used to explain the much shorter, more efficient one.

At the Plantation, as well as the other camps, the walls were alive with the sounds of men urgently tapping out messages.

When it became clear to the men at the Plantation that they were not going home in return for an end to the bombing of Hanoi, they began trying to improve the physical conditions of their captivity. They would never be comfortable—the cells were crowded and unventilated, and the men slept on boards and wore the same clothes day after day—but they could try to keep clean, and they could improvise several other ways to reduce their misery.

In Warehouse Four there was a lieutenant (j.g.) named Tom Hall who gained a reputation among his fellows as an especially gifted improviser. A farmboy from outside of Suffolk, Virginia, who had grown up learning how to doctor animals, fix cars, and make all of the endless repairs necessary to keep a farm running, he knew how to "make do." After graduating from Virginia Tech, he had gone into the navy and learned to fly fighters. He had been stationed on the *Bonhomme Richard,* on Yankee Station, when his F-8 was hit by a SAM. He had gone to afterburner and pointed the plane toward the beach. Over the Gulf of Tonkin, safely out of reach of the patrol boats and fishing junks, he ejected. The rescue helicopter picked him up and flew him back to the carrier, whose captain was waiting to greet him. A photographer caught the moment, and the picture made the papers back in the States.

Like any pilot who has ejected, Hall was ordered to stand down for a day. The following morning, the weather was so bad over North Vietnam that no missions were flown from the ship. The next day Hall was flying again and he caught another SAM. This time he bailed out near Hanoi—and the North Vietnamese got him. That was June 1966.

To the men who shared space with him in North Vietnam, Tom Hall was the perfect roommate. He knew how to be quiet, but when he talked, he always had something interesting to say. He told them stories about life back home on the farm, including one about how his family kept a hummingbird flying free in the house to keep the bugs down. The other pilots loved this story; the idea of a hummingbird in the house was somehow otherworldly.

Hall never got too high or too low. He maintained an even strain, as pilots say, and he looked after his comrades first and himself second. He didn't bitch and he didn't quit and he knew, by God, how to cope. It was Hall who figured out how to ease the problem of the drafty cells in the winter of 1968, when the men would wake up in the morning close to hypothermic and spend the first hour or two of the day trying to warm up. HATS, he tapped through the wall. Use extra cloth or, better, a sock to make a hat. Stretch it until it fits over your head like a watch cap. You lose most of your body heat through your head, he explained, and this would help. The men tried it, and it did help. Nevertheless, it was cold, especially during the night.

MOSQUITO NETS, Hall tapped. When it is below forty outside, he explained, you do not need to guard against mosquitoes, but the net can be turned into a kind of insulation, like the fishnet material that Scandinavians use for underwear. Before you lie down to sleep, wrap your upper body in your mosquito net. Like the hats, the improvised underwear was a help. The men were not exactly warm, but they weren't chilled to the bone any longer.

Tom Hall improvised sewing needles from fish bones, or from pieces of wire picked up in the yard. The POWs could now mend their clothes, and they even amused themselves by learning to do a kind of needlepoint. The favorite pattern was, far and away, the American flag.

Hall was also given credit for discovering that a man could use his sandals, which were cut from old rubber tires, as a toilet seat by laying them across the cold, sharp, dirt-encrusted edges of the bucket before he squatted. This, in the minds of many POWs, was the most inspired bit of improvisation in the entire war.

Another persistent, seemingly unsolvable problem at the Plantation was the rats. They were abundant and they were bold. You could chase them out of your cell during the day, but they returned at night. Men were frequently awakened by the pressure of small feet moving across their chests.

Using items that he scrounged—pieces of metal, string, and an empty tin can—Hall built a working mousetrap that kept his cell rat-free. He could not use the tap code to teach the other men how to build such a trap from odds and ends, but he could tell them how to improvise a substitute for plaster out of brick dust and water and use that to seal the ratholes. The other prisoners went to work plastering the holes, and for a while this worked as well as all of Hall's other ideas. But the rats were not pushovers. They began to gnaw their way through the weak plaster barricades, and soon the men had to struggle to replaster the holes faster than the rats could gnaw them open again.

Once more, Hall came through. The Vietnamese grew a kind of bell-shaped pepper, which they ate with their rations. The pepper was fiercely hot, hotter than any jalapeño the Americans had ever eaten. It was possible to sneak one or two of these peppers out of the mess hall when you were on food detail, and Hall advised the other prisoners to plug the ratholes with them. Checking the holes a day or two later, the men noticed that the rats had tried gnawing through the new plugs but had given up before breaking through. The peppers were too hot even for them.

The rats remained a problem—there were no complete, unequivocal victories for the POWs—but Tom Hall had made it into a fight, and the POWs got their innings.

HOUSEKEEPING WAS HUMDRUM stuff for men who flew supersonic fighters and were accustomed to turning their dirty uniforms over to a laundry run by enlisted men. But it became vastly important at the Plantation and the other camps. The camp was dirty, and sanitation was nonexistent. Spiders, roaches, and flies were everywhere. One man tapped out a message designating the housefly as the national bird of North Vietnam. Keeping clean was important not only for its own sake but because it represented a challenge, however small. It wasn't the stuff of a fighter pilot's dreams, like shooting down a MiG, but under the circumstances it would do.

In their weakened condition, the POWs were prey to all sorts of infections and parasites. They worked hard at keeping their cells, their clothes, and themselves clean. Each man was issued a small bar of lye soap every week, and since it seemed to be almost as abundant as pumpkins, they washed their uniforms vigorously with it when they were taken out to bathe. But they still got sick. Medical lore was dredged up from memory and passed through the wall. When you had diarrhea, you should drink only the broth from your soup and leave any greens or meat it might contain. If you were constipated, you should eat whatever solids were in the soup and leave the liquid. It was not much, but it was a regimen and they followed it.

Boils were a constant, painful problem, as were abscessed teeth. One man remembered a doctor telling him an old piece of medical shorthand—"piss and pus must come out"—so he sneaked razor blades from the shower and used them to lance the boils and open the abscesses. It was painful and messy, but it seemed to work.

Many of the prisoners had been seriously injured when they ejected, and there was a lot of discussion through the wall about how to treat those injuries. What could you do about a broken bone that had not been set properly and was healing crooked?

Al Stafford—one of Stratton's roommates—had suffered a broken upper arm when he was blown out of his plane. The arm seemed to be mending, after a fashion, but he could not raise it to the level of his chest or move it laterally beyond an arc of about 30°. He improvised slings and used his good arm for support, but this only increased the stiffness. He imagined himself returning home—whenever that day came—as a cripple.

Down the line of cells somewhere, another POW learned about Stafford's problem and tapped back that he should begin exercising the arm as much as possible to prevent muscle atrophy and to break up the deposits of calcium that were forming around the break. It was something he'd learned after a football injury.

This led to a debate within Stafford's cell about exercise in general. Should prisoners exert themselves? Dick Stratton, never a man for fitness regimes even before he was shot down, was against strenuous exercise programs. In Stafford's case, he thought it would merely aggravate the injury. As for the other men, he said exercise would burn calories, and they could not afford to waste a single BTU. They were on starvation rations; sit-ups and push-ups would only exhaust whatever small reserves they had. But Stratton was careful not to overexert his authority in this matter. He did not order the men not to exercise strenuously; he merely recommended against it. (Later, he began exercising himself.)

Stafford tried some simple flexing movements. How much worse, he asked himself, could it make his arm? So he would raise it, tentatively, until he reached the point where pain told him to stop. Then he would raise the arm another inch or two, stopping when he could hear something inside begin to tear. It sounded almost like a piece of paper gently ripping. Tears would fill his eyes and he would feel himself growing faint. He would lower his arm until the pain had passed and he had his breath. Then he would slowly raise the arm again, until he reached the same point, and then he would bite down on his back teeth and go another inch, and one more. . . .

After a couple of weeks, he noticed that the arc of mobility had grown by a couple of degrees. So he massaged the arm and kept on. He set goals: Get the arm loose enough that he could use it to drink a cup of water; then enough that he could touch the top of his head. Every day he worked the arm until he could hear that sound of tearing paper and he was on the edge of passing out. The other men in the cell would look away while he was exercising. Now and then, one would say, "How's the arm, Al?"

"Better. Lots better. I can touch my nose."

"That's great, man. Really great. Hang in there."

Other prisoners, desperate for some kind of physical activity, began doing calisthenics. This was tricky, since the sounds of a man running in place or counting off push-ups would alert guards. They would open the cell's little Judas window, wave a finger at the man, and tell him to stop. If he was caught repeatedly, he might be taken up to the headquarters building, which the POWs called the Big House, for interrogation and punishment. Prisoners were to sit quietly in their cells, eat their two bowls of soup a day, come out for a bath and a shave once a week, and otherwise do nothing.

So prisoners who wanted to do calisthenics had to depend on the "clearing system." Along the line of cells, men would watch—and if a guard approached, they would bang on the walls hard enough to alert everyone along the line. When a heavy thud sounded along the wall, men would scramble up from the floor to sit on their bunks with their hands folded in their laps, like subdued children waiting silently in church for services to begin. Between the warning thuds, they did their push-ups and their sit-ups and kept meticulous records of their repetitions. Scores were tapped through the wall, and competitions inevitably followed.

The sit-up count reached into the thousands. A man would fold his blanket into the shape of an exercise mat, get down on his back on the floor, and begin knocking them out with the easy rhythm of a metronome—up and back, up and back, up and back . . . breathe in, breathe out, breathe in, breathe out. . . . Soon the steady, repetitious flexing of his own body would shut out everything else and he would be alert to nothing except movement and the possible thump from a man in another cell, clearing. Up and down . . . six hundred, six hundred one . . . two. . . . Time seemed to slide by when a man was doing his sit-ups. And when he finished, or had to quit, he would feel an overall exhaustion that seemed so much better than the angry tension that grew tighter and tighter inside, like a rope being slowly twisted, when he simply sat on his bunk, hands folded in his lap, waiting for time to pass, feeling his life go by, leaving behind it a trail of . . . nothing.

For some men, calisthenics were insufficient. After thousands of push-ups, tens of thousands of sit-ups, miles of running in place, they wanted something more challenging. For some reason, it seemed essential to start lifting weights.

There were, of course, no weights available, and nothing in the cells even came close. The sawhorses and pallet beds were too big and cumbersome. The only other things in the cells were the buckets. So the physical-fitness fanatics began curling buckets full of human waste to develop their arms. Some days the buckets were heavy and some days they were light. They always stank, but that seemed less and less important to men who had learned to share space with rats and sit on those buckets with absolutely no privacy. They did their curls, concentrating to make the lifting motion smooth and fluid so the contents of the buckets would not slop around too much inside or spill over the edges.

Years later, when he was home, one of the men went to a movie about weight lifting and bodybuilding. The movie was *Pumping Iron,* and it occurred to him that hour after hour, day after day, for almost six years of his life, what he had been doing was pumping shit. It seemed the perfect description.

IT WAS NOT ENOUGH to work on housekeeping, health, and fitness. Even after you had done all you could to keep the cell and yourself clean, exercised until you were exhausted, and taken your turn tapping or clearing, there were still long, empty stretches of time that had to be filled. Somehow, you had to keep your mind occupied; otherwise you would dwell on your situation and sink into a swamp of self-pity. The POWs found they had more resources than they could have imagined for keeping themselves diverted. It came down to discovering what they already knew.

Stafford was on the wall one day when someone from the next cell tapped out a riddle. You are on a path, the message read, and you come to a place where the path goes off in two directions. There is a guard at the head of each new path. If you take one path, you will meet certain death. If you take the other path, you will live. One guard always lies and the other always tells the truth. You do not know which is which, and you may ask only one question of one of them. What is the question that will allow you to proceed safely?

It took a long time for the man in the next cell to tap out that message. It took much longer—months, in fact—for Stafford, who had never been good at math and logic and the other empirical disciplines, to mull over the answer. But this was the point. When one of his roommates, who knew the answer, tried to coach him, Stafford said, "No, goddammit. Don't ruin it. I'll get it."

Like virtually all of the prisoners, Stafford finally gave up and asked someone to tell him the answer—which was simplicity itself. You ask either guard, "If I ask the other guard which is the road to safety, what will he tell me?" And then you take the opposite path. This was the best of many brainteasers that went through the wall.

Killing time was not an altogether new experience for the aviators. They had always had time on their hands while waiting to fly—especially in the days before the war. One way of killing time had been with card games that could be put down before takeoff and resumed when the planes were back down. Ready-room and alert-room bridge games could last for weeks. It took some resourcefulness, however, to get a rubber going in prison when all four players were in different, and not always adjacent, cells.

First, you needed cards. The Vietnamese were not handing any out. Although they were included in Red Cross and other packages sent to the POWs, these were not distributed until very late in the war. So the POWs had to make the cards. Toilet paper was available. A quill could be made from broom straw, ink from ashes and water. The cards were made small so they could be easily concealed.

Next came the fundamental problem of how to play the game. The men who decided to make up a bridge foursome would each arrange their cards the same way. Then the instructions for how to shuffle would be tapped through each wall. Sometimes these instructions would be relayed by a man who did not play bridge but was willing to help keep the game going and do a little tapping to pass the time.

CUT . . . DECK . . . TEN . . . CARDS . . . DEEP

CUT . . . LARGE . . . PILE . . . FIFTEEN . . . CARDS . . . DEEP

PLACE . . . THIRD . . . ON . . . FIRST . . . PILE . . . and so on until the deck was shuffled.

Then every man would deal four hands, pick up the one that was his, and begin the bidding. Once the bidding was complete, the dummy hand would be turned over. The other hands would remain facedown, and as a card was played, the man making the play would identify the card and its place in the original pile by tapping, so the other players could find it without looking at the rest of the cards in the hand. It would have been easy to cheat, but also, under the circumstances, utterly pointless.

A hand of bridge that might have taken ten minutes to play under normal conditions could last for two or three weeks when every play had to be tapped through several walls. Now and then a new man would decline an invitation to play, saying that it couldn't be done, that tapping all the bidding and the rounds and the scorekeeping through several walls would just take too much time. The other men had an answer, which went back to a time when Dick Stratton had been thrown into a totally darkened cell for punishment.

Long periods of light deprivation is known to cause disorientation and severe emotional distress. Stratton had been kept in that cell for nearly six weeks. His only lifeline was the wall and the man on the other side, Jack Van Loan. At first, simply to give Stratton some kind of reference point, Van Loan would estimate the passage of time and give Stratton a hack every fifteen minutes. It was something. Then, as time went on, Van Loan began asking Stratton to explain things to him: books that Stratton had read, courses he had taken in college, anything that he could remember and describe in detail. Eventually they came to the subject of philosophy, and Stratton was trying to tell Van Loan, through the wall, about a course he had taken in existentialism. That word alone was tough, and Van Loan missed it several times. Each time, Stratton would patiently tap it out again. When they had finally gotten that single word straight, Stratton began tapping out the name Kierkegaard. It seemed to take hours. At one point, Stratton tapped out an apology: **SORRY THIS IS TACING SO LONG**

Van Loan tapped back: **DONT WORRY ABT IT XX I THINC TIME IS ON OUR SIDE XX CEEP TALCING**

From then on, whenever a man protested that a bridge game would take too long to tap through several walls of the Warehouse, the man on the other side would tap back: **THATS OCAY XX TIME IS ON OUR SIDE**

Card games and chess were good for filling time, but they were not enough to fully engage the minds of college-educated men accustomed to learning as a routine discipline. So they began memorizing lines from poems or plays that they might have been taught to recite as children and had never forgotten, even if they had to work hard at the job of recall. When a man had the lines, he would tap them out to a prisoner in the next cell, who recited them over and over until he had memorized them himself. The music of the lines, the hard cadences—especially of Kipling—provided a kind of solace.

> *Then it's Tommy this, an' Tommy that, an' "Tommy, 'ow's yer soul?"*
> *But it's "Thin red line of 'eroes" when the drums begin to roll—*

Men who had never cared much for poetry began to crave the verses, waiting eagerly for them to come through the wall. The POWs in one cell were in the midst of learning *The Highwayman,* line by painstaking line, when they were ordered to move. The order came just as they were reaching the climax of the poem and Bess was prepared to "shatter her breast in the moonlight" to warn the highwayman. It was like losing a mystery novel when you are three or four chapters from the end. From their new cell, which had no common wall and could not receive messages by tap code, the men smuggled a message asking what had happened. A message was smuggled back to them—at some risk—and it read: **HIGHWAYMAN AND BESS—KIA**

As in some old, preliterate society, storytelling became an important art. The stories and myths of their generation were often films, so after the evening meal and the order to put up nets and lie down on the hard wooden pallets, it would be time for movies. A cellmate who could remember a film would lie on his bunk and begin patiently narrating the action, scene by scene, going into character for dialogue and adding as much detail to the physical descriptions as he could remember or invent. Many of the men had favorite movies they had seen more than once, so they were able to relate a passable summary. Some had a real talent for the work and, with the help of other men who had seen the movie, could assemble a fairly complete account. Certain movies became very popular. *Dr. Zhivago* was easily the best-loved movie at the Plantation.

Still, there were long stretches of dead, empty time when nothing happened and a man was reduced to simple, mute awareness of his situation. He was hungry. In the summer he was hot and eaten up with skin infections; in the winter, cold and shivering. He was desperately uncertain about the future. He did not know if he would be hauled out for a quiz in ten minutes, still be a captive in ten years.

Almost all of the POWs learned to fantasize. There was a distinction, however, between idle daydreaming and disciplined fantasizing. No one needed to be told that simply crawling under a blanket and dreaming childhood dreams of mother and dog and painless innocence was unhealthy. That kind of random, formless escape would lead a man farther and farther into passivity, self-pity, arid isolation. Instead, when you fantasized, you tried to create real situations and solve real problems. Properly done, a good session of fantasizing would tire you out, leave you with a sense of having accomplished something.

Al Stafford had always loved to sail, so he would sit up straight with his eyes closed and imagine himself out in Chesapeake Bay. He would decide on the season and then try to remember just what the prevailing weather would be. In the summer, when the cell was stifling and full of bugs, he would picture himself out for a winter sail on the bay, with the water the color of lead, the wind blowing whitecaps off the tops of the swells. He saw himself wearing oilskins, and except for a lone freighter moving up the channel, he had the bay to himself. In the winter, while he huddled under his blanket, he would imagine himself stripped down to a bathing suit, skimming past crab boats and other craft scattered across the mild green expanse of the bay.

At the end of an hour or two of sailing, Stafford could taste the salt on his lips and feel the sun on his skin. He sailed for hours and hours. He used real checkpoints and kept a real logbook. "Five knots equals a mile every twelve minutes. . . . I'll be at the Oxford lighthouse by 1610. . . ."

In another cell, farther down the Warehouse, another man played golf. He would spend two hours a day playing a course he remembered hole by hole. He concentrated so hard on his shots that he could feel the tick of the ball when he made contact with the sweet spot. When his mind wandered for a few moments, he would feel the ugly, metallic sensation all the way up his arms and into his shoulders. A goddamned duck hook, he would tell himself, and trudge off into the rough, hoping that he would be able to find his ball and learn not to use too much right hand.

During his golf games, his cellmates left him alone. It was easy to tell when he was playing, because he would be sitting on his pallet in something like a lotus position, with his eyes closed and his lips moving just slightly as he talked himself through the round. Then, after a couple of hours, he would open his eyes and begin to stretch, as though to relieve the tension. One of the other men in the room would say, "How'd you hit 'em today, Jerry?"

"Not bad. I was two under when I made the turn, but I pushed my drive on fifteen, a long par five. Had to play safe out of the rough and double-bogeyed the hole. Then I three-putted seventeen from twelve feet out. Really blew it. So I was one over for the round."

"That's not bad."

"No, it was a good round. Great weather, too."

"So what about the handicap?"

"I'm still sitting on a two."

"Little more time on the driving range and you'll be a scratch golfer."

"Putting green is more like it. That three-putt killed me."

There was only one limit to this kind of fantasizing: You had to know enough about the situation or the task to make it realistic. You could not simply decide you were going to be a professional golfer and imagine yourself in a playoff against Jack Nicklaus if you had never played a round in your life. But if you put yourself into a world that you did know and understand, and you took your time and forced your mind to follow the consequences of every single choice, you could create a world of almost tangible reality.

It was an escape, but it was also a discipline. If you were a golfer and you played every day, you might feel yourself actually getting better. Though he had not seen blue water for two years, since the morning he last crossed the coast of Vietnam at 20,000 feet. Al Stafford felt sure he was a better sailor than he had been when he was shot down. He knew so much more now. He had been through certain situations so many times in his mind that he now did the right thing automatically. It was like the time you spent in a flight simulator on the ground, which prepared you for situations you later encountered in the air.

But even if it was a productive way to use long, empty stretches of time, it was still no substitute for the real thing. When it was too hot and he was too dispirited even to fantasize, Stafford wondered when he would see blue water and feel the wind again—or, in his worst moments, *if* he ever would.

Along the row of cells in the Warehouse, men strained to keep busy, finding the solution in everything from a serious form of make-believe to the most elaborate improvisation. A man named Charles Plumb "played" music on the keyboard of a piano diagramed in brick dust on the floor. He would patiently play the pieces he could remember, practicing until he got them right. Like Tom Hall, Plumb was an innovator. He had grown up in rural Kansas, where he had been an active Boy Scout and 4-H member. Like many boys his age, he had also fooled around with ham radios and had once sent away for a kit to build his own receiver. He remembered enough about it to try building one at the Plantation so he could listen to news from some source other than Radio Hanoi.

The yard at the Plantation was littered with scrap and debris. On his way to a rare and welcome work detail, Plumb would walk in the typical prisoner fashion, head lowered and shuffling his feet dejectedly. Actually, he was looking for wire. He easily found enough for an aerial and a ground.

During interrogations, prisoners used pencils to write out confessions or letters of apology to the camp commander. They routinely pressed too hard and broke the lead. While a guard was sharpening the pencil, the prisoner would sneak the small piece of broken lead into his clothing to smuggle back into his cell. An eighth of an inch of pencil lead set into a sliver of bamboo made a wonderful, highly prized writing instrument. The POWs would carefully hide their pencils against the possibility of a search. Being caught with a pencil brought punishment for breaking the rule against contraband. Worse, the pencil would be confiscated.

For his radio, Plumb used one of these small pencil points as a detector, balancing it on the edges of two razor blades. For the antenna coil, he wrapped wire around a spool that he made from scrap wood, which he shaped by rubbing it against the rough wall of the cell. He built a capacitor from alternating sheets of waxed paper and aluminum foil smuggled from the kitchen or saved from cigarette packages.

This left the earpiece, which required an electromagnet, diaphragm, and housing. A nail served for the electromagnet. The housing was an unused insulator stuck in the wall, probably dating back to the time the French built the camp. He had worked the insulator loose from the wall and was preparing to wrap the nail with fine wire when the guards conducted a search and confiscated all the parts to his radio. He was taken to the Big House, put in the ropes, and forced to write a letter of apology to the camp commander. He never heard the "Voice of America" on his little radio.

While Plumb was busy with one of his projects, his roommate, Danny Glenn, concentrated on designing and building his dream house. Glenn had studied architecture at Oklahoma State before going into the navy and was shot down four days before Christmas 1966. At the Plantation he filled the hours working on the plans and blueprints for the house he promised himself he would build—exactly to his specifications, with exactly the materials he wanted—when he finally got out of North Vietnam and went home. In his cell, he would rough out the plans on the floor, carefully working out the dimensions and noting the placement of headers, joists, and studs. Then he would draw up his materials list, room by room. His lists were exhaustive and specific, down to the precise gauge of the electric wire. The blueprint of a room would stay on the floor for days, then weeks, while he made his corrections and pondered his decisions.

Lying under his mosquito net at night, Plumb frequently was awakened by his cellmate's voice.

"Hey, Charlie?"

"Yeah."

"You asleep?"

"No."

"Listen, if I'm bothering you . . ."

"That's okay. What is it?"

"Well, you know that upstairs bathroom, the little one at the head of the stairs?"

"Uh-huh."

"Well, I've been thinking about it and I've decided to go with Mexican tile. What do you think?"

"I think it would look real good."

"You sure?"

"Absolutely."

"It's not too fancy?"

"No. I'd say Mexican tile would be just right."

"Well, what about the color?"

"Hell, I don't know."

"I was thinking green. That dark green like you see on sports cars. British racing green, they call it."

"I think that would look real good."

"Okay, Charlie. Thanks a lot."

"Sure."

"Goodnight."

In the morning, Glenn would go to his blueprints and materials list and write in green Mexican tile for the upstairs bathroom. Then he would check the dimensions and do the arithmetic to calculate just how many three-inch squares he would need and where he would need to cut to fit. He would memorize as much as he could and make notes in tiny script on a piece of paper from a cigarette package, using one of the contraband pencil points or an improvised pen. Then he would fold the sheet into the smallest possible square and hide it in a crack in the wall, erase the schematic of the room he'd been working on, and start another.

That night, after the mosquito nets were down, he would say, softly, "Charlie, I'm thinking about paneling that family room downstairs. What do you think . . . ?"

Nearly ten years later, after he had come home and started a new life, Plumb got a call at his home in Kansas.

"Charlie, this is Danny Glenn."

"Yeah, Danny, how you doing?"

"Good. How about you?"

"Real good. What's up?"

"Charlie, I want you to come see me. There's something I want to show you."

"Well . . . all right. Where are you?"

"Oklahoma. Let me tell you how to get here."

Plumb wrote down the directions and said he would drive down that weekend.

"Great, Charlie. Can't wait to see you."

Plumb followed the directions and when he made the last of several turns, the one that would take him up to the driveway where he was to turn in, he saw the house. It was the very same house that he had heard described a thousand times and had helped design while his roommate scratched out the plans and prints on the floor of their cell. He stopped the car and studied the house for a long time. It was unbelievable, like something from a dream.

"Hey, Charlie, come on in. Let me show you around."

Everything was there in exact detail. Plumb could walk around the house as if he had lived there all his life. When he came to the end of a hall and opened a door, he knew exactly what would be on the other side, knew where every bathroom was and what kind of tile would be on the floor. Nothing was out of place and nothing had been changed from the way this house was planned, all those years ago.

"It's beautiful," he said. "I can't believe you got everything just right."

"Oh, it was a bitch, let me tell you. They'd stopped making a lot of the materials I had in mind when I designed this baby. I had to go to salvage yards and warehouses all across the Southwest to find some of this stuff. But, by God, I wasn't going to compromise. I had too much invested—you know what I mean."

Plumb understood.

*AUTUMN 1990*

Geoffrey Norman is the author of *Bouncing Back: How a Heroic Band of POWs Survived Vietnam* (1990), from which this article was adapted.

# 45

# The Evacuation of Kham Duc

## By Ronald H. Spector

*Although most Americans of the Vietnam era readily recall the names of such battles as Hue and Khe Sanh, very few would remember Kham Duc. As with so many other battles in so many other wars, there was little in its size or significance to catch the public's attention or spark its memory. Yet neither war nor history gives a warrior the choice to fight and die only in crucial or well-remembered battles. The sacrifices of one fight are no less poignant and final than another. The short, vicious, and confused battle at Kham Duc in May 1968 reminds us of that fact.*

At the beginning of April 1968, U.S. Marines and Air Cavalry troops in Vietnam lifted the siege of Khe Sanh, in one of the largest operations of the war. As the North Vietnamese withdrew from the area of the beleaguered marine base, leaving behind evidence of their heavy losses, a communiqué from the headquarters of the U.S. commander, General William Westmoreland, declared that for the Communists the battle for Khe Sanh had been "a Dien Bien Phu in reverse." Less than two months later, however, U.S. forces were to suffer a sharp defeat at another remote outpost near the Laotian border called Kham Duc—a defeat that was, in a sense, a Khe Sanh in reverse.

The months following the Tet attacks at the end of January had been a time of stress and of calamity not always averted. Early in February, Communist troops, supported for the first time by tanks, overran the Lang Vei Special Forces camp near Khe Sanh, killing 200 of its 500 defenders, including 10 of its more than two dozen American advisers. After the much-publicized fall of Lang Vei, Kham Duc was the last remaining Special Forces camp of I Corps along the Laotian border. Far from the urban centers and coastal farmlands, Kham Duc sat in the center of a mile-wide green bowl in the rugged country of northwestern Quang Tin province. Route 14, the principal north–south road through the border region, ran through the base. Just across that border, ten miles away, the roads and tracks of the Ho Chi Minh Trail extended their fingers south and east, some already reaching Route 14 itself.

Like Khe Sanh and Lang Vei, Kham Duc and Ngoc Tavak—its satellite camp three miles closer to Laos—did not truly block the enemy's infiltration into South Vietnam. The border country was too rugged, the Communists' lateral roads were too numerous, and the camps' garrisons were too small to do that; yet the units holding them kept the Communists under observation and frequently interdicted their movements. Their presence meant that there would always be some sand and gravel thrown into the smoothly meshed gears of the Laotian infiltration system.

Since early April, U.S. Army engineer units had been at work upgrading Kham Duc's runway and constructing a concrete base to support the radio-navigation facility. As the improvements to the base progressed, so did Communist preparations for attack. By late April, U.S. intelligence was reporting large enemy units in the area, including elements of the 2nd Division of the North Vietnamese Army. A prisoner taken on May 3 reported that his unit was planning to attack Kham Duc. Four months before, when Khe Sanh had been similarly threatened, the Americans had poured in reinforcements and air support. Now the Americans again began reinforcing. A battalion task force of the Americal Division, consisting of the 2nd Battalion, 1st Infantry, an additional infantry company, and some supporting artillery, began arriving by air at Kham Duc late on the morning of May 10. Lieutenant Colonel Robert B. Nelson, commander of the 2nd Battalion, took charge of the camp.

Nelson's men joined about 60 army engineers, about 400 Civilian Irregular Defense Group (CIDG) soldiers, and the latter's South Vietnamese and U.S. Special Forces leaders and advisers. Neither as well armed nor as well trained as the North Vietnamese and Viet Cong, the CIDG were mercenaries that the Special Forces recruited and organized from among the various highland, non-Vietnamese tribal, ethnic, and religious minorities. The CIDG's primary mission was surveillance, scouting, patrol, and local security. Although their leaders were sometimes bound to the Special Forces and the government by personal ties or political deals, they were primarily free-lance soldiers, hired as a group on a contractual basis. Their behavior in a crisis varied from cowardice and treachery to stalwart heroism, depending on the specific situation and the tribal group involved.

Even as reinforcements were arriving at Kham Duc, Ngoc Tavak was already under attack. Located on the site of an old French fort, Ngoc Tavak was defended by a 113-man CIDG Mobile Strike Force company, with 8 U.S. Army Special Forces troops and 3 Australian training-team advisers. Thirty-three U.S. Marines manned two 105mm howitzers, which had recently been moved to Ngoc Tavak to interdict nearby North Vietnamese routes and trails. The howitzers were short of ammunition, however, and could be resupplied only by air from Kham Duc.

At about 3:00 in the morning on May 10, the Communists opened their final heavy-artillery and mortar barrage against the base, followed by a ground attack some thirty minutes later. During the height of the action, some of the CIDG troops abandoned their positions and fled toward the compound yelling, "Don't shoot, don't shoot, friendly, friendly." But once inside the compound, these "friendly" troops tossed grenades and satchel charges at the marine positions, causing heavy casualties. Some of the surviving Americans believed they could also hear the distinctive sound of carbines being fired at them by the CIDGs. (Only the CIDGs had carbines; NVA troops carried AK-47s, whose high-velocity rounds sound quite different from those of a carbine.)

The Special Forces commander, Captain Christopher J. Silva, and the commander of the marine battery, Lieutenant Adams, were both badly wounded during the night. As the North Vietnamese attackers penetrated the perimeter and advanced into the eastern end of the camp, the remaining defenders pulled back and called for support from air force gunships and fighter bombers. The defenders believed that some of the wounded were still on the western side of the camp; but as the North Vietnamese closed in, the Americans had no choice but to call for the gunships to blast the western side with their deadly fléchettes (artillery rounds with dartlike metal projections) and cannon fire.

At dawn two Australian warrant officers managed to organize a counterattack by the CIDG troops who were still loyal; they cleared the perimeter and recaptured the howitzer positions abandoned during the nighttime attack. Yet the marines were almost out of shells for their 105s.

Four CH-46 helicopters carrying reinforcements from Kham Duc arrived later that morning, greeted by a hail of fire from the North Vietnamese forces surrounding Ngoc Tavak. The first chopper managed to land safely and unload its cargo of about twenty-five CIDG troops, but as the second approached the landing zone, its fuel line was severed by automatic-weapons fire. The damaged chopper, fuel streaming from the fuselage, settled safely to the ground and unloaded its troops. The third helicopter landed alongside and discharged its reinforcements as the crew of the crippled CH-46 jumped aboard. But as the third chopper was about to lift off, it was hit by a rocket-propelled grenade round and burst into flames. The landing zone was now unusable, and only small UH-1 medevac helicopters could land at the camp to take off the severely wounded. As one medevac chopper came in to hover off a nearby hill, a large number of panicky CIDG soldiers rushed aboard; others held onto the skids as the helicopter lifted off, then fell to their deaths several hundred feet below.

Captain White of the Australian training team, the senior surviving officer, was now in command. Requesting permission to evacuate the camp, he was told to hang on. But with the helicopter pad unserviceable, water and ammunition nearly exhausted, most of the Americans killed or wounded, and the steadiness of the CIDG a doubtful proposition, White believed he had no choice but to abandon the camp before darkness brought renewed attacks. The men destroyed the damaged helicopter and weapons that they could not take with them.

Avoiding the obvious routes to Kham Duc, where the enemy was almost certain to be waiting in ambush, White led his men southeast through heavy jungle to a hill about a mile from Ngoc Tavak, where they hacked out a landing zone. CH-46s quickly swooped in to take the survivors back to Kham Duc.

The loss of Ngoc Tavak had been a costly one. Of the forty-four Americans and Australians at Ngoc Tavak, fifteen had been killed, twenty-three were wounded, and two were missing. Of the hundred-odd CIDG troops, sixty-four were missing or had deserted and thirty were dead or wounded. By the time the dazed and exhausted survivors reached Kham Duc, that camp, too, was under attack.

Scattered mortar fire rained down on the camp on May 11, as the last of the Americal reinforcements and additional supplies were flown into the besieged base. By the end of that day, there was a total of some 1,500 U.S. and CIDG soldiers at Kham Duc, as well as almost 300 dependents of the CIDG troops who had been evacuated from their village near the base. Many of the Americal troops had been sent to reinforce the outposts in the hills surrounding the bowl-shaped valley where the camp was located.

Late on the night of the eleventh, troops of the 1st Vietcong Regiment, 2nd NVA Division, began their final preparations for an assault on Kham Duc. Around 4:00 A.M. the Communists overran the first of the outposts, Number 7, on a hill northeast of the base. By that time, General Westmoreland had already decided to abandon the camp.

Since the arrival of U.S. forces in Vietnam, some of the largest and most stubborn battles had begun as contests for the control of Special Forces camps such as Khe Sanh. Kham Duc had appeared likely to be the next such battleground, with powerful enemy forces converging on the base, U.S. reinforcements arriving, and support and strike aircraft being summoned to aid the defenders.

Yet as U.S. commanders studied the impending battle, they began to have second thoughts. When Colonel Jonathan Ladd, commander of Special Forces in Vietnam, met with the commander of the III Marine Amphibious Force (MAF), Lieutenant General Robert E. Cushman, Jr., he found Cushman unwilling to commit more troops to Kham Duc. Ladd pointed out that strong reinforcements would be needed to hold the camp against an attack by a reinforced North Vietnamese regiment. But Cushman had few uncommitted troops to spare and was concerned about a new threat posed by the buildup of Communist forces in the An Hoa basin area southeast of Da Nang. A reserve CIDG Mobile Strike Force company had already been dispatched to another threatened Special Forces camp, Thuong Duc, located on the main western approaches to Da Nang. Cushman also pointed out that Kham Duc would be difficult to resupply and was beyond the artillery range of friendly supporting bases.

On the afternoon of May 11, Ladd accompanied the deputy commander of Military Assistance Command, Vietnam (MACV), Creighton Abrams, to a meeting with Cushman and Major General Samuel Koster, the Americal Division commander. Koster had now assumed operational control of the Kham Duc battle. At the meeting, the III MAF staff briefed the generals on the situation at Kham Duc. They recommended that the camp be abandoned—or, as they phrased it, "relocated." Colonel Ladd strongly disagreed, pointing out that Kham Duc was the last South Vietnamese outpost of southern I Corps in the western mountains. He also emphasized that it was an important launching site for the super-secret teams innocuously called the Studies and Observation Group, which conducted reconnaissance missions and raids into Laos and other parts of Southeast Asia to observe and interdict lines of communication, capture prisoners, assess bomb damage, and collect intelligence. By 1968, the number of such missions had risen to over 300 a year. Further, Ladd suggested that the Communists might put a Kham Duc victory to propaganda use, especially in view of the opening of peace talks in Paris.

Unmentioned but ever-present during the deliberations were the recent memories of the siege of Khe Sanh. Although American generals had always spoken of the battle with confidence and enthusiasm when addressing Washington or the media, they had found it an anxious and wearing experience, superimposed as it was on the widespread and bloody fights of Tet. Now, with this new "mini-Tet" looming, neither Abrams nor Cushman was inclined to begin another protracted battle. "The decision to evacuate was brought on considerably by the Khe Sanh experience," wrote Westmoreland's operations officer. At the conclusion of the discussions, Abrams instructed Cushman to prepare plans for a withdrawal. Westmoreland approved the decision a few hours later.

By the time word of the decision to evacuate reached Colonel Nelson at Kham Duc, all seven of the hill outposts were under heavy attack. Squads and platoons of American soldiers reinforcing the CIDG troops on the hills fought desperately, supported by C-47 gunships dropping flares to illuminate the area and peppering the attackers with their minicannon. As the outposts were overwhelmed, the defenders directed gunships and artillery fire onto their own positions. A few managed to escape into the Kham Duc perimeter, but many died in the hill outposts.

The fate of the outposts added to the sense of terror and foreboding within Kham Duc. The morning began with a fresh disaster as one of the first evacuation helicopters, an army CH-47, was hit by heavy ground fire as it landed on the runway. The chopper exploded, and its flaming hulk blocked the runway for over an hour. An A-1E fighter also was shot down.

As the sun rose over Kham Duc, burning away some of the morning fog, aerial observers beheld a grim sight: The camp was under almost continuous mortar fire, and heavy ground attacks were taking place against the northwestern perimeter. The burning CH-47 sent clouds of black smoke into the sky. On the nearby hills, radio antennae sprouted above the newly established NVA command posts.

Inside the perimeter, men tensely awaited the ground attack. The enemy mortar barrage increased in intensity, and a near miss showered one squad with shrapnel. An 82mm mortar round scored a direct hit on a nearby mortar manned by CIDG personnel, killing or wounding all three of the crew. Specialist 4 Todd Regon, leader of a mortar team, quickly rounded up some

Americal infantrymen, led them to the pit, and gave them a crash course in mortar firing. Scrambling back to his own mortar position, Regon was astounded to see illumination rounds bursting harmlessly over the daytime battlefield. An instant later the mortar man realized that he had failed to show his infantry trainees the difference between high-explosive and illumination rounds for the CIDG mortar. Despite his grim situation, Regon managed a smile. "This ought to confuse the hell out of the enemy."

As enemy pressure on the base increased, MACV directed all available air support to Kham Duc. Fighters and attack planes from Pleiku, Da Nang, Cam Ranh Bay, and Phu Cat—as well as bases in Thailand—converged on the beleaguered base in answer to the call from the Seventh Air Force commander, General W.W. Momyer, for a "Grand Slam" maximum air effort. An airborne command post in a converted C-130 coordinated the air attacks as dozens of aircraft responded to Momyer's call. At times there were as many as twenty fighters over Kham Duc. Two forward air controllers (FACs) in light planes flew parallel to each other at opposite sides of the Kham Duc runway, each controlling fighter strikes on his side of the field. Traffic was so thick that by late morning the FACs could specifically select fighters based on their load: napalm, cluster-bomb units, 500- or 750-pound bombs, or high-drag bombs.

"We've got a small Khe Sanh going on here," an air force officer at Kham Duc recorded. "I hope we finish it before night comes." The evacuation, when it came, was marked by confusion, panic, and tragedy. Many of the defenders at Kham Duc were not informed of the decision to abandon the camp until many hours after it had been made. The CIDG forces, panicky and on the verge of mutiny or surrender, feared that the Americans would abandon them. Suspicion was mutual, since American troops had heard the stories of CIDG forces firing on other Americans at Ngoc Tavak.

The air force's 834th Air Division, whose giant C-123s and C-130s would have to make the actual evacuation, was also dogged by confusion and last-minute changes. At 8:20 A.M. on May 12, the 834th was alerted for an all-out effort to evacuate the base. Two hours later, fighting at Kham Duc had grown so intense that the Seventh Air Force canceled the evacuation and directed the transports to fly in additional ammunition to Kham Duc. By the time the MACV operations center directed the 834th to resume evacuation operations, around 1:15 P.M., transports were already on their way to Kham Duc loaded with ammunition. Other planes on the ground had to unload their cargo before proceeding empty to Kham Duc to bring out the defenders. To complicate matters further, Colonel Nelson's command post could not communicate with many of the supporting aircraft because the American's radios were incompatible with those used by most of the planes. Messages had to be relayed from the Special Forces command post, whose radios could talk to the planes. At times, the heavy volume of incoming message traffic almost jammed the two available networks. The communications mess made it almost impossible for ground commanders to coordinate transport and helicopter landings with supporting air strikes.

That complete disaster was averted was due largely to the deadly skills of the fighter pilots and their controllers and to the iron nerve and brilliant improvisation of the tactical airlift crews. The first C-130 into Kham Duc landed on the debris-strewn runway at about 10:00 A.M., in a hail of mortar and automatic-weapons fire that punctured a tire and fuel tanks. Lieutenant Colonel Daryl D. Cole's plane, dispatched before the evacuation order had been reinstituted, had a full load of cargo for Kham Duc, but panic-stricken civilians and CIDG troops rushed the plane as soon as it taxied to a stop, preventing either orderly unloading or evacuation. With mortar shells landing ever closer to the aircraft, Cole decided to attempt a takeoff with his overloaded plane, crowded with CIDG personnel and much of the remaining cargo. His first attempt was unsuccessful, and the increased attention that the plane was attracting from NVA gunners convinced the passengers to make a hasty exit. In the meantime, the crew had succeeded in cutting away part of the ruined tire. Dodging the runway debris, with fuel streaming from the wing tanks and under heavy fire, Cole managed to get his stricken C-130 airborne and safely back to Cam Ranh Bay.

Cole was followed by a C-123 piloted by Major Ray Shelton, which loaded about sixty army engineers and Vietnamese civilians in less than three minutes before taking off under heavy enemy fire.

Throughout the day, army and marine helicopters continued to dodge heavy fire to bring in ammunition and evacuate the wounded from Kham Duc. Yet the helicopters could not carry the large numbers of people now desperate to escape from the doomed camp. Only the large transports of the 834th could do that, and since eleven o'clock there had been no planes. Then, around three in the afternoon, a C-130 piloted by Major Bernard L. Bucher landed at Kham Duc. CIDG troops, women, and children swarmed aboard the plane. The CIDG soldiers and their families were convinced that the Americans intended to leave them behind and were in a state of utter panic. Two hours earlier, Special Forces sergeant Richard Campbell had watched in horror and disbelief as a woman and her small child who had fallen while climbing the rear ramp of a CH-46 helicopter were trampled by fear-maddened CIDG soldiers in a rush to board the chopper. Now nearly 200 women and children crowded aboard Bucher's bullet-riddled C-130.

Because he had received heavy fire from the southwest corner of the field on landing, Bucher elected to take off to the northeast. A few minutes before Bucher's takeoff, fighters raked the NVA machine guns on the low ridges north of the runway with loads of cluster-bomb units. The deadly CBUs killed the gun crews, but replacements from nearby enemy positions soon had the guns back in action. Bucher's plane, struck by heavy machine-gun fire, crashed and exploded in an orange ball of flame less than a mile from the runway. There were no survivors of what has to be counted as one of the worst air disasters of this century, and the costliest one in the Vietnam War.

Watching Bucher's crash, Lieutenant Colonel William Boyd, Jr., pilot of the next C-130 into the camp, decided on a steep, sideslipping descent. Just as Boyd's plane was about to touch down, a shell exploded 100 feet ahead on the runway. Pushing his throttle forward, Boyd climbed steeply into the air. Landing successfully on his next try, he loaded about 100 CIDG and American soldiers and took off under heavy fire for Cam Ranh Bay.

The fourth C-130 of the day, commanded by Lieutenant Colonel John Delmore, had been forced to make a second pass to avoid Boyd's takeoff. This time the Communist gunners were ready, and .50-caliber bullets ripped six-inch holes in the sides of the fuselage as the giant C-130, its hydraulic system shot away, bounced along the runway, glanced off the wreckage of the CH-47 destroyed that morning, and plowed into a dirt mound on the side of the runway. Miraculously, the entire crew escaped. A few minutes later Delmore's crippled plane burst into flames.

The remaining C-130 pilots circling above Kham Duc, awaiting their turn to land, had seen Bucher's plane crash and burn, Delmore's wrecked on landing, and two helicopters destroyed by ground fire. The runway was littered with debris and burning wreckage.

Undeterred, Lieutenant Colonel Franklin Montgomery brought his C-130 into Kham Duc, followed by two more C-130s; together, the three planes brought out more than 400 people just as the Seventh Air Force was issuing orders to cancel further landings. As the order was given, Major James L. Wallace's C-130 was able to make a pickup, bringing out the remaining soldiers and civilians.

But in the confusion, according to some reports, another C-130 landed briefly just as Wallace's was taking off. In the mistaken belief that personnel were still on the ground, the three men in the combat control team (CCT), who had been pulled out of the camp that morning after spending two days helping to bring in the Americal Division reinforcements, were now dropped off again—to find themselves alone, surrounded by exploding ammunition dumps and the advancing enemy.

Heavy fire forced the C-130 that had brought the team to fly out before the three men could return to the plane. The airwaves fell silent as the pilot, Major Jay Van Cleeff, radioed that the camp now was not, after all, fully evacuated and ready to be destroyed by air strikes.

On the ground, Major Gallagher and Technical Sergeants Freedman and Lundie took cover in a ditch, began shooting at the enemy—silencing one of the two machine guns firing at them from the sides of the runway—and hoped for a miracle. Lieutenant Colonel Alfred J. Jeanotte, Jr., given cover by fighter aircraft, touched down on the north side of the runway—but the crew couldn't see the three men and had to take off right away because of enemy fire. Once airborne, however, the crew spotted the men running back to their ditch after seeing the rescue plane leave without them. Their position was radioed to the next plane in line to attempt a rescue.

Lieutenant Colonel Joe M. Jackson brought in his C-123 with a side-slipping descent, to make the smallest possible target. Despite sharp objects and holes on the runway, the plane landed safely, rolled as close as possible to the ditch, and swung back around for a departure as the three men raced from their cover and were pulled on board. In less than a minute, with bullets, shells, and even a 122mm rocket striking all around them, the C-123 took off and got away—without a single hole in the plane. Jackson's daring rescue of the last three defenders of Kham Duc earned him the Medal of Honor.

It was over before 5:00 P.M. Communist troops advanced cautiously into Kham Duc and along the runway perimeter as explosions from the burning aircraft and ammunition dumps lit up the twilight sky. The following morning, sixty B-52 bombers, the entire force available in Vietnam, rained 12,000 tons of bombs on the camp, and MACV proclaimed that the enemy had suffered severely. Yet nothing could disguise the fact that Kham Duc had been an American defeat—a Khe Sanh in reverse. Twenty-five Americans had been killed and nearly 100 wounded, and there were several hundred Vietnamese casualties; seven U.S. aircraft and all the camp's heavy military and engineering equipment were also lost. American commanders had vacillated between reinforcing the camp and evacuating it, finally opting for evacuation—under the worst possible circumstances. Command, control, and communications had been confused and often ineffective. General Abrams termed the operation "a minor disaster." "This was an ugly one and I expect some repercussions," wrote the chief of Westmoreland's operations center.

Yet the repercussions were few. Abrams angrily ordered I Corps commanders to review their command, control, communications, and planning, so "that when your command is confronted with a similar imminent problem, appropriate action would be taken so that we would not lose another camp." The general's expression of unhappiness, however, was confined to top-secret messages. No heads rolled; no investigations were launched. Saigon and Washington remained unruffled, barely concerned. The news media, preoccupied with the Communist attacks in Saigon and the peace negotiations in Paris, paid little attention. In a war in which the distinction between success and failure, victory and defeat, had long been blurred, even an unequivocal debacle like Kham Duc could be obfuscated, obscured, and ignored.

*SPRING 1993*

Ronald H. Spector, author of *After Tet: The Bloodiest Year in Vietnam* (1993), is a professor of history and international affairs at George Washington University. He served in Vietnam in the Marine Corps and is currently studying the social and cultural history of naval warfare in the twentieth century.

# 46

# The Christmas Bombing

## By Stephen E. Ambrose

*In a war permeated with controversy, few actions remain more contro-versial than President Nixon's 1972 Christmas bombing of Hanoi. Some critics, then and now, view the bombing as a brutal, immoral, racist action in a brutal, immoral, and racist war. Other critics, while praising the bombing as an effective and precise use of American air power, con-tend that the bombing was long overdue; that an earlier application of such force would have ended in a quick and decisive American triumph over Communism; that, in essence, the war in Vietnam was lost because America had been unwilling to win it. Stephen E. Ambrose argues, how-ever, that to understand and judge the Christmas bombing, we must know the true target: Was it the North Vietnamese leadership, with its refusal to negotiate in good faith? Or was it the South Vietnamese leader-ship, with its continued rejection of a peace agreement?*

Of the many controversies that swirl around the American role in the Vietnam War, one of the most contentious centers on the Christmas bombing of Hanoi in December 1972. This event fol-lowed Henry A. Kissinger's October news conference in which he said, "Peace is at hand," and President Richard Nixon's triumphant reelection in November. It preceded the signing of the armistice in January 1973 and the release of the American POWs.

According to Nixon and his supporters, the Christmas bombing forced the North Vietnamese to make concessions, accept an armistice, and release American POWs. It was a great U.S. victory that brought peace with honor.

According to Nixon's critics, the armistice agreement signed in January 1973 was identical to the one reached in October 1972. The bombing brought no concessions from the enemy, nor was it intended to; its pur-pose was to persuade the South Vietnamese to go along with an armistice to which they were violently opposed. The bombing ended not because the enemy cried "enough" but because American losses of B-52s were becom-ing intolerable. In addition, conservative critics called the bombing an

American defeat that brought a temporary cease-fire at the cost of a free and independent South Vietnam.

Like so much else in the Vietnam War, the issue of the Christmas bombing was divisive and remains so. To the pro-war hawks, it was done with surgical precision, sparing civilian lives; to the antiwar doves, it was terror bombing, pure and simple. These differences in view cannot be reconciled or settled, but they can be examined.

FOR THREE YEARS, KISSINGER, as national security adviser, had been engaged in secret talks with Le Duc Tho in Paris, seeking a negotiated peace. In the spring of 1972 the Communists had launched their largest offensive ever and had almost overrun South Vietnam. Nixon had responded by bombing Hanoi and mining Haiphong Harbor. The offensive was stopped. In October, Kissinger and Le Duc Tho finally reached an agreement. Its basic terms were a cease-fire in place; the return of POWs; total American withdrawal from South Vietnam; and a National Council of Concord and Reconciliation in South Vietnam to arrange elections, its membership to be one-third neutral, one-third from the current government in Saigon, one-third Communist. Nixon was satisfied that this agreement met his conditions for peace with honor.

President Nguyen Van Thieu of South Vietnam, however, felt betrayed. He perceived the agreement as a surrender: It gave the Communists a legitimate role in the political life of his nation, it allowed the Viet Cong to hold on to the territory it controlled in South Vietnam; worst of all, it permitted the North Vietnamese Army (NVA) to continue to occupy the two northern provinces and retain more than 150,000 troops in his country. Thieu absolutely refused to agree to the cease-fire. In early December, Kissinger went to Paris to persuade Le Duc Tho to remove the NVA from South Vietnam; Le Duc Tho adamantly insisted on going through with the October agreement.

On December 13, 1972, Kissinger flew back to Washington to meet with Nixon and an aide, General Alexander Haig, to discuss the options. The doves urged them to make a separate deal with Hanoi for the release of the POWs in return for a total American withdrawal, leaving Thieu to sink or swim on his own. This proposal had no appeal to Nixon and his aides. To abandon South Vietnam now, after all the blood that had been shed, all the money that had been spent, all the uproar that had overwhelmed the American political scene, would be wrong, cowardly, a betrayal. To abandon Thieu would amount to surrendering the fundamental American goal in the war: the maintenance in power of an anti-Communist government in Saigon.

To get Thieu to sign the agreement, and to force Le Duc Tho to give just a bit more, some dramatic action by the United States was necessary. With fewer than 25,000 U.S. troops remaining in South Vietnam, down from a high of 550,000 when Nixon took office, there was no possibility of escalating on the ground. The only real option discussed was to expand the bombing campaign against North Vietnam.

There were, however, powerful arguments against that course. Sending

B-52s over Hanoi meant risking those expensive weapons and their highly trained crews, because the Soviets had been rushing SA-2 SAMs (surface-to-air missiles) to North Vietnam. The SAMs fired a ten-meter-long missile that U.S. airmen ruefully called "the flying telephone pole." Each missile carried a 286-pound warhead with fuses that could be set to detonate close to a target, on impact, or on command. Guided by a radar tracking beam that honed in on its target, they traveled at a speed of Mach 1.5. The range was up to thirty horizontal miles and about eleven miles up. Fighter-bombers could evade the missiles by diving toward them and then veering off sharply, but that technique was not possible for B-52 pilots.

There were other technological problems for the big bombers. Built in the 1950s, they had been designed to drop nuclear weapons over the Soviet Union. They had only four 4.5mm tail guns—and, in any case, the SAMs came on too fast to be shot down. The B-52s' best defense was altitude: They usually dropped their bombs from 30,000 feet. But the SAMs were able to reach almost 60,000 feet.

And there were political as well as technological problems. Because of the strength of the antiwar movement in the United States, the government—under both Lyndon Johnson and Nixon—had imposed many restrictions on targets in the air war, which, naturally, infuriated the airmen. This policy had little effect on public opinion—the doves and foreign critics still charged that the U.S. Air Force was carrying out a barbaric, terrorist campaign—but it was a great help to the North Vietnamese. They knew what was off-limits and could concentrate their SAMs around such predictable targets as railroad yards and radar sites.

The technological advantage was with the enemy; for this reason, Secretary of Defense Melvin Laird, his deputy Kenneth Rush, and the chairman of the Joint Chiefs of Staff, Admiral Thomas Moorer, were opposed to using B-52s over Hanoi, and they so advised the president. Many of Nixon's political advisers were also opposed, because to escalate the bombing after Kissinger's "peace is at hand" statement would drive the Nixon-haters in Congress, in the media, on the campuses, and among the general public into a frenzy.

But something had to be done to convince Thieu that, whatever the formal wording of the cease-fire agreement, he could count on Nixon to come to the defense of South Vietnam if the NVA broke the cease-fire. And Le Duc Tho had to be convinced that, despite the doves in Congress, Nixon could still punish North Vietnam.

That made the bombing option tempting. Although the B-52s were relatively slow and cumbersome, they packed a terrific punch. They carried eighty-four 500-pound bombs in their bomb bays and twelve 500-pound bombs on their wings. They could drop those bombs with relative accuracy, much better than World War II bombers. (The Seventh Air Force commander, General John Vogt, complained that the internal radar systems of the B-52s were "notoriously bad" and that "misses of a thousand feet or more were common." However, in World War II, misses of 1,000 meters—three times as much—had been common.) They flew from secure bases in Guam and Thailand. They had been used with devastating effect in the Battle of Khe Sanh in 1968 and again to stop the NVA spring offensive of 1972. The temptation to use them against Hanoi was great, and growing.

Kissinger tried to resist it. He recommended more bombing south of the 20th parallel, against NVA units that were not as well protected by SAMs as Hanoi was, and reseeding the mines in Haiphong Harbor. On the other hand Haig, always a hard-liner, argued forcefully for an all-out bombing campaign by the B-52s against Hanoi itself.

Nixon later said that ordering the bombing was "the most difficult decision" he had to make in the entire war. But, he added, "it was also one of the most clear-cut and necessary ones." He issued an order on December 14 to reseed the mines, from the air—and also to send the B-52s against Hanoi. He told Kissinger he was prepared "for new losses and casualties and POWs," and explained, "We'll take the same heat for big blows as for little blows."

To Kissinger, the president seemed "sullen" and "withdrawn." Nixon "resented" having to do what he did, because "deep down he was ready to give up by going back to the October draft" of the armistice agreement. His bombing order, according to Kissinger, was "his last roll of the dice . . . helpful if it worked; a demonstration to the right wing if it failed that he had done all he could."

Once Nixon set the policy, public relations became his obsession. John Scali, White House adviser on foreign affairs information policy, put the problem succinctly to Nixon's chief of staff, H.R. Haldeman, in a telephone conversation: "We look incompetent—bombing for no good reason and because we don't know what else to do." On May 8, 1972, Nixon had gone on television to explain his reason for bombing Hanoi and mining Haiphong: It was in response to the Communists' spring offensive. Scali had thought the television appearance unnecessary in May, as the justification for Nixon's strong action was obvious then. But in December, when his critics and even some of his supporters could not figure out his reasons, Nixon refused to go on television to explain his actions.

Kissinger badly wanted Nixon to make a broadcast; he had been urging it for days. But Nixon, according to Kissinger, "was determined to take himself out of the line of fire." Nixon feared that any attempt to rally the people to support more bombing after "peace is at hand" would fall flat.

On the evening of December 14, four days before the bombing was set to begin, Nixon told Kissinger to hold a news conference to explain the status of the negotiations. The president followed up with a five-page, single-spaced memo on December 15 and another of two pages on December 16, instructing Kissinger on what to say. He told the national security adviser to "hit hard on the point that, while we want peace just as soon as we can get it, that we want a peace that is honorable and a peace that will last." Kissinger should admit the U.S. goals had been reached "in principle" in the October agreement, but add that some "strengthening of the language" was needed "so that there will be no doubt on either side in the event that [the agreement] is broken." He should accuse Le Duc Tho of having "backed off" some of the October understandings.

Kissinger should emphasize that with the Christmas season coming on, the president had a "very strong personal desire to get the war settled." But he should also point out that the president "insists that the United States is not going to be pushed around, blackmailed or stampeded into making the wrong kind of a peace agreement." Finally, he should say that "the president will continue to order whatever actions he considers necessary by air and sea"—the only reference to the bombing order, which had already gone out.

In his memos, Nixon was repetitious to a degree unusual even for him, an indication of the strain he was under, due perhaps to the difficulty of his position. As an example of his dilemma, it was the Americans—in response to demands from Thieu—who had backed off the October agreements, not the North Vietnamese. But Nixon could not have Kissinger straightforwardly tell the American people his administration was bombing Hanoi to convince Thieu to sign. Thieu was increasingly seen in the United States as the sole obstacle to peace and thus was increasingly unpopular. On December 15 Senator Barry Goldwater, an Arizona Republican and one of the toughest hawks, said that if Thieu "bucks much more" the United States should proceed with its withdrawal and "to hell with him."

Kissinger held his briefing on December 16 and said what he had been told to say. He stressed the president's consistency, unflappability, firmness, patience, and farsightedness. He mentioned Nixon fourteen times (he had been criticized by Haldeman for referring to the president only three times in his October news conference).

By this time the tension in the Nixon-Kissinger relationship was threatening to lead to an open break. Kissinger was unhappy with his boss because of his interference, and his back-and-forthing, on the negotiations. Nixon was furious with Kissinger for his "peace is at hand" statement, which had raised public expectations to a high level, expectations that were going to be dashed when the bombing began. Nixon also resented the way Kissinger had thrust himself onto center stage, his constant leaks to reporters, and the way the reporters responded by giving Kissinger credit for the huge margin of the election victory. Further, earlier in December *Time* magazine had named Nixon and Kissinger "Men of the Year," with their pictures on the cover; Kissinger correctly feared that Nixon resented having to share the honor.

On December 17, Nixon wrote a letter to Thieu. Usually the president signed drafts of letters to foreign heads of government prepared by Kissinger; in this case, he wrote the letter personally. Nixon had Haig fly to Saigon to hand-deliver it. In the letter Nixon made a threat: Unless Thieu accepted the agreement, the United States would go it alone. "You must decide now whether you want me to seek a settlement with the enemy which serves U.S. interests alone."

Although Nixon himself would do anything possible to avoid a break, the threat was not meaningless because, as Goldwater's statement indicated, Congress might carry it out regardless of the president's wishes. Thieu knew that, and he also knew how to read between the lines of Nixon's letter. After reading it, he told Haig it was obvious he was being asked to sign not a peace agreement but rather an agreement for continued American support.

ON DECEMBER 18, the air force launched its B-52s and fighter-bombers against Hanoi. The orders were to avoid civilian casualties at all costs; for example, a missile-assembly plant manned by Russian technicians in the heart of Hanoi was off-limits, partly because of fear of Soviet casualties, partly to avoid near misses that would devastate residential areas. Still, Linebacker II, as the operation was code-named, greatly damaged railroads, power plants, radio transmitters, and radar installations around Hanoi, as well as docks and shipyards in Haiphong.

It was not Nixon but Johnson who had imposed the restrictions on targets; in fact, they frustrated him. The day after the bombing began, he read a report about targets that had been avoided for fear of civilian casualties, and he called Admiral Moorer. "I don't want any more of this crap about the fact that we couldn't hit this target or that one," Nixon said. "This is your chance to use military power effectively to win this war, and if you don't, I'll consider you responsible." But the armed forces, concerned about their reputation and perhaps doubtful of the effectiveness of area bombing, continued the restrictions.

Nevertheless, a French reporter in Hanoi referred to "carpet bombing," a line repeated by Radio Hanoi. As a result, there was an immediate worldwide uproar and many expressions of moral revulsion. There had been no presidential explanation or announcement of any kind. People everywhere had taken Kissinger at his word, that only a few t's needed to be crossed and a few i's dotted and the negotiations would be wrapped up. The shock when the bombing was announced was even greater than that following the Cambodian incursion of 1970.

The adverse congressional and editorial reaction was unprecedented. Senator William Saxbe, an Ohio Republican, said Nixon "appears to have left his senses." Democratic Senate leader Mike Mansfield of Montana called it a "Stone Age tactic." Democratic senator Edward Kennedy of Massachusetts said it was an "outrage." In an editorial, the *Washington Post* charged that the bombing caused millions of Americans "to cringe in shame and to wonder at their President's very sanity." James Reston, in the *New York Times,* called it "war by tantrum."

Nixon did have supporters, including Governors Nelson Rockefeller of New York and Ronald Reagan of California and Republican senators James Buckley of New York, Howard Baker of Tennessee, and Charles Percy of Illinois. John Connally, former governor of Texas and treasury secretary, called Nixon daily to encourage him and assure him that, regardless of what politicians and the media said, the people were behind him.

That was probably an exaggeration, but not as gross as the exaggerations of Nixon's critics. They charged that he had ordered the most intensive bombing campaign in the history of warfare. That was nonsense. In comparison to the human costs at Dresden, Hamburg, Berlin, and Tokyo—not to mention Hiroshima and Nagasaki—in World War II, the bombing of Hanoi during the Christmas season of 1972 was a minor operation. Under the severe targeting restrictions followed by the air force, civilian casualties were only around 1,500, and at least some of those were caused by SAM missiles falling back on the city after missing their targets. In World War II, a bombing raid that killed fewer than 2,000 German or Japanese civilians was not even worth a minor story in the newspapers, not to mention expressions of moral outrage from opinion leaders and prominent politicians. The Christmas bombing of Hanoi was not terror bombing, as the world had come to know terror bombing in the twentieth century.

Nixon's private response was to personalize it and assign to his critics the lowest possible motives. In his diary he wrote that they "simply cannot bear the thought of this administration under my leadership bringing off the peace on an honorable basis which they have so long predicted would be impossible. The election was a terrible blow to them and this is their first opportunity to recover from the election and to strike back."

That was by no means the whole truth. The most basic cause for the moral revulsion was the nature of the war itself. Few in the United States had protested the firebomb raids of World War II, which set out deliberately to kill civilians. Why the difference three decades later, especially when the air force was doing its utmost to avoid killing civilians? Because from 1942 to 1945, the United States was fighting for its life against a foe who was not only pure evil but also powerful enough to threaten the entire world. In World War II there had been no ongoing negotiations with the Germans and Japanese, only a demand for their unconditional surrender. In 1942–45, the Americans were bombing in order to hasten that surrender.

But in 1972, no one believed that the United States was fighting for its life, or that the NVA could conquer the world, or that there could be no end to the war until Hanoi surrendered; and few believed that more bombing would bring a quicker end to the war.

Despite the protest, Nixon continued to send the B-52s and fighter-bombers, and the battle raged in the sky above Hanoi. If Hanoi was far from being the most heavily bombed city in history, it certainly was one of the best defended. The SAMs shot down six of the ninety B-52s that flew missions on December 20; the following day, two of thirty were destroyed. The air force could not long sustain such losses; on the other hand, the Soviets could not long continue to supply SAMs in such quantity to the North Vietnamese (they were shooting a hundred or more per day at the attackers).

Nixon felt his resolve was being tested; he was determined to prevail. Kissinger, however, broke under the pressure of the protest and began leaking to reporters, especially Reston, word that he had opposed the bombing. This infuriated Nixon. He instructed his aide Charles Colson to monitor all

Kissinger's telephone calls and contacts with the press. The president, according to Colson, "was raving and ranting about Henry double-talking." Colson did as instructed and discovered that Kissinger was calling Reston and others, "planting self-serving stories at the same time he was recommending Nixon be tough on Vietnam."

When Haldeman confronted Kissinger, the national security adviser simply denied the facts. "I have never given a personal opinion different from the president's," he claimed, and said he had not given an interview to Reston. Haldeman got him to admit that he had called Reston on the telephone, just before Reston wrote a column stating that Kissinger had opposed the bombing and implying that Kissinger was the one moderate, sensible man among Nixon's advisers. Kissinger concluded his conversation with Haldeman by suggesting that it was time for the president to give him a vote of confidence: a letter from Nixon giving Kissinger backing and credit for the progress in the negotiations.

Nixon went to his home in Key Biscayne, Florida, for Christmas. He ordered a twenty-four-hour halt in the bombing for the holiday. In his diary he complained he was "more and more" a lonely individual. "It is a question not of too many friends but really too few—one of the inevitable consequences of this position." He received very few Christmas salutations, even from Republicans on Capitol Hill and members of his cabinet. As a result, he told interviewer David Frost four years later, "it was the loneliest and saddest Christmas I can ever remember, much sadder and much more lonely than the one in the Pacific during the war." He did make some telephone calls, including one to Ronald Reagan, who complained about CBS News coverage of the bombing and said that under World War II circumstances the network would have been charged with treason.

The day after Christmas, despite urgings from some of his aides and much of the media that he extend the Christmas Day truce, Nixon ordered the biggest bombing raid yet, 120 B-52s over Hanoi. Five were shot down, but that afternoon Nixon received a message from Hanoi. The Communists, who had evidently exhausted their supply of SAMs, proposed that the talks resume in Paris on January 9. Nixon replied that he wanted technical talks resumed on January 2, and he offered to stop the bombing of Hanoi if the Communists agreed. Hanoi did so.

General Haig was furious. He did not want to stop the bombing when Hanoi was all but on its knees. He was incensed when he discovered that "every single adviser of the president . . . [was] calling the president daily, hourly, and telling him to terminate the bombing." But even Haig realized that Nixon had little choice, because if he continued the bombing after the congressional session began on January 3, "there would have been legislative restrictions which would have been national suicide from the standpoint of ever negotiating a settlement."

Nixon decided to call off the bombing. On December 29 he announced that he had suspended offensive operations north of the 20th parallel and that the Paris talks would resume.

SO WHO WON THE ELEVEN-DAY BATTLE? The North Vietnamese had shot down fifteen B-52s, and eleven fighter-bombers had gone down. Ninety-three American airmen were missing—thirty-one became known POWs. The enemy had fired 1,200 missiles and lost three MiG jets to achieve these results. Some 40,000 tons of bombs had fallen on Hanoi—40 kilotons, or the equivalent of two Hiroshima-size bombs. However, visitors to Hanoi soon after the battle ended, including Americans, all testify that although great destruction was done to military and industrial targets—such as the airfields, railroad network, and factories—residential areas were mostly untouched.

There was no clear-cut winner. Thus, the last American action in the Vietnam War was characteristic of all those that had come earlier—cursed by half measures. From 1964 to 1969 Johnson's actions, as described by Nixon, were always "too little, too late." That had also been true of Nixon's ultimatum in November 1969; of his Cambodian incursion of 1970; of his Laotian operation in 1971; of his May 8, 1972, air offensive; and now of his Christmas bombing. He had taken the heat for an all-out offensive without delivering one. It was not that he did not want to, but rather that it was overwhelmingly obvious the American political system would not allow him to do so.

Nixon called Hanoi's willingness to resume the talks a "stunning capitulation," one presumably brought about by the bombing. But it had been Saigon, not Hanoi, that had created the stalemate in the talks. In his message to Hanoi, Nixon had referred to the October agreements; going back to them represented an American, not a North Vietnamese, concession. Kissinger's reference to "normalization" of relations continued the hints he had been secretly making to Le Duc Tho that when peace came the United States would aid in the reconstruction of North Vietnam, just as it had helped Germany and Japan after World War II.

On December 30 Senator Henry Jackson, a Democrat from Washington, called Nixon to ask the president to go on television and explain that "we bombed to get them back to the table." Nixon passed the message along to Kissinger with a note: "He is right—but my saying it publicly would seriously jeopardize our negotiations."

Nixon had another reason to hesitate to make the claim that Jackson wanted him to make. It would have been extremely difficult to get informed observers to believe that Nixon had bombed Hanoi in order to force North Vietnamese acceptance of terms they had already agreed to. It was much easier to believe that Nixon's real target was not Hanoi but Saigon. And as 1972 came to an end, there was no indication that Thieu was prepared to sign.

On January 2, 1973, the House Democratic Caucus voted 154 to 75 to cut off all funds for Vietnam as soon as arrangements were complete for the withdrawal of American armed forces and the return of the POWs. On January 4 the Senate Democratic Caucus passed a similar resolution, 36 to 12.

Nixon passed the pressure on to Thieu. Initially he tried to do so through Anna Chennault, the widow of General Claire Chennault, whose influence on the right wing of the Republican party was considerable. He had her friend

John Mitchell, his former attorney general, ask her to use her influence with Thieu, but the "Dragon Lady," as she was commonly called, refused. There was irony here. In 1968 Mitchell had persuaded Mrs. Chennault to intervene with Thieu to get him to refuse to help Johnson in his election-eve bid for peace, which if successful might have given Hubert Humphrey the presidency. Now Nixon wanted her to persuade Thieu to cooperate with the president and accept an unsatisfactory peace. She would not.

Nixon again wrote directly to Thieu. The letter, dated January 5, was less threatening than previous ones and contained a more explicit promise: "Should you decide, as I trust you will, to go with us, you have my assurance of continued assistance in the post-settlement period and that we will respond with full force should the settlement be violated by North Vietnam."

Nixon was not in a position to give such a promise. Without congressional appropriations, he could not come to Saigon's aid.

That same day he had a meeting with the leaders of both parties. The atmosphere was cold. He spoke briefly about Vietnam. He said he knew many of the men in the room disagreed with his policies but added that he was determined to persist.

Nixon concluded, "In any event, you have indicated your own positions—some of you—which is in direct opposition. I understand that. I have the responsibility. Gentlemen, I will take responsibility if those negotiations fail. If they succeed, we all succeed."

On January 6 Nixon went to his retreat at Camp David, where he met with Kissinger, who was flying to Paris the next day. The president said that if Kissinger could get Le Duc Tho to go back to the October 8 agreement, "we should take it." Kissinger demurred, but Nixon insisted. He did want Kissinger to get some wording changes so that "we can claim some improvement," but the point was that the war had to end, on whatever terms, in this round of negotiations; otherwise the Ninety-third Congress would force the administration to end it on even worse terms.

The president did agree that Kissinger could threaten the North Vietnamese with a resumption of the bombing of Hanoi if they did not cooperate, but Nixon then warned him that "as far as our internal planning is concerned, we cannot consider this to be a viable option." As for Thieu, Nixon referred to Haig's report of his December visit to Saigon: Thieu was saying that "it is not a peace agreement that he is going to get but a commitment from the United States to continue to protect South Vietnam in the event such an agreement is broken." Nixon said that was exactly right.

JANUARY 9 WAS NIXON'S SIXTIETH BIRTHDAY. In an interview, he gave his formula for living: "Never slow down." He admitted that he had many problems, "but boredom is the least of them."

He also wrote by hand a piece of selfanalysis: "RN approaches his second inauguration with true peace of mind—because he knows that by his actions, often in the face of the most intense sort of criticism, what he is bringing to the world is a 'peace of mind'—that is, a peace formed by the exercise of hard reason and calm deliberation, and durable because its foundation has been carefully laid." Nixon instructed Haldeman to pass the piece along to the staff and called it "an excellent line for them to take" when talking to the press about the president.

That afternoon Nixon got what he called "the best birthday present I have had in sixty years." Kissinger cabled from Paris that there had been "a major breakthrough in the negotiations. In sum, we settled all the outstanding questions in the text of the agreement."

Le Duc Tho had accepted Kissinger's revised wording on the demilitarized zone. But it made no practical difference; the accord that had been reached was basically the same as in October. Kissinger aide John Negroponte was disappointed. He told friends, "We bombed the North Vietnamese into accepting our concession."

Getting the Communists to avow the accord had never been the problem; the problem was Thieu, and that remained. Nixon was eager to have the situation resolved before Inauguration Day, January 20, but he worried that Thieu would refuse to cooperate.

On January 13 Kissinger returned from Paris. He flew down to Key Biscayne to brief the president. They talked until 2:00 A.M. Nixon walked out to the car with Kissinger to say good night and to tell him that the country was indebted to him for what he had done. Nixon later wrote that it is not really a comfortable feeling for me to praise people so openly but "Henry expects it, and it was good that I did so." Kissinger replied it was only Nixon's courage that had made a settlement possible. In his memoirs Kissinger wrote that he felt "an odd tenderness" that night toward Nixon.

The next morning they turned their attention to Thieu. Nixon wrote him another letter and told Haig to fly to Saigon to deliver it. The letter was full of threats: "I have therefore irrevocably decided to proceed to initial the Agreement on January 23, 1973, and to sign it on January 27, 1973, in Paris. I will do so, if necessary alone." There were also promises. If Thieu would sign, Nixon would make it "emphatically clear that the United States recognizes your government as the only legal government of South Vietnam; that we do not recognize the right of any foreign troops to be present on South Vietnamese territory; that we will react strongly in the event the agreement is violated." Of course, there was a big difference between not recognizing the right of the NVA to stay in South Vietnam and requiring the NVA to leave the country when the American armed forces left. Nixon concluded, "It is my firm intention to continue full economic and military aid."

Nixon feared that his words would not be enough, but he was determined to prevail. "Brutality is nothing," he told Kissinger. "You have never seen it if this son-of-a-bitch doesn't go along, believe me." To add to the pressure on Thieu, Nixon had Senators John Stennis, a Mississippi Democrat, and Goldwater warn publicly that if Thieu blocked the agreement he would imperil his government's chances of receiving any further aid from Congress.

Still Thieu would not yield. He sent a letter to Nixon raising the same complaints he had made in October—naturally enough, since it was the same agreement. Nixon replied on January 20 with an ultimatum.

On the public relations front, meanwhile, Nixon was also busy. On January 19 he told Haldeman, "We need to get across the point that the reason for the success of the negotiations was the bombing and the converse point that we did not halt the bombing until we had the negotiations back on track." He instructed Kissinger to brief the staff on the settlement: "The key to this briefing will be to get a lot of people out selling our line." Nixon wanted "an all-out effort with inspired leaks, etc."

On January 20 Nixon was inaugurated for his second term. He had hoped to be able to announce that peace had been achieved, but Thieu's intransigence made that impossible. Under the circumstances, the hoopla that ordinarily occurs at inaugurations was distinctly absent, and Nixon's inaugural address was short and somber.

The parade following the ceremonies was marred by small groups of demonstrators chanting obscenities and throwing eggs and debris, but it was nowhere near as bad as four years earlier. If Nixon had not quite yet brought peace, he had gone a long way toward achieving that objective. The madness and hatred that had been so prominent in 1969 had abated by 1973. Sadly, in part it had been replaced by a bitterness because of the Christmas bombing and a suspicion because of the growing furor over the Watergate break-in. If Nixon deserved credit for the gains, he also deserved blame for the bitterness and suspicion.

ON JANUARY 22 WORD ARRIVED THAT THIEU had finally bowed to the inevitable and consented to the agreement. The following evening Nixon went on television to announce that on January 27 the formal signing ceremonies would be held in Paris. A cease-fire would begin at midnight that day.

After this announcement Nixon met with Kissinger. Nixon said he did not want to have any hatred or anything of that sort toward "our enemies"—by which he meant the American doves, not the Vietnamese Communists. "On the other hand," he continued, Nixon's foes had to recognize that they "are disturbed, distressed, and really discouraged because we succeeded."

Nixon later wondered whether commentators would appreciate what he and Kissinger had accomplished; he decided "probably not." He told Kissinger that every success was followed by a "terrific letdown," and he urged Kissinger not to let it get to him. There were many battles left to fight; he should not be discouraged.

For his part Nixon wrote later that he had expected to feel relief and satisfaction when the war ended, but instead was surprised to find himself with feelings of "sadness, apprehension, and impatience." Kissinger was struck by Nixon's being "so lonely in his hour of triumph."

Beyond the letdown he always felt after a crisis, Nixon had reasons for his negative feelings. In the weeks that followed, he often and vehemently maintained he had achieved peace with honor, but that claim was difficult to sustain. Seven years earlier, when pressed by reporters to explain what kind of settlement he would accept in Vietnam, he had held up the Korean armistice of 1953 as his model. What he finally accepted was far short of that goal.

The Korean settlement had left 60,000 American troops in South Korea; the Vietnam settlement left no American troops in South Vietnam. The Korean settlement left no Communist troops in South Korea; the Vietnam settlement left 150,000 Communist troops in South Vietnam. The Korean settlement had established the 38th parallel as a dividing line, and it was so heavily fortified on both sides that twenty years later almost no living thing had crossed it; the Vietnam settlement called the 17th parallel a border, but the NVA controlled both sides of it and moved back and forth without interference. The Korean settlement had left President Syngman Rhee firmly in control of his country, to the point that the Communist party was banned; the Vietnam settlement forced President Thieu to accept Communist membership on the National Council of Concord and Reconciliation.

Small wonder that Thieu regarded the settlement as little short of a surrender, and feared that the cease-fire would last only until the Americans got their POWs back and brought their armed forces home. Small wonder, too, that he worried about his future, as his army was woefully inferior to Rhee's army (not to mention the NVA).

Thieu did have one asset to match Rhee's: a promise from the American president that if the Communists broke the agreement the United States would come to his aid. But in South Vietnam, in the spring of 1975, that promise proved to be worthless, because by then Nixon had resigned to avoid impeachment. In some part the resignation was brought on by the Christmas bombing. Kissinger's "peace is at hand" promise, followed by Nixon's triumphant reelection, and then by the bombing, created feelings of bitterness and betrayal and led many Democrats to want to punish Nixon. Nixon gave them their excuse with Watergate.

Nixon's defenders assert that had it not been for Watergate, the North Vietnamese would not have dared to launch their offensive in 1975. Or, if they had, that Nixon would have responded with the fury he showed in the spring of 1972, and the American bombing support would have made it possible for the South Vietnamese to turn back the invaders once again.

Nixon's detractors call this scenario nonsense. They assert that all he ever wanted or expected from the cease-fire was a "decent interval" before the NVA overran Saigon. That decent interval was until Nixon had successfully completed his second term. They argue further that Congress was never going to give Nixon the funds to resume bombing in Vietnam and that he knew it, even as he made his promises to Thieu.

No one can know what might have been. Everyone knows what happened.

*WINTER 1992*

---

Stephen E. Ambrose, a historian whose interests include both political and military affairs, is the author of a three-volume biography of Richard Nixon.

# 47

# MIA

## By Marilyn Elkins

*The agony of war lingers long after the guns fall silent. It has always been and always will be so. For the American people, nothing has so clearly demonstrated that cruel fact as the emotional and painful issue of the Vietnam War POW-MIAs. Over 2,000 men remained unaccounted for when that conflict ended. For loved ones of these missing warriors, life now seemed held in suspension. Days of uncertainty turned into months, months into years. The ordeal of Marilyn Elkins, the wife of a navy A-4 Skyhawk pilot, began in October 1966 when the navy declared Lieutenant Frank Elkins, her husband, missing in a flight over Nghe Tinh Province. Her personal odyssey to learn his fate would not end until twenty-three years later.*

Every war has produced some number of men whose remains could not be recovered. In previous centuries, accurate counts of those missing in action (MIAs) were often unobtainable. When Napoleon Bonaparte embroiled Europe in war, for example, soldiers were recruited as armies advanced. The result was huge numbers of men about whom relatives heard nothing and about whose whereabouts the military cared little.

In this century, the numbers of American MIAs have been reasonably well documented: In World War I there were 2,913 of them; in World War II, almost 79,000; in Korea, 8,200; and in Vietnam, 2,273 remain unaccounted for. Since World War II, reported sightings of prisoners of war (POWs)—with attendant claims that Americans are still being held in captivity—have also been common.

At the end of World War II, the Soviets had seized more than 15,000 Americans from German camps and from Soviet-held areas; although they were repatriated, during the late 1940s reports persisted that Americans (including a man wearing a "U.S. Navy" tattoo) were being held in Soviet labor camps. In Korea, the Allied command listed 952 Americans believed to be prisoners of Communist forces; these prisoners' disappearance has never been fully explained. In 1953 a Japanese POW who had been held in the Soviet Union told U.S. officials that he had seen at least a dozen Americans at a labor camp near Khabarovsk. Recently declassified documents indicate that another Japanese POW corroborated this report of

American prisoners; this man insisted that he had also met an American who had been convicted of espionage by a Soviet court and sentenced to imprisonment. Whether these Americans were prisoners from an earlier war or men who disappeared during espionage activities in the Cold War is unclear; on June 13, 1952, a U.S. Air Force B-29 flying a secret mission near the Soviet Union had disappeared near Siberia with twelve Americans aboard.

Declassified Pentagon documents from the 1950s also detail persistent reports by refugees and released prisoners that describe American POWs in both the Soviet Union and China. According to the State Department, some of these reports were "so credible" that in 1956 it demanded an accounting from the Soviets. The Pentagon estimated that the Soviet government was holding at least twelve American prisoners—perhaps from the B-29 and from a navy plane that disappeared over the Baltic in 1950. The Soviets insisted, however, that no Americans were in their prisons. Because Cold War missions were classified, the United States never publicly sought the return of these reported prisoners, and their families were never encouraged to make their concerns public. But the Defense and State departments have admitted that evidence suggests these men may have been captured by the Soviets.

The U.S. Army has a secret archive of alleged sightings under the title "American Citizens Detained in the U.S.S.R." Mark Sauter, an investigative reporter based in Seattle, obtained these records under the provisions of the Freedom of Information Act. The documents detail chilling descriptions of Americans being held—often in poor health—by Communist forces.

Recently, relatives of the two U.S. air crews have begun emulating the activist families of the Vietnam era by organizing pressure groups to look for evidence that Americans were—and may remain—prisoners in the Soviet Union. In only a few months, these families have amassed records of sightings and enlisted the help of senators and congressmen. The Soviet government has already agreed to consider a State Department request for access to archives that may reveal the fate of many alleged Soviet prisoners.

Compared to the numbers of American MIAs from earlier wars, the 2,273 listed from Vietnam seem almost insignificant. The number in relation to the total killed—4 percent—also pales compared to some earlier wars: 5.5 percent in World War I, 27 percent in World War II, and 15.1 percent in Korea. It is insignificant, that is, unless you happen to be related to one of them.

Few of their wives or other family members were prepared for the length of time these servicemen would be listed as either POWs or MIAs; no American soldiers had ever officially been held for more than three and one-half years. While the law provides that a person who has been missing for seven years can be presumed dead, this does not apply to MIAs during a time of war. Americans had never fought in such a long war, and no military policy had been established for such an event. A majority of the MIAs in Vietnam were pilots—America's best and brightest. Exceptional athletes, intellects, and aviators, they had seemed invulnerable. They had not been expected to fall prey to a small, Asian enemy.

CERTAINLY I THOUGHT my husband, U.S. Navy lieutenant Frank Callihan Elkins, was immune to MiGs and SAMs. Married for only nine months, he was twenty-seven and I was twenty-two when his A-4 Skyhawk disappeared during a flight from its vessel, the USS *Oriskany*. I still believed that death was for other people. When I received the notification on October 13, 1966, I had just returned from spending two weeks with Frank in the Philippines and Hong Kong. He had December orders to a test squadron in China Lake, California; I was residing with my parents while I waited out his Vietnam tour. When the casualty assistance officer arrived, I answered the doorbell in a blue floral housecoat, half-awake and half-smiling: I knew that this man would be embarrassed when he learned he had delivered his message to the wrong wife.

The officer told me that Frank had been killed. After making a telephone call to report that he had delivered his message, he returned to say that he had misunderstood the original communication: Frank was only missing. Eager to see this as portentous, I interpreted the whole episode as additional proof that Frank was invulnerable.

Because Frank's father had a serious heart condition, I immediately contacted my brother-in-law and asked him to break the news to his parents. I didn't want them to receive the same misinformation I had. I could not cry but was shiveringly cold, despite the numerous quilts my parents wrapped around me. I seemed to be watching myself participate in conversations, observing these events as though they were happening to someone else.

While official policy demanded that such news be delivered in person by an officer of equal or higher rank, practice—as in my case—sometimes fell short of the ideal. No matter how it bungled the delivery of such news, the Pentagon assumed that families of MIAs in the Vietnam War would maintain the official expected silence—the traditional stiff upper lip that guaranteed a husband's continued military success—as they had done in past wars.

The Korean War was the first one in which the behavior of POWs under stress had been blamed on the prisoners rather than on their captors. Suspected of conspiring with the enemy and succumbing to Communist brainwashing (this was during the McCarthy era), the Korean POW became a symbol of national dishonor, although the number of Americans who chose not to return—twenty-one—was small when compared to the 88,000 Chinese and North Korean prisoners who refused repatriation (more than half of those who fell into American hands).

Consequently, the U.S. military code of conduct used in the 1960s insisted that a captive conduct himself as a fighting man rather than as a powerless prisoner. The code was designed to produce soldiers who could resist torture, remain silent, and attempt escape against overwhelming odds and under brutal conditions. As part of this doctrine, pilots who were being prepared to fly over Vietnam were sent to a week-long survival school in which they were beaten, forced to curl up in a tiny black box for hours, and verbally assaulted if they failed to escape from their "captors." When he returned from this week of "captivity" in March 1966, Frank had bruises on most of his body and slept for a full twenty-four hours from exhaustion. While many of the simulations were classified and therefore not subjects he could discuss, he confided that he had found the solitary confinement most difficult. To occupy his mind during these seemingly endless episodes, Frank had imagined happy scenes from his childhood and of his return home.

I soon found that equal stoicism was expected of military wives. The official policy was to give us as little information as possible so that we could not harm our husbands with any indiscretion. The government ensured our silence through effective manipulation of our concern for our husbands' safety. The navy's telegrams and other communications insisted that because my husband might be "held by hostile force against his will," "for his safety" I should reply to inquiries from outside sources by revealing "only his name, rank, file number, and date of birth." These were exactly the orders given to Frank during his survival training.

Determined not to compromise him in any way, I began a period of intense, silent waiting. My own needs for comforting were subordinated to government policy which, for most of the period of 1966–68, insisted that secrecy was in the MIAs' best interest. Designed to protect national policy without considering their effect on family members, the government's instructions did not include tips on how to survive this silent vigil. No one suggested that I might find psychological counseling helpful. No one offered to explain what Frank's chances for survival might be. No one offered suggestions as to what I should do—except wait in silence. Treatment of MIA wives during the recent Persian Gulf War seems to indicate that this atavistic attitude toward the exigencies of military wives remains relatively unchanged—even though American soldiers now are instructed to give transparently false "confessions," rather than simply remain silent, if they are captured.

I was left in the hands of whatever emotional support I could find—primarily a group of navy wives who generously called me from their homes in California to extend what comfort they could spare from their concern about their own husbands. I now realize how emotionally costly this solace must have been; surely I must have reminded these women that their husbands could suffer Frank's fate at any moment. No wonder they sometimes presented me with unfounded rumors and speculations.

Except for my cousin Shirley, whose husband was also a pilot on the USS *Oriskany,* no one in my immediate family or community knew what to say or do. My parents live on a farm in rural Tennessee; the nearest town, Pikeville, has a population of about 1,000 people. I soon found that even though I had remained silent, most of these people knew about my husband's status and wanted to help. However, no one had provided any of us with a script for appropriate behavior. I couldn't understand why people kept arriving with casseroles, pies, and cakes—rural custom following a death. On the other hand, a friend of my father's who had been a POW in World War II returned home after everyone but his immediate family had given up hope; Clint's experiences, known by everyone in our community, became the repeated "evidence" they could offer that Frank would survive.

But I needed no assurance of that. Within a few weeks I insisted that my father install another telephone line so that I could be reached immediately when Frank came tap-dancing out of the jungle. I was certain that my teenage brothers' constant conversations were responsible for the delay in news about Frank.

On October 26, 1966, fire broke out on the USS *Oriskany,* and many of Frank's friends were killed. One friend, Bill Johnson, had already sent me Frank's diary, which I carefully stored away for Frank; he had kept it with the intention of writing a novel about his Vietnam experience. Bill was killed in the fire, before he could ship the rest of Frank's gear. When the navy finally forwarded Frank's belongings, many items—including the typewriter I had given him and a surprise Christmas gift that I knew he had purchased for me in Hong Kong—were missing. The navy was unhelpful in retrieving these items, which I had embroidered with sentimental significance.

By December I had become accustomed to the fact that my presence often made other people uncomfortable, had lost twenty pounds, and had nearly perfected the role of zombie. I remained intent, however, on fooling myself: I was convinced that I was helping Frank by staring at my special phone, willing it to ring. Finally, my first bout with Crohn's disease, a chronic ailment that is exacerbated by stress, forced me to spend Christmas week in the hospital. My doctor convinced me that I might die if I continued to do nothing but wait. Even I knew my death wouldn't help Frank.

So I decided to get on with plans we had made prior to his disappearance. We both had wanted to become English professors, and I took my first step toward that goal by enrolling in graduate school. A large number of other MIA wives also earned degrees while they waited for their husbands' return. Initially we were not entitled to benefits mandated by the GI Bill because we weren't widows, and we were not allowed to collect our husbands' full salaries; the Defense Department required that a percentage be held in savings. Eventually, when the length of time men were listed as MIA continued beyond that of earlier wars, wives who persisted were given full benefits. But I did not apply because neither my casualty assistance officer nor my monthly updates from the navy informed me that I was eligible. Instead I held part-time jobs to finance my studies.

I was still under government orders not to reveal my husband's status, and so when I was asked about the wedding ring I wore, I'd reply, "My husband's in Vietnam." I often didn't like the immediate response that statement received: an almost instantaneous look of pity, or, rarely, a diatribe about how reprehensible U.S. activities in Vietnam were.

Within a year of Frank's disappearance, the government negotiated with the North Vietnamese to allow wives to send letters and, eventually, packages to their missing husbands. Soon, navy communiqués detailed what could be included in the monthly letters (good news and cheer) and what could not (the war or any other bad news). Last year the navy returned one of my letters; it had "been found" in materials that they received from the North Vietnamese. Speaking encouragingly about Frank's family and my continuing education, the letter closes with this:

What else can I say? I love you and am here waiting. And will be. I do live chiefly by longing, cherishing our past, trusting in our future, but I endure. I keep a thousand experiences to share with you; buy records I know you'll want to hear, books you'll want to read, and clothes I think you'll like. You are the controlling force in my life. I hope you are able to have me with you as much as I have you here. Oh, Frank, I love you so much! I pray I can be worthy of such love.

Rereading these words today, I am embarrassed by how closely they follow navy guidelines. Had he received this letter, I suspect Frank might have found it disconcerting. To anyone who knows my independent nature, it sounds as artificial as the deliberately staged confessions of captured American fliers during the recent Persian Gulf War. Coming from someone who, prior to her marriage, had negotiated an agreement that she didn't have to be the kind of military wife who held squadron teas and luncheons and would be free to pursue a career, this letter sounds suspect. But it illustrates just how fully I had adopted the official government role.

Whenever the government's rules changed, I followed the new orders. Every two months I could send Frank a six-and-a-half-pound package. Suggested contents included toothpaste, playing cards, vitamins, socks, underwear, soap, canned meat, bouillon cubes, raisins, candy, cheeses, and photographs. I remember how apprehensive I was the first time I also included cigars, an item not mentioned on the list.

About once a month I received a letter that detailed any changes of policy. With each letter, the government's insistence on silence about MIAs grew increasingly irritating. Why couldn't I talk about my husband? Why was I being treated as though Frank and I had done something shameful? And although I had been asked to remain silent, information about me was being used by politicians. Many of them were not interested in Frank's fate or mine so much as in furthering their careers. My local congressman, Bill Brock, told a story in his local campaign speeches about my asking him for help (which, following navy guidelines, I had stressed should remain confidential); he colored both my request and the possibility of what he could do to appeal to local voters.

In 1969 I joined the National League of Families of American Prisoners and Missing in Southeast Asia—an organization founded by the families, but fundamentally upholding government policy and receiving government support and encouragement. The league's primary spokeswoman was Sybil Stockdale, the wife of Commander James Stockdale, who was a frequently photographed prisoner and had been the commander of the first air wing of the USS *Oriskany*. She supported the government's argument that we must win the war to free the prisoners. Angered by my congressman's actions, I had written to Allard Lowenstein, the congressman who started the dump-Johnson campaign and who had been a mentor of Frank's at the University of North Carolina, asking for his help and suggestions. I tried to arrange a meeting between Lowenstein and Stockdale, but she refused to cooperate because of his antiwar stance. I have always suspected that her actions were being dictated by government policy, but I have no way of knowing how much official advice she received or followed.

I often resented the rhetoric of war protesters as well. The *Saturday Review* published a letter from a writer who called the first prisoners released by the North Vietnamese in 1969 "obscene biological charades" who wear their uniforms like "the skin of a predator." I responded with a letter of my own, which the magazine also printed. Yet I continued to talk to people like Cora Weiss, co-chair of the left-wing Committee of Liaison, whom I asked for help in establishing communications with the North Vietnamese.

From these disparate sources I tried to piece together a realistic picture, one that would allow me to act in Frank's interest. It became clear to me that the POW-MIA issue was being presented as an excuse to continue an otherwise unpopular war; the missing were being used to justify our increased bombing. Repeatedly calling attention to Hanoi's refusal to abide by the Geneva Convention, President Nixon's speeches included his promise to continue the U.S. presence in Southeast Asia "until the prisoners of war are freed."

Al Lowenstein suggested that my going public might actually help Frank, rather than harm him. He put me in touch with John Siegenthaler, the editor of the *Nashville Tennessean.* (By this time I had moved to Nashville and enrolled at Vanderbilt University in another master's degree program.) Siegenthaler sent Kathy Sawyer to interview me, and she wrote a story that the paper timed to appear on the third anniversary of Frank's disappearance.

The government did not object. For reasons never clearly stated, its policy had changed. After the release of the first three prisoners in 1969, the word went out through our monthly newsletters from the military, through our casualty assistance officers, and through the National League of Families that now we could take our suffering to the public. At league meetings we were asked to conduct letter-writing campaigns to show the Vietnamese what the people in the villages of America thought of their treatment of prisoners. Businessman H. Ross Perot spoke at these meetings, garnering support for his attempts to take food and supplies to the prisoners. The Pentagon encouraged us to woo the media to mobilize world opinion against the North Vietnamese. In an international contest for moral approval and goodwill. our government started calling attention to North Vietnam's refusal to follow the rules of the Geneva Convention.

Kathy's well-written, sensitive articles received a lot of attention, and many of my fellow graduate students seemed shocked to learn that my husband was an MIA. Generally, they were kind and supportive. But I received a number of phone calls from heavy breathers who offered to help me out with my sex life, and others who offered to find Frank for me using a variety of methods that ranged from witchcraft to prayer. When I was interviewed on local television and radio shows, I was surprised by the questions some interviewers and callers asked. They seemed more interested in knowing intimate details about my life than in learning about the MIA situation.

Many people just wanted me to look pretty, vulnerable, and sad; they certainly didn't want me to have a political opinion. Privately, I had felt for some time that the war was wrong—both morally and practically—but I hesitated to express these sentiments because I feared such remarks might have serious repercussions for Frank, or might be used as propaganda tactics against other POWs. So I remained officially silent about my doubts.

In the spring of 1970, encouraged by both our government and the trips other wives had made, I went to Paris. Calling at the North Vietnamese consulate at 2 rue le Verrier, the two translators I had found through the American embassy and I were greeted civilly and allowed to enter. But a Vietnamese gentleman, who never told me his name, insisted that we should "ask President Nixon" about my husband's whereabouts, and he asked us to leave.

I was struck by the contrast between the elegance of the American embassy and the shabbiness of the North Vietnamese consulate. This was my first encounter with Vietnamese people, and I was also humbled by their small physical stature. By comparison, I felt Brobdingnagian, insensitive, and clumsy. The difference in our size seemed, somehow, a metaphor for the war in which America's superior numbers and strength were becoming liabilities.

When I returned to the States, I continued to criticize Hanoi's policy concerning prisoners. But often my speeches, and those of other wives of MIAs, were used for other political purposes. (In fact, the number of MIAs itself was, from the beginning, a highly politicized question. A recent article in the *Atlantic Monthly* claims that of the 2,273 servicemen listed today, the Defense Department has recognized 1,101 as killed in action, since the time of their disappearance. This marks the first time in American military history that registered KIAs were added to the MIA figures.) At a Veterans of Foreign Wars meeting, when the local commander suggested that he and members of the audience should "go over to Arkansas and whip Fulbright's ass for this little lady and her husband," I announced that I was not present to support the continuance of the war in Vietnam or to attack those people who opposed it; I had come only to express my concern about the prisoners. My audience became quiet and unresponsive. No one spoke to me afterward.

The National League of Families meeting held in Washington in July 1970 crystallized my decision to pursue my own course and ignore the one our government was dictating. When Vice President Spiro Agnew made an appearance to address the members, I didn't stand; the rather stout woman beside me started tapping me on the shoulder with her handbag, increasing the force with each tap. At last I stood up, and left—both the meeting and the organization. I had had it with everyone's political agenda. I wanted no part of a group whose allegiance precluded questioning such leaders as Nixon and Agnew.

By this time President Nixon, Defense Secretary Melvin Laird, and other administration officials had escalated the frequency of their claims that we must remain in Southeast Asia to ensure the release of American POWs. The navy was not happy with my public statements that the "identification, treatment, and release of prisoners should be handled as a separate issue."

In March 1971 I decided to move to Paris and make daily visits to the North Vietnamese consulate, vowing to stay until they told me something about Frank's status. Before my departure the navy sent an official to caution me about my action and about any statements that I might make: "The foreign press may misinterpret your remarks if you say anything critical about the war, and you don't want your husband to be hurt by your carelessness." He also advised me to watch out for suspicious people who might want to kidnap me.

So commenced a series of days in Paris that always began with a trip to the North Vietnamese consulate. The French police guarding the consulate would often nudge each other and say, "C'est la femme. Encore, eh?" Usually, a Frenchwoman of about forty-five with blue-black hair and bright red lips, dressed in a white blouse and black skirt, would come to the door demanding in French, "Who's there? What do you want?" I would respond, "It's Madame Elkins. I would like to ask you about my husband." Her "We can't give you any information; go away!" would follow.

Over 200 relatives of POW-MIAs had already come knocking on this door, but I was the first to make it a daily activity. If I knew foreign visitors were likely to be present at the consulate, I would try to time my visit to coincide—making an effort to embarrass the North Vietnamese. Occasionally I would be given admittance and admonished to "go home and tell President Nixon to stop bombing our country. Then you'll get your answer." Sometimes members of the North Vietnamese delegation would yell at me and criticize American bombing; at other times they would apologize and look genuinely moved by my request.

Once I asked the secretary, directly, if Frank was dead. Lowering her eyes, she replied, "Oui." But she would provide me with no additional information. I explained that it would be to her advantage to give me all the information she had on all the men so that President Nixon would have fewer names to use as an excuse for keeping our troops in Vietnam, but she refused. Eventually she began greeting me with "Bonjour, Madame Elkins," but I never obtained the audience I requested with Delegate General Vo Van Sung.

Sometimes I tried to get the secretary to pass him copies of articles that Kathy Sawyer had written about me for the *Tennessean,* notes explaining my position and my plans to return every day, and cards with my address and phone number. Occasionally the secretary would give me pamphlets that restated her instructions to me in English. The details changed, but these conversations always ended with my standing in the shadows before a closed door and saying, "A demain."

Because I had great sympathy and respect for these people, this adversarial role was especially stressful for me. I certainly couldn't blame the North Vietnamese for shooting down Frank's plane when he had been bombing their country. Sometimes I would run into members of the delegation in shops. If I spoke, they usually refused to acknowledge me. I suspect they feared I was a little crazy. Perhaps I was.

Other wives of MIAs or POWs would arrive for short stays in Paris, and I would sometimes accompany them to make their requests. After almost three months, the North Vietnamese delegation must have realized that I was there to stay. They finally admitted me and told me that Frank was dead. But when I asked them to put the information in writing, they refused, saying that all the other wives would then come to Paris and harass them.

By March 1971 the North Vietnamese had begun returning letters addressed to men whose names were not included on the official POW list released to Senator Edward M. Kennedy in December 1970. Stamped "KUONG NGUOI NAHAN TRÁLAI" (this person unknown), my returned letters seemed more official than any information I had received from American sources about Frank. The Defense Department suggested that North Vietnam was reinforcing its contention that the list was complete and final, but insisted that our government would not accept letter or package returns as evidence of the fate of MIAs. Frank Sieverts, an assistant to the secretary of state, maintained that the men's status would not be changed without concrete proof.

My wait for news about Frank continued, and remaining in Paris was more comfortable than returning home. I was relieved to be anonymous, free from people who asked about my husband's status:

"Have you heard anything yet?"

"No."

"Guess you never will, huh? Bless your heart. It's such a pity."

Though well-intentioned, such remarks—sometimes coming from the mouths of complete strangers—always left me fighting back tears. I was also tired of the either-or stance that everyone seemed to insist upon when discussing the war. Simultaneously caring about my husband's return and wanting our troops to withdraw did not seem incongruous to me. I was amazed at how angry hawks could become when I refused to denounce the North Vietnamese, and at how upset doves became when I wouldn't criticize the men who were fighting.

But I had begun to realize that Frank might not return, and I began editing his diary for publication—an act I had not attempted earlier because I believed he would use it himself, as the basis for a novel. Publishing his diary now seemed my responsibility. Editing his writings during 1972, I thought I had finally achieved some catharsis. I hoped that writing its prologue had also provided me with closure. When the book was published in the fall of 1973, I returned to the United States to push its sales—and discovered that the public that had once seemed so eager to know about the war had become largely apathetic. They did not want to be reminded of our national defeat.

Almost a year after the return of the 591 POWs in early 1973, I left Paris for San Francisco. Feeling that I had done all I could to ascertain Frank's fate, I hoped the government would now assume its responsibility for finding him. After all, it had promised to bring him home when the war was over.

Once the war ended, however, public interest in the MIA issue also ended. After the prisoners returned, leadership of the National League of Families shifted from wives to other family members of MIAs. E.H. Mills, the father of Lieutenant Commander James Mills (shot down on September 21, 1966), became the director in 1973, and he was eventually succeeded by his daughter Ann Mills Griffiths. Her fourteen-year reign has produced various critics and at least one splinter group, directed by Dolores Alfond, who insists that Griffiths has responded less to the needs of the families than to those of the government. Many MIA family members now echo my earlier suspicions that the league is basically a government organization. (During the Nixon administration, its long-distance telephone bill was paid out of White House funds.) In February 1991, Colonel Millard Peck, a highly decorated veteran, quit his post as chief of the POW-MIA unit of the Defense Intelligence Agency, contending that the official government "mind-set to debunk" evidence of live MIAs is encouraged by Griffiths, whom he describes as "adamantly opposed to any initiative to actually get to the heart of the problem." He accused Griffiths of sabotaging POW-MIA investigations.

During the mid-1970s the league did little to slow down the speed with which the government began perfunctorily changing MIA status to "presumed finding of death" (PFOD). In December 1976 a House panel determined, later with President Carter's agreement, that no live MIAs remained in Southeast Asia. In March 1977 a presidential commission traveled to Hanoi; it subsequently agreed with a House select committee that the Vietnamese were acting in good faith to "repatriate" the remains of all American MIAs. The government provided wives and family members with no explanation for these decisions. Because they were made by our government, we were simply expected to assume they were trustworthy.

These announcements only confirmed my suspicions that Frank had been used as a pawn. I became convinced that our government would make no more real efforts to recover him—alive or dead. And I realized how powerless I remained.

The navy changed Frank's status to PFOD on October 31, 1977; the telegram arrived at my door in Oakland along with a group of young trick-or-treaters. The following year Frank's family and I held a memorial service for him at the National Cemetery in Wilmington, North Carolina. By 1978 the Pentagon had declared all MIAs to be PFODs, except for Colonel Charles E. Shelton of the air force, who remains listed as a POW for symbolic reasons. His wife took her own life in October 1990. She left no explanation, but friends suggest that her suicide was a result of battling about POW-MIA issues for more than twenty years. To me, her action seems as symbolic as her husband's status. [Editor's note: The last official POW-MIA, Colonel Charles E. Shelton, USAF, was declared dead by the Pentagon in September 1994.]

In 1983 President Reagan announced that the MIAs were a high priority for his administration. He sent delegations to Vietnam, and 150 sets of remains were identified and returned. The military's Joint Casualty Resolution Center at Barbers Point in Hawaii, established in the 1970s, increased its efforts to recover remains and make identifications. In 1985 Vietnam turned over the remains of another five persons believed to be MIAs; in 1988 the first joint American-Vietnamese team uncovered two more sets of MIA remains.

But no one had asked me for additional information about Frank, and by the time another twelve, silent years had gone by I felt sure that I would never know his exact whereabouts. Consequently, I was unprepared for the telephone call I received from the navy in December 1989 asking me if I "happened to have" a copy of my husband's dental X rays.

"No. . . . Why?"

"Well . . . uh . . . we have a piece of a jawbone and some teeth that we think may have belonged to him."

My anger at the unfeeling language obscured my initial shock. How could this stranger choose his words so carelessly, ignoring their possible effect upon me? But his tone of voice indicated that he was not so unfeeling as his choice of words implied. He explained that Frank was only one of several men who were being considered as the possible source for a box of remains that the North Vietnamese had turned over to American authorities in June. I suggested that he contact my husband's family. Then, as I had during the previous twenty-three years, I tried to remain calm as I confronted this latest unexpected reminder of Frank and of my own, irretrievable loss.

On January 22, 1990, exactly twenty-four years from the day I married Frank, the navy notified me that these remains had been positively identified as his. (The bones included those of the torso, legs, and a part of the lower jawbone that seemed to be broken. No bones were available from the rest of the face and head or the feet and hands.) If I regarded the pathologists' reports as "inconclusive," I would have the "option" to arrange for someone else to review the paperwork and remains to provide "quality assurance" of this decision.

A few days later, members of Frank's family and I met with military officials to review their evidence. They explained that the government research group reached their decision based on a combination of evidence. First they looked for the names of all of the men who were listed as having disappeared in the area of Dien Chau District, Nghe Tinh Province—the area from which the bones had been recovered. Using a section of the pelvic bone to determine the age of the person at death, they were able to narrow the possibilities even more. By measuring the torso and leg bones, they were also able to estimate the person's height. Because of the prominent muscle insertion in the bones, the pathologists were certain that the person had had an unusually muscular build. Frank's medical records show that he had a forty-two-inch chest, thirty-one-inch waist, and twenty-two-inch thigh and could military-press 200 pounds; he had begun lifting weights when he was in high school, an activity that he continued. Using information from the computer data base of missing persons' dental records, they narrowed the possibilities to three men. And while they were able to obtain dental X rays on all of the men except Frank, none of their X rays fitted the dental work remaining on the lower jawbone. Although no X rays of Frank's teeth were available, the dental charts showing his fillings and earlier extractions matched those of the jawbone. So he filled the description in every possible way, as did no one else who had disappeared within a fifty-mile radius of the site.

With the recounting of each explanation, I was asked if I wanted to see photographs of the bones or medical records substantiating each claim. At first I could only respond, "I don't know yet. Wait a minute, and I'll let you know." Then I would tell myself that I had to look or continue to doubt their judgment. Each decision to look at the evidence became a little easier, and I managed to get through the afternoon without embarrassing any of us by becoming hysterical. Frank's family told me later that if I had not agreed to look at the photographs they would have done so; they also felt we needed to look to be able to know.

At first I did wonder if the remains were really Frank's. But because I had put no pressure on our government since the early 1970s, its decision to assign them to him, rather than to the husband of a more insistent wife, seems to serve no ulterior purpose. The government had nothing to gain by returning Frank's remains; this made its analysis more convincing to me. I can imagine no other motivation for this vicissitude. Frank and I were just lucky.

Frank appears to have died in the crash of his plane. The fragmentation of the bones and the broken jaw make this the likeliest explanation. The bones were encrusted with dirt since Vietnamese bury the dead directly in the ground without a coffin and then, approximately three years later, after the flesh has rotted away, dig up the bones and place them in a smaller grave. This process also partly accounts for the missing smaller bones. When this ritual was explained to me, it was described as something the Vietnamese do because of their "superstitions" about the dead. I couldn't help thinking that we characterize our own practices in such matters, really no more civilized, as "respect for the dead."

I was touched that the Vietnamese had gone to such trouble to bury someone who had been bombing their country. Their humane customs are partly responsible for my having Frank's remains for reburial. And I was beginning to discover how grateful I was.

FRANK'S WAS ONE of ten sets of MIA remains identified and returned to the U.S. mainland for interment in 1990. They were shipped to Travis Air Force Base and in late February brought home to North Carolina, where our families held a private, quiet interment in the National Cemetery in Wilmington. Knowing the whereabouts of Frank's remains has helped me begin a healing process I was helpless to effect earlier. Unconsciously, I had been unable to forgive myself for "deserting" him, for failing to negotiate the labyrinth of government policies and foreign terrains. My earlier insistence that his final whereabouts did not matter had been dishonest. I had been diminishing the importance of what I could not change. Now I can draw comfort from envisioning his grave site, from having a specific physical location that automatically comes to mind when I think of him. His flesh had already become part of Vietnam, but his bones no longer lie—like those of Thomas Hardy's Drummer Hodge—uncoffined and unmarked beneath "foreign constellations."

*SPRING 1992*

Marilyn Elkins is a professor of English at California State University, Los Angeles. She edited her husband's Vietnam diary, *The Heart of a Man: A Naval Pilot's Vietnam Diary,* which was reprinted by the Naval Institute Press in 1991. She is the author of *Metamorphosising the Novel, Kay Boyle's Narrative Innovations* (1994) and editor of *August Wilson: A Casebook* (1994).

# 48

# The Gulf Crisis and the Rules of War

## By Martin van Creveld

*The 1990–91 Persian Gulf crisis presented clear and multiple violations of the generally accepted rules of war. Iraqi leader Saddam Hussein's first action—an invasion to extinguish an existing country, Kuwait—breached international standards. He followed with the threat to use poisonous gas against any country that moved to liberate and restore Kuwait. Finally, he took hostages from within the international community in Iraq and planted them around potential strategic targets. In response the United States implied that, if hostilities commenced, Saddam Hussein would constitute a legitimate target. Though both Iraqi and American actions threatened accepted rules of war, Martin van Creveld argues that such rules are neither universal nor permanent: Ultimately it is history and not law that determines what is or is not permissible in war.*

As the Persian Gulf crisis unfolded, the rules of war—as understood by most of the world in this last decade of the twentieth century—were violated in many ways. The very first move in the crisis—namely, the use of force by President Saddam Hussein in order to abolish an existing state, change an international boundary, and conquer territory—already constituted a clear violation of existing *jus ad bello*. Adding insult to injury, the Iraqi government then announced that if war broke out it would resort to a weapon prohibited by international treaty: poison gas. Next, foreign citizens belonging to many different nationalities were detained, refused exit visas, and sent to various strategic installations, where they were made to serve as human shields against attack. Finally, and in what many saw as a justified response to these Iraqi moves, the U.S. government dropped hints that if war broke out—and possibly even if it did not—Saddam Hussein (and his mistress) would be among the first targets.

Whatever one may think of these various deeds, threats, and announcements, there is no question that from the opening days of the crisis, much new ground was broken. In spite of Saddam's eventual defeat, precedents were set, some of which will no doubt be followed in the future.

In modern works on strategy, the rules of war—defining what the belligerents may and may not do—are scarcely mentioned. In this respect they differ markedly from medieval books such as Honoré Bonet's *L'Arbre des batailles* and Christine de Pisan's *L'Art de chevalerie,* which mainly discuss not strategy or tactics but the actions one knight may legitimately take against another, as well as how wars should be declared, whether ruses are permitted, and the like.

The reason behind our modern "strategic" indifference to such problems is that we, like Carl von Clausewitz, see war as an instrument of the state, an organization that, unlike medieval principalities, both makes the law and recognizes no judge above itself. Further, the first chapter of Clausewitz's *On War* defines war as an act of violence carried to the utmost bounds; hence, whatever self-imposed restraints a war may admit are "so weak as to be hardly worth mentioning."

There are three interrelated points to be made. First, what is and is not considered acceptable behavior in war is historically determined, neither self-evident nor unalterable. Second, and however regrettable the fact in the eyes of some, the Gulf crisis may well represent a turning point in what is and is not permissible. Third and possibly most important, in ignoring this problem our present-day military historians and strategists are committing a serious error. Far from being merely a weak "philanthropic" (Clausewitz's term) attempt to mitigate the worst horrors, the rules define what armed conflict is all about—even to the point that without them war itself becomes impossible.

To BEGIN WITH the question of what war may—and may not—be waged for: The single document most subscribed to by mankind today is the United Nations Charter. That charter expressly forbids the use of force for altering international boundaries, that is, "aggressive war." This prohibition arose from the Allies' experience with Nazi and Fascist aggression. However, during much of history no such ban existed. Between about 1500 and 1789 in particular, altering frontiers and acquiring territory were the main reasons rulers went to war. They were, in fact, expected to go to war over territory.

Then as now, provinces derived their importance from the demographic and material resources they contained, as well as the strategic position they occupied. And, as now, some kind of juridical justification—often in the form of ancient feudal rights—was usually required if a ruler sought to take over his neighbor's property. However, the idea that territory forms an integral part of the state and cannot be formally conceded under any circumstances had not yet been born.

Instead, provinces were viewed almost as pieces of real estate, to be exchanged among rulers by means of inheritance, marriage, agreement, or force. "My generals have lost a war; I pay with a province," commented Emperor Franz Josef after Austria was defeated by Prussia and Italy in 1866. Governments had the right to dispose of territory without considering the inhabitants' wishes or interests. Since borders were the result of historical accident, they were never regarded as sacrosanct.

The modern idea that borders are inviolable has a curious, somewhat twisted history. The French in the revolutionary years 1793–95 were the first to make the annexation of new territories dependent on popular approval. Every time the citizens' army entered some town or district, it drove out the local "tyrant" and held a plebiscite. The inhabitants would express their burning desire to join the glorious republic; their desire would be acknowledged by the Assemblée Nationale and the act of union itself formally accomplished.

While it is true that most of the territorial changes and the revolution itself were later undone, the new doctrine of self-determination refused to die. Having originated in the womb of democracy, it formed an alliance with nationalism toward the middle of the nineteenth century and acquired a new and strident quality that was frequently anything but democratic. As the nationalist gospel told the story, it was not the fact that certain people lived between the river and the mountain that made them into a nation; on the contrary, it was alleged—if only as a historical fiction—that the people in question had *chosen* to live between the river and the mountain *because* they constituted a nation.

The enlightenment of the eighteenth century had emphasized certain commonalities—reason above all—among all peoples. The new doctrine of nationalism, on the other hand, was interested mainly in the differences that separated one people from another. Beginning in the 1860s, there arose an important school of thought that perceived these differences as bound up with the country, its climate, its physical characteristics, and its history. From this it was but a short step to the idea that a people's material and spiritual lives—the very things that made them a nation—were intimately connected with their territory; hence, every inch of that territory was part of the "sacred" patrimony linking past generations with the future.

The most visible outcome of these developments was a change in the status of territory: Territory became inalienable in principle and increasingly in fact as well. Even when military misfortune compelled a state to sign away a province, as France did Alsace and Lorraine in 1871, the people were supposed to treasure its memory in their hearts, forever looking for the opportunity to restore their ownership.

At Versailles in 1919, nationalism achieved its greatest triumph. The collapse of the old multinational empires was followed by an attempt, led by President Woodrow Wilson, to reconcile might with right by redividing the world in accordance with the principle of self-determination. The redistribution was far from perfect, but once it was completed the victors in particular tended to regard borders as fixed and unalterable. Any attempt to alter them by force—for whatever reason—was labeled "aggression."

And countries that refused to accept this new logic—particularly Germany, Italy, and Japan—were considered "revisionist" disturbers of the peace. Their use of armed force to overrun existing frontiers caused them to be confronted by a coalition consisting of virtually the entire world, and their subsequent defeat, as well as the war-crimes trials, confirmed the principle that aggressive war should not be allowed to overturn the territorial status quo. In his death cell, Alfred Jodl, Hitler's chief operations officer, regretfully recalled the days when wars ended with the exchange of a province or two, after which everybody was friends again.

Since 1945 there have been numerous smaller wars, aggressive and other. Often, particularly in the so-called Third World, where most of these wars took place, the borders separating the countries in question were drawn by the old colonial powers, and were arbitrary and irrational. Yet to date few countries have succeeded in having their attempts to move borders recognized as legitimate by the international community. On only one occasion has an entirely new frontier been carved out by means of war. That was Israel's War of Liberation in 1948–49, and the amount of trouble *that* has led to does not require recounting. The American victory in the Gulf crisis has merely confirmed the rule. Whatever else Saddam Hussein might have done, he probably would *never* have gotten the annexation of Kuwait recognized by any other state, including even his own closest allies.

IN THE EYES OF many people, the most flagrant violation of international law in the Persian Gulf was Saddam Hussein's use of gas in his war against Iran and his threat to use it against Israel and the Allied forces. Our abhorrence is certainly justified, but it ignores the fact that during most of history the employment of asphyxiating agents has been considered perfectly normal and hardly deserving of comment.

Before the modern age, asphyxiating agents, most commonly smoke, were used in siege warfare. All through ancient and medieval times, mining—tunneling under walls to cause their collapse—was one of the most important means available to a besieging army. As mining led to countermining, subterranean encounters ensued. Both sides used combustibles to smoke each other out of their respective galleries.

There were occasional attempts to use smoke in other situations as well. Early modern military handbooks described all kinds of substances—some of them including strange components like snakeskins, bird droppings, and menstrual blood. These peculiar mixtures were to be put in barrels or on carts, set alight, and rolled toward the enemy with the aim of blinding or asphyxiating him, or driving him away with sheer bad smell. Such substances were rarely used, however—not so much for humanitarian reasons as for technological ones: Only limited quantities could be produced; the fuses for igniting them were unreliable; and even if they were ignited, the wind, temperature, and barometric pressure could cause the resulting smoke to spread unpredictably. The substances were therefore most commonly used in siege warfare, where spaces were constricted and considerable concentrations could be achieved.

The rise of the modern chemical industry in the first half of the nineteenth century changed the situation. Noxious substances could now be made to order and in any quantity. From midcentury on, authors discussed new possibilities, either making suggestions to the military—most of which were examined and found impractical—or incorporating them into tales of imaginary wars, as H.G. Wells did.

Chemicals seemed about to turn war into something new, unprecedented, and even more monstrous. As a result, when Czar Nicholas II assembled the First Hague Conference in 1899, all major countries felt obliged to attend. Admiral Alfred Thayer Mahan, acting as America's representative, said he could see no logical difference between blowing up people in a ship, from which they could scarcely escape, and choking them by gas on land. Nevertheless, it was decided to ban poison gas, and the decision was reaffirmed eight years later at the Second Hague Conference.

The use of gas in World War I is well known. The first to employ it were the Germans at Ypres in April 1915. Though this was initially denounced as Teutonic wickedness, within a few months everybody else followed suit and gas became an acceptable weapon. As the British military historian and strategist B.H. Liddell Hart—himself a gas victim—was later to note, as weapons go, gas is relatively humane. The best available data—collected by the son of the inventor—indicate that gas was responsible for only about 3 percent of all casualties in the war; and compared to those wounded by other means, a greater percentage of gas victims recovered.

The threat of gas made it necessary to encumber soldiers with protective gear and obstructed their work. Moreover, using gas against a line of enemy trenches was one thing; drenching entire districts and even provinces, asphyxiating large numbers of noncombatants, for the purpose of mobile operations is another. This may explain why the prohibition on the use of gas was reaffirmed at Geneva in 1937 and observed during World War II.

While the ban has been violated on a few occasions since then—the Egyptians' reliance on gas in Yemen during the sixties comes to mind—by and large it has achieved its purpose and, what is more, created a situation whereby the use of gas is regarded with horror. Either because Saddam Hussein did not dare to use gas or because he did not feel that his situation was sufficiently desperate to require it, the recent Gulf crisis did not witness its employment. All the same, an objective observer will have to admit that Mahan was right insofar as this horror has neither logic nor history to support it.

WHEN SADDAM Hussein announced that Western citizens would not be allowed to leave Iraq but would be held hostage, much of the world was outraged by this violation of the rules of war and, indeed, of the standards of "civilized behavior" in general. Such outrage is certainly justified, but it overlooks the fact that during most of history taking hostages as a guaranty against attack has been a common method of war and diplomacy, at times even more important than strategy.

Greek city-states routinely gave and took hostages from among their most prominent citizens, considering this the best way to guarantee that treaties would be kept and that conquered peoples would not revolt. The practice was continued by Rome. The Greek historian Polybius was the most famous among a group of hostages who, after the destruction of Macedonia in 168 B.C., were taken to Rome; he spent twenty years of his life in the Italian capital. Later during imperial times the Romans (and after them the Byzantines) routinely had the sons of client kings educated in Rome, as was Herod Agrippa, for example. This supposedly imbued them with pro-Roman sentiments while permitting their use as hostages should the need arise.

Throughout ancient and medieval times, the garrisons of besieged towns and fortresses sometimes put captives on the wall and threatened to mistreat or kill them unless the attackers desisted. Medieval princes also continued the practice of giving and taking each other's sons, relatives, and retainers hostage. For example, following the Battle of Poitiers, King John II's brother (Philip of Orléans), his two younger sons (Louis of Anjou and John of Berry), his cousin (Pierre of Alençon), and the dauphin's brother-in-law (Louis II of Bourbon) were detained in England pending the payment of ransom, the surrender of contested territories, and the handing over of certain castles designated as pledges for the execution of the treaty. Similarly, the system by which the sons of vassals were educated in the lords' households continued in force until well into the Renaissance. It permitted those youths to seek advancement and make useful connections and at the same time helped guarantee their fathers' good behavior.

As late as the Thirty Years' War, warfare was conducted not only by states but by independent noblemen, free cities, religious leagues, peasant organizations, and all kinds of freebooters. The Treaty of Westphalia, signed in 1648, finally defined the state as the dominant type of organization that wages war. Thereafter states were understood as abstract organizations possessing independent legal personalities and embracing both rulers and ruled. Their rise led to the idea of government as an institution separate from the people who exercised it, putting an end to the rationale for holding rulers' relatives hostage. Even the most absolute rulers, such as Louis XIV, were increasingly guided by *raison d'état,* not their personal inclinations. As a symptom of changing attitudes, Frederick II on the eve of the Battle of Leuthen (1757) gave express orders that if he was taken prisoner, the war was to be continued as before. The time came when rulers who behaved otherwise were regarded as corrupt, treasonous, or both. This applied as well to their subordinates.

Simultaneously, the late seventeenth century saw the rise of standing armies clearly separate from the civilian population. These armies claimed, and increasingly obtained, a monopoly in the use of legal armed violence. As war was taken out of the hands of the society at large, rulers began to formalize the situation by concluding mutual agreements that obliged them to refrain from involving each other's citizens in war by taking them hostage or by any other means. From these agreements modern international law, as codified by such men as Emmerich von Vattel around the middle of the eighteenth century, evolved. The idea that taking hostages constitutes a contravention of the rules of war dates from this time. The result was that when the Germans took civilian hostages in connection with anti-partisan warfare in Italy, France, and elsewhere during World War II, some of the Germans were subsequently apprehended and punished.

During the past two decades, the convention that forbids hostage-taking has clearly been eroded—for two reasons. First, more and more wars are being waged by organizations that are not states and that do not recognize the distinction between armies and civilian populations. These organizations see no reason to adhere to conventions that states established for their own convenience. Second, when the aim of policy is not war but deterrence, taking hostages, however uncivilized it may appear to modern sensibilities, makes perfect sense. Though Saddam did not carry out his threat of using hostages (or prisoners of war, which is another story) to protect his strategic installations, again it is possible that a precedent has been set, one that may increasingly be followed in the future.

FINALLY, THE Persian Gulf crisis has been remarkable in that both George Bush and Saddam Hussein publicly announced their intention of making the struggle a personal one—either by resorting to subversion in order to kill the opposing leader or by threatening to put him on trial for alleged crimes. Both courses of action fly in the face of modern rules of war, which are based on the fiction that wars are waged by states, not men. Since rulers are supposed to be merely acting on behalf of their states, for some 300 years, between 1648 and 1945, making war *per se* was not considered a crime and was not supposed to be punished. This applied even in cases when the opportunity to punish did present itself, as when Napoleon III was taken prisoner by the Prussians in 1871. He was merely held for a few weeks and then allowed to leave for England, where he died.

States, however, are a comparatively recent invention. During most of history, rulers, not states, waged war, and were supposed to wage war, on their own behalf. As a result, waging war *ad hominem*—against the enemy leaders themselves—was not the exception but the rule. The Book of Joshua describes how the Israelites first stepped on the necks of enemy kings whose cities they had conquered and then put them to death. Alexander, during his Persian campaign, pursued Darius relentlessly, and indeed not before the emperor was dead was Alexander's work of conquest really accomplished. Roman soldiers who killed the enemy commander (who in many cases was the ruler) were rewarded with the *spolia opima,* or first spoils; captured enemy leaders were led along in triumph and then, unless the victor chose to exercise clemency, were killed in public and their bodies subjected to all kinds of outrages.

Insofar as medieval warfare was largely a question of class, most feudal rulers did not approve of common soldiers' killing enemy commanders and on occasion reacted sharply to prevent such acts or to punish them. However, acting among themselves they waged war on one another—and indeed, given the structure of medieval society and the absence of any clear distinction between the private and public domains, it is difficult to see what else they could have done.

In this respect, as in so many others, our modern ideas date from the second half of the seventeenth century. As the idea of the state as an abstract organization emerged, an increasingly sharp line was drawn between the rulers' private personas and their public ones. The latter were legitimate targets; the former were supposed to remain inviolate. During the eighteenth century, princes addressed each other as *monsieur mon frère* even as they went to war. Their families were respected; so, by and large, was the private property of enemy commanders. (Frederick the Great in a fit of pique once demanded that a hunting lodge belonging to an Austrian general be burned, and was rebuffed by his commanders.) When Napoleon besieged Vienna in 1809, he took care to direct his artillery fire away from Schönbrunn Palace, where Princess Marie Louise—the future empress—was known to be lying ill.

By 1914, so strongly entrenched had this particular convention become that the state-assisted assassination of an archduke started a world war. But as far as we know, in neither of the great conflicts of this century were there attempts to wage war by murdering enemy rulers.

Since 1945 a growing number of wars have been waged not by states but by all kinds of other organizations. Since these organizations have not been recognized as governments, their leaders do not enjoy immunity and are often hunted by every imaginable overt and covert means. Originating in modern terrorism, this has begun to extend to interstate conflict as well. Conversely, the leaders of these organizations see no reason to grant immunity to their persecutors, with the result that from the White House to 10 Downing Street, high-profile politicians have taken to turning their residences into fortresses.

Judging by the declarations of both sides in connection with recent events in the Persian Gulf, the idea is spreading that rulers should not enjoy immunity but be held personally accountable for their actions. Whether it will be contained or whether we shall witness a return to earlier historical ideas that did not make the distinction and did not seek to avoid war *ad hominem,* only time will tell.

THE ABOVE BRIEFLY outlines the rules pertaining to the reasons for which war may be made, the weapons that may be used, the question of hostages, and the question of waging war against the leaders themselves. In all four areas, the relevant norms have proved to be neither eternal nor self-evident but the product of specific historical circumstances. Therefore, should circumstances change, so in all probability will the norms. Already as a result of the Persian Gulf crisis it seems that some of the modern rules of war— notably the one that prohibits states from employing violence in order to change international borders—are as strong as ever. Others appear to be on their way out; in October 1990 it was President François Mitterrand who said that France did not take hostages, and in the next sentence placed restrictions on the movements of Iraqi diplomats.

What is more, the four problems discussed here represent only a fraction of a much larger body of conventions and usages. From the dawn of history men, far from discarding all restraint when they went to war, have sought to regulate it and subject it to limitations. Even some of the most primitive societies known to us surrounded armed conflict with rules that defined the way it should be declared and terminated. The same societies also sought to establish procedures by which the two sides could communicate (parleys), ways in which the fighting could be temporarily halted (truces), places that would be exempt from it (sanctuaries), weapons that could not be used (poison arrows), and so on.

Like all rules, those that pertain to war are occasionally—some would say frequently—broken. The purpose of the rules is not, as Clausewitz and most modern "strategists" seem to think, simply to appease the consciences of a few tenderhearted people. Their real function is to protect the armed forces themselves. This is because war, the most confused and confusing of all human activities, is also among the most organized. Armed conflict can be successfully waged only if it involves the cooperation of many men. Men cannot cooperate, nor organizations even exist, unless they abide by a common code. That code should be in accord with the prevailing cultural climate, clear to all, and capable of being enforced. A group of people unclear about just whom it is (and is not) allowed to kill, for what ends, under what circumstances, and by what means is not an army but a mob. Though there have always been mobs, usually when confronted by an effective fighting organization they have scattered like chaff before the wind.

The need for rules of war, however, goes farther than this. War by definition consists of killing, of deliberately shedding the blood of fellow creatures. Killing is an activity no society can tolerate unless it is carefully circumscribed by rules that define what is and is not allowed. Always and everywhere, killing done by certain authorized persons, under certain specified circumstances, and in accordance with certain prescribed rules is saved from blame and regarded as praiseworthy. Conversely, killing that ignores the rules or transgresses them usually provokes punishment— often the killing of the transgressor.

Though societies have differed greatly as to the precise way in which they draw the line between war and murder, the line itself is absolutely essential. Some killers deserve to be decorated, others hanged. Where this distinction is not preserved, society will fall to pieces and war will become mere indiscriminate violence.

So far removed is such uncontrolled violence from war proper that Greek mythology, always a good source of insight, had two different deities to represent them. The patroness of orderly, regular war was the virgin goddess

Pallas Athena. Springing from Zeus's forehead, she was a powerful warrior who is often represented leaning on her spear, her helmet pulled back, lost in thought. The patron of unrestrained violence was Ares, "mad, fulminating Ares," to quote Homer, an outcast among gods and men. Athena was one of the greatest deities; the largest city in Greece, as well as the Parthenon, was named in her honor. Ares, born to the same father, was a minor deity with few worshipers and fewer temples. The *Iliad* tells how Ares on one occasion met Athena in battle and was soundly defeated. Bleeding and trumpeting his pain as he ran from the field, he ascended to Olympus and complained to Zeus—from whom he received scant sympathy.

Though the rules of previous ages differed from our own, then as today those who broke them were sometimes apprehended and brought to justice. Nor was fate necessarily kinder to those, probably the majority, who never stood trial. Western literature as represented by the *Iliad* begins at the point where Agamemnon, the mighty king, is punished by Apollo for violating the law and rejecting the ransom of a young woman he had captured. In later Greek mythology, warriors who desecrated temples or committed other excesses were persecuted by the Erinyes and overtaken by Nemesis, the monstrous goddess of revenge who made a victim's very food inedible. During the Christian Middle Ages, knights who did not respect the rights of monks, nuns, and "innocent people" in general were destined to be hounded by the devil while they lived and to be carried off to hell after they died.

Although the Persian Gulf crisis is over, the possibility still exists that Saddam Hussein and his associates will one day be made to account for their crimes. Meanwhile, it has already become clear that the rules of war—established by European or European-derived states and codifying their own preferred way of engaging in armed conflict—are changing and will continue to change.

*Summer 1991*

Martin van Creveld is a professor of history at the Hebrew University, Jerusalem, and the author of *The Transformation of War* (1991), *Nuclear Weapons and the Future of Conflict* (1993), and *Airpower and Maneuver Warfare* (1994). He is currently working on a volume to be entitled *The Rise and Fall of the State*.

# 49

# Little Wars

## By Thomas B. Allen

*The portrayal of war through the format of a game—whether it be chess, toy soldiers, or Fletcher Pratt's 1930s naval tournaments—has a long tradition. More recently, such games or simulations have taken the form of hobby board games or computer versions of the same, where the players can refight a battle from the past or play out a possible conflict of the future. Although often considered simply for their value as amusement, diversion, or mental exercise, war games can provide a serious means of studying conflict without the negative aspects of real casualties and economic costs. They are, Thomas B. Allen relates, "a way to understand reality by painlessly confronting it." For the Pentagon, the 1990–91 Persian Gulf crisis presented a unique opportunity in American military history: the chance to play a war and fight a war simultaneously.*

At about 7:30 on the morning of August 2, 1990, Mark Herman, a creator of war games, boarded the subway in a Maryland suburb of Washington to head for his office. He had started off late that day and had rushed out of his house without taking his usual quick look at the television. It was only when he happened to glance at the headline on a copy of the *Washington Post* being read by a fellow passenger that he learned that Iraq had invaded Kuwait.

Herman had just suggested to Pentagon customers of his war games that they should play one during an actual crisis. As soon as he reached his office, a Booz•Allen & Hamilton war-gaming think tank, he began making telephone calls. "By ten o'clock," he recalls, "it was decided to go on with my crisis-gaming concept as a crisis was happening, and by two o'clock we were doing it."

Not since World War II had anyone tried the bold maneuver of waging war and playing war at the same time. The previous real-war game had been played, accidentally, on the morning of November 2, 1944, when the staff of the German Fifth Panzer Army met to plan possible new moves in the battle shaping up at the western edge of the Hürtgen Forest.

"The map exercise had hardly begun," an account of the game says, "when a report was received that according to all appearances a fairly strong American attack had been launched in the Hürtgen-Gemeter area"—exactly where the map exercise was being played. General-feldmarschall Walther Model, whom Hitler had frequently called his best field marshal, ordered the players—except commanders of units under attack or directly threatened—to continue playing, using messages from the front as the basis for game moves. Twelve generals and members of their staffs joined Model in merging a game's theory and a battlefield's reality. As one of the generals later recalled, Model "directed that the actual situation be taken for [the] basis of the map maneuver."

At the game table, players decided that a reserve unit, the 116th Panzer Division, had to be thrown into battle. The commander of the 116th, who was playing the game, turned to his operations officers and couriers and issued actual orders that paralleled his gaming orders. "The alerted division," according to German general Friedrich J. Fangor, "was thereby set in movement in the shortest conceivable time. Chance had transformed a simple map exercise into stern reality." The game was ended at noon, when the commander in chief of the Seventh Army "asked to be allowed to return to his command post." The moves of the game, reflected in the moves on the battlefield, sealed off the American penetration.

Mark Herman, well aware of the 1944 game that had come true, saw an incredible opportunity to play a similar one—fighting not merely a battle this time but an entire war. The game was—and still is—classified top secret. The policymakers who assembled that afternoon in a small office building near the Pentagon cannot be identified. Herman does go as far as to say, "There were four men and women sitting around, plus myself and my staff, about eight people crammed in a room, with a table taking most of the space." On the table were the board and markers of a highly successful commercial war game called "Gulf Strike" that Herman had created in 1983—and one that any hobbyist could walk into a store and buy. The game, through a series of scenarios, offered what Herman called an "understanding of the operational alternatives available in the Persian Gulf in the event of widespread conflict." The Pentagon players brought with them the latest intelligence estimates.

The people at the table trusted Herman's judgment and his expertise in an arcane pastime that has become, in the Pentagon as well as in executive boardrooms, a way to understand reality by painlessly confronting it. Herman had originally been brought to the Pentagon by his mentor, James F. Dunnigan, a wisecracking, cigar-puffing creator of such hobbyist war games as "Jutland" and "Normandy," as well as fantasy games such as "Dragonslayer." In 1980 Dunnigan was commissioned to produce a nuclear-war game for Net Assessment, the Department of Defense's tightly guarded agency that then assessed the military strengths and strategic doctrines of the United States and the Soviet Union. His game was known in the Pentagon as SAS, for Strategic Analysis Simulation. (Because "gaming" might sound too frivolous to taxpayers and Congress, the preferred word is "simulation.")

For hobbyists, board games are elaborate playthings. But the best games—the ones that people like Dunnigan and Herman both create and oversee—are more than this. They are accurate, fascinating reenactments of war. They teach players to think under the extreme conditions of war; like autopsies, they have great value in showing the living why certain actions can be fatal. In a game, lessons come cheap.

But in badly run games, players can manipulate reality. Herman calls the practice "jiggering." When he inherited SAS from Dunnigan, for example, he learned that navy players declined to sink aircraft carriers. Herman forced them to admit that a nuclear-tipped missile could destroy a carrier, and he insisted on building that possibility into the game. "I put into this SAS, right off the bat, right to their faces at the briefing, that there are three words that do not belong in the military lexicon: unsinkable, unbreakable, and indestructible," Herman says.

He knew that the members of his Persian Gulf crisis team would play realistically, if only because the setting of the game was so real. "Gulf Strike" was the model. As Herman originally designed the board game in 1983, it looked at two possibilities: a Soviet move into the Persian Gulf and the effect of an Iranian victory in the Iran-Iraq War, which at the time had been going on since 1980. Herman had Iran defeating Iraq and threatening to invade Kuwait and Saudi Arabia.

When Herman's players gathered in 1990, the reality was that Iraq had defeated Iran—"I got that part wrong," Herman admitted about his original game design—and the disintegrating Soviet Union no longer was a potential adversary. In Herman's game, some territory had changed hands after Iran had won; but the game board's entry point for an invasion of Kuwait was the same as the one that Saddam Hussein's troops used. And the question of a U.S. response was the same. Herman had revised the game in 1988 to add Scud and Silkworm missiles. So the players now had a real-life assessment of Iraq's arsenal. The game also specified how U.S. forces would be deployed, if we became involved in the fighting. "I had that part right," Herman says, "down to which units and when they show up. I was right on track with the reality."

The game that the Pentagon policymakers began playing looked at what could happen if Saddam Hussein's forces did not stop in Kuwait but rolled on into Saudi Arabia. Herman, as Control, pushed the players onto three different paths and then made them look at where those paths would lead.

Path One: Iraq consolidates its position in Kuwait. The Gulf Cooperation Council (GCC)—Saudi Arabia, Oman, Qatar, United Arab Emirates, Bahrain, and Kuwait—and the United States and United Nations do not react militarily but enact economic and political sanctions. Path Two: After consolidating briefly in Kuwait, Iraq continues its offensive into Saudi Arabia. There is no GCC or U.S. military response. Path Three: Iraq, after consolidating briefly, goes on the offensive. The GCC defends Saudi territory, and the United States launches a military response.

The game continued into the night and was resumed the next morning. At about 11:00 A.M. on August 3, Herman declared the game finished. The players, aided by Herman, wrote a top-secret report based on treading the three paths. "The report said that if you hold to Path One, then you have a long buildup to take Kuwait back, or you let him have it," Herman recalled. There was a third possibility to Path One: Wait Saddam out, letting him wonder what you do next. Herman did not reveal the assessments of Path Three, the path ultimately taken. But he added, "We said what the big issues were and what the U.S. should be doing. I saw Xeroxed copies of the report all over the Pentagon."

At a game store in Pentagon City Mall, a subway stop away from the Pentagon, staff officers bought the few "Gulf Strike" games in stock. An army colonel ordered forty-eight more, which were rapidly delivered. The game became a unique planning document. In January 1991, when the Persian Gulf air war started, military strategists were using the game in setting up the ground war. Herman was later told that the military players had estimated the ground war would go on for about ninety-six hours. In reality, the ground campaign lasted just four more than that.

Such absolute validation of a war game is rare. A game is not supposed to predict the future. A well-designed game looks to the past, using history as a kind of armature, or framework, of reality. But it is the concept of history that creates the greatest difference between designing a game for a hobbyist and a game for a general. The hobbyist wants the thrill of participating in history and verifying the adage about the past providing lessons for the present. Generals and admirals care less about the past than about what they think modern technology and computer-guaranteed facts can give them in the present or the near future.

Facts, however, are not what drive recreational war games. And it is here that the connection between reality and recreation breaks down. Because there is no history of nuclear war, for example, war gamers must create an artificial nuclear war and then try to make it real with numbers plucked from reality: kilometers, ranges of artillery, sizes of army units, speed of aircraft carriers.

Unlike many military scenarists, the hobbyist is realistic about the chances of victory. A hobbyist game usually has "victory conditions" or a "victory level." As Dunnigan put it in the *Complete Wargames Handbook,* "Victory is often a fairly vague thing in military history. . . . Certain levels of victory have been established through the years. These levels are, in ascending order, draw, marginal victory, substantial victory, decisive victory, overwhelming victory." A general wants unconditional victory; an amateur will settle for an entertainingly realistic war.

Military-model makers know, as an article of faith, that the future cannot be predicted. And yet, without daring to say it aloud, many do want to discover some way to simulate the future. These heretical modelers, like medieval alchemists, are sometimes implicitly encouraged by their orthodox superiors. Military players often try to transform a game board into a kind of Ouija board, so that the game becomes a mystical device that will give them clairvoyance. And indeed, hobbyist games played by military professionals have produced tantalizing examples of a predictable future. An Indochina game that Dunnigan published in 1972 was played in

Thailand by a group of American officials who substituted top-secret information for the game's data, which Dunnigan had found in the *New York Times* and *Newsweek*. Apparently, there was little difference between playing the game with Dunnigan's information and playing with official secrets. The 1973 Arab-Israel War seemed to follow the scenario of "Sinai," an earlier Dunnigan game in which the Egyptians manage to cross the Suez Canal into the Sinai—a maneuver that had seemed extremely unlikely when the game was developed.

THE ENVISIONING of battle through games—as in chess, the Hindu *chaturanga*, and the oriental *go*—is an idea so old and universal that its origins are lost in time. But the idea that real war itself could be waged like a game was well chronicled through medieval times. As chess, which seems to have originated in India, became a European game, the king, queen, castle, knight, bishop, and peasant pawn mirrored the warfare of the time. By the seventeenth century, the game tradition had manifested itself in other forms: military chess and toy soldiers.

In military chess, a German invention, traditional chess pieces evolved into specific battlefield figures, from marshal and colonel to captain and private. While officers learned war at this militarized chessboard, kings and princes played games with tiny soldiers made of silver and gold—and sent real soldiers off to fight highly stylized battles. In the wars of the seventeenth century, armies fought in tight formations, following tactics as formal as the moves of chess. Military theorists saw war as a phenomenon subject merely to rules of logic and mathematics. Of course, field commanders, fighting in the fog of war, knew better.

In 1797, a German tactician, Georg Venturini, created a war game for military schools. Known as the "new *Kriegsspiel* [war game]," it was played on a board whose 3,600 squares represented the terrain along the Franco-Belgian border. A sixty-page rule book governed the game, which was soon eclipsed by another version, this one played by Prussian army officers on realistic maps. In 1824, when the chief of the German General Staff saw the *Kriegsspiel* being played, he exclaimed, "It is not a game at all! It's a training for war!"

Every Prussian regiment was issued the *Kriegsspiel* and encouraged to play it regularly. It became endlessly complex; data from nineteenth-century wars were incorporated into more and more charts and tables. The game became known as "rigid *Kriegsspiel*" to distinguish it from the evolving "free *Kriegsspiel*," which was governed by the verdicts of umpires rather than voluminous rule books. (Mark Herman uses "rigid *Kriegsspiel*" and "free *Kriegsspiel*" in distinguishing between gaming with and without computers. Rigid *Kriegsspiel*, he says, "is what a computer model would be be-cause you program it. Free *Kriegsspiel* allows for clever thought during play.")

As the *Kriegsspiel* became popular, German artisans began producing *Zinnfiguren* (tin figures)—flat, inexpensive soldiers that transformed a royal diversion into a commoners' pastime. Toy soldiers marched through the lives of Goethe and Churchill, of Robert Louis Stevenson and Anatole France, of G.K. Chesterton and H.G. Wells. A pacifist, Wells used his interest in toy soldiers as a way to ridicule war. In *Little Wars,* published in 1913, Wells wrote:

> "Little Wars" is the game of kings—for players in an inferior social position. It can be played by boys of every age from twelve to one hundred and fifty—and even later if the limbs remain sufficiently supple,—and by girls of the better sort, and by a few and gifted women. . . .
>
> You have only to play at Little Wars three or four times to realise just what a blundering thing Great War must be. Great War is at present, I am convinced, not only the most expensive game in the universe, but it is a game out of all proportion. Not only are the masses of men and material and suffering and inconvenience too monstrously big for reason, but—the available heads we have for it are too small.

In Wells's first little war against little soldiers, he fired a spring-powered, breech-loading gun, a "priceless gift to boyhood" that was "capable of hitting a toy soldier nine times out of ten at a distance of nine yards." He loaded the gun with a wooden bullet about an inch long. His first battlefield was a room littered with encyclopedia volumes and other hefty books forming barricades for lead solders to hide behind while players fired at them.

Then as now, war gamers felt compelled to call in experts. Wells's consultant was a British army captain back from the Boer War. The captain speeded up the battle action, but the war itself became more complex, with strict rules about the size and disposition of troops. The new rules led to the question of taking prisoners. "Now, in actual civilized warfare," Wells wrote, "small detached bodies do not sell their lives dearly; a considerably larger force is able to make them prisoners without difficulty. Accordingly we decided that if a blue force, for example, has one or more men isolated, and a red force of at least double the strength of this isolated detachment moves up to contact with it, the blue men will be considered to be prisoners."

Wells preached that playing with soldiers had nothing to do with real war. But his toy soldiers launched not only games for hobbyists but also the enduring relationship between hobbyist games and military games. Elements of Wells's toy-soldier games can be found today in both Pentagon games and the ones sold in hobby shops.

ALTHOUGH GAMING had been practiced spasmodically in U.S. military establishments since the early nineteenth century, not until the 1880s did a specific game receive serious attention. Its rules were set forth in the book *American Kriegsspiel* by William R. Livermore, a major in the U.S. Army Corps of Engineers. The game ushered into U.S. military thinking many ideas that would survive in modern gaming. It involved up to sixteen companies of infantry, with colored blocks for troops (red and green versus blue and orange), and was played using topographical maps. Metal pointers of various kinds indicated the direction of marches and the intensity of the troops' rifle and cannon fire. A pegs-and-holes "firing board" startlingly resembled a data-processing punch card of early computer days. Tables handled questions of firepower and troop movement. As in games today, a roll of dice decided issues that in real war would often be decided by chance.

Attrition formulas were based on data from the Civil War and nineteenth-century European wars: a casualty rate of one man per minute at a range of 500 yards, three per minute at 100 yards. Encounters were called "melees," a word that Wells had also used in *Little Wars.* The complexity of the "American Kriegsspiel" was criticized by an army officer in words that some modern critics would recognize: The game "cannot be readily and intelligently used by anyone who is not a mathematician, and it requires, in order to be able to use it readily, an amount of special instruction, study, and practice about equivalent to that necessary to acquire a speaking knowledge of a foreign language."

In 1889, Major Livermore brought his "American Kriegsspiel" to the five-year-old Naval War College in Newport, Rhode Island, and the war game quickly went to sea. The champion of gaming at the new college was William McCarty Little, retired from the navy as a lieutenant in 1884 because he had lost his sight in one eye from a gun accident ashore. Rear Admiral Stephen B. Luce, founding president of the college, had invited his friend McCarty Little to join the faculty, and in 1886, when Rear Admiral Alfred Thayer Mahan became president and lecturer on naval history and strategy, he encouraged McCarty Little's interest in gaming. Initially, he demonstrated tactics by moving cardboard ships around on sheets of drawing paper. By the time Livermore arrived in 1889 as a lecturer, "Naval Kriegsspiel" was permanently part of the college's curriculum.

The college later inaugurated the "Strategic Naval War Game" and established many of the basic rules of American war gaming. Game fleets were assigned colors. Blue became the permanent color of the U.S. Navy. The Royal Navy was Red; the Canadian, Crimson; the German, Black; the Japanese, Orange. The Naval War College at that time selected America's probable future enemies and, through exercises at sea and games in the war college, plotted the navy's likely battles. A 1911 game at Newport envisioned a war ending with a naval blockade of Japan. Much of the plan, which foresaw the fall of the Philippines, was still accepted doctrine on December 7, 1941.

American war gaming for entertainment did not begin until the 1930s, when normally sensible adults could be found crawling about the floor to deploy lead ships in what became known as "Fletcher Pratt's Naval War Game." This was the brainchild of a writer who, along with his friends, "became a trifle bored with the poker games that were the staple amusement of their gatherings." Pratt, whom someone once called a one-man war college, was a prolific writer on Napoleon, the U.S. Navy, the War of 1812, and the Civil War. He was also a founder of the American Rocket Society, a science-fiction writer, and a journalist who was a war correspondent in World

War II. In the 1930s, he welcomed to his home in New York City fellow writers and visiting army and navy officers who joined him in his naval game.

At first, players aimed flashlights at ships and shot beams of light. Then came toy cannon that fired wooden plugs. Then came "air pistols, with which the contestants retired to another room to shoot at pictured ships on a wall," Pratt wrote. But all the weapons "had the fatal objection of turning the game into one of chance, or the dangerous one of introducing a violent sense of unreality." Game nights originally were stag affairs, like the poker nights. Eventually, though, Pratt wrote, the naval game attracted "nearly as many players of one sex as of the other; and one of the feminine delegation has been praised by a naval officer player as the most competent tactician in the group."

Pratt finally developed a complex formula involving the thickness of armor, the speed, and the number and caliber of guns for each of the ships (originally pictures on a wall, then lead waterline models—cut off at the waterline for easy movement on the floor). As proof of his method, in his 1940 book Pratt used the real-world fate of the *Admiral Graf Spee,* the German pocket battleship fatally damaged in 1939 during a running battle with three Royal Navy cruisers. "Rated on gun-power and armor," Pratt wrote, the *Graf Spee* "should have been more than a match for the three British cruisers; but by the formula here [in his book] they should have beaten her. They did."

In September 1941, about a year after Fletcher Pratt's naval-war-game book was published, a naval game was begun at the Japanese Naval War College in Tokyo. For eleven days, officers of the Imperial Japanese Navy played a game that climaxed with a massive surprise attack on Pearl Harbor. Vice Admiral Chuichi Nagumo, who would lead the real attack, played himself in the game. The Japanese estimated that two-thirds of the U.S. capital ships at Pearl Harbor would be sunk, but at great loss to the attackers. Six carriers took part in the raid during the game, which indicated that U.S. patrols would discover the attack force and sink two or three carriers or otherwise put them out of action. Nagumo, convinced by the game, argued against imperiling the entire Japanese force of large carriers. But he was overruled by Admiral Isoroku Yamamoto, commander in chief of the navy—and chief umpire of the game.

A month before the Pearl Harbor game, officials of the Total War Research Institute had gathered for another game in Tokyo, this one a global political-military game designed to examine a long-term war. Reflecting the reality of the nation itself, the game's Japan was a shifting coalition of often competing interests—the army and the navy, other cabinet members, and industry. According to an account of the game based on a postwar examination of institute records, "The game even included plans for the control of consumer-goods, plans, incidentally, which were identical with those actually put into effect on December 8, 1941 [the date of Pearl Harbor on the Japanese side of the international date line]."

The game started the war on December 15, 1941, when Japan, allied with Germany and Italy, launched surprise attacks on the Philippine Islands and several nations in southeast Asia. (There was no attack on Pearl Harbor, probably because high-ranking officers in the Imperial Navy were then still arguing about such plans.)

But the Japanese players, projecting their game into the future, let wishes conquer sense. While the Soviet Union fought a losing battle against Germany, Japan would invade and seize Siberia. Germany would defeat the Soviet Union and England. The United States was not treated as an important force. (By some accounts of Japanese gaming, one version of a global game had the Japanese, after conquering India, linking up with Germany in a Nazi Middle East.)

The results of the game, presented by the military officers as convincing arguments to political authorities, confirmed Japan's decision to go to war in Southeast Asia.

U.S. war gaming during World War II took the form of what came to be called operations research, whose advocates saw war not as an art but as a science. They discovered, for example, that the mathematical concept of "constant effectiveness ratio" could be applied to warfare. In mathematics, constancy is demonstrable: What happens in one mathematical model happens in others having similar properties. In warfare, constancy means that tactics or solutions discovered in one theater of war can be reproduced in another theater. One study, for example, showed that whether British aircraft laid mines in German sea-lanes or German planes dropped mines in British ports, the effectiveness ratio remained constant: For every sixty mines laid, one ship was sunk.

When the war ended, operations research remained in the U.S. military establishment. The Pentagon's Operations Research Office (ORO), under contract with the Johns Hopkins University, invented "Tin Soldier," a kind of checkers match between opposing tank forces. The tin soldiers moved over the traditional squares of the original war-game battlefield, the chessboard. (When hobbyists began developing games, they discovered that the movement and massing of military units could be better approximated on a hexagonal grid than on a square chessboard grid. The attenuating, multidimensional damage caused by a bomb, for instance, could be better calculated by a formula based on the hexagon. Military gamers picked up the hexagon idea when they began commissioning secret games from the designers of hobby games.) "Tin Soldier" evolved into the "Maximum Complexity Computer Battle," the first computerized analytical war game.

In a typical ORO simulation, twenty or so Red, Blue, and Control players, almost invariably retired army officers, gathered around map tables in large rooms equipped with little more than chairs, game-time clocks, and whirring machines that produced random numbers used in formulas to determine such factors as casualties and targeting effectiveness. Players analyzed potential conflicts in Western Europe, the Middle East, and Southeast Asia. They examined such old problems as logistics and inventory management, playing the same battle again and again, with varying amounts of supplies. They also introduced such new topics as the radiation exposure of tank crews on nuclear battlefields and tactics for newly developed antitank weapons.

Computers quickened the pace of games and changed their nature, pushing them off the tabletop and into the theoretical realm of modeling. A model is a simplified portrayal of something; it could be a formula defining, say, "area fire," or it could be a mathematical representation of, for example, the shipping needed to supply three months of warfare in Europe.

To the ranks of military gamers were added modelers, who would rather analyze phenomena than launch attacks, and who would play at war not in quest of victory but in a mathematical search for a weapon's "measure of effectiveness." At the same time, Project RAND (an acronym for "research and development"), which began during World War II, entered the Cold War as the Rand Corporation. Rand became the nation's major powerhouse for creating strategy in a nuclear world, a world dominated by two nuclear-armed opponents, a world of Blue and Red. The new strategy was built upon operations research but ranged beyond it. Edwin Paxson, a Rand mathematician, called what he did *systems analysis*, an attempt to quantify everything possible in complex operations, such as a Strategic Air Command strike against the Soviet Union. The analyses often took the form of simulation, involving not just pilots but also policymakers. And this evolved into a Rand specialty that quickly spread to the academic community: the political-military war game.

By 1966, a Joint Chiefs of Staff study listed 103 different war games and simulations run by fifty organizations, of which only thirty were military. There was a passionate belief in gaming, in numbers, in simulation, in manipulation of models. To the ultimate believers, if something could be modeled, it could be done in real life. They saw fate as a tangible outcome that could be easily jiggered through mathematics and analysis. American policy mandates could be analyzed and modeled in Washington, and then operators in the real world could shape that policy by working the humble clay of developing countries.

Such projects bewildered and infuriated military officers trained in old and battle-tested ways. Only one high-ranking officer, Vice Admiral Hyman G. Rickover, "the father of the nuclear submarine," dared to criticize openly the rising influence of systems analysis. Testifying before Congress in 1966, he said, "On a cost effectiveness basis the colonists would not have revolted against King George III, nor would John Paul Jones have engaged the *Serapis* with the *Bonhomme Richard,* an inferior ship. . . . Computer logic would have advised the British to make terms with Hitler in 1940."

Rickover also gravely spoke about war itself—especially the war then going on: "A war, small or large, does not follow a prescribed 'scenario' laid out in advance. If we could predict the sequence of events accurately, we could probably avoid war in the first place. The elder Moltke [Count Helmuth von Moltke, chief of the Prussian General Staff (1858–88) and an advocate of war gaming] said: 'No plan survives contact with the enemy.' Are we not relearning that bitter lesson every day in Vietnam . . . ?"

Vietnam was playing out a scenario of limited war—a measurable war, a war that could be logical and reasonable. "As we go back and read the writings of political scientists and systems analysts on limited war," wrote army colonel Harry G. Summers, Jr., "they are noteworthy for their lack of passion. The horror, the bloodshed and the destruction of the battlefield are remarkably absent." Summers circulated a "bitter little story" told during the final days of the Vietnam War:

> When the Nixon Administration took over in 1969 all the data on North Vietnam and the United States was fed into a Pentagon computer—population, gross national product, manufacturing capability, number of tanks, ships, and aircraft, size of the armed forces, and the like.
>
> The computer was then asked, "When will we win?"
>
> It took only a moment to give the answer: "You won in 1964!"

His story haunted the Pentagon, and gaming by computer eventually fell into disfavor. But human gaming—what Mark Herman calls "a table with men and women sitting around"—has endured in the Pentagon and the State Department. "The important aspect of any war game is the players," Herman says. Put good ones around that table and they may well take a path toward reality.

*SUMMER 1994*

---

Thomas B. Allen is the author of *War Games* (1987) and coauthor with Norman Polmar of *Rickover: Controversy and Genius* (1982) and *Code-Word Downfall: The Secret Plan to Invade Japan—and Why Truman Dropped the Bomb* (1995).

# 50

# An Empty Ocean

## By John Keegan

*The aircraft carrier and the submarine emerged from the contests of World War II as the two great weapons of the sea. In the half century since that conflict, both weapons have progressed far beyond the* Essex*-class carriers and* Gato*-class submarines that swept the Pacific clean of Japanese ships by the summer of 1945. Fueled by nuclear power, today's aircraft carriers—such as the nearly 100,000-ton* George Washington*—are the behemoths of the ocean and the quintessence of power projection. At the same time, their nuclear-powered sister ships—such as the attack submarine* Dallas *and the missile submarine* Ohio*—are the sharks of the seas and the epitome of stealth and menace. In the oceans of the future, which of these ships will command the sea? John Keegan first asks and then answers that question.*

By the end of the Second World War, indeed well before its end, the submarine and the aircraft carrier had established themselves indisputably as the dominant weapons of war at sea. Of the two types, it was the aircraft carrier whose rise was the more dramatic. The Soviet Union had built none; the two laid down by Germany and France, the *Graf Zeppelin* and *Bearn,* had not been completed. But the British had seven fleet carriers, five light fleet carriers, and thirty-eight escort carriers, and twenty fleet or light fleet carriers building; the Japanese had two of thirteen fleet carriers and two of eight light fleet carriers still afloat; the United States Navy, which had begun the war with seven carriers, deployed in August 1945 twenty fleet carriers, eight light fleet carriers, and seventy-one escort carriers, providing deck space for nearly 4,000 aircraft of a multiplicity of types—fighter, torpedo, bomber, antisubmarine, and reconnaissance.

The majesty of the American carrier groups maneuvering at sea exceeded even that of the Dreadnought fleets of the First World War. The spectacle of those great floating airfields, which could launch and recover a hundred aircraft in one sortie, steaming upwind at twenty-five knots under the vast Pacific sky, surrounded by cruisers, destroyers, and radar pickets of their air-defense screens, left an indelible impression of grace and power on all who witnessed it. Here, it seemed beyond doubt, was the supreme instrument of command of the sea, unapproachable by surface ships, self-defending against aircraft, and able to strike at will for hundreds of miles in any direction beyond the circle of ocean it directly occupied.

Yet the defeat of Japan was not solely to be ascribed to the aircraft carrier; in the opinion of Prime Minister Hideki Tōjō, the Japanese war leader, the submarine played an equal part in the American victory. Statistics bear out his analysis. Submarines not only destroyed one-third of the Japanese fleet, including two of its last aircraft carriers, they also destroyed much of the Japanese merchant navy. At the beginning of the war, Japan owned 6 million tons of merchant shipping; by its end, that tonnage had declined to 1.8 million, despite the requisition of 800,000 tons by capture and the addition of another 3.3 million from new construction. And this toll of destruction had largely been inflicted by American submarines. By mid-1945 these were operating with impunity in the Sea of Japan itself, and had brought most traffic between the home islands to a halt.

In short, what the German admiral Karl Dönitz had tried but failed to achieve in the Atlantic, the Americans had succeeded in doing in the Pacific. Their submarines had locked a stranglehold about the enemy economy and squeezed it into paralysis. For Japan, to an even greater extent than Britain, was a country dependent upon seaborne imports for its raw materials and means of subsistence. Its population was larger than Britain's, but its agricultural product smaller, as was its domestic production of fuel and basic minerals. America's threat to interdict the import of oil and metals was the pretext Japan had chosen for making war in 1941; America's actual interdiction of their supply in 1945 ensured that, had Japan not accepted defeat by nuclear bombardment, it shortly would have had to concede in any case.

The American submarines that had destroyed Japan's shipping were superior in type to those with which Dönitz had fought the Battle of the Atlantic, being faster on the surface and twice the size, with a larger complement of torpedoes and a greater overall cruising range. The Americans, moreover, had not sought to orchestrate their submarines' operations by radio orders from land and had thereby denied the enemy the opportunity to locate and attack them through intercepts. But these were marginal superiorities. The American submarine of 1945 differed little from the American submarine of 1941. It was still essentially a submersible, able to submerge when need be, but operating to best advantage on the surface as a torpedo boat and losing most of its speed and endurance when it sought invisibility in the deep.

Expert prognosis, had it been sought in 1945, might well have held that the submarine's potential for development lagged far behind that of the aircraft carrier. True, a new submarine—the German Walther boat—had been designed with a closed hydrogen-peroxide fuel system that promised prolonged submerged cruising and high underwater speed for short periods. But no Walther boat had been brought to an operational state, and the experimental models that existed were small. Snorkel boats, ventilated through a breathing tube, were also able to cruise submerged, and therefore virtually undetectable, on their diesels at speeds better than electric motors could deliver. But the snorkel imposed unpleasant pressure changes on the crew as its valve snapped open and shut, which effectively limited underwater endurance, while cruising range was still determined by fuel capacity. The submarine's offensive weapon, moreover, was still the torpedo, of which even the best models were comparatively short-range and inaccurate.

THE AIRCRAFT CARRIER, by contrast, was undergoing sensational improvement. The first "supercarrier," the USS *Forrestal,* was, when launched in 1954, the largest warship in the world. At 86,000 tons, she far outweighed the *Midway* class of 1942, then considered giants at 55,000 tons, and dwarfed the 1931 USS *Ranger,* the first American ship built specifically as an aircraft carrier. The *Forrestal* admittedly carried fewer aircraft than the *Mid-ways,* but hers were jet-powered, little inferior in performance to their land-based equivalents and capable of delivering nuclear weapons.

The U.S. Navy's carriers had acquired their first nuclear-capable aircraft in 1951; with the advent of the supercarriers, the navy put itself at the forward edge of the American strategic system. Supercarriers carrying high-altitude bombers of the Savage, Skywarrior, and Vigilante series, and deployed to the Mediterranean and western Pacific, complemented—in fact, competed with—the air force's Strategic Air Command in holding the Soviet Union at nuclear risk. And the reality of the risk was enormously enhanced in 1958 with the laying down of a carrier that was nuclear-powered, the new USS *Enterprise.* The *Enterprise,* if replenished under way with stores and aviation fuel, could in theory keep to the seas indefinitely, using her mobility to hide from an enemy and using her air group and supporting screen of escorts to defeat any attacker that chanced to find her.

Four years before the keel of the USS *Enterprise* was laid, however, the launching of the USS *Nautilus* had achieved a modernization of the submarine revolutionary enough to challenge the aircraft carrier's supremacy over twentieth-century oceans. For the *Nautilus* was also nuclear-powered, thereby dispensing altogether with the old, bulky, but necessary duplication of engines—electric for underwater cruising and petroleum-fueled for surface travel. In addition, she was capable of the same speed—more than twenty knots—below and above the surface. Her considerable size, over 3,000 tons, and her advanced air-purification system allowed her, moreover, to remain submerged for days at a time.

The *Nautilus,* in short, realized the dream of the submarine pioneers, being a true submarine and not merely a submersible boat. But she was not yet a dominant weapon of war. Her armament consisted of conventional torpedoes, and though she would certainly have eluded the escorts that fought the Battle of the Atlantic and slaughtered any convoy the escorts sought to protect, she did not in herself represent the "war deci-sive" weapon into which Dönitz had hoped to transform the U-boat. Pitted against a high-speed carrier group and its formidable array of anti-submarine aircraft, the *Nautilus* would not necessarily have inflicted crippling losses, and her own survival might have been at risk.

In the next decade, however, the successors to the *Nautilus* grew in size, power, and capability. The experimental USS *Triton,* of 5,500 tons, circum-navigated the globe submerged in 1960. The *Skipjack,* first of a class of nuclear-powered attack submarines, achieved an underwater speed of thir-ty knots and regularly dived below 1,000 feet. Trials with the Regulus mis-sile mounted in the USS *Halibut* also proved the submarine's ability to launch nuclear-capable missiles, though the *Halibut* had to surface to do so, as the Regulus was a relatively primitive subsonic, air-breathing weapon.

With the launching of the first of the *George Washington* class in 1959, a year after the start of the nuclear supercarrier *Enterprise,* half measures in the revolutionizing of the submarine disappeared and it moved in a single step to the first rank among units of naval power. The *George Washington* was unquestionably a capital ship, if that dated term still had validity; indeed, she exceeded the capital ship's status, being an instrument of national strategy at the direct disposal of the head of state. For the *George Washington* represented a marriage between two dynamic technologies: that of the true submarine and that of the long-range ballistic nuclear mis-sile. The boat deployed no specifically marine weapon at all, no gun, and no torpedoes. Her armament consisted of sixteen Polaris missiles, representing a new seaborne element in the United States' nuclear deterrent system to be launched, if at all, not at the direction of the boat's captain but only by specific instructions from the president of the United States.

The *George Washington* was the first of a ballistic-missile fleet that was to grow to forty-one units, a figure fixed by Soviet-American agreement in 1972. Meanwhile the direct descendants of the *Nautilus,* now known as nuclear attack submarines, were also multiplying. By 1980 they numbered nearly a hundred, of which the most advanced achieved underwater speeds of thirty knots—faster than all but the fastest escorts—and dived to below 1,000 feet. At such depths conventional antisubmarine weapons, even if motor-propelled to increase their rate of descent, were erratically effective; the attack submarine's own counterescort weapons, particularly the wire-guided torpedo, were actually more effective. And escorts laid themselves open to counterattack if they used active sonar, in which a sound signal is sent out to locate and bounce off underwater targets; while passive sonar, which simply monitors through sonar equipment the noise of surface ship movements without sending signals, did not expose a submerged sub-marine to retaliation.

Passive sonar could, of course, also be used by surface escorts to detect submarines below the surface; but so rapidly could a submerged nuclear-propelled submarine maneuver that a precision attack, by either motor-propelled depth charge or guided torpedo, was an uncertain means of achieving a hit. Antisubmariners consequently reckoned only two weapons as dependably effective against their adversary: One was the nuclear-warhead torpedo, in the American form called the Subroc, a rocket-propelled diving missile that killed a submarine by creating large over-pressures in a wide area of sea; the other was the wire-guided torpedo fired from either an aircraft, a submerged mine, or another submarine.

But potentially the deadliest instrument of antisubmarine warfare is the submarine-hunting submarine. Submarine captains are alarmed by aircraft because they lack the means with which to bring them under attack even if alerted to their presence by active sonar echoes (aircraft-borne passive sonar betrays itself not at all). But aircraft are relatively feeble antisubmarine weapon platforms, as they must track their prey by indirect means. Typically they find targets by dropping patterns of sonar buoys that retransmit echoes to the parent aircraft, and by dunking sonar transponders—instruments set to react to a predetermined signal—into the sea surface. An attack submarine, by contrast, can chase its quarry through the sea's depths, hiding in the "cone of silence" created by the quarry's propeller wash, where the quarry submarine's sonar cannot detect it.

The significance of the developing dialectic between submarine and antisubmarine is nowhere better demonstrated than in the growing diversification of submarine types. Forty years ago, in the aftermath of World War II, all submarines were "attack" vessels, dedicated to attacking surface ships. By 1960 the class had separated into three: ballistic-missile submarines, belonging to the "central strategic system" of the nuclear powers; nuclear attack submarines designed to win another "Battle of the Atlantic" should it break out; and conventional submarines for operations in confined waters. The third type has today almost disappeared from the naval order of battle of advanced states. The second continues to increase its underwater speed, safe limit of submersion, and offensive power; boats of the later *Los Angeles* class, for example, travel at thirty-five knots, dive to nearly 1,500 feet, and mount submarine-launched cruise missiles as well as torpedoes, which give them strategic as well as tactical capability. The first and truly strategic type has begun to diversify in a highly significant manner. The American *Ohio* class mounts twenty-four intercontinental missiles and displaces 19,000 tons, as against the sixteen shorter-range missiles and 8,000 tons of the earlier *Lafayette* class; the Soviet *Typhoon* class, mounting twenty missiles, displaces 29,000 tons, considerably more than any of the Dreadnoughts that fought at Jutland.

It required little prescience to foresee that submarine types would continue to diversify in exactly the same way as ironclads did in the last century. That diversification was among the most striking of all developments in the naval architecture of steam and iron. The wooden world knew only one category of ship, differentiated by size alone; but size differentiation ensured that the larger were not a threat to the smaller, and vice versa, since the low speed and maneuverability of the heavily gunned ship ensured that she could not bring the more lightly armed one to battle, while the more lightly armed dared not use her superior sailing qualities to challenge a heavier adversary. Frigates, in short, fought frigates, and line-of-battle ships each other.

The coming of the ironclad and of the weapons coeval with the ironclad—particularly the torpedo—altered that stratification. The torpedo boat was designed specifically to challenge the largest ships in an enemy's fleet. Her appearance called forth the torpedo-boat destroyer, which in turn required the multiplication of light cruisers, then of heavy cruisers, and ultimately the creation of the battle cruiser. Fleet actions, in consequence, imposed on admirals a bewildering diversity of ship types to orchestrate. The later addition of submarines and aircraft carriers to the equation, balanced with the time urgency and space variables of battle, compounded difficulties.

These difficulties are now threatening to transfer themselves underwater, as the efficient parts of fleets progressively acquire diverse submarine forms: larger and smaller ballistic types, cruise-missile types, mixed cruise-missile attack types, and pure attack types, all of them nuclear-powered. Tennyson's image of "the nations' airy navies grappling in the central blue" now threatens to be replaced as a vision of the future by something akin to an underwater Jutland, involving huge, variegated submarine fleets and beset by difficulties of command and control.

FOR THE WEAKNESS of modern submarine operations is the problem of communication, both to submerged submarines from the surface and between one submerged submarine and another. It is a problem that scientists are still struggling to solve. Surface-to-submarine communication is possible when the submarine deploys a large enough trailing aerial, though that limits its maneuverability and restricts its depth-keeping; intersubmarine communication, because of the conductivity of water, is intrinsically undirectional and insecure. The consequence is that submarine fleets, though undoubtedly the most powerful instruments of naval forces ever sent to sea, are unamenable to either tactical or strategic control. And as the history of naval warfare is essentially the story of an effort to impose first tactical and then strategic control over fleets, it is clear that admirals have far to go before they can assume with some degree of certainty the powers of command exercised by predecessors on ironclad and wooden-wall ships.

Yet command of the sea in the future unquestionably lies beneath rather than upon the surface. If that is doubted, let the doubter contemplate for the briefest moment the record of the only naval campaign fought since 1945, that of the Falklands in 1982. From it two salient facts stand out: that the surface ship can barely defend herself against high-performance, jet-propelled aircraft; and that she cannot defend itself at all against the nuclear-powered submarine. Traditionalists would undoubtedly invoke "special circumstances" to argue otherwise. They would argue that the eleven out of twenty-seven British surface warships sunk or damaged by Argentine aircraft bombs or guided missiles were hit in exceptional circumstances: These included the narrowness of the Falkland Sound, in which the escorts had to cover the landing of the task force's embarked troops; and the constriction of the 200-mile "exclusion zone" that the British declared around the Falklands, within and around which the fleet operated.

That the fleet's freedom of action was limited by its need to land and support its embarked troops is undeniable. But what traditionalists overlook in arguing constriction as an explanation of losses is that almost all naval battles, throughout the history of war at sea, have been fought in close proximity to land. The deep oceanic encounters of the Pacific War—and only the battles of Midway and the Philippine Sea occurred far out at sea—remain exceptional events.

Even in the vastness of the Pacific in the Second World War, most encounters took place close to the mainland, to large islands, or to archipelagoes—that holds true of Pearl Harbor, the battles of the Java and Coral seas, Savo Island, the eastern Solomons, the Santa Cruz Islands, Guadalcanal, the Bismarck Sea, Leyte Gulf, and Iwo Jima and Okinawa. The same is true of all the naval battles of the First World War, including the distant actions of Coronel and the Falklands. All nineteenth-century naval battles—Navarino, Sinope, Lissa, Manila Bay, Tsushima—were fought in confined waters. And the record of action in "classical" naval operations between the wooden-wall ships of Britain, Holland, France, and Spain discloses the same pattern. Only Admiral Richard Howe's Glorious First of June victory against the French in 1794, which was fought 400 miles from the mainland, ranks as a deep-sea engagement. All the other "decisive" battles between ship-of-the-line navies—including the Armada fight, the Texel, Beachy Head, Barfleur, the Saints, Camperdown, Cape St. Vincent, the Nile, Copenhagen, and Trafalgar—were fought close to or within sight of land, or actually directly offshore.

Indeed, it was not until the appearance of the submarine and the aircraft carrier that deep-sea operations acquired strategic point. Thitherto, the intrinsic difficulty of locating an enemy fleet or profitable concentrations of merchant shipping in great waters had always argued for the necessity of bringing on fleet engagements as close to home, or to major overseas bases, as possible. That logic was reinforced by the fact that most naval operations were an adjunct of land warfare and that fleets had to hold close to the operational areas of the armies they were supporting. The aircraft carrier and the long-range submarine altered the terms of that argument. The first, by taking to sea what essentially was an instrument of land warfare, the airplane, opened up the possibility of striking over a wider area of strategic space than any admiral had previously sought to dominate. The second, by its power to establish broad lines of surveillance across sea routes deep within the ocean, confronted surface navies with the need to fight at a greater distance from land than ever before.

Between the upper pincer of the aircraft carrier and the lower of the submarine, the conventional surface ship of whatever size—battleship, cruiser, escort—awaited an inevitable constriction. Without the protection of the carrier-borne aircraft, it could not survive in a surface engagement;

equally, it could not safely engage its submarine enemy unless aircraft were at hand—at first to keep that enemy submerged, later to enlarge and reinforce its own capacity to detect and attack the submarine keeping to the deeps. The ultimate effect of the operation of these two pincer jaws has been to bring them into immediate opposition: The conventional surface ship has now been made a marginal instrument of military force, while the submarine and the aircraft carrier directly challenge each other for command of the sea.

What shall be the outcome? Proponents of the one or the other are each convinced that their favored weapon commands the future. Maritime air-power enthusiasts emphasize the degree of risk at which the submarine is held by the antisubmarine aircraft and cite the carrier group's formidable ability to defend itself through the deepening of its escort screen against torpedo and missile attack. Submariners counter that the escort screen is no stronger than its component units; that they are themselves surface ships (though some are also attendant attack submarines); and that those surface escorts are vulnerable to sustained submarine assault. The destruction of the carrier group's heart, the carrier itself, must come by inexorable process, and the long reign of the surface capital ship will then be ended.

Foresight is the riskiest of all means of strategic analysis. It must nevertheless be said that the vision of the submariner is intrinsically the more convincing. For it is with the submarine that the initiative and full freedom of the seas rest. The aircraft carrier, in any realistic scenario—operating in great waters or amphibious support close to shore—will be exposed to a wider range of threat than the submarine must face. In a shoreward context it risks attack not only by carrier-borne aircraft but also by land-based aircraft, land-based missiles, and the submarine itself. And the experience of the Falklands rubs home how menacing only two of these elements proved to be: The Argentine land-based aircraft and land-based missiles inflicted losses that narrowed the British aircraft carriers' protective screen of escorts to the slenderest of margins; had the Argentines been able to deploy either an effective carrier or offensive submarine effort—or both—against the task force, it would have been driven into retreat.

The British attack submarines, by contrast, operated at will, sinking the Argentine navy's largest conventional surface ship, driving its aircraft carrier and the whole of its escort fleet ignominiously into harbor, and risking in the process no effective retaliation whatsoever. That the Argentine navy was an ineffective antisubmarine force does not invalidate the conclusion to be drawn from the encounter. Given equal numbers and an equivalent allocation of ship types between the two fleets, it would have been the Royal Navy that operated at a disadvantage, with inevitably disastrous consequences for the outcome of the expedition to the South Atlantic. It would have suffered all the losses that it did; and to them would have been added the sinkings that a nuclear attack submarine force would certainly have inflicted.

The era of the submarine as the predominant weapon of power at sea must therefore be recognized as having begun. It is already the instrument of ultimate nuclear deterrence between the superpowers, holding at risk their cities, industries, and populations as it circles their shores in its relentless oceanic orbit. It is now also the ultimate capital ship, deploying the means to destroy any surface fleet that enters its zone of operations. Five hundred years ago, before the sailing-ship pioneers ventured into great waters, the ocean was an empty place, the only area of the world's surface in which men did not deploy military force against each other. In a future war the ocean may appear empty again, swept clear both of merchant traffic and of the navies that have sought so long to protect it against predators. But the ocean's emptiness will be illusory; for in its deep, new navies of submarine warships, great and small, will be exacting from each other, as Rudyard Kipling described it in *A Song of England,* "the price of admiralty."

*AUTUMN 1988*

For many years senior lecturer at Sandhurst, John Keegan is now the defense editor for the *Daily Telegraph* in London. His most recent book is *A History of Warfare* (1993).

# 51

# A Short History of United Nations Peacekeeping

## By Paul Lewis

*With the disintegration first of the Soviet Empire and then of the Soviet Union itself, the armed forces of the United States faced a new and confusing world. Who would be the probable enemy or enemies of the future? What types of conflicts might be expected? Would the roles and missions left from the Cold War remain true for the future? With the recent experiences of Somalia, Rwanda, Bosnia, and Haiti, would American military forces become increasingly concerned with peacekeeping rather than war-fighting capabilities? Paul Lewis, with his summary of United Nations blue-helmet efforts in the past, provides a possible foretaste of how American military forces might be used in the future.*

The decrepit houses lining the narrow deserted street that cuts through the center of Nicosia have been transformed into miniature fortresses, with windows bricked up except for rifle slits and sandbags blocking doorways. This is the "Green Line," a narrow band of no-man's-land that divides the Mediterranean island of Cyprus into watertight Greek and Turkish sections. On one side the houses are full of armed Greek Cypriot soldiers, while on the other, just ten feet away, they hold units of the Turkish army who keep bayonets on their rifles at all times and a bullet in the breech. The only pedestrians moving on the street are the young Canadian infantrymen who patrol every hour or so—sometimes on foot, sometimes in white jeeps—wearing the distinctive blue helmets of United Nations peacekeepers.

Time has been frozen here since Turkey invaded Cyprus eighteen years ago, cutting the island in half, and a U.N. peacekeeping force moved in between the combatants to supervise the truce. In a deserted café the overturned cups and plates are just as the customers left them in 1974 when they fled before the advancing troops. Dust and debris cover the unused cars in a dealer's showroom, now transformed by the years into vintage collector's items.

These days the street is usually quiet. But the U.N. patrols check constantly that neither side is improving its position by adding another sandbag, moving into an empty house, or even altering the size of a flag. When they do find infringements, the Canadian officers have only the power of friendly persuasion to get them reversed. Every now and again, tensions flare up, with the soldiers trading insults and baring their backsides at each other across the street. Then the peacekeepers put their lives on the line, marching in under both sides' guns in an effort to calm the passions unleashed by centuries of hatred between Christian Greek and Muslim Turk.

THE UNITED NATIONS Peacekeeping Force in Cyprus—known by the acronym UNFICYP—is just one of twelve such peacekeeping operations currently under way in every part of the world involving over 25,000 soldiers at a cost that now promises to run into billions of dollars. From the high mountains of Kashmir to the deserts of the Persian Gulf and the steaming jungles of El Salvador and Angola, these blue-helmeted "soldiers without enemies" have carved out an impressive role for themselves monitoring cease-fire agreements, disarming rebel groups, and preserving law and order in troubled lands, often so that the local population can decide their own future through the ballot box.

It is taxing work for soldiers who, against all their tradition and training, find themselves conducting nonviolent operations beyond the orders of their government in politically sensitive situations that require reserves of calm, tact, impartiality, and good humor. Often unarmed, they may use force only when attacked. Some 812 peacekeepers from forty-three countries have died on duty.

Today, with the end of the Cold War, the great powers are increasingly working through the Security Council to resolve civil wars and other conflicts around the globe, and the demand for U.N. peacekeeping operations is growing just as their nature is becoming more complex and challenging. Since 1988, when Blue Helmets past, present, and future were collectively awarded the Nobel Peace Prize for their arduous and often dangerous work, the United Nations has taken on thirteen new peacekeeping commitments, the same number as during the first forty years of its existence. The number of U.N. soldiers and police deployed in the field jumped from 11,500 in January 1992 to 44,000 by the end of May. The world peacekeeping bill will jump from $421 million in 1991 to an anticipated $2.7 billion this year.

PEACEKEEPING is found nowhere in the United Nations Charter. Its invention is often credited to Secretary-General Dag Hammarskjöld, who jokingly called it "chapter six and a half" of the Charter—meaning that it fell between chapter 6, which calls for the peaceful resolution of disputes, and chapter 7, which empowers the Security Council to reverse aggression by military might if negotiations fail—as it did to drive North Korean forces out of South Korea in 1950 and the Iraqis from Kuwait in 1991.

But some scholars trace the concept's origins as far back as the fifth century B.C. when the Greek city-states of the Delian League jointly policed the Aegean Sea. Medieval popes sought to impose the "Truce of God." And the eighteenth century produced a flurry of utopian schemes for preserving peace, which prompted Frederick the Great to remark sarcastically to Voltaire, "The thing is most practicable; for its success all that is lacking is the consent of Europe and a few similar trifles."

The clearest precedent for present-day peacekeeping, however, probably lies in the arrangements the defunct League of Nations made to monitor the plebiscite that returned the Saar to Germany in 1935. Some 3,200 troops from Britain, Italy, Sweden, and the Netherlands, together with a police contingent, were sent in under the command of a British general—but wearing their normal uniforms—to preserve law and order while the citizens of the Saar determined their future.

Though the word *peacekeeping* was not yet in vogue, the force was described as "a peace force, not a fighting force," and was ordered to exercise strict impartiality. As with modern-day peacekeeping operations, the soldiers sought to avoid force, cooperated closely with the civilian authorities, and relied on high-visibility patrolling to maintain order. A similar operation was planned in connection with a proposed referendum on the future of Vilnius, but in the end the referendum never took place.

THIS NOVEMBER, as the heat fades on the plains around Rawalpindi, Pakistan, Brigadier General Jeremiah Enright of the Irish army will move down to his winter headquarters there from a cool summer retreat high up in the mountain peaks at Srinagar, India, making the same journey that generations of British proconsuls made before him when they returned from the hill stations to the administrative centers of the Raj at the end of each summer. But as current commander of the small United Nations military observer force on the India-Pakistan border, General Enright is also making an important symbolic statement about the political evenhandedness that is central to the peacekeeper's role as he tries to maintain the truce between these two long-standing Asian rivals.

The ink was barely dry on the San Francisco Charter and its new doctrine of collective security when the whole Indian subcontinent erupted into bloody chaos as the Muslim north split away from independent India to form Pakistan. Meanwhile the United Nations stood by, paralyzed by the failure of political will that was to characterize so much of its next forty years.

Left free to decide whether to join a new Pakistan or a diminished India, Kashmir's traditional Hindu rulers opted for the latter, despite their subjects' Muslim majority. Subsequently, unrest broke out there. After a truce was eventually negotiated, the United Nations in 1949 sent a small force of military observers to monitor that high cease-fire line. It was an operation that, like similar previous missions in Greece, Palestine, and Indonesia, became a model for the many such truce-monitoring exercises the U.N. would undertake in the decades ahead.

The United Nations quickly learned that its credibility as peacekeeper depends on treating both sides with strictest equality. So if General Enright keeps cool during the hot summer months in the mountains of Kashmir on the Indian side of the border, he must spend his winters on the Pakistani side.

Curiously, the League of Nations' experiment with peacekeeping in the Saar found no echo in the San Francisco Charter. Instead the founding fathers concentrated on devising a mechanism that would enable them to put their armed forces at the disposal of the Security Council to enforce peace and reverse future aggressions if countries refused to settle their disputes peacefully. Cold War rivalries quickly ensured that their plan for a team of world policemen, as Franklin Roosevelt called them, would be still-born. But this did not stop the United Nations from being drawn almost immediately into a series of local disputes, which laid the foundations for its future peacekeeping role.

The fact that peacekeeping was not found in the Charter proved useful because it gave the secretary-general and the Security Council flexibility in designing operations to suit the particular circumstances of each crisis. On the other hand, it also allowed the Soviet Union to question the legitimacy of operations that it thought favored Western interests and to refuse to pay for them. In 1947 the United Nations assigned military officers to the Special Committee on the Balkans (UNSCOB), sent to investigate Communist infiltration of Greece from neighboring Balkan states—an operation that planted the first seeds of Soviet opposition to the organization's peacekeeping role. After the Soviet Union vetoed such an overtly anti-Communist action in the Security Council, the United States created a precedent it was to follow several times in the future, most notably during the Korean War, by seeking authorization instead from the General Assembly, which the West then controlled.

In August 1947 the Security Council set up a good-offices committee, assisted by a team of military observers, to end the fighting that began after Indonesia sought to break free from the Netherlands and claim its independence. The committee was disbanded in 1951 when the Dutch finally withdrew.

The largest of these early observer missions—and the first true U.N. peacekeeping operation, unambiguously under the control of the secretary-general—was the United Nations Truce Supervision Organization (UNTSO). This force of over 500 military observers was sent to Jerusalem in 1948 to supervise a truce called for by the U.N. Security Council after the first Arab-Israeli war broke out. Israel had been attacked by its neighbors, Egypt, Jordan, Lebanon, and Syria, within hours of its creation. UNTSO was given a flexible mandate that has allowed it to remain in existence to the present, with its members often redeployed to help with other peacekeeping activities in the region, although its strength is now down to about 300. Thus, within four or five years of its creation, the United Nations established a clear precedent for deploying military observer forces in trouble spots around the world, sometimes in a fact-finding role but increasingly to monitor truces while efforts were made to find a permanent political solution. Its early operations already showed other trends found in later peacekeeping missions. The U.N. observers gradually built up a reputation for impartiality, and the secretary-general slowly established a solid measure of operational control.

Although the observers in Greece had been told to show "strict impartiality," U.S. State Department officials were still telling Congress in 1949 that the American representatives on all four of these early missions were under the "administrative" authority of the United Nations but American "operational" command. But member states increasingly came to accept the secretary-general's argument that such forces must be independent and impartial to win moral influence with the parties to a dispute, and this required them to take their day-to-day orders from him, with a broad mandate defined by the Security Council. In 1948 the General Assembly even agreed to give the secretary-general a worldwide communications system of his own.

The United States also emerged as a strong supporter of such operations during these early years, agreeing to pay 30 percent of their costs and lending generous logistical assistance. In Indonesia, for example, the United Nations relied on the U.S. consulate in Batavia and an American communications vessel for its radio links with U.N. headquarters in New York.

But Moscow was becoming increasingly wary of the organization's expanding peacekeeping role and the control the secretary-general exercised over these operations, which the Soviets felt served Western interests more than their own by stabilizing troubled parts of the developing world.

And it is significant that to this day, successive secretaries-general have entrusted day-to-day operational control of peacekeeping missions first to an American, Ralph Bunche, and then to two senior British officials, Sir Brian Urquhart and, after his retirement, Marrack Goulding.

THE YOUNG MALAYSIAN MAJOR drove the air-conditioned white Toyota Land Cruiser with its black United Nations insignia across the desolate moonscape of a modern battlefield. Villages had been reduced to little more than a brick-colored stain in the churned-up desert sand; nearby were the blackened stumps of palm trees. Piles of empty shell cases, tank tracks coiled like huge snakes, and the half-buried, burned-out hulks of armored vehicles dotted the scene. Observers, perching perilously on high steel towers, scanned the enemy's lines through binoculars. Occasional clumps of green camouflage netting marked artillery batteries, and every few miles a squadron of Iraqi tanks was drawn up in a perfect square.

An immense wall of earth and sand, some thirty feet high and running the length of the Fao peninsula, marked the Iraqi front line against the Iranian army. Brandishing aloft a big blue-and-white U.N. flag, the officer shepherded his party up concrete steps to the top. Iraqi soldiers stood every ten yards, rifles in hand, inside a narrow trench running along the top of the wall, with bigger guns in hollowed-out emplacements every hundred yards. Steps wound down to the soldiers' sleeping quarters deep inside the earthen wall. The view was out across the Shatt-al-Arab, choked with the rusting hulks of sunken cargo ships resting on the bottom of the channel, to the piles of sandbags on the farther shore that marked the Iranian front line. Nothing stirred on that warm spring morning.

The year was 1989, and the truce ending the bitter eight-year Iran-Iraq war was some six months old. About 400 U.N. officers, members of the United Nations Iran-Iraq Military Observer Group (UNIIMOG), were monitoring a 700-mile front line that stretched from the burning deserts of the Gulf to the snow-covered mountains of Kurdistan. Their task was still the classic one of overseeing a cease-fire agreement and preventing either side from improving its military position while, somewhere else, diplomats searched for a political solution that has still not come. (UNIIMOG was withdrawn in February 1991, with the consent of both parties; a few observers remain.) But holding the ring between the two mightiest armies in the Middle East, armed with the most sophisticated weaponry that petrodollars can buy, is clearly a far cry from those earlier little observer teams tramping through the swamps of Indonesia and over the mountains of Greece and Kashmir.

That morning the old Shatt-al-Arab hotel at Basra, where these peace-keepers were headquartered, had shuddered to the distant rumble of artillery fire as the Iraqi guns opened up in an effort to keep the Iranian army from flooding areas of no-man's-land to force back their forward observation posts. Iran replied with a barrage of mortar shells. Clearly the scale of operations and the risks involved were greater than anything undertaken in Kashmir or Greece. Peacekeeping had entered a new, more assertive phase.

The Suez crisis of 1956 marked the opening of this more assertive period, which saw the mounting of major operations in the Middle East, the Congo, and Cyprus. What had started with small, unarmed observer missions to oversee a truce was now evolving into much larger and more structured operations involving deployment of army units numbering thousands of men to serve as buffers between contending armies. The peacekeepers' responsibilities grew more complex as they were required to patrol borders, maintain law and order, and manage day-to-day developments in an international crisis.

By the fall of 1956, it was clear that the U.N. efforts to maintain the armistice between Israel and its Arab neighbors were collapsing; violence flared along Israel's borders with Egypt, Syria, and Jordan. In July, Egypt had nationalized the Suez Canal, after the West canceled financing for the Aswan High Dam. On October 29, following a number of armed clashes, Israel invaded Egypt through the Sinai with the avowed intention of cleaning out Palestinian guerrilla bases.

Two days later, working to a prearranged plan, Britain and France started bombing Egyptian airfields after demanding that Egypt and Israel withdraw ten miles from their side of the canal so that the invasion force could take back control of it.

But this force was still five days' sailing from Suez, giving opponents of their scheme time to organize a massive campaign of political resistance. The idea of sending in a U.N. force had been raised by the then secretary-general, Dag Hammarsjköld, at the very start of the crisis. And by November 3, as the strength of the opposition to their action became clear, even Britain and France were suggesting that their forces should join such a U.N. operation when they reached the canal.

Twelve years later U.N. peacekeepers were to pull the world back from a nuclear confrontation between the superpowers in this very same region. But this time the U.N. job was to provide a face-saving cover behind which Britain, France, and Israel could retreat from the Suez fiasco.

On November 4 the General Assembly formally asked Hammarskjöld to negotiate a cease-fire and explore the novel idea of deploying a nonviolent U.N. military force not just to monitor a cease-fire but to ensure the withdrawal of the invading British, French, and Israeli forces and preserve peace. For the West, this would remove any pretext for a rumored Soviet incursion into the region.

Speed and improvisation were needed. Curious problems arose that required imaginative solutions. With three foreign armies fighting on Egyptian soil, the U.N. troops needed clear identification, particularly as the peacekeeping contingent Canada offered would be wearing British battle dress. Berets of the same light shade of blue as the U.N. flag was the agreed solution—until it was discovered that these would take months to manufacture. So the United States quickly spray-painted thousands of army helmet liners the right shade of blue and shipped them to Suez. The "blue helmet," or *"casque bleu,"* was born.

With no logistical pipeline to the area, the United Nations solved its supply problems by buying food and equipment on ships blocked in the canal by the fighting. This first 6,000-strong United Nations Emergency Force maintained a buffer zone in the Gaza strip and Sinai between the Egyptian and Israeli forces. But in what was later to seem a costly mistake, Israel confined deployment to Egyptian soil and did not allow the Blue Helmets into territory it controlled.

Its size and complexity, as well as the speed with which it went in, made UNEF I the model for several subsequent operations. And its success—it kept the peace in the area for ten years and guaranteed freedom of movement through the Suez Canal—encouraged Hammarskjöld to take a deeply pragmatic approach to peacekeeping, even rejecting a call from Secretary of State John Foster Dulles for a standing force because he feared this might "freeze a pattern of action." The United Nations had improvised once; it wanted to be able to do so again. Above all, the U.N. involvement in Suez showed for the first time that even though countries might fear becoming involved in another Korean War, they were prepared to deploy substantial forces under the U.N. flag to keep the peace in troubled areas with the consent of the parties to the crisis.

But this first emergency force in the Middle East ended in controversy and, many would say, failure when on May 16, 1967, President Gamal Abdel Nasser of Egypt abruptly demanded its withdrawal from Egyptian territory, confronting the new secretary-general, U Thant, with an agonizing dilemma. All the omens suggested Nasser wanted the force out because he planned to send his soldiers to help Syria stage a new confrontation with Israel.

Many have said U Thant should have refused to withdraw and summoned the General Assembly or Security Council into emergency session to discuss what was clearly a threat to peace. Whether either body would have been able to agree on concrete action to avert war in the climate of Cold War paralysis affecting the United Nations in those days remains questionable. But if Israel had allowed the force to be deployed in its territory, the secretary-general would have found it easier to play for time and resist Nasser's demand.

In the end, after first warning Egypt in bellicose language that the force had a right to remain on its soil, Canada abruptly withdrew its contingent when Nasser said he could no longer guarantee their safety. Left without logistical support or aircraft, U Thant had no option but to withdraw his peacekeepers. Israel responded promptly with the massive preemptive strike that started the Six-Day War.

In 1958, within two years of UNEF's formation, the United Nations began its long peacekeeping association with Lebanon when it dispatched the 600-strong United Nations Observer Group in Lebanon (UNOGIL) to investigate complaints that Egypt and Syria (both then known as the United Arab Republic) were infiltrating guerrillas into that troubled country. But by the end of the year, the internal situation in Lebanon appeared stable and UNOGIL was disbanded.

The largest, costliest, and most complex peacekeeping operation by the standards of its time resulted from the chaos in the Congo (now Zaire) after Belgium granted it independence in 1960. Within days the army mutinied, law and order broke down, Belgium sent troops back to protect its citizens, the copper-rich province of Katanga seceded under Moise Tshombe, and, overwhelmed by chaos and confusion, President Joseph Kasavubu and Prime Minister Patrice Lumumba sent a joint telegram to the United Nations appealing for help. But the U.N. involvement in the Congo became increasingly controversial as its forces had to deal not just with Katanga's secession but with a full-scale civil war between supporters of the pro-Western President Kasavubu and those of the Moscow-oriented Prime Minister Lumumba. And Soviet frustration with U.N. peacekeeping reached new peaks as it watched Lumumba's downfall while France, Britain, and the United States showed themselves lukewarm about suppressing Katanga's secession.

Meanwhile, financial problems plagued the operation—a foreshadowing of things to come. For opposite reasons, the Soviet Union and France refused to pay their shares of the costs, almost bankrupting the organization and forcing it to issue bonds to stay afloat. The United States retaliated by threatening to deprive the Soviet Union of its General Assembly vote in 1964, a move that might have broken up the U.N. had a compromise not been found.

At the time the Congo operation seemed a disaster that had almost cost the United Nations its existence. The world body had intervened directly for the first time in a chaotic internal crisis and found itself out of its depth. Today, in retrospect, the operation seems to have been more successful than was thought at the time. It helped maintain the unity of present-day Zaire, averted an East-West confrontation in Africa, provided a wealth of valuable peacekeeping experience, and showed that U.N. peacekeeping techniques can dampen and ultimately extinguish a state of anarchy and civil war.

Although Hammarskjöld's and U Thant's running of the Congo operation annoyed the Soviet Union, ruffled French feathers, and precipitated a major financial crisis, the United Nations went ahead with new, smaller operations in a number of countries, at the rate of about one a year between 1962 and 1965. In 1962 it dispatched forces to help administer West New Guinea (West Irian) as the Dutch handed over their last Pacific colony to Indonesia. The following year U.N. observers were in Yemen trying to oversee a fragile cease-fire between royalists and republicans. It also attempted to play a role following America's military intervention in the Dominican Republic to block a leftist government from coming to power. And in 1965 it increased its presence in and around Kashmir after fighting flared up again. Peacekeeping, clearly, had survived the Congo.

THE YEAR 1964 saw the start of an altogether more sophisticated and controversial exercise with the creation of the United Nations Peacekeeping Force in Cyprus, which is still in place today. After the island achieved independence in 1960 under a constitution that Britain, Greece, and Turkey guaranteed, intercommunal violence broke out on Cyprus between the Greek majority and the Turkish minority, arousing fears that Greece and Turkey, both NATO members, would be drawn into a war over the island's future.

Plans to deploy the first-ever peacekeeping force involving NATO members collapsed because of resistance from Archbishop Makarios, the island's Greek president. The Security Council then agreed in 1964 to deploy some 6,500 soldiers and policemen in a constabulary force throughout the island, which largely succeeded in restoring law and order. However, the Soviet Union, which had little interest in averting stresses within the NATO alliance and was certainly not going to pay money for doing so, insisted that the force be financed by voluntary contributions so that it would not be required to contribute to its upkeep.

The U.N. role in Cyprus changed dramatically after Turkey invaded the island in 1974, following a coup against the government of President Makarios, and divided it into separate Greek and Turkish states. This caused the Blue Helmets to revert to a classic peacekeeping operation, monitoring the cease-fire between the two armies deployed on either side of the "Green Line," which bisects the island.

The United Nations sought a peacemaking role as well on Cyprus, appointing a resident mediator between Greeks and Turks and launching many diplomatic initiatives. But progress has been minimal so far, prompting some critics to complain that the force is really perpetuating the crisis, not solving it, by keeping the island divided into separate communities that have had no contact for over a generation.

This year, as the operation passed its twenty-eighth birthday, three of the troop contributors—Austria, Denmark, and Canada—have warned that they are losing patience and might soon pull out unless there is progress toward a political solution. The new U.N. secretary-general, Boutros Boutros-Ghali, Egypt's former deputy prime minister, warned the Security Council that he will propose shutting down the operation altogether later this year unless the two sides compromise.

PEACEKEEPING went into remission between 1967 and late 1973, when not a single new operation was mounted, although existing ones continued. But the joint Egyptian-Syrian attack against Israel on October 6, 1973, shattered the calm, leading to the creation of two new forces: the second United Nations Emergency Force (UNEF II), in 1973, which acted as a buffer between Israeli and Egyptian forces along the Suez Canal; and the United Nations Disengagement Observer Force (UNDOF), in 1974, which served much the same purpose between Israel and Syria on the Golan Heights. For the first time, U.N. peacekeepers played a critical role in pulling the world back from the brink of a nuclear confrontation between the United States and the Soviet Union.

The opening of the war on Yom Kippur, the holiest day of the Jewish year, brought stunning reversals for Israel, as Syria penetrated the Golan Heights and Egyptian forces pushed across the Suez Canal deep into the Sinai. But the United States rushed in fresh military supplies, enabling Israel to launch a counterattack; as a result, its forces encircled the Egyptian Third Army in the Sinai and crossed the Suez Canal to threaten Port Said. On October 22, in an impressive display of joint statesmanship, the United States and the Soviet Union won Security Council approval for a resolution calling for a self-executing cease-fire between the belligerents, after a flying visit to Moscow by Henry Kissinger.

In his autobiography, *A Life in Peace and War*, Sir Brian Urquhart recalls that he was hardly popular when he pointed out to the Americans that in the United Nations experience such unsupervised cease-fires seldom worked. And he was proved right, with almost catastrophic consequences. The next day the Israelis broke the cease-fire by taking up new positions, to the fury of Egypt and Moscow. Although temporarily restored that night, the cease-fire collapsed again the next day when the Israelis started fighting again with the Egyptian Third Army. The precarious relationship that Washington and Moscow had established just three days before was in jeopardy, along with their unsupervised cease-fire arrangement.

Egyptian president Anwar Sadat asked the United States and the Soviet

Union to intervene directly. But Washington refused to send troops to deal with Israel, while the Soviet Union began preparations to come to Egypt's aid. President Nixon, determined to stop the Soviet Union from getting a military toehold in the Middle East, responded with a DefCon 3 alert, putting American forces everywhere on the highest state of alert in peacetime conditions. The superpowers seemed poised for confrontation in the explosive Middle East. "It was probably the most dangerous situation confronting the world since the Cuban missile crisis of October 1962," the United Nations writes in its history of peacekeeping, *The Blue Helmets.*

But the peacekeepers rushed to the rescue, as Urquhart has described in detail in his autobiography. Yugoslavia and the nonaligned members of the Security Council demanded rapid deployment of a new force to separate Egyptian and Israeli forces. That averted the risk of a direct superpower clash. But at American insistence, troops from the five permanent Security Council members were excluded from the new peacekeeping mission, denying Moscow the possibility of sending forces to the Middle East under U.N. guise. Kissinger later placated Moscow by asking it to send thirty-four Soviet officers to the Truce Supervisory Operation instead, a gesture that for the first time gave the Soviet Union a constructive role in a peacekeeping operation and set a precedent for superpower cooperation in the Middle East. The United States also agreed to include a Polish contingent in the new emergency force as part of the logistical support unit—to the consternation of the Canadian government, which traditionally provided logistical support for peacekeeping operations and was reluctant to share the honor.

The new emergency force soon made a reality of the cease-fire in the field. It resupplied the surrounded Third Egyptian Army with badly needed food and water through Israeli lines, and its members even got into fistfights with Israeli soldiers who were trying to dismantle the U.N. roadblocks. It administered a wide buffer zone between the two sides. And it organized the "Kilometer 101 talks" that eventually rescued the marooned Third Army. It also monitored the partial Israeli withdrawals from the Sinai between 1974 and 1976. The Security Council allowed its mandate to lapse in 1979, as Egypt and Israel agreed to recognize each other in a political settlement that finally brought lasting peace to that part of the region. (The Camp David accords had foreseen a role for U.N. observers, but Arab and Soviet opposition blocked that.)

Once the cease-fire had been secured on the Suez front and superpower confrontation avoided, Kissinger switched his attention to stabilizing the situation on the Golan Heights through deployment of another U.N. peacekeeping effort there. While Syria wanted only an observer group, Israel demanded a large-scale force to act as a buffer against the Syrian army. The compromise, hammered out by Kissinger in five weeks of shuttle diplomacy, was the United Nations Disengagement Observer Force. This provides for a central buffer zone between the two belligerents that is occupied only by U.N. forces, buttressed by a "limited-armaments zone" on each side where the two sides agree to restrict deployment of offensive weapons.

Syria had difficulty accepting the new force at first, and there were many early disputes over such matters as the United Nations force's blowing up unused fortifications in the buffer zone and checking Syrian vehicles entering its area. But its presence probably helped prevent renewed fighting in the area in 1978, when Israel invaded Lebanon and later accused Syria of deploying missiles in the Bekáa Valley. At the height of the missile dispute, Israel and Syria each quietly asked UNDOF to verify that the other side was not preparing for an attack by moving forces into the limited-armaments zone.

ON MARCH 11, 1978, a Palestine Liberation Organization terror squad left southern Lebanon by boat, landed undetected in Israel just north of Tel Aviv, commandeered a bus on the Haifa–Tel Aviv road, and ended up in a firefight with Israeli security forces in which thirty-seven Israelis died. The attack brought to a climax mounting Israeli anger over the frequent assaults Palestinians had been making against Israel since the early 1970s from southern Lebanon. Defense Minister Ezer Weizman ordered the army to cross the border into Lebanon, where it quickly overran most of the territory south of the Litani River except the city of Tyre. But this Israeli invasion also threatened to torpedo the Camp David peace process on normalizing relations between Egypt and Israel. President Sadat could not afford to recognize Israel if it was occupying part of another Arab state.

The United Nations had thought about deploying a peacekeeping force in southern Lebanon to decrease the constant clashes between Israeli forces and the PLO forces based there, but it dismissed the idea as impractical because neither side seemed interested in a truce. But the United States, anxious to salvage the Camp David talks, brushed aside such reservations and pushed the Security Council into approving the United Nations Interim Force in Lebanon (UNIFIL), ostensibly to oversee Israel's withdrawal from the south. An Israeli plea that the United States wait until Prime Minister Menachem Begin arrived in Washington the next day was rejected, thus ensuring Israeli opposition to the deployment from the start.

Meanwhile, Lebanon removed a provision from the resolution giving the force the right to exclude armed personnel from its zone, which would have put a brake on Palestinian guerrilla operations there. This in turn gave Israel justification for establishing a security zone in southern Lebanon, under the control of its Christian Lebanese allies after its own forces had withdrawn. As a result of these restrictions on its activity, UNIFIL has proved anything but interim—existing to this day, without being able to stop or even significantly reduce the endemic violence in the region. The force had to stand aside in 1982 when Israel launched another large-scale armed incursion into Lebanon. And it was humiliated again in February 1992 when an Israeli armored column punched through its roadblocks on its way to punish Hezbollah guerrilla groups.

The Lebanese operation illustrates how little U.N. peacekeeping forces can do when the parties to a conflict are not seriously interested in stopping their fighting—a lesson the organization was to learn again years later when it tried to promote peace in Yugoslavia. As a result of its ineffectiveness, the U.N. force in Lebanon has been plagued by poor morale. Its soldiers, aware that they are virtually powerless to stop the hostilities, put survival first. And governments sending troops have often undercut the U.N. commander by giving their forces special instructions to stay out of danger and minimize casualties.

THE UNITED NATIONS launched no further peacekeeping operations for a decade, but these were still eventful years for the peacekeeping concept because they witnessed the beginning of the end of the Cold War and the radical shift in Soviet policy that paved the way for the resurgence of peacekeeping in the 1990s. As East-West tensions eased, the Soviet Union under Mikhail S. Gorbachev came to see the United Nations as a cornerstone of its new foreign policy and realized that the world organization could play a useful role in helping the Soviet Union extricate itself from conflicts around the globe that it could no longer afford. Thus, at a time when the Reagan administration was still denigrating the United Nations as an enemy of American values and refusing to pay its dues, the Soviet Union announced in 1987 that it would start paying off all its own unpaid obligations to the world organization—which then amounted to some $200 million.

By 1988 the United Nations was sending a fifty-officer mission to monitor the Red Army's retreat from Kabul as Moscow pulled out of its long Afghan adventure, opening the way for a flood of new peacekeeping operations over the following years. With the Soviet Union and the United States now trying to resolve conflicts that they had previously sought to exploit, the U.N. peacekeeping role began to change. Increasingly these operations became more complex exercises in political reconciliation, with the United Nations sending in soldiers, policemen, and civilian administrators to oversee peace plans worked out by the parties to a dispute who had finally agreed to settle their differences through the ballot box.

Of the thirteen peacekeeping operations set up before Cold War tensions started fading in 1988, all but one were of the traditional kind, in which a U.N. force oversees a truce while efforts are made to find a political solution to the underlying conflict. But eight of the thirteen launched since then have been new-style operations, set up to help implement a political settlement already negotiated by the peacemakers. The United Nations has increasingly found itself in the business of creating the conditions in which free and fair elections can be held. This means the peacekeepers have been expected to disarm guerrillas, confine regular forces to barracks, preserve law and order, and monitor election campaigns. In 1989, for example, it set up the United Nations Observer Group in Central America (ONUCA) to monitor the agreement that Costa Rica, El Salvador, Guatemala, Honduras, and Nicaragua had made to cease aid for guerrilla movements in the region. But its mandate was then expanded to permit it to help in the voluntary disarming of the Nicaragua contra forces while a separate U.N. civilian operation supervised free elections. The United Nations subsequently took on very similar responsibilities under the agreement that ended the long civil war in El Salvador.

The same year, after protracted diplomatic efforts by the United States, Cuba began a staged withdrawal of the 50,000 troops it had sent to Angola to help the nominally Marxist government there against the South African–backed UNITA rebels of Jonas Savimbi. In exchange, South Africa agreed to give independence to the southwest African territory of Namibia, which it had administered since shortly after World War I.

The result was the United Nations Angola Verification Mission (UNAVEM), a sixty-member observer team monitoring the Cuban pullout, and the United Nations Transition Assistance Group (UNTAG), a far more sophisticated year-long mission that organized Namibia's first free elections to choose the government that would lead it to independence.

While typical of the new style of peacekeeping operation, in which the U.N. presence in a country is part of an agreed political solution to a dispute, the Namibian mission also illustrated a trend that was to assume increasing importance in the 1990s: mounting concern about their cost. Although ultimately deemed a success, the Namibian operation got off to a rocky start after cutbacks in the military component of the U.N. teams. This attempt to save money infuriated African leaders who feared that a smaller U.N. presence would allow South Africa to manipulate the elections.

But fewer soldiers also meant fewer patrols along the Angolan border. As a result, a heavily armed party of some 300 SWAPO guerrillas successfully infiltrated the country, only to be gunned down by the South African army instead of being stopped and disarmed by the United Nations on the frontier. After that incident, however, the operation proceeded more smoothly, with the United Nations successfully disarming the SWAPO guerrillas, monitoring the local police, and keeping the regular army confined to barracks while it organized free elections.

In late 1991 and early 1992, the United Nations was committed to four major new peacekeeping operations, and there was serious concern that the demand for its services as the breakup of the Soviet Union unleashed a new wave of old ethnic tensions would outstrip its members' willingness to meet the bill. In Cambodia, the United Nations was starting the biggest of the new-style peacekeeping operations it had ever undertaken, deploying some 20,000 soldiers, police, and administrators to oversee the operations of this war-torn nation, disarm the dreaded Khmer Rouge and the other parties in that country's twenty-two-year civil war, and organize free elections. Simultaneously, in Western Sahara, a U.N. operation was organizing a referendum to decide on that territory's future. Meanwhile, a large force was deployed in Croatia in the hope that a cease-fire would hold while the European Community countries tried to broker a political settlement to the Yugoslav civil war. But it quickly spread to other former parts of the federation, particularly the republic of Bosnia and Herzegovina, and the United Nations found itself unable to stem the violence. Finally, at the urging of the secretary-general, the United Nations negotiated a fragile cease-fire in Somalia, then made plans to deploy observers to monitor the cease-fire, as well as a force of military guards to supervise the distribution of food and humanitarian supplies to a country that had slipped into almost total anarchy.

These four new operations, together with the eight others under way in different parts of the world, have produced what can only be described as a crisis over the future of United Nations peacekeeping. The crisis shows itself most clearly in financial terms, with the international community's peacekeeping bill expected to jump from some $421 million in 1991 to almost $3 billion in 1992. But the new republics that succeeded the Soviet Union have been unable to pay anything at all, while the United States, paralyzed by the onset of a presidential election year, has fallen deeply into arrears, owing $112.3 million in unpaid peacekeeping dues and a further $555 million to the regular U.N. budget.

Meanwhile, deep-seated ethnic animosities have continued to flare up in the Balkans, elsewhere in Eastern Europe, in Central Asia, and in many parts of Africa, suggesting that while the Cold War might be over, the world still faces a new wave of low-intensity ethnic conflicts that could create a growing demand for peacekeeping. At the same time, the manifest success of many U.N. peacekeeping operations has produced an upsurge of interest among academics and other experts in this aspect of the organization's work, as well as a flood of ideas and proposals for strengthening it. Some have favored giving the United Nations a kind of rapid-deployment force, which could be rushed in to quell conflicts as soon as they erupt. Many hope member countries will earmark troops and matériel on a standby basis for peacekeeping tasks so the secretary-general will always have forces at the ready. There also have been suggestions for more preventive peacekeeping, for instance by deploying observers along the frontier of a country that feels threatened. Paradoxically, at the very moment the United Nations appears to be standing at the verge of bankruptcy, its prestige and the public's interest in its work have never been higher.

The secretary-general's reaction to the crisis has been to call a halt to all new peacekeeping operations as of the spring of 1992, saying the organization lacks the resources to take on any more crises. If France and Germany really want to expand the Yugoslav operation across the entire territory of the former federation, they have been told, they will have to find the men and money themselves.

At the same time, the United Nations has also urged regional organizations to do more to put out brushfires in their areas of the world. In the former Yugoslav federation, for example, the United Nations secured a limited truce in Croatia and sent in monitors but handed the peacemaking process over to the European Community, which continued its efforts to organize a conference to negotiate a settlement between the newly independent republics and the remainder of Yugoslavia. Similarly, the United Nations arranged the initial truce in Somalia and agreed to send in monitors. But the task of finding a long-term solution to the anarchy and tribal violence plaguing that country was given to the organization of African Unity, the League of Arab States, and the Organization of the Islamic Conference. In the crisis in Haiti, it was the Organization of American States that tried to find a political solution.

This approach is in strict conformity with the United Nations Charter, according to which the states of a particular region should try to settle their differences peacefully before taking disputes to the Security Council. In addition, regional organizations such as the European Community and the Arab League have far more money and other resources than the United Nations at present. And while they may lack experience in dispute resolution, as the secretary-general has argued, experience is gained only by trying.

Meanwhile, the emphasis at the United Nations is switching subtly away from classic, costly peacekeeping operations toward what is known as "preventive diplomacy," or expanding the secretary-general's "good offices." This means that instead of sending in the Blue Helmets to clean up the mess after a fight has begun, the secretary-general will try to keep the belligerents from coming to blows in the first place—clearly a less expensive solution. To this end, Dr. Boutros-Ghali is seeking to consolidate the many separate offices that the United Nations and its specialized agencies maintain around the world into single establishments, which could also serve as his ears and eyes in future trouble spots.

Nevertheless, the U.N. peacekeeping operations continue. Some, such as those in Central America, Cambodia, and Western Sahara, will end once the agreed political solutions have been put in place and their tasks are finished. In other parts of the world, the U.N. peacekeeping role is still ahead of its peacemaking function, and the Blue Helmets must continue their difficult, lonely task with no terminal date in sight. That is why General Jeremiah Enright will be rotating his headquarters again this year with the onset of winter in Srinagar, while his peacekeeping monitors continue a vigil over the mountains of Kashmir that began forty-four years ago.

*AUTUMN 1992*

**Paul Lewis is the United Nations correspondent for the *New York Times*.**

# Bibliography

## Editor's Suggested Readings

Anyone who has read even a few of the articles in this volume quickly begins to realize the wealth of available material in the area of American military history. It is a rich and tempting bounty, and I hope that the following list will help those readers who wish to slake their appetite for more. Any attempt at a definitive list would be unwieldy and likely unwanted in a volume of this type. Instead, I have compiled a list of basic works that combine excellent scholarship and outstanding readability. They are also books that, in over two decades of teaching, I have found especially stimulating and helpful. Many contain outstanding bibliographies of their own. In scanning this list, however, a reader needs to keep in mind the inherent imbalance within the writing of American military history. An overwhelming abundance of books exists for the Civil War and World War II, while a relative paucity exists in other periods, such as the Quasi-War with France or the Philippine-American War, a problem mirrored in this volume, too. For the bibliophiles among us, thankfully that means there are more than ample topics for the historians of the future.

### Reference Works
Burns, Richard. A *Guide to American Foreign Relations since 1700* (1983).
Dupuy, R. Ernest, and Trevor Dupuy. *The Harper Encyclopedia of Military History: From 3500 B.C. to the Present* (1993).
Higham, Robin. A *Guide to the Sources of United States Military History* (1975). *Supplements* (1981, 1986, 1993).
Jessup, John E., and Robert W. Coakley. A *Guide to the Study and Use of Military History* (1979).
Wintle, Justin. *The Dictionary of War Quotations* (1989).

### General Histories
Beach, Edward. *The United States Navy: 200 Years* (1986).
Brodie, Bernard. *War and Politics* (1973).
Futrell, Robert F. *Ideas, Concepts, Doctrine. Basic Thinking in the United States Air Force* (1989). 2 vols.
Hagan, Kenneth. *This People's Navy: The Making of American Sea Power* (1991).
Heller, Charles E., and William A. Stofft, eds. *America's First Battles, 1776–1965* (1986).
Higham, Robin. *Air Power: A Concise History* (rev. ed. 1988).
Kennett, Lee B. A *History of Strategic Bombing* (1982).
Millett, Allan. *Semper Fidelis: The History of the United States Marine Corps* (rev. ed. 1991).

Millett, Allan, and Peter Maslowski. *For the Common Defense: A Military History of the United States* (rev. ed. 1994).

Millis, Walter. *Arms and Men: A Study in American Military History* (1956).

Natty, Bernard C. *Strength for the Fight: A History of Black Americans in the Military* (1986).

Perret, Geoffrey. *A Country Made by War: From the Revolution to Vietnam: The Story of America's Rise to Power* (1989).

Sprout, Harold, and Margaret Sprout. *The Rise of American Naval Power, 1776–1918* (rev. ed. 1967).

Utley, Robert M., and Wilcomb E. Washburn. *The American Heritage History of the Indian Wars* (1977).

Weigley, Russell F. *The American Way of War: A History of United States Military Strategy and Policy* (1973).

———. *History of the United States Army* (rev. ed. 1984).

COLONIAL PERIOD

Ferling, John E. *Struggle for a Continent: The Wars of Early America* (1993).

Leach, Douglas E. *Arms for Empire: A Military History of the British Colonies in North America, 1607–1763* (1973).

———. *Flintlock and Tomahawk: New England in King Philip's War* (1958).

———. *Roots of Conflict: British Armed Forces and Colonial Americans, 1677–1763* (1986).

AMERICAN REVOLUTION

Billias, George Athan, ed. *George Washington's Generals* (1964).

———. *George Washington's Opponents: British Generals and Admirals in the American Revolution* (1969).

Davis, Burke. *The Campaign That Won America: The Story of Yorktown* (1970).

Dwyer, William M. *The Day Is Ours! November 1776–January 1777: An Inside View of the Battles of Trenton and Princeton* (1983).

Flexner, James Thomas. *Washington, the Indispensable Man* (1974).

Higginbotham, Don. *The War of American Independence: Military Attitudes, Policies, and Practice, 1763–1789* (1971).

Morison, Samuel Eliot. *John Paul Jones, a Sailor's Biography* (1959).

Robson, Eric. *The American Revolution in Its Political and Military Aspects, 1763–1783* (1955).

Royster, Charles. *A Revolutionary People at War: The Continental Army and American Character, 1775–1783* (1979).

Wallace, Willard M. *Appeal to Arms: A Military History of the American Revolution* (1951).

EARLY NATIONAL PERIOD

DeConde, Alexander. *The Quasi-War: The Politics and Diplomacy of the Undeclared War with France, 1797–1801* (1977).

Kohn, Richard H. *Eagle and Sword. The Federalists and the Creation of the Military Establishment in America, 1783–1802* (1975).

Smelser, Marshall. *The Congress Founds the Navy, 1787–1798* (1959).

Tucker, Glenn. *Dawn Like Thunder: The Barbary Wars and the Birth of the U.S. Navy* (1963).

WAR OF 1812

Brooks, Charles B. *The Siege of New Orleans* (1961).

Coles, Harry. *War of 1812* (1965).

Fowler, William M. *Jack Tars and Commodores: The American Navy, 1783–1815* (1984).

Hickey, Donald R. *The War of 1812: A Forgotten Conflict* (1989).
Lord, Walter. *The Dawn's Early Light* (1972).

### MEXICAN WAR AND THE FRONTIER

Bauer, K. Jack. *The Mexican War, 1846–1848* (1974).
Coffman, Edward M. *The Old Army: A Portrait of the American Army in Peacetime, 1784–1898* (1986).
Eisenhower, John S. *So Far from God: The U.S. War with Mexico, 1846–1848* (1989).
Goetzmann, William H. *Exploration and Empire: The Explorer and the Scientist in the Winning of the West* (1966).
Morison, Samuel Eliot. *"Old Bruin": Commodore Matthew C. Perry, 1794–1858* (1967).
Prucha, Francis Paul. *The Sword of the Republic: The United States Army on the Frontier, 1783–1846* (1968).
Utley, Robert M. *Frontiersmen in Blue: The United States Army and the Indian, 1848–1865* (1967).

### CIVIL WAR

Coddington, Edwin B. *The Gettysburg Campaign: A Study in Command* (1968).
Cozzens, Peter. *This Terrible Sound: The Battle of Chickamauga* (1992).
Davis, William C. *Jefferson Davis. The Man and His Hour* (1991).
Foote, Shelby. *The Civil War, a Narrative* (1958–74). 3 vols.
Fowler, William M. *Under Two Flags: The American Navy in the Civil War* (1990).
Hattaway, Herman, and Archer Jones. *How the North Won: A Military History of the Civil War* (1983).
Linderman, Gerald F. *Embattled Courage: The Experience of Combat in the American Civil War* (1987).
McPherson, James M. *Battle Cry of Freedom: The Civil War Era* (1988).
Oates, Stephen B. *With Malice toward None: The Life of Abraham Lincoln* (1977).
Royster, Charles. *The Destructive War: William Tecumseh Sherman, Stonewall Jackson, and the Americans* (1991).
Sears, Stephen W. *George B. McClellan: The Young Napoleon* (1988).
———. *Landscape Turned Red: The Battle of Antietam* (1983).
Thomas, Emory M. *Bold Dragoon. The Life of J.E.B. Stuart* (1986).
———. *The Confederate Nation, 1861–1865* (1979).
Wiley, Bell Irvin. *The Life of Billy Yank, the Common Soldier of the Union* (1952).
———. *The Life of Johnny Reb, the Common Soldier of the Confederacy* (1943).
Wilkinson, Warren. *Mother, May You Never See the Sights I Have Seen: The Fifty-seventh Massachusetts Veteran Volunteers* (1990).

### CLOSING OF THE FRONTIER

Utley, Robert M. *Cavalier in Buckskin: George Armstrong Custer and the Western Military Frontier* (1988).
———. *Frontier Regulars: The United States Army and the Indian, 1866–1891* (1973).
———. *The Lance and the Shield: The Life and Times of Sitting Bull* (1993).

### SPANISH-AMERICAN WAR AND EXPANSION

Abrahamson, James L. *America Arms for a New Century: The Making of a Great Military Power* (1981).
Cosmas, Graham. *An Army for Empire: The United States Army in the Spanish-American War* (1971).
Gates, John Morgan. *Schoolbooks and Krags: The United States Army in the Philippines, 1898–1902* (1973).

Linn, Brian McAllister. *The U.S. Army and Counterinsurgency in the Philippine War, 1899–1902* (1989).
Seager, Robert, III. *Alfred Thayer Mahan: The Man and His Letters* (1977).
Spector, Ronald H. *Admiral of the New Empire: The Life and Career of George Dewey* (1974).
Trask, David. *The War with Spain in 1898* (1981).

### WORLD WAR I
Coffman, Edward M. *The War to End All Wars: The American Military Experience in World War I* (1968).
Ferrell, Robert H. *Woodrow Wilson and World War I, 1917–1921* (1985).
Kennett, Lee B. *The First Air War, 1914–1918* (1991).
Morison, Elting E. *Admiral Sims and the Modern American Navy* (1942).
Smythe, Donald. *Pershing, General of the Armies* (1986).
Trask, David F. *The AEF and Coalition Warmaking, 1917–1918* (1993).

### BETWEEN THE WORLD WARS
Buckley, Thomas H. *The United States and the Washington Conference, 1921–1922* (1970).
Copp, DeWitt S. *A Few Great Captains: The Men and Events That Shaped the Development of U.S. Air Power* (1980).
Hurley, Alfred F. *Billy Mitchell: Crusader for Air Power* (1964).
Leutze, James R. *Bargaining for Supremacy: Anglo-American Naval Collaboration, 1937–1941* (1977).
Melhorn, Charles M. *Two-Block Fox: The Rise of the Aircraft Carrier, 1911–1929* (1974).
Miller, Edward S. *War Plan Orange. The U.S. Strategy to Defeat Japan, 1897–1945* (1991).
Reynolds, Clark G. *Admiral John H. Towers: The Struggle for Naval Air Supremacy* (1991).

### WORLD WAR II
Ambrose, Stephen E. *D-Day: June 6, 1944: The Climactic Battle of World War II* (1994).
———. *Eisenhower.* Vol. I: *Soldier, General of the Army, President-Elect, 1890–1952* (1983).
Blair, Clay. *Silent Victory: The U.S. Submarine War against Japan* (1975).
D'Este, Carlo. *Decision in Normandy* (1983).
Feifer, George. *Tennozan: The Battle of Okinawa and the Atomic Bomb* (1992).
Frank, Richard. *Guadalcanal* (1990).
Gray, J. Glenn. *The Warriors: Reflections of Men in Battle* (1959).
Hastings, Max. *Overlord: D-Day and the Battle for Normandy* (1984).
Heinrichs, Waldo H. *Threshold of War: Franklin D. Roosevelt and American Entry into World War II* (1988).
James, D. Clayton. *The Years of MacArthur* (1970–85). 3 vols.
Kahn, David. *Seizing the Enigma: The Race to Break the German U-Boat Codes, 1939–1943* (1991).
Keegan, John. *Six Armies in Normandy: From D-Day to the Liberation of Paris* (rev. ed. 1994).
Knox, Donald. *Death March: The Survivors of Bataan* (1981).
Larrabee, Eric. *Commander-in-Chief: Franklin Delano Roosevelt, His Lieutenants, and Their War* (1987).
Leinbaugh, Harold P., and John D. Campbell. *The Men of Company K: The Autobiography of a World War II Rifle Company* (1985).
Lewin, Ronald. *The American Magic: Codes, Ciphers and the Defeat of Japan* (1982).

MacDonald, Charles. *Company Commander* (1947).

Mauldin, William. *Up Front* (1945).

McFarland, Stephen L., and Wesley Phillips Newton. *To Command the Sky: The Battle for Air Superiority over Germany, 1942–1944* (1991).

Morison, Samuel Eliot. *The Two-Ocean War. A Short History of the United States Navy in the Second World War* (1963).

Morton, Louis. *The Fall of the Philippines* (1953).

Perret, Geoffrey. *There's a War to be Won: The United States Army in World War II* (1991).

———. *Winged Victory: The Army Air Forces in World War II* (1993).

Pogue, Forrest. *George C. Marshall* (1963–87). 4 vols.

Prange, Gordon. *At Dawn We Slept: The Untold Story of Pearl Harbor* (1981).

———. *Miracle at Midway* (1982).

———. *Pearl Harbor. The Verdict of History* (1986).

Reynolds, Clark G. *The Fast Carriers: The Forging of an Air Navy* (1968).

Rhodes, Richard. *The Making of the Atomic Bomb* (1986).

Ryan, Cornelius. *The Longest Day: June 6, 1944* (1959).

Sledge, E.B. *With the Old Breed at Peleliu and Okinawa* (1981).

Spector, Ronald H. *The Eagle against the Sun: The American War with Japan* (1985).

Weigley, Russell F. *Eisenhower's Lieutenants. The Campaigns of France and Germany, 1944–1945* (1981).

Weinberg, Gerhard L. *A World at Arms: A Global History of World War II* (1994).

Wohlstetter, Roberta. *Pearl Harbor: Warning and Decision* (1962).

KOREAN WAR AND COLD WAR

Appleman, Roy E. *East of Chosin: Entrapment and Breakout in Korea, 1950* (1987).

Blair, Clay. *The Forgotten War: America in Korea, 1950–1953* (1987).

Boettcher, Thomas D. *First Call: The Making of the Modern U.S. Military, 1945–1953* (1992).

Brodie, Bernard. *Strategy in the Missile Age* (1959).

Brugioni, Dino A. *Eyeball to Eyeball: The Inside Story of the Cuban Missile Crisis* (rev. ed. 1991).

Dalfiume, Richard M. *Desegregation of the U.S. Armed Forces: Fighting on Two Fronts, 1939–1953* (1969).

Herken, Gregg. *The Winning Weapon. The Atomic Bomb in the Cold War, 1945–1950* (1980).

Hoopes, Townsend, and Douglas Brinkley. *Driven Patriot: The Life and Times of James Forrestal* (1992).

Isenberg, Michael T. *Shield of the Republic: The United States Navy in an Era of Cold War and Violent Peace* (1993).

Leffler, Melvyn P. *A Preponderance of Power. National Security, the Truman Administration, and the Cold War* (1991).

Marshall, S.L.A. *Pork Chop Hill: The American Fighting Man in Action, Korea, Spring, 1953* (1956).

———. *The River and the Gauntlet: Defeat of the Eighth Army by the Chinese Communist Forces, November, 1950, in the Battle of the Chongchon River, Korea* (1953).

May, Ernest R. "Introduction: NSC 68: The Theory and Politics of Strategy," in *American Cold War Strategy: Interpreting NSC 68* (1993).

Potter, E.B. *Admiral Arleigh Burke* (1990).

Rees, David. *Korea: The Limited War* (1964).

Smoke, Richard. *National Security and the Nuclear Dilemma: An Introduction to the American Experience* (rev. ed. 1987).

Toland, John. *In Mortal Combat: Korea, 1950–1953* (1991).

VIETNAM WAR

Braestrup, Peter. *Big Story: How the American Press and Television Reported and Interpreted the Crisis of Tet 1968 in Vietnam and Washington* (1977).

Clodfelter, Mark. *The Limits of Air Power: The American Bombing of North Vietnam* (1989).

Davidson, Phillip B. *Vietnam at War: The History. 1946–1975* (1988).

Halberstam, David. *The Best and the Brightest* (1972).

Herring, George C. *America's Longest War: The United States and Vietnam, 1950–1975* (rev. ed. 1986).

Moore, Harold G., and Joseph L. Galloway. *We Were Soldiers Once . . . and Young: Ia Drang, the Battle That Changed the War in Vietnam* (1992).

Palmer, Bruce. *The 25-Year War: America's Military Role in Vietnam* (1984).

Sheehan, Neil. *A Bright Shining Lie: John Paul Vann and America in Vietnam* (1988).

Spector, Ronald H. *After Tet: The Bloodiest Year in Vietnam* (1993).

Summers, Harry G., Jr. *On Strategy: A Critical Analysis of the Vietnam War* (1982).

PERSIAN GULF WAR

Atkinson, Rick. *Crusade: The Untold Story of the Persian Gulf War* (1993).

Freedman, Lawrence, and Efraim Karsh. *The Gulf Conflict, 1990–1991: Diplomacy and War in the New World Order* (1993).

Gordon, Michael, and Bernard E. Trainor. *The Generals' War* (1994).

Hallion, Richard P. *Storm over Iraq: Air Power and the Gulf War* (1992).

Woodward, Bob. *The Commanders* (1991).

# Credits

"Mrs. Benedict Arnold," adapted from *Benedict Arnold: Patriot and Traitor* by Willard Sterne Randall, © 1990. Reprinted by permission of the author. • "How Lincoln Won the War With Metaphor," adapted from *Abraham Lincoln and the Second American Revolution* by James M. McPherson, © 1991. Reprinted by permission of Oxford University Press, New York. • "'Lord High Admiral of the U.S. Navy,'" adapted from *Partners in Command: The Relationships Between Leaders in the Civil War* by Joseph T. Glatthaar, © 1993. Reprinted by permission of The Free Press, a Division of Simon & Schuster, Inc., New York. • "Civil War Cavalry: Missed Opportunities," adapted from *Battle Tactics of the Civil War* by Paddy Griffith, © 1989. Reprinted by permission of Yale University Press, New Haven, Conn., and The Crowood Press, Marlborough, Wiltshire, England. • "Last Stand," adapted from *Cavalier in Buckskin: George Armstrong Custer and the Western Military Frontier* by Robert M. Utley, © 1988. Reprinted by permission of the University of Oklahoma Press, Norman, Okla. • "Belleau Wood: One Man's Initiation," adapted from *In Many a Strife: General Gerald C. Thomas and the U.S. Marine Corps, 1917–1956* by Allan R. Millett, © 1993. Reprinted by permission of Naval Institute Press, Annapolis, Md. • "Bywater's Pacific War Prophecy," adapted from *Visions of Infamy: The Untold Story of How Journalist Hector C. Bywater Devised the Plans that Led to Pearl Harbor* by William H. Honan, © 1991. Reprinted by permission of the author. • "They Can't Realize the Change Aviation Has Made," adapted from *The Borrowed Years, 1938–1941: America on the Way to War* by Richard M. Ketchum, © 1989. Reprinted by permission of Random House, Inc., New York. • "Kimmel's Hidden Agenda," adapted from *War Plan Orange: The U.S. Strategy to Defeat Japan, 1897–1945* by Edward S. Miller, © 1991. Reprinted by permission of Naval Institute Press, Annapolis, Md. • "Truman Fires MacArthur," adapted from *Truman* by David McCullough, © 1992. Reprinted by permission of Simon & Schuster, Inc., New York. • "The Invasion of Cuba," adapted from *Eyeball to Eyeball: The Inside Story of the Cuban Missile Crisis* by Dino A. Brugioni, © 1991. Reprinted by permission of Random House, Inc., New York. • "That's Ocay XX Time Is on Our Side," adapted from *Bouncing Back* by Geoffrey Norman, © 1990. Reprinted by permission of Houghton Mifflin Co., New York. • "The Evacuation of Kham Duc," adapted from *After Tet: The Bloodiest Year in Vietnam* by Ronald H. Spector, © 1993. Reprinted by permission of The Free Press, A Division of Simon & Schuster Inc., New York. • "The Christmas Bombing," adapted from *Nixon: Ruin and Recovery 1973–1990* by Stephen E. Ambrose, © 1990. Reprinted by permission of Simon & Schuster, Inc. New York. • "The Gulf Crisis and the Rules of War," adapted from *The Transformation of War: The Most Radical Reinterpretation of Armed Conflict Since Clausewitz* by Martin van Creveld, © 1991. Reprinted by permission of The Free Press, a Division of Simon & Schuster, Inc., New York. • "An Empty Ocean," adapted from *The Price of Admiralty: The Evolution of Naval Warfare* by John Keegan, © 1988. Reprinted by permission of Viking Penguin, Inc., New York.

# Index

# Index

# Index

# About the Author

Calvin L. Christman is a professor of history at Cedar Valley College and an adjunct professor at the University of North Texas. In addition, he serves as a National Security Fellow for the Institute for Advanced Technology at the University of Texas, Austin, and as an associate chairman of the Inter-University Seminar on Armed Forces and Society. He is a contributor to *A Guide to the Sources of United States Military History* and *Calculations: Net Assessment and the Coming of World War II* and has published articles on military history in *Military Affairs, Diplomatic History, Mid-America,* and *The Americas.*

The **Naval Institute Press** is the book-publishing arm of the U.S. Naval Institute, a private, nonprofit society for sea service professionals and others who share an interest in naval and maritime affairs. Established in 1873 at the U.S. Naval Academy in Annapolis, Maryland, where its offices remain, today the Naval Institute has more than 100,000 members worldwide.

Members of the Naval Institute receive the influential monthly magazine *Proceedings* and discounts on fine nautical prints and on ship and aircraft photos. They also have access to the transcripts of the Institute's Oral History Program and get discounted admission to any of the Institute-sponsored seminars offered around the country.

The Naval Institute also publishes *Naval History* magazine. This colorful bimonthly is filled with entertaining and thought-provoking articles, first-person reminiscences, and dramatic art and photography. Members receive a discount on *Naval History* subscriptions.

The Naval Institute's book-publishing program, begun in 1898 with basic guides to naval practices, has broadened its scope in recent years to include books of more general interest. Now the Naval Institute Press publishes more than seventy titles each year, ranging from how-to books on boating and navigation to battle histories, biographies, ship and aircraft guides, and novels. Institute members receive discounts on the Press's nearly 400 books in print.

For a free catalog describing Naval Institute Press books currently available, and for further information about subscribing to *Naval History* magazine or about joining the U.S. Naval Institute, please write to:

Membership & Communications Department
U.S. Naval Institute
118 Maryland Avenue
Annapolis, Maryland 21402-5035
Or call, toll-free, (800) 233-USNI.